MASTER THE

John W. Crum, Ph.D.

2002

AP* U.S. HISTORY

T E S T S

TEACHER-TESTED STRATEGIES AND

TECHNIQUES FOR SCORING HIGH

ARCO

THOMSON LEARNING™

Australia • Canada • Mexico • Singapore • Spain • United Kingdom • United States

An ARCO Book

ARCO is a registered trademark of Thomson Learning, Inc., and is used herein under license by Peterson's.

About Peterson's

Founded in 1966, Peterson's, a division of Thomson Learning, is the nation's largest and most respected provider of lifelong learning online resources, software, reference guides, and books. The Education Supersite[SM] at petersons.com—the Web's most heavily traveled education resource—has searchable databases and interactive tools for contacting U.S.-accredited institutions and programs. CollegeQuest[®] (CollegeQuest.com) offers a complete solution for every step of the college decision-making process. GradAdvantage[TM] (GradAdvantage.org), developed with Educational Testing Service, is the only electronic admissions service capable of sending official graduate test score reports with a candidate's online application. Peterson's serves more than 55 million education consumers annually.

Thomson Learning is among the world's leading providers of lifelong learning, serving the needs of individuals, learning institutions, and corporations with products and services for both traditional classrooms and for online learning. For more information about the products and services offered by Thomson Learning, please visit www.thomsonlearning.com. Headquartered in Stamford, Connecticut, with offices worldwide, Thomson Learning is part of The Thomson Corporation (www.thomson.com), a leading e-information and solutions company in the business, professional, and education marketplaces. The Corporation's common shares are listed on the Toronto and London stock exchanges.

For more information, contact Peterson's, 2000 Lenox Drive, Lawrenceville, NJ 08648; 800-338-3282; or find us on the World Wide Web at: www.petersons.com/about

ISSN: International Standard Serial Number information available upon request.
ISBN: 0-7689-0738-1

Printed in the United States of America

10 9 8 7 6 5 4 3   03 02

CONTENTS

PART THREE

Acknowledgments

Thanks are due to the following for permission to reprint copyrighted material:

The Art Institute of Chicago, for reprint of *American Gothic,* by Grant Wood. Reprinted by courtesy of the Art Institute of Chicago. All rights reserved.

The Atlantic Monthly, for quotes from "What Substitute for War," by Charles Lindbergh, *The Atlantic Monthly*, February, 1940; and "The Road Not Taken," by David Cohen, *The Atlantic Monthly,* March, 1940. Copyright © 1940 by The Atlantic Monthly Co. Reprinted with permission.

The University of Chicago Press, for the quote from *An American Primer,* edited by Daniel Boorstin. Copyright © 1966 by Daniel Boorstin. Reprinted by permission of The University of Chicago Press.

The College Board, for statistics from *The History Examinations of the College Board* 1980/82. Copyright © 1980 by College Entrance Examination Board; and for quotes from *Advanced Placement Course Description: History*. Copyright © 1993 by College Entrance Examination Board, New York. Reprinted by permission of The College Board.

The Curtis Publishing Company, for the cartoon from the *Saturday Evening Post,* January 8, 1938. Reprinted from the *Saturday Evening Post* © 1938 by The Curtis Publishing Company.

E. P. Dutton, Inc., for quotes from *Seventy Years of Life and Labor: An Autobiography* by Samuel Gompers. Copyright © 1925 by E.P. Dutton, Inc., © 1953 by Gertrude Gleaves Gompers. Reprinted by permission of E.P. Dutton, Inc.

Michael S. Henry and *The Social Studies,* for quotes and a chart from, "The Advanced Placement American History Examination: How Has It Changed?" *The Social Studies,* July/August, 1987. Reprinted with permission of the Helen Dwight Reid Educational Foundation. Published by Heldref Publications, 4000 Albemarle St., N.W., Washington, D.C. 20016. Copyright © 1987.

Herblock, for the cartoon from Herblock Cartoons, *The Washington Post,* October 6, 1966. Copyright © 1966 by Herblock in *The Washington Post.* Reprinted by permission of Herblock Cartoons.

Michael Katz, for the chart from *The Irony of Early School Reform,* by Michael Katz. Copyright © 1968. Reprinted by permission of Michael Katz.

Richard P. McCormick, for charts from "New Perspectives on Jacksonian Politics," by Richard P. McCormick, *American Historical Review,* LXV, January, 1960. Reprinted by permission of Richard P. McCormick.

Prentice-Hall, Inc., for the chart, "Population Composition of Major Cities, 1910," from *The Evolution of American Urban Society,* by Howard P. Chudacoff. Copyright © 1975. Reprinted by permission of Prentice-Hall, Inc.

Reader's Digest, for quotes from "Pro and Con: Should We Act to Curb Aggressor Nations?" March, 1939. Reprinted by permission of *Reader's Digest* © 1939.

Arthur M. Schlesinger, Jr., for the map, "The Populous States in 1890," from *The Rise of the City,* by Arthur M. Schlesinger, Sr. Copyright © 1933. Reprinted by permission of Arthur M. Schlesinger, Jr.

Stanford University, for the quote from *The Man in the Street,* by Thomas A. Bailey. Copyright © 1948. Reprinted by permission of Stanford University.

James T. Stewart, for quotes from "America Looks at War," by Raoul de Roussy de Sales, *The Atlantic Monthly,* February, 1940. Reprinted by permission of James T. Stewart.

Preface

As a teacher I owe a great debt of gratitude to several sources of inspiration. I have worked with hundreds of fellow AP teachers from all over the United States. Over the years I have encountered a deep devotion to scholarship and teaching and a high degree of competence. I have been most fortunate to teach at Mount Pleasant High School, a public high school in Wilmington, Delaware. Our school is well known for the strength of its academic program, the quality of the faculty, and the friendly interaction between the students and the faculty. I must thank the thousands of students who have challenged and stimulated me in the classroom. I am especially grateful to three colleagues from my early career in the Social Studies Department—Robert Emrich, David Menser, and Albert Clark—and, now, late in my career, to the present members of the department—David Bradley, David Cooper, Kurt Crock, Robert Limmina, David Needs, Michael Prince, and Michael Pullig. Their advice, support, and congeniality over the years has meant much to me. It is hard to imagine more stimulating and supportive fellow workers.

Most of all I want to thank my wife and our two daughters for their faithful encouragement, patience, and tolerance. My debt to them is beyond mere words. They have sacrificed much to support my academic pursuits. I have won many awards and much recognition as a teacher, but no joy compares to that which has come from being a husband and a father. For all these reasons I want to thank my wife, Karen, and our daughters, Laurette and Leslie.

J.W.C.

Introduction

The College Board Advanced Placement Program is an opportunity to achieve excellence. The AP program provides high school students the opportunity to earn credit and advanced standing from the college of their choice. The College Board contracts with Educational Testing Service to construct, administer, and grade the advanced placement examinations. The tests are scored as 5, 4, 3, 2, or 1. Most colleges and universities grant college credit for scores of 3, 4, or 5.

The College Board estimates that perhaps a fourth of all the nation's college-bound high school students are able to do freshman-level work. It takes more effort than the usual high school course, but the results are well worth it. Such work can enrich your mind and boost your self-confidence. In the final analysis it is your education, your opportunity, your achievement, and your reward. Don't shortchange yourself in effort or in achievement.

Introduction: About AP United States History

U.S. History AP Examination: What to Expect

STRUCTURE OF THE EXAMINATION

The U.S. History AP examination is a rigorous three-hour examination. It will be one of the most difficult examinations you will ever prepare for. Whereas almost every college course you will take is a semester course, the AP examination covers a year's worth of effort and content. This is not meant to scare you; thousands and thousands of students have done very well on the U.S. History AP examination. It is, however, an examination that demands and deserves your best effort.

Part One of the examination consists of 80 multiple-choice questions. You have 55 minutes for Part One; at the end of the 55-minute period, the multiple-choice questions and your machine-scored answer sheet are collected. You are not able to refer to the multiple-choice questions for facts and ideas to include in your essays.

Part Two, the essay section, is divided among one document-based essay question (DBQ) and two essay questions that you select from a list of four. Every student must answer the DBQ, which is question number 1. You are given 6 to 12 documents to analyze in order to answer a question relating to a particular historical circumstance, event, issue, or theme. For your second essay, you select either question 2 or 3 to answer a question covering the period from colonization to Reconstruction. For your third essay, you select from questions 4 and 5 to answer a question covering the period from Reconstruction to the present. You have a total of 130 minutes to write your three essays. Included in this 130-minute period are 15 minutes dedicated to the document-based question: to read the documents, analyze the documents, and outline your DBQ essay. It is recommended that you use 5 minutes to outline each essay, leaving you with 40 minutes to write the DBQ and 30 minutes to write your two essays selected from each pair. The entire examination takes three hours and five minutes: the 55-minute multiple-choice section, the 15-minute reading period for the document-based question, and the 115-minute essay section.

SPECIFICATIONS FOR THE EXAMINATION

The specifications for the multiple-choice questions are arranged by topic as follows: 35 percent are political history and government questions, 35 percent are social history, 15 percent are diplomatic history, 10 percent are economic history, and 5 percent are intellectual and cultural history. The chronological specifications are as follows: 15 percent from the 1607–1789 period, 45 percent from the 1790–1916 period, 30 percent from the period of 1917 to the present, and 10 percent are a mix of questions from among these time periods, known as cross periods. Few topics before 1607 appear in the multiple-choice questions.

The document-based essay question could come from anywhere in the entire range of U.S. History. Beginning with the 1996 U.S. History AP examination, the Test Development Committee has begun to announce the general area of the next year's DBQ. This announcement is made following the administration of the AP examination. For example, in 1995 the committee announced that the DBQ topic for 1996 would come from the fifty-year period between 1850 and 1900. The time period from which the DBQ will come will be published annually in the *AP Course Description for History*, popularly known among AP teachers as the "Acorn Book." This publication is sent each year to the AP Coordinator for your school, the Educational Testing Service and College Board contact person at your school to whom all the AP materials are mailed.

The College Board U.S. History Test Development Committee, which makes up the examination each year, is well aware of the difficulties AP teachers have trying to adequately cover the history of the United States from the Second World War to the present. You should be aware, however, that the committee is emphatically interested in extending the range of the essay questions through to the present. While this is not a current events course, neither is it one that ends with the Second World War. Of the four essay questions that follow the DBQ on each AP examination, you select two to answer, one from each pair. Generally speaking, you will find that, adding the DBQ to the four essay questions, the five essay questions will be distributed among the topical categories used to describe the multiple-choice questions: political and governmental history; social history; diplomatic history; economic history; and intellectual or cultural history. However, please remember that since political history and social history constitute 70 percent of the specifications for the multiple-choice questions, more than one political or social history essay question may appear. An essay question is rarely concerned with only the colonial era or the period after 1970. For example, you may be asked to illustrate the assertion that presidents are rarely successful in both domestic policy and foreign policy. The instructions might direct you to write on one twentieth-century president and one late-nineteenth-century president. Questions recently appeared, however, on the rise and decline of the Puritans, on the characteristics of religion in the colonial era, and on the election of 1968. You should be aware that the colonial era is defined as ending in 1789.

GRADING THE EXAMINATION

The U.S. History AP examination is a tough, discriminating examination. It is designed to differentiate among the students who take the examination. The average score for the multiple-choice section is 55 to 60 percent correct. You must prepare for the psychological shock of taking a test and feeling that you probably correctly answered only 6 out of every 10 questions. Most students think of themselves as failures if their scores are 60 percent. On this AP examination, 60 percent may be just fine. After you read the 400 multiple-choice questions in this book, you will understand! Each AP examination contains equators, multiple-choice questions that have been given on previous exams. The equators tell the statisticians how this year's group of test-takers compares with those from previous years. That information is included in the eventual decision on where to draw the lines to determine a score of 5, 4, 3, 2, or 1.

Each multiple-choice question is worth 1.125 points for a total of 90 points for the 80 questions. The document-based essay and the second and third essays are each graded on a scale of 0–9. The DBQ essay is 45 percent of the essay portion and the other two essays are each 27.5 percent, or 55 percent of the essay portion. The DBQ score and the two essay scores are multiplied by a weighted factor to give a point total on a 90-point scale. The essay potential score of 0–90 and the 0-90 potential score on the multiple choice section add up to a 0–180 scale. Based on what the statisticians tell College Board officials about the comparison of this year's group of test-takers with those of previous years, plus information gathered during the week-long grading of the essays by a group of AP high school teachers and college professors, the Chief Reader in U.S. History (employed by the College Board, not ETS, Educational Testing Service) decides where to draw the lines on the 0–180 scale to determine the 5, 4, 3, 2, or 1 score. There is no predetermined range of scores nor a predetermined percentage of scores. The Chief Reader's primary concern is to maintain the high standards historically associated with the U.S. History AP examination.

The grading process begins long before the almost 500 U.S. History graders gather to grade the essays. Experienced graders meet for several days to determine the standards for grading each essay. The 0–9 scale is condensed to a working scale of 0–1, 2–4, 5–7, and 8–9. For example, the essay standards delineate the desired qualities of a 5–7 essay. A grader recognizes an essay as a 5–7 essay and then decides whether it is a fair, good, or well-done essay within that range; in other words, 5, 6, or 7.

This oversimplified look at the essay grading procedure is intended to illustrate several points. First, the person grading your essay is well qualified. Second, you are judged against a standard; this is not the place for creating a new form of written communication. Third, you are competing with established national standards of excellence; the harder you work to prepare, the better you will do. Don't think of the 0–1, 2–4, 5–7, and 8–9 categories as grades such as F, D, C, B, and A. The scores rank the essays. The average document-based essay score is around 4.5. The average score for the second essay and the third essay is lower. A different grader grades each of the three essays. The 0–9 scale is not a bell-shaped curve, but a pear-shaped curve. Therefore, anything you do to improve your writing of essays is certain to reap dividends. The standards are established on the 0–9 scale to string out the scores of the students taking the examination. As in many endeavors in life, the top is less crowded than the bottom! Work toward putting yourself in the top. Expect a difficult examination and prepare diligently.

AFTER THE EXAMINATION

The AP examinations are given in May. At your first AP examination for the year, you will receive a booklet containing your identification number and information about reporting AP scores to your college. You may at that time designate which colleges you wish to receive your scores. If you are not a senior, you must initiate the procedure for reporting your scores the following year.

Give careful consideration to the AP policies at colleges you wish to attend. Each academic department within the college or university sets its own standards and policies. Every college catalog contains the school's AP philosophy policy statement, but each department controls that department's policy. Check with the departments concerned to substantiate the disposition of your hard-earned AP scores.

The AP program was designed by secondary schools and colleges to prevent duplication of introductory-level courses. It grew out of student and university complaints that the first-year college courses repeated the content of high school courses. The AP program established a means by which to validate the achievement of freshman college-level knowledge. When a college receives your score, it determines what that score means within the context of its programs and requirements. Depending upon the college or university, there are eight different approaches to your AP score:

1. Credit given in the major field of the examination
2. Credit given, but you must take an upper-level course in that department
3. Credit given, but you must pay for the credit hours
4. Credit given, but the credits are subtracted from the total needed for graduation; in essence, the credits come from your electives outside your major and minor fields

5. Credit given for only one introductory course in the major but not for both; for example, credit given for U.S. History to 1877 or U.S. History since 1865 but not for both

6. No credit given

7. No credit given; advanced standing given, but you must take an upper-level course in that department

8. Combining three or four AP scores gives you sophomore standing; you skip the freshman year and begin college as a sophomore

CLEP EXAMINATION

If your AP score is too low to qualify for college credit, you have another opportunity before you enroll in the appropriate college introductory course. The College Board also offers the College-Level Examination Program, or CLEP. This program was originally designed for the older student entering college. Through individual reading and experience, such a student may feel that he or she already knows the level of material offered in the introductory course. CLEP provides a test to determine proficiency. If you feel that you just missed qualifying for an acceptable AP score, investigate the possibility of taking the U.S. History CLEP examination at your college or university. The examinations are administered early in the semester. Each college establishes its own procedures, fees, and so forth. A few summer hours each day with a good U.S. history textbook to complement your AP course work may bring success. Don't be afraid to ask, and don't be afraid to risk the effort.

AP Course Survival Skills

GETTING THE FACTS

You need two tools for studying and writing history: facts and concepts. No shortcut exists for acquiring a body of factual information. You must work at it! You need facts about individuals, ideas, relationships, groups, conditions, and major societal forces to support the arguments you present. Because history suffers from too many facts, you as a student must select only the appropriate and significant ones to support your concepts.

Always cluster your facts around a concept. A concept is an idea, scheme, or design used to group facts. Be able to elaborate upon each concept with at least three to five factual supports. Don't just touch upon a concept or compile a list of facts. Synthesize the facts and concepts. Use the concept as a frame for a canvas and the facts as details to create the painting.

Use concepts to organize your thoughts toward achieving high-level thinking skills of analysis, synthesis, evaluation, and interpretation. Most essay questions invite or force you to answer within the concepts raised in the question, "The Populist Party foolishly sought political solutions to economic problems. Assess the validity of this statement." What were those economic problems, what were the political solutions proposed, and how does the element of foolishness fit in?

One approach to answering the question is the following outline, which first describes the political solutions before addressing the economic problems. This question divides into two major conceptual areas: political and economic. The wording of the question asks you to comment on the foolishness of the political solutions and why these political solutions did not solve the farmers' economic problems.

I. **Political Solutions**

    A. Sought political reforms designed to make government more responsive to the people

        1. Direct election of senators

        2. Referendum

ROAD MAP

- *Getting the Facts*
- *Reading a Textbook*
- *Reading a Secondary Source*
- *Taking Lecture Notes*

3. Initiative

(Foolishness: They assumed that their demands would lead to a more sympathetic hearing for their problems, yet farmers were becoming a smaller percentage of the population. Farming was changing from a way of life to a business.)

B. Sought political reforms to break the close alliance between the government and big business and the favoritism shown by the government for the rich and powerful

1. Governmental ownership of railroads, telephones, and telegraphs

2. Municipal ownership of public utilities

3. Long haul, short haul discrimination

4. Morgan rescue of the U.S. Treasury

5. Income tax amendment

C. Political reforms to ease the farmers' economic plight

1. Reduce mortgage rates

2. Easement for debt

3. Free silver

4. Stop favoritism of high tariff

(Please remember that this is only a conceptual outline. All or most of the following facts fit under the concept of free silver: Civil War inflation, greenbacks, Granger Movement, Greenback Party, bimetallism, demonetization of silver, Crime of '73, Gresham's law, Bland-Allison Act, cheap money, 16-1, Cross of Gold speech, Bryan vs. McKinley.)

II. Economic Problems

A. Expansion of agriculture

1. Acreage cultivated doubled

2. Increased number of farms

3. Great increases in production

4. Increased number of tenant farmers

(Yet paradoxically the percentage of farmers relative to the rest of the population declined. There were too many marginal farmers, and their political, social, and economic status declined.)

B. Application of machinery to farming

1. New sources of machines and power

2. Costs too high for marginal farmers

C. Application of science to farming

1. New methods for fertilizing

2. Prior tradition of government aid for farmers: Morrill Act, Hatch Act

   (Farming changed from a way of life to a business. The farmers were victims of their own success. They grew too much, overproducing for the new expanded world market in which they now sold their goods.)

III. Conclusion

Society was changing, the agriculturally based society and isolated island communities were disappearing, farmers becoming seen as hayseeds, Jefferson's noble yeoman gone. Federal government had played a role in the expansion of agriculture, and therefore the farmers demand for governmental aid did not suggest a new departure. The new image (not reality) of laissez-faire, however, worked against the farmers' hopes for political solutions.

In addition, by the 1890s the farmers problems were unsolvable by political proposals. The 1890s was a period of party realignment that ended the third party system. Farmers counted for less politically in the new party system emerging.

You may look at the concepts roughed out in this outline, and think that you could never duplicate it. You can with practice, practice, practice! Study to master both facts and concepts. After reading an assignment, think about the concepts involved. The key to answering any essay question is to organize it conceptually. The way to be prepared to organize an essay is to have *already* thought in terms of the concepts surrounding the topic. The first step in answering an essay question is to decide what concepts apply and how you are going to organize an answer. Outline your answer conceptually and fill in the facts to support your concepts. Part of the judgment of your essay is the quality and quantity of factual support. Note that quality of facts is listed first because appropriate and significant facts count more than related facts.

A historian doing research builds from the empirical to the conceptual to the general. He (or she) assembles a collection of facts based upon detective work. Then he brainstorms through the material, conceptualizing it first one way, then another, and selects the method that presents the story best. After sufficiently digesting and analyzing the facts and concepts, he recounts the history in his own words.

A student must answer an essay question in the opposite way that a historian researches history. Identify the concepts and generalizations in the question, then assemble the appropriate facts. Unlike the historian doing research, you select the facts and concepts. The essence of answering an essay is to provide a firm conceptual framework with adequate factual support.

When you encounter an essay question, decide what concepts are appropriate. "The North didn't win the Civil War, the South lost it. Explain." How many ways can a nation lose a war? The South could have lost for political, economic, diplomatic, or military reasons. Politically the South suffered a lack of cohesion, a bad governmental structure for waging a war, poor leadership, division of goals and means, and the burden of simultaneously creating a new government. Economically the South suffered from a lack of resources, the overwhelming might of the North, too few banks, mismanagement of resources, too little industry, and structural defects such as a poor railroad system. Diplomatically the South proved unable to gain allies, to find an outlet for its cotton, or to receive recognition as a nation. Militarily the South may have pursued outdated military strategy and tactics, lacked a unified command structure, and been hampered by too little attention to organization and discipline. You ideally should select at least three to five major concepts for answering the question with three to five facts supporting each concept. Which concepts you select is determined by which concepts you understand well enough to write about and which concepts you feel you have sufficient facts to support. A conceptually sound essay without factual support is inadequate. A conceptually weak essay with excellent facts is also inadequate. Always ask yourself: What are my conceptual arguments and are they factually supported?

You might consider some of the following economic concepts for an essay question dealing with economics: competition, scarcity, supply and demand, resource allocation, opportunity cost, technology, invention, industrialization, interdependence, conservation, and land use patterns. A question concerning an increasing or decreasing economic role for the federal government should include a consideration of the simple question of who gained and who lost from the shift in policy. Which individuals, classes, sections, regions, leaders, parties, ideas, or forces won? The decision to create the Interstate Commerce Commission in 1887 was a victory for something over something even if it was a hollow victory. Think and analyze before you write. You otherwise run the risk of writing the following: "And so, to solve some kind of problem they created the ICC, and lived happily ever after." What problem? Who is they? Lived happily ever after? Such writing is so easy to grade!

You might include some of the following concepts for a question concerning beliefs and ideas: values, sovereignty, equality, liberty, natural rights, attitudes, ideology, cultural conflict, liberty versus order, religion, myth, individualism, and moral beliefs.

Decide what political concepts apply to a political question. Three great ideas—liberty, equality, and fraternity—dominated both the French Revolution and its subsequent historiography. One cannot write anything on the French Revolution that ignores these ideas. An American historian once reduced the period of the Confederation and Constitution to four concepts: nation-making, federalism, the creation of a new colonial system (Northwest Ordinance, equal status for new states), and the reconciliation of liberty and order. Suppose you were asked the political significance of the era of the Articles of Confederation and the Constitution. Any essay including these four concepts backed by strong factual support certainly captures the significance of the Confederation and Constitution period. After you know what concepts to organize your answer around, no essay question is difficult. You may not get the highest grade, but you are certain to pass, and pass high.

If a question asks for the causes of something, be aware of the diverse explanatory concepts that surround the general concept of causation. Differentiate between long- and short-run causes. Remember that most events have multiple causes, and assign relative weight or significance to a few. That is, identify one as the major cause, a second as the second most important, and lump the rest together as contributing causes. Don't forget failure as a cause, since the new in history often springs from the defects of the old. Certainly one of the causes of the adoption of the Constitution was the failure of the Articles of Confederation.

Cause questions implicitly or explicitly invite elaborating on results. Try to define how the results relate to the causes. Did the causes change over a period of time so that the results were influenced by new factors? One difficulty with cause-and-result questions is the problem of success. Don't make the mistake of reading history backward. Try to evaluate the results against the goals and intentions. Sometimes the situation changes, and creates new problems or new goals. Toward the end of the Vietnam War, for example, the United States refused to agree to a ceasefire until the North Vietnamese agreed to return all our prisoners of war. The safe return of our POWs was not a goal at the beginning of the war! During the course of the war, we redefined what we considered an acceptable ending of our involvement in Vietnam.

Many subconcepts are attached to the concept of change, a frequent theme in history essay questions. First, don't forget the power of the twin forces of stability and inertia. Continuity characterizes human society more than change. Use the concept of continuity to refine and specify the elements of change you discuss. There are many types of change: social, political, economic, cultural, policy; different speeds of change, such as revolutionary and evolutionary; and planned and unplanned change. Be aware of the possibility of different reactions for different aspects of society to events and ideas. Liberty and equality moved the Founding Fathers to independence, but not to freeing their slaves. Change implies the word "new." Identify the consequences of change, new policies, new goals, and new organizations. Change occasionally throws off the new, and returns to a former policy or accents features of an older policy. Change can look backward as well as forward.

Finally, be alert to apply a model of change. Throughout your study of American history you will encounter various models to explain historical phenomena. The most famous is probably Crane Brinton's *The Anatomy of Revolution*. Brinton studied the English, American, French, and Russian revolutions, and identified stages and events common to all of them. In the initial stages of each revolution, the intellectuals transfer their allegiance from the old government to a new revolutionary ideal. For example, in the American Revolution the ideal is liberty and independence. Each revolution contains a period during which two governments coexist, the old authority (British colonial authorities) and the new revolutionary government (Sons of Liberty and Continental Congress). The uninterested citizen is torn between the two governments, whereas the dedicated revolutionary easily gives his allegiance to just one. This period in a revolution is called *dvoevlastie,* an untranslatable Russian word that means dual power and dual sovereignty, two governments, both powerful and both legitimate. This aspect of Brinton's model makes the 1773–1776 period much clearer. Don't superficially and indiscriminately apply models, however. Make sure your model applies and illuminates or don't use it.

READING A TEXTBOOK

Your textbook is the chief source for the building blocks, the facts and concepts, of American history. A good knowledge of American history provides the background for seeing how people, events, and ideas fit into the larger picture. There is no easy way to acquire a body of factual knowledge. The process is initially frustrating, but as you learn more history you begin to be able to relate ideas and events to one another. You might study the New Deal reforms of the 1930s as if something like this had never happened before in American history, or you can recognize that attacks on the money trust, attempts to regulate big business, and efforts to mitigate the suffering of the poor are all concepts with deep roots in American history. The first approach is like beginning the study of a foreign language. The second is like curling up on the sofa with an old friend.

Read your textbook assignments as soon as they are assigned. Many students make the mistake of thinking that since only reading is involved they can read two or three chapters at once. Reading a chapter is not the same as studying a chapter, and not the same as understanding a chapter. Look for generalizations, explanations, and interpretations as you read. Textbook authors do not hide their topic sentences; they are usually the first sentence in each paragraph.

Never simply begin reading a textbook. First look through the entire assignment—notice the chapter title, the subheadings, and all the picture captions, cartoons, graphs, and so forth. Become familiar with the topic before you read. Second, skim the assignment. Put a piece of white paper or a card on the page and go down a column in ten seconds. You will pick up a few words or phrases. Now read the assignment. You might even read one subsection at a time. Next, skim it again. This approach is preferable to reading the entire assignment twice. Concentrate when you read. Reading only words is a waste of time. If someone asks you what you have read when you finish you should be able to say more than simply "fifteen pages." You might as well have read it backward!

Recent research on reading comprehension indicates that those who learn material keep going over and over it until they understand. Don't get discouraged. Comprehension rates differ from student to student. Another technique is to read the first and last paragraphs of the assignment. Still another is reading the first sentence of each paragraph before or after reading the assignment. Teachers do students a disservice by calling it a "reading assignment." For the student it is a "study and mastery assignment."

READING A SECONDARY SOURCE

You will occasionally encounter a secondary source: a journal article, a monograph, or an interpretation. The author usually hits you between the eyes with his thesis: "This author believes that..." "In this article I will prove that..." "One cannot escape the conclusion that slavery was an unprofitable economic burden on the South."

Ask yourself: What is the author trying to prove? Most secondary source arguments are so emphatically stated that they are overstated. What are the author's assumptions? What is his point of view? How does this source compare to other sources you have read? Teachers assign secondary sources to illustrate a point of view on a disputed concept. Ask yourself what the concept is and what point of view is represented. This is the stuff from which essay questions spring.

An article that concludes that colonial Boston was becoming less economically and socially democratic as the Revolution approached states only that. Rural Massachusetts may well have been quite democratic in land distribution, social democracy, political rights, etc. The first source does not exclude the second interpretation. Of course, both points of view enliven an essay, "How Democratic Was Colonial America?" Be critical as you read; be an active participant in the study of history.

TAKING LECTURE NOTES

Use a pen; pencil notes smear.

Read all textbook assignments and additional reading before, not after, the lecture. A lecture organizes the material around a particular theme with specific factual support. The emphasis and organization may be new to you, but the facts and the topic should not be. You run the risk of missing significant points while you puzzle over what a Sacco and Vanzetti is (a new car, camera, book?). Listen intently to the beginning and end of the lecture for a restating of the thesis and how it relates to the other history you have been studying. Ask yourself: What are the major concepts around which the lecture is based? For example, most textbooks do not discuss the First, Second, Third, etc., Party Systems. The presidential candidates and the parties obviously do not change, just the organizational scheme.

As soon as possible after the lecture, read your notes to see if they make sense. You will probably find that you left holes, intending to go back to fill in the material later. Notetakers often write furiously as the lecturer says, "There are three main reasons for the failure of the Articles of Confederation." You write down only two! He moved on to another topic before you finished all three. It will do little good to open your notebook the night before an examination if you discover gaps in your notes. By going over your notes within a few hours you forestall many potential problems. Leave spaces periodically to allow room for amplification and for facilitating a visual retention of the material. Check the spelling of historical terms immediately. To believe a student is doing his best is difficult when his essay on Gilded Age politics spells the word as "Guilded" or "Gilted."

At the end of each lecture you should summarize the lecture in your notebook in a three-by-five inch box. The outline for the Populism essay question, "What are Facts and Concepts" ("The Populist Party foolishly sought political solutions to economic problems. Assess the validity of this statement.") would look as follows:

pol reforms	a) more dem, dir of sen, ref, init
	b) anti big bus, RR, tel, tel (govt owned) pub util, long, sh, Morgan Bonds, income tax
	c) eco-mort, debt, 16-1, lo tariff, inflation, B-A Act, Granger laws
eco probs	a) expan-acreage, farms, production, tenants
a business	b) new costs-mach, hurt marginal farmers
	c) new use of science-govt sponsored Morrill, Hatch
changes	TJ's quote, hayseed, la-faire att, 3rd Party System ending, symbol, election of 1896, free silver

Reread your notes again and again; commit the boxed summary to memory. Specific numbers regarding the increase in farm acreage and the number of farms are impressive when you use them to support the concept of an overexpanded agricultural system. A boxed summary links quality facts to quality concepts. Periodically review as if you were studying for an examination. In preparing for essay exams concentrate on understanding the concepts. When studying for multiple-choice questions you need more precise knowledge. One key to multiple-choice is to ask yourself as you study: "What is the significance of ...?" It is not enough to know what the Morrill Act did; what was the significance of the Morrill Act?

Pay attention to chronology. Anchor your knowledge with a few dates and be able to place events, people, and ideas in proper chronological order.

How to Write an Essay

THE ESSAY AS AN OPPORTUNITY

An essay examination is an opportunity to display thinking, organizing, and writing skills. Practice thinking when you study. Only through effort do you learn the highest forms of intellectual activity: generalizing, analyzing, interpreting, and evaluating.

An essay gives you the freedom to make a statement in a unique way, but first you must have an argument worth writing and reading. Avoid the temptation to write everything you know or to tell a pleasant story.

An essay allows you to demonstrate your ability to organize material. Everyday conversation is disorderly; writing should not be. Think through and organize answers to practice essay questions. Take a second look at your creation the next day. While working on a project we frequently feel profound, but Monday's masterpiece is often Wednesday's drivel. If possible, give yourself time to reflect on your written work.

The words used in an essay must do more than just communicate. Don't write *about* a subject; write to persuade. Be careful of abstract words such as democracy, progress, success, and individualism. Certain abstract words carry a wide range of definitions and connotations. Take the time to define an abstract word to yourself even if you do not incorporate the definition into your essay. It helps you focus on that aspect of the word the essay question intends.

Use adjectives to convey the amount of generality or specificity needed for a particular sentence. "Merchants led the revolt against Great Britain." "Urban merchants extensively engaged in imperial trade led the revolt against the newly enforced British navigation acts." The first of these two sentences is vague, the second specific. Now look at another sentence. "The U.S. has a democratic government." You could have written that sentence in fourth grade! Is it a parliamentary democracy, representative democracy, direct democracy, or imperfect democracy? Do you mean political, economic, social, or religious democracy? Do you mean democratic in results or in opportunity? Often a single adjective sufficiently describes a noun; for example, "fascist leaders," or "marginal farmers."

The third opportunity offered by essay tests is the opportunity to write. Watch the adults in your life. A major difference between those who are successful and those who are not is their ability to express themselves by written means. Learning how to write concisely gives you an advantage, and the only method of learning how to write is to write. Mastering writing is hard work, and must be redone each generation. Even the children of Ph.Ds must learn punctuation and vocabulary usage. Concentrate on mastering the basics. Nothing you ever learn matches the supreme sense of self-confidence you feel knowing that you know how to write. Knowledge is power; mastering the communication of knowledge is exhilarating power.

RULES TO FOLLOW IN WRITING ESSAYS

After you have decided what you want to write, the writing of an essay is a race among the amount of paper you have, the clock on the wall, the ink in your pen, and the muscles in your hand. First, know your history; second, organize your thoughts; third, present your arguments; and fourth, support them.

Taking a test is scary. Allay those fears by adequate study. If you have studied, you know more than you think, and your initial sense of panic is unjustified. Budget your time, for you have plenty. Delay writing your essay for approximately one-fifth to one-fourth of the allotted time. (For a fifty minute test do not write for at least ten minutes.) If you have more than one essay, outline all your answers before you write a single essay. If you are given a choice, choose your questions carefully after reading the directions and the wording of each question. Think about the question. Do you understand it? Watch for absolute words—never, all, only, every, and so forth. Quickly begin to jot down ideas and facts about all the questions you are answering. Don't forget to number your answers correctly.

Make conceptual arguments in your essay, provide factual support, and move on. Some students pound a single point, believing that constant restating adds to an essay. Avoid lengthy discussion of minor or peripheral material.

When you are finished, briefly read your essay and check for grammatical errors and misspellings. The omission of a single word may change the meaning of your essay. A student occasionally begins an essay with one argument, realizes he has better support for the opposite viewpoint, and changes the remainder of the essay without changing the introduction. For example, he answers an essay on slavery as the sole cause of the Civil War by agreeing with the statement in the introduction and proving that there were multiple causes in the body of his essay.

ORGANIZING YOUR ESSAY

The first rule of organizing an essay is understanding that there are no standard patterns of organization to follow in cookbook fashion. The nature of the material, the purpose of the essay, and the potential grader determine the pattern of organization. Many teachers insist upon a five paragraph format—introduction, three well developed paragraphs, and a conclusion. The wording of some questions, however, does not fit the five paragraph pattern. "In the 1790s, the infant United States was confronted by the hostile policies of the two European superpowers. Assess the validity of this statement." You might organize your answer around at least three broad conceptual points, being careful to include both Great Britain and France. Or you could use a four paragraph format, one for each nation in the body of your essay, and incorporate some concepts within the introduction and the conclusion.

Organize your answer according to the key words in the question—list, compare, contrast, define, discuss, illustrate, explain, defend, differentiate, outline, summarize, and assess. An essay is written in the form of a thesis or argument defending a position or point of view. Substantiate concepts with specific facts. Concrete details should fit in with one another and with the appropriate concepts. Stalin died March 5, 1953. Broke your train of thought, didn't it? An inappropriate fact thrown into an essay in order to impress a grader with your depth of knowledge usually has the opposite effect.

A question often permits choice in organization. "In the 1790s, Great Britain and France interfered with our domestic politics, violated our neutral rights, and prevented us from achieving our foreign policy goals. Assess the validity of this generalization." One approach is to write three paragraphs in the body of your essay, one for each conceptual generalization concerning domestic politics, neutral rights, and foreign policy goals. Suppose you feel weak in one area, though, such as violation of our neutral rights. Do you want a skimpy, two sentence paragraph sandwiched between two healthy paragraphs? An alternative is to organize the answer around the two countries rather than the three concepts.

In the first approach you discuss the concept itself, and trace it through British and French policies. Along the way you should introduce distinctions between these nations and explain shifts in policy. This organization is an effective method to emphasize differences between something that initially seemed similar. For example, the degree of French interference in our domestic affairs far exceeded Great Britain's. Be careful to remember to focus constantly on the concept.

In the second approach the focus is on France rather than on French violations of our neutral rights or on French interference with our domestic politics. You should treat the three concepts in the same order within both your French and British paragraphs. If you begin the French paragraph with the violation of our neutral rights, begin the British paragraph the same way. A disadvantage of this organization is that it may leave the grader wondering if you answered the question.

Answering an essay question requires a plan. In order to answer an essay you must first understand what is being asked. The first five things to do in answering an essay are to read the question, read the question, read the question, read the question, and read the question. Like reading problems in mathematics, the phrasing is what gives students trouble. Underline the key words or phrases in the question.

Approach an essay with this format: "It is suggested that ... however ... because...." Suppose you were asked, "Slavery was the sole cause of the Civil War. Assess the validity of this statement." In your analysis, say to yourself, *it is suggested* that slavery was the sole cause of the Civil War; *however,* this is only partially true (or is true, or isn't true) *because* of the following reasons. Address the validity of the statement conceptually and support your *however* with *because* concepts and facts.

Outline an answer before writing. Use a topic, phrase, or sentence outline, whichever you prefer, but watch the time. If you are unorganized, jot down on scrap paper all the concepts and facts pertaining to the answer, and then organize the essay. The final picture doesn't emerge by itself; you must outline because otherwise your essay will resemble the transcript of a monologue. In conversation you keep talking until the listener gets your point, but in writing you don't have the advantage of watching facial expressions to determine if the reader understands.

The sequence of conceptual points should be carefully planned. Put conceptual assertions in their approximate order of difficulty, with the most complex or interesting either at the end, to finish your essay on a high note, or at the beginning, to get the grader's attention.

Each one of your conceptual points should reveal something about the central topic. Your basic assumptions must be as explicit as possible. Be sure not to contradict assumptions.

Test generalizations by thinking of exceptions and counterarguments. The essay grader knows the counterarguments; therefore, you must address them. Either explain the counterarguments fully or put them in a subordinate clause. "The argument that slavery would have died naturally west of the 100th meridian is a hypothesis that assumes slavery was primarily tied to cotton culture. It was instead a racial institution...." This proves that you understood, considered, and dismissed that argument because you had a better explanation.

THE BEGINNING PARAGRAPH

Introductory paragraphs are difficult to write. A good beginning paragraph has a clear, precise topic sentence that unequivocally states your main idea. Precision is crucial in the beginning paragraph. Don't be too broad, including ideas that the essay will not address, or too narrow, omitting ideas or limiting your eventual scope. Let your introduction lead into the body of your essay. You may state your thesis by rewording the question in the form of an argumentative statement.

History students frequently link their essay to inappropriate, if authoritative, historiography. If the question asks what caused the Civil War, do not build your essay around the remark that the Civil War began with the initial arrival of blacks in 1619 because you have assumed the responsibility for filling in the years between 1619 and 1861. Argue instead that the institution of slavery created political and economic differences too profound for compromise, or that the existence of blacks, emphasizing slavery as a racial system rather than a system of labor, was the root cause of the war. Either statement is more precise than the mere arrival of blacks. Historians who begin with that argument continue to develop it; students usually have difficulty filling in the intervening years. Constantly ask yourself: What does the question ask, what is my thesis, is my thesis manageable?

THE CONCLUDING PARAGRAPH

The concluding paragraph is your last impression on the grader. A conclusion should strengthen your essay, not undermine it. Don't hastily throw a conclusion together. Think about what you have written. If the essay is long, write a brief summary of your main points. Avoid a mere recapitulation of your essay, but don't introduce new ideas. Another possible ending is to elaborate briefly on your thesis in the introduction.

You may introduce new material in a conclusion if you are not making a new conceptual point. After carefully describing specific causes of the Civil War, you might make some short comments on the causes of war in general. Move from the specific to the general. "The Civil War, like all wars, illustrates man's inability to compromise. Emotion renders compromise either impossible to achieve or impossible to sustain. Moral righteousness and practical politics cannot coexist."

Another exception to the rule against introducing new material is the essay that describes the aftermath or result of something. An essay describing the achievements of blacks during Reconstruction might end on a negative or positive note. For instance, racial equality was written into the Constitution although later ignored. "The civil rights laws represented a deferred promise of equal rights. The South slumbered until injustices awakened the North to effective intervention to give blacks minimum legal equality. What might have been in the 1860s was achieved by the bitter struggles of the 1960s. The second Reconstruction completed the promise of the first."

End an essay strongly. Don't confess that your essay probably is not worth reading. A conclusion is not the place for apologies for inadequate preparation, acknowledgement of exceptions to your thesis, or concession to opposing ideas. Deal with possible contradictions to your thesis in the body of the essay. Leaving objections out until the end suggests that you just thought of the points and threw them in, like a cook throwing a missing ingredient on top of a half-baked cake. Don't end an essay with a smiley face, "The End," or a dramatic signature. These give the impression you are trying to get by on personality instead of knowledge.

Nine Sample Student Essays with Grader Comments

Formerly all the essays on the U.S. History AP examination were graded on a scale of 0 to 15. Now all the essays are graded on a 0–9 scale. In actual practice the 0–9 scale is divided into the following categories: 0–1, 2–4, 5–7, and 8–9. Categories assist the grader in quickly assessing an essay and then judging where that essay fits within the category. For example, if the essay falls in the 5–7 category, is it a 5, 6, or 7? Essays are arrayed along the full breadth of the scale in order to differentiate, in the final analysis, between the good student and the truly outstanding student. The graders consider a 7 to be a very good essay, but not as well-written or as well-organized as an 8–9 essay.

No matter what skills you have at this moment, you can learn to write essays in the upper range of the 5–7 category. If you know your history, you can write an acceptable essay by following the rules and guidelines. If you do not know U.S. history, no level of style or grammar will hide your ignorance.

THREE STUDENT ESSAYS—THEODORE ROOSEVELT VERSUS WOODROW WILSON

The first three student essays that follow were written to answer the question below. Look at the standards that follow the third essay, then read the essays and the grader's comments and explanation of the standards.

> *"Theodore Roosevelt and Woodrow Wilson differed greatly, but both were effective presidents." Assess the validity of this statement by comparing Theodore Roosevelt and Woodrow Wilson as presidents.*

ROAD MAP

- *Three Student Essays— Theodore Roosevelt Versus Woodrow Wilson*
- *Six Student Essays— Women's Movement Since 1945*

FIRST STUDENT ESSAY

(1) Woodrow Wilson and Theodore Roosevelt were both good presidents, but in their own ways. They both avoided certain things that could cause controversial and hazardous situations or pressure. They both started out as conservatives, but as things went on, they went their own ways. They didn't necessarily turn away from conservatism, though just taking their own separate parts.

(2) The Presidents were somewhat equal as conservatives. Both spent their early lives in a relatively secure family, although Wilson went through a long spell of poverty and frustration. They both went along with their party tradition of laissez-faire. Both of them stood for the general good welfare of the country—the middle class. Both were against, though they didn't come right out and say it, labor and the Populist movements. They were suspicious of the trusts because they were a problem to politics, but either didn't know exactly what to do. They eventually converted to the progressive views.

(3) Even though Wilson and Roosevelt were both conservative and eventually progressive, the difference was in their way of doing it. Wilson, as an early conservative, was a man who believed in reasoned philosophy of politics. As opposed to Wilson, Roosevelt without much patience pressed toward violence. The early Wilson left himself enough room for reform in his philosophy, though nothing more than a shift of emphasis. Roosevelt on the other hand, didn't leave himself a "reform cause." Roosevelt stuck with what had been there with him, he was not a man of many changes. Wilson went forward with the new, though at the same time he combined the old with the new.

(4) In the end, they both switched to progressivism because that philosophy had more opportunity for their political careers. They both reached progressivism from different ways. Roosevelt was prompted by ambition to a violent change in language. Wilson simply used his "reform cause."

(5) All in all, they were two men who were alike as far as conservativism and progressivism were as concepts. But how it was done, was a different story. Roosevelt, who seemed like the stubborn type, for instance fighting against trusts, who muscled through things, though stayed out of sticky situations. Wilson was a man of reason, who could sit down and figure it out, but he could be tough, when needed.

Comments on the First Student Paper

1st Paragraph: The question doesn't ask if the two were "good" Presidents. Use "effective," "innovative," or "ineffective"; that is, any word is more powerful than "good." You are free to agree, to disagree, or to agree partially with the wording of a question. This paper does not take a strong stand; it has no thesis statement. The writer suggests differences between the two, but "own ways," "certain things," and "as things went on" do not present the differences as concepts. This paragraph illustrates the weakness of using too many pronouns in writing. The essay writer knows what the pronouns refer to, but the grader does not. If this student knows what he means, he is not communicating this knowledge. You will not get the benefit of the doubt from the grader.

A grader assumes a grade of 5 when he begins to read an essay. This first paragraph gives the impression that this is no more than a 1–2 range essay. Do first impressions count? Of course they do!

2nd Paragraph: This paragraph illustrates a fatal trap of writing—a pleasant story pleasantly told. "Once upon a time there were two presidents who loved their mothers, believed in goodness, the middle-class, and the American way, and so they became Progressives." There is no transition from the first paragraph to the second. After concluding that the two had taken "their own separate parts," he begins by labeling them "somewhat equal," a contradiction. Their early lives are insignificant unless the student relates them somehow to their later careers as presidents, which he does not. The student has a weak understanding of their differing economic philosophies, the New Nationalism and New Freedom, and no sense of change over time in their economic thinking. If both men were for the middle class, anti-labor, and anti-Populist, the student should explain apparent contradictions such as the Clayton Act and the Coal Strike of 1902. He displays no sophistication on the antitrust issue. This is an excellent opportunity to bring up the question of the degree to which Roosevelt's trustbusting reputation was deserved. He doesn't.

3rd Paragraph: Once again a grader senses a missed opportunity. Where is the sense of growth and change over time for the two politicians? This is also an opportunity to address the question of how conservative the Progressive movement was. Was it a liberal or conservative movement? Based on this paper we shall never know. This student suggests that the two differed in methods but not goals, but this difference could be much more fruitfully developed. "Violence" is a poor word choice for describing Roosevelt. Wilson's "reasoned philosophy of politics" looks interesting conceptually, but this point is not supported factually. As shown by what? Wilson is credited as being more innovative, a man who "combined the old with the new." As shown by what, where, how? Here is a missed opportunity to emphasize their respective policies toward tariffs, banking, trusts, and leading Congress. The writer implies that Roosevelt was more conservative in his methods, but the point is undeveloped.

4th Paragraph: This paragraph repeats much of the earlier drivel. Does the writer really believe that these two presidents embraced Progressivism only to help their political careers?

5th Paragraph: The writer never defines or describes conservatism or Progressivism. At the end of the essay the grader must wonder if the student understands these two concepts. He does seem to know that Roosevelt avoided sticky issues such as the tariff, currency, and banking, but they are not stated. The description of Wilson as a leader who "could be tough, when needed" deserves examples as illustrations.

The grade for this paper is a 2 only because the writer understands too much to put him in the 0–1 range. It is a poor essay. Please note that the numbers in the margin are used only to help you coordinate the student essay and the grader's comments. Never number your paragraphs.

SECOND STUDENT ESSAY

(1) In analyzing the similarities and differences of foreign and domestic policies of Theodore Roosevelt and Woodrow Wilson, one invariably finds that there were many more differences than similarities in their ideas and actions.

(2) Comparing the ideas of these two men as presidents, one finds that they didn't agree on too much. However, there were two important things they did agree on. First, in domestic policy, both these men tried desperately to be extreme trust-busters. They were very against the big companies ruling everything and running the "little guy." However, instead of "trust-busting" they ended up more regulating them. On the subject of foreign policy, they both wanted to get rid of the man who called himself President of Mexico, Huerta. They felt he was only hurting the common masses and Wilson even went so far as to support the constitutionalists (Presidential rebels) to try to build a new, more solid Mexican government.

(3) Between these two men, the differences were enormous. First, in domestic policy, Woodrow Wilson acted on issues that Teddy Roosevelt wouldn't touch because they were "too much trouble." Wilson attacked the bankers and started the Federal Reserve and he wanted lower tariffs through the Underwood-Simmons Act. He was very economy-minded. Roosevelt however, was more into things like conservation that weren't such a public issue. Also, Roosevelt was into New Nationalism to regulate monopolies while Wilson was into New Freedom to destroy them.

(4) In foreign policy, Roosevelt was a vicious go-getter. He frequently used his "big stick" and violently jumped right into foreign affairs. In his corollary to the Monroe Doctrine, he showed this by stating the U.S. should play "policeman" and use intervention in foreign affairs and he acted on this by being the mediator in the Russo-Japanese War. On the other hand, Wilson was thoroughly disgusted by "big stickism." He believed in "watchful waiting" and a foreign policy of helpfulness to more than 30 other nations. We can see their ideas on foreign policy and how to handle sticky situations were oceans apart.

(5) In conclusion, seeing the results of the work of these two men, it is a matter of opinion whether one favors Roosevelt's "go get' em" attitude or Wilson's conservative waiting. These two men, who had basically the

same background, obviously had many differences. However, it seems these differences benefited America's domestic and foreign policies at the time in innumerable ways. Both men felt they were doing the right thing and truly worked for the good of America. One cannot say Wilson's or Roosevelt's policies were better because they were just too different. No matter how different they were, though, they seemed to have come to good ends.

Comments on the Second Student Paper

1st Paragraph: This student begins with an excellent thesis statement that promises to address both domestic and foreign policies and to prove that there were more differences than similarities. She will support this thesis by referring to specific ideas and actions. What a positive beginning!

2nd Paragraph: The euphoria fades because of the awkward organization of the second paragraph. It has a thesis, which is preferable to having none. After finishing the first paragraph by stating that there were more areas of disagreement, though, she begins the second paragraph by stating the areas of agreement. The student seems to understand Wilson's eventual adoption of Roosevelt's regulatory approach toward trusts, but supplies no specifics. Mixing domestic and foreign policies is an awkward organizational scheme, but it is within the student's premise that their ideas differed. Their respective Mexican policies are poor choices for illustrating differences in foreign policy. The student's knowledge of Roosevelt's comments on Mexico is quite impressive, since this information is not found in most textbooks. The ultimate weakness of this paragraph is the student's use of only two factual supports to prove major areas of agreement existed between the two men.

3rd Paragraph: The organizational awkwardness continues. This paragraph addresses the differences between the two. The factual quality has improved. The student knows that Wilson attacked issues Roosevelt backed away from. The specifics are much better than the first essay, but one wonders what "economy-minded" means to the student. Roosevelt did emphasize conservation, but calling conservation not much of a public issue is incorrect. Finally, the succinct characterization of the New Freedom and the New Nationalism is accurate, but deserves elaboration on the eventual outcome after Wilson won in 1912. The wording detracts from the facts; politicians are not "into" their programs.

4th Paragraph: This paragraph compares the methods used by the two presidents to achieve their foreign policies. The factual support is correct, but it is handled with only minimum adequacy. The U.S. added the Roosevelt Corollary to the Monroe Doctrine. But where, why, for what reasons, how was it received, what other issues did it raise? Wilson pursued "watchful waiting" in regard to Mexico. Does the student believe it aptly describes Wilson's foreign policy everywhere? It could be so used, but she misses the opportunity.

5th Paragraph: In the conclusion, as in the rest of the essay, there are too many fuzzy general statements and too few specific facts. The student fails to take a definite stand. This paper illustrates what graders call "a touch." The student "touches" on facts and concepts without development and explanation. The following lists the factual points the student "touched" without elaborating on them or weaving them together: trustbusting, Huerta, banking and Federal Reserve, lower tariffs and the Underwood-Simmons tariff, conservation, the New Nationalism and the New Freedom, big stick, Roosevelt Corollary, Russo-Japanese War, and watchful waiting.

The grade for this essay is a 4.

THIRD STUDENT ESSAY

(1) In comparing the foreign and domestic policies of Theodore Roosevelt and Woodrow Wilson, while in office, the general evidence seems to prove that the policies of these two men greatly differed from one another and the similarities between the two were minimal.

(2) Domestic policy was one of Woodrow Wilson's strong points. He passed much legislation and was very aggressive. Theodore Roosevelt on the other hand passed only a mere amount of legislation and was rather withdrawn. When Roosevelt took office a sweeping reform movement had just begun, it went from stamping out corruption at the municipal level to solving the great national problems growing out of the industrialization and urbanization of the nineteenth century. Roosevelt sought to head the movement while at the same time tempering it with "sane leadership." Legislation passed under Roosevelt consisted of the Hepburn Act in 1906, which increased the power of the Interstate Commerce Commission to regulate the nation's railroads. The Pure Food and Drug Act of 1906 prohibited the manufacture and sale of adulterated foods. A federal Meat Inspection Act was also passed. Roosevelt created the Inland Waterways Commission in 1907 and he also enforced the Sherman Antitrust Act against major corporations. Roosevelt never touched three areas while in office: banking, tariff, and antitrust.

(3) On the contrary Woodrow Wilson not only attacked these three but solved them. He did so with such legislation as the Underwood-Simmons Tariff Act of 1913 which effected the first sizable reduction of custom rates since the Civil War and provided for a permanent graduated income tax. The Federal Reserve Act of 1913 reorganized the American banking and currency systems and placed them under the control of the Federal Reserve Board appointed by the President. The Clayton Anti-trust Act of 1914 legalized labor unions, peaceful pickets, boycotts, and strikes while it limited the use of labor injunctions. The Federal Trade Commission Act was also passed under Wilson in 1914. It provided for the supervision and regulation of interstate trade.

(4) As for foreign affairs the situation is the reverse. Roosevelt was the aggressor. He was quick to take sides and he liked other countries to be

aware of the power of the U.S. and the fact that the U.S. was ready and willing to fight to protect itself and its possessions. Woodrow Wilson conversely took the stand of neutrality. He preferred peace and did not intervene unless absolutely necessary and then only if compromise was not possible. While Roosevelt was in office he strengthened the army and navy and started construction of the Panama Canal. He added a corollary to the Monroe Doctrine making the U.S. virtually responsible for seeing that the Latin American countries met international obligations. Roosevelt demonstrated strength by the diplomatic method he used to get the Panama Canal, by U.S. actions during the Venezuela blockade in 1902, by the Alaskan boundary dispute in 1903, and also by sending the Great White Fleet on a peaceful tour of the world. Roosevelt did mediate twice, once he intervened and it resulted in the Treaty of Portsmouth between Russia and Japan in 1905. The second was in the 1906 dispute between European powers at the Algeciras Conference. Roosevelt won the Nobel Peace Prize in 1906.

(5) While Wilson was in office he kept the U.S. neutral for his entire first term even though World War I had broken out. Wilson watched and waited. He was moderate and considerate. His main desire was to maintain peaceful relations with foreign countries without the threat or use of violence. He displayed this through his willingness to submit differences with Mexico to mediation and his demand for repeal of the Panama Canal toll exemptions and by his proposal to apologize to Colombia and to pay an indemnity of $25,000,000 for the seizure of the Panama Canal Zone. This last was defeated by the Senate. Even when the U.S. had to enter World War I Wilson wanted not only "victory" but world peace. Wilson made a proposal for world peace that included a League of Nations. For this idea and effort he was awarded the Nobel Peace Prize in 1919.

(6) In conclusion, the foreign and domestic policies of these two men greatly differed based on the above information. Roosevelt was much more aggressive in foreign than in domestic policies. He was not afraid of war and liked to make his military strength known. Wilson on the other hand was much more domestically aggressive rather than foreignly aggressive. He worked on solving domestic problems such as tariffs, banking, and antitrusts while remaining neutral as much as possible on foreign affairs. The two men were similar in only a few ways; both had strong ambition, steady nerves, flexible scruples, and tenacity. Both men won Nobel Peace Prizes that dealt with keeping peace.

Comments on the Third Student Paper

1st Paragraph: Compare this thesis statement with the first two papers; it is much stronger.

2nd Paragraph: This paragraph begins by correctly labeling Wilson as a stronger legislative leader than Roosevelt. The student makes the common mistake of stating that the president passes legislation, which detracts somewhat because Congress passes our laws. The president may be for, against, or lukewarm toward a piece of legislation. Roosevelt is correctly called cautious in style and tone. While he was the first Progressive president, the student realizes that the Progressive movement predated him. He realizes that the Progressive movement was a response to problems generated by urbanization and industrialization. Roosevelt did proudly congratulate himself for bringing sane leadership to Progressivism. Remember, he used the derisive term "muckrakers" even though the public accepted the term without his connotation. The Hepburn Act is an example of an impressive quality fact; the date and specifics are included. The other factual support is correct and equally impressive. The student is aware of Roosevelt's caution in banking, tariff, and antitrust. The only flaw in this otherwise excellent paragraph is that the first two sentences give the impression that the paragraph will center on Wilson rather than Roosevelt.

3rd Paragraph: Note the excellent transition from the second to the third paragraph. This whole paragraph presents impressive factual range and depth, especially the detailed knowledge of the Clayton Act.

4th Paragraph: The student sees a reversal in the positions of two men in foreign affairs. Roosevelt is characterized by aggression and Wilson by neutrality. This paragraph contains too many generalizations, such as "the U.S. was ready and willing to fight to protect itself and its possessions." As shown by? Quickly glance at the third paragraph. Specific facts in the fourth paragraph are fewer, but the paragraph is still well done. The student is aware that Roosevelt built up the army as well as the navy. Every student knows the Great White Fleet, but few know Elihu Root's contributions and the subsequent reorganization of the army. The remainder of the paragraph is well done. It needs only a few more specifics.

5th Paragraph: This is an excellent paragraph. The student details Wilson's methods and goals with quality and quantity facts. The Mexico policy could be developed in more depth. The Panama Tolls dispute and the apology to Colombia is impressive, as is the understanding of the larger implications in the League and world peace issues.

6th Paragraph: The concluding paragraph is awkwardly written. It could be strengthened by returning to the original question and emphasizing the effectiveness of the two presidents in domestic affairs and foreign policies. Instead, the student emphasizes the "aggressiveness" of the two, and concludes the essay around a concept that he used to organize his thoughts to differentiate between the two men. The original question asked for both differences and effectiveness. The student should have addressed both briefly in his conclusion.

The grade for this essay is an 8. It was a 9 before the last paragraph.

GRADING STANDARDS

The grading standards for this essay question are as follows:

"Theodore Roosevelt and Woodrow Wilson differed greatly, but both were effective presidents." Assess the validity of this statement by comparing Theodore Roosevelt and Woodrow Wilson as presidents.

8–9
- balanced treatment of both presidents
- good coverage of foreign and domestic policies
- concepts, each supported by 4–5 facts
- analyzes the question by focusing on events, personalities, programs, and political philosophies
- explains similarities and differences
- well written, well organized

5–7
- some imbalance, but deals with both presidents
- may emphasize either foreign or domestic more, but mentions both
- 2–3 concepts or 2 done very well, with 2–3 facts for each
- some analysis, mentions events, personalities, programs, or political philosophies
- attempts to explain similarities and differences
- may contain a few errors

2–4
- imbalance, generalized treatment of both presidents, with weakness in regard to one president
- little consideration of either domestic or foreign for one (or both) presidents
- little or poor conceptualization—few specific facts, weak facts, or inappropriate facts
- similarities and differences muddled or not addressed
- major errors, such as puts Federal Reserve under Roosevelt, Northern Securities case under Wilson

0–1
- generalized discussion, a rambling essay
- conceptualization missing, few facts, little substance
- major errors
- rather inept

Errors startle an essay grader and raise doubts about the student's level of knowledge. When faced with errors, the grader questions his or her assumptions as to the meaning of general, unexplained statements by the student. Errors cause a grader to withhold credit for knowledge not explicitly demonstrated. An accident of haste is easy to recognize. Writing 1812 instead of 1912 is not a major error. Writing "the Guilded Age" instead of "the Gilded Age" causes chuckles. Every grader recognizes that a student is under extreme pressure.

Major errors are significant, however, and keep a student from getting above the lower end of the 5–7 category at best. Confusing the Underwood-Simmons Tariff and the Payne-Aldrich Tariff is significant if you are using the tariff issue to illustrate a major point. If you are just mentioning Wilson's attack on the "triple wall of privilege" and mislabel the tariff, the damage is less significant. Errors are evaluated within the total context of the argument in your essay. Incorrect dates, faulty chronology, and factual mistakes are not as significant as an incorrect emphasis.

A grader wonders about the student who claims that the La Follette Seamen's Act was a major part of Wilson's Progressive legislation. The grader says to himself, "Is that all you are going to mention?" The student need not worry if he or she mentions the La Follette Seamen's Act as typical of the era, as part of the Wilson administration, or as an example of Progressive legislation pushed through without strong presidential support. All three descriptions are accurate enough.

In short, there are errors and there are errors. Minor errors are not held against you, but they slow the adding of points for you. Major errors cast doubts on your essay and cause the grader to wonder how much you really understand. You no longer get the benefit of the doubt. Reduce your potential for errors by adequate study and clear writing.

SIX STUDENT ESSAYS—WOMEN'S MOVEMENT SINCE 1945

The first set of essays contained only three essays; this one contains six. By carefully studying the differences and nuances between the six essays, you can get a better understanding of what separates an average essay from a poor one, and the excellent essay from the average.

The six essays that follow were written to answer the question below. Look at the standards that follow the ninth essay, read the essays, and then read the grader's comments and explanation of the standards.

"What were the issues, successes, and failures for the women's movement from 1945 to the 1980s?"

FOURTH STUDENT ESSAY

(1) Since the 1920s, the women's movement has been a typical American reform movement and like many others, it has shared the same triumphs, setbacks, and heavy opposition. From the days of Lucretia Mott and Susan B. Anthony, the women's movement has taken different goals and routes to amend its aims. In the early twentieth century, women marched in the streets just as civil rights marchers did in the 1960s amid obscentities being yelled at them, violence being perpertrated on them, hate-filled policemen and sexists cursing and kicking them, etc., how-

ever they kept pursuing at it. The methods that each of the women's movements have used have ranged from having patrons sign petitions and trying to influence high and powerful VIPs to speak on behalf of the cause just as many labor and other special interest movements have, to marching and protesting in the streets as all other groups have. The goals of the women's movement have been to achieve better and equal status in American society. They have done this by lobbying for admendments similar to the 19th admendment which gave them the right to vote. The tactics that have been common for this group have been to play off powerful opponents, in this case powerful male chauvanists and sexists to increase there own stance just as a few astute civil rights officials played off conservative Democrats and Republicans to augment their own programs and purposes. The tactics suceeding in some cases that are somewhat in concurrence with the women's movement like the 1973 Roe v. Wade decision that legalized abortion by a divided supreme court.

(2) However, for the women's movement opposition has been a huge adversary. There are many women as well as men who feel that a women cannot and should not be granted certain priviledges as men have. Phyllis Schlafly, one of the leading antifeminist crusaders in the country today has joined thousands of conservative men and women that have been successful enough to block ERA ratifications by the Senate more than once. Along with Schafly there were those who argued that if this women's movement was enacted, that means private facilities meaning men and women would be no more and other arguments that come into play against this movement. Overall, the women's movement like all of the other movements has as the Virginia Slims advertisement says, "come a long way, baby" but women still have many doors that are still closed off to them. But has gained much freedom that at one time was denied to them and to the movement itself.

Comments on the Fourth Student Paper

1st Paragraph: The student begins by digging a hole for himself. Why waste so much time on introductory material before 1945? Does the student not know enough to write on the question itself? A flag comes up in the second sentence, "to amend its aims." Whatever he means by this, it isn't clear. Oh, my, two misspellings—obscenities and perpetrated. What is "it" that women "kept pursuing at it"? Marching? Was marching an issue, success, or failure? He is straying too far from the question. The sentence on the methods of the women's movement and the previous sentence combine to suggest that this student intended to write on any reform question by generalizing about all reform movements.

Finally, a hint of substance in the sentences on goals and the Nineteenth Amendment, although he misspells amendment. The last two sentences in this paragraph are gibberish. Note the "there" and "suceeding." He seems to know that Roe v. Wade (the date is impressive) came out of a divided court, but says nothing about what this has to do with the tactics of the movement, let alone its successes or failures.

My initial reaction to this essay was to ask myself, and by implication the student, "Does it matter that you took a course in American History or that you read the textbook?" Is this not an essay you could have written the second day of school? Other than three names, a well-known court case, and the Nineteenth Amendment, what is in here that shows more than the general knowledge of any reasonably intelligent person?

It is clear that this student has basic knowledge about the topic, but little else.

2nd Paragraph: Now on to the opposition. Is opposition the same as failure? You might write the topic sentence for the paragraph using a portion of the wording of the question: "However, opposition to the women's movement doomed many of its goals to failure." The ERA was blocked in state legislatures, not in the U.S. Senate. He doesn't understand how amendments are ratified, or how to spell privileges.

Knowing Phyllis Schlafly is impressive, although he may mean two different people, based on the changing spelling. The final sentence, the last opportunity to make an impression, doesn't even have a subject!

Overgeneralized and trite, this essay falls into the 0–1 range, probably a 1 because he knows some specifics.

FIFTH STUDENT ESSAY

(1) The women's movement of today is very strong and very positive, however, their movement in 1945 and the 1950s had it's weak points. During the decade between the 1940s and 1950s the women's movement digressed. Fewer women were enrolled in college, fewer women were becoming Ph.D.'s. The United States, unlike many other countries, did not put a great deal of value on our children. This greatly affects the women's fight for equality because they are the sex that produces children and the child is therefore naturally linked with women. This situation is carried to a less severe case today because we know that children are the responsibility of both parents and we acknowledge this, early Americans did not. The child was the mother's.

(2) The women's movement was helped and hindered by the feminists. Many feminists organizations were formed to help women achieve their equality, but as time progressed, the groups were beginning to be taken over by the radical feminists. This takeover drove membership down and took away from the feminists' power. The issue of abortion also played a big part in the women's movement. When a women wanted an abortion, she was supposedly killing a human life; this was her right as a woman, and since this was a woman's issue, the feminist groups must have wanted to support it. This was not necessarily true. All of this tended to drive a wedge between the feminist groups, diminishing their

power and their drive to achieve equality for women. Equality for women is very important to women, but to others it was not and therefore did not receive a great deal of support.

(3) The women's movement of today is aided greatly because of the longer life expectancy of women. In earlier years women would become old enough to have children and barely get them through college when they died. Today women have their children and get them through college and still have twenty or more years to do whatever they would like. Some pursue a career and a few even go back to school themselves. The role of the female, as well as, her equality has come a long way since 1945, Jimmy Carter even brought up the issue of drafting women for non-combat purposes, but was turned down.

Comments on the Fifth Student Paper

1st Paragraph: If you learn nothing else from reading these essays and comments, please remember to answer the question that was asked. Is this paragraph an introduction to an answer, or does it focus on issues, failures, or successes? The grader can't be sure. Some facts on the women's movement are interwoven with some very elementary biology lessons, but there is little here of substance. The facts need concepts to put them in touch with the question. This paragraph gives the impression that the student may know something about this topic. She may not, however, understand the topic conceptually.

2nd Paragraph: This paragraph illustrates the essay's lack of a sense of change over time. It is almost as if the years since 1945 all have the same characteristics. There were differences among women over tactics, but this essay doesn't develop or explain them. The writer seems to just take them for granted. She hints that abortion was not initially an important issue for the women's movement, but she never develops the consequences for the drive for the ERA. The split among the movement's advocates was not as significant as the rise of a solid opposition bloc, the grass roots Right-to-Life Movement, which linked with antifeminists to stop the ERA just short of success. The defeat of the ERA has to be the movement's greatest failure, but we shall never know from this essay.

3rd Paragraph: This paragraph ends the essay, but it doesn't conclude the essay. Was President Carter's proposal a success or failure for the women's movement? Actually, it was never an issue for women. They never advocated the draft for women, but after the issue was raised, women's groups reluctantly supported it. So does that make it a success or failure, or a non-issue? The other information is roughly correct, but how does it relate to any concept in regard to the question?

The grade for this essay is a 3.

SIXTH STUDENT ESSAY

(1) The women's movement since 1945 has gone through several stages and has often become very confused. After the Second World War, many women still worked or wanted to work, but the baby boom often led to the return of women to their homes. In the 1950s, people like Doris Day glorified and honored the housewife with her sweetness and innocence. At the same time, Marilyn Monroe convinced everyone to be as curvaceous and flirtatious as possible. Freud tried to convince women to stay home with the children, as did Dr. Spock. So many confused images for women to follow!

(2) In the 1960s, more and more women went to college. Unfortunately, most dropped out before graduation to marry. It seems that college was the place to find a promising man for a husband.

(3) Women had the right to vote now, and most of the everyday American women were satisfied. Of course, there are always radicals, and as was the case of Black Americans, radicals began to stir things up and the women's movement was split. These new radical women wanted to erase the distinction between men and women. Women won the right to be drafted. This failed when President Carter called a draft and Congress wouldn't let women be drafted after Russia invaded Afghanistan. Women won the right to murder fetuses in Roe v. Wade when the Supreme Court legalized abortion. The abortion issue caused Phyllis Schafley and her anti-ERA movement to join with the Right-to Life anti-abortion movement.

(4) By this time, most American women had dropped out of the women's movement. They had only wanted equal pay for equal work. The movement lost its momentum and is basically nonexistent today.

Comments on the Sixth Student Paper

This concise essay teasingly displays more understanding than it develops. This is a student who studies hard, understands the women's movement, and knows how to say much in a short space; however, this student never ties the conceptual points together. The general chronological framework is the organizational theme more than the issues, successes, or failures of the women's movement. The worst feature is the emotional reference to murder in regard to abortions. A good essayist keeps himself and his own emotions out of an essay. Think of an essay as a reasoned argument rather than an emotional argument, especially if you do not know the grader well. A good grader also keeps his emotions out of the grading process. Help him. I hope Phyllis Schlafly knows how to spell her name. Most of us do not!

This essay has too much information for the 2–4 category. It is just barely a 5.

SEVENTH STUDENT ESSAY

(1) The women's movement can be seen to have had its roots in the civil rights' movement activity of the 1950s and 1960s. The objective of the women's movement was by liberation a woman would gain influence and power. The way the women would gain influence and power is through their job standing. Women discovered that men, both white and black, obtained the top policy positions while women were delegated to the menial types of chores. They recognized the importance of militant, well-publicized pressure groups in an effort to bring about change. Beginning in the 1940s, America witnessed a period of transformation and readjustment. Men were being sent home from war. This conflicted with women's new task of working outside of the home. Men returned with the ideas of the wife in the home while the husbands returned back to their normal jobs. Women had enjoyed working outside of the home and many women remained in the workforce. *Generation of Vipers* stated that women in the household were stripping men of their masculinity and *Lost Generation* was stating that more women were not staying at home. Freud, on the other hand, stated that the only way women could achieve satisfaction was through childbirth. This is the belief that many women moved away from during the beginning of the women's movement. In the period of the 1950s there was the outstanding baby boom. With more children in the household, this made the decision easier for women to remain in the household. There was a large emphasis in this time period on housewife and motherhood. Some 60% of all women attending college dropped out before earning their degree. The emphasis was to go to school and find a husband. After early marriage the women were expected to have children, and support their husbands' careers. Magazines and movies in this time period also depicted women's innocence. Women like Doris Day portraying innocence and Debbie Reynolds' sweetness was the typical stereotype of that time. Marilyn Monroe with no character was another famous actress who portrays a popular stereotype. Magazines also emphasized the housewife role. "Good Housekeeping" and "Ladies Home Journal" stressed the housewife as the hero. A new fascination with sex constructed the "Playboy" magazine. A new mode of style for clothing was also emphasized. Straight skirts, suits, shoulder pads, skinny waists, large breasts, and high heels were the new form of fashion. Women still remained at the bottom of the social scale performing their "pink collar" jobs in the clerical and secretarial areas. Women's main purpose in this time period was to play your cards right and land the right man and be his object of desire.

(2) The 1960s brought about another change in the women's movement. At least half of all women worked. Although working in "women's jobs," they earned only 63¢ to the males' $1. The Civil Rights Act of 1964 started the prohibition of discrimination on the basis of gender. As day care centers emerged more women with preschool children remained in the outside work of the home. The National Organization for Women

emphasized fair pay, equal opportunity, and also for the development of a new egalitarian form of marriage. Books like the *Feminine Mystique* offered arguments supporting women by stating that women didn't have the special ability to raise children and women don't have to stay home. The greatest impact on the feminist movement occurred with the invention of the pill. Women could now control their bodies and plan children around their lives.

(3) The decade of 1970 to 1980 placed even more emphasis on feminism. There was a continuing struggle for existence and equal opportunity; however, the facts told a different story. More women were working but there remained no equal pay for equal work. Women were only earning only 58¢ for every $1 of their male counterpart. With the greater existence of day care, almost 45% of women with preschool children have entered the workforce. Women have also attained some political appointments. G. Ferraro ran for the vice-presidency and the first woman to be appointed to the Supreme Court, Sandra Day O'Connor, among other women in the mayoral and senatorial races. In this time period we also see a deterioration of the movement. Magazines such as MS which placed an emphasis on ideas such as abortion and forums for the improvement in the feminist movement conflicted largely with Good Housekeeping, which stressed domestic issues, house decorating, and often sexual fantasies.

(4) With the passage of the ERA which stated equal pay for equal work and stated that no one shall be denied any rights by basis of sex the feminists from New York, who became known as radicals got a little out of control. Most of them were lesbians, communists, and socialists. They stressed that fundamental change of the individual's identity was necessary. With the decision like Roe v. Wade, which declared abortions legal, was the final dividing point among the feminists and also the declaration of the equal draft, brought the movement to somewhat of an end. Although the women's movement was never unified, until the decade of 1974 to 1984 women continued to vote their fundamental civil rights and values.

Comments on the Seventh Student Paper

1st Paragraph: This verbose essay makes a grader want to get out the scissors. The first paragraph is too long. It is difficult to see the conceptual theme. The student seems to lay the groundwork for the women's movement in the Second World War and the rise of black civil rights activity. Many statements, however, just float over the page. One gets the impression that this paragraph could be cut into individual sentences and pasted together in any order. It is a collection of facts rather than a paragraph. The information is excellent and correct; but a grader can't help but feel sorry for what could have been much better said.

2nd Paragraph: This paragraph repeats the mistakes of the first. The factual information is correct, but the theme of "change" is too weak to form the paragraph around. Change in what direction, toward what, away from what, or led by whom? A much better topic sentence would read as follows: "In the 1960s many factors combined to revitalize the women's movement, with women playing a more significant role." A subtheme of the paragraph would be the accomplishments of the decade: the birth control pill, the Civil Rights Act of 1964, and the formation of the National Organization for Women. Two of these achievements, the pill and the Civil Rights Act, were not due to the women's movement. Better organization would have greatly strengthened this information. As it is, this paragraph is conceptually weak.

3rd Paragraph: The reference to feminism is puzzling. After reading the paragraph it is clear that the student should have written: "In the decade from 1970 to 1980 there was a continuing struggle for equal opportunity; however, the facts told a different story." The reference to more emphasis on feminism was not developed. The student instead paints a picture of some small victories and continuing difficulties. Again, good information in a conceptually weak paragraph.

4th Paragraph: This paragraph unravels and deteriorates. The student leaves the grader guessing. Does he really understand the issues, successes, and failures of the women's movement or has he instead merely listed events and ideas associated with the women's movement? The ERA was passed by Congress but never ratified by the required number of states. There was a New York feminist group that legally took the nickname "The Feminists" and gave the movement a radical image. Internal disputes and division over goals weakened the women's movement. He understands this, but says it poorly. What a sad way to end an essay. Compare this essay with the previous one. If we could combine this information with the previous essay's conceptualization—wow!

The grade for this essay is a 6 or 7, depending on how the grader values the quality of the factual information. I would call it a strong 6.

EIGHTH STUDENT ESSAY

(1) The women's movement since 1945 has been a successful reform movement. This can clearly be seen by evaluating the issues, failures, and the degree of success for the women's movement.

(2) In the 1940s, women were looked upon as being the root of evil in society if they decided to get a job outside of the home. In the 1950s, women were seen as "the perfect housewife" who was willing and able to do whatever her husband and children needed her to do. This ideology has put women back many years, thus the 1960s and 1970s have been major turning points here in the United States.

(3) Women in the United States have more rights than any other women on the globe. Still though, women have been trying to work towards the goal of "equal opportunity" in the United States. Women, to some extent

have achieved this goal with such acts as the Civil Rights Act of 1964. This act was intended to give the black minority the civil rights they deserved with a stipulation of "no discrimination of race, color, or creed." The addition of "sex" gave women the leverage which they needed to band together and fight for equal rights.

(4) The way in which women have achieved their current status is by banding together and forming organizations. NOW and ERA are both prominent organizations formed to further the advancement of women. NOW is the National Organization of Women and was created with the intent to get legislation passed for equal rights for females. ERA is the equal rights admendment, this is the admendment that was not ratified, and which would have constitutionally guaranteed women equal rights (the 5th and 14th are supposed to already guarantee this).

(5) The Supreme Court case, Reed v. Reed was a success for women. It dealt with the distribution of an estate of a teenager in Idaho. The mother had custody of the child and therefore wanted to be executor of the estate (instead of the husband, from whom she was separated). The court found in favor of the woman.

(6) Women have also gotten more rights and have exercised these by becoming directly involved with the political system, such as Geraldine Ferraro as a vice presidential running mate, and some have written books, such as Gloria Steinem, for the advancement of women today.

(7) There have been hindering effects placed on women from the 1940s up to the ERA movement in present day America. The 1940s placed women at the root of problems if she entered the work force. Followers of Freud stated that women felt inferior to men, not because they didn't have equal rights, but because women wanted to be like men. The only way women could lay this envy of males to rest was to have sons.

(8) The 1950s brought with it fiction dealing with the housewife heroine and nonfiction literature which dealt with childbearing and cooking and cleaning tips. This era also brought movie stars devoid of character (Marilyn Monroe), sweet and innocent (Debbie Reynolds), or the all-American girl (Doris Day). These stereotypes hindered the advancement from the home to the work force and instead glorified the housewife in her station wagon waiting at the train station for her husband.

(9) Unfortunately a few left-wing radical groups such as WITCH, Women's International Terrorist Conspiracy from Hell, and COYOTE, Cut Out Your Old Tired Ethics, a group of prostitutes, and other groups called for the destruction of the national government and the family, while still others felt that women should not live with men. One organization, The Feminists, a New York radical group, with this legal nickname, was often confused with feminists who were working towards the advancement of women's issues. The typical female voter is 47 years old, and radical issues are simply not going to attract her support.

(10) The degree of success of the women's movement has mixed responses. Women have gotten more rights than in the 1940s, both constitutionally and societal, but other incidents in recent years set back the ERA.

Abortion legalization in the Supreme Court case Roe v. Wade pitted both pro-lifers and anti-ERAers together to destroy the ERA movement. The Afghanistan crisis in which women would have been drafted also set back the ERA movement. Therefore, the degree of success is mixed. Women have more time to enjoy their life now, not like the early 1900s when a woman got married at 22, had children until 32 and died at 51. Today woman are finishing college, and instead of trying to marry a doctor, are becoming doctors themselves. In 1950 only about 40% finished college, the rest dropped out and got married. Therefore, the woman's movement since 1945 has been a successful reform movement.

Comments on the Eighth Student Paper

1st Paragraph: This paragraph immediately shows this essay's major defect: the paragraphs are too short. The first two paragraphs should be joined together, as they are naturally.

3rd Paragraph: After suggesting in the first two paragraphs that he will follow a chronological approach, the student sets off on a topical approach. What he writes is correct, but it leaves the grader puzzled as to conceptual organization. One should never puzzle a grader!

4th Paragraph: In addition to organizational difficulties, the student needs help with transition. Transition is the smooth flow from one paragraph to the next. Paragraph three and paragraph four could be interchanged. Read them both ways. This should never be. Your paragraphs should logically build toward your conclusion, piling up evidence in a sequential manner. Two small errors—the spelling of amendment, and NOW, which is the National Organization *for* Women—also detract from the paragraph.

5th Paragraph: Now we are degenerating into the pleasant story pleasantly told. "And so a woman named Reed sued a man named Reed over their child's estate." So what? What is the significance of this case? That the wife won? No, no, no! This is the first Supreme Court decision in history that stated that a state law could not discriminate in favor of a male without a compelling reason. You cannot discriminate against a woman because she is a woman. What a missed opportunity to conceptually develop his argument. This paragraph should have been tied together with the second half of the fourth paragraph to develop a superb outline of the changing constitutional position for women in the 1970s. The ERA failed, but there were constitutional victories.

6th Paragraph: What is the tie between more rights and increased political awareness, or political activity, or political visibility. None of these have come about as a result of increased rights. Does this student believe that before Gloria Steinem women were not allowed to write books? Fuzzy thinking and writing fails to get you the benefit of the doubt in the grader's mind. There is no real excuse for a one sentence paragraph. Unless it is a dramatic turning point in your essay, avoid the single sentence paragraph. It belongs more to fiction writing.

7th and 8th Paragraphs: The next two paragraphs drift back to a chronological theme. The information is correct but the writing is conceptually weak. These paragraphs paint a picture more than they argue a position. Rather than "hindering effects" the student should have used stronger language. "Expectations, stereotypes, and self-image hindered the women's movement in the 1940s and 1950s." Merge the two paragraphs with this sentence replacing the first one in paragraph seven. Read it this way—it sounds much better.

9th Paragraph: "Unfortunately" in the first sentence is the only clue that the student feels that the women's movement took a wrong turn by becoming more radical. At the end of the paragraph the grader clearly understands this, but a grader should not have to wait until the end of a paragraph to catch your conceptual point. Let's replace the single word "unfortunately" with a new sentence: "In the 1960s and 1970s the women's movement unfortunately became more radical, alienating many of its advocates and potential supporters."

10th Paragraph: The first sentence is awkward; almost any rewording will improve it. The rest of this paragraph is good, although it violates the general rule that new information should not be introduced in the concluding paragraph.

This paper is a strong 7 or just barely an 8 due to the inconsistency in its conceptual organization. Overall, it is actually stronger.

NINTH STUDENT ESSAY

(1) The women's liberation movement from 1945 to 1985 faced many issues, successes, and failures. Women were not out to change American society greatly, but were simply seeking equal status, equal pay for equal jobs, and the right to have equal access to jobs as well.

(2) In the late 1940s and early 1950s women were seen as solely housewives and mothers. Those women who wanted to leave their homes and work were looked down upon. The book, *The Generation of Vipers*, which came out in the early 1940s, said that women were trying to strip men of their masculinity. Law suits involving discrimination were lost in court because women should clearly know that their place was in the home, not outside of it. There was even a book which helped women to plan all of their household duties in such a way that they were still able to pick up their husbands at the commuter railroad station. Many women went to college to drop out and get married. In 1950, 50% of the women enrolled in college dropped out to get married. They went to college to get their MRS degree. However, at the same time there were women who left their homes to work and even liked it.

(3) One of the major forces for change in any society is technology. In the 1960s the birth control pill brought about big changes. For the first time women were able to organize and plan when they wanted to have children. They no longer had to plan their life around surprises, birth could be prevented, and this allowed a new freedom for women. Simultaneously society's morals were changing outside of marriage and sexual activity lost its former bad connotations. Women began taking advantage of the new means of birth control and many women lived alone and worked outside of the home.

(4) The women's movement achieved occasional goals in conjunction with the civil rights movement. In 1964 the Civil Rights Act passed, and this seemed to be a step in the right direction for females. Southern conservatives inserted the word "sex" into the Civil Rights Act as an amendment to the original bill to make the bill so ridiculous that it would never pass. If black civil rights couldn't be stopped, then link it to female civil rights and doom the whole idea! However, the bill passed. The Civil Rights Act gave the "go-ahead" for many cases to go to court for inequality. For example, Sally Reed was separated from her husband and was living with and taking care of their son. The son died, and the small estate went to her husband according to Idaho law. She fought this, and the U.S. Supreme Court ruled that such a law was unconstitutional. This was the first Supreme Court case that ever ruled that discrimination against women was unconstitutional.

(5) A new awareness arose among women with many new magazines emerging such as MS, which was highly feminist. Gloria Steinem, the editor of MS magazine, went as far to say that "marriage is a form of prostitution." These magazines contributed to a radicalization in the women's movement.

(6) In 1979 President Jimmy Carter tried to pass a law which would allow the United States to draft women into the army. If women wanted to be equal, then we might as well take them up on it. Here is another example where women started to get themselves into issues which they did not initiate, and once again, as with Roe v. Wade, the women's movement started to lose many followers. The draft was not passed, but it initiated a change of heart in more conservative women.

(7) By the mid 1960s the women's movement started to become a radical movement, just like what happened to the blacks, and many conservative women dropped out. Radical groups such as COYOTE, Cut Out Your Old Tired Ethics; WITCH, Women's International Terrorist Conspiracy from Hell; and the New York Radical Women, who were nicknamed "The Feminists," were started. It seemed that the women's movement had turned into a movement of lesbians, socialists, and radicals.

(8) A curious characteristic of the women's movement was that many of its successes and failures had little to do with the actions of the organized women's movement. For example, abortion had never been much of an issue. But, once the Supreme Court ruled in Roe v. Wade that women

had the right to abortions during the first six months of pregnancy, the movement had to endorse the ruling because it philosophically fell under their abstract assertions that women had the right to control their own lives. Out of the opposition to the abortion decision emerged the Pro-Life Movement which linked up to Phyllis Schlafly's anti-ERA organization to create a formidable opponent for the now narrowly defined and radical women's movement.

(9) Yes, women have come a long way, but it is still a fact that college graduates who are women receive less income than high school graduates who are men. And, furthermore, for the same job, the same qualifications, men receive higher incomes than women. Overall, women had many successes, then faced with unexpected issues the movement turned radical, and radicalism, simply, isn't the answer.

Comments on the Ninth Student Paper

1st Paragraph: This introductory paragraph needs to be strengthened and lengthened somewhat. He gives the impression that he will concentrate on equal status, equal pay, and equal access. But the following paragraphs do not develop these themes. Instead, the next three paragraphs emphasize self-image, the role of technology, and the parallel influence of the civil rights movement. This paragraph needs one more sentence, such as: "The early women's movement fought off the image of the dutiful housewife and was stimulated by two concurrent but unrelated developments: the invention of the birth control pill and the growth of civil rights for blacks."

2nd, 3rd, and 4th Paragraphs: Some excess verbiage pads these paragraphs, but they are well done.

5th Paragraph: This looks like the paragraph of a student who has just panicked because he glanced at the clock. This paragraph would be better joined to the seventh paragraph. Note the similar themes of the radicalization of the movement.

6th Paragraph: Buried in the middle of this paragraph is a profound concept that should have been the conceptual focus. It is the idea that the women's movement became entangled in issues not on their agenda. Both abortion and the draft were two such issues that alienated many conservative and moderate supporters. This paragraph is poorly constructed. Before you write any paragraph always ask yourself—what is my conceptual point and how am I going to prove it?

8th Paragraph: This paragraph and paragraph six should be merged. Note the clear conceptual statement alluded to in paragraph six.

9th Paragraph: Not a bad ending; he sees some successes, some failures, and yet some issues remain. This is clearly the best paper; it is a weak 9. An essay doesn't have to be perfect to get a 9.

GRADING STANDARDS

The grading standards for this essay question are as follows:

"What were the issues, successes, and failures for the women's movement from 1945 to the 1980s?"

8–9
- balanced treatment that explicitly addresses all three concepts—issues, successes, and failures
- uses 4–5 facts to support each concept
- analyzes the question by focusing on changes over time, cause and effect, and nuances in successes and failures
- coverage of the whole period
- well written, well organized

5–7
- may be imbalanced, may explicitly or implicitly address all three concepts uses 2–3 facts to support each concept
- awareness of changes over time and cause and effect
- may superficially cover some parts of the 1945-to-the-1980s period
- may contain minor errors of fact not significant to the essay

2–4
- imbalanced, generalized treatment of the question
- may not address, even implicitly, one of the concepts
- conceptually weak
- few specific facts, weak facts, or inappropriate facts
- major errors of fact

0–1
- generalized discussion of the question
- conceptualization missing, few facts, little substance
- major errors
- rather inept

Don't make the mistake of assuming that an essay grader merely counts the number of facts in an essay. The standards use phrases such as "2–3 facts." But some facts are better than others. Some are more appropriate than others. Some illustrate a point better than others.

What counts is the way in which the facts support the particular conceptual argument you are making in that paragraph. An essay is an argument. A paragraph is part of your overall argument. A fact is a descriptive illustration to buttress that particular part of your overall argument. An essay grader does not simply count the facts in an essay. Each fact is evaluated within the context of the paragraph. Don't assume that the grader will understand the connection between the Boston Massacre and the beginning of the Revolutionary War. You assume that responsibility.

The Ten Types of History Essay Questions

1. CHANGE OVER TIME

Q "The period from 1783 to 1815 was a period of evolution to economic maturity for the infant United States. Assess the validity of this view."

This type of question asks you to measure the degree of change over a period of time. First ascertain what you are assessing. Next identify the key words. Did other major events occur within these dates that had an impact on the period? Why did the question select these dates? Do they mark turning points, beginnings, ends, dramatic shifts, or a convenient time period? Remember to cover the entire period of the question. If it asks for 1783–1815, do not concentrate on the 1790s. Change over time assumes that something changed over the time period. It is possible some ideas or policies did not change.

Q "Between 1790 and 1870 the economic growth of the United States was significantly stimulated by governmental aid. Assess the validity of this statement."

What is meant by governmental aid—tariffs, internal improvements, public land policy, land grants to railroads, subsidies, Bank of the U.S., and so forth? The key words are the dates, economic growth, stimulated, and governmental aid. Why pick these dates? What is meant by "stimulated"? What governments are involved—state, local, or national? What does the phrase "economic growth" mean? Was the stimulus uneven, sporadic, or even counterproductive? Why the use of "significantly"? Could the governmental aid have been insignificant? Were factors at work stimulating the economy other than governmental aid?

2. CAUSE AND EFFECT

Q "Why did the United States enter the First World War?"

In this question be sure to balance immediate and long range causes. How are the causes related? Can you group them under broad ideas? An essay on the American entry into the First World War should not begin with the

ROAD MAP

- *Change over Time*
- *Cause and Effect*
- *Compare and Contrast*
- *Define and Identify*
- *Statement, React to It*
- *Evaluation*
- *A Statement from a Particular Viewpoint*
- *Given Framework*
- *Problem–Solution*
- *Answer and Include*

German resumption of unrestricted submarine warfare in January 1917, but do not find causes too far back in history. If you blame the initial arrival of blacks in 1619 for the Civil War, you have given yourself the responsibility for filling in the years between 1619 and 1861.

Nothing is so simple that it has one cause. Always answer cause and effect questions with multiple causation. Rank the relative importance of the causes and explain your choice. Include the consequences of ideas, actions, and events to emphasize the effect. A discussion of the causes of the Civil War should conclude that it resolved the dilemma of slavery in the territories. Remember feedback from the effect to the cause. The original system for electing the president produced the tie vote in the electoral college of 1800. The procedure changed. The 1800 election result ended that cause of a tie in future electoral college votes.

Q "What caused the Civil War?"

Think of broad categories for causes and decide which categories to emphasize and which facts to emphasize within each category. A good answer considers the following: slavery in the territories; the clash of economic systems; Southern nationalism versus Northern dominance; race, slavery, and the future of blacks in America; Northern abolitionism and Southern reaction; and the failure of democracy or the triumph of democracy. Conclude your essay with a look at the broad issues resolved by the Civil War and a peek at new issues raised by the struggle.

3. COMPARE AND CONTRAST

Q "Compare and contrast Jacksonian Democracy and Jeffersonian Democracy."

To contrast is to compare with respect to differences. "Compare" emphasizes likenesses over differences. In a sense, therefore, "compare and contrast" is redundant. No matter how the question is phrased, though, the student must include both similarities and differences in a "compare," "contrast," or "compare and contrast" question. Often students concentrate on only half of the question. Ask yourself what is comparable among the choices given. Are there obvious differences or similarities? Do you organize the answer by developing a description of each separately or by linking both for each concept? A fresh approach is needed if the question is phrased in a manner you never considered. For example, compare Jacksonian Democracy and Populism, or compare and contrast colonial immigration with nineteenth century immigration.

Q "Compare and contrast three colonies—Virginia, Pennsylvania, and Massachusetts."

Create a list of conceptual comparisons. Decide which are the most important and defend them well. You should consider the following: motives of the founders; influence of climate and geography; economies; political systems; closeness to the British colonial ideal; religions; morals; social structure; and education systems. All of these conceptual ideas are significant enough to require a separate paragraph. Some should be grouped together, however, according to the wording of the question, your degree of knowledge, and the amount of time. Two paragraphs that cover religion and the economy merely introduce the subject. Strive for a broad range of concepts to compare and contrast.

4. DEFINE AND IDENTIFY

Q "Discuss Jacksonian Democracy."

Ask yourself what were the traits, leaders, characteristics, origins, results, or issues involved. A define and identify question is often worded as "describe" or "discuss." "Discuss Jacksonian Democracy" does not mean telling a series of pleasant stories about Jackson. Zero in, and define and identify Jacksonian Democracy through its origins, leaders, characteristics, issues, and policies. Sometimes a define and identify question is limited to one or two qualities. To answer the question, "What were the characteristics of colonial religion?" you must identify, define, and explain the characteristics. In response to the question, "What were the results of Reconstruction?" you should carefully define Reconstruction, and include the issues that had an impact on the results of Reconstruction.

Of all the possible wordings that are used, "define and identify" most easily degenerates into a pleasant narrative. Remember that defining and describing means ranking and explaining the traits, characteristics, results, issues, origins, or leaders. Jackson's attack on the Bank of the United States may be a symbol of Jacksonian Democracy or an aberration. To write that Jackson attacked the Bank is not enough. Why did he? What did he or his supporters gain? What beliefs did the attack illustrate?

5. STATEMENT, REACT TO IT

Q "Presidents are rarely successful in both foreign and domestic policy. Assess the validity of this statement."

These questions are usually worded as statements followed by either "explain," or "assess the validity." You may react to the statement as valid, invalid, or partially valid. Avoid the trap of the simplistic answer, which blandly declares with little support the statement valid or invalid. The best answers select the partially valid choice, address the opposite position, or state a strong support.

Q "Slavery was the sole cause of the Civil War. Evaluate this statement."

If you defend the statement, define slavery broadly and consider its ramifications broadly. The best essays discuss slavery as one cause and then discuss other causes. Remember to look for key words in the statement. In this example it is "sole." If you disagree with the statement, do not write an analysis of the causes of the Civil War and ignore the issue of slavery. You may justify other causes, but do not neglect slavery as a cause.

6. EVALUATION

Q   "Pick three of the following and evaluate their effectiveness as political leaders."

George Washington

John C. Calhoun

Thomas Jefferson

Henry Clay

John Quincy Adams

Daniel Webster

Evaluation questions are worded as "evaluate," "assess the significance," or "assess the validity." You control your answer because you determine the conceptual criteria and factual support. A quick path to an "F" on this essay is to write in the "it was good, it was really good, or it was bad" mode. "Evaluate" or "assess" demands an evaluation, not an evasion. "Evaluate Jacksonian Democracy" means that you decide what criteria to use to evaluate Jacksonian Democracy. Do not glibly stamp Jacksonian Democracy as "good."

Q   "Was colonial society democratic?"

You must first deal with the ambiguous word "democratic." Carefully create a workable definition of democracy. Next, identify conceptual categories for your evaluation of colonial democracy—religious, political, social, and economic. A good essay suggests that some aspects of colonial society were democratic, some were not, and changes occurred throughout the colonial period.

7. A STATEMENT FROM A PARTICULAR VIEWPOINT

Q   "Defend British policies during the period from 1763 to 1776."

The secret to this question is to place yourself in the asked-for position. In order to do that you must clearly understand the view stated and be able to defend it. These questions frequently confuse students momentarily because the question may be worded in a manner that the student has never considered.

Q   "According to a radical historian, what have been the foreign policy objectives of the United States in the twentieth century?"

Do you know the basic tenets of the radical critique of American foreign policy? If so, this may be easy; otherwise ...! An answer to this question emphasizes the aggressive, expansionist, and imperialistic nature of our foreign policy; the elite control of decision making; our antidemocratic posture; and our internal oppression of workers and minorities. Even if you disagree with the radical critique of our foreign policy, do not forget that your primary purpose is to answer the question. The question tests your knowledge, not your patriotism. Do not make the mistake of writing a critique of the radical critique instead of answering the question. Add a statement to your conclusion that gives your opinion in a discreet manner if you wish. For example, write, "The radical critique of twentieth century foreign policy more aptly applies to communist nations than to the United States."

8. GIVEN FRAMEWORK

Q "The powers of the President grew because of war and foreign crises. Evaluate this statement."

A given-framework question limits your range of conceptualization because you must write within the defined framework. Otherwise, a long essay proudly submitted may be returned with a single terse comment, "You failed to answer the question." You may disagree with the statement that the powers of the president have expanded because of war and foreign crises, but that places upon you the burden of showing that war and foreign crises did *not* cause the growth of presidential power. You cannot answer the question by stating the opposite, that domestic problems are the primary cause for the growth of presidential power. That approach fails to address the question.

Q "The United States displayed all the typical characteristics of a new nation during the early republic, 1789–1823. Assess the validity of this view."

This framework suggests that the experiences of the infant United States have a modem counterpart in the nascent nations of the Third World. Either make a brief reference to new Third World nations in your conclusion or introduction or sprinkle remarks throughout your essay. An adequate answer includes the attempts to avoid superpower struggles, expand the economy, achieve neutrality, spread our unique ideology, and expand our territory.

9. PROBLEM-SOLUTION

Q "What causes of the Civil War were resolved by the Civil War and Reconstruction?"

In a problem-solution question, a defined problem leads to a proposed solution that then resolves the problem, generates new problems, or both.

The chief difficulty for a student is accurately identifying the relationship between the problem and the solution. The second difficulty is judging if the solution resolved the issue.

Q   "The Progressive movement solved problems that rose from industrialization. Discuss this statement."

What aspects of the Progressive movement concerned themselves with industrialization? An adequate answer includes political manipulation of legislatures, inspection of products, safety of workers, maldistribution of wealth, neutrality in labor disputes, control of Wall Street, antitrust, etc. In an essay you should evaluate the solutions, and identify those that were successful and those that led to new problems, such as meat inspection laws aiding the consolidation of the meat-packing industry.

10.   ANSWER AND INCLUDE

Q   "Analyze the relative importance of three of the following as contributing to the Civil Rights movement."

Gunnar Myrdal, *An American Dilemma*
The desegregation of the armed forces
Brown v. Board of Education
African American demographic changes

I constructed this example to illustrate a point. If you have never heard of Myrdal's *An American Dilemma* and you are not sure what is meant by demographic changes, this question is not for you, even if you thought you were prepared to answer an essay on the civil rights movement. The wording of the question doesn't give you much leeway. Can you answer the question by adequately covering two and including at least some references to a third event? You may be able to get minimum credit if you write, "A minor factor that paved the way for the civil rights movement was intellectuals raising issues that forced white Americans to confront the status of African Americans. For example the book *Black Like Me* showed...." (You knew *Black Like Me,* but not *An American Dilemma.*) This is preferable to ignoring a third event, especially if you know the remaining two events well. Be certain to weave the three events, ideas, or forces together in an essay answering each part of the question. Don't fall into a trap this format invites—writing three unconnected paragraphs. In this example you were asked the relative importance of each as contributing factors. Pull everything together and incorporate additional events, people, and forces to answer the question. Take the phrase "three of the" out of the question to focus on the question.

Q   "Identify and analyze the issues separating the United States and the Soviet Union during the Cold War as illustrated by three of the following."

NATO and Warsaw Pact

The Korean War

The Berlin Wall

The nuclear arms race

Without the number this question becomes, "Identify and analyze the issues separating the United States and the Soviet Union during the Cold War." Think of the listing as intended to jar your memory as to what the issues could be. The Berlin Wall is not an issue, not until you explain the real and symbolic forces that it illustrated. This approach will force you to write on the issue conceptually, incorporating the Berlin Wall factually as support and illustration to buttress your conceptual points. In many respects "Answer and Include" is simply one of the first nine types of questions illustrated here, with the additional provision requiring you to include certain events or ideas.

Historiography and the Essay

Two historians using the same facts may come to two different interpretations of a historical event. Contemporary British and American views of the battles of Lexington and Concord would obviously differ because the two sides held different assumptions. Any two historians several years later would also hold different assumptions and produce different historical accounts. Decades later other historians declare that the previous historians only perceived part of the truth. Generation after generation rewrites history and theoretically comes closer to the truth. In actuality, each historian reflects his time. The study of changing historical interpretations, shifting emphasis, and different methodologies is called *historiography*.

Students in survey courses need to know some historiography but should never sacrifice a firm grounding in the fundamental facts and concepts of American history for more depth in historiography. You run the risk of name-dropping in your writing and of citing authoritative sources as a substitute for your own analysis. To explain the breakdown of the federal political system in the 1850s is better than to state, "Craven blames the coming of the Civil War on the breakdown of the political system." How? When? Where? As shown by?

Historiography helps you to understand the assumptions behind the conceptual statements made by historians. For instance, many intellectuals were distressed by the inability to secure a peaceful world after the First World War. Disillusioned by war as a means of obtaining any political or diplomatic goal, they reasoned that war itself was often unnecessary and counterproductive. Historians with these assumptions found in the 1850s a "blundering generation" of politicians who were too stupid and petty to avoid the needless tragedy of the Civil War. The Second World War taught a different lesson. Some evils are so monstrous, they stated, that society is justified in suffering great numbers of casualties in order to eradicate the evil. Hitler was such an evil, and slavery was also. The Civil War tragedy of 600,000 dead soldiers, formerly perceived as having died needlessly, became the triumph over a monstrous evil. They did not die in vain. Nothing about the ending of slavery was unnecessary or blundering.

ROAD MAP

- *Progressive Historiography*
- *Consensus Historiography*
- *New Left Historiography*
- *Diplomatic Historiography: Nationalists*
- *Diplomatic Historiography: Realists*

The summaries that follow explain the chronology and assumptions underlying three schools of historiography concerning domestic politics (Progressive, Consensus, and New Left), and three schools of historiography for foreign policies (Nationalist, Realist, and Radical). Be leery of a fatal trap for students: Summarizing a historian's viewpoint in one or two sentences is impossible. Include historiography in your writing if you wish, but don't substitute it for your own analysis. Use historiography to support your arguments. Remember that historians hold varying opinions of the correctness of other historians' ideas. Unless the question directly asks about historiography, make it a minor part of your essay if you use it at all.

PROGRESSIVE HISTORIOGRAPHY

Three different schools of historians have emerged in the twentieth century. The first, the Progressive school, named for the Progressive reform era, dominated historiography from the early twentieth century to the end of the Second World War. Like the writings of most intellectuals, the themes of the Progressive historians reflected the issues and concerns of their time. The Progressive movement was a collection of reforms designed to adjust to changes brought on by industrialization and urbanization. A second influence upon these historians was the rise of the social sciences—economics, sociology, psychology, and so forth—as separate fields of study. Historians borrowed heavily from these new fields for insights into history, correcting what they saw as the overemphasis on political history. Progressive historians hoped for the social and political betterment of the society of their time and made no effort to hide their loyalties. They championed liberal, democratic, and progressive ideas and causes. The solution to almost every problem was more democracy, and the way to the golden age was through the secret ballot. The people would prevail because they were the embodiment of goodness. Finally, to the basic assumptions of the Progressive historians add one philosophical characteristic of the era, a belief in progress.

Progressive historians stressed the differences between competing groups, sections, and classes. American society was an arena of competing social and economic forces. First one, then the other gained control in cycles of reform and reaction. The dominant theme was class and sectional conflict. Clearly defined turning points marked the ascension of one group and the defeat of the other. All of the following were used to represent our polarized history: rich vs. poor, interests vs. people, haves vs. have-nots, privileged vs. less privileged, aristocracy vs. democracy, debtors vs. creditors, East vs. South and West, labor vs. big business, Jeffersonianism vs. Hamiltonianism, democracy vs. oligarchy, liberalism vs. conservatism, and agrarianism vs. capitalism.

The central role in American history was played by the frontier or by social or economic forces. Historian Frederick Jackson Turner stressed "The

Significance of the Frontier in American History." Carl Becker argued that the American Revolution was a question of home rule and who shall rule at home. The colonists revolted from Great Britain and fought among themselves for control of the new American governmental institutions. The Constitution marked the temporary victory of the conservatives over the democrats, temporary in the sense that the struggle was to resurface in American history again and again.

The most famous Progressive historian was Charles Beard. In 1913 Beard shocked conservatives with his *An Economic Interpretation of the Constitution*, which asserted that the Constitution represented the triumph of large property interests over the interests of small farmers. The Constitution that every school child was taught to revere was antidemocratic. No scholarly historical book had ever provoked the debate Beard's did. He carefully worded the title of his book, using "An" rather than "The." He accepted the possibility that he may not have researched and written "The" definitive economic explanation of the origins of the Constitution. Therefore he used "An," allowing "The" for future use. Whatever definitive explanation a future historian would make would be economic. Of that Beard was certain.

CONSENSUS HISTORIOGRAPHY

After the Second World War a new school emerged of historians who stressed that the shared ideas of Americans were more important in our history than conflicts among them. They believed that Americans possessed a much narrower range of divisive issues and conflicts compared with other peoples of the world. We had had conflicts, but our domestic disputes had never approached the nastiness of European uprisings and revolutions. The bloody reign of terror in the French Revolution had no comparable American counterpart. Patriots battled Tories during the American Revolution but not with guillotines.

The Consensus historians, or Neoconservatives as they were sometimes called, unabashedly celebrated the accomplishments and achievements of American democratic capitalism. A key word used to describe them is continuity. They rejected much of the periodicalization of American history, and studied ideas that crossed over the typical political periods. Consensus historians saw in American culture common traits, expressed in the longevity and durability of our institutions. In a world of constantly changing political ideas, governments, and constitutions, they asked, why has our political system endure? Dumb luck? No, features in the American national character have shaped our history, and given it a unique stability and homogeneity. The cement holding us together is our widespread prosperity and universal acceptance of the principles succinctly summarized in the first parts of the Declaration of Independence and the Constitution.

Consensus historians believed that American society by the 1950s had achieved an unmatched state of widely dispersed affluence. In short, we had no have-nots, or so few that they were insignificant in our history. Political power had always been widespread because of liberal suffrage laws. Americans fought through the ballot, not to achieve the ballot. As a people we all endorse the same egalitarian fundamentals, they said. Our political struggles have always been within the center rather than between left and right extremists.

Consensus analysis of economic forces ignored the emphasis by Progressive historians upon the role of individuals. For them institutional factors shaped and molded our economy. The Robber Barons became entrepreneurs, innovators in new fields. Men like Rockefeller and Carnegie brought order to the chaos of oil refining and steel production. Their methods may have led to monopoly, but they also led to efficiency. Carnegie, for example, lowered the price of steel from seventy-five dollars a ton to fourteen dollars. What passes for conflict between the haves and have-nots in American history is really competition between competing groups of businessmen or entrepreneurs.

For the Progressive historian the struggle for political power was the struggle for control of the one institution, the federal government, capable of giving one group of entrepreneurs an advantage over another. Raising or lowering the tariff helped or hurt depending upon your economic interests. Approaching from a different level of economic analysis, Consensus historians ignored individuals to concentrate upon the larger economic factors such as the growth of urban markets, the rise of research and development, the rise of the corporate organization, and the rise of advertising.

Much of their political writing directly or indirectly tried to address a perplexing question of American society. Every industrial nation has developed a strong worker, labor, or socialist political party or parties. Why not us? Louis Hartz suggested that American political development took place within the framework of the ideas of European politics but outside their actual conditions. The debates between our liberals and conservatives were really debates among liberals because we had never had the extreme conservatives and leftists of Europe. We don't have deeply felt political issues, he said, because we don't have deep political thought on either end. In this past year, how many evenings did you spend intensely discussing political issues? Constant political discussion sharpens differences, clarifies thinking, and leads to more deeply held convictions. Our political culture doesn't generate truly divisive issues, because we disagree on only minor questions of ends or means, according to Hartz. Daniel Boorstin has suggested that Americans are not an idea-oriented people. The key to understanding American society is pragmatism. We don't think, we do.

Critics disliked several features of Consensus historiography. Their writings perpetuated the myth of American uniqueness that carried with it the implication of superiority. There was little need to study other nations. The history of the United States developed the way it did only because of Americans. In defense of the Consensus historians, consider the impact of both the Second World War and the rise of the Cold War upon intellectuals. Without our superb arsenal of industry we would have never won the Second World War. Thank God for Rockefeller and Carnegie. Our moral and economic superiority over the communists was a self-evident truth in the 1950s.

In the Consensus view ideas of pragmatism, abundance, and liberalism had a life of their own. They never sprang from, or were associated with, any class struggle or decisive event. The interesting parts of American history were missing. The peaks and valleys of American history were smoothed out by the single-theme emphases.

Finally, if man is not influenced by economic needs and desires, what motivates him? What causes him to join a group to contest the control of the political apparatus? Richard Hofstadter's *The Age of Reform* suggested that concern over rising or declining status, or "status anxieties," lay behind the irrational addiction to Populism, Prohibition, and McCarthyism. Consensus historians borrowed from the social sciences even more than had the Progressives to explain motives. They occasionally selected complex and controversial theories upon which to base their explanations. Many psychologists do not share Hofstadter's faith in borrowed theories of status. Even a lifetime may not be enough to master an academic field such as history. Borrowing from another academic field carries risks, but also may offer unusual insights.

NEW LEFT HISTORIOGRAPHY

Great changes accompanied America's transition into the 1960s. The 1950s had been characterized by a general agreement on national goals, by a secure self-confidence, and by an easy categorization of other nations into good guys and bad guys. In the late 1950s our smug self-assurance dissolved in successive waves of polarization over the issues of racism, imperialism, and poverty. The seeming reemergence of conflict in current events stimulated a reexamination of conflict in American history.

The new champions of the theme of conflict in our history constituted an approach termed the "New Left." The "new" theoretically differentiates them from the unimaginative, Socialist Party orientation of the old left of the 1930s and 1940s. The "left" signifies an orientation toward methods and concepts that focus on the masses and their experiences, "history from the bottom up," as it is called. Unlike the old left, the New Left avoids the preconceived molds of Marxist theories, which distorted the facts to fit a foreign doctrine. The historians of the New Left demand the inclusion of those features of our history that explain how we came to be a violent, racist, repressive society. We don't need imported nineteenth-century theories to find what is discreditable in our history because we have plenty if we don't mince words. We need a "usable past," one that realistically includes all of our bad features. We need to break from the textbook view of American history. Otherwise we can't begin to understand and deal with the poverty, racism, and repression of today.

The renewed emphasis on conflict and polarization was fed by the civil rights struggle. Early New Left historians wrote on the depth of American racism and the pervasiveness of slavery. The rediscovery of poverty and the War on Poverty of Lyndon Johnson's administration both stemmed from the same source, Michael Harrington's *The Other America*, a detailed look at scenes unknown to most middle- and upper-class Americans. Unrest over the draft and the war in Vietnam, impatience with the pace of civil rights, and the examples of political assassinations combined to produce explosions of violence in the cities in the 1960s. The final ingredient convulsing American society was the emergence of the women's movement. Women and minorities destroyed the homogenized image of "consensus" America. The new emphasis was on our pluralism, the existence of many different peoples, ethnic groups, and races. Each aspect of this pluralism deserved representation in our history. We are not a melting pot, but a stew of race, class, gender, and ethnicity.

DIPLOMATIC HISTORIOGRAPHY: NATIONALISTS

All nations pursue foreign policy objectives consistent with their own self-interest. Foreign policy is normally an offshoot of domestic policies, needs, and goals. You are already familiar with the Nationalist approach, for it is found in almost every textbook. Nationalist historians believe that American foreign policy combines a realistic concept of self-interest with generous support of other nations' goals of democracy, self-determination, and economic prosperity. A commitment to high ideals characterizes a successful foreign policy, a record of which we should be proud.

After the American Revolution, Lafayette returned to France with a framed copy of the Declaration of Independence. He placed it off center on a wall. The empty space was reserved for a hoped-for French document granting similar rights. In similar fashion our Declaration of Independence and Constitution have inspired people all over the world and well they should, for these documents epitomize the aspirations of all mankind, not just Americans. Our foreign policy has given expression and substance to these ideas, a record of unselfish idealism unequaled in the history of the world.

We have, admit the Nationalists, made a few mistakes in our foreign policy, such as taking the Philippines and keeping it as a colony. But we rectified our error by generously preparing it for independence and economic stability. We built roads, bridges, schools, and so forth. Independence came on July 4, 1946, symbolizing the aspiration of all people of the world for self-rule. We may have been an imperialist power, but we were a good imperialist power, prepared from the start for the eventual end of our control.

The assumptions underlying the Nationalist evaluation of American foreign policy were succinctly summarized by a European newspaper during the celebration of the United States bicentennial. The newspaper confessed that although it had often been critical of the United States, what the world needed was more rather than fewer countries like the United States of America.

DIPLOMATIC HISTORIOGRAPHY: REALISTS

The Realist school of historical interpretation emerged as a criticism of what it saw as wide swings in twentieth century foreign policy. We sought to "make the world safe for democracy" during the First World War. Ten years later we rejected world leadership and withdrew into a cocoon of isolationism. Both extreme swings, say the Realists, were not in our best self-interest. The United States has too often regarded itself as a special nation not bound by the same rules and consequences as others. Our victory in the Spanish-American War was due to God, claimed McKinley and many history books. Realist historians are more apt to accept Bismarck's contemporary analysis, "God watches over fools, drunks, and the United States of America." We were lucky!

Realists criticize both the assumptions behind American foreign policy and the mechanism for conducting it. The American people have mistakenly assumed that much of our history turned out the way it did because we wanted it to. We avoided European wars in the nineteenth century because we chose to stay out. Actually, none were fought. The long period of peace in our history is abnormal, considering the history of other nations. The safe nineteenth century and the security of two oceans gave us the erroneous opinion that war was abnormal and peace normal. Therefore, any interruption of peace is due to evil people, nations, or isms.

We don't fight wars; we cleanse the world of evil. For foolish, idealistic, and moral reasons we periodically go on crusades like the knights of old. Our success rate is better than theirs, but the consequences may be worse.

Realists castigate American foreign policy for ignoring the timeless lessons of history. The key element preserving the peace among nations is a balance of power, in which every nation's existence is maintained in a shifting, interlocking stability of conflict and tension. Wars occasionally break out, but they are always limited to a nation's foreign policy objectives, which stem from her self-interests. A nation goes to war to gain territory, protect markets, etc., not just to win. War is not the same as the World Series. The United States, claim the Realists, too often goes to war to win, and forgets objectives consistent with its own self-interest.

One of the great mistakes of war is unconditional surrender. It creates power vacuums and sucks us into future conflicts. Before the Second World War Japan kept order in the Far East. Since the Second World War we have kept order in Korea, Vietnam, and Taiwan with mammoth military defense budgets. Has Japan suffered from no longer shouldering this burden? Please notice what is missing in this analysis. There are no statements of right and wrong, moral and immoral, good and evil. Realists reject this line of thought. We can't right every wrong, defend everyone, and correct all injustice. So we simply do what is best for us. A chastised Japan would have been better for the United States than a defeated Japan.

Our sense of specialness has led us to believe that we are an example to the world. Our political practices, economic prosperity, and eternal ideals place us above the normal fray of shortsighted nations. For example, the Soviet Union spoke for the Soviet Union only; we speak for all mankind. We have been shocked on occasions in the twentieth century to discover that some people did not understand how special we are. Stung by criticism, we have withdrawn. This vacillation between intense moralistic crusades and indifferent, self-righteous isolation characterizes our foreign policy. The only way to avoid such swings is to remove the masses and emotion from the decision-making process.

Realists boldly assert that foreign policy is not a matter for public debate. The self-interest goals of any nation clearly establish themselves. The conduct of foreign policy should rest in the hands of professional diplomats who coldly assess the immediate and the long-range consequences of potential policies, and keep in mind the self-interest goals of all the nations involved in a dispute. Realists accept the world as it is and suggest realistic policies. The difficulty for Realists lies in the fact that democracies do occasionally become emotionally aroused. Sometimes the leaders of a government mold public opinion, but sometimes they are moved by it.

DIPLOMATIC HISTORIOGRAPHY: RADICALS

Radical diplomatic historians believe that American foreign policy is controlled by our industrial and economic elite who guide our foreign policies in order to gain new economic markets and resources. In the process the public is manipulated, misled, or propagandized into believing that foreign policy objectives are matters of national rather than corporate or elite concern. The rallying cry of democratic ideals and national security masks the real purpose. The masses fight; the elite gains.

In the nineteenth century, the blood lust for land and resources swept away Mexicans, Indians, and Spaniards. The enlargement of national territory was imperialism, the grabbing of colonies, in disguise. As the twentieth century dawned, a new type of imperialism sought to establish economic hegemony over the Caribbean and Latin America. Occasionally U.S.

military might has protected American business adventures abroad. By the middle of the twentieth century the United States expanded and influenced or controlled vast areas of the world for markets and resources. Businessmen do not like instability. Thus, say Radical historians, the economic power elite has enlisted the United States government in its efforts to prevent small nations from controlling their own resources or from keeping these resources to themselves. The United States, claim the Radical historians, is now the opposite of what it was in its beginning. It is now the most antiprogressive and antirevolutionary nation in the world. The Declaration of Independence has been shelved.

What has caused the United States to assume this stance? Foreign policies stem from domestic needs, goals, and images. Radical historians feel primarily that our foreign policies mirror our domestic policies and distract attention from the real issues. What we need is a domestic policy that seeks solutions to the plight of our deprived and disadvantaged classes. We must reduce the power of the elite to provide more for the lower classes. By redistributing income within the United States the domestic economy could absorb the goods produced by our economy for foreign markets and make much of our imperialism unnecessary.

Radical historians are not Marxists, but they accept the tone and direction of leftist writers. The raw power of the upper classes within American domestic politics is muted, but shines through in the execution of our foreign policy, they say. If you seek the extent to which the power elite will go to enhance or maintain their position, study American foreign policy; it reveals the worst features of the elite control of American society.

As students of history it is important that you understand the difficulties facing Radical historians. To my knowledge no Radical historian has ever found a letter or document written by a member of the power elite establishing a clear relationship between the adoption of a specific foreign policy and the economic objectives of a specific corporation or business. Their case would benefit greatly from a 1940 letter, say, to the stockholders by a major steel corporation urging a flood of letters to their congressmen asking for war in order to increase stock dividends. An old adage among historians is "no documents, no proof, no history." Without documents history writing cannot be supported on the minute, footnote level.

Radicals, however, sense an overall tone and orientation toward American society that is expressed in most of our institutions such as churches, corporations, governments, universities, foundations, and so on. It is this larger feel for American society upon which their historical assumptions rest.

Radical historians have been influenced by Lenin's adaptation of Marx's theory of class struggle. Marx postulated a capitalist society in which the capitalists would progressively squeeze the workers through longer hours and lower pay, which would lead to more and more dissatisfaction. Eventually the workers would revolt in a great socialist revolution, end capitalism, and inaugurate socialism. This two-sentence summary of Marx's writings is quite oversimplified! In many ways Marx was a prisoner of his time, the mid-nineteenth century. What he did not foresee was the rise of the middle class, the development of labor unions, and the growth of the welfare state, all of which undermined Marx's prophecy.

Early in the twentieth century, Lenin, who later led the Russian communist revolution, added to Marx's scenario of revolution. Lenin theorized that the capitalists, sensing a rising cauldron of trouble, would try to divert domestic dissatisfaction by pursuing an imperialistic foreign policy in the hope that nationalism would suffocate worker dissatisfaction. Imperialism therefore is not just the greedy thrust of the power elite, but represents the dying gasp of the capitalist class who clutch at straws as they sink lower and lower into the consequences of the mess they themselves created and into a defeat they cannot avoid. To a sincere Marxist capitalist, imperialism is an encouraging sign that the capitalist society can no longer sufficiently suppress its own workers. Now you understand why so much communist propaganda criticizing the United States uses the phrase "imperialist."

Hardly any American Radical historian is a Marxist. As a group, however, they do share a belief that American society has been too little concerned with the disadvantaged and too much concerned with an aggressive foreign policy. The key word is aggressive. Firm believers in protecting American society and protecting American interests, they argue that a more peaceful, understanding, and cooperative foreign policy must replace the policies we have historically pursued. Their general criticisms of our foreign policy are clearer than their specific prescriptions for what they would do if they could determine our foreign policy. Only a small number of historians of American foreign policy are Radical historians, but their influence exceeds their number. They force all students of history to think, to defend, to analyze, and to reexamine. Any scholar must understand the arguments of the other side. Understanding the assumptions of Radical historians doesn't make you a radical, just as understanding a football playbook doesn't make you a football player.

Always be alert to the philosophical assumptions an author may have. This short summary of the schools of historiography will help you analyze writings by historians.

The Essentials
of U.S. History

PART

2

PREVIEW

Chronological Time Periods

HOW TO USE THIS CHAPTER

The units that follow break U.S. history into ten chronological time periods: 1607–1763, 1763–1783, 1783–1800, 1800–1840, 1840–1877, 1865–1900, 1900–1920, 1920–1940, 1940–1960, and 1960 to the present. An additional unit discusses the Constitution.

Each unit begins with the *Major Themes and Ideas* for that period. These themes come from former AP essay questions and the traditional essay questions historians associate with the era. You should be able to write an essay on at least three or four themes under each subsection of the *Major Themes and Ideas*. The themes and ideas are the concepts you must understand in order to be able to grasp the significant issues of the era.

Next comes the *Major Terms and Concepts* for the unit. This is the key factual information for the period. Learn these terms, but not in a mere recognition manner. To know that Langston Hughes was a black poet is not enough. When did he write? What did he write? What is his significance? Constantly ask questions as you go through each term under the *Major Terms and Concepts*. Your goal is to acquire enough understanding and knowledge to be able to organize your thoughts and to explain a point of view in an essay. Few of the AP multiple-choice questions are recognition questions. Most require extensive knowledge and understanding of the terms and concepts involved.

The next section gives brief summaries of the *Supreme Court Cases to Know*. The Court cases often focus on the issues of the era and illuminate these issues because of the Court's need to come to a decision.

Readings for Depth and Historical Interpretation provides a short bibliography of readings. You do not have time for an extensive list. This carefully developed list balances depth and interpretation. It was not compiled in the same manner as a bibliography for a term paper. These lists give you the depth needed for a deeper understanding of the conceptual issues for the period under study. Neither extensive nor exhaustive, the list is just very useful.

Each unit ends with a *Sample Outline* that illustrates what to do in order to prepare for an essay question on some part of that topic. As you work your way through the chapter you will realize that the outlines differ greatly. Some are more conceptual, others more factual. The difference is deliberate and is designed to show the range of approaches of studying for a major essay examination.

ROAD MAP

- *1607–1763*
- *1763–1783*
- *The Constitution*
- *1783–1800*
- *1800–1840*
- *1840–1877*
- *1865–1900*
- *1900–1920*
- *1920–1940*
- *1940–1960*
- *1960–1990s*

UNIT ONE: 1607–1763

Major Themes and Ideas

Colonization

1. How careful European plans for various colonies were altered by the reality of the American environment
2. Compare and contrast three colonies.
3. Explain and illustrate the growing differences between the Southern, New England, and Middle colonies.
4. There were two Souths: the Chesapeake society and the Carolinas.

Puritans and Religion

1. Characteristics of the Puritan experiment
2. How successful were the Puritans as a "City upon a Hill"?
3. Characteristics of religion in colonial America

Slavery and Indians

1. Interaction between Europeans and Native Americans (Indians)
2. Origins of slavery

Great Britain and the Colonies

1. Nature of the British political heritage we inherited
2. Events in Great Britain that had an impact on the colonies
3. The slow evolution from separate colonies to unity by 1763
4. Economic and political relationships between Great Britain and the colonies to 1763
5. British control through economic and political measures to 1763
6. Competition between Great Britain and France: causes, strengths of each, consequences
7. Impact of the Colonial wars on the colonies and on their relationship with Great Britain

Colonial Institutions

1. Role of slavery and indentured servanthood in the colonial economy
2. Mercantilism and the colonies
3. The great issues of the seventeenth century were theological, those of the 18th political.
4. Between 1607 and 1763 Americans gained control over their own economic and political institutions.
5. Growth of democracy in the colonial era: social, political, economic, and religious
6. Social mobility in the colonial era
7. The intellectual life of the colonies was more American than European.
8. Benjamin Franklin as a perfect example of an eighteenth century American

Major Terms and Concepts

Discovery

best known explorers, countries they sailed for, areas explored

Columbus, reasons

Spanish Armada, 1588

know the order of colonization of the colonies in North America

New England

Mayflower Compact

William Bradford

contrast Pilgrims and Puritans

Massachusetts Bay colony

Cambridge Agreement

Puritan migration

Church of England

John Winthrop, his beliefs

Separatists, Non-Separatists

Calvinism

Congregational church, Cambridge Platform

contrast Puritan colonies with others

Anne Hutchinson, antinomianism

Roger Williams, Rhode Island

covenant theology

voting granted to church members, 1631

Half-Way Covenant

Brattle Street Church

Thomas Hooker

Saybrook Platform

Fundamental Orders of Connecticut

Massachusetts school law

Harvard founded

New England Confederation, 1643

King Philip's War

Dominion of New England

Sir Edmund Andros

Southern Colonies

joint stock company

Virginia: purpose, problems, failures, successes

headright system

John Smith

John Rolfe, tobacco

slavery begins

House of Burgesses

Cavaliers

Bacon's Rebellion

Culpeper's Rebellion

Georgia: reasons, successes

James Oglethorpe

Carolinas

John Locke, Fundamental Constitutions

Charleston

staple crops in the South

Middle Colonies

Pennsylvania, William Penn

liberal land laws in Pennsylvania

Holy Experiment

1701 Frame of Government

New York: Dutch, 1664 English

patroon system

Peter Stuyvesant

Five Nations

crops in the middle colonies

New York City and Philadelphia as urban centers

Leisler's Rebellion

Benjamin Franklin

John Bartram

Religion in the Colonies

Pennsylvania, Maryland, Rhode Island— founders

established churches

Great Awakening

Jonathan Edwards, *Sinners in the Hands of an Angry God, A Careful and Strict Enquiry into...That Freedom of Will*

George Whitefield (pronounced Whitfield)

William Tennent

Gilbert Tennent

Old Lights, New Lights

Lord Baltimore

Maryland Act of Toleration

deism

Huguenots

SPG, Society for the Propagation of the Gospel (in Foreign Parts)

The Colonial Economy

mercantilism: features, rationale, impact on Great Britain, impact on the different colonies

North–South economic differences

Navigation Acts of 1650, 1660, 1663, 1696

admiralty courts

triangular trade (it wasn't very triangular!)

merchants/markets

consignment system

Molasses Act, 1733

Woolens Act, 1699; Hat Act, 1732; Iron Act, 1750

Currency Act, 1751 (applied to Massachusetts)

Currency Act, 1764 (extended to all the colonies)

Colonial Society

Salem witch trials

primogeniture, entail

quitrents

indentured servants

Poor Richard's Almanac(k)

Phillis Wheatley

Anne Bradstreet

Colonial Politics

Magna Carta, 1215

Petition of Right, 1628

Habeas Corpus Act, 1679

Bill of Rights, 1689

Board of Trade (of the Privy Council)

Robert Walpole

"salutary neglect"

the Enlightenment

theories of representative government in legislatures: virtual representation, actual representation

rise of the lower house

proprietary, charter, and royal colonies

colonial agents

town meetings

John Peter Zenger trial

Glorious Revolution, 1688

John Locke, his theories

a democratic society or not?

Great Britain versus France

land claims, squabbles in North America: where, why, over what

changes in land claims of 1689, 1713, 1763

differences between French and British colonization

why Great Britain eventually won

Queen Anne's War (War of Spanish Succession)

Treaty of Utrecht, 1713

War of Jenkin's Ear

King George's War (War of Austrian Succession)

French and Indian War, Seven Years War, Great War for Empire

Francis Parkman

Albany Plan of Union, Benjamin Franklin

General Braddock

William Pitt

Fort Pitt, Fort Duquesne

Wolfe, Montcalm, Quebec—the Plains of Abraham

Treaty of Paris, 1763

Pontiac's Rebellion

Proclamation of 1763

Readings for Depth and Historical Interpretation

Democracy in Colonial America

1. James A. Henretta, "Economic Development and Social Structure in Colonial Boston," *William and Mary Quarterly,* January 1965, pp. 75–92. Henretta uses two Boston tax lists—for 1687 and 1771—and quantitatively compares the two Bostons. He concludes that the 1771 Boston was decidedly less democratic.

2. Kenneth A. Lockridge and Alan Kreider, "The Evolution of Massachusetts Town Government, 1640–1740," *William and Mary Quarterly,* October 1966. The authors dispute the traditional view of the town meeting as the citadel of democracy. Until the end of the colonial era the town meeting was run by the selectmen through consensus politics, not democracy.

3. Charles Sydnor, chapter on "County Oligarchies" in *Gentlemen Freeholders: Political Practices in Washington's Virginia.* Sydnor deems the Virginia of George Washington's era an oligarchy run by church vestries and county courts. Who served in the legislature didn't matter.

4. Robert E. Brown, *Middle-Class Democracy and the Revolution in Massachusetts, 1691–1780.* Brown's thesis is in his title. Massachusetts in the colonial era was a middle-class democracy. The land ownership requirement for suffrage, inherited from the Old World to restrict voting, actually gave suffrage to eighty percent of the adult male population because land ownership was so widespread. The colonists fought Great Britain in the revolution to preserve the democratic society they already possessed.

5. Oscar Handlin, "The Significance of the Seventeenth Century," in James Smith, ed., *Seventeenth-Century America: Essays in Colonial History.* Handlin explains the seventeenth-century development of a decentralized, mobile society with a sense of mission which led to an institutional looseness and the creation of a new social order.

6. Kenneth Lockridge, *A New England Town, The First Hundred Years, Dedham, Massachusetts, 1636–1736,* contains several chapters that trace the changing politics over this hundred-year period. You should also see Michael Zuckerman, "The Social Context of Democracy in Massachusetts," *William and Mary Quarterly,* October 1968, pp. 523–544, which argues that a democratic elite led by consensus. Is this democracy?

7. A good recent comparison of Virginia and Massachusetts is found in Timothy Breen, *Puritans and Adventurers: Change and Persistence in Early America.* Breen compares social values, social institutions, and the transfer of these institutions to different Americas from what was in actuality different Englands.

Origins of Slavery

1. The economic argument, that the Southern need for a labor supply was the primary reason for the institution of slavery, is found in Oscar and Mary Handlin, *Race and Nationality in American Life,* pp. 7–28. A much more complete analysis is in Peter Kolchin, *Unfree Labor: American Slavery and Russian Serfdom,* "Introduction: The Origin and Consolidation of Unfree Labor," pp. 1–46. To continue the study of slavery after its establishment, see Allan Kulikoff, *Tobacco and Slaves: The Development of Southern Cultures in the Chesapeake, 1680–1800.*

2. Carl N. Degler, Chapter 1, "Black Men in a White Men's Country," in his *Out of Our Past.* Degler sees the existence of prejudice as the significant attitudinal source in the early development of slavery.

3. Winthrop Jordan, Chapter 2, "Unthinking Decision, Enslavement of Africans in America to 1700," in his *The White Man's Burden; or,* the longer book, *White Over Black.* (One has the footnotes, one doesn't.) The enslavement of blacks was an "unthinking decision" resulting from a variety of factors—racism, labor need, a

general debasement of blacks, English concepts of blackness, and the African's heathen status.

4. Edmund S. Morgan argues a more social and cultural explanation. Black slavery arose as part of a long term attempt to create a stable social order, which ultimately became the basis of the development of unique ideas of freedom and equality for whites. See the last four chapters in Edmund S. Morgan, *American Slavery, American Freedom: The Ordeal of Colonial Virginia,* or, the essence of his arguments in "Slavery and Freedom: The American Paradox," *Journal of American History,* June 1972.

5. For white servitude, indentured servants, see Richard Hofstadter, *America at 1750: A Social Portrait*, pp. 33–65.

Religion in the Colonies

1. Edmund S. Morgan, *The Puritan Dilemma: The Story of John Winthrop*, pp. 84–95. Gives the political thought of John Winthrop and the conversion of the charter into a government in 1631.

2. Daniel J. Boorstin, "A City Upon A Hill: The Puritans of Massachusetts Bay" in his *The Americans: The Colonial Experience.* Boorstin sees the Puritans as a practical people, community builders who were not preoccupied with religious dogma.

3. Carl Degler, section from Chapter 1, "Were the Puritans 'Puritanical'?" in his *Out of Our Past*. Degler finds a different group than that found by nineteenth-century moralists.

4. Richard Bushman, "Awakening," in his *From Puritan to Yankee: Character and the Social Order in Connecticut, 1690–1765*. The chapter on the Awakening helps explain the transition of the Puritan into a Yankee as the old social and religious order broke down in the face of economic and social changes.

5. The Puritan church in one town is the focus of Kenneth Lockridge, *A New England Town, the First Hundred Years, Dedham, Massachusetts, 1636–1736*. Both persistence and change coexisted. See the chapter on "The Heart of Perfection: The Church."

6. The Great Awakening and its impact is in Richard Hofstadter, *America at 1750: A Social Portrait*. See the chapters on "The Awakeners" and "The Awakening and the Churches."

7. Patricia U. Bonomi, *Under the Cope of Heaven: Religion, Society, and Politics in Colonial America,* carries the story of religion throughout the colonial period. The interplay of politics and religion in the Great Awakening and the Revolution explains "The Foundation of American Religious Culture" (last chapter) by the Revolution:

Sample Outline

What were the chief characteristics of religion in colonial America? Since this question doesn't set a terminal date for the colonial period, you must decide the chronological end of your outline. You may use 1763, 1775, 1783, or 1789. Be sure to carry your outline to a conclusion chronologically. Your outline should prepare you to be able to answer any question about any aspect of colonial religion.

Religion in the Colonial Era

I. Characteristics of Religion

    A. Important motive behind several colonies

        1. Freedom from religious persecution (not religious freedom)

           a. PA: Penn, 1682, Quakers

           b. RI: Roger Williams, from Massachusetts

           c. MD: Lord Baltimore, Catholics

d.   SC and NJ experiments

2.   Combat spread of Catholic powers in Spain and France

3.   French Huguenots

B.   Colonial religion part of the continuing debate dating from the Reformation

1.   Role of ministers, number of sacraments, organization of the church, liturgical service, hierarchy, Presbyterians, Congregationalists, Quakers, antinomianism, Arminianism

2.   Changes in England: Bishop Laud, Charles I, 39 Articles, Civil War, Levellers, Puritan Commonwealth, Test Act (1673), Toleration Act (1689), Glorious Revolution

C.   Influence of Puritanism

1.   Source of significant ideas—education for Bible reading, Harvard—ministers, higher law, moral codes

2.   City upon a hill, an example of a sense of mission

3.   Covenant theology: boost to the idea of a covenant between government and governed

D.   Union of church and state

1.   Established churches in 9 colonies (tax supported)

Anglican: NY, MD, VA, NC, SC, GA

Congregational: Mass., Conn., NH

Quakers: PA (for all practical purposes)

2.   Roger Williams: RI separate to preserve the purity of church, not state

3.   Fear of tyranny of church and state, SPG (Society for the Propagation of the Gospel in Foreign Parts) seen as a conspiracy

4.   Anne Hutchinson exiled for doctrinal belief that faith more important than good works

E.   Overwhelmingly Protestant

1.   Of 3142 church buildings in 1775 only 56 Catholic churches and 5 Jewish synagogues—more than 98% Protestant

2.   Called "Penal Period" by Catholic historians; all colonies had anti-Catholic laws at one time

3.   U.S. now more than 20% Catholic, 3% Jewish

II.   Changes in the Colonial Period

A.   Multitude of religions

1.   Too many for any one church to control, although Mass and Pa significant; Roger Williams, Anne Hutchinson, Mary Dyer

2.   Four largest, Congregational, Presbyterian, Anglican, Baptist, were only 21%, 19%, 16%, and 16% of total population.

B.   Calvinistic

1.   Emphasis on evangelical Calvinism

2. The individual's direct personal relationship to God rather than the church's corporate one

3. Emotion, not doctrine

C. Influence of the Great Awakening

1. Reinvigorated Calvinistic influence—society seen as egalitarian

2. Jonathan Edwards, *Sinners in the Hands of an Angry God ... Freedom of Will*

3. William and George Tennent

4. George Whitefield from Great Britain

5. Colleges established to train ministers

6. Controversies within denominations—New Sides, Old Sides; New Lights, Old Lights

7. Missionaries to Indians

D. Many unchurched

1. Many never attended church (in Phila. only 18 churches in 1776, for 40,000 people)

2. Few churches or missionaries in backwoods areas

3. Deism widespread among upper classes

E. Colonial religion contributed to the rise of political liberty.

1. James I: "No Bishop, No King." Democratic churches led to a demand for democratic governments.

2. Puritan franchise to church members seemingly restrictive, but was very democratic

3. Concept of natural laws, natural rights fed by deism

4. Weak church organization and control spurred individualism. Calvinism emphasized significance of individual rather than corporate body.

5. Disestablishment came only because it proved too difficult to establish a single church. Disestablishment came with Revolutionary War, VA Declaration of Rights (1776); VA Act for Establishment of Religious Freedom (1785) after much debate and effort to establish an official church.

6. Religious freedom not original desire (MD Act of Toleration for only those who believed in the Trinity) but ended up as such. (Don't confuse religious freedom and freedom from religious persecution.)

UNIT TWO: 1763–1783

Major Themes and Ideas

The Coming of the American Revolution

Be aware that it is possible to think of the "Revolution" in three ways: the War for Independence, 1775–1783; the period from 1763–1783; or the period from 1763 to the writing of the Constitution. Be sure your essay fits the meaning of the wording of the question.

1. The victory over France led to the American Revolution.

2. The long- and short-run causes of the American Revolution

3. Colonial assemblies as leaders against Great Britain

4. The Revolution fomented by changes in British colonial policy in the 1763–1776 period

5. The Revolution was brought on by tight economic controls and loose political controls.

6. Economic factors caused the Revolution.

7. The ideas and accusations in the Declaration of Independence

8. Support two different interpretations by historians on the causes of the American Revolution.

The American Revolution

1. The American Revolution as an event in European history

2. Was the Treaty of Paris (1783) a victory for the U.S.?

3. What did the participants in the American Revolution seek to preserve in American society?

4. In what ways and how had the thirteen separate colonies become similar by the time of the Revolution?

5. There were 21 British colonies in the New World. Why didn't all of them revolt?

6. The American Revolution as a democratic revolution turned into an aristocratic government by the Constitution

7. Why did great political thinkers and leaders develop in the slave South?

8. The American Revolution as a question of home rule and who should rule at home

9. The American Revolution as a revolutionary event: consider the economic and social changes associated with the Revolution.

10. Was the Revolution avoidable?

Major Terms and Concepts

Great Britain versus France

Review Unit One terms and concepts on this topic.

Coming of the American Revolution

> writs of assistance
>
> James Otis
>
> Pontiac's Rebellion
>
> Proclamation of 1763
>
> Paxton Boys
>
> Navigation Act, 1651 (a temporary act)

Navigation Act, 1660: renewed the provisions of the 1651 act; trade in English ships; enumerated articles to be sold only to England

Navigation Act, 1663: European trade through England first, then to colonies; strengthened in 1673

Navigation Act, 1696: created Board of Trade and Plantations to enforce navigation acts

Grenville's program

Sugar Act, 1764: modified Molasses Act,

1733

Currency Act, 1764: extended Currency Act of 1751, that applied only to Mass., to all the colonies

vice-admiralty courts

non-importation

virtual, actual representation

Stamp Act

Virginia Resolves

Stamp Act Congress, 1765

Patrick Henry

Sons of Liberty

internal taxes

external taxes

Declaratory Act, 1766

Quartering Act (called the Mutiny Act by the British)

Townshend Acts, reaction

John Dickinson, "Letters From a Farmer in Pennsylvania"

Massachusetts Circular Letter

Sam Adams

The Association

repeal of the Townshend Acts, except tax on tea

Boston Massacre, 1770

Crispus Attucks

John Adams

Carolina Regulators

Battle of the Alamance

Gaspee incident

Governor Thomas Hutchinson of Mass

committees of correspondence

Lord North

Tea Act, East India Company

Boston Tea Party, 1773

Coercive Acts (or Intolerable Acts, or Repressive Acts)

Boston Port Act

Massachusetts Government Act

Quebec Act

First Continental Congress, 1774

Suffolk Resolves

Galloway Plan

Continental Association

Lexington and Concord, April 19, 1775

Paul Revere, William Dawes

Second Continental Congress

George Washington

Battle of Bunker Hill (Breed's Hill)

Olive Branch Petition

Thomas Paine, *Common Sense*

natural rights philosophy

John Locke, *Second Treatise of Government*

George III

Richard Henry Lee's Resolution of June 7, 1776: "These united colonies are, and of right ought to be, free and independent states."

Committee on Independence: Thomas Jefferson, Benjamin Franklin, John Adams, Roger Sherman, and Robert Livingston

July 4, 1776 and the Declaration of Independence. Read it and know the ideas in the preamble.

Somerset case (in Great Britain)

Quock Walker case—Mass.

Revolutionary War

John Adams

Abigail Adams

Mercy Otis Warren

Edmund Burke

Lafayette

George Rogers Clark

Benedict Arnold

Robert Morris

John Paul Jones

Bonhomme Richard and the *Serapis*

Conway cabal

French Alliance of 1778, reasons for it

major battles: Saratoga, Valley Forge

Yorktown, Lord Cornwallis

League of Armed Neutrality

Treaty of Paris, 1783

negotiators: Benjamin Franklin, John Adams, John Jay

French and British intrigue over U.S. boundaries

social impact of the war

primogeniture, entail

disestablishment, Virginia Statute of Religious Freedom

new state constitutions (Mass new constitution adopted by popular vote)

Newburgh conspiracy

Articles of Confederation: powers, weaknesses, successes

Readings for Depth and Historical Interpretation

The American Revolution and the Civil War are two of the most studied and least understood events in American history. We know what happened; what we don't know is why both happened and what they mean in the broader context of American history. Additional readings on the American Revolution provide some depth and understanding. Complete understanding takes more than a lifetime.

American Revolution

1. Robert B. Downs, "Clarion Call for Revolution: Thomas Paine's *Common Sense*," in *Books That Changed America*. Downs calls *Common Sense* "the American best-seller of all time in relation to population." Probably every fifth American owned a copy of *Common Sense*. This source summarizes Paine's ideas and place in American history.

2. Carl Becker, "Provincial Parties and Party Politics, 1700–1769," in his *The History of Political Parties in the Province of New York, 1760–1776*. Becker sees the American Revolution as two struggles—one against the British for independence and another between the privileged and the unprivileged for control of the state government. "The first was the question of home rule; second was the question ... of who should rule at home."

3. J. Franklin Jameson, *The American Revolution Considered as a Social Movement*. Originally published in 1926, Jameson sees accompanying the Revolution deep and permanent social and economic changes in the patterns of landholding, church-state relations, restrictions on slavery, changes in inheritance laws, etc.

4. Crane Brinton, *The Anatomy of Revolution*. This 1938 book uses four revolutions—the American, French, English, and Russian—to study the phenomenon of revolutions. It is difficult reading, but immensely rewarding for the serious student of history.

5. Gordon S. Wood, "Rhetoric and Reality in the American Revolution," *William and Mary Quarterly,* 1966. Wood reviews the various interpretations for the causes of the American Revolution, and discusses the difficulty involved in trying to link ideas and behavior.

6. Robert E. Brown, *Middle-Class Democracy and the Revolution in Massachusetts, 1691–1780*. Brown claims that Massachusetts in the colonial era was already a middle-class democracy because the land ownership requirement for the right of suffrage gave the right to vote to over 80 percent of the adult white males. Because the colonists fought against Great Britain to preserve the already existing democratic society, ours was a conservative revolution.

7. Robert A. Gross, *The Minutemen and Their World,* is a superb book that looks at life in Concord, Massachusetts, before and during the American Revolution. The outside world intruded upon a community already under stress, further straining the social and political fabric. This is Jameson's argument at the microlevel.

8. The difficulties involved in raising an army are well presented in John Shy, "Mobilizing Armed Force in the American Revolution," in John Parker and Carol Urness, eds., *The American Revolution: A Heritage of Change.* Another article on the loyalists is also good.

Sample Outline

The American Revolution as an intellectual and ideological revolution

I.   **Looking Backward, 1776 to 1760 in Retrospect**

   A.   John Adams: "There seems to be a direct and formal design to enslave America."

   B.   Thomas Jefferson in 1774: "[though] single acts of tyranny may be ascribed to the accidental opinion of a day ... a series of oppressions begun at a distinguished period and pursued unalterably through every change of ministers too plainly proves a deliberate and systematical plan of reducing us to slavery."

   C.   Changes in self-perception and changes in our image of Great Britain

      1.   America seen as the citadel of natural rights

      2.   Long American identification with and sympathy for the Whig opposition to the British government

      3.   America was the last defense of traditional English liberties and rights. (Note that early appeals were to Parliament until the colonists realized that Parliament sided with the stupid, corrupt, or evil ministers. Then the appeal was to the king until the colonists realized the king, the ministers, and Parliament were all of a single mind.)

      4.   The entire British government and society increasingly seen as corrupt; America viewed as crude, but morally superior; slow realization that our inferiority was really our superiority.

II. **Specific British Acts of Tyranny (part of the long "series of oppressions" and the "direct and formal design")**

   A.   The early acts

      1.   Writs of assistance widely thought to be illegal (Mass. high court had to ask if they were legal because the court was uncertain itself. Almost all colonial lawyers thought them to be unconstitutional.)

      2.   Proclamation of 1763 a logical British answer to Pontiac's Rebellion, but had adverse impact on land speculators and colonial land claims in a society that increasingly thought of itself as crowded

      3.   Revenue laws

         a.   Sugar Act, 1764, cut rates of Molasses Act of 1733, but now strictly enforced

         b.   Currency Act, 1764, forbade issuing of paper money by colonies, hindering trade

         c.   Stamp Act, 1765, to be affixed to 54 different types of documents, from 1¢ to $10 to set a precedent for internal taxes. (The amounts to be raised were small, why did the British push for it?)

         d.   Stamp Act Congress: Unity forced England to back down; Declaratory Act passed, ignored by colonists

      4.   The attack on the principle of representative government

         a.   Suspension of the NY legislature for protesting against the Quartering Act

b. Suspension of Mass. legislature for circular letter urging resistance to Townshend Acts

B. Corruption in Great Britain

1. John Wilkes: a radical denied his seat in Parliament after election and imprisoned

2. His supporters gathered at St. George's Fields, beside King's Bench Prison, to protest and see him; British army dispersed mob (attacked by a standing army)

3. Wilkes's friend, Colonel Barre, condemned government's action. (Wilkes-Barre, PA, was named for them.)

4. Paoli, leading a revolution in Corsica, asked England for aid, and was instead lured from his revolution by British money and gifts (Paoli, PA. named for him).

5. Significance of these events: British government opposed to representative government and republican ideals; preferred old monarchical principles

6. Boston Massacre (1770) similar to St. George's Fields massacre (Note the terminology. A few deaths become a massacre when fighting tyranny.)

C. Confirmation of prior suspicions

1. 1770–1773 a period of calm with isolated events—Alexander McDougall, NYC, Sons of Liberty leader imprisoned; Gaspee burned, British revenue ship

2. Committees of correspondence active

3. Slow development of *dvoevlastie* (see p. 14)

4. Boston Tea Party, 1773, 342 chests of tea

5. British response: Coercive Acts (Intolerable Acts or Repressive Acts)

a. Closed port of Boston

b. British troops could be quartered anywhere at colonial expense.

c. Mass town meetings restricted to one a year

d. British officials to be tried in English rather than American courts

6. Quebec Act passed to appease Canadian French Catholics and retain their loyalty (very successful in long run); angered Americans, extended Canada's border to Ohio River, jeopardized colonial land claims and extended area of hated Catholicism. (The colonists unfairly linked the Quebec Act to Intolerable Acts.)

7. Intolerable Acts led to First Continental Congress.

III. Reflections on Events Since 1763

A. First Continental Congress asked for redress of grievances, yet they denounced every British action taken since 1763.

B. Church of England's SPG sent missionaries to Indians, yet they stayed in Boston area where there had been no Indians for 100 years.

C. Since 1763 there had been a large increase in the number of British officials in the colonies—why?

D. New policy of tenure for judges caused reduced effect of popular pressure on judges.

E. Vice-admiralty courts to try violation of navigation acts (no longer a jury of your peers, your fellow anti-Britishers)

F. Shift of location of trials from Mass to Nova Scotia

IV. The Revolution in American Thinking

A. The Revolution erupted at the end of a long period culminating in the development of uniquely American political, social, and intellectual ideas.

B. The intense political debate from 1763–1776 convinced Americans that American society and institutions were not only different from, but better than their British counterparts.

C. Americans became convinced that traditional English liberties could only survive on the pure American republican continent.

D. Thus, the commitment to a moralistic, optimistic, regenerative republic

E. All that was left after this realization was for the Second Continental Congress to assume the power to govern, which it did.

THE CONSTITUTION

Dividing Power Between the Federal Government and the State Governments

Federal Powers Only

1. Regulate foreign commerce
2. Regulate interstate commerce
3. Coin money
4. Establish post offices
5. Control naturalization and immigration
6. Grant patents and copyrights
7. Declare war and peace
8. Admit new states
9. Fix standard weights and measures
10. Raise and maintain an army and navy
11. Govern the District of Columbia
12. Conduct foreign relations
13. Set uniform laws for bankruptcy

Federal and State Powers

1. To tax, to borrow, and to spend money
2. To control the militia
3. Both governments could now act directly on individuals

Limitations on the Federal Government

1. Bill of Rights guarantees for individuals
2. No ex post facto laws
3. No bill of attainder
4. Appropriation for the military limited to two years
5. May not suspend habeas corpus except in a crisis
6. May not favor one port over another
7. No taxes on exports
8. May not grant titles

State Powers Only

1. Conduct elections
2. Establish qualifications for voters
3. Provide local governments
4. Ratify amendments to the Constitution
5. Regulate contracts, wills
6. Regulate intrastate commerce
7. Provide education
8. Levy direct taxes (before the Sixteenth Amendment permitted the federal government to levy direct taxes)
9. Exercise police power over the public's health, safety, and morals
10. Maintain integrity of state borders—no change without approval of states involved

Limitations on State Governments

1. No ex post facto laws
2. No bill of attainder
3. May not enter into a treaty, alliance, or confederation
4. May not grant letters of marque and reprisal
5. May not impair contracts
6. May not print money or emit bills of credit
7. May not levy export or import taxes
8. May not wage war (unless invaded)

Federalism

Federalism is composed of two independent levels of government, the federal and the state. The powers granted to the federal government are called delegated or enumerated powers. All powers not granted to the federal government and not specifically prohibited to the states are reserved powers belonging to the states.

The elastic clause, Article I, Section 8, Clause 18, is the source of the debate over loose and strict construction of the Constitution. The Founding Fathers inserted the elastic clause into the Constitution because they realized that they could not think of everything. The Constitution clearly grants the power to print money. Does that include the power to purchase ink and paper? The elastic clause solved that problem. But what of questions in more ambiguous areas? The federal government may collect taxes. Can it create a national bank to deposit its tax revenues? Or build a warehouse to house merchandise before customs duties are collected? Defining the edges of federal and state intrusions upon one another is a never-ending process. In some new areas the federal and state governments have expanded the scope of their shared powers through grants such as federal aid for building highways.

It's interesting to learn what the Founding Fathers did not argue about. The areas of agreement are rarely mentioned, and yet, probably nowhere else in the world would a group of government makers have accepted the following without at least serious argument:

1. The principle of representative government

2. A single executive (Plural executives are common in history. Within a short time the French Revolution produced a multiple executive, the Directory.)

3. A bicameral legislature (Many national legislatures are unicameral, and almost all products of revolutions are unicameral. Franklin wanted a unicameral legislature, since Pennsylvania had one.)

4. A means to amend the Constitution in the future (This was a confession that their work was imperfect.)

5. A fixed time for elections, limiting terms of office

6. Two governments, a federal and a state, with overlapping powers and each having a legislature, an executive, and a judiciary

7. The supremacy of the national government over state governments (Perhaps the Articles of Confederation could have been strengthened.)

Sections of the Constitution

Preamble

It gives the purposes of the Constitution although it is not technically part of the Constitution. Read it.

Article I: Legislature

TERMS—KNOW THE FOLLOWING:

    logrolling

    riders

    quorum

    seniority

    committee system

    majority leader

    majority whip

    minority leader

    minority whip

    gerrymander

YOU SHOULD KNOW:

    how a bill becomes a law

    that each House judges the qualifications of its members

    that members of Congress may not hold another federal office

    that members of Congress are free from arrest for anything said on the floor of Congress

HOUSE OF REPRESENTATIVES

> 2-year terms, 25 years old at least, 435 members, based on population
>
> Speaker of the House presides
>
> limited debate because of size, except that they may reorganize themselves into the Committee of the Whole (technically a committee) for long debate
>
> brings impeachment charges
>
> All money bills must originate in the House

SENATE

> 6-year terms, 30 years old at least, two per state
>
> Vice-president is presiding officer, and may vote in a tie
>
> President pro tempore normally presides
>
> unlimited debate, filibuster, closure (cloture)
>
> originally elected by state legislatures
>
> serves as a court and jury for impeachment
>
> approves or rejects presidential nominations
>
> approves or rejects treaties

Article II: Executive

> 4-year term, no limit on reelection, 35 years old at least, citizen for at least 14 years
>
> Twenty-second Amendment limited the president to two terms

The president and the vice-president were elected by the electoral college, which was designed to insulate the selection process from the people. Electors were selected by state legislatures, and each state had the same number of electors as it had total senators and representatives. The winner was the man (or woman) with the most votes named on over one half of the electoral ballots. The vice-president was the one with the second highest number of votes, provided that he (or she) was also named on over one half of the ballots. If no one received a majority the House of Representatives, voting by states, selected the president; the Senate selected the vice-president. Note that in either case the states are equal in power. The Founding Fathers expected four out of every five presidential elections to end in the House of Representatives. If each elector independently selected his choice for the two best men for president,

the chances of a majority of electors naming one of the same choices would be very slim. Thus, most elections would go to the House of Representatives. The rise of political parties altered the operation of the electoral college. Electors began to pledge that they would vote for a certain candidate if selected as an elector. Party loyalty negated the original intention of the electoral college mechanism.

The electoral college system has come under criticism from many sides. It has many advantages, though, and should not be hastily abandoned. It produces a clear winner. If we depended on a national popular vote the recounting might drag through courts for years. The electoral college also reminds us that this is a federal system. States do count for something other than serving as administrative units for the federal government's programs.

The president's powers, as described by Clinton Rossiter in *The American Presidency,* are as follows:

CONSTITUTIONAL RESPONSIBILITIES

> Chief of state—the ceremonial head of the government
>
> Chief executive—responsible for carrying out laws
>
> Commander in chief—commander of the armed forces
>
> Chief diplomat—As Truman said in 1948, "I make American foreign policy."
>
> Chief legislator—presents a legislative program to Congress and exerts leadership, signs legislation

UNOFFICIAL RESPONSIBILITIES

> Chief of party—leads his party as a politician
>
> Voice of the people—the molder and voice of public opinion
>
> Protector of the peace—responds to emergencies with aid and comfort
>
> Manager of prosperity—the Employment Act of 1946 gives the president the responsibility for the state of the economy. (Even if this law didn't, the voters would.)
>
> World leader—the leader of the coalition of free nations

Article III: Judiciary

The Constitution established the Supreme Court and described its powers but left all the details to Congress. The Judiciary Act of 1789 created the federal court system with district courts and circuit courts. Section 2 of Article III describes the original jurisdiction cases for federal courts. These suits begin in the federal courts. Another jurisdiction the courts possess is over appellate cases, which are appealed from lower court decisions. This article specifically defines treason as an overt act witnessed by two other persons. The Founding Fathers were well aware of the ease with which the charge of treason had been used to smear in the past. Treason is such an odious crime that the accused is popularly convicted by just the accusation. The Founding Fathers wanted a clear act, not a thought or a profane expression, with two witnesses. You may, in this country, discuss many ideas with impunity as long as you don't actually do something. Discussing the ease and desirability of overthrowing the government might get you some strange glances from your neighbors. Discussing the same ideas while loading your shotgun will get you in deep trouble.

Terms—know the following:

> common law
>
> statute law
>
> civil law
>
> equity law
>
> admiralty and maritime law
>
> martial law
>
> international law
>
> canon law
>
> majority opinion
>
> minority opinion or dissenting opinion
>
> concurring opinion

Article IV: Interstate Relations

Section 1 is the "full faith and credit" clause. This clause means that court decisions and legal actions in one state are valid in others. Once married, you do not have to remarry if you move to another state.

A corporation chartered in one state is a corporation in the other 49 states. This article provided for the extradition of criminals and runaway slaves and the reciprocal exchange of the benefits of citizenship. New states may be added to the original 13. This sounds so logical to us today that we do not appreciate how revolutionary it was. The Northwest Ordinance of 1787 and the Constitution admitted new states on equal footing with the older states and guaranteed that the power and influence of the original states would be diluted. Virginia had one-thirteenth of the vote in the first Senate and 10 of the 65 members of the first House of Representatives. Virginia's power in the present Congress is much less. This article also guarantees a republican form of government for each state and federal protection against invasion and domestic violence.

Article V: The Amendment Process

Amendments can be *proposed* by a two-thirds vote of each house of Congress or by a special convention called by Congress upon the request of two-thirds of the state legislatures. Amendments can be *ratified* by three-fourths of the state legislatures or by conventions in three-fourths of the states. Only the Twenty-first Amendment (repeal of prohibition) was ratified by the latter method. The Seventeenth Amendment passed Congress only after it became clear that the states would actually use the convention method to propose an amendment. Since the Articles of Confederation demanded unanimous consent for amendments, the Founding Fathers wanted to make amending the Constitution easier but still prevent emotional issues from easily changing the supreme law of the land.

Article VI: Supremacy Clause

All federal and state judges and officials must take an oath to support the Constitution. According to the Constitution, it is the supreme law of the land, followed by treaties, federal laws (and now federal regulatory agency directives), state constitutions, state laws, and local laws. For example, if a treaty and a state law conflict, the treaty takes precedence.

Article VII: Ratification

The Constitution went into effect when it was ratified by special conventions in nine states. Rhode Island and North Carolina disapproved of the Constitution. You should take a long look at the order of ratification and the closeness of the vote in many states. As the ninth state to ratify approached, the crux of the ratification vote lay in Virginia and New York. If they did not join, the whole endeavor was in jeopardy.

State	Vote	Date
1. Delaware	unanimous	Dec. 7, 1787
2. Pennsylvania	46 to 23	Dec. 12, 1787
3. New Jersey	unanimous	Dec. 18, 1787
4. Georgia	unanimous	Jan. 2, 1788
5. Connecticut	128 to 40	Jan. 9, 1788
6. Massachusetts	187 to 168	Feb. 7, 1788
7. Maryland	63 to 11	Apr. 28, 1788
8. South Carolina	149 to 73	May 23, 1788
9. New Hampshire	57 to 47	June 21, 1788
10. Virginia	89 to 79	June 26, 1788
11. New York	30 to 27	July 26, 1788
12. North Carolina	194 to 77	Nov. 21,1789
13. Rhode Island	34 to 32	May 29, 1790

Amendments to the Constitution

THE BILL OF RIGHTS—FIRST–TENTH AMENDMENTS, all passed in 1791

FIRST AMENDMENT: freedom of religion, speech, press, assembly, and freedom to petition the government

SECOND AMENDMENT: right to bear arms (in order for states to maintain a militia. This was not meant to guarantee an individual's right to bear arms.)

THIRD AMENDMENT: no quartering of troops in private homes

FOURTH AMENDMENT: specific search warrants required

FIFTH AMENDMENT: rights of the accused, indictments required, double jeopardy, self-incrimination, due process, just compensation

SIXTH AMENDMENT: speedy and public trial, to be confronted by witnesses, ability to call your own witnesses

SEVENTH AMENDMENT: trial by jury

EIGHTH AMENDMENT: excessive bail, cruel and unusual punishment

NINTH AMENDMENT: All rights not enumerated are retained by the people.

TENTH AMENDMENT: All powers not delegated are retained by the states.

ELEVENTH AMENDMENT, 1798: Individuals may not sue states.

TWELFTH AMENDMENT, 1804: Electors cast separate ballots for president and vice-president. If there is no winner the House selects the president and the Senate the vice-president. (This amendment prevented the recurrence of the results of the election of 1800.)

CIVIL WAR AMENDMENTS—THIRTEENTH, FOURTEENTH, FIFTEENTH

THIRTEENTH AMENDMENT, 1865: abolishes slavery

FOURTEENTH AMENDMENT, 1868: Blacks became citizens. Confederate leaders were not eligible for public office; Confederate debt was void; and (Southern) states would have their representation in Congress reduced proportionately if they denied (blacks) voting rights. This amendment confers dual citizenship—you are a citizen of the United States and of your state. Section 1 has been interpreted as applying all the rights in the Bill of Rights, which applied only to the federal government, to the state governments. The "due process" clause and the "equal protection of the laws" clause have been part of many significant court suits.

FIFTEENTH AMENDMENT, 1870: Black suffrage guaranteed.

PROGRESSIVE AMENDMENTS—SIXTEENTH, SEVENTEENTH, EIGHTEENTH, NINETEENTH

SIXTEENTH AMENDMENT, 1913: legalizes the income tax

SEVENTEENTH AMENDMENT, 1913: direct election of senators, instead of by state legislatures

EIGHTEENTH AMENDMENT, 1919: Prohibition

NINETEENTH AMENDMENT, 1920: women's suffrage

TWENTIETH AMENDMENT, 1933: Lame duck sessions of Congress were abolished, and inauguration date was changed from March 4 to January 20. Under the older timetable newly elected congressmen did not meet until thirteen months after their election in November. This amendment eliminated the session of Congress that met from December to March, after the November elections had possibly replaced some congressmen.

TWENTY-FIRST AMENDMENT, 1933: repealed prohibition

TWENTY-SECOND AMENDMENT, 1951: two-term limit for the president

TWENTY-THIRD AMENDMENT, 1961: presidential electoral votes for the District of Columbia

TWENTY-FOURTH AMENDMENT, 1964: poll taxes prohibited

TWENTY-FIFTH AMENDMENT, 1967: presidential disability and succession

TWENTY-SIXTH AMENDMENT, 1971: suffrage for eighteen-year-olds

Separation of Powers

The separation of powers and the checks and balances system prevent any person or group from gaining control of all three branches of government. They diffuse power. In addition, the federal nature of our government puts us under two executives, the president and a governor; two legislatures, Congress and a state assembly; and two judiciaries, the federal and state courts. As an ambassador once said, "Anyone who thinks he knows exactly how and where a decision is made in America is crazy." The levels of government and the diffusion of power and responsibility do exactly what they were intended to do—prevent centralization and dilute authority. The three most important powers of government are lodged mainly in three separate branches: legislative power—power to make laws; executive power—power to enforce laws; and judicial power—power to interpret laws.

One of the most difficult concepts for students to understand is that the Founding Fathers intended to create a slow, deliberate government. They valued debate and rational decisions more than haste. The popular will is often frustrated by the slow machinery, but the Constitution is the oldest continuous form of government in the world. The government doesn't work quickly, but it seems to work well.

Checks and Balances

President versus Congress

1. May veto legislation
2. Suggests legislation
3. Party leader
4. Molds public opinion
5. May call a special session
6. Commander in chief

1. May override a veto by a two-thirds vote
2. Investigates executive branch
3. Has control over appropriations
4. Declares war
5. House only may impeach President
6. Senate only is court and jury for impeachment

7. Chief diplomat

8. Salary may not be raised or lowered

7. Senate only ratifies appointments

8. Senate only ratifies treaties

Congress versus Judiciary

1. Creates inferior courts and their jurisdiction

2. Determines the number of Supreme Court judges

3. May specifically restrict court review of a piece of legislation*

4. May propose a constitutional amendment to negate a court decision

5. House only may impeach judges

6. Senate only is court and jury for impeachment

7. Senate only ratifies presidential

1. Interprets laws and treaties

2. Judicial review of laws (when the issue comes up in a court case)

3. Lifetime tenure

Judiciary versus President

1. Interprets laws and treaties

2. Judicial review of presidential actions (when the issue comes up in a court suit)

3. Lifetime tenure

1. May pardon

2. Appoints judges (with Senate approval)

3. May refuse to enforce a court order

* Several colleagues inquired about the basis for number three. The reference is to "the exceptions clause of the Constitution," Article III, Section 2, Clause 2, " ... the supreme Court shall have appellate Jurisdiction, both as to Law and Fact, with such Exceptions, and under such Regulations as the Congress shall make." In the debate over the repeal of the Judiciary Act of 1801, following Jefferson's victory over John Adams, the Federalists in Congress never denied the right to use this clause to modify the Supreme Court's appellate jurisdiction. The best example of a decision under this clause occurred on March 27, 1868, when the Radical Republicans in Congress repealed an 1867 law, which conferred upon the Supreme Court the right to hear certain appeals involving habeas corpus. In Ex Parte McCardle (also spelled McArdle), 1869, the Supreme Court acknowledged Congress' right to define and to limit its appellate jurisdiction by unanimously declaring that no appeal from a federal Circuit Court under the repealed act of 1867 was reviewable.

Scholars still argue over the meaning of "the exceptions clause" within the context of the whole Article III and the subsequent evolution of constitutional law and practice. See Raoul Berger, *Congress* v. *The Supreme Court*, 1969, and section four of Sarah Baumgartner Thurow, editor, *E Pluribus Unum: Constitutional Principles and the Institutions of Government*, 1988.

Congress and Voting

Study the following list. Students often confuse the majorities needed for legislative actions.

ACTIONS REQUIRING ONLY A MAJORITY VOTE

- raising taxes
- appropriations
- declaring war
- adding to the national debt
- instituting a draft
- House only—impeachment charges

ACTIONS REQUIRING A TWO-THIRDS MAJORITY

- overriding a presidential veto
- proposing amendments to the Constitution
- expelling a member of Congress (a two-thirds vote in only that one house of Congress)
- Senate only—ratifying treaties
- Senate only—acting as a jury for impeachment
- Senate only—ratifying presidential appointments to executive branch positions, the judiciary, and federal agencies

ACTIONS REQUIRING A THREE-FOURTHS MAJORITY

- three-fourths of the states must approve a proposed constitutional amendment

UNIT THREE: 1783–1800

Major Themes and Ideas

Confederation and Constitution

1. Enlightenment concepts and the Constitution

2. How critical was the "critical period"?

3. Compare and contrast the Declaration of Independence, the Articles of Confederation, and the Constitution.

4. Did the Constitution reject the principles of the Declaration of Independence?

5. The Constitution came from American experiences.

6. The Constitution came from European ideas and concepts.

7. Origins of the ideas of separation of powers, written constitutions, and federalism

8. Areas of agreement at the Constitutional Convention

9. Amendments; reasons for them

10. Historiography of the Constitution

11. Bill of Rights: provisions and meanings

12. Slavery and the Constitution

Domestic Issues of the 1790s

1. Failure of the Constitution led to political parties.

2. Development of political parties

3. Liberty versus order in the 1790s

4. United States as a typical new nation

5. Hamilton's economic program

6. Thomas Jefferson versus Alexander Hamilton

7. Differences between the Democratic-Republicans and the Federalists

8. Different concepts of the role of government in the 1790s

9. Compare 1763–1776 with 1783–1800 in regard to the relationship between the central government and the colonies or states.

10. Significant elections: 1796, 1800

11. The Revolution of 1800

12. Loose versus strict construction as a matter of sectional or political interest

13. Why is George Washington ranked as a great president?

Foreign Policy Issues in the 1790s

1. Trace relations with France to 1800.

2. Trace relations with Great Britain to 1800.

3. Trace relations with Spain to 1800.

4. Basis of our foreign policy: economic motives, moral principle, or political motives?

5. Was our foreign policy successful?

6. This period as the beginning of isolationism

7. Foreign policy differences: Federalists and Democratic-Republicans

8. Motives and nature of westward expansion in the 1790s

Major Terms and Concepts

Articles of Confederation

Maryland, cession of western land claims

strengths, weaknesses of the Articles of Confederation

new state constitutions during the Revolutionary War and after

primogeniture, entail

disestablishment

Pennsylvania militia routs Congress, 1783

Northwest posts

Land Ordinance of 1785

Northwest Ordinance, 1787

proposed Jay-Gardoqui Treaty, 1785

Shays' Rebellion

Annapolis Convention, 1786

1780s depression

Noah Webster

Writing the Constitution, Ratification

Philadelphia Convention

delegates: Alexander Hamilton, George Washington, Benjamin Franklin

Montesquieu, *The Spirit of Laws*

John Locke, *Second Treatise of Government*

Hobbes

James Madison, "Father of the Constitution"

Great Compromise

VA Plan, NJ Plan, Conn. Compromise

checks and balances—examples

North-South compromises

slavery and the Constitution: slave trade, three-fifths clause

procedures for amendments

Beard thesis, his critics

Fiske, *The Critical Period of American History*

Antifederalists

supporters of the Constitution

opponents of the Constitution

Patrick Henry

Sam Adams

George Mason, Bill of Rights

the ratification fights, especially in MA, NY, and VA

The Federalist Papers, Jay, Hamilton, Madison

The Federalist, number 10

Politics in the 1790s

Bill of Rights adopted, 1791

President George Washington

Vice-president John Adams

Judiciary Act, 1789

Secretary of the Treasury Hamilton

Secretary of State Jefferson

Secretary of War Knox

Attorney General Randolph

Hamilton's program: ideas, proposals, reasons for it

Tariff of 1789

Bank of the U.S.

national debt, state debt, foreign debt

excise taxes

Report on Manufactures

implied powers, elastic clause, necessary and proper clause

loose, strict interpretation of the Constitution

location of the capital: logrolling, D.C.

Residence Act

Major L'Enfant, Benjamin Banneker

Whiskey Rebellion

Washington's Farewell Address

election of 1796: President Adams, Vice-president Jefferson

new states: VT, KY, TN

Federalists and Democratic-Republicans (Democrats) or Jeffersonians or Republicans

party leaders and supporters

programs

philosophies

foreign proclivities

Society of the Cincinnati

Democratic Societies

Alien and Sedition Acts

Virginia and Kentucky Resolutions

doctrine of nullification

election of 1800, tie, Jefferson and Burr

Revolution of 1800

Jefferson's Inaugural Address

Twelfth Amendment

second Great Awakening

Gilbert Stuart

Charles Willson Peale

Foreign Affairs in the 1790s

French Alliance of 1778

French Revolution

Citizen Genêt

Neutrality Proclamation

XYZ affair, Talleyrand undeclared naval war with France

Convention of 1800

British seizure of American ships

"Rule of 1756"

Northwest posts

Jay's Treaty

Washington's Farewell Address

Pinckney's Treaty (San Lorenzo), right of deposit at New Orleans

Spanish intrigue in the Southwest

James Wilkinson

"Mad" Anthony Wayne, Battle of Fallen Timbers

Treaty of Greenville, 1795

Barbary pirates

Court Cases to Know

The first three cases are significant because they all dealt with judicial review before the Constitution was written. Many constitutional scholars believe that the Founding Fathers understood and approved of the concept of judicial review, but some believe the opposite. These cases are extensively discussed in Gordon S. Wood's *The Creation of the American Republic, 1776–1787*. The quotes that follow are from Wood's book.

1. *Rutgers* vs. *Waddington*, 1784

This case involved a clash between a legislative law and common law, which includes the law of nations, the prevailing international law. The New York Trespass Act of 1783 prohibited military authorization of the use of abandoned property. The prevailing law of nations permitted using abandoned property during wartime. In addition, in the Treaty of Paris of 1783, which ended the Revolutionary War, the two sides renounced all previous damage claims. The judges in the case carefully skirted the issue of ruling the New York Trespass Act illegal. When the legislature passes a law that is unreasonable, the duty of the court is "to give their *intention* its proper effect." After all, the judges concluded, the legislators did not really mean to void the law of nations because they never said they intended to do so.

2. *Trevett* vs. *Weeden*, 1786-1787

The Rhode Island legislature passed legislation to force merchants to accept paper money. The merchants closed their shops in protest. In his arguments for Weeden, a merchant, the defense attorney asserted that the judge's responsibility was to "reject all acts of the legislature that are contrary to the trust reposed in them by the people." Since the people themselves are the source of the creation of the legislature, the responsibility of the judiciary, itself a creation of the people, is to prevent the legislature from exceeding their original responsibilities. The people may constitutionally change the legislature's responsibilities; the legislature may not constitutionally change the legislature's responsibilities.

3. *Bayard* vs. *Singleton*, 1787

This court case preceded the Philadelphia Constitutional Convention. In this North Carolina case, the North Carolina Supreme Court declared a state law void. It is the clearest application of judicial review in this period.

Supreme Court Cases to Know

The abbreviation for versus in Supreme Court cases is (v.). The abbreviation for versus in all other cases is (vs.).

1. *Chisholm* v. *Georgia*, 1793 (individuals suing states)

Two citizens of South Carolina sued Georgia in the Supreme Court. The court accepted the case and handed down a decision for the South Carolinians, who were acting as agents for a British creditor. Georgia refused to participate in the case. The case angered many, who saw it as an infringement on the sovereignty of the states. According to English common law, a sovereign power (Georgia) could not be sued without its permission. The Eleventh Amendment ended such suits.

2. *Ware* v. *Hylton*, 1796 (treaties and state laws)

This case involved a conflict between the 1783 Treaty of Paris and a 1777 Virginia statute hindering British creditors in their attempt to recover debts owed by Americans. In the treaty the United States pledged not to impede British attempts to secure payment of debts. The court ruled that, as specified in the Constitution, treaties overruled state laws.

Readings for Depth and Historical Interpretation

Constitution

1. Richard Hofstadter, "The Founding Fathers: An Age of Realism," *The American Political Tradition*. Hofstadter surveys the political and economic thinking of the Founding Fathers and finds them to be realistic in their appraisal of their fellow man and astute in devising a form of government to serve as an arena for economic self-interest.

2. Charles A. Beard, *An Economic Interpretation of the Constitution,* 1913. Beard argues that economic interests and motives led the Founding Fathers to create a Constitution to protect and to promote their own economic interests. Read the summary of his argument in the last few pages of the book. The best refuting of the economic interpretation is Henry Steele Commager, "The Constitution: Was It An Economic Document?" *American Heritage,* December, 1958.

3. Gordon S. Wood, "The Worthy Against the Licentious," and "The Federalist Persuasion," in his *The Creation of the American Republic, 1776–1787*. Wood sees fundamental social differences between the Federalist and Anti-federalist visions of society. In many respects this is an updating of the Progressive era dichotomy.

4. Cecelia Kenyon, "Men of Little Faith: The Anti-Federalists on the Nature of Representative Government," *William and Mary Quarterly,* January 1955. Kenyon focuses her attention on the opponents of the ratification of the Constitution. She does not see the Anti-federalists as democratic defenders against a conservative aristocratic group favoring centralized authority. They were men with little faith in majority rule, a large country, representative democracy, and so forth.

5. John P. Roche, "The Founding Fathers: A Reform Caucus in Action," *American Political Review,* December 1961. Roche sees the members of the Constitutional Convention as "superb democratic politicians" who understood the political realities of their day. Practical politics and compromise rather than abstract theory hammered out a consensus on what should be in the Constitution.

6. One factor in winning the ratification of the Constitution was Shays' Rebellion. The rebellion was the reaction of subsistence farmers against an intruding commercial-oriented society. See the first chapter, "The Two Worlds of New England," in David P. Szatmary, *Shays' Rebellion: The Making of an Agrarian Insurrection.*

7. The fragility of the American sense of national identity is the theme in John M. Murrin, "A Roof Without Walls: The Dilemma of American National Identity," in Richard Beeman, Stephen Botein, and Edward C. Carter, eds., *Beyond Confederation: Origins of the Constitution and American National Identity*.

8. As losers in the ratification fight, the Antifederalists have been poorly understood. Their best defense is found in *What the Anti-Federalists Were For*, by Herbert J. Storing and Murray Dry, especially the conclusion, pp. 71–76.

Politics in the 1790s

There are three decades in American history that you must understand. The 1790s is the first. If you understand the events and issues of the 1790s you understand much of American history preceding this decade and many subsequent developments. The other two decades are the 1850s and the 1930s.

1. J. A. Carroll, "George Washington," Stephen G. Kurtz, "John Adams," and Morton Borden, "Thomas Jefferson," in Morton Borden, ed., *America's Eleven Greatest Presidents*. This book looks at eleven presidents and their times, and it is worth having so as to facilitate understanding of this complex decade.

2. Richard Hofstadter, "Thomas Jefferson: The Aristocrat as Democrat," *The American Political Tradition*. A thorough, brief discussion of Jefferson's political philosophy in theory and in practice.

3. John C. Miller, "The Quarrel Between Hamilton and Jefferson," in his *The Federalist Era, 1789–1801*. An excellent summary of the dispute between Hamilton and Jefferson. Upset by the early quarrel between Hamilton and Jefferson, Washington asked the two men to explain the reasons for their dispute. They both replied in letters written on September 9, 1792. They are reprinted in Frederick Prescott, ed., *Alexander Hamilton and Thomas Jefferson: Representative Selections*, published in 1934. A local college library should have a copy.

4. James MacGregor Burns, *The Deadlock of Democracy: Four-Party Politics in America*, pp. 27–46. This contains an analysis of Jefferson and Madison as political party leaders in and out of the presidency. Madison was the weaker president because he was constrained by his political theories. Jefferson was the better practical politician in the presidency.

Sample Outline

Development of Political Parties in the 1790s

I. Continuity from the Revolutionary War?

   A. Revolutionary War organizations tended to be ad hoc interest groups and factions more certain of what they didn't want than what they did.

   B. Radical and conservative labels make little sense—not much of a range

II. Political Parties in the 1790s

   A. Essentials of a political party

      1. Elaboration of *ideology* in platforms and newspapers

      2. Growth of a party structure, *organization* within the states

      3. Recruitment of party *leadership* at different levels

      4. Enlistment of a *cadre* of faithful party workers

      5. Development of party *loyalty* among the electorate

6. All this provided an institutional complexity and stability that earlier political forms lacked.

B. Issues

1. Great consensus on the basic tenets of American republican ideology

2. Men and their policies were at fault, not the Constitution.

3. Each party believed the other threatened the survival of its vision of the future of the United States.

4. The disputes centered around the dramatic personalities of Hamilton and Jefferson.

5. Those in office regarded themselves as the embodiment of the national will.

   a. Federalist approach was plebiscitarian.

   b. Federalists called Republicans "Democrats" as a smear tactic. Republicans proudly accepted the name.

6. Disputes arose over basic constitutional, economic, and diplomatic policies, and the relative powers of the states and the federal government.

C. A period of trials for the new nation revealed sharp disagreements and accented differences. Examples include the Whiskey Rebellion, undeclared naval war, Alien and Sedition Acts, VA and KY Resolutions, Jay's Treaty, and disunion schemes in the West.

III. Hamilton's Program

A. Nonpartisan beginnings

1. Madison, in *The Federalist Papers,* stated, "Among the numerous advantages promised by a well constructed Union, none deserves to be more accurately developed than its tendency to break and control the violence of faction (party). The friend of popular governments never finds himself so much alarmed for their character and fate, as when he contemplates their propensity to this dangerous vice."

2. Hamilton: The "poison" of faction would menace the republic.

3. Washington: "A frightful despotism" would be erected "on the ruins of Public Liberty" if parties ever developed in this country.

4. Jefferson: "If I could not go to heaven but with a party, I would not go there at all."

B. Debt—foreign, national, state

1. Hamilton's proposal to refinance at par to present bondholders; Madison opposed—original owners

2. Refinancing of state debt to strengthen union and increase centralization. State position depended on size of debt and if already paid off, but division tended to be North-South.

3. Assumption of state debts traded for Northern support for national capital located on the Potomac River after ten years in Philadelphia.

C. Bank proposal

1. Sectional voting, North 33-1, South 6-19

2. On this issue, Hamilton and Jefferson wrote explanations of loose and strict construction.

D. Excise tax on whiskey

1. 25% of net price, North 28-6, South 7-15

2. To raise revenues, impress westerners with Federal power

3. Eventually led to Whiskey Rebellion; 12,600-man army raised to put down rebellion.

4. Jefferson: "An insurrection was announced and proclaimed and armed against, but could never be found."

E. Hamilton wanted a protective tariff; revenue tariff passed.

F. Report on Manufactures

G. Arguments over Hamilton's program form the first ingredients in the platforms of the parties.

IV. Split over Foreign Policy

A. French Revolution: dominating event of the decade

1. Initial enthusiasm waned as excesses and terror appeared; disagreement over what the French Revolution symbolized.

2. John Adams: "Ours was resistance to innovation; theirs was innovation itself."

3. Jefferson: "The liberty of the whole earth was depending on the issue of the contests, and ... rather than it should have failed, I would have seen half the earth devastated."

B. Complications caused by the Treaty of 1778

1. Citizen Genêt

2. Washington's Neutrality Proclamation, 1793

C. Great Britain: Northwest posts, neutral commerce rights violated, impressment

D. Jay's Treaty: event around which differences crystallized

1. Provisions of the treaty: posts surrendered by June 1796; East Indian ports opened to U.S. ships; minor and limited concessions on U.S. trade with West Indies (so offensive that this part was removed before ratification); acceptance of paper (unenforced) blockades; commissions in the future to resolve border disputes

2. Senate controlled by Federalists; treaty passed

3. House controlled by Dem-Reps tried to block treaty by withholding appropriations ($90,000). (The first congressional caucus in history was a Republican meeting for strategy on this issue.)

E. Election of 1796: caucus used to select candidates for president (note: initial organization is at top); Washington's Farewell Address warns against parties. Adams, president; Jefferson, vice-president

V. Alien and Sedition Acts

A. XYZ affair

   1. Negotiators sent: Charles Pinckney, Elbridge Gerry, John Marshall, bribes, Talleyrand

   2. A Republican disaster when they forced the president to make public the negotiations; war fever; undeclared naval war with France. Federalists gain twenty seats in next election.

B. Alien and Sedition Acts

   1. Most immigrants joined Republican Party; most famous, Albert Gallatin.

   2. Naturalization Act: 5 to 14 years for citizenship

   3. Alien Friends Act: remove aliens in wartime

   4. Alien Act: president may order out of the country all aliens suspected of "treasonable activities."

   5. Sedition Act: illegal to falsely criticize the government

      a. For example, two Republican newspaper editors wrote, "No Stamp Act, No Sedition, No Alien Bills, No Land Tax; downfall to the tyrants of America, peace and retirement to the President, long live the Vice-president and the Minority; may moral virtue be the basis of civil government."

      b. One convicted for violating the Sedition Act received 6 hours in jail and a $5 fine; the other, 18 months and a $400 fine

   6. Virginia and Kentucky resolutions protested. Written by Madison (VA) and Jefferson (KY), the resolutions are an overreaction to the Alien and Sedition Acts, not a party doctrinal statement in favor of nullification and states' rights. The issue was liberty, not constitutional doctrine.

C. Federalist Party hurt by two factors:

   1. Adams's peace with France in undeclared naval war

   2. Adams pushed Hamilton's supporters out of the cabinet in a split between Hamilton and Adams.

D. Election of 1800: crystallization of the party platforms, established party organizations

   1. The "tie": Jefferson, 73; Burr, 73

   2. House controlled by Federalists decided winner.

   3. 35 ballots before tie was broken. Federalists finally accept Jefferson because they distrust Burr.

E. The election of 1800 is seen as the acceptance of the decision of the electorate and the toleration of an opposition. In truth, both parties pursued an approach to become the only party and only embodiment of the national will (which each believed themselves to be).

VI. Parties in the 1790s

A. Each feared tyranny, but expected it from a different source.

1. Federalists: mobs, the majority in the House

2. Republicans: executive branch and Senate

B. Party debate clarified thinking and sharpened policies and led to policies and institutions in the 1790s that were well thought out.

UNIT FOUR: 1800–1840

Major Themes and Ideas

Politics

1. Did Jefferson out-federalize the Federalists by stealing their ideas?

2. Decline and death of the Federalist Party

3. Era of Good Feelings

4. Forces for nationalism

5. Marshall and his Supreme Court decisions

6. Supreme Court as a partisan body, acting in the interests of one party, section, or ideology

7. Differences and similarities between Jeffersonian and Jacksonian Democracy

8. Compare Jefferson and Jackson in regard to courts and criticism of the judiciary.

9. What was Jacksonian Democracy?

10. What caused Jacksonian Democracy to develop?

11. Compare the Second Party System with the First.

12. Rise and development of political parties in the Jacksonian era—economic, social, and geographical characteristics and leaders

13. Immediate and long range consequences of the split between Jackson and Calhoun

14. The issues that divided the supporters and opponents of the Constitution divided the Whigs and the Jacksonian Democrats.

15. Hamilton's economic program created the political issues for the next fifty years.

16. Loose or strict interpretation of the Constitution was used to defend the economic, political, and constitutional positions of various regions between 1800 and 1840.

17. Trace sectional tensions, 1800–1840.

18. Give the positions, rationale, issues, and spokesmen for the sections on the following political topics: tariff, banking, internal improvements, expansion, and slavery.

19. The Federalists and the Whigs represented the same classes, ideologies, attitudes, sections, and political philosophies.

20. Clay, Calhoun, and Webster reflected the interests of their sections between 1810 and 1850.

21. Significant elections: 1824, 1828, 1832, and 1840

Foreign Policy

1. Trace relations with Great Britain and France from 1800 to 1815.

2. Trace our relations with Spain to 1824.

3. War of 1812 as a second War for Independence

4. Foreign policy united and divided Americans between 1800 and 1824.

5. Explain the changes in the historiography of the War of 1812.

6. The interests of the West were satisfied by neither the Jeffersonians nor the Federalists between 1789 and 1815.

7. Our border adjustments, 1800–1824

8. Provisions and impact of the Monroe Doctrine

Economy

1. Clay's American system

2. Was Jacksonianism an attack on privilege?

3. Bank War: its enemies and defenders, veto message, laws from 1800 to 1865 on banking

4. Changes in federal land laws and policies

5. Role of state and federal governments in promoting economic growth, 1800–1860

6. Changes in the economy in transportation, labor, and industrialization

7. Impact of changes and improvements in transportation on the direction and extent of population movement and trade patterns

8. United States as an underdeveloped nation in 1840

Reform and Intellectual Movements

1. Identify the motives, methods, leadership, goals, and accomplishments for any reform.

2. Status and goals of the women's movement

3. An era of the common man?

4. Transcendentalism: why, what was it, leaders

5. Reform characterized by perfectionism, distrust of established institutions, and uncompromising impatience

6. Social mobility in American society

7. Era was one of the establishment of political, economic, and cultural independence from Europe.

8. Compare the First and Second Great Awakenings.

9. Strengths and weakness of democracy as illustrated by abolitionism and the women's movement.

Major Terms and Concepts

Jeffersonians and Period to the War of 1812

election of 1800

Revolution of 1800

President Jefferson, Vice-president Burr, Secretary of Treasury Gallatin

Jefferson's inaugural address, "We are all Federalists, we are all Republicans."

Federalist control of courts and judges, midnight judges

Justice Samuel Chase

Tripolitan War

Treaty of San Ildefonso

Louisiana Purchase: reasons, Jefferson and loose construction

Toussaint L'Ouverture

Federalist opposition to Louisiana Purchase

Hamilton-Burr duel

Burr expedition, treason trial

Lewis and Clark, Pike, Major Long, their observations

Berlin Decree, 1806; Milan Decree, 1807

Polly case, Essex case

orders-in-council

impressment

Chesapeake-Leopard affair

Embargo of 1807, opposition

Nonintercourse Act

Erskine Agreement

Macon's Bill No. 2

Tecumseh

War Hawks

causes of the War of 1812

Why war against Great Britain rather than against France?

Federalist opposition to the War of 1812, why?

naval engagements in the War of 1812

Fort McHenry, Francis Scott Key, Star Spangled Banner

events of the war: Perry, Lake Erie, D.C., New Orleans

Jackson's victory at New Orleans

New England's merchants, critics of the war, Essex Junto

Hartford Convention, resolutions

treaty negotiators: John Quincy Adams, Albert Gallatin, Henry Clay

Treaty of Ghent, provisions

neutral rights issues end with the defeat of Napoleon

Nationalism and Sectionalism to 1828

war increased nationalism, economic independence

second Bank of the U.S. a reversal of Jeffersonian ideas

Tariff of 1816 protective

Bonus bill veto

Rush-Bagot, Great Lakes

Convention of 1818

panic of 1819

West Florida, 1810

Jackson in Florida, Rhea letter

purchase of Florida

Transcontinental Treaty (Adams-Onis Treaty
or Step Treaty or Florida Treaty)

Quadruple Alliance, Holy Alliance

George Canning

Monroe Doctrine: origins, provisions, impact

Era of Good Feelings

Chief Justice John Marshall: decisions

Missouri: Tallmadge Amendment, Thomas
Amendment, Missouri Compromise,
provisions

Clay's American System, ideas

growth of industry in New England, textiles

Samuel Slater

Robert Fulton, Clermont

Eli Whitney, cotton gin, interchangeable
parts

Boston Associates, Lowell, MA

Daniel Webster

National (Cumberland) Road

internal improvements

Erie Canal, DeWitt Clinton

new states

federal government's land policy: 1796,
1800, 1804, 1820

New England's opposition to cheap land

John Quincy Adams as Secretary of State:
FL, Monroe Doctrine

election of 1824: popular vote, electoral vote,
House vote: Jackson, Adams, Crawford,
Clay

"corrupt bargain"

Panama Conference

Tariff of Abominations

Vice-president Calhoun: South Carolina

Exposition and Protest, nullification

Jacksonian Democracy

Jacksonian Revolution of 1828

age of the common man

Jacksonian Democracy: characteristics

franchise extended

spoils system

National Republicans

caucus system, national nominating conventions

kitchen cabinet

Cherokee Indian removal, trail of tears

Worcester v. *Georgia,* 1832; and *Cherokee
Nation* v. *Georgia,* 1831

Whigs: origins, policies

Maysville Road veto

election of 1832, Anti-Masonic Party

Clay, bank recharter bill, Nicholas Biddle

veto message

Jackson's removal of deposits, Roger B.
Taney, pet banks, Loco-Focos

Chestnut Street to Wall Street

Foote Resolution, Webster-Hayne Debate

Peggy Eaton affair

Calhoun resigns as vice-president

South opposes protective tariffs (Tariff of
Abominations) nullification, SC Exposition
and Protest

Jefferson Day dinner: toasts and quotes

Clay: Compromise Tariff of 1833, Force Bill

Calhoun splits with Jackson

Martin Van Buren, the Albany Regency

Specie Circular, 1836

Charles River Bridge decision, Chief Justice
Roger B. Taney, general incorporation laws

panic of 1837

Dorr's Rebellion

Independent Treasury Plan

election of 1840: candidates, characteristics

rise of the second party system

Pre-emption act, 1841

Tariff of 1842

Reform: Social and Intellectual

Transcendentalism

Transcendentalists

Ralph Waldo Emerson

Henry David Thoreau, *Walden,* "On Civil Disobedience"

Orestes Brownson

Margaret Fuller, *The Dial*

authors and their works:

James Fenimore Cooper, *The Last of the Mohicans*, *The Spy*, *The Pioneers*

Herman Melville, *Moby Dick*

Nathaniel Hawthorne, *The Scarlet Letter*

Edgar Allan Poe

Washington Irving

Henry Wadsworth Longfellow

Walt Whitman, *Leaves of Grass*

Alexis de Tocqueville, *Democracy in America*

Hudson River school of art

millennialism, Millerites

"the burned-over district"

Charles G. Finney

Mormons, Joseph Smith, Brigham Young, Utah

Brook Farm, New Harmony, Oneida Community, Shakers, Amana Community

lyceum movement

some reforms successful, some not—why?

Dorothea Dix, treatment of the insane

rise of labor leaders

National Trades Union

Commonwealth vs. Hunt

criminal conspiracy laws and early unions

Oberlin, 1833; Mt. Holyoke, 1836

public education, Horace Mann

American Temperance Union

Ten Nights in a Bar-Room, Timothy Shay Arthur

Maine law, Neal Dow

Irish, German immigration

nativism; Samuel F.B. Morse, *Imminent Dangers to the Free Institutions of the United States through Foreign Immigration, and the Present State of the Naturalization Laws*

women, their rights, areas of discrimination

Lucretia Mott

Elizabeth Cady Stanton

Seneca Falls, 1848

Emma Willard

Catharine Beecher

"Cult of True Womanhood": piety, domesticity, purity, and submissiveness

women's movement, like others, overshadowed by antislavery movement

American Peace Society

prison reform: Auburn system, Pennsylvania system

Supreme Court Cases to Know

1. *Marbury* v. *Madison,* 1803 (judicial review)
In March 1801, Secretary of State James Madison refused to give William Marbury a commission as a justice of the peace for Washington, D.C., after the previous presidential administration had authorized the commission. Marbury sued under a writ of mandamus to obtain his commission. The Court's decision, written by Chief Justice John Marshall, dismissed Marbury's suit because he had sued under a writ of mandamus, and the Constitution did not include such writs within its listing of the powers of the Supreme Court. The Judiciary Act of 1789 authorized the Supreme Court to issue a writ of mandamus, but, claimed Marshall, Congress could not enlarge the powers of the Supreme Court. Therefore, Section 13 of the Judiciary Act of 1789 was unconstitutional. This case is significant because it is the first time the Supreme Court declared an act of Congress unconstitutional. The second did not occur until the Dred Scott case.

2. *Fletcher* v. *Peck,* 1810 (contracts and state laws)

This case was the first to declare a state law void as a violation of the Constitution. Influenced by bribes, the corrupt Georgia legislature sold land to specu-lators. The outraged public elected virtually a new legislature at the next election, and the new legisla-ture rescinded the previous sale. The case involved the legality of the sale of a tract of land made before the second legislature rescinded the original trans-action. Chief Justice John Marshall wrote the deci-sion. The Georgia legislature could not interfere with a lawfully executed contract. No matter how the original land speculators had obtained the land grant, Fletcher had made a legal, contractual pur-chase with which the legislature could not interfere. The contract clause of the Constitution overrode the state law.

3. *Martin* v. *Hunters Lessee,* 1816 (federal appel-late jurisdiction over state courts)

This case asserted that the Supreme Court had appellate jurisdiction over state court decisions. Concurrent federal and state jurisdiction did not make the state and federal courts equal, and state judges must decide cases according to "the su-preme law of the land," the Constitution. Supreme Court appellate jurisdiction of state court cases ensures a uniformity of constitutional decisions.

4. *Dartmouth College* v. *Woodward,* 1819 (con-tracts and state laws)

In 1816 the state legislature of New Hampshire took over Dartmouth College. The board of trustees sued to regain control. Was the original charter granted in 1769 a contract within the meaning of the contract clause of the Constitution? The Supreme Court ruled that it was. The charter of a private corporation was protected by the Constitution and could not be altered by the people through their legislature.

5. *McCulloch* v. *Maryland,* 1819 (the elastic clause and federal state relations)

The state of Maryland levied a tax on the Baltimore branch of the Bank of the United States. The cashier of the Bank refused to pay the tax. The case raised the question of the constitutionality of the 1791 act of Congress that created the Bank, and the question of whether a state could tax the federal government. Marshall's opinion supported the loose construc-tion theory of the Constitution. "Let the end be legitimate, let it be within the scope of the Consti-tution, and all means which are appropriate, which are plainly adapted to that end, which are not prohibited, but consist with the letter and spirit of the Constitution, are constitutional." The act of Congress creating the Bank was constitutional. In answering the second question the Court ruled that "the power to tax is the power to destroy." Think of the logic of taxation. The annual tax on the Balti-more branch was $15,000. Once the principle of state taxation of the Bank was admitted, though, what is the difference, in principle, between a $15,000 tax and a $483 billion dollar tax? A tax is a tax, but the second tax puts the bank into bank-ruptcy! Therefore, the Maryland tax was unconsti-tutional.

6. *Cohens* v. *Virginia,* 1821 (federal jurisdiction over state cases involving federal rights)

The Cohens were arrested and fined for selling lottery tickets in Virginia. They had sold Washing-ton, D.C., lottery tickets authorized by Congress, the government for the District of Columbia. The Cohens appealed their conviction. Marshall ruled that the Supreme Court possessed the power to review state court decisions to see "whether that judgment be in violation of the Constitution or the laws of the United States," in this case the act of Congress authorizing the D.C. lottery.

7. *Gibbons* v. *Ogden,* 1824 (federal control of interstate commerce)

This is the first case decided under the commerce clause. Two steamboat operators clashed over their respective charters to control steamboats in New York City harbor. One had a charter from the federal government; the other had a monopoly grant from the state of New York. The decision affirmed exclu-sive federal control of interstate commerce even in the absence of federal legislation or action.

8. *Cherokee Nation* v. *Georgia,* 1831; *Worcester* v. *Georgia,* 1832 (state laws, treaties, and Indians)

These two cases are part of the long struggle by Georgia to push the Cherokee Indians westward. The federal government had much earlier promised to support Georgia's efforts. The Cherokee tried to stop a Georgia declaration that the laws of the Cherokee were null and void. The Court ruled in the first case that while it lacked jurisdiction, the Cherokee Nation was a "domestic, dependent, nation" possessing some sovereignty, and not a foreign nation. In the second case, Marshall ruled that the laws of Georgia had no force within the territorial boundaries of the Cherokee Nation. President Jackson, no admirer of Marshall, reportedly said, "John Marshall has made his decision, now let him enforce it." In this clear clash between state law and the federal government, the president sided with the state of Georgia.

9. *Charles River Bridge* v. *Warren Bridge,* 1837 (contracts and the community's rights)

The Charles River Bridge Company sued to prevent the state of Massachusetts from authorizing the construction of a new bridge across the Charles River. Was its original charter a contract, an implied, vested, perpetual agreement? Chief Justice Roger B. Taney, in his first significant decision, ruled that no charter granted to a private corporation permanently vested rights that might harm the public interest. Taney wrote, "the continued existence of a government would be of no great value, if by implications and presumptions, it was disarmed of the powers necessary to accomplish the ends of its creation; and the functions it was designed to perform, transferred to the hands of privileged corporations." (Try to imagine the situation if the Charles River Bridge Company still owned the only permitted bridge across the Charles River.)

The rights of the community supersede a broad interpretation of the private rights of a corporation. "While the rights of property are sacredly guarded, we must not forget that the community also have rights...." It is not the duty of the legislature to specify what the corporation charter does not say.

10. *Commonwealth vs. Hunt,* 1842 (a union's right to organize)

This Massachusetts decision ruled that trade union organization and strike tactics were legal. Traditional interpretations considered unions illegal under the conspiracy laws of English common law. This decision did not immediately open a new era for labor unions; many judges continued to consider unions to be illegal.

Readings for Depth and Historical Interpretation

Foreign Policy

For issues in diplomatic history you are advised to concentrate on reading for depth rather than for acquiring various historical interpretations. Read for better understanding of the chronology and the complexities of foreign policy. Almost every student in American history can write in an essay that prior to the War of 1812 the British violated our neutral rights. How many include a paragraph on the "Rule of 1756," detailing one aspect of British violations? Strengthen your understanding of diplomatic history by reading relevant sections in standard diplomatic history textbooks.

Diplomatic History Textbooks

1. Samuel Flagg Bemis, *A Diplomatic History of the United States.* Thomas Bailey, *A Diplomatic History of the American People.* Robert H. Ferrell, *American Diplomacy.*

2. Dexter Perkins, *A History of the Monroe Doctrine.* The author is considered the authority on the Monroe Doctrine. The first two chapters describe the origins and meaning of the Monroe Doctrine.

Overviews of the Period

1. Marcus Cunliffe, *The Nation Takes Shape*: 1789–1837. An excellent survey of the period, it focuses on conflicts such as nationalism and sectionalism, conservatism and democracy, and so on.

2. Alexis de Tocqueville, *Democracy in America*. This is a classic in American literature. Bear in mind as you read *Democracy in America* that it is an aristocratic Frenchman's sympathetic analysis of democracy rather than of America. Read sections of the book or see the selections and commentary in Robert B. Downs, *Books That Changed America*.

Jackson and Jacksonian Democracy

With some misgivings I recommend books and articles for Jackson and Jacksonianism. If you read everything written about this subject you will add to your knowledge but not necessarily to your understanding. This period is confusing. No historical interpretation or emphasis seems to exclude other interpretations, but simply piles on top of them. This period aptly exemplifies the old adage, "History is what historians say it is." Part of the source of the confusion is that Jackson and Jacksonian Democracy may be two separate entities having little to do with one another.

1. John William Ward, *Andrew Jackson: Symbol for an Age*. Ward uses three ideas—Nature, Providence, and Will—to study the period and to describe how Jackson came to symbolize these concepts in myth and fact. Intellectual history at its liveliest, you will never forget the images of Jackson.

2. Marvin Meyers, "The Old Republic and the New: An Introduction," and "The Restoration Theme: On Jackson's Message," in his *The Jacksonian Persuasion: Politics and Belief*. Meyers claims that Jacksonian Democrats in this era yearned for earlier republican virtues such as integrity, morality, frugality, and simplicity. They looked backward, not forward.

3. Richard P. McCormick, Chapter 7 in his *The Second American Party System: Party Forma-*
tion in the Jacksonian Era*. A thoughtful analysis of the forces behind the creation of political parties in this period, it separates reality from the myths of Jacksonian politics.

4. Arthur M. Schlesinger, Jr., *The Age of Jackson,* especially the chapters "Jacksonian Democracy as an Intellectual Movement" and "Traditions of Democracy," which include a discussion of Jeffersonian Democracy. Schlesinger defines liberal reform as the periodic attempt by "other sections of society to restrain the power of the business community." He sees the origins of Jacksonian Democracy in the lower economic classes and challenges Frederick Jackson Turner's theme of Jackson as a western revolt.

5. Bray Hammond, Chapters 12–15, *Banks and Politics in America From the Revolution to the Civil War*. Richard Hofstadter, "Andrew Jackson and the Rise of Liberal Capitalism," in his *The American Political Tradition*. Robert V. Remini, *Andrew Jackson and the Bank War: A Study in the Growth of Presidential Power*.

The first two selections argue that Jacksonian Democracy was the successful struggle by one group of entrepreneurs against an entrenched, privileged business group identified with the Bank of the United States. Hammond summarizes it as a struggle between Wall Street and Chestnut Street, the Philadelphia site of the Bank. Remini sees the Bank War as a political phenomenon, a factor in party development and in the increase in presidential power.

6. Edward Pessen, *Jacksonian America: Society, Personality and Politics*. Pessen is an excellent source for differentiating between the Whigs and the Jacksonians. See the chapter "The Rise of Major Parties: Democratic and Whig Theory and Practice." A very readable survey of the period, it also includes his studies of social mobility in Jacksonian America. He found increasing inequality, not a rise in democracy. For a brief summary of the issues of the era, see the chapter "Reflections on Political Issues of the Era." Another source for his social mobility thesis is Edward Pessen, "The Egalitarian Myth and the American Social Reality: Wealth, Mobility, and Equality in the 'Era of the Com-

mon Man'," *American Historical Review,* 1971.

7. Daniel Walker Howe, *The Political Culture of the American Whigs,* looks at the Whig Party; see especially, "The Whigs and Their Age," and "Conclusion," the Whig legacy in American politics.

Reform

1.   Barbara Welter, "The Cult of True Womanhood: 1820–1860," *American Quarterly,* Summer 1966. Welter describes the creation of the image of the ideal middle-class woman complete with the four cardinal virtues—piety, purity, submissiveness, and domesticity.

2.   John L. Thomas, "Romantic Reform in America, 1815–1865," *American Quarterly,* Winter 1965. In his analysis of the reform impulse, Thomas emphasizes the reliance upon individual conversion as a method for achieving reform. Difficult reading but insightful.

3.   Paul Johnson, *A Shopkeeper's Millennium: Society and Revivals in Rochester, New York, 1815–1837.* Johnson shows the religious ferment in action in Rochester, the impact of Charles Finney's revivalism, and evangelical Protestantism.

4.   Ellen DuBois, *Feminism and Suffrage: The Emergence of an Independent Women's Movement in America, 1848–1869*, traces the women's movement in the two decades after the Seneca Falls convention, a period of both accomplishment and disappointment. Another way to trace the women's movement is through Elizabeth Cady Stanton. See Lois Banner, *Elizabeth Cady Stanton: A Radical for Women's Rights*, which carries the story to 1900.

Sample Outline

The Age of Reform

I.   Defining Reform

  A. Reform and revolution: Revolution implies a thorough revision of the institutions of society; reform is more of a patching approach to the ills of society.

  B. Heredity and environment: Reforms tend to come in periods of greater faith in environment as an influence on individuals.

  C. Perfectibility: A key characteristic of this reform era was the belief in the perfectibility of man and the doctrine of progress, a desire to perfect human institutions, a belief in the worth of the individual, and a compassionate humanitarianism.

II. Characteristics of the Reform Impulse

  A. Part of the Romantic literary stress on the natural, the simple, the ordinary

  B. Reformers tended to be optimists.

  C. Reformers displayed an extraordinary sense of obligation and stewardship and religious conviction.

  D. They saw science and reason as complementing religion, not contradicting it, but did not have the supreme faith in reason characteristic of the Enlightenment.

  E. Catholic in their concerns and interests, they recognized the complexity and interdependence of society, and were well aware of similar reforms in Europe.

  F. Reformers tended to come from the well-to-do and middle-class. Politically they tended to be old Federalists, Whigs, and anti-Jackson.

G. This was a period of institutional instability. (Colonial society had been balanced, with measured economic development, a slow trend toward equality, and social order and stability.) Economic individualism eroded this, and led to instability and to the proliferation of the chief mechanism of reform—the voluntary association.

H. An emphasis on institutional solutions to social problems—the asylum, the custodial school—in an urban society that was deteriorating. What was needed was regimentation, punctuality, precision.

I. Not all reform aimed toward progress and goodness.

   1. Nativism: an attempt to Americanize a newly pluralistic society

   2. Temperance: leaders narrow and bigoted, Dow

J. Variety of reforms: Reformers sometimes fought one another for attention, funds, workers, and so on.

K. They may have worked in a local area, but their goals were national in vision.

L. Motivation? a displaced elite? a displaced class without function? impose their values?

III. Example: Education Reform

A. Prior to the 1830s

   1. Colonial schools: high literacy rate, few public schools, dame schools, transitory teachers

   2. Schools: little preparation for world of work

   3. English tradition: nondenominational charity schools designed to build character

   4. Sunday school: Their emphasis and purpose changed from 1815 to 1840 from teaching fundamental skills to teaching religion, from serving the poor to serving everyone.

   5. Lancaster system, monitorial school

   6. Regular schools: 60-plus kids per room

B. Behind the impulse for educational reform

   1. Change in the conception of childhood, from miniature adults to children in a plastic, malleable stage

   2. Education seen as the key to progress, to democracy, and to individual fulfillment

   3. Changes in the family and the role of the wife due to Industrial Revolution

C. Issues of educational reform

   1. Tuition: Does it make one a better parent? How to attract the lower classes? (Formerly, the "rate schools" were free except for special tax on parents.)

   2. Great concern for the future of urban society, how to break the cycle of poverty

   3. Social control: the breakdown of institutional controls, the school as a custodial institution, discipline (in one school in Boston—65 floggings per day out of 400 students in the school). Should these methods continue?

   4. Local control versus larger (state), the benefits of uniformity versus local control

5. Teaching teachers—unspecialized schools?

6. Separate schools for blacks? Roberts case in Boston. In St. Louis the black schools had numbers, not names, and no black teachers.

7. Since no compulsory attendance laws yet, how to attract the middle class? What range of subjects offered in the high school?

8. Male or female teachers? A feminization of the teaching faculty. Mann quote: "The greater intensity of the parental instinct in the female sex, their natural love of the society of children, and the superior gentleness and forebearance of their dispositions—all of which lead them to mildness rather than severity, to the use of hope rather than fear as a motive of action, and to the various arts of encouragement rather than to annoyances and compulsion, in their management of the young."

9. Catholics: How to attract them into the public school? In NYC—from 2% to 19% of the population; which Bible to use? Differences found in St. Louis: Catholic schools, foreign-born teachers, emphasis on absolute values; public schools, native-born teachers, emphasis on a functional education. In 1844, NJ was the first state to put secular education in its constitution.

D. Horace Mann, the father of public education

1. Appointed Secretary to the MA State Board of Education in 1837; influential through his twelve annual reports—little regard for educational theory, practical and useful information

2. "I have faith in the improvability of the race—in their accelerating improvability."

3. The means of education: "On schools and teachers I rely more than on any other earthly instrumentality, for the prosperity and honor of the state, and for the reformation and advancement of the race. All other reforms seek to abolish specific ills; education is preventive." The public common school is "the greatest discovery ever made by man."

4. Moralistic, he believed that most problems were moral. Favorite words: Man, Duty, God. One of his last statements was, "Be ashamed to die until you have won some victory for humanity."

E. Results

1. Reformers could not imagine a workable pluralistic society of different cultures, values, and traditions.

2. Gains not uniform: Of 320 high schools in 1860, 167 were in just three states—NY, Ohio, and Mass

3. Laid the basis for great expansion after Civil War

UNIT FIVE: 1840–1877

Major Themes and Ideas

Slavery and Abolitionism

1. Trace the history of blacks and slavery from 1619 to the Fifteenth Amendment.

2. "Mind of the South" (Wilbur Cash wrote a book by that title, *The Mind of the South*.)

3. Slavery from the viewpoint of the slave, the slaveholder, and the nonslaveholding white Southerner

4. The issue of slavery in the territories involved an imaginary slave in a place not suited for slavery.

5. Slavery as a threat to white northern labor

6. Compare the black struggle to achieve freedom with the abolitionist struggle to free slaves.

7. Southern justifications for slavery

8. Blacks in the North, 1790–1860

9. William Lloyd Garrison: hero or villain of the antislavery movement?

10. South fought to keep from becoming what the North had become, a democratic society.

11. Trace sectionalism from 1810 to 1850 through the careers of Clay, Calhoun, and Webster.

12. Northerners objected not to slaves but to the political and economic power and influence slavery gave the slaveholder in the national government.

13. There were many reforms in the 1830s; by the 1850s abolition was the only reform.

14. Why was abolition disreputable in the 1830s and acceptable by the 1850s?

15. Slavery dominated all aspects of Southern life: political, economic, social, and intellectual.

Civil War and Reconstruction

1. Event, person, or place as a symbol of North-South division, such as bleeding Kansas, John Brown, or the Crittenden Compromise

2. Role of the Supreme Court in the Civil War and Reconstruction

3. Breakdown of both the Whig and Democratic parties in the 1850s and the rise of the third party system

4. Struggle between the president and Congress for dominant political power within the federal government, 1850–1868

5. Accomplishments and failures of Reconstruction

6. States' rights from 1790 to 1860 for all the sections

7. Civil War: triumph of American democracy over European aristocracy

8. Why did black male suffrage come before white female suffrage?

9. The 1850s: a decade of political sectionalism and economic nationalism

10. When did the Civil War become inevitable and why?

11. What causes of the Civil War were resolved by the Civil War and Reconstruction?

12. The North and the South compromised in 1820, 1833, 1850, and 1877. Why was compromise impossible in 1860?

13. Did the North win the Civil War or the South lose it?

14. Outline events of the 1850s.

15. Historiography of the causes of the Civil War

16. Compare the elections of 1852, 1856, and 1860.

17. Was the Republican Party consistent in its policies from the 1850s to 1877?

18. Decade of the 1850s as a period of major battles within rather than between parties

19. The issues of the Civil War were similar to those of the American Revolution.

20. Lincoln: a hero to blacks?

21. Why is Lincoln ranked as a great president?

22. Why did Lincoln, who opposed social and political equality for blacks, eventually free the slaves?

Economy

1. Role of the state and national governments in promoting economic growth

2. Trace land policy changes.

3. Trace changes in the economy in transportation, money, labor, banking, sectionalism, and commerce.

4. Republican legislation passed during the Civil War—triumph of Clay's American System and beginnings of industrial growth

5. Economic changes in American society drew the Northeast and the Northwest closer while driving the South from both.

6. Industrialization in the United States

7. Trace the history of the corporation as a business institution.

8. Compare Southern black slavery and Northern wage slavery.

9. The South: an underdeveloped economy in the antebellum period

10. Southern economic grievances against the North

11. North-South economic differences before the Civil War that continued unresolved after it

12. Trace the history of the union movement from 1790 to 1860.

Expansion and Foreign Affairs

1. Principles that caused territorial expansion between 1815 and 1860

2. Slavery and territorial expansion as causes of the Civil War

3. Impact of Manifest Destiny on both foreign affairs and domestic politics

4. U.S. policy toward Latin America was dishonorable but produced good results.

5. The Civil War began with the Mexican War.

6. Principles of the Monroe Doctrine and how these principles were put into practice from 1823 to 1895

7. Compare policies toward California, Texas, Cuba, and Oregon.

8. Manifest Destiny grew out of Jacksonian Democracy.

9. Why was Oregon annexed peacefully, but not Texas?

10. Trace the history of the Oregon Territory to annexation.

11. Use Texas to illustrate the characteristics and consequences of American foreign policy from 1830 to 1850.

12. Trace relations between Great Britain and the United States from 1830 to 1875.

13. The diplomacy of the Civil War was based on consistent principles.

14. The opening of trade relations with China and Japan illustrates significant themes in American foreign policy.

15. Compare the foreign policies of Jefferson and Polk.

Black History

1. Supreme Court, Congress, and the president and the position of blacks in American society, 1850–1900

2. Compare the social and political gains made by blacks during Reconstruction with those during the second Reconstruction, and during the 1950s and 1960s.

3. Outline developments in the history of blacks between 1865 and 1912.

Major Terms and Concepts

Manifest Destiny

Great American Desert

"Manifest Destiny"

Horace Greeley

Senator Thomas Hart Benton

Stephen Austin

Texas War for Independence

Santa Anna

Alamo

San Jacinto

Sam Houston

Republic of Texas

annexation of Texas, joint resolution under
    President Tyler

election of 1844: candidates, issues, third
    party's impact, Liberty Party

reoccupation of Texas and reannexation of
    Oregon

54° 40' or Fight!

James K. Polk

Slidell mission to Mexico

Rio Grande, Nueces River, disputed territory

General Zachary Taylor

Mexican War: causes, results

spot resolutions

Stephen Kearny, John C. Fremont, General
    Winfield Scott

Nicholas Trist

Treaty of Guadelupe Hidalgo provisions

All Mexico movement

Mexican Cession

Webster-Ashburton Treaty

Caroline and Creole affairs

Aroostook War

John Jacob Astor

Oregon fever

Willamette Valley

Oregon territory

49th parallel

election of 1848: Cass, Taylor

Wilmot Proviso

Joseph Smith

Brigham Young, Mormons, Great Salt Lake

Gadsden Purchase

hegemony

Economy

Samuel Slater

"transportation revolution"

Eli Whitney, interchangeable parts

cotton gin (short for engine)

Erie Canal

National Road (Cumberland Road)

Commonwealth vs. Hunt (MA case)
    Boston Associates

Lowell factory, factory girls

Cyrus McCormick, mechanical reaper

Elias Howe

ten-hour movement

clipper ships

Cyrus Field

Robert Fulton, steamships

Samuel F.B. Morse, telegraph

Walker Tariff, 1846

Independent Treasury system, Van Buren
    and Polk

Slavery and the South

American Colonization Society

cotton gin

abolitionism

sectionalism

William Lloyd Garrison

The Liberator

American Antislavery Society

Theodore Weld

Theodore Parker

the Grimké sisters

Elijah Lovejoy

Wendell Phillips

Nat Turner's insurrection

David Walker, Walker's Appeal

Sojourner Truth

Gabriel Prosser

Denmark Vesey

Frederick Douglass

Tredegar Iron Works, Richmond, Virginia

mountain whites in the South

Prigg v. *Pa,* 1842

personal liberty laws

"King Cotton"

Free Soil Party

The 1850s

John Sutter

forty-niners

California applies for admission as a state

Compromise of 1850: provisions, impact

Fugitive Slave Law

Anthony Burns

Ableman v. *Booth*

Webster's 7th of March speech

Nashville Convention

Henry Clay

John C. Calhoun

underground railroad

Harriet Tubman

Uncle Tom's Cabin, Harriet Beecher Stowe

election of 1852: end of the Whig Party

Perry and Japan

Ostend Manifesto

Kansas-Nebraska Act, 1854

birth of the Republican Party

Stephen A. Douglas

popular sovereignty

36° 30' line

election of 1856: Republican Party,
   Know-Nothing Party

"bleeding Kansas" and Lawrence

"Beecher's Bibles"

John Brown's raid

Pottawatomie massacre

New England Emigrant Aid Company

Sumner-Brooks affair

Lecompton Constitution

Dred Scott decision

Chief Justice Roger B. Taney (pronounced
   Tawny)

Lincoln-Douglas debates of 1858 during
   Illinois senatorial campaign

Freeport Doctrine

panic of 1857

George Fitzhugh, *Sociology for the South, or
   the Failure of Free Society*

Hinton Helper, *The Impending Crisis of the
   South*

Lincoln's "house divided" speech

John Brown, Harpers Ferry raid

election of 1860: candidates, parties, issues

Democratic Party conventions: Baltimore,
   Charleston

John Bell

John Breckinridge

Republican Party: 1860 platform, supporters,
   leaders

Buchanan and the secession crisis

Crittenden Compromise proposal

Civil War

border states

South's advantages in the Civil War

North's advantages in the Civil War

Fort Sumter

Bull Run

Monitor and the Merrimac

Lee, Jackson

Grant, McClellan, Sherman, Meade

Vicksburg, Gettysburg, Antietam, Appomattox

Jefferson Davis, Alexander Stephens

Northern blockade

cotton versus wheat

Copperheads

Congressman Clement L. Vallandigham

suspension of habeas corpus

Republican legislation passed in Congress after Southerners left: banking, tariff, homestead, transcontinental railroad

conscription, draft riots

Emancipation Proclamation

Charles Francis Adams

Great Britain: Trent, Alabama, Laird rams, "continuous voyage"

election of 1864: candidates, parties

financing of the war effort by North and South

Clara Barton

Reconstruction

Lincoln's ten percent plan

assassination of April 14, 1865

John Wilkes Booth

Ex parte Milligan

Radical Republicans

Wade-Davis bill, veto, Wade-Davis Manifesto

Joint Committee on Reconstruction (Committee of Fifteen)

Reconstruction acts, 1867

state suicide theory

conquered territory theory

the unreconstructed South

black codes

Texas v. *White*, 1869

Thaddeus Stevens

Charles Sumner

Andrew Johnson

Freedmen's Bureau

General Oliver O. Howard

Ku Klux Klan

Civil Rights Act

Thirteenth Amendment

Fourteenth Amendment and its provisions

Fifteenth Amendment

Tenure of Office Act

impeachment

Chief Justice Chase

Secretary of War Stanton

scalawags, carpetbaggers

purchase of Alaska

Secretary of State William Seward

Napoleon III

Maximilian in Mexico

Monroe Doctrine

Ulysses S. Grant

Treaty of Washington

Secretary of State Hamilton Fish

election of 1872; Liberal Republicans, Horace Greeley

election of 1876: Hayes and Tilden

Compromise of 1877 provisions

Solid South

sharecropping, crop lien system

segregation

Hiram R. Revels

Blanche K. Bruce

Supreme Court Cases to Know

1. *Prigg* v. *Pennsylvania,* 1842 (fugitive slaves and federal-state powers)

Pennsylvania tried to prohibit the capture and return of runaway slaves within the state, a direct challenge to the federal government's fugitive slave law of 1793. The state law was declared unconstitutional because the return of fugitive slaves was a federal power as specified in Article IV, section 2 of the Constitution. Many Northern states responded by prohibiting state officials from assisting anyone pursuing runaway slaves (called personal liberty laws).

2. *Dred Scott* v. *Sandford,* 1857 (citizenship and slaves)

This complex case raised three questions: (1) Was Dred Scott a citizen? If he wasn't, he could not sue in a federal court. In other words, did the Supreme Court have jurisdiction to hear the case? (2) Could Congress exclude slavery from the territories? Since territories are controlled by Congress, who exercised a responsibility to represent all the people of the United States, could Congress restrict citizens of one section from taking their slaves into the territories? (3) If slaves are property, is the owner not protected by the Fifth Amendment from being deprived of his property without compensation?

Dred Scott was owned by an army doctor who took Scott into Illinois and part of the Wisconsin territory. Slavery had been outlawed in these two areas by the Northwest Ordinance and Illinois law and by the Missouri Compromise of 1820. Scott sued for his freedom based on the argument that residence on free soil made him a free man. The case quickly became a test case, with the doctor's widow selling Scott to her brother, Sanford, in New York (misspelled Sandford in official legal documents). The involvement of two different states forced the case into the federal courts.

All the judges wrote separate opinions in the case, which caused the debate to go on long after the decisions. The majority held that Scott was not a citizen; free blacks or slaves could not be citizens of the United States. They could be granted state citizenship. (The Fourteenth Amendment clearly granted dual citizenship to abolish this aspect of the case.) The judges could have ended their explanation here, and they hoped to do so. Two Northern Supreme Court judges, however, announced their intention to write long dissenting opinions against the majority, and the majority was forced to refute the hostile dissents. But the majority itself was so divided in its reasoning that all the majority judges wrote separate opinions. In answering the other two questions the Taney court declared the Missouri Compromise null and void because it prohibited a citizen of the United States from taking his property (slaves) into the territories. Southerners smiled; Northerners bristled with contempt. Dred Scott's owner freed him and his family.

3. *Ableman* v. *Booth,* 1859 (a state challenge to federal authority)

Booth, a Wisconsin abolitionist editor, was arrested by the federal government for helping a fugitive slave escape from the custody of a federal marshal. The Wisconsin Supreme Court issued a writ of habeas corpus to release him. The federal authorities refused to recognize the validity of the writ of habeas corpus.

Chief Justice Taney wrote the unanimous decision asserting that a court or judge that goes beyond the limits of its jurisdiction exercises "nothing less than lawless violence." The issue was now federal supremacy, not the fugitive slave laws. Northern reaction paralleled the earlier Virginia and Kentucky Resolutions.

4. *Ex parte* Merryman, 1861 (president's war powers)

This is not technically a Supreme Court case. Early in the Civil War an unruly Baltimore mob attacked Union soldiers passing through the city. Under President Lincoln's orders the army suspended habeas corpus and declared martial law. John

Merryman, a Southern sympathizer, was among those arrested. The federal circuit judge, who happened to be Chief Justice Roger B. Taney, issued a writ of habeas corpus that the army refused to accept. The only recourse left to Taney was to write to the president criticizing his usurpation of the power of Congress (Article I, section 9). Lincoln never directly replied. When Merryman was no longer a potential threat to the war effort he was quietly released.

5. Prize Cases, 1863 (president's war powers)

In April 1861, Lincoln declared a blockade of Southern ports before Congress met to react to secession. Captured ship owners sued to recover their property and claimed that in the absence of a declaration of war by Congress the president was powerless. The Court, by a 5–4 margin, upheld the blockade from the date it was first proclaimed. Under his powers as commander in chief the president had to respond to an insurrection that had become a war "without waiting for Congress to baptize it with a name."

6. *Ex parte* Milligan, 1866 (constitutional rights during war)

Lambdin Milligan, a citizen of Indiana, was arrested for subversive activities in support of the Southern cause during the Civil War. He was tried, convicted, and sentenced to die by a military court in Indiana in spite of the fact that the Indiana civilian court system was functioning. Milligan's appeal to the Supreme Court raised the question of the dividing line between civil and military control over civilians during wartime. The Supreme Court ruled that while the Constitution permitted the suspension of habeas corpus, it did not suspend the judicial powers of federal courts. Military tribunals could be established, but when the federal courts were "open and ready" no other court could claim jurisdiction. "The Constitution of the United States is a law for rulers and people, equally in war and in peace, and covers with the shield of its protection all classes of men, at all times, and under all circumstances." Milligan sued for damages for false imprisonment. A jury awarded him five dollars.

7. *Mississippi* v. *Johnson,* 1867 (separation of powers)

This case involved the attempt by the state of Mississippi to force the president to stop enforcing the Reconstruction acts on the grounds that the acts were unconstitutional. Can the Supreme Court stop the president from carrying out an act of Congress?

"The Congress is the legislative department of the government; the President is the executive department. Neither can be restrained in its action by the judicial department; though the acts of both, when performed, are in proper cases, subject to its cognizance."

The Court had earlier issued the doctrine of political question to avoid involvement in Dorr's Rebellion (*Luther* v. *Borden,* 1849). This doctrine simply stated that the issue was a political question to be resolved at the polls or in the legislature.

8. *Texas* v. *White,* 1869 (nature of the Union)

This case involved the legality of the sale of U.S. federal government bonds in the possession of the Texas government, which were sold after the state seceded. The case hinged upon the question of whether or not a state could leave the Union. The Court said secession was constitutionally impossible. "The Constitution, in all its provisions, looks to an indestructible Union, composed of indestructible states.

"When, therefore, Texas became one of the United States, she entered into an indissoluble relation. All the obligations of perpetual union and all the guarantees of republican government in the Union, attached at once to the State. The act which consummated her admission into the Union was something more than a compact; it was the incorporation of a new member into the political body. And it was final. The union between Texas and the other states was as complete, as perpetual, and as indissoluble as the union between the original States."

Readings for Depth and Historical Interpretation

Slavery

1. Kenneth Stamp, *The Peculiar Institution*. An early attack on Ulrich B. Phillip's older view that slavery would have died eventually if left alone and was a benign paternalistic institution, a schoolhouse of civilization for primitive Africans. Stamp painted a picture of rebellious slaves, and destroyed the myth of the contented happy slave.

2. John Blassingame, *The Slave Community,* especially the revised and enlarged edition. Blassingame looks at slavery through the eyes of black slaves, history seen from the bottom up. He studies the "African heritage, culture, family, acculturation, behavior, religion, and personality." Also see the early chapters on slave songs and tales in Lawrence W. Levine, *Black Culture and Black Consciousness: Afro-American Folk Thought from Slavery to Freedom.*

3. Herbert G. Gutman, *The Black Family in Slavery and Freedom,* 1750–1925, and his updated observations, "The Black Family in Slavery and Freedom: A Revised Perspective," in *Work, Culture, and Society in Industrializing America.* Gutman attacks the myth of the maternalistic black family existing in and coming out of slavery. Considering the impediments, slave families were remarkably durable and resilient.

4. Eugene D. Genovese, *The World the Slaveholders Made.* Or see "The Slave South: An Interpretation," *Science & Society,* December 1961, pp. 320–337, which is also in *The Political Economy of Slavery.* A Marxist scholar, he sees a precapitalist society in the South dominated economically, politically, and socially by an aristocratic class of planters. Within the context of the master-slave relationship, the slaves fought back to the best of their ability.

5. Richard Hofstadter, "John C. Calhoun: The Marx of the Master Class," in *The American Political Tradition.* A good explanation of the political thought of America's most original political thinker. Hofstadter explores the economic foundations of Calhoun's ideas.

6. Stanley Elkins, *Slavery, A Problem in American Institutional Life.* See also the introduction in Ann J. Lane, *The Debate Over Slavery: Stanley Elkins and His Critics.* Elkins explains the Sambo image of slaves as arising out of the no-exit situation of slavery, which caused slaves to revert to infantile behavior patterns.

7. For the abolitionists, see Ronald G. Walters, *American Reformers,* 1815–1860, or James Brewer Stewart, *Holy Warriors: The Abolitionists and American Slavery.*

8. To understand slavery from the viewpoint of the slave, see the contemporary autobiography by an escaped slave, Frederick Douglass, *Narrative of the Life of Frederick Douglass,* or Nathan Huggins, *Slave and Citizen: The Life of Frederick Douglass.*

Economy, 1790–1860

1. George R. Taylor, *The Transportation Revolution,* 1815–1860. Uses changes in transportation to illustrate fundamental changes in the American economy in this period.

2. Louis Hartz, *Economic Policy and Democratic Thought: Pennsylvania, 1776–1860.* Using Pennsylvania as a case study, Hartz shows that state governments often intervened in the economy to direct economic affairs. He destroys the myth that laissez-faire aptly describes governmental policy in this era.

3. Douglass C. North, "Acceleration of U.S. Economic Growth, 1815–1860," in his *Growth and Welfare in the American Past: A New Economic History.* See also North's *The Economic Growth of the United States,* 1790–1860. North uses the newer approach of statistical analysis to look at economic growth.

4. Richard Hofstadter, "Andrew Jackson and the Rise of Liberal Capitalism," in *The American Political Tradition.* Hofstadter covers the Bank War and introduces students to the entrepreneurial school of interpretation.

5. John F. Kasson, *Civilizing the Machine: Technology and Republican Values in America, 1776–1900.* See pages 55–106, on the response to the model factory town of Lowell, Massachusetts.

6. Sean Wilentz, *Chants Democratic: New York City and the Rise of the American Working Class, 1788–1850,* especially the introduction, for urban economic developments in this period. Another source for understanding the working class is Bruce Laurie, *Working People of Philadelphia, 1800–1850,* pages 3–30; or, his "'Nothing on Compulsion': Life Styles of Philadelphia Artisans, 1820–1850," *Labor History,* 1974.

7. Constance McL. Green, *Eli Whitney and the Birth of American Technology,* is a biography of Whitney's double impact on the economy through the cotton gin and interchangeable parts.

The 1850s and the Coming of the Civil War

1. Charles and Mary Beard, *The Rise of American Civilization.* The war was caused by competition between economic interest groups fighting for control of the federal government. The two major economic groups—industrialists and planters—just happened also to be divided geographically.

2. James G. Randall, "The Blundering Generation," *Mississippi Valley Historical Review,* June 1940. The 1850s generation blundered into a needless and unnecessary war because they were not intelligent political leaders. They played on emotions to gain votes rather than face the issues.

3. Avery Craven, *The Coming of the Civil War,* or "The 1840s and the Democratic Process," *Journal of Southern History* XVI, 1950. Agitation over slavery led to mistaken and false sectional images. The fanaticism of the abolitionists was critical in causing the war (as well as irresponsible).

4. Arthur M. Schlesinger, Jr., "The Causes of the Civil War: A Note on Historical Sentimental-

ism," *The Partisan Review,* October 1949. The needless war and the blundering generation critics miss a major point. Some moral evils are so great that their destruction is worth the deaths of thousands. Slavery was such a moral evil. Schlesinger had been influenced by the experiences of World War II.

5. David M. Potter, *The Impending Crisis,* 1848–1861, is the finest overview of this decade. He tries to see the issues and events as Americans saw them at the time, unaware that the Civil War was coming.

6. Two articles address the question of the differences between the North and the South. The first sees few real differences; the second concludes that the South possessed a distinct and separate identity because the North was different. Edward Pessen, "How Different from Each Other Were the Antebellum North and South?" *American Historical Review,* December 1980, and James M. McPherson, "Antebellum Southern Exceptionalism: A New Look at an Old Question," *Civil War History,* September 1983.

Reconstruction

1. Kenneth Stamp, "The Tragic Legend of Reconstruction," *Commentary,* January 1965. Summarizes the Dunning school interpretation of Reconstruction and shows how the revisionists have challenged the older interpretation. Places the older interpretation within the context of that era's intellectual thought.

2. Carl Degler, "Dawn Without Noon," in *Out of Our Past,* latest revised edition. Summarizes the recent revisionist historical views of Reconstruction.

3. William A. Dunning, *Essays on the Civil War & Reconstruction.* A reprint of the 1897 book. The original statement by one who saw Reconstruction as a tragic era.

4. John Hope Franklin, *From Slavery to Freedom.* Black history by a noted black historian. He emphasizes the positive black achievements during Reconstruction.

5. C. Vann Woodward, *The Strange Career of Jim Crow,* third and revised edition. Wood-

ward links the first Reconstruction to the second, the civil rights movement in the 1950s and 1960s. He sees segregation as a product of the politics of the Populist revolt, not the Reconstruction era.

6. E. Merton Coulter, *The South During Reconstruction, 1865–1877.* A more modern (1947) summary of the Dunning interpretation.

7. James MacGregor Burns, *The Workshop of Democracy,* sees the political challenge as too great for the leadership in and out of Congress to successfully meet. See pages 51–70. Lincoln's assassination removed him from the scene, but Stephen B. Oates, *Abraham Lincoln: The Man Behind the Myths,* paints a picture of Lincoln as an evolving and adjusting politician of principle, whose ideas about Reconstruction were not as opposed to those of the Radicals as most texts present.

8. August Meier, "Afterword: New Perspectives on the Nature of Black Political Leadership during Reconstruction," pages 393–405, in Howard Rabinowitz, ed., *Southern Black Leaders of the Reconstruction Era.* Meier looks at a group that has been the subject of intensive recent research, providing information about the second tier of black leaders. Another source is *Black Leaders of the Nineteenth Century,* edited by Leon Litwack and August Meier. Included are Richard Allen, Nat Turner, Harriet Tubman, Frederick Douglass, and black Reconstruction leaders.

9. For overviews of the Reconstruction era, see Eric Foner, *Reconstruction: America's Unfinished Revolution*, 1863–1877, or Michael Perman, *Emancipation and Reconstruction*, 1862–1879.

Sample Outline

Reconstruction confuses students. This period in American history can be organized around many different themes. One theme is the North versus the South, or the Civil War continued. Among the salient points in this emphasis are the triumph of Northern economic interests; the North first aiding blacks in the South and then losing interest and commitment; and the question of which came first, Southern intransigence or Radical Republican laws. A second theme looks at Reconstruction as either a success or a failure, with an emphasis on the differing viewpoints of the Dunning school of historians and the revisionist historians. A third view concentrates on the South, seeing the essence of Reconstruction in the ongoing struggle between Southern whites and the former slaves. A fourth method for viewing Reconstruction is through the contest between Congress and the president over the issue of civil rights for blacks. This viewpoint is outlined below.

Meaning of Reconstruction
Congress versus President over Issue of Civil Rights

Two concepts are central to Reconstruction: (1) the demand of Congress that the president recognize the prerogative of Congress (the powers of Congress are listed first in the Constitution because legislative power is paramount); and (2) the demand of Congress to somehow guarantee civil rights for blacks.

I. **Presidents Take Charge**

   A. The relationship between Lincoln and Congress created a residue of ill will.

   1. Beginning of the Civil War: Lincoln did not call a special session of Congress from April to July.

   2. President suspended habeas corpus, suppressed newspapers, and issued arrest order for Congressman Vallandigham.

3. President issued Emancipation Proclamation, Jan 1, 1863.

4. Question of Lincoln's commitment: once spoke of colonizing blacks outside the U.S., and of letting South work out details of black-white relations after the war

5. President's Reconstruction Plan

  a. When 10% of all ex-Confederates take oath of allegiance and agree to support Thirteenth Amendment, states may set up a state government.

  b. TN, AK, and LA did.

6. Congressional reaction—Wade-Davis bill, July 1864—asserted Congressional control of Reconstruction, pocket vetoed by Lincoln. Wade-Davis Manifesto, August 1864, blasted Lincoln.

  a. Majority (not 10%) must take loyalty oath

  b. Must repudiate Confederate debt

  c. Similarities to Lincoln: accept Thirteenth Amendment, high Confederate officials disenfranchised.

  Quote from Wade-Davis Manifesto: The President "must understand that our support is of a cause and not of a man; that the authority of Congress is paramount and must be respected; that the whole body of the Union men of Congress will not submit to be impeached by him of rash and unconstitutional legislation; and if he wishes our support, he must confine himself to his executive duties—to obey and execute, not make the laws—to suppress by arms armed rebellion, and leave political reorganization to Congress."

B. Election of 1864 and Andrew Johnson

  1. Republican Party dissolved; Union Party with former Republican from North as president, former Democrat from South as vice-president

  2. Second Inaugural Address conciliatory

  3. Lincoln assassinated April 14, 1865. Johnson takes over.

  4. Johnson's Reconstruction Plan: South abolish slavery, accept Thirteenth Amendment, repudiate Confederate debt, disavow secession.

  5. Congress not in session April to December 1, 1865

  6. All but Texas accepted Johnson's terms for return

  7. South unrepentant in spirit: black codes

  8. In November election for Congress, South elected many ex-Confederate leaders, who arrogantly demanded Congressional seniority back. Congress kicked them out.

II. Congress Takes Charge

A. Seized control of Reconstruction policy

  1. Joint Committee on Reconstruction (Committee of Fifteen): Thaddeus Stevens, Benjamin Wade, Charles Sumner

  2. Theoretical question of control over South: territorial status or state suicide theory

3. Motives: protect program of Republican Party (banking, tariff, RR, Homestead Act) to ensure its future

4. "Radical" tag a misnomer; all but handful opposed Johnson

5. Thaddeus Stevens, September 6, 1865, advocated 40 acres and a mule.

6. General Sherman issued Order No. 15: 40,000 land titles to freedmen for 485,000 acres seized

7. Southern Homestead Act, July 1866 (expired January 1, 1867) extended principle of 1862 Homestead Act to public lands of AL, MS, AK, LA, and FL. It was open to all who did not support the Confederacy. It failed; their land was inferior, and freedmen lacked capital for equipment.

B. Congress and president fight over civil rights and Reconstruction policies

1. February 1866: Freedmen's Bureau extended, vetoed, and passed over veto.

2. April 1866: Civil Rights Act passed, vetoed, and passed over veto.

3. Fourteenth Amendment proposed and sent to states. All Southern states but TN refused to ratify.

4. In the Congressional elections of 1866, Radicals won over two-thirds of seats.

C. Congress in control

1. March 1867 Reconstruction Act: Ten Southern states divided into five military districts (the "sinful ten" who rejected the Fourteenth Amendment).

2. To reenter the Union they had to write new state constitutions, guarantee black suffrage, and ratify the Fourteenth Amendment.

3. By election of 1868, only three had not accepted these terms—VA, TX, MS.

4. In 1868 election Republican Grant narrowly wins. Democrats win two Southern states, LA and GA; Radicals claimed only because blacks were not allowed to vote.

5. Fifteenth Amendment proposed to guarantee black vote.

D. Congress handcuffs Supreme Court

1. No appeals to courts allowed under Reconstruction acts

2. Number of SC judges reduced to prevent Johnson from appointing one if vacancy occured

E. Assuring a Republican Party future

1. Impeachment part of Congress vs. president battle over civil rights

2. Tenure of Office Act: Secretary of War Stanton was in charge of five military districts, and therefore control of this office meant control of Reconstruction policy.

3. Trial ended 35–19; failed by one vote, two-thirds needed.

4. Pliant Grant wins presidency.

5. VA, TX, and MS accepted Fifteenth Amendment and were readmitted.

     6. GA readmitted after being put again under military rule for anti-black measures.

  F. After 1870

     1. Southerners and Conservatives gradually regained control of individual Southern states.

     2. General Amnesty Act, 1872, issued for all but 500 top ex-Confederates.

     3. Republicans still worked to protect blacks and civil rights: Ku Klux Klan Acts, Civil Rights Act, 1875.

III. Reconstruction and Civil Rights

  A. Putting the commitment to equal rights in perspective

     1. The U.S. was the first major nation to commit itself to equal rights for all.

     2. In later quest for equality, blacks appealed to the national government to obey established national laws rather than to change them.

  B. Reasons for the failure to secure civil rights

     1. The push for black equality required interference with local governments on a massive scale. The weakness of the Radical program was this dependence on national intervention.

     2. Black vote supported on principle and on Republican dependence on black vote. As the second weakened, so did the first.

     3. Difficult to ensure legal and constitutional racial equality in a society that did not popularly believe in the equality of the races in any sense. The popular belief in the equality of the races is a mid-20th-century concept.

UNIT SIX: 1865–1900

Major Themes and Ideas

Politics in Late Nineteenth Century

1. Characteristics of the third party system

2. Characteristics of politics in the late nineteenth century

3. Compare and contrast Democratic and Republican parties: base of support, policies, successes, and so forth.

4. Relative powers and influence of Congress, presidents, and Supreme Court

5. History of political reform movements and why they failed

6. Who in this period deserves to be called a statesman, and why?

7. Compare Cleveland with any other period politician.

8. Presidents are rarely successful in both foreign policy and domestic policy. Assess this statement in regard to Johnson and Grant.

9. Pivotal election of 1896

Business

1. Is the Robber Baron nickname deserved?

2. Changes in the economy from 1865–1900 in transportation, agriculture, labor force, and industry

3. Did the Civil War stimulate or retard industrialization?

4. Rise of corporations, trusts, pools, and holding companies

5. Social mobility and businessmen (their origins)

6. Antimonopoly movement to the 1930s

7. The 1890s as a decade of economic, political, and social crises

8. Factors that promoted industrialization

9. Which shaped the economy more, individual businessmen or market forces?

10. Trace shifting Supreme Court decisions in regard to the regulation of railroads and industry.

11. Money question as an economic and political problem

12. This period, 1865–1900, as a period of governmental intervention in the economy, not of laissez-faire

13. The role and significance of technological innovations

Labor

1. Characteristics of different unions—NLU, Knights, AFL, ARU—differences, successes, failures, leaders, reasons for directions they took

2. Changing workplace conditions: wages, hours, safety

3. Compare and contrast the Haymarket Square riot, the Homestead strike, and the Pullman strike.

4. Why were American workers unreceptive to socialist doctrines?

5. Attitude of government, state and federal, toward labor unions to 1914

Urbanization

1. Explain the location and growth of specific cities.

2. Impact of new immigrants on cities

3. Rise of spectator sports

4. Explain James Bryce's observation that city governments were "the one conspicuous failure of the United States."

5. Advantages and disadvantages of urban life

6. Gilded Age as an era of "conspicuous consumption" (Thorstein Veblen's phrase)

7. Reciprocal relationship between technology and urban growth

8. Reformers' attempts to address problems of poverty, housing, and health

9. Municipal governments: why were they so bad, why so frustrating to reformers?

10. Women's Movement, 1848–1900

11. Churches' attack on social and economic problems

12. Rise of urban transportation

13. Reactions to immigration: pre-Civil War, Civil War to 1920s

14. Urbanization reflected in art and literature

Social and Intellectual Movements and Ideas

1. What did intellectuals criticize in American society?

2. Darwinism and church leaders

3. Darwinism created and justified new thought.

4. Impact of Darwinism on scientific thought

5. Compare and contrast Henry George and Edward Bellamy.

6. Higher education: role of individuals and governments

7. *Progress and Poverty* and *Uncle Tom's Cabin* were two of the three top-selling books of the nineteenth century. Evaluate their themes and impact.

8. Competition and laissez-faire as ideals and as realities

9. Characteristics of literature and art in the late nineteenth century

10. The Social Gospel as a religious movement

11. Causes of the increasing inequality of wealth and solutions proposed by intellectuals

Blacks

1. Outline developments in the history of blacks, 1865–1912.

2. Compare and contrast the treatment of immigrants, blacks, and Indians.

3. Race as the central issue in Southern life, 1865–1900

4. Southern whites reestablished political control after Reconstruction and modernized the Southern economy.

5. Rise of Jim Crow

6. Booker T. Washington versus W.E.B. DuBois

The West and Populism

1. Populism urged political solutions to economic problems.

2. Why did Populism fail, or did it?

3. Problems facing farmers

4. Compare and contrast the Grange, the Farmers' Alliance, and Populism.

5. Compare Populism and Jacksonianism or Jeffersonianism.

6. Connect Southern Populism and the rise of racism.

7. Compare the Southern agricultural systems before and after the Civil War.

8. Why was the Great Plains settled last?

9. What brought a speedy end to the frontier?

10. Economic and political consequences of the closing of the frontier

11. Theories of Frederick Jackson Turner

12. Myth of the cowboy

13. What factors removed the Plains Indians?

14. Evolution of federal land policy toward Indians to 1924

15. Farmers versus the railroads and industry

16. The significance of federal government policies in developing the West

Major Terms and Concepts

Politics in Late Nineteenth Century

Ulysses S. Grant

Whiskey Ring

"waving the bloody shirt"

Ku Klux Klan

Secretary of State Hamilton Fish

Treaty of Washington, 1871

Liberal Republicans: Carl Schurz, Horace Greeley

panic of 1873, depression

election of 1876: candidates, electoral commission

Compromise of 1877

Solid South

greenbacks, Ohio Idea

Specie Resumption Act

Greenback-Labor Party

Pendleton Civil Service Act

Chester A. Arthur

election of 1884: James G. Blaine, Grover Cleveland

Stalwarts, Roscoe Conkling

Half-Breeds

Mugwumps

"Rum, Romanism, and Rebellion"

high tariffs

treasury surplus

pensions, GAR

secret ballot (Australian ballot)

Cleveland's 1887 annual address

election of 1888: candidates, issues

Benjamin Harrison, Billion Dollar Congress, Czar Reed

McKinley Tariff

election of 1892: candidates, issues

Morgan bond transaction

Wilson-Gorman Tariff

Dingley Tariff

Business

laissez-faire

Adam Smith, *The Wealth of Nations*

Union Pacific Railroad, Central Pacific Railroad

Crédit Mobilier

"Robber Barons"

John D. Rockefeller

Standard Oil Company

horizontal consolidation

Andrew Carnegie

Henry Clay Frick

vertical consolidation

Charles Schwab

Thomas A. Edison

Alexander Graham Bell

Leland Stanford

James J. Hill, Great Northern Railroad

Cornelius Vanderbilt, New York Central Railroad

Bessemer process

United States Steel Corporation, Elbert H. Gary

Mesabi Range

J. Pierpont Morgan

Gustavus Swift

Philip Armour

James B. Duke

Andrew Mellon

"stock watering"

Jay Cooke Co.

Jay Gould and Jim Fiske

pools, trusts

rebates

depression of 1873

holding companies

Fourteenth Amendment's "due process clause"

Interstate Commerce Act, Interstate Commerce Commission

long haul, short haul

Sherman Antitrust Act, 1890

Labor

National Labor Union, William Sylvis

Knights of Labor: Uriah Stephens, Terence Powderly

American Federation of Labor (AFL)

Samuel Gompers

collective bargaining

injunction

strikes, boycotts

closed shop

blacklist, yellow dog contracts

company unions

Great Railroad strike, 1877

Haymarket Square riot

John Peter Altgeld

Homestead strike

Pinkertons

American Railway Union

Pullman strike, 1894

Eugene V. Debs

Richard Olney

Danbury Hatters strike

Urbanization

George Washington Plunkitt

"honest graft"

Boss Tweed

Tammany Hall

Thomas Nast

"new immigration"

Dillingham Commission Report, 1911

streetcar suburbs

tenements

Jane Addams, Hull House

Denis Kearney

Chinese Exclusion law, 1882

American Protective Association

literacy tests

James Bryce, *The American Commonwealth*

John A. Roebling, Brooklyn Bridge

Louis Sullivan

Frank Lloyd Wright

Ashcan school

Armory Show, 1913

Anthony Comstock

Social and Intellectual Movements and Ideas

Charles Darwin, *Origin of Species*

Social Darwinism

Andrew Carnegie, *The Gospel of Wealth*

Herbert Spencer

William Graham Sumner, *What Social Classes Owe to Each Other*

Henry Ward Beecher

Rev. Russell Conwell, *Acres of Diamonds*

Dwight L. Moody

Rev. Josiah Strong

Lester Frank Ward

Social Gospel

Salvation Army, YMCA

Walter Rauschenbusch

Washington Gladden

Rerum Novarum, 1891

Charles Sheldon, *In His Steps*

Mary Baker Eddy

Chautauqua movement

Johns Hopkins University

Charles W. Eliot, Harvard

Josiah Willard Gibbs

Morrill Act, 1862

land grant colleges, A&M, A&T, A&I

Hatch Act, 1887

Edward Bellamy, *Looking Backward, 2000-1887*

Henry George, *Progress and Poverty*

the single tax

"Gilded Age"

nouveau riche

William James

pragmatism

E.L. Godkin, editor of *The Nation*

William Dean Howells

Henry James

Stephen Crane

Hamlin Garland

Bret Harte

Mark Twain

The Gilded Age, Mark Twain and Charles Dudley Warner

Horatio Alger's books for youth

James McNeill Whistler

Winslow Homer

Joseph Pulitzer

William Randolph Hearst

Susan B. Anthony

Elizabeth Cady Stanton

Carrie Chapman Catt

Alice Paul

Women's Christian Temperance Union (WCTU)

Francis Willard

Carry A. Nation

Clara Barton

Blacks

Mississippi plan

Bourbons or Redeemers

New South, Henry Grady

Joel Chandler Harris

Slaughterhouse Cases

Civil Rights Act, 1875

Civil Rights Cases, 1883

sharecropping, crop lien laws

lynching

Booker T. Washington, Tuskegee Institute

Atlanta Compromise

George Washington Carver

W.E.B. DuBois

"talented tenth"

Plessy v. *Ferguson,* "separate but equal"

Jim Crow laws

disenfranchisement, *Williams* v. *Mississippi,* 1898

grandfather clause

Niagara Movement

Springfield, Ill., riot, 1908

NAACP

The Crisis

The West and Populism

Great American Desert

Homestead Act, 1862

Oliver H. Kelley

Granger Movement

Granger laws

barbed wire, Joseph Glidden

Indian Appropriations Act, 1871

Plains Indians

Chivington massacre

Battle of the Little Big Horn

Chief Joseph

Battle of Wounded Knee

Helen Hunt Jackson, *A Century of Dishonor*

Dawes Severalty Act, 1887

Frederick Jackson Turner, frontier thesis

safety valve thesis

Comstock Lode

"Crime of 1873"

Bland-Allison Act

Sherman Silver Purchase Act

bimetallism

"Coin" Harvey

free silver

16 to 1

depression of 1893

Coxey's army, 1893

repeal of the Sherman Silver Purchase Act, 1893

Farmers' Alliance

Ocala Demands, 1890

Populist Party platform, Omaha Platform, 1892

Tom Watson

James B. Weaver

"Pitchfork" Ben Tillman

Mary Ellen Lease

"Sockless" Jerry Simpson

Ignatius Donnelly

William Jennings Bryan

"Cross of Gold" speech

election of 1896: candidates, issues

Marcus Hanna

Gold Standard Act, 1900

Supreme Court Cases to Know

1. Legal Tender Cases, 1870, 1871 (federal monetary powers)

During the Civil War the Union government issued paper money, called greenbacks, and made them legal tender, meaning that they were considered money for all public and private debts. Even if one refused to accept a greenback when it was offered, the debt was still legally considered to have been paid. (Read a modern dollar bill.) Many in this period believed that paper money had to be backed by specie. When the first case, *Hepburn* v. *Griswold,* was decided in 1870, a 5–4 Court majority ruled the Legal Tender Acts of 1862 and 1863 unconstitutional in regard to contracts made before the passage of these acts. The decision implied that later contracts might be invalid, and it jeopardized the circulation of $350,000,000 in greenbacks. Within a year President Grant appointed two new judges to the Supreme Court. The two new judges joined three of the dissenters from *Hepburn* v. *Griswold* to declare the Legal Tender Acts constitutional in a new suit for all debts, whether previous or subsequent to the first Legal Tender Act. The cases involved in the 1871 second suit were *Knox* v. *Lee* and *Parker* v. *Davis*. Grant was incensed at the Hepburn decision and frankly solicited the opinions of his new appointees before submitting their names to the Senate for confirmation. These cases clearly illustrate how the Supreme Court can become involved in current political issues.

2. Slaughterhouse Cases, 1873 (the privileges and immunities clause)

The three suits in the Slaughterhouse cases were the first under the Fourteenth Amendment. Both the majority opinion and dissenting opinions molded the interpretation of the Fourteenth Amendment for decades. The Louisiana Reconstruction state government granted a monopoly to one corporation for butchering livestock in New Orleans, and put more than one thousand butchers out of business. The butchers claimed this act violated the Fourteenth Amendment, abridging their "privileges and immunities" as citizens of the United States. In a 5–4 decision the Court ruled a sharp distinction between state privileges and rights and federal privileges and rights. The Fourteenth Amendment protected only the latter; it offered no protection against state infringement. Most rights of citizenship are state, not national. The Court narrowly interpreted the Thirteenth, Fourteenth, and Fifteenth amendments as designed solely for freeing slaves and establishing citizenship rights for blacks.

The dissenting opinions of two judges foreshadowed the future emphasis of the first clause of the Fourteenth Amendment. The due process and equal protection clauses became the heart of the amendment's later interpretations, which made the guarantees in the Bill of Rights applicable to the states. Read the first section of the Fourteenth Amendment.

3. *Bradwell* v. *Illinois,* 1873 (women and the professions)

Myra Bradwell, wife of a prominent Chicago lawyer, studied law in her husband's law office. In 1868 she began to publish the *Chicago Legal News,* a weekly paper specializing in state and municipal court cases and state legislation. Within a short time she was recognized as an expert on state and local law. After she passed the bar exam she applied to the Illinois Supreme Court for admission to the bar. She was rejected on the grounds that she was a married woman and therefore not legally able to sign contracts without her husband's consent to each contract! She and her husband appealed to the United States Supreme Court claiming that her "privileges and immunities" of citizenship had been denied. As with the *Minor* v. *Happersett* case, the Court ruled that the right to practice law was not a right of citizenship.

Women reformers were incensed at a concurring opinion that served as a legalistic justification for excluding women from professional careers. Judge Joseph P. Bradley wrote that "the civil law, as well as nature herself, has always recognized a wide difference in the respective spheres and destinies of man and woman. Man is, or should be, woman's protector and defender. The natural and proper timidity and delicacy that belongs to the female sex evidently unfits it for many of the occupations of civil life. The constitution of the family organization, which is founded in the divine ordinance, as well as in the nature of things, indicates the domestic sphere as that which properly belongs to the domain and functions of womanhood. The harmony, not to say identity, of interests and views which belong or should belong to the family institution, is repugnant to the idea of a woman adopting a distinct and independent career from that of her husband." Myra Bradwell was finally admitted to the bar in 1890.

4. *Minor* v. *Happersett,* 1875 (suffrage for women)

Mrs. Virginia Minor sued in federal court in St. Louis claiming that she had been deprived of one of her "privileges and immunities" by being denied suffrage. In a unanimous decision the Court ruled that suffrage was not a right of citizenship.

5. *Munn* v. *Illinois,* 1877 (state regulation of business)

This case involved an Illinois state law limiting maximum rates for the storage of grain in privately owned grain elevators. One of the so-called Granger laws, it grew out of the 1870 revision of the state constitution, which empowered the legislature to regulate the storage of grain. Munn and his partner were fined $100 for charging higher rates and for operating without a license. He sought relief from his conviction on the grounds that it violated the due process and equal protection clauses of the Fourteenth Amendment and on the grounds of exclusive federal regulation of commerce. Chief Justice Waite wrote the 7–2 majority opinion asserting that the public has always had a right to regulate business operations in which the public has an interest. "Property does become clothed with a public interest when used in a manner to make it of public consequence, and affect the community at large. When, therefore, one devotes his property to a use in which the public has an interest, he, in effect, grants to the public an interest in that use, and must submit to be controlled by the public for the common good, to the extent of the interest he has thus created. He may withdraw his grant by discontinuing the use; but, so long as he maintains the use, he must submit to the control...." Justice Waite recognized that all regulation carries the potential for abuse, but cautioned, "For protection against abuses by legislatures the people must resort to the polls, not to the courts."

6. Civil Rights Cases, 1883 (discrimination against individuals)

In a decision consistent with the Slaughterhouse Cases, the Supreme Court narrowly defined the civil rights guaranteed by the Fourteenth Amendment in the Civil Rights Cases. The Civil Rights Act of 1875 made it a crime for any individual to deny full and equal use of public conveyances and public places such as hotels, trains, railroads, theaters, and restaurants. The Court declared that the Fourteenth Amendment protected individuals from state action, not individual action. "The wrongful act of an individual unsupported by any such state authority, is simply a private wrong, or a crime of that individual. ..." Discouraged, Congress did not pass another civil rights act until 1957.

7. *Wabash, St. Louis & Pacific RR Co.* v. *Illinois,* 1886 (states and the commerce clause)

Popularly known as the Wabash Case, this decision is significant because it added to the push for the Interstate Commerce Act of 1887. An Illinois law prohibited the infamous practice of different rates for long and short haul traffic. The Court ruled that states could regulate only intrastate commerce, not interstate commerce. Since the federal government had not yet begun to regulate railroads crossing state lines, the railroads were legally beyond control. Compare this decision to the Munn case.

8. *U. S.* v. *E. C. Knight Co.,* 1895 (monopolies, manufacturing, and commerce)

This was the first significant case under the Sherman Antitrust Act. The E.C. Knight Co. controlled 98 percent of the nation's manufacture of sugar. The Court ruled that monopoly control of manufacturing was not the same as monopoly control of commerce. The Sherman Antitrust Act restricted commerce, not manufacturing. Within a short time the Court broadened the definition of commerce by introducing the concept of "stream of commerce."

9. *Pollock* v. *Farmers' Loan and Trust Co.,* 1895 (the income tax)

Actually several cases, the Pollock suit challenged the constitutionality of the income tax imposed by the Wilson-Gorman Tariff, 1894. Income taxes had been in use for thirty years, but the Court now found them to be a violation of the Constitution, which requires direct taxes to be apportioned by population. The Court decided that a tax on rental income and a tax on personal property were both direct taxes. The Sixteenth Amendment negated this decision and specifically permitted income taxes.

10. In re Debs, 1895 (labor and injunctions)

During the Pullman strike in 1894, the Pullman Company obtained an injunction under the Sherman Antitrust Act. After refusing to comply, the union's leader, Eugene V. Debs, was arrested for contempt of court. Debs' writ of habeas corpus to the Supreme Court was denied on the basis of a broad interpretation of the commerce clause and the federal government's obligation to deliver the mail. Justice Brewer wrote, "The strong arm of the national government may be put forth to brush away all obstructions to the freedom of interstate commerce or the transportation of the mails." Critics and cynics wondered why "the strong arm of the national government" did not move as swiftly against monopolies.

11. *Plessy* v. *Ferguson,* 1896 (separate but equal)

One-eighth black, Homer Plessy was fined for refusing to leave a railroad car restricted to only whites. Louisiana state law required "separate but equal" facilities. The Fourteenth Amendment ensured political equality, not social equality. "We consider the underlying fallacy of the plaintiff's argument to consist in the assumption that the enforced separation of the two races stamps the colored race with a badge of inferiority. If this be so, it is not by reason of anything found in the act, but solely because the colored race chooses to put that construction upon it." According to the Court, separate was not second-class citizenship. The legislature could do only so much to ensure civil rights. "Legislation is powerless to eradicate racial instincts or to abolish distinctions based upon physical differences, and the attempt to do so can only result in accentuating the difficulties of the present situation. If the civil and political rights of both races be equal one cannot be inferior to the other civilly or politically. If one race be inferior to the other socially, the Constitution of the United States cannot put them upon the same plane."

In a stinging dissent Justice Harlan laid the foundation for the arguments that overturned the Plessy decision in *Brown* v. *the Board of Education of Topeka, Kansas,* 1954. "Our Constitution is color-blind, and neither knows nor tolerates classes among citizens. In respect of civil rights, all citizens are equal before the law. The humblest is the peer of the most powerful. The law regards man as man, and takes no account of his surroundings or of his color when his civil rights as guaranteed by the supreme law of the land are involved. It is, therefore, to be regretted that this high tribunal, the final expositor of the fundamental law of the land, has reached the conclusion that it is competent for a state to regulate the enjoyment by citizens of their civil rights solely upon the basis of race."

Readings for Depth and Historical Interpretation

Politics and Overviews of Period

1. Robert H. Wiebe, *The Search for Order: 1877–1920.* A good introduction to the link between economic issues and politics. Wiebe also assesses the impact of the expanding transportation system upon social values. He sees the destruction of the small town "island communities."

2. Vincent P. De Santis, "The Republican Party Revisited, 1877–1897," in H. Wayne Morgan, ed., *The Gilded Age: A Reappraisal.* De Santis analyzes the strengths and weaknesses of the two major political parties. He finds not a disgusting period devoid of values but "an era of party stalemate and equilibrium."

3. Ari Hoogenboom, "Spoilsmen and Reformers: Civil Service Reform and Public Morality," in H. Wayne Morgan, ed., *The Gilded Age: A Reappraisal.* Hoogenboom dispassionately looks at the Gilded Age's reputation for corruption. Its sordid image was due as much as anything else to the articulate and quotable reformers of the era who often took part in the "political corruption" of the spoils system.

4. Richard Hofstadter, "The Spoilsmen: An Age of Cynicism," in his *The American Political Tradition.* This is the traditional view of the era's politics. Woodrow Wilson summarized the politics as "No leaders, no principles: no principles, no parties."

5. Richard Hofstadter, "William Jennings Bryan: The Democrat as Revivalist," in his *The American Political Tradition.* This is a good source for the confusing politics of free silver and the election of 1896.

Business

1. Matthew Josephson, *The Robber Barons,* pp. 264–280. Josephson popularized the "Robber Baron" nickname in his 1934 book. The date is significant, for businessmen were not popular in the 1930s. In this section Josephson portrays John D. Rockefeller as a ruthless, conspiratorial businessman who callously brushed away competitors.

2. John Tipple, "The Robber Baron in the Gilded Age: Entrepreneur or Iconoclast?" In H. Wayne Morgan, ed., *The Gilded Age: A Reappraisal.* Tipple weaves together the Robber Baron image and the rise of the corporation as an instrument to conduct business activities. The corporation was "a supralegal abstraction above the traditional laws of the land," which undermined "American institutions and individualistic values by rendering them impotent. ..."

3. Harold Livesay, *Andrew Carnegie and the Rise of Big Business.* Livesay looks at Carnegie the businessman and finds the secret of his success in his obsession with cutting costs. The key to profits was not high prices but efficient production and lower prices. This book presents an image that certainly differs from *The Robber Barons. Also see his American Made: Men Who Shaped the American Economy,* especially Cyrus McCormick, Andrew Carnegie, Thomas Edison, and Henry Ford. The products of a market mentality, these men were exceptional because of their ability to create and inspire an organization.

4. Alfred D. Chandler, Jr., "The Beginnings of Big Business in American Industry," *Business History Review,* Spring, 1959, or *The Visible Hand: The Managerial Revolution in American Business,* or "The Large Industrial Corpo-

ration and the Making of the Modern American Economy," in *Institutions in Modern America: Innovation in Structure and Process,* ed. by Stephen Ambrose. Market forces—marketing, purchasing, processing—and changes in the structure of industry—the corporation with its autonomous divisions—molded and shaped industrial expansion. Few individuals are mentioned in Chandler's analysis. Not only is the Robber Baron image incorrect, he states, it is not even applicable.

5. Glenn Porter, *The Rise of Big Business, 1860–1910,* is a brief and excellent overview of industrialization and economic changes.

Labor

1. Stephan Thernstrom, "Newburyport and the Larger Society," in his *Poverty and Progress: Social Mobility in a Nineteenth Century City,* or "Urbanization, Migration, and Social Mobility in Late Nineteenth-Century America," in Barton J. Berstein, ed., *Towards a New Past: Dissenting Essays in American History.* Thernstrom introduces the concept of social mobility, movement up or down the social class ladder. Before Thernstrom historians too frequently assumed easy movement up the ladder. This study found a more static society.

2. Harold Livesay, *Samuel Gompers and Organized Labor in America.* Livesay's book portrays Gompers as an effective labor leader but only for elite skilled workers. Gompers stuck to his union principles, and generally ignored the plight of the unskilled mass production workers.

3. Carl Degler, the last two sections of "Machines, Men, and Socialism," in *Out of Our Past.* Degler summarizes the rise of unions and addresses the intriguing question of the absence of a strong socialist movement among American workers. We are the only industrial nation without a viable socialist movement.

4. Herbert G. Gutman, "Work, Culture, and Society in Industrializing America, 1815–1919," *American Historical Review,* June 1973. This article is difficult reading but full of insight.

During this one-hundred-year period successive waves of immigrants shaped the culture of American workers and determined our business values.

5. Herbert Gutman, *Work, Culture, and Society in Industrializing America,* contains the above article and an insightful look at "Class Composition and the Development of the American Working Class, 1840–1890."

Urbanization

1. Oscar Handlin, *The Uprooted,* or *Boston's Immigrants. The Uprooted* is a more general account of immigration, which includes the European background. *Boston's Immigrants* looks at the Irish in Boston: their arrival, economic and social adjustment, conflicts, and group identity.

2. Jane Addams, *Twenty Years at Hull House.* This autobiographical account by America's premier social worker covers the years from 1889 to 1909. She presents an insider's look at immigrant life, municipal corruption, and urban poverty in Chicago.

3. Carl Degler, *Out of Our Past.* The first half of the chapter, "Alabaster Cities and Amber Waves of Grain," is devoted to developments in the cities in the late nineteenth century.

4. John Bodnar, *The Transplanted,* especially the chapter, "The Rise of an Immigrant Middle Class." Bodnar tries to lift the history of immigration out of the "old-new" and ethnic molds. He sees the immigrants as peasants confronting modernity and capitalism as families, while also interacting with the new urban and economic forces of class, culture, and ideology.

5. John Higham, *Strangers in the Land: Patterns of American Nativism, 1860–1925.* Higham looks at the American reaction to immigration. The last few chapters on the 1920s are especially insightful. Also see his chapters on "The Immigrant in American History," and "The Politics of Immigration Restriction," in John Higham, *Send These to Me.*

6. Alexander B. Callow, Jr., *The Tweed Ring,* pp. 76–88. Callow describes the New York City

government, with comments on urban governments in this era. James Bryce, an English observer, called our municipal governments "the one conspicuous failure of the United States."

Social and Intellectual Movements and Ideas

1. Edward Bellamy's *Looking Backward, 2000–1887,* in Robert B. Downs, *Books That Changed America.* Bellamy's *Looking Backward* inspired millions of readers in the late nineteenth century. He offered hope that the vicious cycle of unending competition between individuals would somehow be replaced by a more cooperative society.

2. Michael Zuckerman, "The Nursery Tales of Horatio Alger," *American Quarterly,* 1972, or John G. Cawelti, "From Rags to Respectability: Horatio Alger," in his *Apostles of the Self-Made Man.* Either of these two articles help put Horatio Alger into perspective. Alger's message was never rags to riches. His heroes achieved respectability and exhibited the virtues of what we would call the team player and the organization man.

3. John F. Kasson, *Civilizing the Machine: Technology and Republican Values in America, 1776–1900,* pages 183–234. Kasson looks at the utopian and critical novels that appeared in the last two decades of the nineteenth century.

4. Eleanor Flexner, *Century of Struggle: The Women's Rights Movement in the United States,* covers the women's movement for the entire nineteenth century.

Blacks

1. Booker T. Washington, *Up From Slavery,* and W.E.B. DuBois (he Anglicized the pronunciation, so don't pronounce "DuBois" as if it were French), *The Souls of Black Folk.* (Both these books are in a paperback, *Three Negro Classics,* along with James Weldon Johnson's *The Autobiography of an Ex-Colored Man.*) The dispute between Booker T. Washington and

W.E.B. DuBois is best followed by reading their philosophies in their own words to compare their differences.

2. C. Vann Woodward, "Capitulation to Racism," in his *The Strange Career of Jim Crow.* Woodward details the rise of extreme Southern racism due to the decline of three restraining forces in the late nineteenth century: "Northern liberalism, Southern conservatism, and Southern radicalism."

3. Two other sources for differentiating between Washington and DuBois are found in "The Challenge to Washington's Leadership," Samuel R. Spencer, Jr., *Booker T. Washington and the Negro's Place in American Life,* and August Meier, *Negro Thought in America, 1880–1915: Racial Ideologies in the Age of Booker T. Washington.*

4. Leon Litwack, *Been in the Storm So Long: The Aftermath of Slavery,* is stronger on the Reconstruction era, but it continues black history to 1900. Leon Litwack also wrote a book that describes the racial animosities of the earlier half of the nineteenth century, *North of Slavery: The Negro in the Free States, 1790–1860.*

The West and Populism

1. Walter Prescott Webb, "The Frontier as a Modifier of Institutions," in his *The Great Frontier,* which summarizes significant points in his famous book, *The Great Plains.* Webb's *The Great Plains* illustrated the impact of environment upon institutions. The Plains region changed and modified settlers as much as they modified it. Among changed institutions were the six-gun, fences, transportation, and laws about water usage.

2. Dee Brown, *Bury My Heart at Wounded Knee.* This is a popular history of the Indian wars as seen from the Indian point of view.

3. Frederick Jackson Turner, "The Significance of the Frontier in American History," in Robert B. Downs, *Books That Changed America.* Frederick Jackson Turner is considered one of the most preeminent historians in the United States. His essay on the significance of the

frontier has dominated historical writing on the West since 1893. He revolutionized the writing of history by reversing the emphasis on the "germ theory" on the European origins of American institutions. To him, frontier experience shaped America's institutions more than our ancient political and constitutional principles.

4. Paolo E. Coletta, "Greenbacks, Goldbugs, and Silverites: Currency Reform and Policy, 1860–1897," in H. Wayne Morgan, ed., *The Gilded Age: A Reappraisal*. This is an excellent short summary of a topic that mesmerizes students—the money question.

5. John D. Hicks, *The Populist Revolt,* especially the chapters entitled "The Grievances" and "The Populist Contribution." This 1931 book still remains the most comprehensive and sympathetic treatment of the Populists. You should also find a copy of the 1892 Omaha Platform of the Populist Party and read it carefully.

6. Richard Hofstadter, "The Folklore of Populism," in his *The Age of Reform*. Hofstadter is critical of the Populists and balances Hicks' sympathetic portrayal. Hofstadter paints a picture of status anxieties and harebrained schemes instead of genuine economic problems confronting the Populists.

7. Carl Degler, *Out of Our Past*. The second half of the chapter entitled "Alabaster Cities and Amber Waves of Grain" summarizes the plight of the farmers and describes the Populist Party revolt.

8. Lawrence Goodwyn, *The Populist Movement* (which is an abridged version of *Democratic Promise: The Populist Movement in America*). Goodwyn sees the Populist movement as a democratic political movement. Another source along this same vein is James Turner, "Understanding the Populists," *Journal of American History,* September 1980. Turner also sees the Populists as within the mainstream of American political protest movement, part of a traditional American political response.

9. Henry M. Littlefield, "The Wizard of Oz: Parable on Populism," *American Quarterly,* Spring 1964, will absolutely delight students. Littlefield argues that the book on which the popular movie was based is a thinly veiled parody of Populism.

10. Julie Roy Jeffrey, *Frontier Women: The Trans-Mississippi West,* 1840–1880, and Joanna L. Stratton, *Pioneer Women: Voices from the Kansas Frontier*. These two books fill a void in reminding students that the westward movement was often a family affair, frequently filled with the hardships of frontier life, temperance crusades, suffrage efforts, sod houses, and civilizing the frontier.

Sample Outline

Urban America changed dramatically between 1850 and 1900. Waves of immigrants flooded the cities; mass transit systems sorted the population; and industrialization created new and different types of employment. The modern city emerged from this interaction between mass man and mass technology. One word of caution: Urbanization and industrialization occurred at the same time in the United States, but they are different, if parallel, historical movements. The fact that they occurred at the same time had momentous consequences for the nature of our cities. European cities differ drastically from American cities because urbanization preceded industrialization in Europe.

Much of the information in this outline is from Howard P. Chudacoff, *The Evolution of American Urban Society,* an excellent survey of our urban history.

Urbanization

I.   **The Old City**

   A.   Until the 1850s the compact city centered around the waterfront.

B. Walking city up to the 1850s

C. Land use was mixed; commercial, residential, industrial—all intermingled.

D. People relatively integrated, little segregation by immigrant or occupational group

E. Lure of the city

    1. Easy reception to novel ideas

    2. A person could lose one's past.

    3. Tendency of urbanites to look the other way when ambition took a dishonest turn

    4. Even today the average age of farmers is in the fifties.

II. Changing the Old City: Growth of Mass Transit

A. Omnibus: By 1833, 80 in NYC, each drawn by two horses, capacity of twelve passengers; 180 in 1837; 260 in 1847; 683 in 1853 serviced 120,000 daily.

B. Commuter railroad, 1859, 40 trains daily between Philadelphia and Germantown at a cost of 15¢ to 25¢ (too much for laborers who made only $1 a day).

C. Streetcars from horse-drawn to mechanical by 1873; cable cars in Chicago and San Francisco featured a continuous wire cable (a break halted the whole system); trolley cars: Frank Sprague, Richmond in the 1880s. By 1890, 5,700 animal-powered, 500 cable, 1,260 electric. By 1902, 250 animal, 22,000 electric.

D. Streets getting too crowded

    1. Elevated railroads came into use because 600 died in accidents in Philadelphia in just one year. 8,000 railroad street crossings existed in Philadelphia alone.

    2. Subway; 1897 in Boston; 1904 in NYC

E. Streets were mostly unpaved. In 1880 NYC, Boston, and Philadelphia combined didn't have 10 miles of asphalt. By 1900 extensive roads existed. (Revulsion over power of urban transit systems and political corruption led to cries of reform, one feature of the Progressive movement.)

F. Consequences

    1. Transit sorted people and land uses. In 1850 the borders of Boston were 2 miles from the central business district; in 1900, 10 miles.

    2. Decentralization of economic functions, with multiple commercial districts

    3. Fine social and economic distinctions between neighborhoods; the ideal of the single-family dwelling and the small community setting. Note such pastoral names as Woodside and Shipley Farms.

    4. Emergence of rings or zones around the city; central business district, poor, middle class, wealthy suburbs

    5. Speed and punctuality became urban habits, and mobility made the ideal of the stable community impossible.

III. Changing the Old City: Industrialization

A. Economic specialization, mass production, mass consumption, and mass distribution of goods and services

B. Urban imperialism, the drive for hinterland economic markets; competition among cities such as St. Louis and Chicago; NYC, Philadelphia, and Baltimore; San Diego and LA

C. Specialization among industrial cities

   1. Large unskilled labor force led to mass production industries. Philadelphia, textiles; NYC, clothing (At one time NYC had 10 percent of the nation's manufacturing total.)

   2. Exploited nearby industries: Milwaukee, beer; Minneapolis, flour

   3. Nearby resources: Cleveland, coal and iron; Dallas, oil; Denver, minerals

   4. Technological advances: Akron, tires; Detroit, automobiles; Dayton, cash registers

IV. Changing the Old City: Immigration

A. From 1860 to 1920, population living in U.S. cities rose from 6.2 million to 54.3 million.

B. Internal immigrants: Rural Americans, or "buckwheats," escaped the isolation and loneliness of farms.

C. First wave of immigrants: 1840s to peak in 1880s; Irish Catholics, German Catholics and Protestants, English, some Scandinavians

   1. Drinking habits: beer, ale, wine were introduced. (Rum and whiskey were traditional American drinks.)

   2. Religion; 1840–90, 5.5 million Catholics entered. Of 3,142 church buildings in 1775, only 56 were Catholic; by 1870, 40 percent of all churchgoers were Catholic.

   3. American innovation of the ethnic parish for Catholics

   4. Squabbles: Know-Nothings; Bible reading in public schools

D. Second wave from 1880s to 1920, like earlier wave, featured mostly poor and peasants, but the numbers were greater. Catholics from Italy and Poland, Jews from Russia and Eastern Europe (Russian draft for the army was for 21 years' service.)

   1. Larger numbers: 1880–1890, 5.2 million; 1900-1910, 8.8 million

   2. Much ethnic conflict among Catholics

   3. Jews: conflict between German and Russian Jews, and among Orthodox, Conservative, and Reform Jews

E. Characteristics of immigrants

   1. Loss of self-identity led to emphasis on nationalism after arrival.

   2. Many came only to earn money, and hoped to return home. From 1900 to 1910 an estimated 30–40 percent went home.

   3. Lived in older urban areas, such as NYC's Lower East Side

F. Blacks: In 1890, 90 percent lived in rural South; by 1900, 32 cities in the North and West

UNIT SEVEN: 1900–1920

Major Themes and Ideas

Foreign Policy

1. Organize U.S. foreign policy from 1865 to 1900 by (1) geographic region—Far East, Latin America, Caribbean, Europe; (2) American motives—economic, moral, Monroe Doctrine, balance of power among European nations, dominance in the Caribbean; (3) influence of domestic politics on foreign policy.

2. Imperialism: characteristics, sources, nature, causes, impact, results, compared to European imperialism

3. Link Reconstruction, Populism, and imperialism.

4. Compare and contrast the old and new Manifest Destiny.

5. Debate over the Treaty of Paris

6. Open Door: myth or reality?

7. Roosevelt's foreign policy

8. Wilson's foreign policy

9. U.S. policy toward Mexico and Cuba, 1890s to 1930s

10. The U.S. pushed around smaller nations, 1865 to 1914.

11. U.S. policy in the Far East: Balance Japan and protect China.

12. Causes of U.S. entry into the First World War and its attempts to remain neutral

13. Give several contrasting interpretations of U.S. entry into the First World War.

14. Defeat of the Versailles Treaty; immediate and long-run consequences

15. Who was responsible for the defeat of the Versailles Treaty?

16. War and the threat of war united and divided Americans in the 1898 to 1920 period.

17. Compare the foreign and domestic policies of William McKinley and his vice-presidential successor, Theodore Roosevelt.

Progressive Movement

1. Compare and contrast the Populist and Progressive movements.

2. Compare Progressivism and Jacksonianism.

3. Social, economic, political, and intellectual sources of Progressivism

4. Goals of Progressivism; successes, failures

5. Compare the political philosophies of Progressivism, Conservativism, and Socialism.

6. Progressives as the new Federalists: Compare Hamilton's program and Progressivism.

7. Progressivism as an answer to the problems raised by immigration and urbanization

8. Progressivism as the have-nots against the haves: role of labor unions, immigrants, blacks, women, and urban poor

9. Charles Beard's *An Economic Interpretation of the Constitution* as a reflection of its times

10. There was not one but many parallel "Progressive movements."

11. What did Progressivism seek to preserve in American life?

12. Corporations and unions both wanted governmental protection but not governmental regulation.

13. Trace the regulation of big business and court interpretations from the Interstate Commerce Act to *U.S.* v. *United States Steel Corporation* in 1920.

14. Trace the long history of a reform such as prohibition, women's rights, or banking.

15. Supreme Court interpretations and changing economic and social conditions, 1890–1920

16. Significant elections: 1900, 1912, 1920

17. Struggles within the parties, 1900 to 1912

18. Compare and contrast the programs and administrations of Theodore Roosevelt and Woodrow Wilson: banking, railroads, trusts, tariffs, etc.

19. Presidencies of Taft, Roosevelt, and Wilson: real differences or differing philosophies of the office of the president

20. Compare Congress versus Johnson with Congress versus Wilson.

21. First World War both helped and hurt blacks and labor.

22. Compare the domestic impact of the First and Second World Wars.

23. Progressivism—a liberal or conservative movement?

Major Terms and Concepts

Imperialism

James G. Blaine, Pan-Americanism

Venezuelan boundary dispute

Bering Sea seal controversy

"yellow journalism"

Josiah Strong, *Our Country*

Captain Alfred Thayer Mahan

Samoa, Pago Pago

Virginius

reconcentration policy

de Lome letter

Maine explodes

Assistant Secretary of Navy Theodore Roosevelt

Commodore Dewey, Manila Bay

Cleveland and Hawaii

Queen Liluokalani

annexation of Hawaii

Rough Riders, San Juan Hill

Treaty of Paris, 1898

American Anti-Imperialist League

Philippines, Guam, Puerto Rico

Walter Reed

Insular Cases

Teller Amendment

Platt Amendment

protectorate

Aguinaldo, Philippine insurrection

Secretary of State John Hay, Open Door Notes

spheres of influence

Boxer Rebellion

extraterritoriality

most favored nation clause

election of 1900: candidates, issues

Roosevelt's Big Stick diplomacy

U.S.S. Oregon

Clayton-Bulwer Treaty

Hay-Pauncefote Treaty

Hay-Herran Treaty

Hay-Bunau-Varilla Treaty

Panama revolution

Panama Canal

Goethals and Gorgas

Venezuelan crisis, 1902

Drago Doctrine

Roosevelt Corollary

"Colossus of the North"

Dominican Republic

Russo-Japanese War, Treaty of Portsmouth

San Francisco School Board incident

Elihu Root

Gentleman's Agreement

Great White Fleet

Root-Takahira Agreement

Lansing-Ishii Agreement, 1917

Progressivism

democracy, efficiency, pragmatism

"muckrakers"

Henry Demarest Lloyd, *Wealth Against Commonwealth*

Thorstein Veblen, *The Theory of the Leisure Class*

Jacob Riis, *How the Other Half Lives*

Lincoln Steffens, *The Shame of the Cities*

Frank Norris, *The Octopus*

Ida Tarbell, *History of the Standard Oil Company*

John Spargo, *The Bitter Cry of the Children*

David Graham Phillips, *The Treason of the Senate*

Charlotte Perkins Gilman, *Woman and Economics*

John Dewey, *The School and Society,* "progressive education," "learn by doing"

Oliver Wendell Holmes, Jr., Supreme Court

Margaret Sanger

Edward Ross

Richard Ely

initiative, referendum, recall

direct primary

Australian ballot (secret ballot)

Tammany Hall

Sixteenth, Seventeenth, Eighteenth, and Nineteenth Amendments

Charles Evans Hughes

Triangle Shirtwaist Co. fire

WCTU, Women's Christian Temperance Union

Anti-Saloon League

Square Deal

Newlands Reclamation Act, 1902

Forest Reserve Act, 1891

anthracite coal strike, 1902, George F. Baer

Elkins Act, 1903, rebates

Hepburn Act, 1906

Mann-Elkins Act, 1910

"trustbuster"

Northern Securities Co. case

Meat Inspection Act

Upton Sinclair, *The Jungle*

Pure Food and Drug Act

conservation conference, 1908

panic of 1907

election of 1908: candidates, issues

Mark Hanna

scientific management, Frederick W. Taylor

Wisconsin, "laboratory of democracy"

Robert M. La Follette

regulatory commissions

Jane Addams, Hull House

Florence Kelley, consumerism

home rule for cities

Tom Johnson, Sam (Golden Rule) Jones, Brand Whitlock, Hazen Pingree

city manager plan, commission plan

William Howard Taft

Department of Labor (from 1903 Department of Commerce and Labor, Bureau of Corporations also in 1903)

Payne-Aldrich Tariff, 1909

Ballinger-Pinchot controversy

Uncle Joe Cannon, Old Guard

Senator George Norris

rule of reason: Standard Oil case, American Tobacco case

"dollar diplomacy"

Secretary of State Knox

Manchurian railroad scheme

Roosevelt's Osawatomie, Kansas, speech

Taft-Roosevelt split

Bull Moose Party

Woodrow Wilson, New Freedom

Theodore Roosevelt, New Nationalism

Herbert Croly, *The Promise of American Life*

election of 1912: Wilson, Roosevelt, Taft, Debs—issues

Eugene V. Debs, Socialist Party

Daniel DeLeon, IWW, Wobblies, "Big Bill" Haywood

Pujo Committee

Federal Reserve Act

Underwood-Simmons Tariff

income tax

Federal Trade Commission, cease and desist orders

Clayton Antitrust Act, labor's Magna Carta

Secretary of State William Jennings Bryan

arbitration treaties

Panama Tolls dispute

Colonel House

Louis Brandeis, "Brandeis brief"

La Follette Seaman's Act

Federal Highways Act, 1916

Adamson Act, 1916

Smith-Lever Act, Smith-Hughes Act

Virgin Islands purchased

Jones Act, 1916 (Philippines)

Jones Act, 1917 (Puerto Rico)

Mexican Revolution, Diaz, Huerta, Carranza

Mexican migration to the U.S.

"watchful waiting"

ABC Powers

Pancho Villa, General Pershing

Archangel expedition

First World War

"sick man of Europe," Ottoman Empire, Balkan Wars

Triple Entente: Allies

Triple Alliance: Central Powers

loans to the Allies

British blockade

Lusitania, Arabic pledge, Sussex pledge

election of 1916: Hughes, Wilson, issues

unrestricted submarine warfare

Zimmermann Note

Russian Revolutions, 1917, March and Bolshevik

war declared, April 1917

"Make the world safe for democracy"

Creel Committee

bond drives

War Industries Board

Bernard Baruch

Herbert Hoover, Food Administration

Espionage Act, 1917; Sedition Act, 1918

Eugene V. Debs imprisoned

AEF

selective service

black migration to Northern cities

aims of Allies and U.S. at peace conference

wartime manpower losses

Fourteen Points

congressional elections of 1918

Versailles Conference, Versailles Treaty

U.S. Versailles delegation

Big Four: Wilson, Lloyd George, Clemenceau, Orlando

League of Nations

collective security

new nations, self-determination

reparations

mandate system

Article 10 (often written Article X) of the Versailles Treaty

Article 231 of the Versailles Treaty

Senate rejection, Senator Henry Cabot Lodge, reservations

"irreconcilables": Borah, Johnson, La Follette

Red Scare, Palmer raids

strikes: 1919, coal, steel, police

inflation during the First World War

election of 1920: candidates, issues

brief depression, 1920–1921

Supreme Court Cases to Know

1. Insular Cases, 1901, 1903, 1904 (constitutional rights in territories)

Three appeals to the Supreme Court—*Dorr* v. *U.S., Downes* v. *Bidwell,* and *Hawaii* v. *Mankichi*—raised questions concerning the extent to which constitutional rights were bestowed automatically upon the natives in newly acquired territories. The Supreme Court slowly worked out a new judicial position for the Constitution. Some rights are fundamental and applied to all American territory. Other rights are procedural and should not be imposed upon those unfamiliar with American law. Congress must determine which procedural rights applied in unincorporated territories. The Constitution did not follow the flag.

2. Northern Securities Case, 1904 (antitrust laws)

At the turn of the century three financial giants—J.P. Morgan, James J. Hill, and E.H. Harriman—fought for control of the railroads running west from Chicago to the Pacific coast. Frustrated in their separate efforts, they joined forces to create the Northern Securities Company, which owned a majority of the stock in both the Northern Pacific and the Great Northern railroads, which together owned enough stock to control the Burlington Railroad. A single holding company thus controlled the entire transportation network for one quarter of the nation. The Supreme Court ruled 5–4 that the Northern Securities holding company violated the Sherman Antitrust Act. The company was a "trust," not just a stock company. Owning the stock of competing railroads violated the Sherman Antitrust Act.

3. *Lochner* v. *New York,* 1905 (due process and state police power)

The state of New York passed a law to limit bakery and confectionary workers to only 60 hours a week or 10 hours per day. Lochner, who owned a bakery in Utica, was arrested for violating the law. The case involved a contest between the due process clause of freedom of contract and the state's police power to guard the health, safety, and morals of its people. In a 5–4 decision the Court held that the Fourteenth Amendment protected individuals against "an unreasonable, unnecessary and arbitrary interference with the right of the individual to his personal liberty." These criteria put judges in the position of legislators. Unreasonable and arbitrary laws are easier to identify than unnecessary laws, which are a matter of philosophical opinion. "Due process" had historically meant procedures to guarantee a fair trial. The Supreme Court now used "due process" to protect property from unreasonable, unnecessary, and arbitrary legislation.

Justice Holmes's dissent became the majority viewpoint after the 1937 case of *West Coast Hotel* v. *Parrish.* He said in 1905, "This case is decided upon an economic theory which a large part of the country does not entertain. ... The Fourteenth Amendment does not enact Mr. Herbert Spencer's [a famous proponent of Social Darwinism] *Social Statics. ...*A constitution is not intended to embody a particular economic theory, whether of paternalism and the organic relation of the citizen to the State or of laissez faire. It is made for people of fundamentally differing views, and the accident of our finding certain opinions natural and familiar or novel and even shocking ought not to conclude our judgment upon the question whether statutes embodying them conflict with the Constitution of the United States."

4. *Muller* v. *Oregon,* 1908 (due process and state police power)

This case is famous for the novel arguments presented by Louis Brandeis, who was later appointed to the Supreme Court. Oregon limited women to only 10 hours of labor in factories and laundries. Curt Muller owned a laundry in Portland, and based on the Lochner decision he refused to comply with the law. His appeal eventually reached the Supreme Court. In defense of the Oregon law, Brandeis presented only two pages of legal arguments and over one hundred pages detailing statistics and opinions from various commission reports on the adverse impact of long hours on the health of women. In a unanimous decision the Court accepted the economic and social arguments in the "Brandeis brief." Brandeis argued that the law must come out of facts, not abstract logic. The majority opinion in Lochner cited the "common knowledge" that baking was not a difficult occupation. Brandeis undermined any potential opinion that the health of a nation's female population was not a legitimate governmental concern. The Court found that "in order to preserve the strength and vigor of the race ... [a] woman's physical structure, and the functions she performs in consequence thereof, justify special legislation restricting or qualifying the conditions under which she should be permitted to toil."

5. Danbury Hatters' Case, 1908 (*Loewe* v. *Lawlor*) (antitrust laws and labor unions)

Unable to secure union recognition at the Danbury Hatters Company owned by Loewe and others, the hatters' union instituted a boycott against the company's hats. The unanimous Supreme Court decision held the boycott to be a violation of the Sherman Antitrust Act, and required triple damages against the union for the amount of normal income lost due to the boycott. Labor unions were shocked. They found partial exemption from antitrust laws in the Clayton Act.

6. *Standard Oil of New Jersey* vs. *U.S.*, 1911; *U.S.* v. *American Tobacco Co.*, 1911; and *U.S.* v. *United States Steel Corporation*, 1920 (antitrust laws)

In three cases the Supreme Court differentiated between a "good" trust and a "bad" trust, putting into interpretation a widespread popular view that bigness was not synonymous with badness, and that large corporations were part of modern society. The Court took responsibility for determining if a specific trust was good or bad, the "rule of reason." Standard Oil of New Jersey was dissolved under the Court's "rule of reason." The American Tobacco Company was bad, but not too bad, and so it was forced to reorganize to stimulate competition. The United States Steel Corporation didn't have to be dissolved; it was a "good" trust. The antitrust laws applied only to "bad" trusts.

7. *Hammer* v. *Dagenhart,* 1918 (child labor laws)

The Keating-Owen Act of 1916 tried to stop child labor by excluding the products produced by child labor from interstate commerce. Dagenhart sued, asking for an injunction to permit his two sons to continue working to supplement the family's income. The Court ruled 5–4 that Congress had overstepped its authority. The Court narrowly defined the commerce power of Congress. "Over interstate transportation, or its incidents, the regulatory power of Congress is ample, but the production of articles intended for interstate commerce is a matter of local regulation." The Court evoked a doctrine that came to be known as "dual federalism," the idea that Congress could not intrude into the powers reserved to the states by the Tenth Amendment. "In interpreting the Constitution it must never be forgotten that the nation is made up of states, to which are intrusted the powers of local government. And to them and to the people the powers not expressly delegated to the national government are reserved."

8. *Bailey* v. *Drexel Furniture Co.*, 1922 (child labor laws)

Unable to use the commerce clause to prohibit child labor, Congress used its power to tax in order to impose a heavy fine upon the profits of companies employing child labor. In an 8-1 decision the Court decided that the tax attempted to regulate an area reserved for the states rather than to tax to raise revenue. Not until *U.S.* v. *Darby* in 1941 were child labor laws found to be constitutional.

9. *Schenck* v. *U.S.*, 1919 (radicals and the First Amendment)

Schenck, an official of the Socialist party, was arrested and convicted for violation of the Espionage Act of 1917 because he and other socialists had distributed leaflets to draftees urging them to resist. On one side of the leaflet was a copy of the Thirteenth Amendment, which outlawed slavery or involuntary servitude. Schenck claimed he was protected by the First Amendment freedom of speech and press. The opinion by the unanimous Court announced Justice Holmes' "clear and present danger" test. Every act must be judged according to the circumstances. No freedom is absolute; First Amendment questions were a matter of "proximity and degree," and the nation was at war. He included his often-quoted remark that freedom of speech "would not protect a man in falsely shouting fire in a theatre and causing a panic."

10. *Abrams* v. *U.S.,* 1919 (radicals and the First Amendment)

The Abrams case involved the Sedition Act of 1918, an amendment to the Espionage Act of 1917. Five Russian immigrants were convicted for distributing antiwar propaganda. Justice Holmes, who wrote the opinion in the Schenck case, dissented from the 7–2 decision. Holmes recognized that "the United States constitutionally may punish speech that produces or is intended to produce a clear and imminent danger that it will bring about forthwith certain substantive evils that the United States constitutionally may seek to prevent. The power undoubtedly is greater in time of war than in time of peace because war opens dangers that do not exist at other times." In a brilliant plea for freedom of speech and press he wrote, "when men have realized that time has upset many fighting faiths, they come to believe even more than they believe the very foundations of their own conduct that the ultimate good desired is better reached by free trade in ideas—that the best test of truth is the power of the thought to get itself accepted in the competition of the market, and that truth is the only ground upon which their wishes safely can be carried out."

Readings for Depth and Historical Interpretation

Origins and Essence of Progressive Movement

1. George E. Mowry, "Political America," and "The Progressive Profile," in his *The Era of Theodore Roosevelt and the Birth of Modern America,* 1900–1912. Mowry describes the intellectual political currents in the Progressive era.

2. Richard Hofstadter, "The Status Revolution and Progressive Leaders," in his *The Age of Reform.* Both Mowry and Hofstadter see the Progressive movement as a revolt by the middle class. Hofstadter added the view that the middle class was primarily motivated by status anxieties over their relative decline in American society.

3. J. Joseph Huthmacher, "Urban Liberalism and the Age of Reform," *Mississippi Valley Historical Review* (now the *Journal of American History*), 1962. Huthmacher argues that lower-class immigrant urbanites formed a significant source for the Progressive impulse. They knew from experience the evils that needed correction.

4. David P. Thelen, "Social Tensions and the Origins of Progressivism," *Journal of American History,* 1969. The Progressive movement grew out of the railroad and corporate arrogance of the 1890s and the social tension generated by the depression of the 1890s. He attacks Hofstadter's status revolution thesis.

5. Lincoln Steffens, *The Shame of the Cities;* Upton Sinclair, *The Jungle;* Jane Addams, *Twenty Years at Hull House;* and Frederick Winslow Taylor, *The Principles of Scientific Management* in Robert B. Downs, *Books That Changed America.* Four of the twenty-five books Downs identified as influential were written in the Progressive era. This provides a quick look at these influential works.

6. Gabriel Kolko, "Introduction" and the first section of the "Conclusion," in his *The Triumph of Conservatism.* Kolko sees a different perspective in the Progressive movement, the fight against "political capitalism," the effort by big business to use governmental power to protect and to expand their profits. The interventionist government served business, not reform. This argument represents a different and unusual perspective for students.

7. Jill Conway, "Women Reformers and American Culture, 1870–1930," *Journal of Social History,* V, 1971–1972, pp. 164–175. Conway shows the persistence of stereotypes among women that hindered women reformers and reform for women.

8. Richard McCormick, *The Party Period and Public Policy: American Politics from the Age of Jackson to the Progressive Era.* McCormick's first three chapters summarize the recent political historiography—ethnocultural interpretations, the realignment synthesis, and the social analysis of political his-

tory. He also has an interesting chapter on "Political Parties in American History." Also see his "The Discovery that Business Corrupts Politics: A Reappraisal of the Origins of Progressivism," *American Historical Review,* April 1981. McCormick tries to tie together the diversity of both the reform effort and the effort of historians to describe and define Progressivism.

9. Paul Boyer, *Urban Masses and Moral Order in America, 1820–1920.* Boyer reminds us that the attempt to impose moral standards on the city's population had long roots in American history. The Progressive Movement was not the first to try or the first to fail to satisfy its sponsors.

10. William H. Chafe, *The Paradox of Change: American Women in the 20th Century* (a revision of *American Woman: Her Changing Social, Economic, and Political Roles, 1920–1970*). Chafe's first three chapters focus on "Politics and Ideology" from 1848 to 1940. The next three cover "Women and the Economy" from 1900 to 1940. Both sections provide sources of information on the women's movement in the Progressive era.

Theodore Roosevelt and Woodrow Wilson

1. Richard Hofstadter, "Theodore Roosevelt: The Conservative as Progressive," and "Woodrow Wilson: The Conservative as Liberal," in his *The American Political Tradition.* An excellent introduction to these two progressives.

2. Richard Lowitt, "Theodore Roosevelt," and E. David Cronon, "Woodrow Wilson," in Morton Borden, ed., *America's Eleven Greatest Presidents.*

3. Arthur S. Link, "The New Nationalism Versus the New Freedom," in his *Woodrow Wilson and the Progressive Era, 1910–1917.*

4. John M. Cooper, Jr., *The Warrior and the Priest: Woodrow Wilson and Theodore Roosevelt.* You may guess who is the warrior and who is the priest. Cooper's book is an excellent source for differentiating between these two Progressive presidents.

Foreign Policy

1. Alfred T. Mahan's *The Influence of Sea Power upon History, 1660–1783,* in Robert B. Downs, *Books That Changed America.* Mahan is credited with popularizing the idea that sea power lies behind every great nation.

2. Frederick Merk, "The Rise and Fall of Insular Imperialism," and "Mission," in his *Manifest Destiny and Mission in American History.* Merk compares the two thrusts of Manifest Destiny.

3. Walter La Feber, *The New Empire: An Interpretation of American Expansion, 1860–1898.* Chapter One, "Years of Preparation, 1860–1889," summarizes American foreign policy in this period. Pages 407–417 summarize his basic argument that American foreign policy was primarily economically motivated, as contemporary socialists charged.

4. George F. Kennan, *American Diplomacy, 1900–1950.* Chapters One, Two, and Three criticize the Spanish-American War and American policy in the Far East. Kennan belongs to the Realist school of foreign policy historians who criticize the crusading morality of our foreign policy.

5. Dexter Perkins, "The Policeman of the West: The Evolution of the Roosevelt Corollary," in his *A History of the Monroe Doctrine.* Provides a look at the Caribbean policies of Roosevelt.

6. Richard Hofstadter, "Cuba, the Philippines, and Manifest Destiny," in *The Paranoid Style in American Politics and Other Essays.* Hofstadter argues that there was a psychic crisis in the 1890s, a mass sense of frustration and fear that sought relief through a foreign crusade in Cuba.

First World War and Versailles

1. Arthur S. Link, *Woodrow Wilson and the Progressive Era, 1910–1917.* The chapter entitled "From Peace Without Victory to War" covers the U.S. entry into the First World War.

2. George F. Kennan, *American Diplomacy, 1900–1950,* gives the Realist historians' view of the mistakes made by U.S. foreign policy in regard to the First World War and the Versailles Treaty.

3. Thomas A. Bailey, *Woodrow Wilson and the Great Betrayal.* "The Supreme Infanticide" puts most of the blame for the defeat of the Versailles Treaty on Wilson's failure to make adjustments in his creation.

4. Selig Adler, *The Isolationist Impulse: Its Twentieth Century Reaction.* The first chapter traces the history of isolationism since the Revolutionary War. The second chapter summarizes the factions that formed the basis for the isolationist sentiment after the First World War.

Sample Outline

Political Philosophies in the Progressive Era

I. **Political Climate in 1900**

   A. World of change: economic and technological, new scientific and religious ideas, growth of big business and organized labor, urbanization

   B. Various political ideological groups developed. Two had been present in politics for previous 25 years.

   C. The third ideological group felt the full impact of the new ideas and intellectual forces and rapidly changing conditions. This group came to be called the Progressives.

   D. Differentiating political philosophies

   1. Radical (Socialist in this era) refers to advocating drastic revolutionary changes in society and in the government.

   2. Conservative refers to preserving the existing order; that is, conserving rather than changing.

   3. Reactionary refers to desiring to move society backward into a past society, usually idealized.

   4. Liberal refers to advocating changes in society's institutions to reflect changing conditions.

   5. These terms refer to means as well as ends; one can pursue radical goals by conservative means, for example, socialists running for political office in a democratic political system.

II. **Conservative Creed**

   A. Nature of man

   1. Frail creatures unable to withstand evil impulses. Life was a "succession of pitiful compromises with fate."

   2. With the present uncertain and the future unknowable, the only way to prevent anarchy, chaos, and disaster was to cling to the time-tested methods of the past. "God Almighty made men and certain laws which are essential to their progress in civilization and Congressmen cannot break these natural laws without causing suffering."

   3. Inequality: Interested in protecting the rights of the outstanding contributor to society; inequality was natural because the average man contributed little to progress.

   4. The masses were political junk. Democratic systems of government led to demagogues.

   B. Nature of progress

   1. Application of natural (divine) laws was the key to progress. It was beyond the capacity of mankind to devise improvements.

   2. Reason could not solve any political problem because the reasoner never gets all the premises into his thinking.

3. Man could only discover God's laws, not change them—Social Darwinism. Progress was God's process, which took generations, not years or days. The quest for property was man's progress.

III. Radical Rationale

A. Nature of man

1. Nothing was evil in human nature.

2. Society was the teacher, creating the experiences for each individual's life; tabula rasa.

3. Man was a mirror that reflected his environment, chiefly his material environment. (This is pre-1917 socialist thinking.)

B. Nature of progress

1. Scientific: Man was a creature of his economic class, which had evolved according to the scientific laws of evolution.

2. Inevitable: It was only a matter of time before progress instituted the classless society. 1904 Socialist Party platform: "The Socialist program is not a theory imposed upon society for its acceptance or rejection, it is but the interpretation of what is sooner or later inevitable."

IV. Progressive Profile

A. Nature of man

1. The conservative was pessimistic, the Progressive optimistic.

2. Deep faith in man and his ability to better his station on Earth; used phrases like "the beautiful people," "the essential nobility of man," "In the end the people are bound to do the right thing, no matter how much they fail at times."

3. A free individual: Man must be free to develop to his fullest capacity as an individual and to bring benefits to society. Many Progressives opposed all organizations hampering the free individual—parties, unions, big business, and so on.

4. Democracy: not just a belief, but a faith; the right to choose is more important than the ability to choose wisely. "Democracy is a soul satisfying thing." The solution to most problems was more effective democratic methods.

5. Dichotomy of economic beliefs:

   Some Progressives favored a return to laissez-faire economics; feared the federal governmental bureaucracy as well as trusts; aim was to preserve individualism: Wilson, New Freedom. (Its original philosophy was to break up the industrial system with antimonopoly laws.)

   Other Progressives wanted to face the economic realities of the time and have national regulation of national industries to preserve and protect individualism: Roosevelt, New Nationalism. (Accept the industrial system and regulate it.)

6. Christian ethics: In attacking society's problems, the solution was to amend the system. In dealing with the individuals who need reform, the solution was to preach Christian ethics and to tolerate no exceptions: juvenile courts, juvenile offenders,

Judge Benjamin Barr Lindsey. The movement had a righteous and evangelical character, "a political carnival of purity."

B. Nature of progress

1. Man was neither chained to his past (as the conservative believed) nor riding automatically into the predetermined future (as the socialist believed).

2. Man was a free agent who controlled his own destiny.

3. Inequality caused injustice and most of the evil in the world. If inequality could be wiped out, the result would be a more honest, neighborly, helpful, and capable individual. (Read the Boy Scout oath, for the BSA was founded in this period.)

4. By improving the basic building block of society, the free individual, society as a whole would improve and progress.

5. Malleable homo sapiens: Central to the Progressives was the idea that man, more good than evil, had the power through his moral sense and intellect to change his environment and himself.

UNIT EIGHT: 1920–1940

Major Themes and Ideas

The Twenties

1. Harding and the twenties as the end of Progressivism

2. What aspects of Progressivism survived into the twenties?

3. Were the twenties "golden" for agriculture, labor, and business?

4. Coolidge's quote in regard to union-business relations: "The man who builds a factory builds a temple; the man who works there worships there."

5. The twenties as an age of nonconformity: blacks, feminists, literary criticism, sexual customs

6. The twenties: an assault by rural and small-town America against urban America

7. The dark side of the twenties: immigration, KKK, Scopes, prohibition

8. Alienation as a literary theme in the twenties

9. The twenties as an era of transition

10. Individuals that best exemplify the twenties

11. The issues and results of the presidential elections of 1920, 1924, and 1928

12. Causes of the Great Depression

13. Compare the criticisms of American society writers made in the twenties with those made in the thirties.

The Thirties

1. Compare Hoover's and Roosevelt's response to the Depression.

2. Compare the role of the federal government in the economies of the twenties and thirties.

3. The twenties were pro-business; the thirties were anti-business.

4. Compare Progressivism and the New Deal.

5. Compare and contrast the first and second New Deals.

6. Relate aspects of the New Deal to previous reform movements in regard to antimonopoly, labor, banking, agriculture, taxation, and relief.

7. The New Deal was revolutionary.

8. The New Deal was a conservative program.

9. The New Deal helped the rich more than the needy.

10. Successes and failures of the New Deal

11. Supreme Court and the New Deal

12. Impact of the Depression on segments of the economy: corporations, workers, farmers, middle class, and so on.

13. Impact of various New Deal programs and agencies on American society

14. Rise of the welfare state

15. Countervailing powers theory: Big government and big labor checked big business.

16. Explain the critics: Townsend, Coughlin, Long, leftists, conservatives.

17. What ended the reform effort by the late 1930s?

18. Reform would have come without a depression because reform in American history is the periodic readjustment of aspects of the economy.

19. Compare the labor movement of the 1930s with the labor movement of the late nineteenth century.

20. Why did the Socialist Party fail to become a serious factor in American politics?

Major Terms and Concepts

The Twenties

election of 1920: candidates, issues, vice-presidential candidates

Normalcy

Esch-Cummins Transportation Act

Harding scandals: Charles Forbes, Harry Daugherty, Secretary of Interior Fall, Teapot Dome, Harry Sinclair

Harding's death, Coolidge takes over

Bureau of the Budget

Secretary of Treasury Mellon, tax cuts

Senator George Norris, Muscle Shoals

election of 1924: candidates, Robert La Follette, Progressive Party

McNary-Haugen Bill, vetoes

Federal Farm Board

election of 1928: candidates, personalities, backgrounds

Bruce Barton, *The Man Nobody Knows,* 1925

H. L. Mencken, editor of the magazine, *The American Mercury*

"the Lost Generation"

F. Scott Fitzgerald, *The Great Gatsby*

Sinclair Lewis, *Main Street, Babbitt*

Theodore Dreiser, *An American Tragedy*

Ernest Hemingway, *A Farewell to Arms*

T.S. Eliot, *The Waste Land*

Sigmund Freud's theories

KDKA, Pittsburgh

Prohibition, Volstead Act, Al Capone

KKK

fundamentalists

Immigration Acts, 1921, 1924, quota system

Sacco and Vanzetti case

Leopold and Loeb case

Billy Sunday

Scopes trial, Clarence Darrow, William Jennings Bryan

Henry Ford, the Model T, Alfred P. Sloan

Cecil B. de Mille

The Jazz Singer

Rudolph Valentino, Charlie Chaplin

new woman, flappers

Harlem Renaissance, Langston Hughes

James Weldon Johnson

Marcus Garvey, Universal Negro Improvement Association

Charles Lindbergh, *Spirit of St. Louis*

Babe Ruth, Jack Dempsey

Foreign Policy

Twenty-One Demands

Lansing-Ishii Agreement

Versailles Treaty

Washington Disarmament Conference

Five Power Treaty, Four Power Treaty, Nine Power Treaty

5-5-3-1.75-1.75 ratio

World Court

reparations

Dawes Plan, Young Plan

Kellogg-Briand Treaty

Hoover Administration

causes of the Depression

Depression as an international event

Fordney-McCumber Tariff, 1922

Hawley-Smoot Tariff, 1930

Reconstruction Finance Corporation, RFC

Bonus Army

"Hooverville"

Clark Memorandum

London Naval Conference

Hoover Moratorium, 1931

Manchuria, Hoover-Stimson Doctrine

Mexico's nationalization of oil

Ambassador Morrow

Good Neighbor Policy

Norris-La Guardia (anti-injunction) Act, 1932

election of 1932: candidates, issues

Roosevelt and New Deal

Twentieth Amendment

Wickersham Commission

Twenty-first Amendment

"bank holiday"

Hundred Days

"relief, recovery, reform"

Brain Trust

Emergency Banking Relief Act, 1933

Glass-Steagall Banking Reform Act, 1933

Gold Clause Act, 1935

Federal Deposit Insurance Corporation (FDIC)

National Industrial Recovery Act (NIRA)

National Industrial Recovery Administration (NRA), "The Blue Eagle," Hugh Johnson

Agricultural Adjustment Act (AAA), second AAA, 1938

Soil Conservation and Domestic Allotment Act, 1936

Civilian Conservation Corps (CCC)

Federal Emergency Relief Administration (FERA)

Civil Works Administration (CWA)

Public Works Administration (PWA), Harold Ickes

Works Progress Administration (WPA), Harry Hopkins, Federal Arts Project

Home Owners' Loan Corporation (HOLC)

Federal Housing Authority (FHA)

Securities and Exchange Commission (SEC)

Tennessee Valley Authority (TVA), Senator Norris

Rural Electrification Administration (REA)

National Youth Administration (NYA)

Indian Reorganization Act, 1934

recognition of the USSR, 1933

section 7a of the NRA

Wagner Act, 1935

National Labor Relations Board (NLRB)

Fair Labor Standards Act: maximum hours and minimum wage

Congress of Industrial Organizations (CIO), John L. Lewis

sit down strikes

dust bowl, Okies, John Steinbeck, *The Grapes of Wrath*

Frances Perkins, Secretary of Labor

Eleanor Roosevelt

Keynesian economics

deficit spending

monetary policy, fiscal policy

Revenue Act, 1935

Liberty League

coalition of the Democratic Party: blacks, unions, intellectuals, big city machines, South

Huey Long, Share the Wealth, Gerald L.K. Smith

Father Charles Coughlin

Dr. Francis Townsend

election of 1936: candidates, issues

Literary Digest poll

second New Deal

Social Security Act

"court packing" proposal

Chief Justice Charles Evans Hughes

"conservative coalition" in Congress

Robinson-Patman Act, 1936

Miller-Tydings Act, 1937

Hatch Act, 1939

Supreme Court Cases to Know

1. *Adkins* v. *Children's Hospital,* 1923 (minimum wage laws)

From the 1890s to the 1930s the Supreme Court frustrated congressional and state regulatory efforts. It invalidated many acts under the freedom of contract doctrine and the due process and equal protection clauses of the Fourteenth Amendment. As the government for the District of Columbia, Congress passed an act in 1918 creating a Minimum Wage Board, authorized to establish minimum wages for women and children working within the District of Columbia. Several female employees at Children's Hospital were fired because the hospital did not want to pay the minimum wage for these jobs. Their suit claimed that their individual freedom of contract had been abridged; the Court agreed, 5–3. "In making ... contracts, generally speaking, the parties have an equal right to obtain from each other the best terms they can as the result of private bargaining.... There is, of course, no such thing as absolute freedom of contract. It is subject to a great variety of restraints. But freedom of contract is, nevertheless, the general rule and restraint the exception; and the exercise of legislative authority to abridge it can be justified only by the existence of exceptional circumstances." Chief Justice Taft's dissent challenged the Court's assumption of legislative powers.

2. *Gitlow* v. *New York,* 1925 (radicals and the First Amendment)

This case involved the arrest of Benjamin Gitlow, an official of the Communist Party, for the violation of New York's criminal anarchy law. The Court upheld the conviction, 7–2. The real significance of the case is that the majority asserted for the first time that the guarantees in the Bill of Rights also apply to the states because of the Fourteenth Amendment.

3. *Schechter Poultry Corp. v. U.S.,* 1935 (constitutionality of New Deal programs)

This "Sick Chicken Case" unanimously found the National Industrial Recovery Act unconstitutional. Under the act the NRA was directed to establish codes for each industry in partnership with industries and unions. If the industry did not establish its code, the NRA could impose one. This last feature of the law violated the Constitution because it granted legislative powers to the executive branch. The act also exceeded the government's interstate commerce authority by attempting to regulate the killing of chickens for market, which the Court found to be an intrastate activity. Chief Justice Hughes rejected the argument that a national emergency justified the NRA. "Extraordinary conditions do not create or enlarge constitutional power. The Constitution established a national government with powers deemed to be adequate, as they have proved to be in war and peace, but these powers of the national government are limited by the constitutional grants. Those who act under these grants are not at liberty to transcend the imposed limits because they believe that more or different power is necessary."

4. *U.S.* v. *Butler,* 1936 (constitutionality of New Deal programs)

This decision was the second to declare an important New Deal program, in this case the Agricultural Adjustment Act, unconstitutional. The law used the federal government's taxing power as a means to regulate production. As such, it exceeded the powers of the federal government by invading state jurisdiction. In this decision the court resurrected the doctrine of "dual federalism," the concept that the states and the national government were equals, and that the Tenth Amendment limited the delegated powers given to Congress. In his dissent Justice Stone blasted the conservatives on the Court. "Courts are not the only agency of government that must be assumed to have capacity to govern."

5. *NLRB* v. *Jones and Laughlin Steel Corp.,* 1937 (interstate commerce and control of labor)

Many students mistakenly believe that most bitter strikes involve wage demands. The most disruptive strikes have actually involved union recognition, the industry's acquiescence in the union's right to represent the workers and to engage in collective bargaining. The National Labor Relations Board was established to supervise and conduct elections for workers deciding upon union representation. In a 5–4 decision, the Court upheld the constitutionality of the Wagner Act creating the NLRB. The Court broadly defined commerce, asserting Congress's right to legislate broadly in the "stream of commerce" because commerce was more than mere transportation. "Although activities may be intrastate in character when separately considered, if they have such a close and substantial relation to interstate commerce that their control is essential or appropriate to protect that commerce from burdens and obstructions, Congress cannot be denied the power to exercise that control."

6. *West Coast Hotel* v. *Parrish,* 1937 (due process and state police powers)

This 5–4 decision upheld state regulation of wages and hours for women and children. The Court reversed the decision in *Adkins* v. *Children's Hospital* by putting the contract clause into a different perspective. "The Constitution does not speak of freedom of contract. It speaks of liberty and prohibits the deprivation of liberty without due process of law. In prohibiting that deprivation the Constitution does not recognize an absolute and uncontrollable liberty. Liberty in each of its phases has its history and connotation. But the liberty safeguarded is liberty in a social organization which requires the protection of law against the evils which menace the health, safety, morals, and welfare of the people. Liberty under the Constitution is thus necessarily subject to the restraints of due process, and regulation which is reasonable in relation to its subject and adopted in the interests of the community is due process."

7. *U.S.* v. *Darby Lumber Co.,* 1941 (commerce and wages and hours)

This case expressly overruled *Hammer v. Dagenhart.* The Darby Lumber Company was charged with violating the federal Fair Labor Standards Act of 1938, which established minimum wages and maximum hours for workers engaged in interstate commerce. The unanimous decision enlarged the definition of interstate commerce to include the production of goods for commerce, not just the transportation of goods. "The motive and purpose of a regulation of interstate commerce are matters for legislative judgment upon the exercise of which the Constitution places no restriction and over which the courts are given no control."

8. *U.S.* v. *Curtiss-Wright Export Corp.,* 1936 (president's control over foreign policy)

In 1934, Congress empowered the president to prohibit the sale of military supplies to Bolivia and Paraguay, who were engaged in a war that threatened the peace of the whole of South America. Bolivia purchased its entire air force of thirty-four planes from the Curtiss-Wright Export Corporation prior to the congressional resolution. In violation of President Roosevelt's proclamation the Curtiss-Wright Corporation tried to smuggle fifteen airplane machine guns into Bolivia. When the case reached the Supreme Court, the key question involved the legality of the congressional grant of legislative power to the president. The previous year the NIRA had been declared unconstitutional in the Schechter Sick Chicken Case on the same grounds. In a 7–1 majority opinion the Court differentiated between domestic and foreign policy. The Court ruled that the president has a "degree of discretion and freedom from statutory restriction which would not be admissible were domestic affairs alone involved." As President Harry Truman later said, "I am American foreign policy."

Readings for Depth and Historical Interpretation

The Twenties

1. Frederick Lewis Allen, "The Revolution in Manners and Morals," in his *Only Yesterday*. This contains delightful comments and examples of the social revolution of the twenties. Another source is William Leuchtenburg, "The Revolution in Morals," in *The Perils of Prosperity, 1914–1932*.

2. H.L. Mencken's *Prejudices* in Robert B. Downs, *Books That Changed America*. Mencken, the supreme iconoclast in American journalism, gives you a new definition of satire. He was called "the most powerful private citizen" in the nation by the *New York Times*. He had a great impact on the literary giants and intellectuals of his era and much later.

3. Arthur S. Link, "What Happened to the Progressive Movement in the 1920's?" *American Historical Review*, 1959. Link argues that many features of Progressivism survived into the 1920s.

4. Irving Bernstein, "The Worker in an Unbalanced Society," in his *The Lean Years: A History of the American Worker, 1920–1933*. Bernstein destroys the image of the twenties as a golden age for workers; "the serious maladjustments within the economic system fell upon them with disproportionate weight."

5. Two sources for the social history of the decade highlight the Harlem Renaissance and the beginning of beauty contests. Nathan Huggins, *Harlem Renaissance*, and the relevant chapters in Lois Banner, *The American Beauty: A Social History through Two Centuries of the American Idea, Ideal, and Image of the Beautiful Woman*.

6. Kenneth Jackson, *The Ku Klux Klan in the City, 1915–1930*, sees the Klan as a typically American movement rather than an aberration. For a full history of the various Klans in American history, see David Chalmers, *Hooded Americanism: The First Century of the Ku Klux Klan*, which covers the story from the 1870s to the 1970s.

7. William E. Leuchtenburg, "Epilogue," in his *The Perils of Prosperity, 1914–1932*. Leuchtenburg summarizes the decade of the twenties.

8. John Kenneth Galbraith, "Cause and Consequence," in his *The Great Crash, 1929*. Galbraith explains the causes and consequences of the 1929 crash, which ushered in the Great Depression.

The New Deal

1. Otis Graham, *An Encore for Reform: The Old Progressives and the New Deal*, pp. 172-186. Graham compares the Progressive movement and the New Deal by asking what old Progressives thought of the New Deal. He found most Progressives opposed to the New Deal, suggesting significant differences between the two reform movements.

2. Richard Hofstadter, "Herbert Hoover and the Crisis of American Individualism," and "Franklin D. Roosevelt: The Patrician as Opportunist," in his *The American Political Tradition*. Hofstadter compares Hoover and Roosevelt as political leaders.

3. James MacGregor Burns, "President of All the People?" and a section of chapter 18 subtitled "Roosevelt as a Party Leader," in his *The Lion and the Fox*. These two sections address the subject of FDR as a political leader.

4. Arthur M. Schlesinger, Jr., "The Ideology of the Second New Deal," "The Politics of the Second New Deal," and "The Roosevelt Coalition," in his *The Politics of Upheaval*. Schlesinger compares the First and Second New Deals. Major characteristics, "the techniques employed, the economic presuppositions, the political style, the vision of the American future itself" all changed.

5. Douglass C. North, "War, Prosperity, Depression, and War, 1914–1945," in his *Growth and Welfare in the American Past: A New Economic History*. North looks at statistical data to ask the question "Was the New Deal a Social

Revolution?" His investigation of its policies in regard to employment, economic growth, and income redistribution indicates that it was not revolutionary.

6. Carl Degler, "Was It a New or Old Deal?" in his *Out of Our Past*. Degler surveys historical opinions and offers his own assessment "that traditional as the words may have been in which the New Deal expressed itself, in actuality it was a revolutionary response to a revolutionary situation."

7. Richard Hofstadter, "The New Departure," and "The New Opportunism," in his *The Age of Reform*. Hofstadter sees the New Deal as unlike any previous reform movement in American history, "different in its ideas and its spirit and its techniques." The New Deal was a "drastic new departure" in American reform.

8. William E. Leuchtenburg, "The Roosevelt Reconstruction: Retrospect," in his *Franklin D. Roosevelt and the New Deal, 1932–1940*. Leuchtenburg looks at FDR and the New Deal and pronounces the New Deal to be a "half-way revolution."

9. Paul Murphy, "Franklin Roosevelt," in Morton Borden, ed., *America's Eleven Greatest Presidents*. Murphy looks at the New Deal and FDR's leadership in the Second World War, an often neglected area in assessing FDR.

10. Harvard Sitkoff, ed., *Fifty Years Later: The New Deal Evaluated,* is a collection of essays looking at various topics on the New Deal—race, politics, economy, women, legacy, and achievements.

11. The full flavor of the human impact of the Great Depression and the New Deal is available in two journalistic sources: Studs Terkel, *Hard Times,* and Caroline Bird, *The Invisible Scar.*

Sample Outline

One theme around which to organize the 1920s is the urban-rural cultural conflict. Urban values and institutions triumphed in the twenties. The 1920 census revealed that a majority of Americans lived in urban areas, and rural areas sensed that they were losing out to the new culture, the urban culture. Farmers and small-town dwellers by this period thought of themselves as hicks, hillbillies, and hayseeds; they were proud of their rural heritage, yet beginning to feel inferior. In the twenties, rural America fought to reassert its values in an urbanizing nation.

The Twenties as a Decade of Cultural Conflict

I.   Threats to the Old Order

  A. Changing standards of morality

   1. Behavior: new codes for dancing and dress—Charleston, thinner clothes, juvenile look, sleeveless dresses

   2. Double standard: A change in attitudes occurred toward expectations for behavior in regard to sexual standards for men and women. Now women began to assert publicly their right to imitate male standards. Only affection was necessary for sex.

  B. Reasons for changing standards

   1. First World War: The maxim "eat, drink, and be merry" often appears after wars. The First World War had the highest ratio of those killed and injured to participants of any war. Small matters of morality seemed less important after this carnage.

   2. Women: greater independence, less parental supervision, Nineteenth Amendment. They joined the labor force in large numbers, and more lived alone.

3. Impersonality of urban areas

4. Automobile: sudden capability to escape supervision

5. Freudian psychology filtered down to the popular level in the 1920s. The message that came down said repressed desires lead to mental illness.

II. Manifestations of Cultural Conflict

A. Ku Klux Klan: five million members strong in over twenty states, especially Indiana and Oregon. More of a small-town, fraternal, patriotic defense of the old order than an anti-black organization; they hated Jews, Catholics, blacks, immigrants, and unions. Oregon required all children to attend public schools, not parochial schools.

B. 1924 Democratic Party Convention in Madison Square Garden: one-hundred three ballots were required to nominate a presidential candidate, John W. Davis, and a vice-presidential candidate, Charles W. Bryan, brother of William Jennings Bryan. A huge fight over platform statement denouncing the Klan passed by fewer than five votes.

C. Fundamentalism: The Scopes trial in Dayton, Tenn., concerned the teaching of the theory of evolution. William Jennings Bryan aided the prosecution; Clarence Darrow, the defense. Bryan testified that the world was created in 4004 B.C. and the flood occurred in 2348 B.C.

D. Nativism: laws of 1921 and 1924, fear of radicals, competition among workers, unions for it, feeling those here insufficiently Americanized, patriotism of First World War, new influx after the war, scientific racism, Army I.Q. tests. First 1910, then 1890 used as a base for immigration quotas.

E. Al Smith campaign: NYC, Tammany Hall, a wet, Catholic, son of immigrants, accent, strong rural and Southern vote against him

F. Prohibition: WCTU, Anti-Saloon League, Eighteenth Amendment, Volstead Act, job safety, attacks on the urban saloon. Immigrant drinking was seen as a cause of poverty. Anti-union because saloons seen as union meeting places. Anti-German war spirit, speak-easies, bootleg liquor. Al Capone in one year made $110 million and was responsible for 110 deaths.

G. Hero worship: Lindbergh, a small-town boy, beat the corporations as the "Lone Eagle." Individualism was not dead. Babe Ruth was an orphan, a man who didn't follow the organization rules, yet he was successful and an individual.

H. Fear of radicals: Red Scare, Palmer raids. President Coolidge wrote an article for the *Saturday Evening Post,* "Are the Reds Stalking Our College Women?"

I. Marcus Garvey and UNIA. Popularity was a response by urbanized Southern blacks to the harshness of Northern life; Chicago race riot, 1919.

III. Age of Social Insecurity

A. Technology caused drastic changes.

1. Car: In 1919, one of every sixteen people owned a car; in 1929, one of five; Model-T.

2. Films: weekly average attendance in 1922, 40 million; by 1930, 115 million

3. Radio: WWJ, Detroit, and KDKA, Pittsburgh; in 1930, 612 stations. In 1920, $10 million in radios & parts; by 1930, $400 million

B. Nicknames for the twenties: The roaring 20s, The Jazz Age, The Flapper Age, The Golden Age, Normalcy; summarized as "We never had it so good."

C. The verdict of literature was more harsh. "The Lost Generation" was disillusioned with the war and materialism.

1. T.S. Eliot, *The Waste Land*

2. Sinclair Lewis, *Babbitt, Main Street*. In 1930 Lewis gave a scathing Nobel Prize acceptance speech attacking the literary establishment.

3. H.L. Mencken, editor of the magazine *The American Mercury*

4. Dreiser's *An American Tragedy*. The dream of success slips away.

D. Popular literature not harsh

1. "Confession" magazines have their beginning.

2. Bruce Barton, *The Man Nobody Knows,* popular view of Christ as a super businessman

UNIT NINE: 1940–1960

Major Themes and Ideas

Foreign Policies

1. Compare isolationism after the First World War with leadership of the Western world after the Second World War.

2. Compare and contrast American foreign policy in the twenties and thirties with American foreign policy in the fifteen years after the Second World War.

3. The impact of communism upon both foreign and domestic affairs in the two decades after the Second World War

4. Was the Cold War inevitable?

5. Compare American neutrality before the First World War with American neutrality before the Second World War.

6. Compare and contrast the foreign policies of Truman and Eisenhower.

7. Historiography of the Cold War

8. Was FDR ineffective in his foreign policy from 1933 to 1941?

9. How consistent was U.S. policy toward China from 1900 to 1949?

10. Impact of the Spanish-American War, the First World War, and the Second World War on our commitments and security in Asia and the Pacific Ocean

11. Trace the changes in the Monroe Doctrine in the twentieth century.

12. American foreign policy from 1945 to 1960 was controlled by the ghost of Woodrow Wilson.

13. League of Nations, World Court, and United Nations: success and failures

Domestic Policies

1. Compare and contrast the experiences of various groups—labor, blacks, business, farmers—following the First and Second World Wars.

2. Disputes among black leaders over goals, methods, and the degree of integregation

3. 1950s as an era of social anxiety

4. Reasons for and consequences of black migration from the rural South to the urban North in the twentieth century

5. Supreme Court and social change in the period from 1920 to 1965

6. Civil rights movement to 1960

Presidency

1. Power of the presidency: foreign crises, economic depressions, and social conflicts

2. Power of the presidency: war and the threat of war

3. Historians love to rank presidents; compare and contrast three presidents since 1928.

4. Analyze the connection between previous administrations and presidential election campaigns and the election results for 1912, 1920, 1932, 1952, 1960, 1968, 1976, and 1980.

5. Why is FDR ranked as a great president?

6. Compare the foreign and domestic policies of Franklin Roosevelt and his vice-presidential successor, Harry Truman.

Major Terms and Concepts

Second World War

Montevideo Conference

Rio de Janeiro Conference, 1933

Buenos Aires Conference, 1936

Lima Conference, 1938

Declaration of Panama, 1939

Act of Havana, 1940

Jones Act, 1916

Tydings-McDuffie Act, 1934, Philippines

Nye Committee

"merchants of death"

neutrality legislation: 1935, 1936, 1937

Spanish Civil War, Franco

Ethiopia

Mussolini

Japan attacks China, Chiang Kai-shek

Panay incident

"Quarantine speech," 1937

Hitler, Nazism

Munich Conference, appeasement, Neville Chamberlain

Austria annexed

nonaggression pact between Germany and USSR

invasion of Poland, blitzkrieg

Axis powers

"cash and carry," revision of neutrality

fall of France

America First Committee

isolationism, Charles Lindbergh

Committee to Defend America by Aiding the Allies

Smith Act

Tojo

destroyer deal

election of 1940: candidates, issues

"lend lease," March 1941

Atlantic Charter, August 1941

Pearl Harbor, December 7, 1941

Japanese relocation

bond drives

War Production Board

Office of Price Administration (OPA)

War Labor Board

General Eisenhower, General MacArthur

genocide, "Final Solution"

second front

D-Day, June 6, 1944

Stalingrad

Winston Churchill

Casablanca Conference, 1943

Cairo Conference, 1943

Teheran Conference, 1943

"unconditional surrender"

Okinawa

Battle of the Bulge

Manhattan Project

J. Robert Oppenheimer

atomic bomb

Hiroshima, Nagasaki

Cold War

Yalta Conference

Potsdam Conference

partitioning of Korea, Vietnam, Germany

Charles de Gaulle

Winston Churchill, "Iron Curtain" speech

Stalin

Bretton Woods Conference

Dumbarton Oaks Conference

San Francisco Conference, 1945, and UN Charter

UN: Security Council, General Assembly, Secretary-General

Atomic Energy Commission

superpowers

socialism, communism

satellites

Nuremberg trials

Department of Defense created

Voice of America, CARE

Yugoslavia, Marshal Tito

Czechoslovakian coup

containment, George F. Kennan

Truman Doctrine

Marshal Plan

Point Four

Israel created, 1948

Berlin blockade

North Atlantic Treaty Organization (NATO)

Warsaw Pact

Southeast Asia Treaty Organization (SEATO)

Central Treaty Organization (CENTO)

Australia, New Zealand, U.S. (ANZUS)

collective security

fall of China, Mao Tse-tung

State Department "White Paper," 1949

Chiang Kai-shek, Formosa

Quemoy, Matsu

Korean War, limited war

Truman-MacArthur controversy

Gandhi

Dien Bien Phu

Vietnam, Ho Chi Minh

Bricker Amendment

John Foster Dulles

"massive retaliation"

brinksmanship

preemptive strike

Khrushchev, 1955 Geneva Summit

Hungarian revolt, 1956

Nasser, Suez Canal crisis

peaceful coexistence

Eisenhower Doctrine

Common Market

Organization of American States (OAS)

U-2 incident

Castro's revolution

Bay of Pigs

Alliance for Progress

Cuban missile crisis

ICBM

Domestic, 1940s and 1950s

Revenue Act of 1942

G.I. Bill of Rights, 1944

Office of War Mobilization and Reconversion

extension of OPA vetoed

postwar inflation

baby boom

Employment Act of 1946

Taft-Hartley Act

Sen. Robert A. Taft

"right-to-work" laws

1948 election: candidates, issues

Dixiecrats, J. Strom Thurmond

Progressive Party, Henry Wallace

Fair Deal

Americans for Democratic Action (ADA)

National Security Act, 1947, 1949

House Un-American Activities Committee (HUAC)

McCarthyism, Senator Joseph McCarthy

Alger Hiss

McCarran Internal Security Act, 1950

Julius and Ethel Rosenberg

Twenty-second Amendment

1952 election: candidates, issues

Ike and Modern Republicanism

"fiscal management"

Reinhold Niebuhr

Ayn Rand, *The Fountainhead*

McCarran-Walter Immigration Act, 1952

Department of Health, Education and Welfare (HEW)

Interstate Highway Act

St. Lawrence Seaway

Landrum-Griffin Act

Jimmy Hoffa

AFL-CIO merger

Alaska, Hawaii

Sputnik

National Defense Education Act (NDEA Act)

"military-industrial complex"

Black History

A. Philip Randolph

Fair Employment Practices Committee

Detroit race riots, 1943

Gunnar Myrdal, *An American Dilemma*

rural and Southern to urban and Northern

To Secure These Rights

desegregation of the armed forces, 1948

Korean War

"separate but equal"

Brown v. *Bd. of Education of Topeka*

Thurgood Marshall

Rosa Parks, Montgomery bus boycott

Rev. Martin Luther King, Jr.

Little Rock, Ark, crisis

Civil Rights Act, 1957

Civil Rights Act, 1960

literacy tests, grandfather clause, poll taxes, white primaries

Supreme Court Cases to Know

1. *West Virginia State Board of Education* v. *Barnette,* 1943 (flag salute in school)

In a 1940 case, *Minersville School District* v. *Gobitis,* the Supreme Court upheld the expulsion from school of two Gobitas children (misspelled in official legal documents) who refused to salute the flag. The Gobitas family belonged to Jehovah's Witnesses, who believe the First Commandment directs them to worship no other god. The Court upheld the school board, 8–1. Just three years later the Court reversed itself, 6–3, in a similar case from West Virginia. Through various legal contortions, students expelled from school for refusing to salute the flag were declared delinquents, subject to imprisonment in reform schools. Many local and state school boards felt the Gobitis decision sanctioned broadly based attacks on Jehovah's Witnesses, and the members of the Supreme Court were shocked at the consequences of that decision. Thus, their reversal is less dramatic than it seems. (Ironically, the decision was announced on Flag Day, June 14th.) The majority opinion reflected the atmosphere of 1943, which differed from the war preparation and uncertainty of 1940. In 1943 we knew we would eventually win. The Court strongly defended the First Amendment. "If there is any fixed star in our constitutional constellation, it is that no official, high or petty, can prescribe what shall be orthodox in politics, nationalism, religion, or other matters of opinion or force citizens to confess by word or act their faith therein."

2. *Korematsu* v. *U.S.,* 1944 (war powers and civilians)

Korematsu was arrested and convicted for noncompliance with the military order that moved all people of Japanese ancestry from the West Coast into relocation centers after the attack on Pearl Harbor. The Court upheld the action in a 6–3 decision based upon a broad interpretation of the nation's war powers. In his dissent Justice Jackson explained Korematsu's dilemma. He "was convicted of an act not commonly a crime ... being present in the state whereof he is a citizen, near the place where he was born, and where he lived all his life. Even more unusual is the series of military orders that make this conduct a crime. They forbid such a one to remain, and they also forbid him to leave. They were so drawn that the only way Korematsu could avoid violation was to give himself up to the military authority." Fred Korematsu had tried to enlist in the army, but was rejected because of ulcers. He then spent his life savings of $150 to learn welding to help the war effort. Instead he was arrested.

3. *Smith* v. *Allwright,* 1944 (blacks and voting in primaries)

Texas Democrats limited membership in their political party to only whites. This tactic negated the black vote because whites fought their internecine battles in the party primaries, and then almost all of them voted for the Democratic candidates in the general election. The Court ruled that this practice violated the Fifteenth Amendment. The Texas state government gave parties complete control of the primary procedures, but this attempt to evade state responsibility was unconstitutional. "When primaries become a part of the machinery for choosing officials, state and national, as they have here, the same tests to determine the character of discrimination or abridgment should be applied to the primary as are applied to the general election."

4. *Dennis* v. *U.S.,* 1951 (radicals and constitutional rights)

Decided in the middle of the McCarthy era, this case upheld the conviction, 6–2, of eleven leaders of the Communist Party for violating the 1940 Smith Act. The case revived the division among judges over the "clear and present danger" and the "bad tendency test" in regard to subversive activities. The "clear and present danger" doctrine announced in *Schenck* v. *U.S.* stated, "The question in every case is whether the words used are used in such circumstances and are of such a nature as to create a clear and present danger that they will bring about the substantive evils that Congress has a right to prevent. It is a question of proximity and degree."

The "bad tendency test" formulated in the decision of *Gitlow* v. *U.S.* was based upon a government's inherent right of self-preservation. A government could restrict any freedom of speech or press that had the tendency to injure the government.

In the majority opinion in the Dennis case, the Court declared, "Whatever theoretical merit there may be to the argument that there is a 'right' to rebellion against dictatorial government is without force where the existing structure of the government provides for peaceful and orderly change."

5. *Youngstown Sheet and Tube Co.* v. *Sawyer,* 1952 (president's powers)

After a long, bitter dispute between the United Steelworkers Union and the steel companies, a strike date was announced. Various federal agencies intervened unsuccessfully to settle the strike. The nation was engaged in the Korean War, a limited war that had not been declared. The Korean War was technically a police action, not a war. Truman ordered Secretary of Commerce Sawyer to take possession of the mills for the federal government. The steel companies sued to regain control, and won in a 6–3 decision. The majority judges wrote six different opinions. Two common threads held that the president received no grant of power from Congress authorizing him to so act, and even in his capacity as Commander in Chief he could not seize property. Neither Congress nor the Constitution supported the seizure, and Truman quickly and quietly complied. The union went on strike.

6. *Sweatt* v. *Painter,* 1950 (blacks and "separate but equal" education)

Several cases over the years foreshadowed judicial disenchantment with the "separate but equal" Plessy doctrine. Two cases were announced the same day in 1950. The first, *McLaurin* v. *Oklahoma State Regents,* ended the segregation against a black student after admission to the state graduate school. He had been assigned his own cafeteria table, his own library table, and an entire row in his classrooms.

Sweatt was denied admission to the University of Texas Law School solely on the basis of race. After he had filed suit, the state government hurriedly put together a "separate but equal" law school for blacks. In a unanimous decision the Court found the two schools unequal, denying Sweatt the equal protection of the laws. The two schools especially differed in "those qualities which are incapable of objective measurement but which make for greatness in a law school. Such qualities, to name but a few, include reputation of the faculty, experience of the administration, position and influence of the alumni, standing in the community, traditions and prestige. It is difficult to believe that one who had a free choice between these law schools would consider the question close."

7. *Brown* v. *Board of Education of Topeka, Kansas* 1954 (blacks, education and the equal protection clause)

In 1951 Oliver Brown filed suit on behalf of his daughter, Linda, who was bused to a black school over twenty blocks away. Another elementary school for whites only was five blocks away. Three other cases—from South Carolina, Virginia, and Delaware—were also filed at this time. This is one of the most significant cases ever decided by the Supreme Court. Recognizing the impact of this case, the Court entertained arguments from all quarters. Fifty-one *amici curiae*, "friends of the court," briefs were filed along with those involved in the case. The majority opinion, 8-0, relied heavily on sociological and psychological factors as well as legal arguments. Segregation had to end. "We conclude that in the field of public education the doctrine of 'separate but equal' has no place. Separate educational facilities are inherently unequal." The Court did not order immediate compliance, but instead directed lower courts to implement the order "with all deliberate speed." This speed was lacking for a number of years.

Readings for Depth and Historical Interpretation

Domestic, 1940s and 1950s

1. Richard Kirkendall, "Harry Truman," in Morton Borden, ed., *America's Eleven Greatest Presidents*. This book was originally entitled *America's Ten Greatest Presidents*. The addition of Harry Truman changed the title. Most known for his foreign policies, Truman avoided the massive economic depression that everyone expected. Truman made decisions that determined our Cold War foreign policy for decades.

2. Arthur M. Schlesinger, Jr., "Introduction," and "Freedom: A Fighting Faith," in his *The Vital Center*. The book was originally written in the late 1940s as a clarion call for liberals to revitalize liberalism in order to confront the challenge of socialism and communism. Schlesinger updated his book in the 1960s.

3. Richard Hofstadter, "The Pseudo-Conservative Revolt—1954," in his *The Paranoid Style in American Politics*. Hofstadter sees McCarthyism as part of the American tradition of the conspiracy theory of history. Status anxieties motivated those behind McCarthyism, which was a reappearance of the same impulses behind Populism.

4. Richard H. Rovere, "What He Was and What He Did," in his *Senator Joe McCarthy*. Rovere gives a hostile assessment of McCarthy and McCarthyism. The sense of fear that lay behind McCarthyism is evident in "Year of Shock" (1949), in Eric Goldman, *The Crucial Decade—And After*. Also see "American Politics and the Origins of 'McCarthyism," by Robert Griffith, in *The Specter: Original Essays on the Cold War and the Origins of McCarthyism*, edited by Robert Griffith and Athan Theoharis.

5. Norman Graebner, "Eisenhower's Popular Leadership," *Current History*, October 1960, a contemporary assessment of Eisenhower's administration. Other evaluations of Ike's presidency are in Alonzo L. Hamby, *Liberalism and Its Challengers: FDR to Bush*, and, Fred Greenstein, *The Hidden Hand Presidency: Eisenhower as Leader*. A revisionist view of Ike that upgrades him is "The Ike Age," by Stephen Ambrose, *New Republic*, May 9, 1981.

6. John Kenneth Galbraith, *The Affluent Society*, in Robert Downs, ed., *Books That Changed America*. Galbraith added a phrase to our economic thinking. In his book, Galbraith castigated economists for continuing to emphasize production for personal consumption in a society that neglected public communal needs. For a look at what Galbraith meant, see "The Baby Boom and the Age of the Subdivision," and "The Drive-in Culture of Contemporary America," in Kenneth T. Jackson, *Crabgrass Frontier: The Suburbanization of the United States*.

7. Douglass C. North, "Current Economic Problems in Historical Perspective, 1945–1965," in his *Growth and Welfare in the American Past: A New Economic History*. North looks at the historical economic background of the role of government, poverty, balance of trade, full employment, economic growth, and so on.

Second World War and Cold War

1. For the Second World War itself, see Studs Terkel, The Good War: An Oral History of World War Two, and John M. Blum, V Was for Victory.

2. Walter La Feber, "Before Pearl Harbor," Current History, August 1969. La Feber traces U.S. Far Eastern policy for the fifty years before the Second World War.

3. George F. Kennan (Mr. X), "The Sources of Soviet Conduct," Foreign Affairs, 1947, also in his American Diplomacy, 1900–1950. This is the original argument for the policy of containment, written by George F. Kennan under the pseudonym "Mr. X."

4. Arthur M. Schlesinger, Jr., "Origins of the Cold War," Foreign Affairs, October 1967. Schlesinger puts most of the blame for the beginning of the Cold War on the Soviets and Stalin. He updated his original position in "Why the Cold War?" in The Cycles of American History.

5. Gar Alperovitz, "How the Cold War Began," The New York Review of Books, March 23, 1967. Alperovitz puts most of the blame for the beginning of the Cold War on the United States and Truman.

6. William A. Williams, The Tragedy of American Diplomacy, pp. 164–177. A leftist critique of the origins of the Cold War, it puts most of the blame on the long-term nature of our capitalist economy.

7. The decision to actually drop the atomic bomb, and what it meant as a policy, has been the subject of many inquiries. The two best are Martin J. Sherwin, "The Atomic Bomb and the Origins of the Cold War: U.S. Atomic-Energy Policy and Diplomacy, 1941–45," American Historical Review, October 1973, and, "The Decision to Drop the Bomb: The Uses of Models in History," in James Davidson and Mark Lytle, After the Fact, volume II.

Sample Outline

Second World War in Historical Perspective

I.   Impact of the War on Domestic America

The war brought increased coordination between business, labor, and government. Two new institutions were admitted into the inner circle of power—higher education and the scientific community.

A. Stimulus to the economy

1. War contracts aided big business.

a. Introduction of tax write-offs

b. Cost plus fixed fee contracts

c. Two-thirds of war contracts (total of 117 billion) went to corporations in the top 100; GM got 8 percent.

d. Economic concentration; 500,000 small businesses disappeared during the war.

e. Number employed in iron and steel rose by 500,000; transportation up 2,600,000.

f. Big corporations had first option to buy government surplus facilities after the war.

2. Labor union membership grew from 8.5 million in 1940 to 15 million in 1945.

3. Agriculture

     a. Total output increased 50 percent during the war.

     b. Concentration increased.

     c. Value of machinery used increased from 3.1 billion in 1940 to 6.5 billion in 1945.

B. Permanent changes in government

    1. Numbers in federal bureaucracy grew from 1 million in 1940 to 3 million in 1945.

    2. New agencies: CIA, NRC, Department of Defense

C. Higher education and the scientific community

    1. Universities received big contracts for scientific research; MIT, 117 million; Cal Tech, 83 million; others were Harvard, Columbia, U of Cal, Johns Hopkins, U of Chicago.

    2. Higher Ed science joined the military-industrial complex. For example, synthetic rubber: After Japan captured 97 percent of the source of U.S. supply of rubber, the federal government spent 700 million to develop synthetic rubber, and gave corporations the patents for small fee. Before the war the U.S. was the largest importer of rubber; after the war it was the largest exporter of synthetic rubber.

D. Social impact of the war

    1. Blacks served in large numbers.

    2. Same number of women worked in 1950 as in 1945.

    3. 14.5 million served in armed forces.

    4. The internal movement of our population during the war was greater than the total number of immigrants who entered the United States.

    5. Many day care centers and child care centers

    6. Large juvenile delinquency rates in 1950s among those who were young children during the war

    7. Pollutants show up for the first time: DDT, plastics, smog in L.A.

II. Second World War in Worldwide Perspective

A. Change from a European-centered world to a world stage; from 1500 to 1945 European nations had dominated the world, but this was no longer true.

B. Change from international balance of power politics to balance of terror. Atomic weapons undermined a viable use of balance of power.

C. Before the war eight nations were considered more or less equal—U.S., Germany, Japan, Great Britain, France, China, Italy, and USSR. After the war three were defeated, three exhausted, and only two were left. (Since 1945 we have seen the slow resurrection of the six defeated and exhausted nations rather than any decline of the U.S.)

D. From alliances to superpowers: Instead of alliances for collective security, superpowers now provide a nuclear shield for their satellites.

E. Superpowers' needs

    1. Large land mass

  2. Large population

  3. Advanced economy and technology (not necessarily a high standard of living)

  4. Possession of deliverable atomic bombs

  5. Autonomy in foreign policies

F. Confrontation of "isms": Military losses in Second World War were USSR, 7.5 million, U.S. 291,000; the war was primarily fought as a war between the isms of Germany and USSR.

G. From old to new imperialism

  1. Old imperialism was political and economic.

  2. New imperialism is military and ideological.

H. Resurgence of Africa and Asia

  1. End of the old imperialism brought independence to many new nations and much confusion in some (Congo).

  2. Soviet propaganda effective as part of anti-imperialism effort; United States often unfairly linked to European imperialists.

  3. Race as an issue complicated the end of imperialism. (1950s marked the beginning of the popular acceptance of the concept of racial equality.)

I. The speed of technological change has gone from evolutionary to revolutionary, in part speeded up by the war effort.

UNIT TEN: 1960–1990S

Major Themes and Ideas

Foreign Policies

1. Containment policy in the Eisenhower, Kennedy, and Johnson administrations

2. What were the immediate and long-range consequences of the Vietnam War?

3. Continuing themes and new departures in foreign policy since 1960

4. Did the "military-industrial complex" lead us into the Vietnam War?

5. Vietnam killed the Great Society.

6. Consistency in American foreign policy in the 1960–1985 period

7. Compare and contrast the foreign policies of two presidents from 1960 to the present.

8. What developments from 1945 to 1975 called the global preeminence of the United States into question?

Social Change

1. New patterns of black leadership since 1960

2. Is American society becoming more egalitarian?

3. Trace the issues, leaders, goals, turning points, successes, and failures of the women's movement.

4. Counterculture movement and changing American values

5. The 1960s as an era of alienation

6. Immigration legislation to the 1980s

7. Leftist criticism since 1960

8. Social issues: crime, elderly, poverty

9. Compare the civil rights movement for blacks in the North and South.

10. Compare the Great Society and the New Deal.

11. Compare the goals and strategies of the women's suffrage movement and feminism since 1945.

Politics and Political Issues

1. Pivotal elections: 1968, 1972, 1976, 1980, 1984

2. Why did presidents from 1960 to 1980 serve less than two full terms?

3. Trace the increase and decrease of military programs and social programs as reflected in the federal budgets since 1960.

4. Federal budget since 1960: Keynesian economics, monetary policy, fiscal policy, deficits, priorities

5. What happened to the antitrust movement in the 20th century?

6. What in the past ten years will become part of future history books and why?

7. Compare the foreign and domestic policies of John F. Kennedy and his vice-presidential successor, Lyndon B. Johnson.

Major Terms and Concepts

Blacks

Brown v. *Board of Education of Topeka, Kansas*

Montgomery bus boycott

Rev. Martin Luther King, Jr.

Southern Christian Leadership Conference

National Association for the Advancement of Colored People (NAACP)

Urban League

Congress of Racial Equality (CORE)

Student Nonviolent Coordinating Committee (SNCC)

sit-ins, freedom rides

"I have a dream" speech

March on Washington, 1963

Medgar Evers

Adam Clayton Powell

H. Rap Brown

Malcolm X

Stokely Carmichael

Black Panthers

Black Muslims

Angela Davis

black power

Twenty-fourth Amendment

Watts, Detroit race riots

Kerner Commission on Civil Disorders

de facto, de jure segregation

white backlash

Robert Weaver

Thurgood Marshall

Civil Rights Act of 1964, public accommodations section of the act

Voting Rights Act, 1965

Civil Rights Act, 1968

Vietnam

geography: Gulf of Tonkin, North Vietnam, South Vietnam, Thailand, Laos, Cambodia

Ho Chi Minh

Viet Cong

Dien Bien Phu

Geneva Conference, 1954

National Liberation Front (NLF)

Gulf of Tonkin Resolution, 1964

demilitarized zone (DMZ)

domino theory

Tet offensive

Kent State incident, Jackson State incident

Daniel Ellsberg, Pentagon Papers

My Lai, Lt. Calley

Hanoi, Haiphong

Senator Fulbright

bombing of Laos and Cambodia

Vietnamization

Paris Accords, 1973

1960s

election of 1960: issues, candidates, "missile gap"

"impeach Earl Warren"

Miranda decision, Escobedo decision

Gideon v. *Wainwright*

Baker v. *Carr*

Rachel Carson, *Silent Spring*

New Frontier

Kennedy and the steel price rollback

Peace Corps, VISTA

Berlin Wall

Common Market

Trade Expansion Act, 1962

Nuclear Test Ban Treaty, 1963

Lee Harvey Oswald, Warren Commission

Bay of Pigs

UN in the Congo

"flexible response"

Cuban missile crisis

Alliance for Progress

Dominican Republic, 1965

Salvador Allende

Panama Canal treaties

Students for a Democratic Society (SDS)

"flower children"

Charles Reich, *The Greening of America*

election of 1964: LBJ, Goldwater

Great Society

Office of Economic Opportunity

War on Poverty

Elementary and Secondary Act

Medicare

abolition of immigration quotas

Department of Housing and Urban Development

John Birch Society

New Left

Robert Kennedy

election of 1968: candidates, issues

Czechoslovakia invaded

Chicago, Democratic Party Convention riot

Richard Nixon's "Southern strategy"

Governor Wallace

moon race, Neil Armstrong

Sunbelt versus Frostbelt (or Rustbelt)

Betty Friedan, *The Feminine Mystique*

National Organization for Women (NOW)

Equal Rights Amendment (ERA)

National Women's Political Caucus

Ralph Nader, *Unsafe at Any Speed*

1970s

Nixon, "New Federalism"

Spiro T. Agnew, his resignation

"revenue sharing"

wage and price controls

Nixon versus Congress

Watergate

Committee for the Reelection of the President

election of 1972: candidates, issues

White House "plumbers"

Sen. George McGovern

Sen. Edmund Muskie

Watergate tapes

H.R. Haldeman, John Ehrlichman, John Dean, John Mitchell

impeachment proceedings

SALT I Agreement

detente

China visit, 1972

recognition of China

War Powers Act, 1973

Six Day War, 1967

Yom Kippur War

Henry Kissinger, "shuttle diplomacy"

Twenty-fifth Amendment

Twenty-sixth Amendment

Chicanos

Cesar Chavez

Warren Burger appointed, 1969

American Indian Movement (AIM), Wounded Knee

multinational corporations

Arab oil embargo

Organization of Petroleum Exporting Countries (OPEC)

balance of trade, trade deficits

Alaska pipeline

The Imperial Presidency

Gerald Ford

Nixon pardon

"stagflation"

SALT II

election of 1976: candidates, issues

Jimmy Carter

amnesty

Panama Canal Treaty

Camp David Accords

Egypt-Israel Peace Treaty: Menachem Begin, Anwar Sadat

Palestinian Liberation Front, (PLO), Yasser Arafat

Department of Energy

Department of Education

Iranian crisis, the Shah, Ayatollah Khomeini

1980s and 1990s

Afghanistan, 1979–1989

Olympic boycott, 1980

election of 1980: candidates, issues

John Anderson

Economic Recovery Tax Act, 1981 (tax cut)

Reaganomics

supply side economics

Sandra Day O'Connor

Lech Walesa, Solidarity

Three Mile Island

Secretary of Interior James Watt

Love Canal, Niagara Falls, NY

Times Beach, Missouri

EPA, Environmental Protection Agency

"New Federalism" proposals, 1982

deregulation—AT&T, airlines, trucking

NEH, National Endowment for the Humanities

Title IX of Education Amendments, 1972

Betty Friedan, *The Second Stage,* 1981

defeat of the ERA

Phyllis Schlafly

Falkland Islands War

civil war in Lebanon, Israel moves into Southern Lebanon

Grenada, 1983

El Salvador, Duarte, ARENA Party

Nicaragua—Somoza family, Sandinistas, Contras, Ortega

Arias Peace Plan in Central America

Iran-Iraq War

"Star Wars," SDI, Strategic Defense Initiative

Third World debt

election of 1984: candidates, issues

Geraldine Ferraro

AIDS (acquired immune deficiency syndrome)

"Moral Majority"

Rev. Jerry Falwell

Vietnam Veterans Memorial, 1982

Agent Orange

Challenger disaster, 1986

Tax Reform Act, 1986

The "Teflon Presidency"

HUD scandals

LBOs (leveraged buy-outs), "junk bonds," corporate "raiders"

insider trading: Michael Milken, Ivan Boesky

savings and loan industry deregulated, Charles Keating, "Keating Five"

nuclear freeze movement

Iran-Contra affair, Irangate

Col. Oliver North

Tower Commission Report

Panama, Gen. Noriega, drug-trafficking indictment, conviction

South Africa, apartheid, Nelson Mandela, F. W. DeKlerk

Marcos, Philippines, Corazon Aquino

Duvalier, Haiti

Middle East—Persian Gulf, West Bank

Gorbachev, glasnost, perestroika

Col. Qaddafi, Libya

INF Treaty, 1987 (Intermediate-Range Nuclear Forces Treaty)

Black Monday, 1987, Stock Market crashes

Rev. Jesse Jackson, Rainbow Coalition

election of 1988: candidates, issues

George Bush

holes in the "Iron Curtain"

Berlin Wall falls

S&L bailout, Resolution Trust Corporation

Gramm-Rudman-Hollings Act

national debt triples from 1980 to 1989, 908 billion to 2.9 trillion

Clean Air Act, 1990 (also one in 1970)

William J. Bennett, "drug czar"—Office of National Drug Control Policy

Tiananmen Square, Beijing

Germany reunited, 1990

Nicaragua, Pres. Ortega defeated in a free election

August, 1991, attempted coup in Moscow, Gorbachev, Boris Yeltsin

U.S., Soviet cutbacks in ICBMs

from the Soviet Union to the Commonwealth of Independent States, CIS, 1991

difficulties between Russia and the new republics

Saddam Hussein, Iraq invades Kuwait

UN Security Council Resolution 661 (trade embargo on Iraq)

Desert Shield, Gen. Colin Powell

UN Security Council Resolution 678 (authorizes use of force, Iraq must withdraw from Kuwait by Jan. 15, 1991)

Gulf War, Operation Desert Storm, Gen. Schwarzkopf

SCUD missiles, Patriot missiles

revolts in Iraq: Shi'ites in South, Kurds in North

Family Support Act, 1988, "workfare"

education—multiculturalism versus politically correct

MTV

1991 Civil Rights Act

Clarence Thomas nominated to Supreme Court, Anita Hill, Congressional hearings

baby-boom generation hits middle age

gentrification

increased Asian, Hispanic immigration

"gridlock," Congress versus the president

election of 1992: candidates, issues, Ross Perot

bombing of World Trade Center

European Community & European Free Trade Association join to become the European Economic Area on Jan. 1, 1993

GATT, General Agreement on Tariffs and Trade

North American Free Trade Agreement, NAFTA

disintegration of Yugoslavia, "ethnic cleansing," Bosnia, Serbia, Croatia

peace-keeping operation in Bosnia begins, 1995

PLO: Israel Peace Treaty, 1993, Arafat, Rabin

Somalia

Whitewater

Clinton's health plan

corporate downsizing

"greenhouse effect"

Republican victory in 1994 Congressional election, control of House & Senate, Newt Gingrich, Bob Dole, "Contract with America"

intervention in Haiti

Oklahoma City bombing, 1995

Gen. Powell withdraws from the 1996 Republican nomination race

Million Man march on Washington, DC, 1995, Louis Farrakhan

Rabin assassinated, 1995

budget showdown between Congress and president

election of 1996: candidates, issues

Supreme Court Cases to Know

1. *Mapp* v. *Ohio,* 1961 (Bill of Rights and the states)

This case was the first of a series of decisions that extended the Fourteenth Amendment to protect citizens against state infringement. The Supreme Court used the "due process" clause to make the Bill of Rights apply to state officials. The Mapp case overturned a state court conviction based on evidence obtained by an unreasonable search and seizure. (Since 1914 the Supreme Court had barred federal use of illegally obtained evidence.)

2. *Gideon* v. *Wainwright,* 1963 (right to counsel)

Gideon was arrested in 1961 for breaking into a poolroom. He asked for a court-appointed lawyer because he could not afford one. Florida law provided lawyers for penniless defendants only in capital crimes, which carried a possible death penalty. The Supreme Court decided that legal counsel must be provided for all persons charged with a felony. In 1972 the Court extended the right to counsel to anyone charged with misdemeanors, a lesser category of crimes, in a decision in regard to Jon Argersinger, another Floridian, *Argersinger* v.

Hamlin. Argersinger was sentenced to 90 days in jail for carrying a concealed weapon.

3. *Escobedo* v. *Illinois,* 1964 (right to counsel)

In a 5–4 decision the Supreme Court ruled that the police must honor an arrested person's request that a lawyer be present during a police interrogation. The constitutional guarantee to be represented by counsel extends to the period prior to actual indictment.

4. *Miranda* v. *Arizona,* 1966 (rights of the accused)

The Miranda decision culminated the 1960s trend toward protecting the rights of the accused. In a 5–4 decision the Supreme Court stated that an arrested person must be told that he has the right to remain silent; that whatever he says may be used against him; that he has the right to be represented by a lawyer; that if he cannot afford a lawyer one will be provided; and finally, that he is permitted one telephone call to obtain a lawyer or to contact someone to make arrangements for him to arrange for a lawyer and bail proceedings. The Supreme Court justices were heavily criticized for coddling criminals. In a rare comment before a convention of chiefs of police, one justice stated that in America it is supposed to be difficult to arrest and convict someone.

5. *Engel* v. *Vitale,* 1962; *School District of Abington Township* v. *Schempp,* 1963 (religion and public schools)

The first case struck down a prayer composed by the New York State Board of Regents, the state public education authority. The second ended the reciting of the Lord's Prayer and the daily reading of ten Bible verses. The Court held that under the Constitution religion is "too personal, too sacred, too holy" for governmental sanction. Religion is a personal matter; government is a public matter.

6. *Baker* v. *Carr,* 1962; *Wesberry* v. *Sanders,* 1964; *Reynolds* v. *Sims,* 1964 (legislative reapportionment)

Beginning with the *Baker* v. *Carr* case, the Supreme Court ended the old practice of apportioning legislative districts to overrepresent rural areas. The boundary lines for both houses of the state legislatures and for congressional districts must reflect the principle of "one man, one vote" as much as possible. Before the *Baker* v. *Carr* case, federal courts avoided reapportionment arguments as "political questions" to be resolved by the legislatures and the voters.

7. *Heart of Atlanta Motel* v. *U.S.,* 1964 (discrimination in public accommodations)

The Civil Rights Act of 1964 outlawed discrimination in schools, employment, and voting. It also outlawed discrimination in public accommodations, or areas frequented by the public. The Supreme Court upheld the constitutionality of this section of the Civil Rights Act of 1964, and ended the argument that a proprietor had the right to refuse service on the basis of race in his own establishment.

8. *Swan* v. *Charlotte-Mecklenburg Board of Education,* 1971 (public schools and integregation)

Southern school districts tried every conceivable method, even closing schools for a year, to avoid desegregating their public schools. In this opinion the Supreme Court sanctioned virtually any method to achieve desegregation, including busing, redrawing district boundary lines, racial balancing, and so on. This decision ended seventeen years of Southern legal subterfuge to avoid the Brown decision.

9. *Bakke* v. *Board of Regents,* 1978 (reverse discrimination)

This reverse discrimination case involved a claim by a white, Allan Bakke, that he was the victim of discrimination. The Civil Rights Act of 1965 prohibited discrimination based upon race, but in order to compensate for the collective results of previous discrimination practices, the University of California at Davis reserved sixteen of its hundred openings for medical school specifically for non-whites. Objective scores and measurements of Bakke's potential put him outside the 84 slots for whites, but higher than the successful applicants for the sixteen non-white positions. In a 5–4 decision the Court upheld both Bakke's admission and the university's use of race to ensure a diverse student body.

10. *Reed* v. *Reed,* 1971 (discrimination based on sex)

This case was the first of a series of sex discrimination decisions. Idaho state law prescribed that the father be given preference over the mother in a dispute over administering the estate of a deceased child. The Reeds were separated when their child died, leaving an estate less than a thousand dollars. The Supreme Court ruled that if both parents were equally qualified the state could not give men preferential treatment; state law had to serve "a compelling government interest" in differentiating between men and women.

11. *Doe* v. *Bolton,* 1973; *Roe* v. *Wade,* 1973 (the abortion cases)

These two cases struck down Texas and Georgia state statutes prohibiting abortions. The Court found such laws to be an infringement on rights to privacy protected by the Ninth and Fourteenth Amendments. The Court limited state legislation by defining three stages of pregnancy and specifying when and which state restrictions were legal.

These two cases illustrate a weakness within our political system. Our political system works because it facilitates compromises at many different levels before a policy decision is actually rendered. When the issue involved is a moral issue, however, or is seen by many as a moral issue—abortion or slavery—compromise becomes difficult, if not impossible. Moral right and wrong leaves no middle ground for compromise. Half-right is the same as half-sinful; something is either sinful or it is not, especially to those who know that they are morally in the right. Our political system does not handle deeply felt moral issues well.

12. *U.S.* v. *Nixon,* 1974 (executive privilege and judicial review)

The Constitution established three separate, distinct branches of government—legislative, executive, and judicial. Presidents have long claimed executive privilege or presidential immunity, claiming that the other two co-equal branches are limited in their right to order the president to do something. When subpoenaed, President Jefferson refused to testify personally at Aaron Burr's treason trial, instead sending written testimony. While common sense says that some areas of executive concern should be sheltered from judicial compulsion, such as military and diplomatic secrets, the Constitution itself does not explicitly mention the concept of executive privilege or presidential immunity.

During the Watergate investigation the special prosecutor asked the White House to turn over certain specific tape recordings concerning seven administration officials indicted for obstruction of justice. The president refused, citing executive privilege. By an 8–0 vote the Supreme Court ordered the tapes handed over. Because the tapes were relevant to an ongoing criminal investigation, "the fundamental demands of due process of law in the fair administration of criminal justice" outweighed the president's "generalized interest in confidentiality." The president did not possess an absolute privilege of immunity from each and every judicial process. If no need exists to protect national security, legitimate judicial needs outweigh any absolute executive privilege. For the first time the power of judicial review was used directly against a president rather than against executive branch officials.

13. *Diamond* v. *Chakrabarty,* 1980 (patent laws and new life forms)

In a decision with monumental possible consequences for the future, the Supreme Court in 1980 declared that a genetically created new bacteria could be patented. Chakrabarty's new bacteria broke down crude oil components to facilitate the control of oil spills. The Supreme Court ruled that manmade forms of life can be patented because they are "not nature's handiwork."

14. *Immigration and Naturalization Service* v. *Chadha*, 1983 (legislative veto)

Over the years Congress has been frustrated by its inability to maintain influence over executive branch policies as Congress had delegated some regulatory duties to executive branch agencies. The "legislative veto" was a provision inserted into laws concerning regulatory agencies that reserved to Congress the right to review and to veto proposed regulatory agency actions. In essence, Congress gave away some of its responsibility to oversee policy decisions, but it still wanted to intervene occasionally to direct policies. The Supreme Court voided the legislative veto as a violation of the principle of separation of powers. Both the "line item veto" sought by every president, and the "legislative veto" pushed by Congress, are attempts by each branch of the federal government to assert more influence over what it sees as an unwieldy, inefficient competing branch.

15. *Texas* v. *Johnson,* 1989; *U.S.* v. *Eichman,* 1990 (flag burning)

Desecration of the American flag, the very symbol of our nation and our heritage, angers many Americans. As a constitutional issue, however, flag burning is protected by the right of free speech. The Texas case declared the state's anti-flag-burning law unconstitutional. In the second case the following year the Supreme Court declared unconstitutional a federal flag-desecration law. "Punishing desecration of the flag dilutes the very freedom that makes this emblem so revered." Most Americans are able to understand freedom of speech as an abstraction, but the exercising of that right often angers them. The volume of mail that senators and representatives received from constituents over flag burning exceeded that of any other issue.

16. *Webster* v. *Reproductive Health Services,* 1989; *Rust* v. *Sullivan,* 1991 (abortion cases)

In the Webster case concerning abortion rights, the Supreme Court upheld major features of a Missouri law, in effect chipping away at the Roe decision's unlimited right to an abortion during the first six months of pregnancy. The Supreme Court upheld a ban on the use of state facilities for abortions and a prohibition against state employees performing abortions. These two parts of the law primarily affected the poor, because they applied to public hospitals.

Wealthier women could always use more expensive private facilities. Another provision required physicians to test whether a post-twenty-week-old fetus could survive outside the womb. Remember, the Roe decision had said that states could not limit or regulate during the first six months, or twenty-four weeks. In the second case, *Rust* v. *Sullivan*, the Supreme Court upheld an administrative regulation forbidding federally funded clinics from providing abortion services or even mentioning the possibility of abortion to a patient, in spite of the Court's admission that for eighteen years the statute upon which the administrative interpretation was based had not been so interpreted.

17. *Miller* v. *Johnson,* 1995 (racial gerrymandering)

The percentage of minority Congressmen has never been as high as the percentage of minorities in the population. Blacks, therefore, have long complained that underrepresentation in legislatures essentially reduces the significance of issues important to minorities. For example, no African-Americans served in Congress from 1901 to 1928; one from 1928 to 1945; and only two from 1945 to 1959. Between 1871 and 1973 no black from Georgia served in Congress. As a remedy, some states, such as Georgia, tried to draw Congressional voting districts to create an almost certain "black" Congressional district. Georgia's redrawing put three blacks in Congress. Conservative critics sued. The Supreme Court ruled that states may not make race the "predominant factor" when drawing legislative boundaries. The Court stated that "racial gerrymandering, even for remedial purposes, may balkanize us into competing racial factions; it threatens to carry us further from the goal of a political system in which race no longer matters—a goal that the fourteenth and fifteenth Amendments embody, and to which the nation continues to aspire." The problem of underrepresentation persists; racial gerrymandering as a possible solution is out.

Readings for Depth and Historical Interpretation

Politics

1. Alonzo L. Hamby, *Liberalism and Its Challengers: FDR to Bush.* Hamby's book covers political developments throughout this whole period.

2. William L. O'Neill, *Coming Apart: An Informal History of America in the 1960's,* and Allen J. Matusow, *The Unraveling of America: A History of Liberalism in the 1960's.* These are both excellent sources for the kaleidoscope that was the 1960s—the civil rights movement, the New Left, Black Power, the Vietnam War, and the elections. One book that concentrates on the protests is Milton Viorst, *Fire in the Streets: America in the 1960's.*

3. James Giglio, *The Presidency of John F. Kennedy,* and David Burner, *John F. Kennedy and a New Generation.* Students are still fascinated by the Kennedy presidency; both these books are excellent.

4. Theodore White, *Breach of Faith,* pp. 322–343. Also see Walter Karp, "The Hour of the Founders," and Vance Bourjaily, "The Final Act," both in *American Heritage,* June/July, 1984. These three sources explain the Watergate scandal, with Bourjaily taking a retrospective look after a decade had passed.

5. Rachel Carson, *Silent Spring,* in Robert Downs, ed., *Books That Changed America.* This book alerted the nation to the disastrous impact of pesticides and insecticides, especially DDT, on the balance of nature. The continued story is in Samuel P. Hays, *Beauty, Health, and Permanence: Environmental Politics in the United States, 1955–1985.*

6. Lou Cannon, *The Role of a Lifetime,* is the best overview on the Reagan years, in spite of the fact that it is early for definitive treatments of the Reagan presidency. A critical look is Garry Willis, *Reagan's America: Innocents At Home.*

Women's Movement

1. Nancy Woloch, *Women and the American Experience.* This is the best history of American women. Also see Mary Ryan, *Womanhood in America: From Colonial Times to the Present.*

2. William H. Chafe, *The Paradox of Change: American Women in the 20th Century.* The last third of this book covers the era since the Second World War.

3. William L. O'Neill, *Feminism in America: A History,* is the history of an idea. (This is a revised edition of *Everyone Was Brave*).

4. J. William T. Youngs, *Eleanor Roosevelt: A Personal and Public Life.* In many respects Eleanor Roosevelt's life mirrored the major changes that affected women in the twentieth century. Shy and introverted, she became more than the wife of a man who became a politician; she became a public figure in her own right.

5. James Davidson and Mark Lytle, "From Rosie to Lucy: The Mass Media and Images of Women in the 1950s," in *After the Fact,* volume II. This explores the way that television depicted women and what it tells us about women and television.

6. Betty Friedan, "The Problem That Has No Name," and "The Happy Housewife Heroine," in *The Feminine Mystique.* This book was the catalyst for the women's movement.

7. Two good collections of articles that cover the whole span of American women's history are Jane DeHart Mathews and Linda Kerber, eds., *Women's America: Refocusing the Past,* and Jean E. Friedman, Mary Jane Capozzoli, and William G. Shade, eds., *Our American Sisters: Women in American Life and Thought.*

8. Steven Mintz and Susan Kellogg, *Domestic Revolutions: A Social History of American Family Life,* is the best family history. Also see Carl Degler, *At Odds: Women and the Family from Revolution to the Present.* For a look at the changing definitions of family violence, see the introduction and conclusion in Linda Gordon's study of Boston from 1880 to 1960, *Heroes of Their Own Lives: The Politics and History of Family Violence.*

Civil Rights Movement

1. John Hope Franklin and August Meier, eds., *Black Leaders of the Twentieth Century*. Among the leaders found here are the following: Booker T. Washington; Ida Wells-Barnett; W.E.B. DuBois; James Weldon Johnson; Marcus Garvey; A. Philip Randolph; Mary McLeod Bethune; Adam Clayton Powell, Jr.; Martin Luther King, Jr.; Malcolm X; and Whitney M. Young, Jr.

2. Gunnar Myrdal, *An American Dilemma*, in Robert B. Downs, *Books That Changed America*. A Swedish scholar, Myrdal was invited to study the status of blacks in American society. The dilemma in our society was the gap between American ideals and racial practices. This book helped the later push for desegregating the armed forces and public schools.

3. John Hope Franklin, "The Postwar Years," and "The Black Revolution," *From Slavery to Freedom: A History of Negro Americans*. Franklin summarizes the black civil rights movement.

4. Harvard Sittoff, *The Struggle for Black Equality, 1954–1980*. His introduction is an excellent brief summary of the issues, events, and achievements of the civil rights movement.

5. Stephen B. Oates, *Let The Trumpet Sound: The Life of Martin Luther King*, and David Garrow, *Bearing the Cross*. These are the two best books on the life of Martin Luther King, Jr., and the Southern Christian Leadership Conference. King was not without his opponents within the black community. For an alternate point of view, see Malcolm X, *The Autobiography of Malcolm X*, a critic of the nonviolent approach.

Foreign Affairs, 1960s and 1970s

1. John W. Spanier, "The Challenges of the 1960s," in *American Foreign Policy Since World War II*. This chapter, a broad introduction to the 1960s, also includes a comparison of the Korean and Vietnam wars, Latin America, Castro, and Africa.

2. C. Vann Woodward, "The Age of Reinterpretation," *American Historical Review*, October 1960. Woodward sees events and changes in the 1945–1960 period as forcing historians to look at previous interpretations of American history. For example, the rise of missiles makes clear the extent to which our history has been shaped by the security provided by two oceans.

3. Arthur M. Schlesinger, Jr., *The Cycles of American History*, "National Interests and Moral Absolutes." Schlesinger looks at American foreign policy and how these two orientations influence our policy decisions.

4. William Appleman Williams, Thomas McCormick, Lloyd Gardner, and Walter LaFeber, *America in Vietnam: A Documentary History*, covers all aspects of the Vietnam War. Especially see LaFeber's "The Rise and Fall of American Power, 1963–1975." Other sources are James Thomson, Jr., "How Could Vietnam Happen? An Autopsy," *Atlantic Monthly*, April 1968, and Walter LaFeber. "The Last War, the Next War, and the New Revisionists," *Democracy*, January 1981.

5. Leslie Gelb, "Vietnam: The System Worked," *Foreign Policy*, 1971; or Leslie Gelb and Richard Betts, *The Irony of Vietnam: The System Worked*. Both of these sources are good for a defense of American policy and decisions in regard to Vietnam.

6. If you want a long look at the Vietnam War, see the following: George C. Herring, *America's Longest War: The United States and Vietnam, 1950–1975;* Frances Fitzgerald, *Fire in the Lake: The Vietnamese and the Americans in Vietnam*, which explains the cultural conflict between the Americans and the Vietnamese; Stanley Karnow, *Vietnam: A History*, which accompanies the television series; and Ron Kovic, *Born on the Fourth of July*, a personal account of transition from enthusiastic recruit to antiwar veteran.

7. Walter LaFeber, *Inevitable Revolution: The United States in Central America*. The first chapter traces American policy from Thomas Jefferson to the Good Neighbor Policy. The rest concentrates on policy since 1940.

Sample Outline

The organization of this outline comes from two books that are well worth reading: Clinton Rossiter's *The American Presidency* and Theodore Sorensen's *Decision Making in the White House*. You will also benefit from Arthur M. Schlesinger, Jr.'s *The Imperial Presidency*.

The Presidency in the Twentieth Century

I. **Constitutional Responsibilities**

  A. Chief of state

    1. Most nations divide their leadership positions in two: a head of government (prime minister) and a head of state (queen, president). The United States combines both positions in the same office.

    2. Figurehead

    3. Symbolic embodiment of the United States

  B. Chief administrator or chief executive

    1. Runs the executive branch of government, executes laws, carries out laws and court directives.

    2. Oversees millions working in the executive department (Ballinger-Pinchot controversy under Taft).

    3. Hampered and limited by the rise of regulatory agencies—now more than 1800 beyond the president's immediate control—Federal Reserve Board, Interstate Commerce Commission, Federal Trade Commission.

    4. Agencies are often controlled by interest groups. An example is Kolko's argument on Meat Inspection Act, 1906. He argues that the Progressive movement included a successful attempt by big business to eliminate competition in the guise of reform.

    5. Carter tried to streamline the bureaucracy but encountered much inertia.

    6. Kennedy complained that he spent half of his time trying to get people to do what they were supposed to be doing.

    7. Beginning with the 1921 Budget and Accounting Act, many responsibilities have passed from Congress to the president.

    8. Nixon: revenue sharing and New Federalism shifted more responsibilities back to the states.

    9. Executive Order 8248 (FDR, 1939) created the Executive Office of the President, putting some agencies within the White House—Bureau of the Budget, National Security Council, Central Intelligence Agency, Council of Economic Advisors. (Note that older cabinet organization has become less important.)

  C. Commander in chief

    1. For all practical purposes the president controls the army, navy, air force, marines, and coast guard.

2. Lincoln expanded original definition to include powers over civilian matters considered to be militarily significant.

3. Second World War greatly expanded scope of CIC powers. FDR claimed the right to "take measures necessary to avert a disaster which would interfere with the winning of the war." Examples: stabilized prices by controls, Japanese removal, Truman's dismissal of General MacArthur

4. Congress retains sole power to declare war, but technology and the need for speed puts many military options under the president's practical control: Teddy Roosevelt and Great White Fleet, Manhattan Project, nuclear response.

5. Attempts to restrict the president include Wilson and arming of merchantmen, Ludlow Amendment, Neutrality Acts, Bricker Amendment, two-term limitation, War Powers Act, 1973.

6. The president is also restricted by budget fights with Congress and the need for two-thirds Senate approval for treaties.

7. Executive orders often are used to implement CIC goals and diplomatic goals. (An executive order is based on the president's authority and theoretically is in force only to the end of that president's term. As a practical matter, most executive orders are irreversible.) Examples: FDR and destroyers for bases deal, Truman and desegregation of armed forces.

8. Real change in CIC role came in August 1945. The bomb brought massive retaliation, preemptive strike, and nuclear shield under the president's power.

9. Before the Second World War we had no bases overseas outside of American territory. Now we have more than 400.

10. Since 1940 a major long-run change in our society is the permanent military presence during peacetime.

D. Chief diplomat or chief of foreign policy

1. The single voice of American foreign policy. As Truman said, "I am American foreign policy." The president controls negotiations of treaties, such as SALT I, SALT II, Yalta Conference, and summit conferences.

2. Limited by Congressional control of funds and Senate ratification of treaties. Examples: Roosevelt and Great White Fleet, neutrality acts in 1930s, Wilson and Versailles Treaty

3. May boldly lead: Teddy Roosevelt and Panama Canal, Russo-Japanese War mediation; Truman-Marshall Plan, Point Four, NATO, Cold War, recognition of Israel, decision to intervene in Korea; Carter's peace initiative in the Middle East; Nixon's visit to China; JFK's Alliance for Progress, Peace Corps

4. May follow public opinion rather than mold it: FDR and Quarantine speech; Washington Disarmament Conference in 1920s; FDR in 1940–41; Wilson in 1914–17

5. May ignore public opinion or previous conventional policies: LBJ and Vietnam; Nixon and bombing of Cambodia; Wilson and Watchful Waiting; nonrecognition of USSR from 1917 to 1933

E. Chief legislator

1. Most major pieces of legislation now originate in the White House. The president takes the legislative initiative such as the State of the Union Address, budget message, and presenting a program. Examples: FDR and 100 Days; LBJ and Great Society; Wilson and tariff, banking, and antitrust legislation

2. President rarely gets all he wants: FDR and court packing plan.

3. President has lost historic confrontations with Congress: Truman and OPA extension, Taft-Hartley Act.

4. Must veto an entire bill, no line item veto.

F. Chief judicial officer

1. Appoints all federal judges. Memorable examples: Wilson, Louis Brandeis; LBJ, Thurgood Marshall; Reagan, Sandra Day O'Connor

2. Limitations: FDR and court packing plan, Nixon and appointment of Southerners to Supreme Court

3. Length of judicial service means a president's influence may extend for years after his own term.

4. Part of election politics: "Impeach Earl Warren." Wallace in 1968 hoped to throw the presidential election into the House to exchange his support for the power to veto appointment of Supreme Court judges.

II. Unofficial Positions

A. Chief of party

1. Taft's fight with Teddy Roosevelt for control of Republican Party machinery in 1912

2. FDR was the most successful broker of political coalitions.

3. Kennedy went to Dallas in November of 1963 to smooth over infighting among Texas Democrats.

4. Patronage jobs distributed

5. Involved in Congressional party politics: Taft, Uncle Joe Cannon, Old Guard versus George Norris and Progressive Republican insurgents

B. Molder of public opinion, or voice of the people

1. Commands immediate attention of the media

2. Successes: LBJ in pushing for civil rights, Reagan's image in news conferences, FDR in fireside chats, Harding as a symbol for Normalcy

3. Failures: Wilson's push for joining the League of Nations; Nixon's attempt to quiet Watergate

4. Especially powerful in foreign affairs: FDR and Atlantic Charter; Carter and Olympic boycott; Wilson and "Make the world safe for democracy."

5. Creates commissions to publicize issues: LBJ and Kerner Commission on Civil Disorders; Truman and civil rights report, To Secure These Rights; T. Roosevelt and conservation conference, 1908

6. Sometimes forced by public opinion to act, for example, Eisenhower in Little Rock, Ark, 1957

C. Chief of the economy, or manager of prosperity

1. Public has always blamed the president for economic hard times.

   a. Pujo Committee under Taft was established to study financial concentration on Wall Street.

   b. Politics and ideology sometimes dictate response: Hoover and Hawley-Smoot Tariff; T. Roosevelt and Northern Securities case and Anthracite Coal strike, 1902.

2. Hoover was the first to assume responsibility for intervening in the economy to reverse downturns with the RFC; FDR assumed total responsibility; JFK and steel price rollback; Truman lost to steel companies; Bush and Savings & Loan industry

3. Employment Act of 1946 created legislative foundation for giving the president responsibility for maintaining full employment; Council of Economic Advisors.

4. President, Congress, and agencies control through fiscal policy (spending and taxing policies) and monetary policy (controlling the amount of money and credit in circulation), and through general policies toward the economy. Kennedy and Reagan cut taxes to stimulate the economy; Federal Reserve Board, SEC, FDIC, JFK and Trade Expansion Act of 1962; dollar diplomacy

5. Responds to emergencies, natural and man-made, such as floods, riots, strikes, to maintain order in our society: Hoover and the Bonus Army

D. Leader of free nations or president of the west

1. From 1815 to 1914 U.S. stayed out of European wars only because there were none.

2. Teddy Roosevelt asserted hegemony over Caribbean and Central America through the Roosevelt Corollary, Panama Canal; later, dollar diplomacy.

3. Wilson: Fourteen Points, Leage of Nations, World Court

4. 1920s—U.S. abdicated; 1930s—West leaderless

5. Second World War—FDR, Churchill, Stalin. By 1945 only two major countries were left.

6. Collective security: NATO, SEATO, CENTO, ANZUS, UN

7. Bipartisan foreign policy

8. Frustrating responsibility: de Gaulle, Suez Canal crisis, 1956; Eisenhower Doctrine; Vietnam; Korea; Bay of Pigs; Cuban missile crisis; Iran-Contra affair

9. Reagan, "The Cold War is over."

III. Limits on the Power of the President

A. Limits on permissibility

1. Must follow Constitution, international law; hampered by policies of our allies (French in Indochina; OAS and Cuban missile crisis)

2. Limited by his own judgment of action being accepted by military, Congress, public, allies, and so forth.

B. Limits on resources

1. Money, manpower, time to respond

2. United States is a superpower, but is not equally powerful everywhere. In 1968 the *Pueblo,* a U.S. spy ship, was captured off North Korea. We protested in the UN because within a few hours we could fly 25 jet fighters to the scene whereas North Korea could fly 625 comparable jet fighters.

3. Dropping an atomic bomb is not a viable option; our nuclear arsenal is more of a defense shield.

4. Unwillingness to commit resources: Hoover-Stimson Doctrine in Manchuria

C. Limits on time

1. Political timing of proposals may be dictated or hindered by events: Sputnik and education.

2. In early period of Cuban missile crisis, almost all advisors urged an all-out attack on Cuba. Kennedy waited, and decided on a blockade to give Soviets time to react.

3. Advisers frequently divided

4. Twenty-second Amendment limits time to carry out proposals, because a president is a lame duck after election to a second term.

D. Limits of previous commitments

1. Traditional party stands and constituencies

2. Treaties and laws

3. Past record in foreign policies, as abrupt changes may be unsettling

4. Existing precedents on what presidents have done in similar situations

5. Commitments made by subordinates in diplomatic situations, and promises to senators and congressmen

6. Political party platforms rank lowest of any commitments.

E. Limits on available information

1. Flow of information to presidents varies with personal style. JFK and LBJ absorbed much public media information; Nixon and Reagan preferred short summaries from their staffs.

2. Usually too much information, except for foreign affairs

Documents and the Document-Based Question

DOCUMENTS AND THE STUDY OF HISTORY

Documents are the building blocks of history. History rests upon evidence supplied by documentary proof. In the words of an old saying among historians, "no documents, no proof, no history." The analysis and evaluation of documents is the starting place for all historians. You had better be honest, for documents will be used by future historians to reevaluate your judgments.

To master the study of history you must master the study of documents. This task is not burdensome. History comes alive when you read a diary. You begin to understand that the characters in history are human beings with human weaknesses. For example, Andrew Jackson held his cabinet meetings on Tuesdays because he considered Tuesday to be his lucky day. The struggle of a sturdy pioneer woman leaps out from this terse diary notation: "Got up at five, cut wood, cooked breakfast, cleaned stove, nine o'clock, delivered my son." In its finest moments history erases the years separating the experiences of human beings, and we become closer observers of one another.

The observations of eyewitnesses to an event are termed *primary sources*. Primary sources do not have to be original. A copy of the Declaration of Independence is a primary source because it exists in the same wording as the original.

Writing based upon the study of primary documents is a secondary source. A historian investigating the evolution of municipal governments from 1650 to 1825 reads various collections of laws for the colonies and early states. On the basis of reading primary sources, the historian writes an interpretation explaining how municipal government changed from being mostly interested in promoting trade to being primarily interested in providing municipal services such as police protection, sewer drainage, clean water, and fire protection. The resulting book, *The Municipal Revolution in America: Origins of Modern Urban Government, 1650–1825*, by Jon C. Teaford, is a secondary source.

Beyond the secondary source is the tertiary or third-level source. You are all too familiar with this example, the textbook. No author can read all the primary and secondary sources in American history! A historian tries to absorb as much history as possible while writing a textbook. Any textbook is by its very nature inadequate in terms of absolute correctness of all factual information and conceptual interpretation. Even if the author became aware of new historical discoveries and interpretations, years may pass before the new ideas appear in the textbook. Rewriting time, publisher's costs, printing schedules, market purchasing cycles, and dozens of other intrusions combine to create a time lag between the arrival of new ideas and information and their appearance in standard textbooks. It's easy to add a few pages for the latest presidential election; it's much harder to rewrite a section on reform in the 1830s.

The advantage of the tertiary source is that it gives you a general idea of the particular topic you are interested in. Secondary sources give specific detailed information if you can find a secondary source on your topic. Primary sources give you the opportunity to be a historian and to experience all the excitement and challenge the historian feels when analyzing and synthesizing data.

Working with documents is exciting, provided you maintain a dash of skepticism. Being critical of what you see, you must be prepared to test the credibility and authenticity of the document. Many times the simple explanation is sufficient. Be prepared, though, to look beyond the obvious.

The first test of authenticity, called *external criticism,* tests the date of the document. Was that particular technology of papermaking known at that time? Chemical and carbon dating tests pinpoint the period when a document was written. Be leery of the 1876 centennial time capsule that contains a photocopy of the Declaration of Independence. Other questions must be asked. Were the expressions and literary style appropriate for the period? (Would you believe an archaeological dig that unearthed a gold ring stamped 752 B.C.?) Finally, are the facts corroborated by other sources? You should doubt the authenticity of letters dated December 15, 1821, West Virginia, because West Virginia was not a state until 1863. A letter dated November 1492 in which Columbus refers to his discovery of the continent of South America would be suspect, for he died not knowing he had discovered a continent. For years historians smiled at the fable of George Washington and the cherry tree, an inspirational story concocted by a minister long after Washington's death. Then came the discovery of European pottery depicting Washington and his cherry tree. Carbon dating put the pottery in the 1790s! Was there some truth to the story? Was the story transmitted orally long before the old minister wrote it down? We may never know, because there is insufficient proof.

Another area of concern involves possession. How did the document come to be located where it is now? Is the known travel route believable? A collection of correspondence between Dorothea Dix and James Buchanan recently was found in a trunk in the attic of one of Dix's descendants. This sounds plausible, but your attic doesn't. Every year gullible tourists in the Middle East buy "ancient" coins from their guides. Such transactions are illegal, but the guide found it last week while plowing his field and his grandmother needs money for an operation and, well, you know the rest. Most documents and artifacts are carefully cataloged in an archival collection, and, similar to prized breeding animals, documents have pedigrees.

Everyone possesses a style of writing. We all have pet expressions and particular words we use repeatedly. A knowledgeable investigator can read a newly discovered manuscript and confidently pass judgment on its author. Today computer technology is just as knowledgeable. Three supporters of the adoption of the Constitution in 1788—John Jay, Alexander Hamilton, and James Madison—wrote a series of unsigned essays to convince several states, especially New York, to ratify the Constitution. The collection of eighty-five essays is called *The Federalist Papers*. We unfortunately didn't know who wrote some of the essays. Enter the computer, which counted and analyzed the frequency of certain words in the essays. The computer designated the probable author of all of the essays, including many substantiated by other sources. Whether we know it or not, we all have style.

A second area of investigation is termed *internal criticism*. Was the observer in a position to know or to observe? Was the observer knowledgeable in the area of his observation? Could he be biased? Any lawyer or judge will tell you that eyewitness testimony is often the least reliable evidence. A classic psychology class experiment involves the sudden disruption of the class by a group of thugs who run in to attack the professor at a lectern. The class watches in horror as the attackers flee. All of a sudden the professor jumps up and tells everyone to write down what happened. The variety is unbelievable!

Another test asks if the document matches other statements made by the author. This aspect is tricky. Fifty campaign speeches may not reveal as much as a single private letter, and all you can do is make an imperfect judgment. In the late nineteenth century businessmen frequently quoted on Abraham Lincoln's birthday a widely circulated Lincoln speech praising the free enterprise system. Lincoln scholars could not locate any copy of or reference to the speech in Lincoln's public or private papers. Confronted with the possibility of fraud, one distributor of the speech blurted that this was the speech Lincoln would have said if he had said something on the topic. In this case the speech's usefulness outweighed its truthfulness.

Reading a document demands critical analysis. Documents contain facts and opinions from which *you* draw an inference. Even primary sources are biased. King George III's comments on the truthfulness of the Declaration of Independence were probably unprintable.

Even simple documents present problems. For instance, newspapers tell us much about the life of ordinary people, but a study of the newspapers in the 1850s in Hamilton, Canada, revealed that less than one percent of the city's population was mentioned in the local newspaper within a one-year period. Obviously there is much the newspaper doesn't tell us. In another case, restored homes give us a taste of life in another period, yet many are constantly torn down in the name of progress. Why were particular houses preserved? Do they represent the typical home of the period? (I once visited a restored home in a small town in the South. The guide proudly described the home as typical, with three floors for the family and a fourth floor for the slaves. Since seventy-five percent of the white families in the South did not own slaves, this house was hardly "typical.")

Ideology plays a role in determining what is printed. Before Hitler invaded the Soviet Union in June 1941, the great enemies of the Soviet Union were the capitalist powers. After the German invasion, the United States suddenly changed from ideological enemy to potential ally. You can imagine the entry under Franklin Roosevelt in Soviet encyclopedia editions before and after June 1941. In the United States, portraits on first-class stamps portray the heroes of the incumbent administration. Democrats produce Democratic heroes; Republicans, Republican heroes. Ideology is never as insidious a factor in our politics as in the former Soviet Union, but it is present. Watch films and newsreels produced during wars. The other side makes propaganda films; we produce patriotic films. Such are the passions of war.

Another difficulty with documents is misinterpretation. A slaveowner listening to his slaves singing while picking cotton announced smugly that his slaves were happy. He should have listened to the words. The words of one song exhorted slaves to "follow the drinking gourd." (The Big Dipper points to the North Star, the route north for a runaway slave.) You may have heard the sad tale of the "Master gone away," in the "Blue-tailed Fly." The master's horse threw him after the slave stuck a burr under the saddle, and the same slave sadly laments his master's inexplicable death when his favorite horse bolted. Some listen to a slave song and find contentment and happiness; some find a message of rebellion and resistance. The song is the same, but not the response of the listener. Be alert.

TYPES OF DOCUMENTS

Documents and physical evidence surround us. Your personal history appears in diaries, memorabilia from grade school, photographs, and a favorite stuffed animal or doll. Society's documents range from official records to printed matter to physical remains to domestic furnishings to a wide variety of miscellaneous objects.

Visit a local public archive, a depository of governmental records. The variety of official records is astonishing. You may find any of the following: church records, court records, census records, cabinet meetings, voting records, city records, state records, police records, hospital records, legislative records and journals, city council minutes, collections of laws, surveys, government publications, diplomatic messages, and maps of municipal sewer lines. Printed material includes the following: speeches, pamphlets, campaign literature, essays, newspapers, books, magazines, autobiographies, city directories, telephone directories, novels, and poems. Manuscripts include letters, diaries, contracts, wills, estate inventories, ship's bills of lading, ship's passenger lists, or warehouse inventories.

Society itself produces physical remains for the historian. Among society's physical evidence are the following: building remains, wells, inscriptions, machinery, aqueducts, roadways, architectural styles, monuments, restored homes, farm equipment, pyramids, fortifications, and sculptures. The inside of a house might include pottery, furniture, cross-stitching, vases, weapons, appliances, cooking utensils, and photographs. Your list of potential sources for information is hardly exhausted. Don't forget coins, maps, films, newsreels, videotapes, folk songs, legends, tapes, records, and stamps.

Finally, the site of a historical event itself is a living document. You learn new definitions of devotion and courage by walking the path of Pickett's charge during the battle of Gettysburg. Harpers Ferry, Virginia, a restored town, is not much different from what it was that autumn night in 1859 when John Brown tried to incite a slave uprising. Textbooks brand Brown's effort a failure, in part because so few slaves joined him. Local historians at Harpers Ferry add a different ingredient to this tale. After the Civil War many former slaves in the area said that they had been waiting in the nearby hills for a sign of success before joining Brown. If you sit on the hillside above Harpers Ferry, you can almost hear the runaway slaves whispering in the hills. You gain a new sense of both what was and what might have been.

ADVANCED PLACEMENT DOCUMENT-BASED QUESTION

An essay question based upon documents is a special kind of essay question. A normal essay question requires you to respond to the wording in the question. A document-based question requires you to answer a question by using documentary evidence and your knowledge of the time period or the events alluded to in the question. One example of a document-based question is comparing four different pictures of the battle of Lexington, drawn by four different generations. How did the pictures change? Why did they change? Which is more accurate? Another example of a document-based question is the inquiry methodology. Students receive a number of documents that they use to synthesize a conceptual hypothesis. In the previous example the questions guide the conceptualization. In the inquiry method the students are free to ask whatever questions they wish concerning the documents, and their own questions determine the path of their analysis.

A special type of question is the AP examination document-based question. Whereas early versions invited information beyond that presented in the documents, the present questions demand additional information and understanding. Using only the documents is not enough. Now a student must be able to display historical knowledge of the time period in addition to using the documents to answer the question.

The most important step in answering a document-based question is to read the question. You are answering the question, not the documents. If you are to use the documents to answer the question, you had better understand the question first.

Bring to your analysis of the documents a tentative hypothesis to answer the question. If a question asks if the Articles of Confederation provided for an effective government, you should say to yourself, in some ways it did and in some ways it did not. As you read each document, look for information to support either point of view. Don't take a simplistic point of view to answer a question. Most questions in history are more complex than they seem at first. Was colonial society becoming more democratic between 1750 and 1780? A simple "yes" or "no" is insufficient. A more sophisticated conceptual framework suggests that in some ways it was and in some ways democracy may even have regressed in some manner.

Suspend your judgment as you read the documents, and be prepared to modify it. In 1984, the document-based question concerned the validity of characterizing President Herbert Hoover as a conservative and President Franklin D. Roosevelt as a liberal. The question invites you, even demands you, to challenge this simple characterization. Do it.

Document-based questions are often change-over-time questions. In a change-over-time question, a sense of chronology is important and a sense of change (or not) is mandatory.

Document-based questions often suggest a means for organization of your essay. Does the question ask for factors or categories? If so, organize your paragraphs by means of these factors or categories. One document-based question asked students what concerns—political, practical, moral, and constitutional—shaped Indian policy between 1789 and Andrew Jackson's presidency. A good answer considers all four concerns. Another directed students to consider the federal government's commitment to laissez-faire in the late nineteenth century by referring to policies in regard to antitrust, interstate commerce, and land grants to railroads. Address the three areas.

If you do not feel comfortable enough to write a full paragraph on one of the factors or concerns, combine two in one paragraph, but don't ignore a factor.

Pay close attention to the organization of the document-based question. Many documents have "tags." The tag tells you the source of the document. Read the tag before you read the document. Understanding an unfamiliar document is easier if you know the author is, say, Karl Marx. Look at the tag for information about the author, such as a title (Senator, Reverend); a position (Senate Whip, president of the VFW, delegate to the Articles of Confederation Congress); a particular point of view he or she may represent (labor, South, business, upper class, Republican Party); and a date indicating chronological development.

Certain document-based questions contain "notes" explaining what happened chronologically between two documents or groups of documents. Others contain "historical settings" that present the historical background by relating events leading to the topic of the question. Read the notes and historical setting for information. Use information in the historical setting for your essay if necessary for transition or if you have linked it to your conceptual theme. Don't merely rephrase the historical setting and the notes. Neither the notes nor the historical setting constitute the answer to the question.

Advanced Placement graders have found over the years that students have a tendency to overemphasize the first document, Document A. It is *a* document, not *the* document. Consider all the documents in answering your question. No one document in a document-based question is absolutely necessary. An excellent answer may refer to several documents implicitly.

As you read each document, ask yourself what facts, ideas, or concepts are expressed in the document? Try to get at least one idea from it. If it doesn't make sense to you, skip it and go back to it later. Look for contradictions or tensions between documents, and be prepared to explain them. As mentioned above, the 1984 document-based question asked students to react to the common characterization of Hoover as a conservative and Franklin Roosevelt as a liberal. One document contained a Roosevelt speech in which he said, "I am that kind of conservative because I am that kind of liberal." Either FDR was schizophrenic or the definitions of liberal and conservative vary from person to person and situation to situation. (It is the latter.) Whereas the students were not required to wrestle with the definition of liberal and conservative in their essays, the better papers tried to come to grips with the contradictions in the two words.

Be skeptical as you read. Be a detective. Ask yourself: Is the document reliable, is there corroboration, and is the source biased? What are the author's underlying assumptions? An abolitionist writing about John Brown differed from a Southerner's report on the raid. Could the source have been designed with posterity more in mind than contemporaries? Woodrow

Wilson, assessing blame for the defeat of the Versailles Treaty, played the role of the prophet by foreseeing the Second World War. Finally, the context of references is important. Don't project modern values into the documents. The reference to tyranny in the Declaration of Independence doesn't make King George III a fascist or a totalitarian dictator.

HOW TO ANALYZE DOCUMENTS

Many of the following examples are based upon former Advanced Placement document-based questions. The principles of how to analyze documents apply to any document.

I. Visuals

    A. Pictures and photographs

        1. Subject: What person, event, or subject is represented?

        2. Time and place: When and where is the subject taking place?

        3. Point of view: Is the artist or photographer trying to convey a particular point of view? (economic and cultural activities in San Antonio in 1849; a view of Greeley, Colorado, showing orderliness and prosperity in contrast to an earlier groundlevel view)

        4. Emotional impact: What is the general impression?

        5. Form of expression: What kind of picture—drawing, painting, etc.—is it?

        6. Any symbolism present: Justice blindfolded in a John Brown lithograph with the Virginia state flag in the background with the state motto, "Thus always to Tyrants." Painting, "The Bridge," by Joseph Stella, a mass of entangling wires and cables, some forming church-style windows (technology a new religion?)

    B. Cartoon

        1. Who are the characters in the cartoon? Are they realistic or exaggerated? What are their expressions? Are the characters or other things labeled?

        2. What symbols—flags, Uncle Sam, unemployed, etc.—are there?

        3. What is the overall idea or impression of the cartoon?

        4. Title or caption

    C. Poster

        1. Who published it, for what possible reasons? (It may reflect a biased view.)

        2. Title

        3. Intended for what audience?

4. Purpose of the poster or the evidence

D. Diagrams and flowcharts

1. They are used to summarize an important idea and to illustrate the idea's parts or components.

2. Check the title.

3. Examine the parts.

4. Labels

E. Maps

1. Maps deal with a specific time period.

2. A map focuses on a specific topic, event, or development in history, often a change-over-time illustration (Compromise of 1850).

3. Places the subject in a specific location

4. Check the title.

5. Check the key or legend. (Western U.S. and geographic features)

6. Remember the differences between geographic maps and electoral vote maps.

F. Charts

1. They usually illustrate a relationship between two subjects. Decide what those two subjects or ideas are (time and voting, residence and prohibitionist leadership, population and money supply) and their relationship (increases, decreases, no change, directly or indirectly related).

2. Check title and category titles.

3. Are the numbers percentages or absolute? Don't refigure the numbers. (It is stupid to claim that twins born to a family of four represent a 100% increase in the number of children in the family. The chart-makers used the numbers, either absolute or percent, to convey an idea, not to teach mathematics.)

4. Be careful: Large money and population figures are often given in abbreviated form such as thousands. Thus, a 62,000 population figure may really be 62,000,000.

5. Were the changes illustrated significant? (65% to 67% is not.)

6. Remember that the chart illustrates a trend for only a specific period.

7. Remember the possible influence of major events on the time period indicated (voting statistics in 1770–1790 and the Revolutionary War).

8. Be aware of the chart with a collapsed *X*- or *Y*- axis (1770–1775, 1784–1792). It is intended to indicate that an insignificant period was purposefully left out of the chart.

G. Graphs

1. Read the key.

2. Notice the title.

3. Look for dates.

4. Graphs use statistical data to present historical comparisons or changes over time. (Black versus White school enrollment, 1860–1930)

5. Circle or pie graph: Each circle represents the total quantity, such as 100% of the population. Note that the portions of the circle represent a percentage.

Bar graph: read both axes. One usually represents a percentage or quantity and the other usually a time period. Note that the bars are drawn to scale to make a comparison. Be alert that the bars in a graph may represent different subgroups; check the legend.

Line graph: Read both axes. Unlike a bar graph, which shows a subject at a specific time, a line graph can show trends over every part of the time period, and often shows several trends at once.

II. Printed Materials

A. Newspapers

1. Editorial or article (abolitionist sympathizer Horace Greeley on John Brown's raid). You should be aware that before the twentieth century it is hard to differentiate between an article and editorial opinion.

2. Interview

3. Evidence of the newspaper's economic or political bias (urban, rural, South, *Wall Street Journal*)

4. Letter to the editor

5. Be aware that an editorial or article may either reflect mass opinion or be an attempt to influence or to create mass opinion.

B. Magazine or pamphlet

1. Same checks as under newspapers

2. What is the normal audience of the magazine *McCall's, Field and Stream*?

C. Book

1. Is it contemporary or not, an eyewitness to an event or second-hand comment (Frank Norris's *The Octopus*)?

2. A disinterested observer (*Uncle Tom's Cabin;* James B. Weaver, *A Call to Action*)

3. Politically partisan, based on evidence or opinion?

4. Remember that the preface is a personal statement.

5. Novels can be symbolic.

6. A review of a book is the reviewer's opinion, not the author's.

7. A recollection of an event long after it happened (Eisenhower recalling a meeting with President Truman three years earlier).

8. Memoirs—a selective and personal view that is rarely self-critical.

9. Is the author a foreign observer? (Harriet Martineau's observations of American society and manners)

D. Poem

1. Poems are meant to use language as art rather than to give information.

2. They usually illustrate a spiritual or symbolic view of a period, event, or idea.

III. **Personal Documents**

A. Speech

1. To what audience? What office or position does the speaker hold? (Booker T. Washington's 1895 Atlanta Compromise speech to the white South)

2. Rough draft (It may be more truculent.)

3. Official speech or informal (inaugural address, State of the Union Address)

4. Campaign speech (FDR versus Hoover)

5. Ask yourself, based on what you know about the speaker, is this a view you would expect him to take, such as Andrew Carnegie's opposition to the Treaty of 1898?

B. Letter

1. Official or personal

2. To a subordinate or a superior

3. What is the relationship between the two people?

4. Private or public (John Adams to his wife)

5. From an organization (VFW on immigration)

6. Is the date significant (a letter to a delegate during the Constitutional Convention, or a letter written during Shays' Rebellion)?

C. Diary

1. Personal

2. After or before the fact

3. Remember that a diary is usually not self-critical.

4. Merely observations or evidence of partisan viewpoint?

IV. **Political Documents**

A. Party platform

1. A presidential candidate may or may not agree with the platform.

2. A political platform is often a compromise document, although third-party platforms are more truculent.

3. A convention declaration such as Seneca Falls, 1848, may describe present conditions, indicate a degree of stridency, or show the organization's goals and expectations, such as the Populist Party platform, 1892.

B. List of groups supporting legislation

1. What organizations are represented?

2. Is there any pattern to support or opposition, any common characteristics (South, urban, immigrant, slave states, Midwest, former Populist states)?

3. Are there any surprises or unusual alliances (Carnegie and Bryan in opposition to the Treaty of 1898)?

V. Public Records

A. Laws, proclamations, executive orders

1. Why was the law passed; what does it represent? Remember, laws are passed as solutions to a problem, as the representation of a group's ideal (prohibition), as a guide for future behavior (Puritan laws on church attendance), or as a response to public pressure for what is perceived as a problem (Sherman Antitrust Act). Is it a veto message? What reasons are given for the veto? (Jackson and BUS recharter veto)

2. Some laws are more symbolic in their passage than in their enforcement (Volstead Act, Sherman Antitrust Act).

3. Commentary on the laws similar to a textbook on laws (Blackstone's *Commentaries on the Laws of England*)

4. Federal, state, or local law?

5. Legislative resolutions are not binding; they just express a sentiment (Va and Ky resolutions, SC legislature endorses Calhoun's Exposition and Protest).

B. Court decision

1. Does it declare a law unconstitutional, and if so, what new problems does it create (Dred Scott)?

2. Does the decision support the views of a particular section, party, or class (NRA)? (Charles River Bridge decision and Jacksonians)

3. Was the decision enforced or obeyed (Brown, Indian removal)?

4. Was there a narrow or broad interpretation in the decision?

5. Note the division in the decisions: 5–4, 9–0, 6–3. Was it close?

6. Trial transcript—Scopes trial, Darrow versus Bryan

C. Legislative debate, Congressional Record, speech in Congress, testimony before a congressional committee

1. Was the speech for constituent consumption or for colleagues?

2. Any other evidence of influence of the speaker among his colleagues? (Henry Clay would be more respected than George M. Dallas.)

3. Is the person known for other activities (Carnegie and the Treaty of 1898)?

4. What point of view or organization does a person testifying before Congress represent (a railroad vice-president testifying on long-and short-haul rate differentials)?

D. Government agency report

1. Federal, state, or local?

2. How does it reflect the general tone of government at the time (1920s versus 1930s)?

3. Be aware that agency reports are rarely critical of themselves.

4. A report may be intended to lay a basis for future expansion in scope or powers or increased funding.

E. Others

1. Diplomatic correspondence such as instructions from the secretary of state to treaty negotiators or correspondence to Congress or an official about ongoing negotiations (Polk on the justice of British claims to Oregon)

2. Official letters (from the Rhode Island state assembly to Congress)

3. Treaties—provisions, how do the provisions compare with prior agreements, or cause future consequences (Yalta Agreements)?

4. Ship passenger lists—look for patterns or characteristics of the group: ages, gender imbalance, individuals or families, conditions of leaving, did both swear allegiance to the Church of England? (Puritans and early Virginia colonists)

DOCUMENT-BASED QUESTIONS FROM PREVIOUS AP EXAMINATIONS

Previous document-based questions have covered a wide range of topics in American history. The best way to prepare for a DBQ is to study American history. You should also remember that the DBQ is, in reality, a document-based essay question. All the rules for writing good essays apply to the DBQ.

Some DBQs require a student to use a specific act or action as a basis for generalizing about the ideas and events surrounding that action. Past DBQs have asked students to explain the reasons for the 1924 Immigration Act, the reasons for the approval of the Treaty of Paris in 1899, and the reasons for the defeat of the Versailles Treaty following the First World War. All these questions require some awareness of the forces at work in Congress. Another DBQ looked at the factors involved in the Jacksonian Indian removal. The defeat of the Crittenden Compromise proposal in 1860 was the basis of another question. A recent DBQ used the dropping of the atomic bomb in 1945 as a focal point for the military and diplomatic history of the Second World War and the postwar period, 1939–1947.

A different type of DBQ asks a student to be aware of the events and characteristics of a period. Such DBQs concerned the evolving differences between the Chesapeake colonies and the New England colonies up to 1700; the era of the Articles of Confederation; the issues of the 1790s; the correctness of the Jacksonians' view of themselves as the guardians of economic opportunity, individual liberty, and political democracy; the beginning of the Civil War; agrarian discontent in the late nineteenth century; the conflicting strategies of Booker T. Washington and W.E.B. DuBois in confronting racism and poverty in the late nineteenth and early twentieth centuries; the rise of Prohibition in the Progressive era; and cultural conflict in the twenties.

A third type of DBQ centers around a concept in a particular period of history. One DBQ looked at democracy in the colonial era. Another used laissez-faire in the late nineteenth century as a focus. Still another asked for changes in the status of middle-class women over a century. One recent DBQ used the concept of geographic determinism (without calling it that) to ask about the impact of the natural environment in shaping the westward movement from the 1840s to the 1890s. In each case the student must understand the concept and the historical period. Any good American history student should have a firm understanding of the different forms of democracy, the theory and practice of laissez-faire, the role of status and social class, and the reciprocal relationship between the environment and economic activity. Finally, one DBQ tested the student's knowledge of the political philosophies of liberalism and conservatism, using Franklin D. Roosevelt and Herbert Hoover as a focus.

Three Sample Document-Based Questions

The instructions in the AP examination booklet state that you must include additional information from the period in your essay answering the document-based question. As in any essay there are two different levels of factual and conceptual information. There are quality facts and concepts, and quantity facts and concepts. Not all of them are equal in importance. For example, a student might include the Sumner-Brooks affair in an essay on the causes of the Civil War, but forget to include slavery in the territories, the Dred Scott decision, the rise of the Republican Party, and other issues. Make certain you have covered the most significant concepts and provided quality facts to buttress your conceptual points.

FIRST SAMPLE DBQ

Suggested writing time—45 minutes

Percent of Section II score—45

Directions: The following question requires you to construct a coherent essay that integrates your interpretation of Documents A–N *and* your knowledge of the period referred to in the question. High scores will be earned only by essays that both cite key pieces of evidence from the documents and draw on outside knowledge of the period.

1. "American foreign policy leading up to involvement in the Second World War was greatly influenced by the continuing debate over the 'lessons' of the 1914–1929 period." Assess the validity of this statement by considering the issues of American foreign policy in the period from 1914 to 1929 and the appropriateness of these "lessons" to the period from 1930 to 1941.

Document A

Fifteen years ago came the Armistice and we all thought it was to be a new world. It is! But a lot worse than it was before.

Ten million men were killed and many more maimed, fifty billion dollars' worth of property destroyed, the world saddled with debts.

And for what? Would it have been any worse if Germany had won? Ask yourself honestly. No one knows.

Is this old world as safe for democracy as it was before all these lives were lost?

Source: editorial, William Allen White, Kansas editor, 1933

Document B

American newspapers said in 1921 that the only American book 'supremely popular' in Europe was Uncle Sam's pocketbook; in 1923 that we had become a leading member of the 'League of Donations'; in 1928 that Europe counted too much on being 'Yank-ed' out of economic difficulties; in 1932 that our being expected to 'succor' Europe suggested too strongly 'sucker'; in 1933 that whenever an international conference met 'to get at the bottom of things,' one of the things is Uncle Sam's pocket.

Source: Thomas A. Bailey, *The Man in the Street,* 1948

Document C

"Samuel! You're not going to another lodge meeting!"

Source: The Saturday Evening Post, January 1938

Document D

Mr. Con Says No:

"Outraged by Nazi barbarism and Japanese megalomania, we are already emotionally drifting, as in 1914–17, toward the same maelstrom. Since Munich, American anti-dictatorship sentiment is just as hot as anti-German sentiment in 1916. England is again casting sheep's eyes at us—witness Churchill's short-wave radio appeal to America, Eden's recent visit, recent English mutterings about maybe paying a little on the war debt. In the name of saving freedom our liberals are again deserting anti-military principles. In sum, we are already hard at what Charles A. Beard, most distinguished of American liberal historians, calls the 'demonology' of naîvely splitting the world into blacks and whites and letting our emotions warp us into betting everything on the side of the angels. They were queer angels in 1919—witness the peace treaties they drew up. Also, in 1931, when they ran out cynically on American efforts to get Japan to respect the Kellogg treaty outlawing war. Also when they permitted the rape of Ethiopia."

Source: "Pro and Con: Should We Act to Curb Aggressor Nations?"
Readers Digest, March 1939

Document E

Mr. Pro Says Yes:

"Parallels with 1914–17 are miserably misleading here. Immature sympathies, Allied propaganda, interests with a financial stake in the Allied cause, had a lot to do with involving us then. Now the hard core of the matter is a natural horror at the bloody rape of China, the sadistic persecutions in Germany. There is no need for artificial propaganda against dictators. The brute facts of their behavior are an irresistible call to action."

Source: "Pro and Con: Should We Act to Curb Aggressor Nations?"
Readers Digest, March 1939

Document F

Some of the factors at work 25 years ago are now present in much greater force; others are absent or are replaced by factors powerfully at work in the opposite direction. The first and the most overwhelming difference of all is, of course, the fact that we now have the experience of the past 25 years behind us. This clearly works both ways. It has given us a knowledge of modem war, a horror of and disillusion with it and a desire to have none of it, unlike anything we knew in 1914. It has also given us memories—of the blood shed at St. Mihiel and the Argonne, of the victory parade through the Arc de Triomphe, of the Hall of Mirrors at Versailles—that link our emotions, our policies and in a real sense our national interests much more closely with France and Great Britain than they were linked a quarter of a century ago. It has given us a conscious place upon the world stage of which we were at that time unaware, and a far more vivid sense of the degree in which any great war in Europe must affect the United States.

Source: Walter Millis, "1939 Is Not 1914." *Life,* November 6. 1939

Document G

The new war is raising much the same detailed issues as did the old, but against this different background they come with a different impact and so far, at least, they have been handled differently. Once more we have acquiesced as the British have snuffed out our trade with Germany, and it seems certain that we shall be even less inclined than before to embarrass the Allied war effort by insisting upon its restoration. But the trade itself is of much less relative importance to us than was our trade with the Central Powers in 1914....

Even if a desire for the business and a wish to give further assistance to the Allies should break down the cash and carry restrictions and the Johnson act, there would still be the bitter memories of past foreign lending to discourage the rebuilding of a war-supply industry on credit. And even if a considerable industry of the sort should nevertheless develop, it might have no great effect in urging us on into war. Businessmen and bankers now know by hard experience what it means to resign the rushing profits of neutrality for the colossal taxation and rigorous controls of wartime. Few things seem to me more certain than that, if the United States does become a belligerent, it will not be for business reasons or under the impulse of an industrial and financial community which probably has more ground than any other group to dread the social and economic dislocations that full-scale participation in a great war must bring.

Source: Walter Millis, "1939 Is Not 1914," *Life* November 6, 1939

Document H

During the first six weeks of the war—(Americans) gave the impression of struggling desperately against an inner urge to succumb to some force stronger than themselves.... This attitude was not so much one of normal abhorrence for a form of human activity which is extremely unpleasant, to say the least, as of mystic dread, as if going to war were a sin. One of the basic elements of Americanism—which is a permanent diffidence and protest against Europe as a whole—found a new expression: in spite of the desire to see Hitler defeated, and in spite also of the general conviction that the Allies had to go to war to achieve this end, the very fact that war existed in Europe reawakened the traditional tendency of the Americans to condemn Europe en bloc because it was at war.

Source: Raoul de Roussy de Sales, French journalist, "America Looks at the War." *The Atlantic Monthly,* February 1940

Document I

In other words, strenuous efforts were made to demonstrate, now that the fight was on, that not one side alone should be blamed, and to remind the Americans that the French and the English were greatly responsible, through their past errors, for having produced Hitler and therefore the war.

The attitude of the liberals was the most interesting of all. Any man who adopts a certain philosophy of life has to pay for it. The liberal bears a cross just like the fanatic, but the cross of the liberal is particularly troublesome because it means living most of the time in a maze of totally insoluble problems.

The liberals all over the world, but particularly in America, are bearing their cross of confusion with increased uneasiness these days. The flower of American intellect, they led the world crusade against Hitler and Fascism. Bravely they accepted the eventuality of war. Freedom, they said, is worth dying for. They sang the glory of the Ethiopians and of the Chinese. They wept over Austria. They mourned the treachery that lost Spain to Franco and Czechoslovakia to Hitler. When the showdown approached, last August, they began to waver. The cross of confusion weighed on their shoulders.

Source: Raoul de Roussy de Sales, French journalist, "America Looks at the War," *The Atlantic Monthly,* February 1940

Document J

The present war is a continuation of the old struggle among western nations for the material benefits of the world. It is a struggle by the German people to gain territory and power. It is a struggle by the English and French to prevent another European nation from becoming strong enough to demand a share in influence and empire.

The last war demonstrated the fallacy of sending American soldiers to European battlefields. The victory we helped to win brought neither order nor justice in its wake, and these interminable wars continue unabated and with modern fury. We cannot impose a peace by force upon strong nations who do not themselves desire it, and the records of both sides show little indication of such a desire, except when it is to their own material advantage. Whether one reads a history of England, Germany, or France, the wish for conquest, when opportunity arose, has always overshadowed the wish for peace.

Source: Charles A. Lindbergh, "What Substitute for War?" *The Atlantic Monthly,* February 1940

Document K

What meaning has the European war for us in 1940? Compare 1914–1917 with the period 1939–1940. Now, as then, most of the world is at war. Again we are neutral; again our neutrality is tilted to favor one side; again we contemplate the consequences to ourselves if that side should lose. What are some of those consequences?

... We must look ahead to the time when Britain and France may be crushed, and a large part of the world may fall under the dominance of Nazi Germany and Soviet Russia.

... We will not, we say, fight unless our vital interests are attacked. It follows, therefore, that the possible disappearance of Britain and France, along with their empires, is not a vital interest of America. Remember how Britain acted from 1931 to the end of 1939. Manchuria was no vital interest of hers. It was in distant Asia, and Japan would be reasonable. Ethiopia, Spain, Austria, Czechoslovakia, were not vital interests of Britain. The destruction by Hitler of the treaties of Locarno and Versailles, and the march into the Rhineland, were merely the whimsies of an unpredictable and dangerous man who might do unpredictable and dangerous things if he were asked—or compelled—to conform to the canons of Western civilization, one of which is a decent respect for the opinion of mankind. Such a policy—or lack of it—is, as we now know, suicidal. In a close-knit, interdependent world it is the equivalent of saying that if my neighbor is being murdered I must refrain both from helping him and from calling the police. After all, the homicide is private to the murderer and the dead man's family, and any intervention on my part means the abandonment of an 'objective attitude' whose preservation is more important than the preservation of life or the law or even, eventually, my own safety.

Source: David L. Cohn, "The Road Not Taken," *The Atlantic Monthly,* March 1940

Document L

If the British Empire, with all the weight of its democratic economic power and its military strength and naval force, should fall, the United States would be alone in a warlike world.... If war is not checked and thwarted in Great Britain, war will come inevitably to the United States. Because our first line of defense lies around the coast of Britain, in this crisis, we should turn to Great Britain in her hour of danger and agony with such neighborly help as public opinion in the United States may seem legally to justify.... Whoever is fighting for liberty is defending America.

Source: speech, William Allen White, Kansas editor, 1940

Document M

Last week a Gallup poll pointed up a major shift in U.S. opinion. A 1937 poll had reported that 64% of U.S. citizens thought it had been a mistake for the U.S. to go into World War I; only 28% thought not. To the same question last week, 42% thought that U.S. entrance into World War I had not been a mistake, 39% still believed it was.

With the beginning of the Blitzkrieg, U.S. opinion on its part in World War I began to change. Many a circumstance, many a circumstantial report did much to remind U.S. citizens that the cause fought for 23 years ago was strikingly familiar to the cause being fought for in Europe today. Many have come to believe that the U.S. mistake was made, not in winning the war, but in losing the peace.

Source: Time magazine, December 23, 1940

Document N

The President of the United States of America and the Prime Minister, Mr. Churchill, representing His Majesty's Government in the United Kingdom, being met together, deem it right to make known certain common principles in the national policies of their respective countries on which they base their hopes for a better future for the world.

First, their countries seek no aggrandizement, territorial or other.

Second, they desire to see no territorial changes that do not accord with the freely expressed wishes of the peoples concerned.

Third, they respect the right of all peoples to choose the form of government under which they will live; and they wish to see sovereign rights and self-government restored to those who have been forcibly deprived of them.

Fourth, they will endeavor, with due respect for their existing obligations, to further the enjoyment of all States, great or small, victor or vanquished, of access, on equal terms, to the trade and to the raw materials of the world which are needed for their economic prosperity.

Fifth, they desire to bring about the fullest collaboration between all nations in the economic field with the object of securing for all improved labor standards, economic adjustment and social security.

...

Eighth, they believe that all of the nations of the world, for realistic as well as spiritual reasons, must come to the abandonment of the use of force. Since no future peace can be maintained if land, sea or air armaments continue to be employed by nations which threaten, or may threaten aggression outside of their frontiers, they believe, pending the establishment of a wider and permanent system of general security, that the disarmament of such nations is essential. They will likewise aid and encourage all other practicable measures which will lighten for peace-loving peoples the crushing burden of armaments."

Source: The Atlantic Charter

In answering the document-based question on the "lessons" of the 1914 to 1929 period, you should, before reading a single document, make two columns. Into the first should go the issues of the early period, into the second those of the later period. After rereading the question five times note that the question concerns the "issues," not necessarily the events. Better answers organize around collective security, neutrality, disarmament, relations with Europe, and so on. As you read through the documents, put issues and events in the appropriate columns in abbreviated form. After you are done, look at the columns to see what outside information you can add. The following are mentioned fleetingly or not at all: Washington Naval Disarmament Conference; Five, Four, and Nine Power Treaties; World Court; Quarantine Speech; Panay incident; Dawes and Young Plans; specifics of the 1930s neutrality acts; America First Committee; Lend-Lease; destroyers deal, and so forth.

DBQs are graded on a 0–9 scale. The best essay using only the documents usually receives a score no higher than a 3–4, and often it is much lower. What I am telling you is simple: Bring in outside information; follow the instructions. You may use some issues and events outside the time period if you can relate them to the period. For example, "Unlike the period after the Second World War, no forum such as the United Nations existed to impose meaningful sanctions on aggressors. The League of Nations was toothless." These sentences indicate your awareness of the comparative effectiveness of the two world organizations.

SECOND SAMPLE DBQ

Suggested writing time—45 minutes

Percent of Section II score—45

Directions: The following question requires you to construct a coherent essay that integrates your interpretation of Documents A–N *and* your knowledge of the period referred to in the question. High scores will be earned only by essays that both cite key pieces of evidence from the documents and draw on outside knowledge of the period.

2. "Between 1880 and 1915 labor leaders voiced sharp disagreement over the proper goals and strategies workers should follow to improve their position in American society." Assess the validity of this statement by contrasting the different goals and strategies advocated by labor leaders between 1880 and 1915. Include an assessment of their vision of the future of American society and the degree of success their approach achieved between 1880 and 1915.

Document A

Question, a senator: I was only asking in regard to your ultimate ends.

Answer, Strasser: We have no ultimate ends. We are going on from day to day. We are fighting only for immediate objects— objects that can be realized in a few years.

Question, a senator: You want something better to eat and to wear, and better houses to live in?

Answer, Strasser: Yes; we want to dress better and to live better, and become better off and better citizens generally.

Question, a senator: I see that you are a little sensitive lest it should be thought that you are a mere theorizer. I do not look upon you in that light at all.

Answer, Strasser: Well, we say in our constitution that we are opposed to theorists, and I have to represent the organization here. We are all practical men.

Source: testimony by Adolph Strasser, President of the Cigar Makers' Union and a founder of the American Federation of Labor, before a U.S. Senate Committee, 1883

Document B

The many must act, and they must act together in a system of cooperation that will stop the grinding process.

Under the competitive system labor has no share in what it develops. It has to take what the master deals out to it; but once it receives a share in what it creates, industry will become part of him who produces, and the secret of content is found.

Source: Terence V. Powderly, *Thirty Years of Labor,* 1889

Document C

It has always been, and is at the present time, my policy to advocate conciliation and arbitration in the settlements of disputes.... Thousands of men who have become disgusted with the ruinous policy of the strike, as the only remedy for ills we complain of were drawn to us because we proclaimed to mankind that we had discarded the strike until all else had failed.... No matter what advantage we gain by the strike, it is only medicating the symptoms; it does not penetrate the system, and therefore fails in effecting a cure.... You must submit to injustice at the hands of the employer in patience for a while longer. Bide well your time. Make no display of organization or strength until you have every man and woman in your department organized, and then do not strike, but study, not only your own condition, but that of your employer. Find out how much you are justly entitled to, and the tribunal of arbitration will settle the rest.

Source: Terence V. Powderly, quoted in a publication by the Missouri Bureau
of Labor Statistics and Inspection, 1887

Document D

The two movements were inherently different. Trade unions endeavored to organize for collective responsibility persons with common trade problems. They sought economic betterment in order to place in the hands of wage-earners the means to wider opportunities. The Knights of Labor was a social or fraternal organization. It was based upon a principle of cooperation and its purpose was reform. The K. of L. prided itself upon being something higher and grander than a trade union or political party.

Source: Samuel Gompers, *Seventy Years of Life and Labor: An Autobiography,*
1925

Document E

John D. Rockefeller's great fortune is built upon your ignorance. When you know enough to know what your interest is you will support the great party that is organized upon the principle of collective ownership of the means of life....

Now, we Socialists propose that society in its collective capacity shall produce, not for profit, but in abundance to satisfy human wants; that every man shall have the inalienable right to work, and receive the full equivalent of all he produces.

Source: Eugene V. Debs, *Debs: His Life, Writings and Speeches,* 1908

Document F

It is well known that the Knights of Labor was not instituted with the view to action in the matter of regulating wages. The objects included education, the bettering of the material condition of the members by means of such schemes as co-operation, etc., and the elevation of labor by legislation through political action, but not taken, however, in a partisan way. The plan of the organization did not include the management of strikes or aught else pertaining to wages and terms of labor, and it is not surprising, therefore, that the machinery has not proven equal to those occasions, when the Knights went outside of their original objects. It would be a blessing to all concerned if the Knights of Labor shall resolve to first principles and devote undivided attention thereto.

Source: National Labor Tribune, July 7, 1883

Document G

The working people find that improvements in the methods of production and distribution are constantly being made, and unless they occasionally strike, or have the power to enter upon a strike, the improvements will all go to the employer and all the injuries to the employees. A strike is an effort on the part of the workers to obtain some of the improvements that have occurred resultant from bygone and present genius of our intelligence, of our mental progress. We are producing wealth today at a greater ratio than ever in the history of mankind, and a strike on the part of workers is, first, against deterioration in their condition, and, second, to be participants in some of the improvements.

Source: Samuel Gompers, President of the American Federation of Labor, testimony before a House of Representatives Committee, 1899

Document H

The "pure and simple" trade union of the past does not answer the requirements of today, and they who insist that it does are blind to the changes going on about them, and out of harmony with the progressive forces of the age....

A modern industrial plant has a hundred trades and parts of trades represented in its working force. To have these workers parcelled out to a hundred unions is to divide and not to organize them, to give them over to factions and petty leadership and leave them an easy prey to the machinations of the enemy. The dominant craft should control the plant or, rather, the union, and it should embrace the entire working force. This is the industrial plan, the modern method applied to modern conditions, and it will in time prevail.

Source: Eugene V. Debs, *Debs: His Life, Writings and Speeches,* 1908

Document I

The advocates of the so-called industrial system of labor organizations urge that an effective strike can only be conducted when all workmen, regardless of trade, calling or occupation, are affected. That this is not borne out by the history of strikes in the whole labor movement is easily demonstrable. Though here and there such strikes have been temporarily successful, in the main they have been fraught with injury to all. The so-called industrial system of organization implies sympathetic strikes, and these time and experience have demonstrated that as a general proposition they should be discarded, while strikes of particular trades or callings have had the largest number of successes and the minimum of defeats.

Source: Convention Declaration, AFL, 1903

Document J

The Socialist party is to the workingman politically what the trade union is to him industrially; the former is the party of his class, while the latter is the union of his trade.

The difference between them is that while the trade union is confined to the trade, the Socialist party embraces the entire working class, and while the union is limited to bettering conditions under the wage system, the party is organized to conquer the political power of the nation, wipe out the wage system and make the workers themselves the masters of the earth.

Source: Eugene V. Debs, *Debs: His Life, Writings and Speeches*, 1908

Document K

I want to tell you, Socialists, that I have studied your philosophy; read your works upon economics, and not the meanest of them; studied your standard works, both in English and German—have not only read, but studied them. I have heard your orators and watched the work of your movement the world over. I have kept close watch upon your doctrines for thirty years; have been closely associated with many of you, and know how you think and what you propose. I know, too, what you have up your sleeve. And I want to say that I am entirely at variance with your philosophy. I declare it to you, I am not only at variance with your doctrines, but with your philosophy. Economically, you are unsound; socially, you are wrong; industrially, you are an impossibility.

Source: Samuel Gompers, speech, AFL convention, 1903

Document L

Teacher of important and much-needed reforms, she [Knights of Labor] had been obliged to practice differently from her teachings. Advocating arbitration and conciliation as first steps in labor disputes she had been forced to take upon her shoulders the responsibilities of the aggressor first and, when hope of arbitrating and conciliation failed, to beg of the opposing side to do what we should have applied for in the first instance. Advising against strikes, we have been in the midst of them. Urging important reforms we have been forced to yield our time and attention to petty disputes until we were placed in a position where we have frequently been misunderstood by the employee as well as the employer. While not a political party we have been forced into the attitude of taking political action.

Source: Terence V. Powderly, 1893

Document M

Resolved, that the A.F. of L. most firmly and unequivocally favors the independent use of the ballot by the trade unionists and workers, united regardless of party, that we may elect men from our own ranks to make new laws and administer them along the lines laid down in the legislative demands of the A.F of L., and at the same time secure an impartial judiciary that will not govern us by arbitrary injunctions of the courts, nor act as pliant tools of corporate wealth. That as our efforts are centered against all forms of industrial slavery and economic wrong, we must also direct our utmost energies to remove all forms of political servitude and party slavery, to the end that the working people may act as a unit at the polls at every election.

Source: Convention Declaration, AFL, 1897

Document N

Hillquit: Then, inform me upon this matter: In your political work of the labor movement is the American Federation of Labor guided by a general social philosophy, or is it not?

Gompers: It is guided by the history of the past, drawing its lessons from history, to know of the condition by which the working people are surrounded and confronted; to work along the lines of least resistance; to accomplish the best results in improving the condition of the working people; men and women and children, today and tomorrow and tomorrow—and tomorrow's tomorrow; and each day making it a better day than the one that had gone before. That is the guiding principle and philosophy and aim of the labor movement—in order to secure a better life for all.

Source: debate between Samuel Gompers, President of the American Federation of Labor, and Morris Hillquit, Socialist Party official, before a Senate Committee investigating industrial relations, 1914

The labor leaders DBQ gives you four conceptual points around which to organize your essay: goals, strategies, vision of the future, and degree of success. You could also organize your essay around the different approaches advocated. The only difficulty with this organizational scheme is that you must be certain to contrast the four. The four approaches to improving the position of workers in American society were the American Federation of Labor, the Knights of Labor, the American Railway Union, and the Socialist Party. Gompers and Strasser are identified with the AFL; Hillquit and Debs (in Document E) are associated with the Socialist Party. Powderly is never clearly identified with the Knights of Labor; this association on your part is an example of the minimum level of outside information demanded by the DBQ. The toughest labor leader and program to remember is the American Railway Union, the short-lived industrial union led by Eugene Debs before he became a socialist. Understanding the differences between Debs before and after the Pullman strike, which destroyed the American Railway Union, is considered significant outside information by the grader. Good American history students are already prepared to differentiate clearly between the approaches to unionism advocated in this period. They already know the four approaches. This DBQ will simply jog their memories. Since every student must do the DBQ, should you encounter one you don't feel quite knowledgeable about, quickly check the sources for the documents before reading a single document. The sources alone will help conceptualize your approach to reading the documents for information and ideas.

Before you begin reading the documents and after you have read the question five times, you should jot down the four concepts on a piece of scrap paper. As you read each document you should categorize the documents under the appropriate concept. Document A, for example, gives the goals of the AFL, usually summarized as "pure and simple" trade unionism, or "more." As one historian once explained, the AFL never argued over how to bake the pie, they just argued over how to slice it and how large a piece they should get. Unlike the Socialist Party, the AFL was never an anticapitalist movement.

Much of the outside information in the labor leaders DBQ should concern the degree of success. Notice that you must supply outside information about the great capitalists and the major strikes. Some of the outside information to include is as follows: the 1877 railroad strike, the Homestead strike, the Pullman strike, anarchists, the eight-hour movement, the Haymarket Square riot, the National Civic Federation, Pinkertons, and so forth. An example of outside information beyond the time period that is permissible and adds to your essay is the following: "The AFL opposed organizing all the workers in an industry under one union. They were forced to face the issue again in the 1930s with the birth of the CIO. Debs was right after all, at least for some industries."

THIRD SAMPLE DBQ

Suggested writing time—45 minutes

Percent of Section II score—45

Directions: The following question requires you to construct a coherent essay that integrates your interpretation of Documents A–L *and* your knowledge of the period referred to in the question. High scores will be earned only by essays that both cite key pieces of evidence from the documents and draw on outside knowledge of the period.

On July 14, 1848, the following announcement appeared in the Seneca (NY) *County Courier*, calling the first pre-Civil War women's rights convention.

Woman's Rights Convention—A convention to discuss the social, civil and religious rights of woman will be held in the Wesleyan Chapel, Seneca Falls, New York, on Wednesday and Thursday, the 19th and 20th of July current; commencing at 10 a.m.
3. "What factors led to the women's rights movement in this era and what goals were women seeking?"

Document A

I now fully understood the practical difficulties most women had to contend with in the isolated household, and the impossibility of woman's best development if in contact, the chief part of her life, with servants and children.... Emerson says: "A healthy discontent is the first step to progress." The general discontent I felt with woman's portion as wife, mother, housekeeper, physician, and spiritual guide, the chaotic condition into which everything fell without her constant supervision, and the wearied, anxious look of the majority of women, impressed me with the strong feeling that some active measures should be taken to remedy the wrongs of society in general and of women in particular. My experiences at the World Anti-Slavery Convention, all I had read of the legal status of women, and the oppression I saw everywhere, together swept across my soul, intensified now by many personal experiences. It seemed as if all the elements had conspired to impel me to some onward step. I could not see what to do or where to begin—my only thought was a public meeting for protest and discussion.

Source: Elizabeth Cady Stanton, *Eighty Years and More*, 1898

Document B

Thus far woman has struggled through life with bandaged eyes, accepting the dogma of her weakness and inability to take care of herself not only physically but intellectually.... But there is now awakened in her a consciousness that she is defrauded of her legiti-

mate Rights and that she never can fulfill her mission until she is placed in that position to which she feels herself called by the divinity within. Hitherto she has surrendered her person and her individuality to man, but she can no longer do this and not feel that she is outraging her nature and her God.... Woman by surrendering herself to the tutelage of man may in many cases live at her ease, but she will live the life of a slave, by asserting and claiming her natural Rights she assumes the prerogative which every free intelligence ought to assume, that she is the arbiter of her own destiny.... Self-reliance only can create true and exalted women....

Source: Sarah M. Grimké, essay, "Sisters of Charity" 1838

Document C

Beloved Sisters—We beg leave to call your attention to the importance of petitioning Congress, at its next session, for the abolition of slavery in the District of Columbia. It has been recommended that a single form of petition for females, should be circulated throughout the state, instead of using different forms in every town and country.... You will oblige us by giving to these petitions as rapid and as extensive a circulation as possible, and returning them with their signatures, to the Secretary of the Female A.S.S. for Muskingham County, as early as the 1st of October. We wish the signatures may be written in a fair legible hand, with their appropriate titles of Mrs. or Miss, that it may appear what proportion of them are adults. ...

Source: Maria A. Sturges, Corresponding Secretary of the Female A.S.S. for Muskingham Co., "Address to Females in the State of Ohio" 1836

Document D

It will scarcely be denied, I presume, that as a general rule, men do not desire the improvement of women. ... I have myself heard men, who knew for themselves the value of intellectual culture, say they cared very little for a wife who could not make a pudding, and smile with contempt at the ardent thirst for knowledge exhibited by some women.

But all this is miserable wit and worse philosophy. It exhibits that passion for the gratification of a pampered appetite, which is beneath those who claim to be so far above us, and may justly be placed on a par with the policy of the slaveholder, who says that men will be better slaves, if they are not permitted to learn to read....

Source: Sarah M. Grimké, essay, "Intellect of Woman" 1838

Document E

... all society was built on the theory that men, not women, earned money and that men alone supported the family.... But I do not believe that there was any community in which the souls of some women were not beating their wings in rebellion. For my own obscure self I can say that every fiber of my being rebelled, although silently, all the hours that I sat and sewed gloves for a miserable pittance which, as it was earned, could never be mine. I wanted to work, but I wanted to choose my task and I wanted to collect my wages. That was my form of rebellion against the life into which I was born.

Source: Charolette Woodward, a 19-year-old who worked at a nearbyglove factory explaining why she attended the Seneca Falls Convention

Document F

Teachers, Massachusetts Public Schools, 1837–1844

	1837 school year	1844 school year
Male Teachers	2370	2529
Female Teachers	3591	4581

Source: testimony by Mr. French, agent of the Boott Mills, before the Massachusetts state legislature, 1845

Document G

"Why, yes: I calculate 'tain't of much account to have a woman if she ain't of no use. I lived up hyur two year, and had to have another man's woman do all my washin and mendin and so on, and at last I got tired o' totin my plunder back and forth, and thought I might as well get a woman of my own. There's a heap of things beside these, that she'll do better than I can, I reckon; every man ought to have a woman to do his cookin and such like, 'kase it's easier for them than it is for us. They take to it kind o' naturally."

I could scarcely believe that there was no more human vein in the animal, and determined to sound him a little deeper.

"And had you no choice made among your acquaintances? Was there no one person of whom you thought more than another?" said I.

"Yas, there was a gal I used to know that was stouter and bigger than this one. I should a got her if I could, but she'd got married and gone off over the Mississippi, somewhar."

The cold-hearted fellow! It was a perfectly business matter with him.

"Did you select this one solely on account of her size?" said I.

"Why, pretty much," he replied; "I reckon women are some like horses and oxen, the biggest can do the most work, and that's what I want one for."

Source: Eliza Farnham, from "Conversation With a Newly-Wed Westerner," in her travel book, *Life in Prairie Land,* 1846

Document H

I was disappointed when I came to seek a profession worthy of an immortal being—every employment was closed to me, except those of the teacher, the seamstress, and the housekeeper. In education, in marriage, in religion, in everything, disappointment is the lot of woman. It shall be the business of my life to deepen this disappointment in every woman's heart until she bows down to it no longer. I wish that women, instead of being walking show-cases, instead of begging of their fathers and brothers the latest and gayest new bonnet, would ask of them their rights ... the same society that drives forth the young man, keeps woman at home—a dependent—working little cats on worsted, and little dogs on punctured paper; but if she goes heartily and bravely to give herself to some worthy purpose, she is out of her sphere and she loses caste. Women working in tailor-shops are paid one-third as much as men. Some one in Philadelphia has stated that women make fine shirts for twelve and a half cents apiece; that no woman can make more than nine a week, and the sum thus earned, after deducting rent, fuel, etc., leaves her just three and a half cents a day for bread.

Source: Lucy Stone, speech, National Women's Rights Convention, 1855

Document I

...it is very well known that thousands nay, millions of women in this country are condemned to most menial drudgery, such as men would scorn to engage in, and that for one-fourth wages; that thousands of women toil at avocations which public opinion pretends to assign to men. They plough, harrow, reap, dig, make hay, rake, bind grain, thrash, chop wood, milk, churn, do any thing that is hard work, physical labor, and who says any thing against it? But let one presume to use her mental powers—let her aspire to turn editor, public speaker, doctor, lawyer—take up any profession or avocation which is deemed honorable and requires talent, and O! bring Cologne, get a cambric kerchief and a feather fan, unloose his corsets and take off his cravat! What a fainting fit Mr. Propriety has taken!

The efficient remedy for this class of evils is education; an equal education! ... If you wish to maintain your proper position in society, to command the respect of your friends now, and husbands and children in future, you should read, read—think, study, try to be wise, to know your own places and keep them, your own duties and do them. You should try to understand every thing you see and hear; to act and judge for yourselves; to remember you have a soul of your own to account for;—a mind of your own to improve. When you once get these ideas fixed, and learn to act upon them, no man or set of men, no laws, customs, or combination of them can seriously oppress you. Ignorance, folly, and levity, are more or less essential to the character of a slave.

Source: Jane Swisshelm, *Letters to Country Girls*, 1853

Document J

Effect of Factory Labor on Females in Boott Mill, No. 2

(effect of work on health)

number where employed	number of females	average age	years employed	improved	as good	not as good
carding room	20	23	5	3	12	5
spinning room	47	28	4	14	29	4
dressing room	25	26	7	2	16	7
weaving room	111	22	3	10	62	39
	203			29	119	55

Source: Horace Mann, Eighth Annual Report of the Secretary of the Board of Education, 1844

Document K

Mr. Mandeville, Tax Collector: Sir—Enclosed I return my tax bill, without paying it. My reason for doing so, is, that women suffer taxation, and yet have no representation, which is not only unjust to one half the adult population, but is contrary to our theory of government. For years some women have been paying their taxes under protest, but still taxes are imposed, and representation is not granted. The only course now left of us is to refuse to pay the tax. We know well what the immediate result of this refusal must be.

But we believe that when the attention of men is called to the wide difference between their theory of government and its practice, in this particular, that they cannot fail to see the mistake they now make, by imposing taxes on women, while they refuse them the right of suffrage, and that the sense of justice which is in all good men, will lead them to correct it. Then we shall cheerfully pay our taxes—not till then.

Respectfully, Lucy Stone

Source: Lucy Stone, letter, 1858

Document L

...it was my privilege to celebrate May day by officiating at a wedding in a farm-house among the hills of West Brookfield, Massachusetts. The bridegroom (Henry B. Blackwell) was a man of tried worth, a leader in the Western Anti-Slavery Movement; and the bride (Lucy Stone) was one whose fair name is known throughout the nation; one whose rare intellectual qualities are excelled by the private beauty of her heart and life.

I never perform the marriage ceremony without a renewed sense of the iniquity of our present system of laws in respect to marriage; a system by which "man and wife are one, and that one is the husband." It was with my hearty concurrence, therefore, that the following protest was read and signed, as a part of the nuptial ceremony; and I send it to you, that others may be induced to do likewise.

Rev. Thomas Wentworth Higginson

While acknowledging our mutual affection by publicly assuming the relation of husband and wife, yet in justice to ourselves and great principle, we deem it a duty to declare that this act on our part implies no sanction of, nor promise of voluntary obedience to such of the present laws of marriage, as refuse to recognize the wife as an independent, rational being, while they confer upon the husband an injurious and unnatural superiority, investing him with legal powers which no honorable man would exercise, and which no man should possess. We protest especially against the laws which give to the husband:

1. The custody of the wife's person.

2. The exclusive control and guardianship of their children.

3. The sole ownership of her personal, and use of her real estate, unless previously settled upon her, or placed in the hands of trustees, as in the case of minors, lunatics, and idiots.

4. The absolute right to the product of her industry.

5. Also against laws which give to the widower so much larger and more permanent an interest in the property of his deceased wife, than they give to the widow in that of the deceased husband.

6. Finally, against the whole system by which "the legal existence of the wife is suspended during marriage," so that in most States, she neither has a legal part in the choice of her residence, nor can she make a will, nor sue or be sued in her own name, nor inherit property.

Source: newspaper, *Worcester Spy,* 1855

Among the factors or causes you could see in this DBQ are the following: (1) the separation of work and home due to industrialization and the accompanying consequences—isolation, rise of the middle class, work outside the home; (2) frustration at the inability to develop intellectually through education; (3) economic concerns limiting or opening careers (women's sphere and teaching), factory working conditions, lack of control over one's own wages, wage discrimination; (4) the influence as example and as activity of the antislavery movement; (5) the general reform atmosphere of this era, transcendentalism and the public school movement; and (6) concern over the contrast between the ideals and the reality of American society—second class status, suffrage, taxation, legal position, and marriage laws. A good answer to this DBQ would develop three to five factors as causes of the women's movement and show how the movement worked to accomplish these goals.

Outside information could come from the issues and events of the antislavery movement, other reforms and reformers, transcendentalism, economic changes and their impact, the "cult of true womanhood," other women as reformers—Lucretia Mott, Dorothea Dix, Margaret Fuller, the public education movement, and political events or issues referred to in the documents, such as the Compromise of 1850 outlawing the slave trade in Washington, DC (Document C). Remember, you must bring in outside information for the DBQ. You know more than you think you do, so stop, get control of yourself, and decide what potential outside information you could use and how you could best use it. Just use it!

The woman's-rights-movement DBQ asks a two-part question: What factors led to the movement and what goals were women seeking? As soon as you read the question you should try to organize your answer. The immediate approach that springs to mind is one paragraph on causes and one on goals, sandwiched between an introduction and a conclusion. The difficulty with this attack is that it assumes an unchanging set of factors and goals. In many movements in history the goals either change over the course of time or the goals acquire a different priority. This is why you need at least a minimum sense of chronology when writing a history essay. Were the factors all of equal weight? Were some more important than others? Did new ingredients appear as the movement gained strength? Were the goals consistent? Did they shift over a period of time?

In selecting your organizational scheme, it would be better to recognize that goals often come out of causes. Something happens to give commitment to the accomplishment of an objective. Therefore, a preferred approach would be to use three to five factors or causes to show what goals were pursued to accomplish these objectives. Arrange your factors in either descending or ascending order of importance (I prefer the first), and include the remaining factors somewhere in your essay. This will show that you are aware of the other factors, that you considered them, and that you relegated them to a minor significance.

Five Sample Multiple-Choice Tests

PART

3

PREVIEW

Chapter

Multiple-Choice Tests Overview

All of the following multiple-choice tests are designed to provide an experience similar to the actual Advanced Placement test, and follow the chronological and topical test specifications for the College Board Advanced Placement examination. The first chart gives the topical specifications for both the AP examination and for the five tests in this book, designated Test A, Test B, Test C, Test D, and Test E.

Topical Content Specifications for the Multiple-Choice Section of the AP Test

Content of Question	AP Test	Test A	Test B	Test C	Test D	Test E
Political History and Government	35%	36%	34%	35%	34%	35%
Social History	35%	34%	36%	33%	35%	34%
Diplomatic History	15%	15%	15%	15%	14%	15%
Economic History	10%	10%	10%	11%	11%	10%

The chronological specifications for the examination are broader than the unit divisions presented in this book. By combining this book's unit designations we approximate the examination's chronological specifications.

Chronological Content Specifications for the Multiple-Choice Section of the AP Test

Chronology	AP Test	Test A	Test B	Test C	Test D	Test E
1607–1789	15%	14%	17%	15%	16%	16%
1790–1914	45%	45%	44%	49%	50%	46%
1915–present	30%	31%	29%	29%	25%	30%
cross periods	10%	10%	10%	8%	9%	8%

The small imbalance is caused by the difference between the dating used for the examination and that used for the units in this book. The College Board Advanced Placement specifications define the colonial period as 1607 to 1789; this book defines it as 1607 to 1783. The College Board Advanced Placement's middle period is defined as 1789 to 1914; this book uses 1783 to 1920. The last College Board Advanced Placement period is 1915 to the present; this book uses 1920 to the present. The five practice examinations almost exactly parallel the Advanced Placement chronological specifications.

The topical content specifications come from two sources. The first is an old College Board publication which analyzed the content specifications for eight different College Board examinations. The second source, the College Board publication, *Advanced Placement Course Description: History,* gives the specifications as follows:

"Both the multiple-choice and the free-response sections cover the period from the first European explorations of the Americas to the present, although the majority of questions are on the nineteenth and twentieth centuries. In the multiple-choice section, approximately one-sixth of the questions deal with the period through 1789, one-half with the period from 1790–1914, and one third with the period 1915–present. Whereas the multiple-choice section may include a few questions on the period since 1970, neither the DBQ nor any of the four essay questions in Part B will deal exclusively with this period."

Reprinted with permission from *Advanced Placement Course Description: History,*
© 1998 by College Entrance Examination Board, New York.

The 1984, the 1988, and the 1996 U.S. History Advanced Placement examinations have been published. Reviewing these examinations is very useful, although the content specifications have changed since the 1984 and 1988 examinations. Review them to gain insight into the type of question you will face, but not for the range within each area of U.S. History. Only the 1996 examination reflects the one you will take in terms of the content range of the questions. As you can see from the chart below, the AP test now includes much more social history. My personal analysis of the topical and chronological content specifications for the three examinations is as follows:

Topical Content Specifications for the Multiple-Choice Section of the 1984, 1988, and 1996 AP Tests

Content of Question	1984 AP Test	1988 AP Test	1996 AP Test
Political History and Government	42%	42%	35%
Social History	13%	12%	34%
Diplomatic History	18%	19%	15%
Economic History	13%	15%	11%
Intellectual and Cultural History	14%	12%	5%

Chronological Content Specifications for the Multiple-Choice Section of the 1984, 1988, and 1996 AP Tests

Chronology	1984 AP Test	1988 AP Test	1996 AP Test
1607-1789	14%	15%	16%
1790-1916	48%	48%	48%
1917-present	30%	30%	31%
cross periods	8%	7%	5%

The most mysterious portion of the AP test is the multiple-choice section. The 80 multiple-choice questions are seen only by the students. This section is collected by the examination proctor prior to beginning the essays and the DBQ. All the multiple-choice tests are shipped back to Educational Testing Service. Every AP teacher or student would love to be able to see all of the multiple-choice questions given over a long period of time. As part of a research project my good friend and AP colleague Dr. Michael Henry of Bowie High School, Bowie, Maryland, was permitted to do exactly that. His review of 2,035 multiple-choice questions given between 1960 and 1984 provides for all of us a rare look at the AP examination.[1] His findings confirmed a long-held theory among veteran AP teachers. The best preparation for the examination is a good course in U.S. History. Sorry, gang, in some parts of life there simply are no shortcuts.

In 1997, Dr. Henry updated his research by analyzing two published AP examinations, 1988 and 1996. He checked to see if the trends and characteristics he identified continued. In his two word summary, "They did." The 1988 and 1996 examinations confirm what experienced AP teachers suspected—STUDY!

Dr. Michael Henry conducted his research to seek any shifts in emphasis among the types of questions or the categories of questions. He devised six different categories, which are as follows:

Primary document questions concerned reading passages from original sources such as diaries, letters, speeches, court cases, treaties, state and national laws, executive agreements, political party platforms and official government documents. Sources were direct quotations at the time the event occurred. They were not paraphrased or secondary accounts or interpretations. These questions featured documents as stimulus materials and were answered by reference to a written passage.

Historiographic questions concerned the history of history. They included passages from historians' works and their interpretations of history. These questions consisted of written passages and paraphrased materials that were interpretations rather than first-hand accounts of historical events or phenomena.

Symbolic representation questions concerned the interpretation of cartoons, graphs, and maps. Questions featured one of these three graphics and could not be answered independently of the specific cartoon, graph, or map.

Arts and humanities questions concerned American literature, architecture, painting and sculpturing. They sometimes referred to a written passage or a picture, but they clearly related to a literary or artistic work.

Social science questions did not include stimulus materials such as reading passages, graphs, cartoons, and maps. They were answered without reference to such data. They concerned concepts, facts and skills from economics, sociology, anthropology, and

---

[1] Michael S. Henry, "The Advanced Placement American History Examination How Has It Changed?" *The Social Studies,* July/August 1987, pp. 159–162.

psychology. They related to such areas as earning a living, taxation, financial issues, industrialization, social groups and social relations.

Traditional questions did not feature stimulus materials such as reading passages, maps, cartoons or graphs and were answered without reference to such data. They concerned historically-oriented political, diplomatic, and military issues.

Since he was permitted to see the old AP tests only under ETS supervision, only Dr. Henry applied this categorization scheme to the questions. Thus, the judgment as to which category to place a specific question was his, and his alone. Another researcher applying the same criteria might have come up with slightly different percentages for the categories. But, in all likelihood, a single researcher consistently applying the same criteria would accurately define and identify any long range trends. This is exactly what Dr. Henry was trying to do and his research sheds great light on the most mysterious part of the U.S. History AP examination—the multiple-choice questions. The following chart summarizes the long-range trends in the multiple-choice questions. Please note that the number of multiple-choice questions on the AP test has changed over the period since 1960.

Distribution of Multiple-Choice Questions by Five-Year Periods, 1960–1984, and for 1988 and 1996

Years	Total No. of Questions	Primary Documents	Historiography	Social Science	Arts and Humanities	Symbolic Representation	Traditional
1960–64	300	118(39.2%)	2(1.0%)	43(14.2%)	4(1.3%)	37(12.3%)	96(32.0%)
1965–69	375	130(34.6%)	1(0.5%)	62(16.5%)	10(2.6%)	55(14.6%)	117(31.2%)
1970–74	375	107(28.6%)	17(4.5%)	59(15.8%)	14(3.7%)	53(14.1%)	125(33.3%)
1975–79	485	108(22.3%)	15(3.1%)	121(24.9%)	25(5.2%)	32(6.6%)	184(37.9%)
1980–84	500	65(13.0%)	8(1.6%)	137(27.4%)	39(7.8%)	39(7.8%)	212(42.4%)
1988–96	180	4(2.3%)	0(0.0%)	60(33.3%)	10(5.6%)	6(3.3%)	100(55.5%)

My summary of Dr. Henry's findings is as follows:

1. As you would expect in an introductory course, historiography is not that important. I have always felt that only four historiographic items must be in the college survey or secondary advanced placement course: Charles A. Beard's *An Economic Interpretation of the Constitution;* the phrase, "the Critical Period"; Frederick Jackson Turner's theories; and the two schools of historiography (but not necessarily the historians) of the interpretations of Reconstruction following the Civil War.

2. The decrease in primary document questions seems to parallel the introduction of the document-based question in 1973. Thus, the real percentage of document questions remained relatively stable over the 1960–1996 period.

3. The increased use of social science questions reflects the rise of two areas of textbook interest not present in 1960, women and minorities. And, in addition, the 1960s and 1970s saw an increase in interest within the history profession in economics, psychology, sociology, urbanization, etc.; in short, in areas influenced by social science concepts. Any good advanced placement textbook now contains sufficient social history to adequately prepare students for this type of question.

4. The increase in the proportion of arts and the humanities questions reflects the influence of American Studies and the emphasis on more interdisciplinary approaches in U.S. history.

5. There are no "fads" or "hot" topics. This is a traditional examination. Don't try to outguess the test developers. Don't say to yourself, "Immigration is a hot political topic this year. I'll bet there will be 15–20 multiple-choice questions on immigration!" You're in for a shock. Please note the increasing emphasis on traditional questions over the whole period, 1960–1996. In the earlier years there were more essay questions and fewer multiple-choice. When the number of multiple-choice questions expanded, the test developers tended to put more traditional questions into the test.

6. After reflecting on his updated review of 2,215 multiple-choice questions, Dr. Henry concluded that the advanced placement test always adhered "to the factual-oriented items that examined students' understanding of historical events, personalities, dates, and specific phenomenon. . . ." Study U.S. history; that's what you will be tested on!!! There are no gimmicks. You have reached the point in your life where your academic potential or raw ability no longer matters. One doesn't take an AP examination on one's ability to figure out the correct answer. It means more to know the correct answer. That only comes from study, and lots of it.

The five complete multiple-choice tests in this book fall well within the guidelines concerning the number of negative questions; that is, questions that use *except, incorrect, but, least, or not*. No more than twenty-five percent of the Advanced Placement examination multiple-choice questions are negative questions. Approximately twenty-two percent of the multiple-choice questions in this book are negative questions. When you encounter a negative question it may help if you reword the question in your mind. If it asks "Which of the following is not," say to yourself, "four of these are." Then identify the four that are true. This turns the question into the more frequently encountered positive wording.

The following breakdown of the five practice tests is provided to permit you to do the multiple-choice questions chronologically. As you study U.S. history in your course, you can use the unit questions for review. At the end of the year, in preparation for the Advanced Placement examination, you may take these multiple-choice tests by units or all at once to duplicate the coming experience. For example, you may want to do all the colonial questions together. Or you may feel that you especially need review in one particular period.

Unit One, 1607–1763

Test A:	1, 8, 11, 33, 43, 47, 52, 56, 74
Test B:	37, 43, 45, 46, 53, 58, 66, 80
Test C:	3, 8, 9, 43, 44, 70, 80
Test D:	20, 43, 46, 56, 60, 64
Test E:	1, 17, 29, 45, 54, 78

Unit Two, 1763–1783

Test A:	50, 64
Test B:	15, 23, 32, 61
Test C:	3, 12, 23, 37, 44, 56
Test D:	2, 6, 8, 37
Test E:	26, 51, 58, 61, 69

Constitution

Test A: 20, 62, 72
Test B: 8, 42, 78
Test C: 64
Test D: 3, 14
Test E: 8, 49

Unit Three, 1783–1800

Test A: 16, 18, 27, 32, 40, 67, 72
Test B: 17, 29, 31, 42
Test C: 1, 12, 16, 30, 48, 50, 57, 76
Test D: 2, 4, 26, 40, 48, 62, 74, 75
Test E: 8, 13, 20, 24, 26, 30, 61

Unit Four, 1800–1840

Test A: 12, 17, 48, 69, 77
Test B: 1, 22, 25, 41, 44, 62, 71, 78
Test C: 1, 5, 14, 18, 25, 26, 39, 42, 61
Test D: 17, 29, 33, 35, 38, 41, 57, 59, 65, 70, 76
Test E: 4, 5, 14, 32, 34, 39, 43, 53, 68, 74, 76

Unit Five, 1840–1877

Test A: 3, 5, 9, 26, 28, 35, 44, 53, 68, 78
Test B: 4, 5, 28, 36, 48, 54, 65, 69, 73, 77
Test C: 4, 6, 22, 29, 34, 41, 46, 72
Test D: 3, 11, 12, 21, 27, 35, 49, 50, 51, 66, 70, 72, 76
Test E: 3, 6, 11, 14, 19, 21, 41, 50, 60, 75

Unit Six, 1865–1900

Test A: 10, 21, 34, 41, 57, 59, 63, 65
Test B: 7, 8, 18, 27, 35, 38, 39, 52, 55, 64, 79
Test C: 2, 7, 17, 19, 20, 31, 36, 45, 52, 58, 63, 65, 68, 71, 78, 79
Test D: 7, 16, 23, 25, 30, 42, 44, 53, 58, 69, 71
Test E: 12, 15, 16, 23, 33, 35, 44, 52, 71, 77

Unit Seven, 1900–1920

Test A: 6, 13, 38, 42, 55, 60, 70, 76
Test B: 9, 13, 50, 55, 57, 68, 75
Test C: 19, 31, 47, 54, 65, 68, 74, 79
Test D: 1, 9, 10, 18, 19, 47, 53, 68, 73, 77
Test E: 7, 25, 28, 47, 67

Unit Eight, 1920–1940

Test A: 4, 14, 24, 36, 39, 75
Test B: 6, 10, 12, 30, 31, 33, 40, 59, 63, 67
Test C: 10, 21, 27, 28, 32, 59, 60
Test D: 13, 28, 39, 45, 80
Test E: 2, 10, 18, 31, 36, 38, 57, 59, 62, 65, 80

Unit Nine, 1940–1960

Test A: 22, 23, 37, 45, 46, 49, 51, 54, 66, 80
Test B: 3, 10, 20, 26, 60, 68
Test C: 33, 38, 49, 55, 66, 73, 75, 77
Test D: 5, 36, 52, 55, 63, 78
Test E: 37, 40, 42, 48, 56, 63, 70, 73, 79

Unit Ten, 1960–1990

Test A: 2, 19, 31, 71
Test B: 11, 16, 19, 24, 34, 39, 49, 70, 74, 76
Test C: 13, 15, 35, 40, 51, 53, 55, 62, 64, 66
Test D: 15, 22, 31, 34, 36, 54, 61, 67
Test E: 27, 37, 64, 70, 72

Cross Periods

Test A: 7, 15, 25, 29, 30, 58, 61, 73, 79
Test B: 2, 10, 14, 19, 21, 24, 31, 39, 47, 51, 56, 68
Test C: 4, 11, 24, 44, 55, 60, 66, 67, 69
Test D: 24, 32, 36, 48, 79
Test E: 9, 22, 37, 46, 55, 66

The four hundred multiple-choice questions in this book were designed to supplement College Board publications that your teacher can order. The College Board "Acorn" book entitled *Advanced Placement Course Description, History* has thirty-five sample multiple-choice questions. Your advanced placement teacher can also obtain a copy of the entire 1988 and 1996 Advanced Placement U.S. History examinations, which contain the one hundred multiple-choice questions given on the 1988 AP examination and the eighty multiple-choice questions given on the 1996 AP examination. Additional materials are available from College Board. *A Student Guide to the AP U.S. History Course and Examination* answers many questions about the AP program, gives sample essays and multiple-choice questions, and explains the grading of the examination. Each year your teacher can obtain the previous year's *AP U.S. History: Free-Response Scoring Guide and Sample Student Answers,* which provides sample essays from the AP exam. Beginning in 1995 the College Board published *Doing the DBQ: Advanced Placement U.S. History, Teaching and Learning with the Document-Based Question.* This book has every DBQ ever given with comments from the authors, two colleagues who are very experienced AP teachers and graders, Luther Spoehr, the Lincoln School, Providence, Rhode Island, and Alan Fraker, Deerfield Academy, Massachusetts. They analyze both the DBQ documents and the student essays written in response to that particular DBQ, giving the pitfalls and challenges of every DBQ given. Finally, any AP teacher, new or experienced, will love the information presented in *Teacher's Guide to Advanced Placement Courses in United States History.* Written by my good friend Eric Rothschild, Scarsdale High School, Scarsdale, New York, this booklet contains sample syllabi from four very successful AP teachers and a college professor, simulation games, bibliographies, and suggestions for presenting and organizing the AP course. All these publications are available from Advanced Placement Program, P.O. Box 6670, Princeton, New Jersey, 08541-6670. There is a charge for all publications. Ask your AP teacher about new developments on the Internet regarding AP. College Board and ETS are using the Internet to expand contact with students and AP teachers. One program provides AP graders who can evaluate your essay and provide feedback, giving you a realistic assessment of the quality of your writing.

None of the subject matter in any College Board publication or the 1984, 1988, or 1996 AP examination is duplicated in this book. By combining the College Board resources and the four hundred multiple-choice questions in this book you can see over six hundred AP-type multiple-choice questions before you take the AP examination in May. It can only help! Explanations of all answers in this book appear at the end of each Sample Test.

Before you begin looking at the multiple-choice questions in this book I must caution you. These questions are designed to teach U.S. history as well as to test U.S. history. They are difficult; some are very difficult. If you take these five tests as a self-evaluation of how ready you are for the AP exam, please be aware that these tests are harder. They are designed to cover U.S. history as stipulated by College Board's AP test specifications. If you know and understand the topics and events and ideas referred to in these tests, you should be ready. On the actual AP exam you should get ten to twelve more correct out of the eighty multiple-choice questions.

SAMPLE TEST A
Answer Sheet

1 Ⓐ Ⓑ Ⓒ Ⓓ Ⓔ	21 Ⓐ Ⓑ Ⓒ Ⓓ Ⓔ	41 Ⓐ Ⓑ Ⓒ Ⓓ Ⓔ	61 Ⓐ Ⓑ Ⓒ Ⓓ Ⓔ
2 Ⓐ Ⓑ Ⓒ Ⓓ Ⓔ	22 Ⓐ Ⓑ Ⓒ Ⓓ Ⓔ	42 Ⓐ Ⓑ Ⓒ Ⓓ Ⓔ	62 Ⓐ Ⓑ Ⓒ Ⓓ Ⓔ
3 Ⓐ Ⓑ Ⓒ Ⓓ Ⓔ	23 Ⓐ Ⓑ Ⓒ Ⓓ Ⓔ	43 Ⓐ Ⓑ Ⓒ Ⓓ Ⓔ	63 Ⓐ Ⓑ Ⓒ Ⓓ Ⓔ
4 Ⓐ Ⓑ Ⓒ Ⓓ Ⓔ	24 Ⓐ Ⓑ Ⓒ Ⓓ Ⓔ	44 Ⓐ Ⓑ Ⓒ Ⓓ Ⓔ	64 Ⓐ Ⓑ Ⓒ Ⓓ Ⓔ
5 Ⓐ Ⓑ Ⓒ Ⓓ Ⓔ	25 Ⓐ Ⓑ Ⓒ Ⓓ Ⓔ	45 Ⓐ Ⓑ Ⓒ Ⓓ Ⓔ	65 Ⓐ Ⓑ Ⓒ Ⓓ Ⓔ
6 Ⓐ Ⓑ Ⓒ Ⓓ Ⓔ	26 Ⓐ Ⓑ Ⓒ Ⓓ Ⓔ	46 Ⓐ Ⓑ Ⓒ Ⓓ Ⓔ	66 Ⓐ Ⓑ Ⓒ Ⓓ Ⓔ
7 Ⓐ Ⓑ Ⓒ Ⓓ Ⓔ	27 Ⓐ Ⓑ Ⓒ Ⓓ Ⓔ	47 Ⓐ Ⓑ Ⓒ Ⓓ Ⓔ	67 Ⓐ Ⓑ Ⓒ Ⓓ Ⓔ
8 Ⓐ Ⓑ Ⓒ Ⓓ Ⓔ	28 Ⓐ Ⓑ Ⓒ Ⓓ Ⓔ	48 Ⓐ Ⓑ Ⓒ Ⓓ Ⓔ	68 Ⓐ Ⓑ Ⓒ Ⓓ Ⓔ
9 Ⓐ Ⓑ Ⓒ Ⓓ Ⓔ	29 Ⓐ Ⓑ Ⓒ Ⓓ Ⓔ	49 Ⓐ Ⓑ Ⓒ Ⓓ Ⓔ	69 Ⓐ Ⓑ Ⓒ Ⓓ Ⓔ
10 Ⓐ Ⓑ Ⓒ Ⓓ Ⓔ	30 Ⓐ Ⓑ Ⓒ Ⓓ Ⓔ	50 Ⓐ Ⓑ Ⓒ Ⓓ Ⓔ	70 Ⓐ Ⓑ Ⓒ Ⓓ Ⓔ
11 Ⓐ Ⓑ Ⓒ Ⓓ Ⓔ	31 Ⓐ Ⓑ Ⓒ Ⓓ Ⓔ	51 Ⓐ Ⓑ Ⓒ Ⓓ Ⓔ	71 Ⓐ Ⓑ Ⓒ Ⓓ Ⓔ
12 Ⓐ Ⓑ Ⓒ Ⓓ Ⓔ	32 Ⓐ Ⓑ Ⓒ Ⓓ Ⓔ	52 Ⓐ Ⓑ Ⓒ Ⓓ Ⓔ	72 Ⓐ Ⓑ Ⓒ Ⓓ Ⓔ
13 Ⓐ Ⓑ Ⓒ Ⓓ Ⓔ	33 Ⓐ Ⓑ Ⓒ Ⓓ Ⓔ	53 Ⓐ Ⓑ Ⓒ Ⓓ Ⓔ	73 Ⓐ Ⓑ Ⓒ Ⓓ Ⓔ
14 Ⓐ Ⓑ Ⓒ Ⓓ Ⓔ	34 Ⓐ Ⓑ Ⓒ Ⓓ Ⓔ	54 Ⓐ Ⓑ Ⓒ Ⓓ Ⓔ	74 Ⓐ Ⓑ Ⓒ Ⓓ Ⓔ
15 Ⓐ Ⓑ Ⓒ Ⓓ Ⓔ	35 Ⓐ Ⓑ Ⓒ Ⓓ Ⓔ	55 Ⓐ Ⓑ Ⓒ Ⓓ Ⓔ	75 Ⓐ Ⓑ Ⓒ Ⓓ Ⓔ
16 Ⓐ Ⓑ Ⓒ Ⓓ Ⓔ	36 Ⓐ Ⓑ Ⓒ Ⓓ Ⓔ	56 Ⓐ Ⓑ Ⓒ Ⓓ Ⓔ	76 Ⓐ Ⓑ Ⓒ Ⓓ Ⓔ
17 Ⓐ Ⓑ Ⓒ Ⓓ Ⓔ	37 Ⓐ Ⓑ Ⓒ Ⓓ Ⓔ	57 Ⓐ Ⓑ Ⓒ Ⓓ Ⓔ	77 Ⓐ Ⓑ Ⓒ Ⓓ Ⓔ
18 Ⓐ Ⓑ Ⓒ Ⓓ Ⓔ	38 Ⓐ Ⓑ Ⓒ Ⓓ Ⓔ	58 Ⓐ Ⓑ Ⓒ Ⓓ Ⓔ	78 Ⓐ Ⓑ Ⓒ Ⓓ Ⓔ
19 Ⓐ Ⓑ Ⓒ Ⓓ Ⓔ	39 Ⓐ Ⓑ Ⓒ Ⓓ Ⓔ	59 Ⓐ Ⓑ Ⓒ Ⓓ Ⓔ	79 Ⓐ Ⓑ Ⓒ Ⓓ Ⓔ
20 Ⓐ Ⓑ Ⓒ Ⓓ Ⓔ	40 Ⓐ Ⓑ Ⓒ Ⓓ Ⓔ	60 Ⓐ Ⓑ Ⓒ Ⓓ Ⓔ	80 Ⓐ Ⓑ Ⓒ Ⓓ Ⓔ

SAMPLE TEST B
Answer Sheet

1 Ⓐ Ⓑ Ⓒ Ⓓ Ⓔ	21 Ⓐ Ⓑ Ⓒ Ⓓ Ⓔ	41 Ⓐ Ⓑ Ⓒ Ⓓ Ⓔ	61 Ⓐ Ⓑ Ⓒ Ⓓ Ⓔ
2 Ⓐ Ⓑ Ⓒ Ⓓ Ⓔ	22 Ⓐ Ⓑ Ⓒ Ⓓ Ⓔ	42 Ⓐ Ⓑ Ⓒ Ⓓ Ⓔ	62 Ⓐ Ⓑ Ⓒ Ⓓ Ⓔ
3 Ⓐ Ⓑ Ⓒ Ⓓ Ⓔ	23 Ⓐ Ⓑ Ⓒ Ⓓ Ⓔ	43 Ⓐ Ⓑ Ⓒ Ⓓ Ⓔ	63 Ⓐ Ⓑ Ⓒ Ⓓ Ⓔ
4 Ⓐ Ⓑ Ⓒ Ⓓ Ⓔ	24 Ⓐ Ⓑ Ⓒ Ⓓ Ⓔ	44 Ⓐ Ⓑ Ⓒ Ⓓ Ⓔ	64 Ⓐ Ⓑ Ⓒ Ⓓ Ⓔ
5 Ⓐ Ⓑ Ⓒ Ⓓ Ⓔ	25 Ⓐ Ⓑ Ⓒ Ⓓ Ⓔ	45 Ⓐ Ⓑ Ⓒ Ⓓ Ⓔ	65 Ⓐ Ⓑ Ⓒ Ⓓ Ⓔ
6 Ⓐ Ⓑ Ⓒ Ⓓ Ⓔ	26 Ⓐ Ⓑ Ⓒ Ⓓ Ⓔ	46 Ⓐ Ⓑ Ⓒ Ⓓ Ⓔ	66 Ⓐ Ⓑ Ⓒ Ⓓ Ⓔ
7 Ⓐ Ⓑ Ⓒ Ⓓ Ⓔ	27 Ⓐ Ⓑ Ⓒ Ⓓ Ⓔ	47 Ⓐ Ⓑ Ⓒ Ⓓ Ⓔ	67 Ⓐ Ⓑ Ⓒ Ⓓ Ⓔ
8 Ⓐ Ⓑ Ⓒ Ⓓ Ⓔ	28 Ⓐ Ⓑ Ⓒ Ⓓ Ⓔ	48 Ⓐ Ⓑ Ⓒ Ⓓ Ⓔ	68 Ⓐ Ⓑ Ⓒ Ⓓ Ⓔ
9 Ⓐ Ⓑ Ⓒ Ⓓ Ⓔ	29 Ⓐ Ⓑ Ⓒ Ⓓ Ⓔ	49 Ⓐ Ⓑ Ⓒ Ⓓ Ⓔ	69 Ⓐ Ⓑ Ⓒ Ⓓ Ⓔ
10 Ⓐ Ⓑ Ⓒ Ⓓ Ⓔ	30 Ⓐ Ⓑ Ⓒ Ⓓ Ⓔ	50 Ⓐ Ⓑ Ⓒ Ⓓ Ⓔ	70 Ⓐ Ⓑ Ⓒ Ⓓ Ⓔ
11 Ⓐ Ⓑ Ⓒ Ⓓ Ⓔ	31 Ⓐ Ⓑ Ⓒ Ⓓ Ⓔ	51 Ⓐ Ⓑ Ⓒ Ⓓ Ⓔ	71 Ⓐ Ⓑ Ⓒ Ⓓ Ⓔ
12 Ⓐ Ⓑ Ⓒ Ⓓ Ⓔ	32 Ⓐ Ⓑ Ⓒ Ⓓ Ⓔ	52 Ⓐ Ⓑ Ⓒ Ⓓ Ⓔ	72 Ⓐ Ⓑ Ⓒ Ⓓ Ⓔ
13 Ⓐ Ⓑ Ⓒ Ⓓ Ⓔ	33 Ⓐ Ⓑ Ⓒ Ⓓ Ⓔ	53 Ⓐ Ⓑ Ⓒ Ⓓ Ⓔ	73 Ⓐ Ⓑ Ⓒ Ⓓ Ⓔ
14 Ⓐ Ⓑ Ⓒ Ⓓ Ⓔ	34 Ⓐ Ⓑ Ⓒ Ⓓ Ⓔ	54 Ⓐ Ⓑ Ⓒ Ⓓ Ⓔ	74 Ⓐ Ⓑ Ⓒ Ⓓ Ⓔ
15 Ⓐ Ⓑ Ⓒ Ⓓ Ⓔ	35 Ⓐ Ⓑ Ⓒ Ⓓ Ⓔ	55 Ⓐ Ⓑ Ⓒ Ⓓ Ⓔ	75 Ⓐ Ⓑ Ⓒ Ⓓ Ⓔ
16 Ⓐ Ⓑ Ⓒ Ⓓ Ⓔ	36 Ⓐ Ⓑ Ⓒ Ⓓ Ⓔ	56 Ⓐ Ⓑ Ⓒ Ⓓ Ⓔ	76 Ⓐ Ⓑ Ⓒ Ⓓ Ⓔ
17 Ⓐ Ⓑ Ⓒ Ⓓ Ⓔ	37 Ⓐ Ⓑ Ⓒ Ⓓ Ⓔ	57 Ⓐ Ⓑ Ⓒ Ⓓ Ⓔ	77 Ⓐ Ⓑ Ⓒ Ⓓ Ⓔ
18 Ⓐ Ⓑ Ⓒ Ⓓ Ⓔ	38 Ⓐ Ⓑ Ⓒ Ⓓ Ⓔ	58 Ⓐ Ⓑ Ⓒ Ⓓ Ⓔ	78 Ⓐ Ⓑ Ⓒ Ⓓ Ⓔ
19 Ⓐ Ⓑ Ⓒ Ⓓ Ⓔ	39 Ⓐ Ⓑ Ⓒ Ⓓ Ⓔ	59 Ⓐ Ⓑ Ⓒ Ⓓ Ⓔ	79 Ⓐ Ⓑ Ⓒ Ⓓ Ⓔ
20 Ⓐ Ⓑ Ⓒ Ⓓ Ⓔ	40 Ⓐ Ⓑ Ⓒ Ⓓ Ⓔ	60 Ⓐ Ⓑ Ⓒ Ⓓ Ⓔ	80 Ⓐ Ⓑ Ⓒ Ⓓ Ⓔ

SAMPLE TEST C
Answer Sheet

1 Ⓐ Ⓑ Ⓒ Ⓓ Ⓔ   21 Ⓐ Ⓑ Ⓒ Ⓓ Ⓔ   41 Ⓐ Ⓑ Ⓒ Ⓓ Ⓔ   61 Ⓐ Ⓑ Ⓒ Ⓓ Ⓔ

2 Ⓐ Ⓑ Ⓒ Ⓓ Ⓔ   22 Ⓐ Ⓑ Ⓒ Ⓓ Ⓔ   42 Ⓐ Ⓑ Ⓒ Ⓓ Ⓔ   62 Ⓐ Ⓑ Ⓒ Ⓓ Ⓔ

3 Ⓐ Ⓑ Ⓒ Ⓓ Ⓔ   23 Ⓐ Ⓑ Ⓒ Ⓓ Ⓔ   43 Ⓐ Ⓑ Ⓒ Ⓓ Ⓔ   63 Ⓐ Ⓑ Ⓒ Ⓓ Ⓔ

4 Ⓐ Ⓑ Ⓒ Ⓓ Ⓔ   24 Ⓐ Ⓑ Ⓒ Ⓓ Ⓔ   44 Ⓐ Ⓑ Ⓒ Ⓓ Ⓔ   64 Ⓐ Ⓑ Ⓒ Ⓓ Ⓔ

5 Ⓐ Ⓑ Ⓒ Ⓓ Ⓔ   25 Ⓐ Ⓑ Ⓒ Ⓓ Ⓔ   45 Ⓐ Ⓑ Ⓒ Ⓓ Ⓔ   65 Ⓐ Ⓑ Ⓒ Ⓓ Ⓔ

6 Ⓐ Ⓑ Ⓒ Ⓓ Ⓔ   26 Ⓐ Ⓑ Ⓒ Ⓓ Ⓔ   46 Ⓐ Ⓑ Ⓒ Ⓓ Ⓔ   66 Ⓐ Ⓑ Ⓒ Ⓓ Ⓔ

7 Ⓐ Ⓑ Ⓒ Ⓓ Ⓔ   27 Ⓐ Ⓑ Ⓒ Ⓓ Ⓔ   47 Ⓐ Ⓑ Ⓒ Ⓓ Ⓔ   67 Ⓐ Ⓑ Ⓒ Ⓓ Ⓔ

8 Ⓐ Ⓑ Ⓒ Ⓓ Ⓔ   28 Ⓐ Ⓑ Ⓒ Ⓓ Ⓔ   48 Ⓐ Ⓑ Ⓒ Ⓓ Ⓔ   68 Ⓐ Ⓑ Ⓒ Ⓓ Ⓔ

9 Ⓐ Ⓑ Ⓒ Ⓓ Ⓔ   29 Ⓐ Ⓑ Ⓒ Ⓓ Ⓔ   49 Ⓐ Ⓑ Ⓒ Ⓓ Ⓔ   69 Ⓐ Ⓑ Ⓒ Ⓓ Ⓔ

10 Ⓐ Ⓑ Ⓒ Ⓓ Ⓔ   30 Ⓐ Ⓑ Ⓒ Ⓓ Ⓔ   50 Ⓐ Ⓑ Ⓒ Ⓓ Ⓔ   70 Ⓐ Ⓑ Ⓒ Ⓓ Ⓔ

11 Ⓐ Ⓑ Ⓒ Ⓓ Ⓔ   31 Ⓐ Ⓑ Ⓒ Ⓓ Ⓔ   51 Ⓐ Ⓑ Ⓒ Ⓓ Ⓔ   71 Ⓐ Ⓑ Ⓒ Ⓓ Ⓔ

12 Ⓐ Ⓑ Ⓒ Ⓓ Ⓔ   32 Ⓐ Ⓑ Ⓒ Ⓓ Ⓔ   52 Ⓐ Ⓑ Ⓒ Ⓓ Ⓔ   72 Ⓐ Ⓑ Ⓒ Ⓓ Ⓔ

13 Ⓐ Ⓑ Ⓒ Ⓓ Ⓔ   33 Ⓐ Ⓑ Ⓒ Ⓓ Ⓔ   53 Ⓐ Ⓑ Ⓒ Ⓓ Ⓔ   73 Ⓐ Ⓑ Ⓒ Ⓓ Ⓔ

14 Ⓐ Ⓑ Ⓒ Ⓓ Ⓔ   34 Ⓐ Ⓑ Ⓒ Ⓓ Ⓔ   54 Ⓐ Ⓑ Ⓒ Ⓓ Ⓔ   74 Ⓐ Ⓑ Ⓒ Ⓓ Ⓔ

15 Ⓐ Ⓑ Ⓒ Ⓓ Ⓔ   35 Ⓐ Ⓑ Ⓒ Ⓓ Ⓔ   55 Ⓐ Ⓑ Ⓒ Ⓓ Ⓔ   75 Ⓐ Ⓑ Ⓒ Ⓓ Ⓔ

16 Ⓐ Ⓑ Ⓒ Ⓓ Ⓔ   36 Ⓐ Ⓑ Ⓒ Ⓓ Ⓔ   56 Ⓐ Ⓑ Ⓒ Ⓓ Ⓔ   76 Ⓐ Ⓑ Ⓒ Ⓓ Ⓔ

17 Ⓐ Ⓑ Ⓒ Ⓓ Ⓔ   37 Ⓐ Ⓑ Ⓒ Ⓓ Ⓔ   57 Ⓐ Ⓑ Ⓒ Ⓓ Ⓔ   77 Ⓐ Ⓑ Ⓒ Ⓓ Ⓔ

18 Ⓐ Ⓑ Ⓒ Ⓓ Ⓔ   38 Ⓐ Ⓑ Ⓒ Ⓓ Ⓔ   58 Ⓐ Ⓑ Ⓒ Ⓓ Ⓔ   78 Ⓐ Ⓑ Ⓒ Ⓓ Ⓔ

19 Ⓐ Ⓑ Ⓒ Ⓓ Ⓔ   39 Ⓐ Ⓑ Ⓒ Ⓓ Ⓔ   59 Ⓐ Ⓑ Ⓒ Ⓓ Ⓔ   79 Ⓐ Ⓑ Ⓒ Ⓓ Ⓔ

20 Ⓐ Ⓑ Ⓒ Ⓓ Ⓔ   40 Ⓐ Ⓑ Ⓒ Ⓓ Ⓔ   60 Ⓐ Ⓑ Ⓒ Ⓓ Ⓔ   80 Ⓐ Ⓑ Ⓒ Ⓓ Ⓔ

SAMPLE TEST D
Answer Sheet

1 Ⓐ Ⓑ Ⓒ Ⓓ Ⓔ	21 Ⓐ Ⓑ Ⓒ Ⓓ Ⓔ	41 Ⓐ Ⓑ Ⓒ Ⓓ Ⓔ	61 Ⓐ Ⓑ Ⓒ Ⓓ Ⓔ
2 Ⓐ Ⓑ Ⓒ Ⓓ Ⓔ	22 Ⓐ Ⓑ Ⓒ Ⓓ Ⓔ	42 Ⓐ Ⓑ Ⓒ Ⓓ Ⓔ	62 Ⓐ Ⓑ Ⓒ Ⓓ Ⓔ
3 Ⓐ Ⓑ Ⓒ Ⓓ Ⓔ	23 Ⓐ Ⓑ Ⓒ Ⓓ Ⓔ	43 Ⓐ Ⓑ Ⓒ Ⓓ Ⓔ	63 Ⓐ Ⓑ Ⓒ Ⓓ Ⓔ
4 Ⓐ Ⓑ Ⓒ Ⓓ Ⓔ	24 Ⓐ Ⓑ Ⓒ Ⓓ Ⓔ	44 Ⓐ Ⓑ Ⓒ Ⓓ Ⓔ	64 Ⓐ Ⓑ Ⓒ Ⓓ Ⓔ
5 Ⓐ Ⓑ Ⓒ Ⓓ Ⓔ	25 Ⓐ Ⓑ Ⓒ Ⓓ Ⓔ	45 Ⓐ Ⓑ Ⓒ Ⓓ Ⓔ	65 Ⓐ Ⓑ Ⓒ Ⓓ Ⓔ
6 Ⓐ Ⓑ Ⓒ Ⓓ Ⓔ	26 Ⓐ Ⓑ Ⓒ Ⓓ Ⓔ	46 Ⓐ Ⓑ Ⓒ Ⓓ Ⓔ	66 Ⓐ Ⓑ Ⓒ Ⓓ Ⓔ
7 Ⓐ Ⓑ Ⓒ Ⓓ Ⓔ	27 Ⓐ Ⓑ Ⓒ Ⓓ Ⓔ	47 Ⓐ Ⓑ Ⓒ Ⓓ Ⓔ	67 Ⓐ Ⓑ Ⓒ Ⓓ Ⓔ
8 Ⓐ Ⓑ Ⓒ Ⓓ Ⓔ	28 Ⓐ Ⓑ Ⓒ Ⓓ Ⓔ	48 Ⓐ Ⓑ Ⓒ Ⓓ Ⓔ	68 Ⓐ Ⓑ Ⓒ Ⓓ Ⓔ
9 Ⓐ Ⓑ Ⓒ Ⓓ Ⓔ	29 Ⓐ Ⓑ Ⓒ Ⓓ Ⓔ	49 Ⓐ Ⓑ Ⓒ Ⓓ Ⓔ	69 Ⓐ Ⓑ Ⓒ Ⓓ Ⓔ
10 Ⓐ Ⓑ Ⓒ Ⓓ Ⓔ	30 Ⓐ Ⓑ Ⓒ Ⓓ Ⓔ	50 Ⓐ Ⓑ Ⓒ Ⓓ Ⓔ	70 Ⓐ Ⓑ Ⓒ Ⓓ Ⓔ
11 Ⓐ Ⓑ Ⓒ Ⓓ Ⓔ	31 Ⓐ Ⓑ Ⓒ Ⓓ Ⓔ	51 Ⓐ Ⓑ Ⓒ Ⓓ Ⓔ	71 Ⓐ Ⓑ Ⓒ Ⓓ Ⓔ
12 Ⓐ Ⓑ Ⓒ Ⓓ Ⓔ	32 Ⓐ Ⓑ Ⓒ Ⓓ Ⓔ	52 Ⓐ Ⓑ Ⓒ Ⓓ Ⓔ	72 Ⓐ Ⓑ Ⓒ Ⓓ Ⓔ
13 Ⓐ Ⓑ Ⓒ Ⓓ Ⓔ	33 Ⓐ Ⓑ Ⓒ Ⓓ Ⓔ	53 Ⓐ Ⓑ Ⓒ Ⓓ Ⓔ	73 Ⓐ Ⓑ Ⓒ Ⓓ Ⓔ
14 Ⓐ Ⓑ Ⓒ Ⓓ Ⓔ	34 Ⓐ Ⓑ Ⓒ Ⓓ Ⓔ	54 Ⓐ Ⓑ Ⓒ Ⓓ Ⓔ	74 Ⓐ Ⓑ Ⓒ Ⓓ Ⓔ
15 Ⓐ Ⓑ Ⓒ Ⓓ Ⓔ	35 Ⓐ Ⓑ Ⓒ Ⓓ Ⓔ	55 Ⓐ Ⓑ Ⓒ Ⓓ Ⓔ	75 Ⓐ Ⓑ Ⓒ Ⓓ Ⓔ
16 Ⓐ Ⓑ Ⓒ Ⓓ Ⓔ	36 Ⓐ Ⓑ Ⓒ Ⓓ Ⓔ	56 Ⓐ Ⓑ Ⓒ Ⓓ Ⓔ	76 Ⓐ Ⓑ Ⓒ Ⓓ Ⓔ
17 Ⓐ Ⓑ Ⓒ Ⓓ Ⓔ	37 Ⓐ Ⓑ Ⓒ Ⓓ Ⓔ	57 Ⓐ Ⓑ Ⓒ Ⓓ Ⓔ	77 Ⓐ Ⓑ Ⓒ Ⓓ Ⓔ
18 Ⓐ Ⓑ Ⓒ Ⓓ Ⓔ	38 Ⓐ Ⓑ Ⓒ Ⓓ Ⓔ	58 Ⓐ Ⓑ Ⓒ Ⓓ Ⓔ	78 Ⓐ Ⓑ Ⓒ Ⓓ Ⓔ
19 Ⓐ Ⓑ Ⓒ Ⓓ Ⓔ	39 Ⓐ Ⓑ Ⓒ Ⓓ Ⓔ	59 Ⓐ Ⓑ Ⓒ Ⓓ Ⓔ	79 Ⓐ Ⓑ Ⓒ Ⓓ Ⓔ
20 Ⓐ Ⓑ Ⓒ Ⓓ Ⓔ	40 Ⓐ Ⓑ Ⓒ Ⓓ Ⓔ	60 Ⓐ Ⓑ Ⓒ Ⓓ Ⓔ	80 Ⓐ Ⓑ Ⓒ Ⓓ Ⓔ

SAMPLE TEST E
Answer Sheet

1 Ⓐ Ⓑ Ⓒ Ⓓ Ⓔ   21 Ⓐ Ⓑ Ⓒ Ⓓ Ⓔ   41 Ⓐ Ⓑ Ⓒ Ⓓ Ⓔ   61 Ⓐ Ⓑ Ⓒ Ⓓ Ⓔ
2 Ⓐ Ⓑ Ⓒ Ⓓ Ⓔ   22 Ⓐ Ⓑ Ⓒ Ⓓ Ⓔ   42 Ⓐ Ⓑ Ⓒ Ⓓ Ⓔ   62 Ⓐ Ⓑ Ⓒ Ⓓ Ⓔ
3 Ⓐ Ⓑ Ⓒ Ⓓ Ⓔ   23 Ⓐ Ⓑ Ⓒ Ⓓ Ⓔ   43 Ⓐ Ⓑ Ⓒ Ⓓ Ⓔ   63 Ⓐ Ⓑ Ⓒ Ⓓ Ⓔ
4 Ⓐ Ⓑ Ⓒ Ⓓ Ⓔ   24 Ⓐ Ⓑ Ⓒ Ⓓ Ⓔ   44 Ⓐ Ⓑ Ⓒ Ⓓ Ⓔ   64 Ⓐ Ⓑ Ⓒ Ⓓ Ⓔ
5 Ⓐ Ⓑ Ⓒ Ⓓ Ⓔ   25 Ⓐ Ⓑ Ⓒ Ⓓ Ⓔ   45 Ⓐ Ⓑ Ⓒ Ⓓ Ⓔ   65 Ⓐ Ⓑ Ⓒ Ⓓ Ⓔ
6 Ⓐ Ⓑ Ⓒ Ⓓ Ⓔ   26 Ⓐ Ⓑ Ⓒ Ⓓ Ⓔ   46 Ⓐ Ⓑ Ⓒ Ⓓ Ⓔ   66 Ⓐ Ⓑ Ⓒ Ⓓ Ⓔ
7 Ⓐ Ⓑ Ⓒ Ⓓ Ⓔ   27 Ⓐ Ⓑ Ⓒ Ⓓ Ⓔ   47 Ⓐ Ⓑ Ⓒ Ⓓ Ⓔ   67 Ⓐ Ⓑ Ⓒ Ⓓ Ⓔ
8 Ⓐ Ⓑ Ⓒ Ⓓ Ⓔ   28 Ⓐ Ⓑ Ⓒ Ⓓ Ⓔ   48 Ⓐ Ⓑ Ⓒ Ⓓ Ⓔ   68 Ⓐ Ⓑ Ⓒ Ⓓ Ⓔ
9 Ⓐ Ⓑ Ⓒ Ⓓ Ⓔ   29 Ⓐ Ⓑ Ⓒ Ⓓ Ⓔ   49 Ⓐ Ⓑ Ⓒ Ⓓ Ⓔ   69 Ⓐ Ⓑ Ⓒ Ⓓ Ⓔ
10 Ⓐ Ⓑ Ⓒ Ⓓ Ⓔ   30 Ⓐ Ⓑ Ⓒ Ⓓ Ⓔ   50 Ⓐ Ⓑ Ⓒ Ⓓ Ⓔ   70 Ⓐ Ⓑ Ⓒ Ⓓ Ⓔ
11 Ⓐ Ⓑ Ⓒ Ⓓ Ⓔ   31 Ⓐ Ⓑ Ⓒ Ⓓ Ⓔ   51 Ⓐ Ⓑ Ⓒ Ⓓ Ⓔ   71 Ⓐ Ⓑ Ⓒ Ⓓ Ⓔ
12 Ⓐ Ⓑ Ⓒ Ⓓ Ⓔ   32 Ⓐ Ⓑ Ⓒ Ⓓ Ⓔ   52 Ⓐ Ⓑ Ⓒ Ⓓ Ⓔ   72 Ⓐ Ⓑ Ⓒ Ⓓ Ⓔ
13 Ⓐ Ⓑ Ⓒ Ⓓ Ⓔ   33 Ⓐ Ⓑ Ⓒ Ⓓ Ⓔ   53 Ⓐ Ⓑ Ⓒ Ⓓ Ⓔ   73 Ⓐ Ⓑ Ⓒ Ⓓ Ⓔ
14 Ⓐ Ⓑ Ⓒ Ⓓ Ⓔ   34 Ⓐ Ⓑ Ⓒ Ⓓ Ⓔ   54 Ⓐ Ⓑ Ⓒ Ⓓ Ⓔ   74 Ⓐ Ⓑ Ⓒ Ⓓ Ⓔ
15 Ⓐ Ⓑ Ⓒ Ⓓ Ⓔ   35 Ⓐ Ⓑ Ⓒ Ⓓ Ⓔ   55 Ⓐ Ⓑ Ⓒ Ⓓ Ⓔ   75 Ⓐ Ⓑ Ⓒ Ⓓ Ⓔ
16 Ⓐ Ⓑ Ⓒ Ⓓ Ⓔ   36 Ⓐ Ⓑ Ⓒ Ⓓ Ⓔ   56 Ⓐ Ⓑ Ⓒ Ⓓ Ⓔ   76 Ⓐ Ⓑ Ⓒ Ⓓ Ⓔ
17 Ⓐ Ⓑ Ⓒ Ⓓ Ⓔ   37 Ⓐ Ⓑ Ⓒ Ⓓ Ⓔ   57 Ⓐ Ⓑ Ⓒ Ⓓ Ⓔ   77 Ⓐ Ⓑ Ⓒ Ⓓ Ⓔ
18 Ⓐ Ⓑ Ⓒ Ⓓ Ⓔ   38 Ⓐ Ⓑ Ⓒ Ⓓ Ⓔ   58 Ⓐ Ⓑ Ⓒ Ⓓ Ⓔ   78 Ⓐ Ⓑ Ⓒ Ⓓ Ⓔ
19 Ⓐ Ⓑ Ⓒ Ⓓ Ⓔ   39 Ⓐ Ⓑ Ⓒ Ⓓ Ⓔ   59 Ⓐ Ⓑ Ⓒ Ⓓ Ⓔ   79 Ⓐ Ⓑ Ⓒ Ⓓ Ⓔ
20 Ⓐ Ⓑ Ⓒ Ⓓ Ⓔ   40 Ⓐ Ⓑ Ⓒ Ⓓ Ⓔ   60 Ⓐ Ⓑ Ⓒ Ⓓ Ⓔ   80 Ⓐ Ⓑ Ⓒ Ⓓ Ⓔ

SAMPLE TEST A

U.S. History

Section I

Time—55 Minutes • 80 Questions

Directions: Each of the questions or incomplete statements below is followed by five suggested answers or completions. Select the one that is best in each case and then blacken the corresponding space on the answer sheet.

1. Which of the following colonial powers exercised the LEAST amount of control over the commercial and political practices in its colonies?

   (A)   Portugal

   (B)   The Netherlands

   (C)   Great Britain

   (D)   France

   (E)   Spain

2. Four of the following contributed to the rise of the women's liberation movement in the 1960s. Which was NOT a factor in the women's movement of the 60s?

   (A)   Women became dissatisfied with their roles in the black civil rights movement.

   (B)   Antiwar protests radicalized women.

   (C)   The number of women in the labor force had greatly increased while job discrimination remained.

   (D)   Dissatisfaction arose over the image of the suburban housewife.

   (E)   Anger grew from the failure to achieve ratification of the Equal Rights Amendment.

3. In the election of 1844

   (A)   Polk narrowly won on a platform of expansion, a lower tariff, and the Independent Treasury system

   (B)   Polk won a large election mandate for Manifest Destiny

   (C)   the Whig Party kept control of the White House

   (D)   Van Buren defeated Clay over the Bank issue

   (E)   Van Buren and Clay agreed to support Manifest Destiny

4. All of the following are considered by historians as causes of the depression in 1929 EXCEPT

   (A)   economic weaknesses in the agricultural sector of the economy

   (B)   maldistribution of income

   (C)   the depressed condition of Europe's economy

   (D)   boom and bust cycles on the stock market

   (E)   harsh federal government regulation of industries

5. She repeatedly risked her life to go into the antebellum South to lead slaves north to freedom, rescuing over 300. When the Civil War began, she volunteered her services as a nurse, a cook, a scout, and a spy. Congress eventually awarded her with a pension. She was

   (A)   Angelina Grimké

   (B)   Sojourner Truth

   (C)   Molly Pitcher

   (D)   Harriet Tubman

   (E)   Harriet Beecher Stowe

6. "Political parties exist to secure responsible government and to execute the will of the people.

"From these great tasks both of the old parties have turned aside. Instead of instruments to promote the general welfare, they have become the tools of corrupt interests which use them impartially to serve their selfish purposes. Behind the ostensible government sits enthroned an invisible government owing no allegiance and acknowledging no responsibility to the people.

"To destroy this invisible government, to dissolve the unholy alliance between corrupt business and corrupt politics is the first task of the statesmanship of the day.

"The deliberate betrayal of its trust by the Republican party, the fatal incapacity of the Democratic party to deal with the new issues of the time, have compelled the people to forge a new instrument of government through which to give effect to their will in laws and institutions.

"Unhampered by tradition, uncorrupted by power, undismayed by the magnitude of the task, the new party offers itself as the instrument of the people to sweep away old abuses, to build a new and nobler commonwealth."

This party platform is from the

(A) Populist Party, 1892

(B) Union Party, 1864

(C) Communist Party, 1932

(D) Progressive Party, 1912

(E) Dixiecrat Party, 1948

7. Traditional United States diplomatic policy, as defined by our first Secretary of State, Thomas Jefferson, was to recognize a new foreign government if the new government satisfied two criteria: first, if the new government was actually in control and capable of fulfilling its international obligations; and, second, if the new government had popular support. Which president departed from this policy twice?

(A) Reagan in regard to El Salvador and Nicaragua

(B) Wilson in regard to Mexico and the Soviet Union

(C) Truman in regard to China and Israel

(D) Theodore Roosevelt in regard to Panama and the Dominican Republic

(E) McKinley in regard to Cuba and the Philippines

Spain   France   Great Britain

8. This map shows European land claims in

(A) 1713

(B) 1763

(C) 1783

(D) 1689

(E) 1500

9. *Uncle Tom's Cabin* by Harriet Beecher Stowe

(A) set off a storm of protest from the South

(B) was written by a Southern woman

(C) initially sold very few copies

(D) told a purposefully distorted story to stir up passions

(E) was published during the debate over the Compromise of 1850

10. In 1872 Charles Loring Brace wrote a book to shock the American people into an awareness of a grave challenge to American society, *The Dangerous Classes of New York and Twenty Years Work Among Them*. Who did Brace see as the most "dangerous" threat to our cities?

    (A) Immigrants

    (B) Atheists

    (C) Youth

    (D) Prostitutes

    (E) Gamblers

11. In the early colonial period a "Separatist" was defined as a person who

    (A) left England to seek economic gain in the New World

    (B) wished to break away from the impure Church of England

    (C) left the Massachusetts Bay colony for religious freedom in Rhode Island

    (D) earned his freedom after working for another person for four to seven years

    (E) had served his apprenticeship

12. When Lincoln met Harriet Beecher Stowe he reportedly said, "So you're the little lady who started the war." Actually an earlier female could also lay claim to that honor. She precipitated a crisis in Jackson's cabinet that forced Vice-President Calhoun out of office and cemented him more deeply into a position as spokesman for the slave South. Who was the earlier woman who also "started the war"?

    (A) Elizabeth Cady Stanton

    (B) Abigail Adams

    (C) Peggy Eaton

    (D) Rachel Donelson

    (E) Mercy Otis Warren

13. This proposed piece of legislation was passed repeatedly by Congress and vetoed by three presidents. It passed in 1897 and was vetoed by the Democrat Grover Cleveland; in 1913, vetoed by the Republican William Taft; and in 1915, vetoed by the Democrat Woodrow Wilson. In 1917 Congress finally had sufficient support to pass the law

over Wilson's second veto. What was this issue that persistently showed up in these years and seemed not to be part of the normal party politics and divisions of the era?

    (A) Free silver

    (B) Monetary reform

    (C) Civil War veterans' pensions

    (D) Literacy tests for immigrants

    (E) Regulation of the food, drug, and meat industries

14. When President Franklin Roosevelt took the oath of office in 1933 the most pressing problem he faced was

    (A) the opposition of Father Coughlin, Huey Long, and Dr. Townsend

    (B) the Manchurian crisis

    (C) Hitler's invasion of Poland

    (D) organizing his Brain Trust

    (E) the banking crisis

15. Which third-party candidate received the highest popular vote and the highest electoral vote for president?

    (A) George Wallace, American Independent Party, 1968

    (B) Eugene V. Debs, Socialist Party, 1912

    (C) James Weaver, Populist Party, 1892

    (D) Robert LaFollette, Progressive Party, 1924

    (E) John Anderson, Independent, 1980

16. Which of the following was NOT associated with our foreign relations with France in the 1790s?

    (A) XYZ affair

    (B) Citizen Genêt

    (C) Undeclared naval war, 1798

    (D) Treaty of 1778

    (E) Barbary pirates

17. Andrew Jackson opposed the Second Bank of the United States for many reasons. Which of the following is NOT a reason why Jackson opposed the Bank of the United States?

(A) The ability of the bank to influence congressmen through loans

(B) The influence of the bank over the lending policies of state banks

(C) The inability of the bank to provide a sound currency

(D) The concentration of the bank's stock in the hands of wealthy individuals in the Northeast and in Europe

(E) The banks being a monopoly and unconstitutional

18. Which political leader endorsed the philosophy that the political and social future of the United States would be more secure if the United States emphasized agriculture instead of industry?

(A) Thomas Jefferson

(B) Alexander Hamilton

(C) Henry Clay

(D) Daniel Webster

(E) Eugene V. Debs

19. In the last half of the twentieth century the terms Sunbelt, Frostbelt, and Rustbelt referred to

(A) shifting coalitions in Congress over the direction of the Cold War

(B) disputes in Congress over the Interstate Highway System

(C) federal emergency aid for national disasters

(D) the population shift out of the Midwest and the Northeast towards the South and West

(E) the dominant weather patterns in the continental United States

20. The Constitution was written to make it difficult for the majority of the population to impress its will on the federal government. Which of the following gave the people the most impact on the federal government?

(A) Length of the term of office for federal judges

(B) Length of the term of office for members of the House of Representatives

(C) Choosing the president by the Electoral College

(D) The method of electing U.S. senators

(E) Having one-third of the Senate elected every two years

21. "When one becomes a member of society, he necessarily parts with some rights or privileges. . . . This does not confer power upon the whole people to control rights which are purely and exclusively private; but it does authorize the establishment of laws requiring each citizen to so conduct himself, and so use his own property, as not unnecessarily to injure another. . . . Property does become clothed with a public interest when used in a manner to make it of public consequence, and affect the community at large. When, therefore, one devotes his property to a use in which the public has an interest, he, in effect, grants to the public an interest in that use, and must submit to be controlled by the public for the common good."

This quotation from the decision by Chief Justice Waite approved a state law to fix maximum rates for railroad grain storage. This 1876 case was

(A) *Muller* v. *Oregon*

(B) *McCulloch* v. *Maryland*

(C) *Lochner* v. *New York*

(D) *Munn* v. *Illinois*

(E) *Cohens* v. *Virginia*

22. "We conclude that in the field of public education the doctrine of 'separate but equal' has no place. Separate educational facilities are inherently unequal. Therefore, we hold that the plaintiffs and others similarly situated for whom the actions have been brought are, by reason of the segregation complained of, deprived of the equal protection of the laws guaranteed by the Fourteenth Amendment." This quotation is from the Supreme Court case of

(A) *School District of Abington* v. *Schempp*

(B) *Brown* v. *The Board of Education of Topeka*

(C) *Plessy* v. *Ferguson*

(D) *Bakke* v. *Regents of the University of California*

(E) *West Virginia Board of Education* v. *Barnette*

23. Which outgoing president warned the nation in a farewell speech to beware of "the military-industrial complex," the result of the need for a sophisticated technological military and the subsequent development of a permanent politically oriented arms industry dependent on military purchases?

    (A) Jimmy Carter

    (B) Richard Nixon

    (C) Harry Truman

    (D) Dwight Eisenhower

    (E) Lyndon Johnson

24. Which work was representative of the Harlem Renaissance?

    (A) Langston Hughes, "Song to A Negro Wash-Woman" and "The Negro Artist and the Racial Mountain"

    (B) W.E.B. DuBois, *The Philadelphia Negro*

    (C) *The Autobiography of Malcolm X*

    (D) Gunnar Myrdal, *An American Dilemma*

    (E) John Howard Griffin, *Black Like Me*

25. Four of the following correctly describe how these states came under the authority of the United States government. Which one is NOT correct?

    (A) Texas: joint resolution by Congress

    (B) Arizona and New Mexico: treaty after a war and then purchase of a small section from Mexico

    (C) Louisiana: purchase from France

    (D) Florida: treaty from Spain

    (E) Alaska: military protectorate, then annexation

26. "Upon these conditions, it is the opinion of the court that the act of Congress which prohibited a citizen from holding and owning property of this kind in the territory of the United States north of the line therein mentioned, is not warranted by the Constitution, and is therefore void; and that neither the plaintiff himself, nor any of his family, were made free by being carried into this territory; even if they had been carried there by the owner, who intended to become a permanent resident."

    Which of the following is NOT true about the Supreme Court case from which the decision quoted above is taken?

    (A) The "act of Congress" referred to was the Missouri Compromise of 1820.

    (B) It is the Dred Scott case.

    (C) The Fourteenth Amendment resolved a problem resulting from this case by making all persons born or naturalized in the United States citizens of the United States and of their state.

    (D) The case grew out of the controversy over enforcement of the Fugitive Slave Act.

    (E) The decision lowered the public's respect for the Supreme Court in the northern states.

27. George Washington once said, "There are combustibles in every state which a spark might set afire." What event in American history was he describing?

    (A) Election of 1796

    (B) Stamp Act

    (C) Shays' Rebellion

    (D) Newburgh conspiracy

    (E) Whiskey Rebellion

28. "Of the thousand things that the _____ has done no balance sheet can ever be made. How it helped the ministers of the church, and saved the blacks from robbery! How it made all show respect for the Negro's rights! How it taught all the people the meaning of the law! It settled neighborhood quarrels, brought about friendly relations between employers and workers, improved education, helped freedmen become landowners, broke up bands of outlaws, taught equal rights, and in such ways carried the light of the North into the dark places of the South."

    What is the author of this 1866 quotation referring to?

    (A) Adoption of the Black Codes

    (B) Freedmen's Bureau

    (C) End of the Jim Crow laws

    (D) Signing of the Emancipation Proclamation

    (E) Period after the *Brown* v. *Bd of Education* decision

29. If the Populists had been transported by magic back into an earlier period of American history they would have most likely joined

    (A) the Ku Klux Klan

    (B) Shays' Rebellion

    (C) the Knights of Labor

    (D) the Whiskey Rebellion

    (E) the Federalist Party

30. Which of the following were generally considered antilabor by organized labor?

    I.   Taft-Hartley Act, 1947

    II. Landrum-Griffin Act, 1959

    III. Fair Labor Standards Act, 1938

    IV. Wagner Act, 1935

    (A) I only

    (B) I and IV only

    (C) III and IV only

    (D) I and II only

    (E) II, III, and IV only

31. All but one of the following are true about the Vietnam War. Which statement is NOT correct?

    (A) Johnson used the domino theory to justify the need for American action.

    (B) In the 1950s the United States supported a dictatorship in South Vietnam.

    (C) The United States did not permit national elections to be held in South Vietnam as specified by the Geneva Accords of 1955.

    (D) The war effort encountered widespread popular opposition within the United States.

    (E) The United States withdrawal in 1973 ended the fighting between North Vietnam and South Vietnam.

32. Which of the following were associated with the Federalist Party in the 1790s?

    I.   They sympathized with Great Britain rather than France in European disputes.

    II. They favored strict interpretation of the Constitution.

    III. They disapproved of the Alien and Sedition Acts.

    IV. Alexander Hamilton and John Adams were two of their party leaders.

    V.   They favored paying the national debt at par to current holders of bonds.

    (A) I, III, IV, and V only

    (B) II and III only

    (C) I, IV, and V only

    (D) II, III, and IV only

    (E) I, III, and IV only

33. The high death rates during travel, the extensive quantity of land, the successive waves of immigrants, the harsh conditions of life, and the hostility of the weather all combined to produce by the end of the period a society that accepted a high degree of social disorder, accepted a high degree of personal risk, and glorified youth and vitality over age and wisdom. What era in American history is described?

    (A) The twenties

    (B) Reconstruction

    (C) The transportation revolution

    (D) The Revolutionary War

    (E) The colonial era

34. "The fact is that a reformer can't last in politics. He can make a show for a while, but he always comes down like a rocket. Politics is as much a regular business as the grocery or dry-goods or the drug business. You've got to be trained up to it or you're sure to fall. . . .

    "I've been studyin' the political game for forty-five years, and I don't know it all yet. I'm learnin' somethin' all the time. How, then, can you expect what they call 'business men' to turn to politics all at once and make a success of it? It is just as if I went up to Columbia University and started to teach Greek. They usually last about as long in politics as I would last at Columbia."

    This quotation represents the viewpoint of a late-nineteenth-century

    (A) big city ward politician

    (B) Populist

    (C) AFL labor organizer

    (D) Progressive

    (E) Chautauqua lecturer

35. "Provided, that, as an express and fundamental condition to the acquisition of any territory from the Republic of Mexico by the United States, by virtue of any treaty which may be negotiated between them, and to the use by the Executive of the moneys herein appropriated, neither slavery nor involuntary servitude shall ever exist in any part of said territory, except for crime, whereof the party shall first be duly convicted." This brief proposal, introduced in Congress by Representative David Wilmot,

    (A) was in retaliation for the gag rule

    (B) became part of the Treaty of Guadelupe Hildago, which ended the Mexican War

    (C) was incorporated into the Compromise of 1850

    (D) stirred a heated debate between North and South over slavery in the territories

    (E) outlawed slavery in California

36. To people living in the decade of the 1920s, which came to symbolize immoral decadence?

    (A) *Muller* v. *Oregon* case

    (B) Sacco and Vanzetti trial

    (C) Scopes trial

    (D) Leopold and Loeb trial

    (E) Sit-down strikes

37. "Red China is not the powerful nation seeking to dominate the world. Frankly, in the opinion of the Joint Chiefs of Staff, this strategy would involve us in the wrong war, at the wrong place, at the wrong time, and with the wrong enemy." This quotation from a speech before a congressional hearing by General Omar Bradley, the Chairman of the Joint Chiefs of Staff, concerned

    (A) U.S. policy in regard to enlarging the scope of the Korean War

    (B) U.S. response to the Japanese invasion of China in the 1930s

    (C) the application of the Hoover-Stimson Doctrine to Manchuria

    (D) U.S. recognition of the government of Taiwan

    (E) the U.S. decision to support the government of South Vietnam

38. "Civilization all through the history of mankind has been chiefly the property of the upper classes, but during the past century civilization has been permeating steadily downward. The leaders of this democratic movement have been general education, universal suffrage, cheap periodicals and cheap travel. To-day the _____ cannot be overlooked as an effective protagonist of democracy. For through it the drama, always a big fact in the lives of the people at the top, is now becoming a big fact in the lives of the people at the bottom. Two million of them a day have so found a new interest in life."

    This quote is from an article by Joseph Medill Peterson in 1907 about the impact of a new technology upon the masses. It was entitled

    (A) "The New Automobile"

    (B) "The Nickelodeons"

    (C) "The Amusement Parks"

    (D) "The Streetcars"

    (E) "The Kodak"

39. Franklin Roosevelt's court-packing plan and his interference in the congressional elections of 1938 both evoked harsh criticism of the New Deal. One result of the uproar was the

    (A) development of new programs to combat the Depression, such as the Agricultural Adjustment Act, the Civilian Conservation Corps, and the Reconstruction Finance Corporation

    (B) creation of two new political parties out of the Democratic Party—the Progressives and the Dixiecrats

    (C) end of the administration's farm price-support program

    (D) creation of a conservative congressional coalition of Southern Democrats and conservative Republicans that effectively blocked liberal legislation

    (E) Supreme Court's invalidation of more New Deal legislation

40. Created in haste, it was a wartime government, "a league of friendship," suffering many pressures from the beginning. It lacked the power to enforce its laws, to tax directly, and to regulate internal commerce. Which government is described?

(A) The colonies during the French and Indian War

(B) Articles of Confederation

(C) The first decade under the Constitution

(D) Northwest Ordinance

(E) League of Nations

41. "Our greatest danger is that in the great leap from slavery to freedom we may overlook the fact that the masses of us are to live by the productions of our hands, and fail to keep in mind that we shall prosper in proportion as we learn to dignify and glorify common labor and put brains and skill into the common occupations of life. . . . No race can prosper till it learns that there is as much dignity in tilling a field as in writing a poem. It is at the bottom of life we must begin, and not at the top. Nor should we permit our grievances to over-shadow our opportunities.

"The wisest among my race understand that the agitation of questions of social equality is the extremist folly, and that progress in the enjoyment of all privileges that will come to us must be the result of severe and constant struggle rather than of artificial forcing. . . . The opportunity to earn a dollar in a factory just now is worth infinitely more than the opportunity to spend a dollar in an opera-house."

These passages represent the philosophy of

(A) Marcus Garvey

(B) Booker T. Washington

(C) Malcolm X

(D) W.E.B. DuBois

(E) Martin Luther King, Jr.

42. In December 1918, ex-President Theodore Roosevelt issued a public statement that said, "Our allies and our enemies and Mr. Wilson himself should all understand that Mr. Wilson has no authority whatever to speak for the American people at this time. His leadership has just been emphatically repudiated by them. Mr. Wilson and his Fourteen Points . . . have ceased to have any shadow of right to be accepted as expressive of the will of the American people." What prompted Roosevelt to make this analysis?

(A) Wilson's stroke negated his ability to lead the nation.

(B) Article X of the Versailles Treaty angered a majority of the Senate.

(C) The Republican Party had just won control of the Senate in an election in which Wilson had appealed to the public to elect Democrats to the Senate.

(D) The isolationists from both parties in the Senate constituted a majority, ensuring defeat of the treaty.

(E) Wilson refused Theodore Roosevelt's advice to include a prominent Republican in the treaty delegation.

43. Which of the following statements concerning the British colonial system prior to 1763 is NOT true?

(A) The colonial system was a secondary concern to Great Britain; British political attention focused more on the many struggles and changes within the British government from 1603 to the 1760s.

(B) The struggle of the British House of Commons for increased power provided a model for the lower houses of the colonial assemblies.

(C) The emergence of a two party system in British politics encouraged the accep-tance of the concept of outspoken opposition to the government.

(D) Responsibility for governing and control-ling the colonies rested clearly and completely in one part of the British government—the Board of Trade.

(E) India was considered to be a more valuable colony than all the North American colonies.

44. Which statement about the Emancipation Procla-mation is NOT correct?

(A) Public sentiment in the North was generally opposed to emancipation early in the war, but Northerners increasingly accepted the idea to speed up the end of the war.

(B)   Lincoln declared the Emancipation Proclamation to add a high moral purpose to the war, originally fought to preserve the Union.

(C)   Lincoln issued the Emancipation Proclamation following the Union victories at the battle of Gettysburg and the battle of Vicksburg in July of 1863.

(D)   The Emancipation Proclamation applied only to those slaves in the areas still in rebellion, or those areas where the Union army was not in control, so in reality it freed no slaves until the North conquered new Confederate territory.

(E)   The Emancipation Proclamation was not consistent with the Republican Party platform of the election of 1860.

45.   After the Second World War, the Soviet Union had difficulty presenting communism as a unified movement, a monolithic workers' international. Which of the following satellites disputed the leadership of the Soviet Union the LEAST while communism lasted?

(A)   China

(B)   Yugoslavia

(C)   Albania

(D)   Hungary

(E)   Cuba

46.   Which of the following is NOT true of life in the Truman and Eisenhower years, the fifteen years after the end of the Second World War?

(A)   The birth rate decreased.

(B)   Television gradually replaced newspapers as the primary source for news.

(C)   For the first time a majority of American families achieved a middle-class lifestyle.

(D)   An increase in material consumption was facilitated by installment purchasing plans.

(E)   The majority of workers worked in white-collar jobs.

47.   The historian investigating the origins of slavery in the colonial period encounters little documentary evidence to establish the date when the two essentials of slavery—lifetime service and inherited status—first appeared. Even less information provides clues as to why black slavery was established. Which of the following has NOT been advanced as an explanation for the development of slavery in colonial America?

(A)   Need for labor

(B)   Inability of Indians to serve as a labor source

(C)   Black slavery in Great Britain as an example

(D)   Prejudice towards blacks

(E)   Heathen status of blacks

48.   It began as a debate over federal land policy and ended as a debate over states' rights and the nature of the federal union. What is described?

(A)   Constitutional Convention, 1787

(B)   Webster-Hayne debate

(C)   Lodge-Wilson debate

(D)   Lincoln-Douglas debates

(E)   Kennedy-Nixon debates

49.   This map shows the

(A)   nations that fought with the United States in the Second World War

(B)   members of NATO, the North Atlantic Treaty Organization

(C)   nations conquered by Axis powers in the Second World War

(D)   members of the Warsaw Pact

(E)   Allies in the First World War

50.   Designed as an attempt to secure the loyalty of the French to their new rulers, this act broke new ground in toleration and statesmanship. Unfortunately for the British, the Americans saw only sinister designs. The act was the

(A)   Treaty of Paris, 1783

(B)   Tea Act

(C)   Statute of Westminister

(D)   Declaratory Act

(E)   Quebec Act

51.   On October 4, 1957, the Soviet Union launched the first man-made satellite, Sputnik (fellow traveler of the earth). The event jolted Americans into doing all the following EXCEPT

(A)   passing the National Defense Education Act, 1958

(B)   pouring more money into the National Aeronautics and Space Administration budget

(C)   taking a critical look at our education system

(D)   putting a special emphasis on improving the teaching of science, mathematics, and foreign languages

(E)   hiring German rocket experts from the Second World War to work on U.S. rocket research

52.   The high wages enjoyed by colonial workers were primarily caused by

(A)   the absence of competition from English craftsmen

(B)   monopolies granted by town councils

(C)   the restrictions of the guild system

(D)   the existence of so much land

(E)   laws against manufacturing

53.   "The North has acquired a decided ascendancy over every department of this Government and through it a control over all the powers of the system. A single section governed by the will of the numerical majority, has now, in fact, the control of the Gov-

ernment and the entire powers of the system. What was once a constitutional federal republic, is now converted, in reality, into one as absolute as that of the Autocrat of Russia, and as despotic in its tendency as any absolute government that ever existed.

"As, then, the North has the absolute control over the Government, it is manifest that on all questions between it and the South, where there is a diversity of interests, the interest of the latter will be sacrificed to the former, however oppressive the effects may be; as the South possesses no means by which it can resist, through the action of the Government."

(A)   This statement was made in support of the Virginia Plan at the Constitutional Convention, 1787.

(B)   This statement is from the preamble to the Populist Party platform, 1892.

(C)   The author of this statement suggested a concurrent majority to protect the interests of the South, 1850.

(D)   This statement was part of the announcement of the Monroe Doctrine, December 2, 1823.

(E)   This statement was written in response to the Alien and Sedition Acts, 1798.

54.   Truman aided the cause of civil rights by

(A)   denouncing Southern support in the 1948 presidential election

(B)   desegregating the armed forces

(C)   integrating the public schools

(D)   ordering nondiscrimination in all defense contracts

(E)   integrating restaurants, movie theaters, and interstate travel

55.   "That the United States hereby disclaims any disposition or intention to exercise sovereignty, jurisdiction, or control over said Island except for the pacification thereof, and asserts its determination, when that is accomplished, to leave the government and control of the Island to its people." This quotation is

(A)   the Teller Amendment

(B)   part of the Treaty of Paris, 1898

(C)   from the Ostend Manifesto

(D)   the Platt Amendment

(E)   the speech in which General MacArthur promised to return to the Philippines

56. "At his entrance before the King, all the people gave a great shout. The Queen of Appamatuck was appointed to bring him water to wash his hands, and another brought him a bunch of feathers, instead of a Towell, to dry them: having feasted him after their best barbarous manner they could, a long consultation was held; but the conclusion was, two great stones were brought before Powhatan: then as many as could layd hands on him, dragged him to them, and thereon laid his head, and being ready with their clubs, to beate out his braines. . . ."

This passage is from

(A)   William Bradford's *The History of Plymouth Plantation*

(B)   Captain John Smith's *The Generall Historie of Virginia*

(C)   Tom Paine's *Common Sense*

(D)   Cotton Mather's *Memorable Providences Relating to Witchcrafts and Possessions*

(E)   Thomas Jefferson's *Notes on Virginia*

57. A violent act aided its creation. Its beginnings were meager. Most successive presidents expanded it to protect their own. It used merit for promotion and was run by a commission. What is described?

(A)   United States Army

(B)   Civil service

(C)   Postal service

(D)   National Aeronautics and Space Administration

(E)   American Federation of Labor

58. Which of the following describes something that happened during the five years after the end of the fighting in both the First and the Second World wars?

(A)   The political party that did not control the White House won control of Congress.

(B)   The United States entered into treaties of alliance with our allies to prevent future wars.

(C)   Postwar conferences were held for writing of peace treaties.

(D)   The United States sent economic aid to rebuild the European economy.

(E)   A depression hindered the transition of the economy from wartime to peacetime.

59. Of the five routes shown, which was the first railroad to be completed?

(A)   Great Northern

(B)   Northern Pacific

(C)   Central Pacific and Union Pacific

(D)   Atchison, Topeka and Santa Fe

(E)   Southern Pacific

60. Which two railroads shown were the target of Theodore Roosevelt's trust busting?

(A)   Southern Pacific and Northern Pacific

(B)   Central Pacific and Union Pacific

(C)   Great Northern and Northern Pacific

(D)   Atchison, Topeka and Santa Fe and the Southern Pacific

(E)   Central Pacific, Union Pacific and the Atchison, Topeka and Santa Fe

61. Ideological overtones frequently colored international athletic events in the twentieth century. Which of the following was LEAST tinged with ideological overtones?

(A)   The 1938 boxing rematch between Joe Louis and Max Schmeling

(B)   The victory by Jesse Owens at the 1936 summer Olympics

(C)   The 1980 summer Olympics in Moscow

(D)   The 1984 summer Olympics in Los Angeles

(E)   The U.S. mens' Olympic basketball victory in 1992, featuring the first American "Dream Team" with NBA players

62.   The first ten amendments to the Constitution, the Bill of Rights, were added to protect

(A)   the states from the power of the federal government

(B)   individual citizens from the power of the federal government and state governments

(C)   individual citizens from the power of the federal government

(D)   individual citizens from the power of the state governments

(E)   minorities from the majority

63.   Horatio Alger wrote over one hundred books aimed at American youth. His message is most accurately described as which of the following?

(A)   Rags to riches is possible for a hardworking young man.

(B)   Rugged individualism is the best philosophy for American business.

(C)   Luck and chance play a major role in the rise from rags to respectability.

(D)   Andrew Carnegie and John D. Rockefeller were examples of the typical business tycoons in terms of their origins and their success.

(E)   The best way to success is to strike out on your own and start your own business.

64.   Which of the following were characteristics of new state constitutions written during the Revolutionary War?

I.   A Bill of Rights was included.

II.   The principles of separation of powers and checks and balances were incorporated.

III. A weak executive was provided for.

IV.   All property qualifications for suffrage were abolished.

(A)   I, II, III, IV

(B)   I, III, and IV only

(C)   II, III, and IV only

(D)   II and IV only

(E)   I, II, and III only

65.   "It occurred to me that woman, having received from her Creator the same intellectual constitution as man, has the same right as man to intellectual culture and development.

"I considered that the mothers of a country mold the character of its citizens, determine its institutions, and shape its destiny.

"Next to the influence of the mother is that of the female teacher, who is employed to train young children at a period when impressions are most vivid and lasting.

"It also seemed to me that if woman were properly educated, some new avenues to useful and honorable employment, in entire harmony with the gentleness and modesty of her sex, might be opened to her."

This statement of purpose envisioned by the founder of a newly created college for women was probably delivered

(A)   in the 1920s, after women received the right to vote

(B)   after the Civil War, reflecting expectations for women from the middle and upper classes

(C)   in the 1960s, following the establishment of the National Organization for Women

(D)   in the early nineteenth century, reflecting the need for female teachers

(E)   after the Revolutionary War, reflecting the spirit of nationalism and self-help in education

66.   The National Security Act of 1947 and the National Security Act of 1949 established which of the following?

I.   National Security Council

II.   Central Intelligence Agency

III. Secretary of Defense

IV.   Joint Chiefs of Staff

V.   House Un-American Activities Committee

(A)   I only

(B)   I and II only

(C)   I, II, and V only

(D)   II and IV only

(E)   I, II, III, and IV only

67.   Secretary of the Treasury Alexander Hamilton proposed that the federal government do which of the following?

    I.   Have a protective tariff rather than a revenue tariff

   II.   Establish a national bank

  III.   Promote the development of industry

   IV.   Pay off the foreign and national debts

    V.   Have the federal governments assume state debts

   VI.   Establish an excise tax

(A)   II, IV, and VI only

(B)   I, II, III, IV, V, and VI

(C)   II, IV, V, and VI only

(D)   II, III, IV, V, and VI only

(E)   I, II, III, V, and VI only

68.   Which of these strategic objectives did the North accomplish last during the Civil War?

(A)   Splitting the Confederacy by gaining control of the Mississippi River

(B)   Blockading Southern ports

(C)   Capturing the Confederate capital of Richmond

(D)   Isolating the South diplomatically, preventing an alliance with a European power

(E)   Splitting the Confederacy by marching through Georgia

69.   In February, 1861, Elizabeth Cady Stanton made an impassioned plea before the New York State Senate's Judiciary Committee to urge passage of a bill. That bill finally passed the New York state legislature, in essentially the same form, over one hundred years later, in 1966. The bill proposed in 1861 concerned

(A)   enlisting women into the armed forces through the draft

(B)   civil rights for minorities

(C)   giving women the right to vote

(D)   providing for female judges for family court cases

(E)   changing the divorce laws to permit divorces on grounds other than adultery

70.   She coined the phrase "birth control" and published a magazine appropriately named *Woman Rebel*. Who was this pioneer advocate of family planning in the Progressive era?

(A)   Jane Addams

(B)   Ida Tarbell

(C)   Frances Willard

(D)   Charlotte Perkins Gilman

(E)   Margaret Sanger

"It's More Than We've Ever Put Out Before"

© 1966 by Herblock in *The Washington Post*

71.   This cartoon suggests that

(A)   the cost for the war in Vietnam deprived cities of needed federal funds

(B)   federal aid to urban areas was inadequate

(C) federal government programs were misdirected, not reaching those who needed them

(D) the public was opposed to federal aid to cities

(E) the financial future for cities would soon be better

72. The electoral college system

(A) worked the way it was envisioned only in the first two elections

(B) foresaw the rise of political parties

(C) was copied from the British parliamentary system

(D) provides for a popularly elected president

(E) was part of the Great Compromise, giving disproportionate representation to the smaller states

73. In *Democracy in America* the French author Alexis de Tocqueville pointed out a potential defect of American democracy, the potential for the abuse of an individual's rights by an emotional democratic majority.

"I know no country in which there is so little true independence of mind and freedom of discussion as in America.... In America, the majority raises very formidable barriers to the liberty of opinion." This role of the tyranny of majority opinion in American history is illustrated by all of the following EXCEPT

(A) the Alien and Sedition Acts

(B) the gag rule in the 1830s

(C) the imprisonment of Eugene V. Debs during the First World War

(D) McCarthyism

(E) antiwar demonstrations against the Vietnam War

74. The majority of people came to America in the colonial period for which of the following reasons?

(A) To seek economic gain

(B) To seek religious freedom

(C) To avoid involvement in European wars

(D) To gain political rights

(E) To pursue the cultural arts

75. Prohibition became part of the Constitution in the Eighteenth Amendment. Many Americans, convinced that a new dawn had arrived, celebrated its arrival. Events in the 1920s illustrated that prohibition was not working, that it produced undesirable results, yet millions of Americans continued to support prohibition.

Who were the strongest supporters of prohibition in the 1920s?

(A) The three Republican presidents

(B) Organized crime figures

(C) Rural Americans and small town residents

(D) Immigrants in big cities

(E) Labor leaders and labor unions

76. Which muckraking novel is NOT correctly linked to the topic of the novel?

(A) *The Jungle*—meatpacking industry in Chicago

(B) *The Octopus*—railroads and farmers

(C) *Wealth Against Commonwealth*—Standard Oil Co.

(D) *The Shame of the Cities*—corrupt urban charities

(E) *The Bitter Cry of the Children*—use of child labor

77. The removal of the Cherokee Indians from Georgia pushed westward an Indian nation that had attempted to assimilate into white culture. In which of the following were the Cherokees the LEAST successful in assimilating into white culture?

(A) Adopting white agricultural methods

(B) Establishing a government based on a written constitution

(C) Adopting white religions

(D) Owning black slaves

(E) Adopting white patterns of land ownership

78. In the period from 1789 to the Civil War, what was the general trend in federal land policy in terms of the price and the minimum number of acres that had to be purchased?

    (A) The price per acre rose and the minimum acreage was reduced.

    (B) The 1789 Homestead Act lowered the minimum acres to 160 and lowered the price to nothing, stimulating the settlement of the West.

    (C) The price per acre decreased and the minimum acreage was reduced.

    (D) The price per acre rose and the minimum acreage increased.

    (E) The price per acre decreased and the minimum acreage increased.

79. Four of the following were Native American (Indian) leaders who led their people in war against white settlers. Which one does NOT belong as a famous Native American (Indian) chief?

    (A) King Philip

    (B) Osceola

    (C) Pontiac

    (D) Sacajawea

    (E) Tecumseh

80. Which congressional investigating committee concluded that American entry into the First World War resulted from the influence of big business and the munitions industry?

    (A) Pujo Committee

    (B) Nye Committee

    (C) McCarthy Committee

    (D) House Un-American Activities Committee

    (E) Kefauver Committee

Answer Key

1. C	17. C	33. E	49. B	65. B
2. E	18. A	34. A	50. E	66. E
3. A	19. D	35. D	51. E	67. B
4. E	20. B	36. D	52. D	68. C
5. D	21. D	37. A	53. C	69. E
6. D	22. B	38. B	54. B	70. E
7. B	23. D	39. D	55. A	71. B
8. D	24. A	40. B	56. B	72. A
9. A	25. E	41. B	57. B	73. E
10. C	26. D	42. C	58. A	74. A
11. B	27. C	43. D	59. C	75. C
12. C	28. B	44. C	60. C	76. D
13. D	29. B	45. E	61. E	77. E
14. E	30. D	46. A	62. C	78. C
15. A	31. E	47. C	63. C	79. D
16. E	32. C	48. B	64. E	80. B

Explanatory Answers

1. **The correct answer is (C).** Spain, France, and Portugal all exercised tight control, in theory, over their colonies. The Netherlands controlled the economy and trade more than the political system. Great Britain exercised the least amount of control in theory and in practice. At one point the colonial-mother country relationship was described as "salutary neglect," or friendly neglect.

2. **The correct answer is (E).** Agitation for an Equal Rights Amendment began in the 1920s after women won the right to vote. The actual Equal Rights Amendment passed Congress only in 1972 and was never ratified by the required number of states. The ERA resulted from the women's movement of the 1960s.

3. **The correct answer is (A).** As the election of 1844 approached, Clay and Van Buren, the expected candidates, both agreed to downplay the volatile issue of expansion. Polk surprised the wily politicians by winning the Democratic nomination, the first so-called dark horse in the presidential sweepstakes. Polk (Democrat) went on to eke out a narrow victory over Clay (Whig) on a platform of expansion, a lower tariff, and the Independent Treasury system.

4. **The correct answer is (E).** The federal regulatory agencies in the 1920s existed more on paper than in reality. Conservatives dominated them, and regulations were laxly enforced. The first four choices are among the many reasons for the Depression of 1929.

5. **The correct answer is (D).** All but one of the women named lived during the antebellum years. Molly Pitcher won fame in the American Revolution when she took her fallen husband's place as a gunner at the battle of Monmouth. The Grimké sisters, Angelina and Sarah, were Southern expatriates who opposed slavery. As former slave owners they added an unusual perspective to the abolitionist movement. Harriet Beecher Stowe wrote *Uncle Tom's Cabin*. Sojourner Truth was a Northern free black who spoke out on abolitionism and women's rights. The courageous former slave who returned to the South nineteen times to lead slaves to freedom was Harriet Tubman. During the Civil War she served as a spy for the Union troops. After the Civil War she established schools for blacks and, later, in New York, the Harriet Tubman Home for Aged Negroes.

6. **The correct answer is (D).** The stinging indictment of both major parties and the "holier-than-thou" attitude stamps the platform as that of the 1912 Progressive Party. Theirs was probably the only presidential nominating convention in American history that sang "Onward Christian Soldiers." The Progressives were fighting evil more than merely seeking public office. The quote lacks the truculence necessary for the Populist platform of 1892, which every student should read.

7. **The correct answer is (B).** Reagan supported the government in El Salvador but not the one in Nicaragua; however, the United States recognized both. Truman recognized Israel in 1948 but not China in 1949. Theodore Roosevelt recognized Panama immediately after the revolution in 1903. Debt repayment, not recognition, was the issue in the Dominican Republic. McKinley took over the Philippines and established a protectorate over Cuba. Wilson refused to recognize the Mexican government under Huerta, and fear of Communism withheld recognition of the Soviet Union in 1917. The United States finally recognized the Soviet Union in 1933 in the hope of increasing trade.

8. **The correct answer is (D).** Jamaica was captured by the English in 1655. By 1713 England owned the Hudson Bay area. After 1763 the French were gone. The year 1783 doesn't fit because the United States had already been established.

9. **The correct answer is (A).** Published in 1852, *Uncle Tom's Cabin* set off a storm of Southern protest. Southerners claimed that the Yankee's book on slavery distorted the facts. Harriet Beecher Stowe had spent just a short time in the slave state of Kentucky but was well read in all the antislavery writings of the period. Her characters were fictional but quite real. To answer her Southern critics, who contended that nothing in *Uncle Tom's Cabin* was based on facts, and that it was in fact "a tissue of lies," Stowe published *A Key to Uncle Tom's Cabin* in 1853. She pinpointed the newspaper accounts, slave narratives, Southern laws, court records, slave codes, and statutes that she used as sources. *Uncle Tom's Cabin* was one of the three best-selling novels of the nineteenth century. (The other two were *Ben-Hur* and *Looking Backward, 2000–1887*.) Her book sold 5,000 copies in two days and over 1.5 million in five years.

10. **The correct answer is (C).** Even then people complained about young people in the cities! Brace wrote, "the class of a large city most dangerous to its property, morals, and its political life are the ignorant, destitute, untrained, and abandoned youth: the outcast street-children grown up to be voters, to be the implements of demagogues, the 'feeders' of the criminals, and the sources of domestic outbreaks and violations of law." He specifically targeted those between 8 and 16–17. Crowded, cramped conditions drove many youngsters out of the house, and the attractions of gangs lured them into the street culture. Sometimes not much changes in history!

11. **The correct answer is (B).** In the religious turmoil of seventeenth-century England, a Separatist wanted to disassociate himself from the Church of England, which was too corrupt and inert ever to correct its many wrongs. The Pilgrims were Separatists; the Puritans were not. The Puritans fought to purify the Church of England either by staying in England to fight or by going to New England to become such a brilliant example of the purified Church that the mother country would imitate New England. This is the "mission in the wilderness" or "city upon a hill" concept. This attitude helps explain why the Puritans would not tolerate shortcomings, for they were rescuing an entire nation.

12. **The correct answer is (C).** Peggy O'Neale married Jackson's Secretary of War, John Eaton. Her questionable background caused socially conscious wives of cabinet members to shun White House social functions. Jackson, remembering his own wife's ill treatment, sided with his old Tennessee friend and his charming young wife. Eventually the entire cabinet was forced to resign in a face-saving gesture. Calhoun clearly saw that the presidency lay beyond his grasp, but not the defense of his beloved South.

13. **The correct answer is (D).** Immigration restriction was increasingly popular in this era. In the twenties it resulted in three different immigration acts, which progressively made it more difficult to enter the United States. This issue cut across party, class, and regional lines and persistently resurfaced. The

presidents all realized that a literacy test would have kept out many of the ancestors of those who now so strongly demanded one!

14. **The correct answer is (E).** On March 4, 1933, thirty-eight states had closed their banks, and in the other states banks were severely restricted. Most historians would jokingly say that the Brain Trust (originally called the Brains Trust) was never organized. There was too much infighting for any semblance of organization. The fervent opposition of Father Coughlin, Huey Long, and Dr. Townsend came after the honeymoon of the Hundred Days. President Hoover and Secretary of State Stimson had wrestled with the Manchurian crisis in 1931–1932. Hitler invaded Poland in 1939, starting the Second World War.

15. **The correct answer is (A).** The winner among this group by far is George Wallace who, in 1968, received 9,906,473 popular votes and 46 electoral votes. The others received the following: Anderson, 5,581,379, and 0; Debs, 900,672 and 0; Weaver, 1,041,028 and 22; and LaFollette 4,822,856 and 13. In the election of 1992 Ross Perot received 19,237,245 popular votes, but he received no electoral votes.

16. **The correct answer is (E).** The Barbary pirates had nothing to do with France. Don't let the 1778 date fool you. We were still allied with France under the Treaty of 1778. The Convention of 1800 finally ended the treaty and the alliance.

17. **The correct answer is (C).** Even its opponents never questioned the Bank's record of providing a sound, stable currency. Despite Chief Justice Marshall's decision in *McCulloch* v. *Maryland*, Jackson considered the Bank of the United States to be unconstitutional. The other three choices were generally acknowledged by everyone at the time. Wealthy bank stockholders and grateful congressmen enjoyed the plums that came their way.

18. **The correct answer is (A).** Clay, Hamilton, and Webster all endorsed industry and commerce over agriculture. Thomas Jefferson wrote in his *Notes On Virginia* (1785) that agriculture was the basis for a republican society. Manufacturing meant dependence on others, urban poor, and unruly mobs. Debs was a labor leader from a much later period.

19. **The correct answer is (D).** Demographic changes in the decades following the Second World War shifted population toward the South and the West. Since Congressional representation is based upon population, with a time lag for reallocation of seats after each census, it was just a matter of time before the demographic changes forced new political alignments among the various geographic regions. In the Congressional fight over national policies and national resources, the Northeast and the Midwest were nicknamed the Frostbelt or Rustbelt. An evaporating technological base, a rusting infrastructure, a dropping population, and lost jobs fed the image of a section on the decline. Conversely, the Sunbelt, stretching from the Atlantic South to Southern California, gained in population, jobs, and military contracts, and it boasted of a booming economy and a bright future.

20. **The correct answer is (B).** Federal judges are appointed for life in order to place them beyond popular control. Although federal judges may be impeached, this mechanism is rarely used. The electoral college was designed to put layers of knowledgeable republicans between the chaotic masses and the chief executive. The electoral college was an undemocratic feature of the Constitution, and the Founding Fathers were quite proud of it. United States senators serve for six years, and one-third of the Senate is up for reelection every two years. The Senate's purpose was to serve as a cooling mechanism for the potentially volatile House of Representatives. All the members of the House of Representatives are elected every two years, making the House the most popularly responsive part of the federal government.

21. **The correct answer is (D).** *Munn* v. *Illinois*, one of the Granger cases, concerned an 1873 Illinois law. Since the case involved intrastate, not interstate, commerce, the state of Illinois had not overstepped its authority and infringed upon that of the federal government.

22. **The correct answer is (B).** The quotation is from the Brown decision, which reversed the "separate but equal" decision of *Plessy* v. *Ferguson*. Both cases deserve a long look. The Schempp case involved school prayer. The West Virginia case concerned saluting the flag. The Bakke case involved reverse discrimination. A white was excluded from admission to a medical school because a certain percentage of admissions were held open for minorities. Bakke scored higher on the entrance exam than the minority applicants, but not high enough to qualify for the admission slots open for whites.

23. **The correct answer is (D).** In a farewell speech on January 17, 1961, Eisenhower raised the specter of "the military-industrial complex." Before 1940 the United States hadn't had a tradition of a standing army, but the days of the instant militia were gone. Thus, a grave fear existed that this new element in American life would somehow change American values over a period of time. As one historian said, by 1960 the United States entered a new age, leaving the age of security. The oceans no longer protected us; missiles could cross the Atlantic Ocean in minutes.

24. **The correct answer is (A).** Langston Hughes is associated with the 1920s Harlem Renaissance, an era when white Americans discovered black poets, novelists, authors, and others. *The Philadelphia Negro*, published in 1899, was a pioneering sociological study of a black neighborhood in Philadelphia. Myrdal's *An American Dilemma*, published in 1944, was a comprehensive indictment of American race relations. *The Autobiography of Malcolm X* (1966) was a statement by an early black power advocate. John Howard Griffin's electrifying *Black Like Me* stunned white America when published in 1960. A white journalist, Griffin medically treated his skin to appear black. A white man inside a black body, he traveled throughout the South and experienced what it meant to be black in the white man's world.

25. **The correct answer is (E).** Alaska was purchased for $7,200,000 from Russia in 1867 after the prodding of Secretary of State Seward.

26. **The correct answer is (D).** The Dred Scott case summarized the irreconcilable issues dividing the North and South in the 1850s. The majority of the court (although all the judges came to their conclusions for slightly different reasons) held that Dred Scott was not a citizen, he was property; therefore, he was not entitled to sue in a federal court because he was not a citizen of the state of Missouri. The Fourteenth Amendment after the Civil War specifically addressed this issue by declaring that "All persons born or naturalized in the United States, and subject to the jurisdiction thereof, are citizens of the United States and of the State wherein they reside." The case had originated in the Missouri courts in 1846, long before the crisis surrounding the Compromise of 1850, the Fugitive Slave Act, and *Uncle Tom's Cabin*. Northerners were shocked at the decision for invalidating the Compromise of 1820, which in many northern minds had become almost sacrosanct, solving the issue of slavery in the Louisiana Purchase territory forever. Northern public opinion of the Supreme Court plummeted.

27. **The correct answer is (C).** Washington was referring to Shays' Rebellion, which disturbed conservatives throughout the country. The Newburgh Conspiracy took place after the Revolutionary War had ended. Some army officers plotted to take over the despicably weak Congress and put George Washington in charge, but Washington put a stop to it. The Whiskey Rebellion was a local event. Shays' Rebellion was also local, but many areas looked ripe for similar uprisings since law and order seemed to be breaking down.

28. **The correct answer is (B).** In the period immediately following the Civil War the Freedman's Bureau improved the lot of thousands of newly freed black slaves.

29. **The correct answer is (B).** Like the Shayites, the Populists believed that the political system was unresponsive and the judiciary was narrowly concerned with enforcing contracts and forcing the payment of debts. The Whiskey Rebellion was caused by taxes.

30. **The correct answer is (D).** Organized labor considered the Taft-Hartley Act and the Landrum-Griffin Act to be antilabor. The Taft-Hartley Act outlawed the closed shop, under which a worker had to belong to a union in order to get a job; permitted states to pass "right-to-work" laws banning the union shop,

under which a worker had to join the union after he got the job; prohibited unions from making political contributions; provided for a sixty-day "cooling off" period after expiration of a union-management agreement (to be declared by the president if he felt the strike could endanger the safety of the public); and prohibited Communists from holding union offices.

Aimed at union corruption, the Landrum-Griffin Act regulated union elections and supervised union finances. Some picketing was restricted, and most secondary boycotts were eliminated.

The Fair Labor Standards Act created the minimum wage and maximum hours concept and also ended child labor in interstate commerce. The Wagner Act gave unions the right to organize and to bargain collectively, and it outlawed a number of antilabor management practices. Also known as the National Labor Relations Act, the Wagner Act established the National Labor Relations Board, empowered to issue cease and desist orders and to adjudicate charges of unfair labor practices.

31. **The correct answer is (E).** Johnson believed the domino theory was valid. Just as a line of dominoes falls over after the first one goes, so would all the countries of Southeast Asia fall to communism. After the final French defeat in Vietnam at Dien Bien Phu in 1954, an international conference in Geneva salvaged something out of the situation. Vietnam was temporarily divided into North and South Vietnam. Within a few years national elections were supposed to determine which single leader would rule Vietnam. The elections were never held in South Vietnam because Ho Chi Minh, the communist hero of the anti-French guerrilla forces, was certain to win. Thus, the United States backed the temporary government of Diem in South Vietnam, a notoriously repressive regime. The United States was eventually drawn into the civil war that developed in Vietnam, which finally ended in 1975, two years after all American troops had left Vietnam. Millions of Americans opposed our participation in the war because our political leaders were unable to convince them that the Vietnam war was essential to our national security.

32. **The correct answer is (C).** The decade of the 1790s is crucial for students of American history. You must know the differences between the Federalists and the Democrats (also called Republicans or Democratic-Republicans or Jeffersonians). The Federalists saw in Great Britain a government and society that the United States should imitate. France represented radical revolution; Great Britain represented stable evolution. Federalists favored a loose interpretation of the Constitution. If it wasn't prohibited, you could do it. The Federalists, or most of them, sponsored the Alien and Sedition Acts to clamp down upon the radical Democratic-Republicans. The Federalist leaders were Adams, Hamilton, Jay, and Pinckney. Hamilton, Secretary of the Treasury under Washington, pushed through Congress his idea to pay the national debt at par.

33. **The correct answer is (E).** All of the clues—such as high death rates, waves of immigrants, harsh conditions of life, and so forth—point to the colonial era.

34. **The correct answer is (A).** The quote is from the delightful little book *Plunkitt of Tammany Hall*, first published in 1905. George Washington Plunkitt, ward boss of the New York City Fifteenth Assembly District, revealed his honest opinions to newspaperman William Riordon. The chapter on reformers in politics is entitled, "Reformers Only Mornin' Glories." Morning Glories are flowers that bloom early in the day and quickly retreat in the heat of the sun.

35. **The correct answer is (D).** The Wilmot Proviso passed the House of Representatives but not the Senate and aroused bitter feelings in the South. The Southern reaction proved to abolitionists that the Mexican War had been a plot to expand slavery. The Compromise of 1850 temporarily resolved the issue of slavery in the territories acquired from Mexico.

36. **The correct answer is (D).** Leopold and Loeb, two college students, killed a stranger for the thrill of it, shocking many who wondered about the continuation of old-fashioned values in the new urban society. Two other events associated with the twenties, the Scopes trial and the Sacco and Vanzetti case, were strong symbols but not of immoral decadence.

37. **The correct answer is (A).** The quote represents the position of Truman and the Joint Chiefs of Staff in response to General MacArthur's suggestion to enlarge the scope of the Korean War by an attack on mainland China. Truman fired MacArthur for insubordination for publicly questioning United States policy in Korea. In this episode MacArthur produced two well-known quotes: "There is no substitute for victory," and "Old soldiers never die; they just fade away." Korea was a limited war, limited in objectives, tactics, scope, and weapons. Many Americans did not accept this new type of warfare. To the president and the Joint Chiefs of Staff, the primary concern was Europe, not Asia; the principal enemy the Soviet Union, not China.

38. **The correct answer is (B).** The new technology was the nickelodeon, the short films that preceded feature films, which began in the next decade. Peterson accurately foresaw the democratizing effect of mass media. Long the privileged possession of the upper class, culture would now expand to encompass the masses through the new "university of the poor," films.

39. **The correct answer is (D).** Southern conservative Democrats and conservative Republicans joined forces to frustrate FDR. The alliance worked because congressional seniority rules put Southerners in charge of many committees. As committee chairmen the Southerners blocked, or forced changes in, liberal legislation. Congressional politics continued to operate this way for over forty years, leading one senator to write a book entitled, *Four Party Politics*. Our nation, he argued, had four parties, not two. They were the Democrats, Republicans, congressional Democrats, and congressional Republicans.

    The AAA was passed in 1933, the CCC in 1933; the RFC had been passed under Hoover in 1932. The Progressive and Dixiecrat split came in 1948 when Truman ran for reelection. The Supreme Court, partially responding to public opinion, began to invalidate fewer New Deal measures. Farm price supports ended much later.

40. **The correct answer is (B).** The government described is the Articles of Confederation. The three powers mentioned—enforcing laws, taxing directly, and regulating commerce—were granted to the federal government under the Constitution. Neither the Northwest Ordinance nor the League of Nations were governments. The colonies did not coordinate their efforts and never had a unified government during the French and Indian War. Remember the proposed Albany Plan of Union?

41. **The correct answer is (B).** These quotations are from the Atlanta Exposition Address by Booker T. Washington in 1895, nicknamed the "Atlanta Compromise." He stressed vocational preparation for eventual full citizenship rather than seeking political and social equality. Booker T. Washington secretly financed lawsuits against Jim Crow laws, but publicly he counseled patience. W.E.B. DuBois offered opposing advice.

42. **The correct answer is (C).** Even after the Republican victory in the congressional election of 1918, Wilson continued on as before. Confident that his cause was just, Wilson failed to make mid-course corrections that might have secured the League of Nations treaty. The war ended November 11, 1918. Despite Democratic party losses, the overwhelming majority of the country and the Senate favored some kind of system of collective security. Teddy Roosevelt was extremely bitter toward Wilson, and his analysis of the situation was personal rather than analytical.

43. **The correct answer is (D).** Many Americans feel insulted when they discover that we were not the most important part of the British colonial system. As a British historian once explained, the British empire was primarily Indian, naval, and then colonial. India, and the quest to secure India, was uppermost. Next came the needs of the navy for ports, supplies, and so forth, and other trade considerations. The imperial system was never systematic, and it was never important enough to be so. The British government underwent momentous alterations in the 1603–1760 period. The era between the accession of James I and George III was characterized by bitter struggles between king and Parliament and within Parliament itself between the House of Commons and the House of Lords. The concept of legitimate opposition developed during this struggle; outspoken disagreement with the

government was not necessarily treason. No one institution within the British government held responsibility for the colonies. That responsibility was diffused throughout many different institutions, such as the Board of Trade, Parliament, the navy, and others.

44. **The correct answer is (C).** It was the battle of Antietam in September, 1862 that led to the Emancipation Proclamation of January 1, 1863.

45. **The correct answer is (E).** Yugoslavia initiated the opposition to Moscow-run international communism. Marshall Tito's native communist guerrillas had liberated Yugoslavia from the Germans, and the Second World War ended with no Soviet troops in Yugoslavia. This permitted the establishment of a strong, nationalist communist government that later rejected Moscow's dictates. Hungary revolted against Soviet rule in 1956, only to be viciously repressed. China proved too large to be a satellite and never was under Soviet domination. Almost more Asian than European, Albania broke with the Soviet Union over ideological differences and sided more with Communist China. Cuba never gave the Soviet Union trouble, except to drain money out of the Soviet treasury to prop up the Castro government and economy.

46. **The correct answer is (A).** The birth rate increased in these years. With the trials of the Great Depression and the Second World War behind them, this generation looked forward to a hopeful future. In such periods of history the birth rate soars, as it did in these years.

47. **The correct answer is (C).** African blacks possessed two distinguishing features, racial color and heathen status, that set them apart from whites. Over a period of time this perception of differences combined with a severe labor shortage, especially in the South, to produce a form of servitude unique to the English. Black slavery never existed in Great Britain before a few slaves were brought from the colonies. Blacks came from a more advanced culture than the American Indians who were impossible to enslave because Indian males simply refused to do a woman's task. To them, death was more honorable.

48. **The correct answer is (B).** The Webster-Hayne Debate in 1830 began over federal land policy. New Englanders sought to slow the sale of western public land because, as population shifted westward, New England's political power dissipated. The South joined the West in a fierce counterattack. Senator Hayne of South Carolina brought up the issue of nullification and the nature of the union. Webster replied that our nation was one of *united* states, not united *states*. It was poor history, but he was probably correct in describing the actual political thinking of the day. He closed his speech with "Liberty and Union, now and forever, one and inseparable." An early draft of the Preamble to the Constitution had begun "We the People of the States of…" and then proceeded to list every one of the states. Gouverneur Morris changed it to "We the People of the United States" for stylistic reasons. Whatever the Founding Fathers meant, by 1830 the United States had changed into a nation populated more by Americans than by Virginians or New Yorkers.

49. **The correct answer is (B).** The map shows a divided Germany, or post-Second World War Germany. The NATO nations are shown. The Warsaw Pact was the Eastern European counterpart to NATO.

50. **The correct answer is (E).** The Quebec Act solved a vexing problem for the British. It secured the loyalty of 60,000 Frenchmen in the new British possession of Canada by guaranteeing the right to practice their Catholic faith. It also rearranged the borders by shifting the southern border of Quebec down to the Ohio River. This seemed logical because the trade orientation of the Great Lakes was through the St. Lawrence River. Since England owned all the colonies involved, the action to them resembled rearranging furniture in one's own home.

Americans had a different perception. Their land claims and original charters (often conflicting) gave them the land north of the Ohio River, and the Quebec Act dampened the area's potential for land speculators. The Quebec Act indirectly attacked representative government by not providing for representative government in Quebec. Anti-Catholics saw ominous threats in the extension of

Catholicism to the Ohio River. To them, the Anglican Church, always dangerously close to Catholicism, had joined papal forces to hem in Protestantism along the coast. From the British point of view, the act was quite successful. French Canadians remained loyal to the British when the colonies rebelled despite intense American efforts to entice the Canadians to join them.

51. **The correct answer is (E).** German scientists were already in the United States. The chief of the German V-2 program, Wernher Von Braun, and over 120 of his colleagues were seized after the Second World War and brought to the United States to run our rocket research program. The four other choices were reactions to Sputnik, especially the feeling that American education needed a boost.

52. **The correct answer is (D).** The difficulty of obtaining land in Europe depressed wages. In America the availability of land raised wages because workers had an alternative. The prevailing system of values encouraged land ownership as the highest form of personal independence and security. Many towns had minimum hours and maximum wage laws for some craftsmen in order to hold down prices. Mercantile restrictions on manufacturing were inconsequential. The guild system belonged more to the Middle Ages.

53. **The correct answer is (C).** This quotation is from Senator John C. Calhoun's last speech to the Senate on March 4, 1850, concerning the Compromise of 1850. A colleague delivered the speech for the dying Calhoun. Several phrases pinpoint the date of the speech: "the North has acquired a decided ascendancy over every department"; a single section has control over "the entire powers of the system"; and "the South possesses no means by which it can resist."

The theory of concurrent majority called for majority approval in both sections on major issues dividing the sections. Against a federal law, a state could use either "state interposition" (nullification) or a state veto that went into effect until overruled by three-fourths of the states meeting in a special convention.

54. **The correct answer is (B).** Truman desegregated the armed forces in 1948 by Executive Order 9981. He never left the Southern Democrats in 1948; they left him to form the Dixiecrat Party. Not until after the Brown case did desegregation of the public schools begin. Movies, restaurants, and interstate travel came later. Franklin Roosevelt had ordered nondiscrimination in defense contracts at the beginning of the Second World War in Executive Order 8802.

55. **The correct answer is (A).** The Teller Amendment was attached to the joint resolution declaring war on Spain in 1898; the United States eschewed any territorial designs on Cuba. Don't confuse the Teller Amendment with the Platt Amendment, part of an army appropriations bill after the Spanish-American War ended. The Platt Amendment, eventually incorporated into the Cuban constitution and into a treaty between the United States and Cuba, made Cuba into a U.S. protectorate.

56. **The correct answer is (B).** John Smith's *The Generall Historie of Virginia* was a rewriting and a retelling (to a great extent) of his earlier *A True Relation of Such Occurences and Accidents of Note as Hath Happened in Virginia*. Comparing the two is interesting. This particular quote is the dramatic passage telling the events that led up to his rescue by Pocahontas. It is missing from the earlier version. Smith apparently spiced up the later version to boost sales.

57. **The correct answer is (B).** Garfield's assassination led to the Pendleton Act, creating the federal civil service system run by the Civil Service Commission. To everyone's surprise, the new president, the former New York spoilsman, Chester A. Arthur, placed nearly ten percent of the federal offices under civil service. Each succeeding president enlarged the coverage to protect some of his own appointments from the incoming administration. The nonpartisan independence of the system benefited from the alternating parties of the next several presidents: Cleveland, Democrat; Harrison, Republican; Cleveland, Democrat; and McKinley, Republican.

58. **The correct answer is (A).** The Republicans captured the House and Senate in 1918 and again in 1946, making life more difficult for Woodrow Wilson and Harry Truman. The United States joined NATO, but rejected the League of Nations with its Article X and overtures from France for a treaty of alliance. Quickly, name the treaty that ended the Second World War! There was no treaty comparable to the

Versailles Treaty that ended the First World War. The United Nations was supposed to tackle those arrangements, but the Cold War got in the way. The United States sent massive aid to Europe after only the Second World War. No depression struck after the Second World War but one did after the First.

59. **The correct answer is (C).** The first transcontinental railroad was the Central Pacific Railroad built eastward to meet the westward construction of the Union Pacific Railroad. They met at Promontory, Utah, in 1869.

60. **The correct answer is (C).** The Northern Securities Company was a holding company that owned three-fourths of the stock of the Northern Pacific and the Great Northern Railroad. The two parallel lines owned most of the stock in the Chicago, Burlington and Quincy, which connected the Northern Pacific and the Great Northern Railroad.

61. **The correct answer is (E).** The only pressure on the "Dream Team" was having to explain why they did not win every game by a greater margin! The 1980 and 1984 Olympics were events in the Cold War. President Carter ordered a boycott of the 1980 Moscow Olympics to show American displeasure at the invasion of Afghanistan. The Soviet Union repaid the insult in 1984 by skipping the Los Angeles Olympics. The frustrated International Olympic Committee ruled that any country skipping two Olympics in a row was permanently out of the Olympics. Jesse Owens soundly defeated his German opponent in the 1936 Olympics in Berlin, much to the consternation of Hitler, who refused to award Owens his medal. In 1938 Louis avenged his only loss by a knockout when he regained the world championship by knocking out Germany's Max Schmeling. Hitler and his crowd were not pleased.

62. **The correct answer is (C).** The Bill of Rights was meant to protect individuals from the federal government. Not until the Fourteenth Amendment and subsequent court interpretations did its guarantees also apply to state governments. Choice (E) is enticing, but the Founding Fathers didn't think in terms of minorities. To them, a minority was what was left over when the majority won an election. No one used minorities in the sense of racial and ethnic minorities.

63. **The correct answer is (C).** Horatio Alger is one of those rarely read, much quoted authors. The heroes in his books were poor boys or orphans who climbed the lower rungs of the ladder of material success, or middle-class children suddenly on their own due to their father's death or misfortune. Alger's heroes attained middle-class respectability, not massive wealth. Carnegie and Rockefeller represent the exception in the nineteenth century, not the norm. Most wealthy business executives started near or at the top. (William Vanderbilt inherited only $90 million: Within a short time he had $200 million.) Alger's heroes worked for someone else. To a great extent Alger praised the character traits of the loyal employee: thrift, punctuality, subservience, loyalty, and so on. The businessmen in Alger's books, like the young heroes, have internalized Christian virtues, which solidify their inner strength and guide their small philanthropic acts. But religion is never worn as a badge of righteousness. The youth in the nineteenth century liked the adventure and luck in Alger's books; their fathers liked the respectable middle-class values of family, charity, and loyalty. Rugged individualism was not a middle-class value.

64. **The correct answer is (E).** The original Constitution did not contain a Bill of Rights, but the state constitutions did. The belief that King George III had corrupted Parliament caused the states to include a system of checks and balances, a separation of powers, and a weak executive. Property qualifications for voting remained. This generation still believed in the "stake in society" theory, that those who owned property in the society should run it.

65. **The correct answer is (B).** These remarks by Matthew Vassar in 1865 illustrate the dominant opinion of the purpose of female education in the post-Civil War era. As befitting her natural responsibilities, a woman should first be trained to be a good wife and mother. If she must work, teaching, which is a form of mothering and nurturing, was the appropriate occupation. Other jobs were also open to women, but she should only work in those positions in "harmony with the gentleness and modesty of her sex." One wonders at the response a pioneer wife would have made to Vassar's remarks.

66. **The correct answer is (E).** The National Security Acts of 1947 and 1949 created the National Security Council to advise the president; the Central Intelligence Agency to coordinate information gathered through espionage; the Secretary and Department of Defense to coordinate the navy, army, and air force; and the Joint Chiefs of Staff to facilitate interservice actions.

67. **The correct answer is (B).** Hamilton proposed all six measures, although Congress did not enact all of his proposals. The first truly protective tariff did not come to pass until 1816. The promotion of industry remained a Federalist attitude but was never a policy of the federal government.

68. **The correct answer is (C).** The capital of Richmond was not captured until near the end of the war.

69. **The correct answer is (E).** The bill in question would have amended the divorce laws to add cruel treatment and willful desertion. Surprisingly, Puritan Massachusetts and Connecticut very early liberalized their divorce laws, diverging from the English practice. The Puritans had a healthy, open attitude toward sex—as long as it was confined to the marriage bed. Unhappy or, more exactly, intolerable marriages were a threat to the community's morals. Unhappy partners could corrupt the morals of others. It was better to dissolve the potential disturbance to the community's peace so that the combatants could find a more suitable partner within a new marriage. At the death of a spouse, the Puritan partner grieved while the ministers began searching. Often within a matter of weeks the widow or widower was remarried! In the period before the Civil War, many states liberalized their divorce laws. New York, however, waited until 1966 to permit divorce on grounds other than adultery. Prior to the Civil War, the New York state legislature had already changed the laws to permit married women to retain their earnings and their own property, both of which had formerly belonged to their husbands.

70. **The correct answer is (E).** Margaret Sanger was the pioneering crusader for birth control. Frances Willard led the Women's Christian Temperance Union for almost twenty years and also lobbied for women's suffrage. Ida Tarbell wrote a scathing exposé of John D. Rockefeller's ruthlessness in building the Standard Oil Company. Jane Addams founded Hull House in Chicago in 1889, launching the settlement house movement in the United States. She branched out from working among the urban poor to women's suffrage and the peace movement and was the co-winner of the Nobel Peace Prize in 1931. Charlotte Perkins Gilman, best remembered for *Women and Economics*, wrote about the need for women to achieve equality in all of its meanings in the new industrial society.

71. **The correct answer is (B).** Lyndon Johnson offered new federal government programs to meet the needs of the cities in his Great Society, but urban problems were growing faster than increased spending for cities.

72. **The correct answer is (A).** The electoral college was not part of the Great Compromise, which established the Senate and House and their respective responsibilities. Some political scientists claim that the electoral college does overrepresent small states because the state's electoral votes are determined by the number of senators and representatives. Since each state is guaranteed two senators, the state's national percentage of the population may be less than its national percentage of the members of Congress. As a practical matter, though, the awarding of all of a state's electoral votes to the winner within that state tends to overemphasize larger states and to actually diminish the importance of smaller states. Americans invented the electoral college system, a unique contribution to government. The aim was to avoid a popularly elected leader because popular election always led to demagoguery or the rise of a personal following such as political parties. Unfortunately for its creators, the electoral college fell victim to partisan political parties after George Washington's first two elections to the presidency.

73. **The correct answer is (E).** The antiwar demonstrators in the 1960s encountered little resistance from the authorities except in a few cases. The overall tone of American society had become open and tolerant. The other four represent intolerant events and periods in American history.

74. **The correct answer is (A).** Americans are much more religious and churchgoing today than they were in the colonial era. Despite the many elementary school stories of religious freedom, the truth is that very few colonists came for that reason. Most came to improve their economic situation.

75. **The correct answer is (C).** Prohibition was to a large degree a small-town and middle-class movement directed against the large cities with their immigrant, working-class populations. Samuel Gompers, the labor leader, called prohibition class legislation, and to a certain extent it was. Labor union leaders opposed prohibition because the saloon was the workingman's relaxation. Organized crime loved prohibition because it provided a ready market for bootleg liquor. Harding, Coolidge, and Hoover were only lukewarm in their support of prohibition.

76. **The correct answer is (D).** In *The Shame of the Cities* Lincoln Steffens exposed corrupt municipal governments. The authors of the other books are as follows: Upton Sinclair, *The Jungle*; Frank Norris, *The Octopus*; Henry Demarest Lloyd, *Wealth Against Commonwealth*; and John Spargo, *The Bitter Cry of the Children*.

77. **The correct answer is (E).** To Indians, land was something to use rather than to own. Land belonged to everyone; thus, the tribal council controlled the land. In white culture, individuals owned land, and each individual controlled the use of his land. This was one aspect of white culture that Indians could not seem to grasp.

78. **The correct answer is (C).** There were six land acts passed between 1785 and 1834. The first two set 640 acres as the minimum unit one had to purchase. The next four acts—1800, 1804, 1820, and 1834—each cut the minimum in half, to 320, 160, 80, and 40 acres. The minimum accepted auction price was set at $1 in 1785, raised to $2 in 1796, and lowered in 1820 to $1.25. The terms of sale at first permitted partial purchase on credit. By 1820, however, the terms were cash. In 1785 one had to buy 640 acres at a minimum of $1 for a total of $640, a sizeable sum in that day. By 1820 one had to purchase only 80 acres for $1.25 per acre; in 1832 only 40 acres. Thus, by 1832 one needed only $50 to purchase land. The Pre-emption Act in 1841 gave squatters the right to purchase land at the minimum auction price. In 1854, the Graduation Act permitted lands unsold at the minimum auction price to be sold below the minimum. Finally, in 1862 the Homestead Act gave 160 acres (320 to married couples) to any settler who lived on the land and improved it. Giving away public land was a culmination of a long trend, not a sudden new departure in policy.

79. **The correct answer is (D).** Sacajawea was the female guide who led the Lewis and Clark Expedition. King Philip (Metacomet) led an uprising against the New England settlements in 1675–1676. Pontiac's Rebellion paralyzed the western Pennsylvania frontier at the end of the French and Indian War. Tecumseh fought with the British against the Americans during the War of 1812. Osceola, a Seminole leader, plagued federal troops for years in central Florida before he was captured through treachery.

80. **The correct answer is (B).** The Pujo Committee, formed in response to the panic of 1907, investigated the "money trust." Many of their investigations bore fruit during the Wilson administration in the Federal Trade Commission, the Clayton Antitrust Act, and the Federal Reserve. The House Committee on Un-American Activities (HUAC) was organized before the Second World War to search for subversives within the federal government. Senator Joseph McCarthy's committee continued the search in the early 1950s and concentrated on ferreting out communists and communist sympathizers in the federal government. In the late 1950s the Kefauver Committee investigated organized crime. The 1934 Nye Committee investigated American bank loans to the Allies and the profits of American arms manufacturers, giving the impression that the "merchants of death" manipulated our entry into the First World War both to protect loans and to make huge profits.

SAMPLE TEST B

U.S. History

Section I

Time—55 Minutes • 80 Questions

Directions: Each of the questions or incomplete statements below is followed by five suggested answers or completions. Select the one that is best in each case and then blacken the corresponding space on the answer sheet.

1. Between 1820 and 1860 five million immigrants arrived in the United States. Most of them came from

    (A) Eastern and Southern Europe

    (B) Germany and Ireland

    (C) Great Britain and Italy

    (D) Poland and Russia

    (E) Poland and Italy

2. One of the characteristics of colonial America was frequent rebellions or uprisings against the political authorities. Which of the following was NOT an uprising in the colonial period?

    (A) Leisler's Rebellion

    (B) Paxton Boys

    (C) Whiskey Rebellion

    (D) Bacon's Rebellion

    (E) The Regulator Movement

3. "When an epidemic of physical disease starts to spread, the community approves and joins in a quarantine of the patients in order to protect the health of the community against the spread of the disease. . . .

    "War is a contagion, whether it be declared or undeclared. It can engulf states and peoples remote from the original scene of the hostilities. We are determined to keep out of war, yet we cannot insure ourselves against the disastrous effects of war and the dangers of involvement. We are adopting such measures as will minimize our risk of involvement, but we cannot have complete protection in a world of disorder in which confidence and security have broken down.

    "If civilization is to survive, the principles of the Prince of Peace must be restored. Trust between

nations must be revived."

On October 5, 1937, the League of Nations found Japan in violation of the Kellogg-Briand Pact and the Nine Power Treaty for its invasion of China. On the same day the president tried to awaken the people in his "quarantine the aggressors" speech. Which president made this speech?

    (A) Herbert Hoover

    (B) Dwight Eisenhower

    (C) Harry Truman

    (D) Theodore Roosevelt

    (E) Franklin Roosevelt

4. The first led to the second in all of the following EXCEPT

    (A) bleeding Kansas led to the Sumner-Brooks affair

    (B) the Compromise of 1850 led to the Nashville Convention

    (C) the Kansas-Nebraska Act led to the birth of the Republican Party

    (D) the Lincoln-Douglas debates led to the Dred Scott decision

    (E) the 1860 secession crisis led to the Crittenden Compromise proposal

5. Most of the canals built in the era of internal improvements, 1815–1850, were built by state and local governments. Most railroads built after this era were funded by private individuals and corporations. How do you explain this difference?

    (A) Private enterprise is always superior to public enterprise.

(B) The canals were only moderately successful financially, prompting most state governments to invest their money elsewhere.

(C) After expanding too rapidly, state governments were caught in the panic of 1837, which forced many states to repudiate their debts and caused them to prohibit the further use of governmental expenditures for internal improvements.

(D) More funds could be raised by private funding, permitting large projects such as railroad lines.

(E) As interstate corporations, railroads came under the control of the federal Interstate Commerce Commission, which prohibited state and local governments from building railroads.

6. Most of the rationale for conservative opposition to the New Deal came from the argument that New Deal programs

(A) raised taxes on the rich

(B) regulated the stock market

(C) diminished the liberty of the individual

(D) favored the wealthy

(E) favored agriculture over big business

7. "Conceding, therefore, in the fullest manner, that colored persons, the descendants of Africans, are entitled by law, in this commonwealth, to equal rights, constitutional and political, civil and social, the question then arises, whether the regulation in question, which provides separate schools for colored children, is a violation of any of these rights.

"In the absence of special legislation on this subject, the law has vested the power in the (local school) committee to regulate the system of distribution and classification (of students).

. . . The committee, apparently upon great deliberation, have come to the conclusion, that the good of both classes of schools will be best promoted, by maintaining the separate primary schools for colored and for white children, and

we can perceive no ground to doubt, that this is the honest result of their experience and judgment."

This quotation is from the Massachusetts court decision in *Roberts vs. City of Boston*, 1849. It foreshadowed a later decision that involved the U.S. Supreme Court case of

(A) *Minor* v. *Happersett*

(B) *Plessy* v. *Ferguson*

(C) *Gideon* v. *Wainwright*

(D) *Korematsu* v. *U.S.*

(E) *Brown* v. *Board of Education*

8. Which of the following is NOT true concerning the relationship between Congress and the federal courts?

(A) Congress has the power to remove a piece of legislation from the jurisdiction of the federal courts.

(B) The Senate must approve the appointment of federal judges.

(C) The House of Representatives may impeach federal judges.

(D) Congress has the power to reduce or increase the number of Supreme Court judges.

(E) A two-thirds vote of both the House of Representatives and the Senate overrides a Supreme Court decision declaring an act of Congress to be unconstitutional.

9. President McKinley officially urged the Senate to accept acquisition of the Philippines for all of the following reasons EXCEPT

(A) we couldn't give them back to Spain

(B) someone else, such as Germany, might take the Philippines if we didn't

(C) the Filipinos were unfit for self-government

(D) we were obligated to Christianize and civilize the Filipinos

(E) the Philippines were a potential source for corporate business profits

10. This graph indicates that

   (A)   New Deal expenditures to fight the effects of the depression caused most of the increase in the national debt

   (B)   the national debt grew mostly because of wartime expenditures

   (C)   the rise in the national debt coincided with the Cold War

   (D)   the national debt increased most when Republican presidents occupied the White House

   (E)   expenditures for welfare and social programs caused the increase in the national debt

11. Which author shocked the American public in a bestseller that warned against the misuse of chemical insecticides and pesticides such as DDT?

   (A)   Rachel Carson

   (B)   Betty Friedan

   (C)   Jonas Salk

   (D)   J. Robert Oppenheimer

   (E)   Ralph Nader

12. How do you explain the hero worship lavished on Charles Lindbergh and Babe Ruth during the 1920s?

   (A)   Both men did something no one else had ever done before.

   (B)   They showed the accomplishments possible through team effort.

   (C)   They demonstrated that individualism was still alive in a modern America dominated by corporations and team players.

   (D)   Their exploits took people's minds off the depression.

   (E)   Both were associated with the isolationist cause to keep America out of Hitler's wars.

13. Many years after the Progressive movement, the Kansas editor William Allen White jokingly remarked, "All we Progressives did was catch the Populists in swimming and steal all their clothing except the frayed underdrawers of Free Silver." Which Populist reform was NOT part of Progressivism?

   (A)   Direct primaries

   (B)   An income tax

   (C)   Direct election of U.S Senators

   (D)   Initiative, referendum, recall

   (E)   Government ownership of railroads

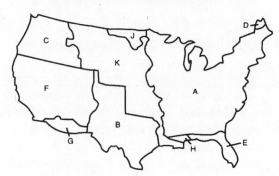

14. Which of the following statements is NOT correct? The U.S. acquired

   (A)   K and G by purchase

   (B)   B by annexation

   (C)   H and E by seizing or by threatening to seize them

   (D)   J and D through negotiated treaties

   (E)   F and C by war conquest

15. By the beginning of the American Revolution,

    (A) Philadelphia had grown to become the second largest city in the British Empire

    (B) one-third of the American population lived in cities along the coast

    (C) New Orleans rivaled New York City in both the value and the volume of American products exported

    (D) Catholics formed a majority of the population of Boston

    (E) free blacks living in northern cities had started to develop distinct residential ghettos

16. Which decade in American history was characterized by the following: Woodstock; Andy Warhol's *Four Campbell's Soup Cans*; Truman Capote's *In Cold Blood*; and Joseph Heller's *Catch-22*?

    (A) 1940s

    (B) 1950s

    (C) 1960s

    (D) 1970s

    (E) 1980s

17. The Treaty of Alliance of 1778 with

    (A) France was officially ended by Washington's Neutrality Proclamation

    (B) France ended with the defeat of the British in 1783

    (C) Great Britain ended when the countries declared war in 1812

    (D) France ended with the Convention of 1800

    (E) France is the only peacetime alliance the United States has ever had

18. "The clear and unmistakable domination of the white race, dominating not through violence, not through party alliance, but through the integrity of its own vote and the largeness of its sympathy and justice through which it shall compel the support of the better classes of the colored race—that is the hope and assurance of the South. Otherwise, the Negro would be bandied from one faction to another. His credulity would be played upon, his cupidity tempted, his impulses misdirected, his passions inflamed. He would be forever in alliance with that faction which was most desperate and unscrupulous. Such a state would be worse than reconstruction, for then intelligence was banded, and its speedy triumph assured. But with intelligence and property divided—bidding and overbidding for place and patronage—irritation increasing with each conflict—the bitterness and desperation seizing every heart—political debauchery deepening, as each faction staked its all in the miserable game—there would be no end to this, until our suffrage was hopelessly sullied, our people forever divided, and our most sacred rights surrendered."

This passage was part of a speech delivered at the Dallas State Fair, October 26, 1887. This speech prophetically foresaw the

    (A) difficulty that the Populists would encounter trying to build up a coalition of poor blacks and poor whites in the South

    (B) conditions of Reconstruction

    (C) impact the Spanish-American War had on Southern racial thinking

    (D) end of school segregation and the use of force, as in the dispatching of federal troops to Little Rock, Arkansas, to integrate public schools

    (E) rise of the Democratic Solid South, the political expression of the unity of whites in the South

19. Which of the following statements is NOT true concerning women in the 1970s compared to those in the 1920s?

    (A) They gave birth to more children, as measured by number of births per thousand fertile women, than in the 1920s.

    (B) There were absolutely and proportionally more women doctors and lawyers than in the 1920s.

    (C) The percentage of women in the labor force was higher than in the 1920s.

    (D) A higher percentage of women graduated from high school and college than in the 1920s.

    (E) There were more women living as single persons in houses and apartments than there were in the 1920s.

20. A rabid anticommunist, he exploited the nation's fear of internal subversion in the early 1950s. His sensational charges of "fellow travelers" and "card-carrying Communists" excited the nation, but his irresponsible charges quickly turned public opinion against him. Who is described?

    (A) Adlai Stevenson

    (B) Douglas MacArthur

    (C) Jimmy Hoffa

    (D) Joseph McCarthy

    (E) Richard Nixon

21. Four of the following tried to restrict the powers of the president. Which does NOT belong with the others?

    (A) Bricker Amendment, 1952

    (B) War Powers Act, 1973

    (C) Hartford Convention, 1814

    (D) Gulf of Tonkin Resolution, 1964

    (E) Ludlow Amendment, 1930s

22. Which tribe of Native Americans was the only one to invent a written alphabet?

    (A) Cherokee

    (B) Apache

    (C) Sioux

    (D) Iroquois

    (E) Cheyenne

23. Which was NOT a result of the French and Indian War (Seven Years' War)?

    (A) France lost Canada.

    (B) Great Britain incurred high war costs.

    (C) Great Britain gained Louisiana.

    (D) Great Britain saw a need to tighten its administrative system.

    (E) Great Britain made a decision to reinvigorate the mercantile system.

24. Some third-party presidential candidates have used a campaign strategy of trying to prevent either major party candidate from winning a majority of the electoral college votes. According to the Constitution, the House of Representatives, voting by states, would then select the next president. The third-party candidates hoped at that time to control a solid bloc of states in one section of the country and to deliver that bloc to whichever candidate was willing to give in to their policies. Which of the following followed this campaign strategy?

    (A) J. Strom Thurmond, 1948

    (B) George Wallace, 1968

    (C) Aaron Burr, 1800

    (D) John Quincy Adams, 1824

    (E) Theodore Roosevelt, 1912

25. List the following in their correct chronological order.

    I. Nullification crisis

    II. Tariff of Abominations

    III. South Carolina "Exposition and Protest"

    IV. Compromise Tariff of 1833

    (A) I, II, III, IV

    (B) I, IV, II, III

    (C) III, IV, I, II

    (D) II, III, I, IV

    (E) I, III, II, IV

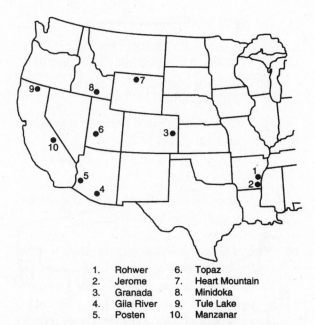

1.	Rohwer	6.	Topaz
2.	Jerome	7.	Heart Mountain
3.	Granada	8.	Minidoka
4.	Gila River	9.	Tule Lake
5.	Posten	10.	Manzanar

26. What are the sites located on this map?

    (A) Areas of innovative suburban growth in the late twentieth century

    (B) Internment camps for Japanese Americans during the Second World War

(C) Locations of confrontations involving the radical labor union, the IWW or "the Wobblies"

(D) Locations of ICBMs, Intercontinental Ballistic Missile sites during the Cold War

(E) CCC camps established during the New Deal

27. In *The American Commonwealth,* James Bryce, a British subject, pointed out the defects of the American political system. He found "a certain apathy among the luxurious classes . . . disgusted by the superficial vulgarities of public life" and "laxity in the management of public business." "The tone of public life is lower than one expects to find in so great a nation." ". . . in no country is the ideal side of public life . . . so ignored by the mass and repudiated by the leaders." City government was "the one conspicuous failure of the United States." Bryce's observations were corroborated in a novel written by Charles Dudley Warner and Mark Twain. What period of American history was Bryce describing?

(A) The Progressive era

(B) The 1920s

(C) The Gilded Age

(D) The 1960s

(E) The years from 1830 to 1860

28. "What, to the American slave, is your Fourth of July? I answer; a day that reveals to him, more than all other days in the year, the gross injustice and cruelty to which he is the constant victim. To him, your celebration is a sham; your boasted liberty, an unholy license; your national greatness, swelling vanity; your sounds of rejoicing are empty and heartless; your denunciation of tyrants, brass-fronted impudence; your shouts of liberty and equality, hollow mockery; your prayers and hymns, your sermons and thanksgivings, with all your religious parade and solemnity, are, to him, mere bombast, fraud, deception, impiety, and hypocrisy—a thin veil to cover up crimes which would disgrace a nation of savages. There is not a nation on the earth guilty of practices more shocking and bloody than are the people of the United States, at this very hour.

"Go where you may, search where you will, roam through all the monarchies and despotisms of the Old World, travel through South America, search out every abuse, and when you have found the last, lay your facts by the side of the everyday practices of this nation, and you will say with me that, for revolting barbarity and shameless hypocrisy, America reigns without a rival."

This stinging speech, entitled "The Meaning of July Fourth for the Negro," was delivered at Rochester, New York in 1852 by

(A) Elijah Lovejoy

(B) Denmark Vesey

(C) Frederick Douglass

(D) Nat Turner

(E) William Lloyd Garrison

29. For the years between 1776 and 1800, which of the following are associated with the shaded area on the map?

I. Northwest Ordinance

II. Land Ordinance of 1785

III. Whiskey Rebellion

IV. Squabbles among the states over western land claims

V. The admission of two of the first three states to join the original thirteen

(A) I, II, IV, and V only

(B) I, III, IV, and V only

(C) I, II, III, and IV only

(D) I, II, and IV only

(E) II, III, and V only

30. The Democratic Party candidate, John W. Davis, received 8,386,503 votes (28.8% of the popular vote) and 136 electoral votes. A third-party candidate, Robert La Follette, received 4,822,856 votes (16.6% of the popular vote) and 13 electoral votes. Who won this election?

(A) Wilson in 1912

(B) Lincoln in 1860

(C) Truman in 1948

(D) Coolidge in 1924

(E) T. Roosevelt in 1912

31. What do the "sick chicken" Schechter decision and Jefferson's opposition to Hamilton's Bank of the United States proposal have in common?

(A) Both involved the "necessary and proper" or elastic clause.

(B) Both involved opposition to direct taxation by the federal government.

(C) Both involved attempts to control inflation through banking.

(D) Both involved the issue of federal control of interstate commerce.

(E) Both involved the question of Congress' illegally delegating its powers to the NRA and to the Bank.

32. Which of the following is in correct chronological order?

(A) Pontiac's Rebellion, Proclamation of 1763, Boston Massacre, Boston Tea Party

(B) Boston Tea Party, Boston Massacre, Stamp Act, Olive Branch Petition

(C) Stamp Act, Proclamation of 1763, Quebec Act, battles of Lexington and Concord

(D) Boston Massacre, Boston Tea Party, Declaration of Independence, Stamp Act

(E) Quebec Act, Townshend Acts, Stamp Act, Stamp Act Congress

33. Which of the following were manifestations of the small town anti-urban impulse of the 1920s?

I. Prohibition

II. Fundamentalism

III. Immigration restriction

IV. Ku Klux Klan

V. Election of 1928

(A) I, II, and III only

(B) I, II, III, IV, and V

(C) II, III, and V only

(D) II, III, and IV only

(E) I, II, III, and IV only

34. In a ringing speech, John F. Kennedy said that those who don't understand what the confrontation between the Soviet Union and the Western democracies was all about should visit "an island of freedom in a Communist Sea . . . a beacon of hope behind the Iron Curtain, an escape hatch for refugees . . . the great testing place of Western courage and will." To what was Kennedy referring?

(A) South Korea

(B) West Berlin

(C) South Vietnam

(D) Laos

(E) Cuba

35. In 1850 the federal government owned 1.4 billion acres of unoccupied land in the West. Including the acreage granted by state governments, the railroads received over 223 million acres in land grants in the next thirty years to encourage the building of railroads. Which of the following statements is NOT true concerning land grants to the railroads?

(A) Corruption of public officials accompanied land grants.

(B) Most of the railroads were built without government funds.

(C) Railroad land grants accomplished the objective of the government—to bring the area under settlement as quickly as possible.

(D)   Granting government subsidies to private industry represented a break with previous laissez-faire practices.

(E)   The federal government paid subsidies based on the terrain the railroad crossed.

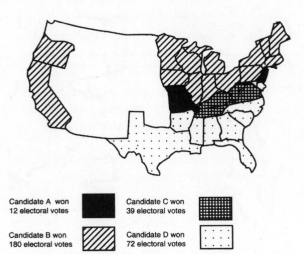

Candidate A won
12 electoral votes

Candidate C won
39 electoral votes

Candidate B won
180 electoral votes

Candidate D won
72 electoral votes

36.   This map shows the election of

(A)   1824

(B)   1860

(C)   1912

(D)   1800

(E)   1948

37.   The Great Awakening in the colonial period

(A)   weakened institutional authority because it preached that a person's future religious destiny lay in his or her own hands

(B)   caused splits among the Presbyterians and the Congregationalists

(C)   challenged patterns of deference to the elite

(D)   was led by George Whitefield and Jonathan Edwards

(E)   was characterized by all of the above

38.   "I am tired of fighting. . . . The old men are all killed. It is the young men who say yes and no. He who led the young men is dead. It is cold and we have no blankets. The little children are freezing to death. My people, some of them, have run away to the hills and have no blankets, no food; no one knows where they are, perhaps freezing to death. I want time to look for my children and see how many of them I can find. Maybe I shall find them among the dead. . . . I am tired; my heart is sick and sad. From where the sun now stands, I will fight no more forever."

These words were spoken by

(A)   General Robert E. Lee after surrendering at Appomattox Courthouse

(B)   Aguinaldo after the U.S. ended the Philippine revolt

(C)   Chief Joseph after the final defeat of the Nez Percé Indians

(D)   William Bradford after the first winter in Plymouth

(E)   General Sam Houston after the Battle of the Alamo

39.   It was the scene of the last major Native American (Indian) battle against the U.S. army in 1890. It was also the site of an Indian protest confrontation in 1973. The site was

(A)   My Lai

(B)   Wounded Knee

(C)   Little Big Horn

(D)   Sand Creek

(E)   Watts

40.   A major difference between the first New Deal and the second New Deal was that the second New Deal

(A)   was much more successful in reducing unemployment

(B)   stressed a closer working partnership with big business

(C)   emphasized a regulated economy more than a planned economy

(D)   supported legislation to secure civil rights for blacks

(E)   was more concerned with revising the banking system

Occupations of fathers of graduates of Chelsea High School, 1858-1864, and of fathers of students entering Somerville High School, 1856-1861.

OCCUPATION	CHELSEA	SOMERVILLE
Upper Middle Class		
Professional and public employee	2	11
Owner of business, store, manufacturing operation, or financial concern (merchant or broker)	19	44
Business employee	3	8
Master, mariner, shipping master, shipwright, shipsmith	5	2
Total	29	65
Middle Class		
Artisan	11	26
Farmer	0	9
Total	11	35
Lower Class		
Operative	0	0
Farm laborer	0	1
Laborer	0	0
Total	0	1
No occupation listed for parent	3	10
Total	43	111

41. Which is the best conclusion to draw from this table?

    (A) Most of the youths of the two towns were illiterate.

    (B) The push to establish high schools came primarily from the working classes.

    (C) Most of the students in elementary schools came from the upper class.

    (D) The availability of high schools in this period represented more a symbolic than a real opportunity for the lower class.

    (E) Young males worked, thus mostly girls were encouraged to go to high school.

42. The Constitution was based upon many sources—the colonial experience, the Revolutionary War, the Articles of Confederation, the imperial relationship, the British example, and political theory. On one topic, the concept of sovereignty, the Founding Fathers

    (A) broke new ground by deciding that sovereignty lay with the people, not the states, and that sovereignty could be divided by the people between the federal government and the states

    (B) provided for the settlement of future disputes by giving the federal courts the power of judicial review

    (C) laid the basis for the Civil War by granting sovereignty to the states similar to that which had been in existence under the Articles of Confederation

    (D) continued the practice of the imperial system by vesting sovereignty in the executive branch

    (E) united the new nation by placing sovereignty under the legislative branch, similar to British political theory

43. The British parliament enacted which of the following to enforce mercantilist theories?

    (A) Half-Way Covenant, 1662; Woolens Act, 1699; Hat Act, 1732

    (B) Navigation Act, 1651; Enumerated Commodities Act, 1660; Staple Act, 1663

    (C) The Fundamental Orders of Connecticut, 1638; Act of Toleration, 1649; Navigation Act, 1651

    (D) Iron Act, 1750; Sugar Act, 1764; Stamp Act, 1765

    (E) Stamp Act, 1765; Quebec Act, 1774; Olive Branch Petition, 1775

44. What period in American history is associated with the following women's fashions—whalebone corsets, bloomers, and long skirts?

    (A) 1920s

    (B) 1840–1860

    (C) 1890s

    (D) 1945–1960s

    (E) 1760s–1780s

45. The existence of the New World offered an opportunity for Europeans to start a society free from the mistakes inherited from the past. One of the themes of colonial history is unfortunately the extent to which the American environment forced changes in careful European plans. Which of the following pairs of colonies most clearly exemplify the extent to which American conditions changed the original plans of the colony's founders?

(A) Connecticut and New Jersey

(B) Massachusetts and Connecticut

(C) Pennsylvania and Massachusetts

(D) Georgia and the Carolinas

(E) Virginia and Pennsylvania

46. There wasn't one but two colonial Souths: the Chesapeake society and the Carolina society. In four of the following respects these two Souths were alike. In which were they NOT alike?

(A) The percentage of black slaves in the labor force

(B) The existence of towns as a focal point for social life

(C) The existence of indentured servants in the labor force

(D) Their fears of a slave revolt

(E) Their dependence on export crops

47. Which best describes our foreign relations or policies for the entire nineteenth century?

(A) American foreign policy frequently became entwined in the issues raised by conflicts between European powers.

(B) Territorial acquisitions increased our overseas possessions.

(C) The United States maintained a small military and naval establishment because of our preoccupation with internal domestic issues, the protection afforded by the oceans, and the existence of weak neighbors on our borders.

(D) Much of our attention went to developing trade with Japan and to partitioning China into spheres of influence.

(E) We protected North, Central, and South America against European conquest.

48. Which is associated with events in the presidential elections of 1848, 1852, and 1856?

(A) The Whig Party virtually disappeared by 1856.

(B) Third parties advocating the end of slavery won electoral votes.

(C) The Republican Party, advocating the extinction of slavery, grew stronger and stronger.

(D) The Democratic Party was swept into the White House in three victories over the Whig Party.

(E) Lincoln's election in 1856 caused South Carolina to secede.

49. One unique American contribution to the entertainment world has been the musical. Who was associated with these great musicals—*Oklahoma!*, *Carousel*, *South Pacific*, *The King and I*, and *The Sound of Music*?

(A) Andrew Lloyd Webber and Tim Rice

(B) John Ford

(C) Stephen Foster

(D) Richard Rogers and Oscar Hammerstein

(E) Cecil B. de Mille

50. Early in his administration, Woodrow Wilson attacked what he called "the triple wall of privilege." He pushed three pieces of legislation through a reluctant Congress to break it. These three highlights of the early Wilson administration were the

(A) Underwood Tariff, Federal Reserve Act, and Clayton Act

(B) Adamson Act, Payne-Aldrich Tariff, and Elkins Act

(C) Volstead Act, act creating the Pujo Committee, and Interstate Commerce Act

(D) Sherman Antitrust Act, Interstate Commerce Act, and Federal Reserve Act

(E) Agricultural Adjustment Act, National Industrial Recovery Act, and Works Progress Administration

51. Which of the following did NOT involve relations between the United States and Cuba?

(A) Ostend Manifesto

(B) Platt Amendment

(C) The *U.S.S. Maine*

(D) Missile crisis, 1962

(E) Roosevelt Corollary

52. "The black men of America have a duty to perform, a duty stern and delicate—a forward movement to oppose a part of the work of their greatest leader. So far as Mr. Washington preaches Thrift,

Patience, and Industrial Training for the masses, we must hold up his hands and strive with him, rejoicing in his honors and glorying in the strength of this Joshua called of God and of man to lead the headless host. But so far as Mr. Washington apologizes for injustice, North or South, does not rightly value the privilege and duty of voting, belittles the emasculating effects of caste distinctions, and opposes the higher training and ambition of our brighter minds—so far as he, the South, or the Nation, does this—we must unceasingly and firmly oppose them."

The author of this passage was

(A) W.E.B. DuBois

(B) Thomas Jefferson

(C) John C. Calhoun

(D) James Madison

(E) Martin Luther King, Jr.

53. In 1620 a ship arrived at Jamestown carrying more than ninety passengers. Each was auctioned off for £ 120 of tobacco, then the tidy sum of approximately $80. They were

(A) black slaves brought from Africa

(B) Irish servants brought from Ireland after the English had taken over Northern Ireland

(C) poor women who agreed to come to become brides

(D) indentured servants bound to work for four to seven years

(E) Indians who had been taken to England to be Christianized, but who refused Christianity; therefore they were being sold as slaves, the first Indians so sold in the British colonies

54. I. "This filthy enactment was made in the nineteenth century, by men who could read and write. I will not obey it, by God." Ralph Waldo Emerson

II. "This momentous question, like a fire bell in the night, awakened and filled me with terror." Thomas Jefferson

III. "On this subject I do not wish to think, or speak, or write, with moderation. . . . I am in earnest—I will not equivocate—I will not excuse—I will not retreat a single inch—AND I WILL BE HEARD." William Lloyd Garrison

These comments were made on the

(A) Fugitive Slave Act; admission of Missouri as a state; subject of slavery in the first issue of *The Liberator*

(B) adoption of the Constitution; secession crisis; irrepressible conflict speech

(C) Dred Scott decision; gag rule; *Sociology for the South*

(D) Dred Scott decision; Underground Railroad; debate on Three-Fifths Compromise

(E) Kansas-Nebraska Act; Nat Turner's Rebellion; John Brown's raid on Harpers Ferry

55. All but one of the following were aspects of urban growth between 1850 and 1900. Which does NOT belong with the other four?

(A) Establishment of professional police forces

(B) Introduction of building codes to prevent disastrous fires

(C) Building of coordinated water and sewage systems

(D) Urban park movement begun by Frederick Law Olmsted

(E) Introduction of the city manager and commission forms of city government

56. Which black American is NOT correctly matched with his or her accomplishment?

(A) Phillis Wheatley—poet during the Revolutionary War

(B) Ralph Bunche—United Nations official who won the 1950 Nobel Peace Prize

(C) Benjamin Banneker—mathematician and surveyor who helped lay out the plans for Washington, DC

(D) Jackie Robinson—first black to play baseball in the major leagues

(E) George Washington Carver—escaped slave who helped other blacks escape via the Underground Railroad

57. Which have been advanced by historians as an explanation for, or as a description of, the Progressive movement?

   I.   The primary aspect of Progressivism was the urban masses who formed the backbone of the voting electorate and who supported reforms to improve the lot of the lower classes.

   II.   The leadership of Progressivism came from middle class urbanites and professionals who had experienced a decline in status with the rise of colossal fortunes.

   III.   Progressivism was a coalition of groups united by rising dissatisfaction with corporate and railroad arrogance.

   IV.   Progressivism was not a reform at all, but "political capitalism" in which conservative businessmen supported "reforms" to use government intervention to consolidate and entrench big business.

   V.   Progressivism was a part of the cyclical patterns of alternating periods of liberal reform and conservative reaction that frequently reappears in American history.

  (A) II and V only

  (B) II, III, and V only

  (C) I, II, and V only

  (D) III and V only

  (E) I, II, III, IV, and V

58. In the 1790s Virginia and Maryland exported 130,000,000 pounds per year. In 1775, 165,000 barrels of another product passed through Charleston and Savannah. New England exported 2,700,000 gallons of its chief product in 1775. These three exports are, respectively

  (A) corn, indigo, and fish

  (B) wheat, naval stores, and molasses

  (C) rice, fish, and wheat

  (D) tobacco, rice, and rum

  (E) tobacco, naval stores, and fish

59. The social reform impulse of the previous decades was lost; the middle class lost its interest. Approximately 200 corporations (out of 300,000 total) controlled one-half of the industrial output. Fed by a series of failed major strikes at the beginning of the decade, labor union membership sank from 5 million to 3 million in ten years. American farm products, whose international market contracted sharply as European farmers recovered, dropped precipitously in price to one-half in just ten years. Which decade in American is being described?

  (A) 1800-1809

  (B) 1920-1929

  (C) 1960-1969

  (D) 1850-1859

  (E) 1890-1899

60. Which was the first wartime conference attended by the three leaders Stalin, FDR, and Churchill?

  (A) Teheran

  (B) Yalta

  (C) Casablanca

  (D) Cairo

  (E) Atlantic Charter meeting

61. Which of the following ideas is NOT found in the preamble to the Declaration of Independence?

  (A) Governments exist to protect their citizens' inalienable rights.

  (B) When a government is oppressive, the people have a right to revolt.

  (C) The government is the servant of the people, not their master.

  (D) Governments are founded on the popular consent of the governed.

  (E) Governments exist to give all people an equal opportunity to share in the wealth of the nation.

62. James Madison asked for a declaration of war against Great Britain in 1812 for four reasons. Which was NOT included in his address to Congress?

  (A) Blockading of American ports

  (B) Impressment of American seamen

  (C) Inciting Indians to attack settlers

  (D) The opportunity to grab part of Canada

  (E) Violation of American neutral rights

63. "At this time, among all the peoples of the world, the group that suffers most from injustice, the group that is denied most of those rights that belong to all humanity, is the black group. . . . We of the UNIA believe that what is good for the other folks is good for us . . . . We [want] a kind of government that will place our race in control, even as other races are in control of their own government. . . . You and I can live in the United States of America for 100 years, and our generations may live for 200 years or for 5,000 more years, and as long as there is a black and white population, when the majority is on the side of the white race, you and I will never get political justice or get political equality in this country."

These words are from a speech by the black leader who founded the Universal Negro Improvement Association (UNIA). Who was this "Black Moses"?

(A) Marcus Garvey

(B) Robert C. Weaver

(C) Thurgood Marshall

(D) A. Philip Randolph

(E) Ralph Bunche

64. In the late nineteenth century numerous protest books appeared that became best sellers. What is the best explanation for the commercial success of *Progress and Poverty; Looking Backward, 2000–1887;* and *Coin's Financial School*?

(A) These works represented a continuation of the Transcendentalist theme in American literature.

(B) These works promoted the popular new idea of socialism.

(C) These works reflected widespread concern over the maldistribution of wealth accompanying industrialization.

(D) These works supported the theme of the Social Gospel.

(E) These works provided insight into the methods of the entrepreneurs which were imitated by small businessmen.

65. "I hastened back to my frightened servants and told them that they had better hide, and then went back to the gate to claim protection and a guard. But like demons they rush in! My yards are full! To my smoke-house, my dairy, pantry, kitchen and cellar, like famished wolves they come, breaking locks and whatever is in their way. The thousand pounds of meat in my smokehouse is gone in a twinkling, my flour, my meat, my lard, butter, eggs, pickles of various kinds-both in vinegar and brine-wine, jars, and jugs are all gone. My eighteen fat turkeys, my hens, chickens, and fowls, my young pigs, are shot down in my yard and hunted as if they were rebels themselves. . . .

"_____ himself and a greater portion of his army passed my house that day. All day, as the sad moments rolled on, were they passing not only in front of my house, but from behind; they tore down my garden paling, made a road through my back yard and lot field, driving their stock and riding through, tearing down my fences and desolating my home—wantonly doing it when there was no necessity for it."

What event or activity was being described in this diary?

(A) The "Trail of Tears," when the Creeks and Cherokees were forced out of their lands in Georgia

(B) General Sherman's march through Georgia in 1864

(C) The army's attack on the Sioux at Wounded Knee in 1890

(D) The federal troops sent by President Cleveland in 1894 to suppress the Pullman strike

(E) British troops during the Boston Massacre in 1770

66. Political theory in the colonial period said that the ideal government was a "mixed government" that contained elements of democracy, aristocracy, and monarchy. The glue that held the mixture together was "deference," which was the belief in

(A) universal suffrage for white males

(B) popular sovereignty

(C) the acceptance of majority rule

(D) yielding to the leadership of the superior upper class

(E) the consent of the governed

Unemployment Statistics, 1929–1939

Year	Total Labor Force	Number Unemployed	Percent Unemployed
1929	49,180,000	1,550,000	3.2
1930	49,820,000	4,340,000	8.7
1931	50,420,000	8,020,000	15.9
1932	51,000,000	12,060,000	23.6
1933	51,590,000	12,830,000	24.9
1934	52,230,000	11,340,000	21.7
1935	52,870,000	10,610,000	20.1
1936	53,440,000	9,030,000	16.9
1937	54,000,000	7,700,000	14.3
1938	54,610,000	10,390,000	19.0
1939	55,230,000	9,480,000	17.2

67. These unemployment statistics indicate that

   (A) the number of new jobs grew by 17.2 percent over the decade

   (B) Hoover's second term was the worst period of the Depression

   (C) New Deal programs helped to counter the effects of the Depression, but did not end them

   (D) the use of Keynesian economics brought the United States out of the Depression

   (E) the economy went downhill after the NRA was declared unconstitutional

68. The first is famous for bitterly opposing Woodrow Wilson's League of Nations. The second, although originally an isolationist, reversed his thinking during the Second World War and became a strong advocate of the United Nations. Who were these two leading Republican senators?

   (A) Charles Evans Hughes and Richard Nixon

   (B) Henry Cabot Lodge and Arthur Vandenberg

   (C) Hiram Johnson and Robert Taft

   (D) William Borah and Harry Truman

   (E) Robert La Follette and Joseph McCarthy

69. Which of the following most accurately describes the relationship between the abolitionists and political parties between 1830 and 1860?

   (A) Since political action proved ineffectual, most abolitionists depended on moral persuasion to advance their cause.

   (B) Enough voters supported the Free Soil Party and the Liberty Party to hold the balance that determined victors in presidential elections.

   (C) Abolitionists infiltrated the major political parties and gained positions of influence, which they used to change their parties' positions to favoring gradual emancipation for slaves.

   (D) Most abolitionists were attracted to the Know-Nothing Party's political position on slavery, which advocated the creation of a new state for blacks in the Appalachian Mountains in the South.

   (E) Disdaining the issue at the national level, abolitionists successfully achieved major victories in voting and civil rights for blacks in the Northern states.

70. A near meltdown occurred in the 1970s at a nuclear power plant at

   (A) *Exxon Valdez*

   (B) Consolidated Edison

   (C) Three Mile Island

   (D) Philadelphia Electric Company

   (E) Love Canal

71. Chief Justice John Marshall asserted that only Congress, not the states, possessed the power to control interstate commerce. The case was

   (A) *Marbury* v. *Madison*

   (B) the Slaughterhouse case

   (C) *McCulloch* v. *Maryland*

   (D) *Cohens* v. *Virginia*

   (E) *Gibbons* v. *Ogden*

72. "If the church cannot bring business under Christ's law of solidarity and service, it will find his law not merely neglected in practice, but flouted in theory. With many the Darwinian theory has proved a welcome justification of things as they are. It is right and fitting that thousands should perish to evolve the higher type of the modern business man. Those who are manifestly surviving in the present struggle for existence can console themselves with the thought that they are the fittest, and there is no contradicting the laws of the universe. Thus an atomistic philosophy crowds out the Christian faith in solidarity. The law of the cross is superseded by the law of tooth and nail. It is not even ideal and desirable 'to seek and to save the lost,' because it keeps the weak and unfit alive. . . .

"The gospel, to have full power over an age, must be the highest expression of the moral and religious truths held by that age. If it lags behind and deals in outgrown conceptions of life and duty, it will lose power over the ablest minds and the young men first, and gradually over all. In our thought to-day the social problems irresistibly take the lead. If the Church has no live and bold thought on this dominant question of modern life, its teaching authority on all other questions will dwindle and be despised. It cannot afford to have young men sniff the air as in a stuffy room when they enter the sphere of religious thought. When the world is in travail with a higher ideal of justice, the Church dare not ignore it if it would retain its moral leadership." This is a statement of the philosophy behind

(A) Social Darwinism

(B) the Social Gospel

(C) the Single Tax

(D) Populism

(E) Fundamentalism

73. The two routes pictured, routes "A" and "B,"

(A) were parts of the Underground Railroad carrying slaves to freedom in Canada

(B) were financed by the federal government to provide internal improvements

(C) were originally vetoed by Andrew Jackson in the Maysville veto

(D) were state projects that stimulated imitation by other states

(E) marked the beginning of the "transportation revolution"

74. "Even though we face the difficulties of today and tomorrow, I still have a dream. . . . I have a dream that one day this nation will rise up and live out the true meaning of its creed: 'We hold these truths to be self-evident, that all men are created equal.'

"I have a dream that one day on the red hills of Georgia the sons of former slaves and the sons of former slaveowners will be able to sit down together at the table of brotherhood. I have a dream that one day even the state of Mississippi, a state sweltering with the people's injustice, sweltering with the heat of oppression, will be transferred into an oasis of freedom and justice.

"I have a dream that my four little children will one day live in a nation where they will not be judged by the color of their skin but by the content of their character. . . .

"I have a dream that one day every valley shall be exalted, every hill and mountain shall be made low, the rough places will be made plain and the crooked places will be made straight, and the glory of the Lord shall be revealed and flesh shall see it together.

"This is our hope."

This speech was delivered by

(A) Stokely Carmichael

(B) Lyndon Johnson

(C) Martin Luther King, Jr.

(D) John F. Kennedy

(E) Malcolm X

75. When the First World War broke out in 1914, Woodrow Wilson asked the American people to be neutral in thought as well as deed. U.S. policy failed to remain neutral because of which of the following?

I. Our foreign policy assumed that American neutral rights would be respected.

II. Our foreign policy assumed that the U.S. government could pursue a truly neutral policy.

III. Allied control of the seas effectively blocked evenhanded trade with belligerents.

IV. Germany was unwilling to accept the sovereignty of the League of Nations.

V. New methods of warfare tainted the image of Germany.

(A) III and V only

(B) I, II, III, and V only

(C) II, III, and IV only

(D) I, II, III, IV, and V

(E) I, III, and V only

76. The "War on Poverty" fought illiteracy and unemployment under Lyndon Johnson. Four of the following kept the "War on Poverty" from achieving victory in the next twenty years. Which did NOT contribute to the demise of the efforts to reduce poverty?

(A) Two basic industries, steel and automobile, switched to more automation and suffered from fierce foreign competition, resulting in increased layoffs.

(B) Millions of illegal immigrants entered the United States from poverty-stricken Mexico and war-torn Central America.

(C) An increase in divorces lowered the living standards for millions of children and women.

(D) Reduced Social Security benefits raised the number of elderly people among the poor.

(E) The Vietnam War diverted the commitment from domestic concerns.

77. The Compromise of 1850 provided for the

(A) establishment of the 36° 30' line to divide slave and free territories

(B) admission of Missouri as a slave state and Maine as a free state

(C) ending of the importation of slaves into the United States as provided by the Constitution

(D) absorption of the Confederate debt after the Civil War

(E) addition of a free state without adding a new slave state

78. The Constitution obligates the federal government to guarantee a republican form of government in each state. Which incident most closely involved the question of "a republican government" within a state?

(A) Populist Party state victories in 1892

(B) Dorr's Rebellion in Rhode Island in 1841–1842

(C) Federal troops sent to the Pullman strike, 1894

(D) Federal takeover of the Arkansas state government during the school integration crisis in 1957

(E) Takeover of automobile plants during the sit-down strikes in the 1930s

79. By the end of the 1880s

    (A) immigrants from Eastern and Southern Europe began to outnumber those from Northern and Western Europe

    (B) Chinese immigration began to increase

    (C) the Irish fleeing the potato famine began to arrive

    (D) most immigrants were becoming farmers

    (E) the first immigration quota act was passed, based on the census of 1890

80. Anne Hutchinson was banished from Massachusetts and excommunicated from the Puritan Church in 1637 because

    (A) she embraced the Quaker ideas of George Fox and William Penn

    (B) she argued that a covenant of works was superfluous because an individual's efforts to gain salvation through good works was by its very nature inadequate in comparison to God's covenant of grace, that is, salvation as a free gift of God

    (C) she defended freedom of religion for all, including Catholics, Quakers, and Jews

    (D) she challenged the political authorities by seeking elected political office, in spite of the fact that women could not vote

    (E) she defended Roger Williams, who argued for a separation of church and state and was banished from Massachusetts

Answer Key

1. B	17. D	33. B	49. D	65. B
2. C	18. A	34. B	50. A	66. D
3. E	19. A	35. D	51. E	67. C
4. D	20. D	36. B	52. A	68. B
5. C	21. D	37. E	53. C	69. A
6. C	22. A	38. C	54. A	70. C
7. B	23. C	39. B	55. E	71. E
8. E	24. B	40. C	56. E	72. B
9. E	25. D	41. D	57. E	73. E
10. B	26. B	42. A	58. D	74. C
11. A	27. C	43. B	59. B	75. B
12. C	28. C	44. B	60. A	76. D
13. E	29. D	45. D	61. E	77. E
14. E	30. D	46. B	62. D	78. B
15. A	31. E	47. C	63. A	79. A
16. C	32. A	48. A	64. C	80. B

Explanatory Answers

1. **The correct answer is (B).** This is the peak period for Irish and German immigration. The Irish fled crowded Ireland and the potato famine. The Germans left poor agricultural conditions and the failed revolution of 1848.

2. **The correct answer is (C).** All these rebellions pitted the lower classes against their superiors. Leisler's Rebellion took place in New York City in the 1690s, a period of turmoil throughout the colonies. Bacon's Rebellion in 1676 has been interpreted as a frontier versus tidewater uprising and as the early forerunner of the spirit of 1776. The Paxton Boys in Pennsylvania and the Regulators in the Carolinas were both frontier protests against colonial governments too preoccupied with Eastern concerns. The Whiskey Rebellion took place in 1795 after the colonial era.

3. **The correct answer is (E).** The president was Franklin D. Roosevelt. The speech is often seen as a turning point in American foreign policy even though the general public remained isolationist in sentiment.

4. **The correct answer is (D).** The Lincoln-Douglas debates took place in 1858 after the Dred Scott decision in 1857. Lincoln nailed Douglas by asking him if he supported both the Dred Scott decision, which Southerners applauded, and popular sovereignty, a term popularized by Douglas. The Dred Scott decision had said slaves could go anywhere; Douglas's answer, called the Freeport Doctrine, was that settlers in the territories could as a practical matter exclude slaves. Douglas's leaning toward popular sovereignty antagonized the South and cost him the nomination of a unified Democratic Party in 1860.

5. **The correct answer is (C).** Don't be fooled by that old myth that laissez-faire has always characterized the U.S. economy. In the pre-Civil War period many state and local governments owned stock in corporations. One historian has characterized the economy in this era as a "mixed economy." The Depression of 1837 disrupted many grandiose projects and reduced the income generated by roads and canals. Many states repudiated their debt in order to escape the financial morass. Burned by this experience, many states prohibited their own governments from investing in corporate stock. Thus the railroads were mostly funded by private sources.

6. **The correct answer is (C).** Conservatives saw in the New Deal a creeping socialism that would put us on the road to serfdom and destroy individual liberty. Read campaign speeches from the 1936 presidential race, especially material from the Liberty League.

7. **The correct answer is (B).** The case of *Plessy* v. *Ferguson* produced the "separate but equal" doctrine and essentially put the stamp of judicial approval on segregation. *Brown* v. *Board of Education* overturned Plessy. *Minor* v. *Happersett* (1875) ruled that voting was not an inherent right of citizenship. Women could be citizens but still be deprived of voting rights. The Korematsu case upheld the removal of the Japanese from the West Coast in the beginning of the Second World War. *Gideon* v. *Wainwright* ensured a poor defendant's right to free counsel in state felony cases.

8. **The correct answer is (E).** There are two methods of overriding a Supreme Court decision declaring an act of Congress unconstitutional. One is to pass an amendment to the Constitution. For example, the Sixteenth Amendment, permitting income taxes, negated the decision in *Pollack* v. *Farmers' Loan and Trust Co.,* which had declared income taxes unconstitutional. The second method is to have the Supreme Court reverse its decision. *Brown* v. *Board of Education of Topeka* overturned the "separate but equal" doctrine in *Plessy* v. *Ferguson*.

The other choices are powers Congress has over the Supreme Court. Article III, section 2, gives Congress the authority to remove a piece of legislation from court review. The Reconstruction Act is an example of this. Congress reduced the number of Supreme Court judges under Andrew Johnson to forestall the possibility that he might make an appointment to the Supreme Court. FDR's court packing plan pressed unsuccessfully for an enlargement of the Supreme Court.

9. **The correct answer is (E).** Economic gain is often offered as a reason for American imperialist expansion, but McKinley did not present it in his address to the Senate. Many industrialists such as Andrew Carnegie opposed acquisition of the Philippines.

10. **The correct answer is (B).** The huge increase in the national debt this century has come from war and the threat of war. Spending for social programs has added very little to the total federal budget deficit.

11. **The correct answer is (A).** Rachel Carson's *Silent Spring* (1962) alerted the world to the dangers of pesticides, especially DDT, which was banned ten years later. Betty Friedan wrote *The Feminine Mystique* (1963), thereby helping to launch the women's movement. Jonas Salk discovered a vaccine for polio. J. Robert Oppenheimer led the Manhattan Project that developed the atomic bomb during the Second World War. Ralph Nader was a driving force behind the consumer revolt of the 1960s. He accused the automobile industry of producing unsafe cars in *Unsafe at Any Speed* (1965).

12. **The correct answer is (C).** Ruth and Lindbergh proved that individualism could still triumph. Corporations sponsored entries in the race to be the first pilot to solo across the Atlantic, but Lindbergh beat them all. Babe Ruth violated every training rule in existence, and some not in existence. The contemporary maxim was "follow the rules and be a team player." Ruth didn't and yet he still excelled. Choice (A) is distracting, for their adulation far exceeded their accomplishments. Lindbergh later became a spokesman for the isolationist cause, and, some would say, the German cause. Ruth did not.

13. **The correct answer is (E).** Populists wanted government ownership of the railroads, but Progressives never did. Progressivism tended to be much more political than Populism. The two key words in Progressivism are efficiency and democracy.

14. **The correct answer is (E).** The Mexican Cession (F) was a prize of war, but the Oregon territory (C) was acquired by treaty from Great Britain in 1846.

15. **The correct answer is (A).** The urban percentage was only five percent. New Orleans would one day rival New York City briefly, but not in 1775. The surge of Catholics entering Boston was far off in the future.

16. **The correct answer is (C).** The rock music festival, Woodstock, and all the other events and books were part of the cultural life of the 1960s.

17. **The correct answer is (D).** The Treaty of 1778, an alliance between France and the United States, ended with the Convention of 1800. After using massive French help to win the Revolutionary War, the United States, following self-interest, avoided helping France in its wars with Great Britain in the 1790s. Washington's Neutrality Proclamation of 1793 wiggled out of our commitment but not out of the alliance. After the undeclared naval war of 1798 further strained U.S.-French relations, it became possible to break off the perpetual alliance of 1778. The United States has had many peacetime alliances since NATO.

18. **The correct answer is (A).** By the 1880s Southern whites almost unanimously supported Democratic candidates in order to negate the black vote and to overwhelm Republicans. Political contests took place during Democratic primaries, not at the general elections, hence the nickname, Solid South. If whites had ever been divided, the beneficiary would have been blacks, who would have found themselves courted by competing groups or classes of whites. This happened during the rise of Populism when lower-class whites sought the support of the predominantly lower-class blacks.

19. **The correct answer is (A).** By virtue of greater access to birth control and abortion, the 1970s produced fewer births per thousand fertile women than did the 1920s.

20. **The correct answer is (D).** Senator Joseph McCarthy, a Republican from Wisconsin, raised eyebrows and passions with his sensational charges of twenty years of treason. The Republican Party found his accusations useful during Eisenhower's 1952 campaign, but its opinion quickly changed when McCarthy added the first year of Eisenhower's administration to the charge of twenty years of treason. The Senate eventually censured McCarthy and his methods, ending his influence.

21. **The correct answer is (D).** The Gulf of Tonkin Resolution in 1964 gave Lyndon Johnson carte blanche authorization to use military force in Southeast Asia. Only two senators opposed this nationalist response to apparent attacks on U.S. destroyers off the coast of Vietnam in the Gulf of Tonkin. Dissatisfaction over the consequences of their grant of power led Congress to pass the War Powers Act in 1973, limiting the time period during which a president could commit American troops to combat situations. The Hartford Convention, the Ludlow Amendment, and the Bricker Amendment all tried unsuccessfully to restrict presidential control of foreign policy.

22. **The correct answer is (A).** Sequoyah invented the 84 letter Cherokee alphabet around 1820. Today approximately 20,000 are able to speak and write it, although for all it is their second language. The adoption of the trappings of civilization was not enough to convince whites that Indians should not be pushed westward. Nothing would have been sufficient.

23. **The correct answer is (C).** The French lost Louisiana in the French and Indian War (Seven Years' War, Great War for Empire) but not to the British. Anxious to end the fighting, France gave Louisiana to her ally Spain, as compensation for Spain's losses. From the American point of view, the two chief results of the war were the cession of Canada to Great Britain and the huge debt the British incurred, forcing a reevaluation of the porous system for collecting customs duties.

24. **The correct answer is (B).** George Wallace knew that he couldn't win the presidency in 1968. He hoped no one would win. His control of the states of the old Confederacy would give him approximately twelve states, half what one of the other candidates would need to win in the House of Representatives. At that point profitable deals were possible.

    The only other third party candidate listed is Strom Thurmond. He sought to deny victory for Truman and to teach the Democrats that they must be more respectful of white Southern feelings on racial issues.

25. **The correct answer is (D).** The South Carolina "Exposition and Protest" was directed against the Tariff of Abominations; the protest followed the tariff. The controversy simmered for several years before leading to the nullification crisis of 1831-1833 resolved by the Compromise of 1833, which included the Tariff of 1833 and the Force Bill.

26. **The correct answer is (B).** Japanese-Americans who lived in the West Coast states of California, Oregon, Washington, and Arizona were interned in these camps, "home" until the army announced the end of relocation in December, 1944. Fear of Japanese attack gripped the West Coast in 1941–1942. The Rose Bowl football game was even moved in 1942 to Durham, North Carolina.

27. **The correct answer is (C).** Mark Twain and Charles Dudley Warner entitled their novel, *The Gilded Age*. To gild means to cover something with a thin layer of gold. The outside looks nice in appearance, but it covers something inferior. The political values and practices of the age earned the title, "The Gilded Age."

28. **The correct answer is (C).** Denmark Vesey was a free black executed in 1822 for plotting a revolt in Charleston, South Carolina. Nat Turner's Virginia uprising in 1831 ended with his hanging. Elijah Lovejoy, an abolitionist newspaper editor, was killed in 1837 trying to defend his printing press against an angry mob. Choosing between Douglass and Garrison is difficult. The speech follows Garrison's truculent vein, but the first paragraph indicates that the speaker feels himself to be outside American society itself, not just American mainstream thought. Hence the choice is Douglass.

29. **The correct answer is (D).** The Whiskey Rebellion took place in Western Pennsylvania in the 1790s. The first states to join the union after the original thirteen were Vermont in 1791, Kentucky in 1792, and Tennessee in 1796, all outside the Northwest Territory.

30. **The correct answer is (D).** La Follette headed the Progressive Party ticket in 1924. The winner was Republican Calvin Coolidge. Republican prosperity and Coolidge's distance from the Harding scandals made him unbeatable. Already occupying the White House after Harding's death also helped.

31. **The correct answer is (E).** For Congress to give its functions and responsibilities to another branch of the government is unconstitutional. Even if another branch can do a more efficient job, Congress cannot relinquish its authority and responsibility. Jefferson argued against the claim that the Bank would facilitate the tax collection function of the federal government. The major reason the Supreme Court ruled against the NRA was that the National Industrial Recovery Act (which created the NRA) delegated legislative powers to an agency under the control of the executive branch.

32. **The correct answer is (A).** The correct order is as follows: Pontiac's Rebellion, 1763; Proclamation of 1763; Stamp Act, 1765; Stamp Act Congress, 1765; Townshend Acts, 1767; Boston Massacre, 1770; Boston Tea Party, 1773; Quebec Act, 1774; Lexington and Concord, 1775; Olive Branch Petition, 1775; and the Declaration of Independence, 1776.

33. **The correct answer is (B).** Prohibition, fundamentalism, and immigration restriction were all small town attacks against corrupt urban America. The Ku Klux Klan is much more complicated because there are actually three klans: the anti-black organization after the Civil War; the pro-smalltown movement in the 1920s; and the anticommunist Klan of the 1950s and 1960s. All contained the same elements, but their emphasis shifted. The 1920s Klan was a fraternalistic glorification of the values of smalltown America. In the election of 1928 Herbert Hoover ran against Al Smith, the son of immigrants, a Catholic, and a wet. Rural America and small town America voted for Hoover to save the United States from a horrible fate!

34. **The correct answer is (B).** All of these were testing grounds of Western courage and will. Two clues indicate Berlin, "an island of freedom" and "behind the Iron Curtain." Berlin was entirely within East Germany. Both Germany and Berlin were divided temporarily after the Second World War into French, British, American, and Soviet zones. The temporary arrangement solidified with the growth of the Cold War. The French, British, and American zones in Germany merged to form West Germany in 1949. Before the Berlin Wall was built, it was possible for an Eastern European to get a passport to visit West Berlin. Once there, one simply took a plane to West Germany and freedom.

35. **The correct answer is (D).** Government grants varied with the terrain, the rougher the terrain the higher the grant. The scandalous Crédit Mobilier was only the most notorious example of political corruption. Contrary to popular myth, private funds built the majority of the railroads. Land grants enticed railroads to build lines across barren prairies. The normal progression elsewhere was for a sufficient population to settle in an area and lure investors into building a railroad to the new settlement. In the Great Plains there never would have been settlement without prior railroad construction. Government policy was to move settlers into vacant lands; the railroads became the means to entice settlers. Once and for all, the prevailing philosophy in nineteenth-century America was laissez-faire; the prevailing practice was government help such as bonds, stock subscriptions, tariffs, and so forth.

36. **The correct answer is (B).** There are few presidential elections in U.S. history in which four candidates received electoral votes. The clear sectional vote indicates that this is the election of 1860. The Republican Lincoln won the North and the Democrat Breckinridge took the South. Bell and Douglas divided the middle.

37. **The correct answer is (E).** The Great Awakening, led by the Rev. George Whitefield (pronounced Whitfield) and the Rev. Jonathan Edwards ("sinners in the hands of an angry God"), swept through the colonies in successive waves beginning in the 1720s. Its message was that each individual should seek salvation. The too highly educated established clergy, involved in tedious doctrinal disputes, had lost their zeal and inspiration and needed to be replaced, reinvigorated, or ignored. Many churches split. The Presbyterians divided internally into the New Lights and the Old Lights; the Congregationalists into the New Sides and the Old Sides. The Great Awakening challenged the established order by emphasizing individualism and deemphasizing the obvious (to some) trappings of God's approval—financial and material success. Not all succumbed to the fever. Whitefield, an Englishman who came to the colonies on seven evangelical trips, could never excite his rational Philadelphia friend, Benjamin Franklin.

38. **The correct answer is (C).** This widely quoted speech was delivered by Chief Joseph after the final defeat of the Nez Percé Indians in 1877.

39. **The correct answer is (B).** Wounded Knee and Sand Creek were both sites of white massacres of virtually defenseless Native Americans or Indians. Wounded Knee, the last major battle between whites and Indians, was the scene of a militant "Red Power" demonstration in 1973 led by members of AIM, the American Indian Movement. The confrontation symbolized the new militant attitude of many young Indian radicals. The Sioux wiped out Custer at Little Big Horn in 1876. My Lai was the site of an American massacre of a Vietnamese village during the Vietnam War. Watts, a black neighborhood in Los Angeles, erupted in 1965, symbolizing black disgust with the pace of civil rights.

40. **The correct answer is (C).** One major characteristic of the second New Deal was the shift from a cooperative, planned partnership approach with big business to a more hostile, regulated approach. The National Recovery Administration belongs to the first New Deal. The Second World War, not the New Deal, solved the unemployment dilemma. The banking crisis was part of the Hundred Days. Despite personal sympathy for the plight of blacks, FDR felt that an open civil rights effort would jeopardize his congressional Southern support for New Deal legislation.

41. **The correct answer is (D).** Choices (A), (B), and (E) may be true, but the chart doesn't provide information to support any of them. Literacy was high in the United States, but most students attended school for a total of only two to five years. The working class was only one source of the push for establishing schools. Many historians also attribute a custodial purpose to the early school reformers; they wanted to keep the students out of the labor market and confined within a caretaker institution. No information indicates the sex of the students. Choice (E) sounds plausible, but we don't know. Choice (C) refers to elementary schools, not high schools.

Another twenty-five years passed before half the lower classes or working classes attended high school, and many more years before half graduated.

42. **The correct answer is (A).** The great contribution the Founding Fathers made to political theory was the idea that sovereignty was divisible. Before the Constitution was written, sovereignty lay with one person (the sovereign), a body such as a council or legislature, or in a class or category of society. The Constitution divided sovereignty, granting some to the states, most to the federal government, and ultimate sovereignty to the people. If the people decide to change their government, they may.

    Some constitutional scholars claim that the Founding Fathers tacitly gave their consent to judicial review. It is one of those historical questions that will probably never be answered. We have all the historical documents that could possibly deal with the question, and a new diary or letter is unlikely.

43. **The correct answer is (B).** This question demands that you understand the theories behind mercantilism. Questions occasionally contain excellent distracters, that is, wrong answers that appear enticing at first glance. In (A) both the Woolens Act and the Hat Act apply, but not the Half-Way Covenant, a milestone in Puritan religious doctrine. In (C) the Maryland Act of Toleration was political and religious while the Fundamental Orders of Connecticut was the first written constitution. The Iron Act and the Sugar Act are enticing in (D), but the Stamp Act was to raise revenue, not regulate trade. None of the choices in (E) are economic or mercantilist.

44. **The correct answer is (B).** The best hint is bloomers, loose-fitting trouser pants extending to the knees popularized by Amelia Jenks Bloomer in the 1850s. These were advocated by women as a relief from inhibiting corsets, crinolines, and petticoats.

45. **The correct answer is (D).** Georgia, the creation of a group of idealists headed by James Oglethorpe, never fulfilled its founders' vision. Liquor and slavery were banned, small farming plots laid out, and a silk industry started. Within a short time everything changed. The Fundamental Constitutions of Carolina (1669) envisioned for North and South Carolina an orderly feudal society complete with serfs, tenants, and nobles. Even after four revisions the Fundamental Constitutions were never put into effect.

46. **The correct answer is (B).** Charleston and Savannah served as urban centers for the lower South. The Chesapeake Bay permitted ships to visit virtually every tidewater plantation for trade purposes. Despite the well-known restoration of Williamsburg, the Chesapeake South lacked urban centers of social and economic vitality.

47. **The correct answer is (C).** There were few European conflicts to get involved in. The Crimean War, Austro-Prussian War, and Franco-Prussian War were short conflicts confined to Europe. We were also not much involved in European imperialism in Africa and the Far East because most of our territorial acquisitions were contiguous to the United States. We did acquire some minor possessions—Guam, Midway, Samoa, Hawaii, the Philippines—but not until late in the century. The United States forced Japan open, but we never parlayed it into much trade because the Japanese didn't want us. The United States played an outsider's role in the partitioning of China.

    Don't be overly impressed by the Monroe Doctrine. After it was announced in 1823 it lay dormant for much of the century. We did chase the French out of Mexico and helped push the British out of part of Venezuela and the Mosquito Coast; but we seemed to many Latin Americans to protect only so that which we could seize. We tried to buy or take Cuba and Santo Domingo (the Dominican Republic), and invaded Canada and Mexico in the nineteenth century.

48. **The correct answer is (A).** Antislavery parties campaigned unsuccessfully in this period. The chief characteristic of the three elections was the death of the Whig Party after 1852 and the sudden birth of the Republican Party in 1854, caused by Northern concern over the Kansas-Nebraska Act. The Republican Party never called for the extinction of slavery. The Whigs won in 1848 with Zachary Taylor. Millard Fillmore became president when Taylor died in July 1850.

49. **The correct answer is (D).** The musicals were the work of the long-time pair Rogers and Hammerstein. Stephen Foster, from the nineteenth century, is best remembered for two songs, "My Old Kentucky Home" and "Camp Town Races." Andrew Lloyd Webber and Tim Rice collaborated on *Jesus Christ Superstar*. John Ford and Cecil B. de Mille were early movie directors.

50. **The correct answer is (A).** Wilson pushed for legislative reforms in tariff, banking, and antitrust laws. Theodore Roosevelt was reluctant to fight Congress on these issues, but Wilson was not.

51. **The correct answer is (E).** The Roosevelt Corollary was directed at the Dominican Republic. Cuba was already a semiprotectorate of the United States by this time.

52. **The correct answer is (A).** Several hints point to W.E.B. DuBois. The first is the opposition to (Booker T.) Washington, who emphasized thrift, patience, and vocational education at Tuskegee Institute. The author emphasizes the importance of voting, attacks the racial caste system of Jim Crow, and proposes the education of the "talented tenth," the upper ten percent of the Negro race. Finally, he urges using "every civilized and peaceful method," including court suits, demonstrations, newsletters, and so on to fight for black civil rights. Booker T. Washington opposed such methods in public, although he secretly helped finance legal challenges to Jim Crow laws.

53. **The correct answer is (C).** The arrival of the "tobacco brides" was eagerly awaited by the lonely Jamestown males. I won't go into details! James Michener's novel, *Chesapeake*, delightfully describes the scene. The women literally auctioned themselves off to the highest bidder, in terms of acres of tobacco. Presumably a large plantation meant a more comfortable and secure life. The scarcity of women negated physical appearance and personal background, both of which left much to be desired. The dangerous voyage, the uncertain future, and instant marriage appealed only to single women who had no future in England or who faced prison. As late as the 1750s women were only 35 to 40 percent of the population in the colonies.

54. **The correct answer is (A).** In the first quote Emerson vented his anger at the Fugitive Slave Act, part of the Compromise of 1850. The second quote was Jefferson's prophetic reaction to the bitterness over the admission of Missouri as a slave state, eventually resolved in the Compromise of 1820. William Lloyd Garrison's first issue of *The Liberator* carried his uncompromising approach to abolition. More quotable than influential, he guaranteed that his position in the abolitionist movement would be overemphasized.

55. **The correct answer is (E).** The city manager and commission forms of government belong to the later Progressive Era. Galveston, Texas, invented the commission form of government after a hurricane struck the city in 1900. Divided responsibility sped recovery. Staunton, Virginia, first used the city manager plan in 1908. Following a disastrous flood in 1910, Dayton, Ohio, adopted the city manager plan, widely publicizing it as an efficient form of municipal government.

56. **The correct answer is (E).** George Washington Carver was a distinguished scientist at Tuskegee Institute, run by Booker T. Washington. Hoping to draw black farmers out of the vicious cycle of cotton production, Carver invented over three hundred products for peanuts, including peanut butter.

57. **The correct answer is (E).** All have been advanced as the causes or characteristics of Progressivism. The following historians are associated with each description: Joseph Huthmacher: urban lower classes; George Mowry and Richard Hofstadter: middle class status; David Thelan: corporate arrogance; Gabriel Kolko: political capitalism; and Arthur Schlesinger, Jr.: alternating cycles of reform and reaction.

58. **The correct answer is (D).** Corn was a major crop in Virginia and Maryland, but tobacco was the chief export. Barrels of rice passed through Charleston and Savannah. Molasses was imported into New England to make rum, the chief export. Fish was also a major New England export, but it was not shipped in gallons!

59. **The correct answer is (B).** It is the 1920s. Progressivism, the middle class social reform movement, never revived after the First World War. A series of failed strikes—the steel industry, the Boston police force, and the Seattle general strike—ushered in a decade of decline for organized labor and a decade of static wages for workers. Finally, American farmers mistakenly measured profit expectations against the lush years of the First World War when European farm output understandably fell off.

60. **The correct answer is (A).** In chronological order, the wartime conferences are the following. The Atlantic Charter meeting in August 1941 took place before U.S. participation in the Second World War. Churchill and FDR issued a statement of principles, and committed themselves to cooperation between the United States and Great Britain. In February 1943 at the Casablanca Conference, FDR and Churchill announced that the war would continue until the unconditional surrender of the Axis powers. In November 1943 FDR, Churchill, and Chiang Kai-shek (Jaing Jieshi) conferred in Cairo on the war against Japan and agreed upon postwar territorial changes in the Far East. In December 1943 FDR and Churchill met with Stalin for the first time. The most important agreement at Teheran was the American and British pledge to finally open a second front against Germany. In February 1945 an ailing FDR met with Stalin and Churchill at Yalta to make arrangements for the postwar world. A call was issued for a San Francisco meeting to establish the United Nations. The Yalta agreements were later heavily criticized as too favorable to the Soviet Union, but one should not read history backwards. At the time the agreements seemed essential. The United States needed Soviet help to defeat Japan, for it was estimated that the war against Japan would go on for two or three more years. The atomic bomb was not even tested until July 16, 1945. Japan's weakness far exceeded expectations. We no longer needed Soviet help, but it was too late to redefine the Yalta agreements. The Soviets were also granted dominance in Eastern Europe, but there was not much else FDR could have done since the Soviet army already occupied the area.

61. **The correct answer is (E).** Reread the Declaration of Independence. Only (E) is missing. Governments exist to provide equality of opportunity in a negative sense of not giving special privileges to a few, but nowhere does the Declaration of Independence assert everyone's right to an equal share of the wealth of the nation. The Declaration is primarily a political document.

62. **The correct answer is (D).** The official declaration didn't mention Canada. Americans were of two minds in regard to Canada: Some wanted to take it, and others wished to invade it as a means of punishing the British.

63. **The correct answer is (A).** Marcus Garvey formed the Universal Negro Improvement Association and the African Communities League in Jamaica in 1914. After moving to Harlem in 1916, Garvey became a symbol of black pride and nationalism. He devised a black, green, and red flag for blacks. His movement foundered after several bad business ventures and his conviction for mail fraud. The other black leaders came after Garvey. A. Philip Randolph organized the Brotherhood of Sleeping Car Porters and Maids in 1925. Robert C. Weaver was the first black cabinet member, appointed secretary of the new Department of Housing and Urban Development in 1966. Thurgood Marshall was the first black appointed to the Supreme Court. Ralph Bunche held several top positions in the United Nations and won the Nobel Peace Prize in 1950 for his work during the Arab-Israeli conflict following the creation of Israel.

64. **The correct answer is (C).** These three represent the most famous and best written protest works. There were thousands of pamphlets, speeches, and other such items, and the vast majority, as in the three works mentioned, addressed the bewildering mystery of how a society could produce simultaneously so much wealth and so much poverty.

65. **The correct answer is (B).** This entry is from the diary of Mrs. Thomas Burge, who lived near Covington, Georgia. After General Sherman captured Atlanta, he marched across Georgia laying waste to the countryside. His army lived off the land, confiscating food and supplies from civilians as they went. Sherman left few friends in Georgia; but his efforts demoralized the South and hastened the end of the war, which was his purpose. Grant and Sherman understood that war had changed; now war was no longer a chess match by professional soldiers but a total war involving everyone on both sides, including civilians. In the twentieth century the involvement of civilians reached alarming heights, noncombatants faring as badly as soldiers.

66. **The correct answer is (D).** Deference was the belief that everyone knew his or her place and acted accordingly. As long as colonists lived in relatively confined areas, everyone knew everyone else, and, therefore, all knew their positions socially and politically. Popular sovereignty, associated with the 1850s, referred to the opportunity for people to decide for themselves the slave or free status of their territories.

67. **The correct answer is (C).** The number of new jobs in the economy is 55,230,000 minus 49,180,000, or 6,050,000, a 12.3 percent growth. Hoover never had a second term. The Schechter "sick chicken" case declared the NRA unconstitutional in 1935. The economy was improving after that date, but the improvement had nothing to do with the decision. FDR never endorsed Keynesian economics; in many respects he remained an old-fashioned fiscal conservative in his thinking. The New Deal brought hope and work to many people in many sections of the economy, but statistics show that the New Deal alone did not solve the problem of unemployment. The Second World War solved it.

68. **The correct answer is (B).** Republican Senator Henry Cabot Lodge helped keep the United States out of the League of Nations after the First World War. Republican Senator Arthur H. Vandenberg helped put the United States into the United Nations after the Second World War.

69. **The correct answer is (A).** National political action proved to be futile and forced abolitionists to depend on moral persuasion. The Know-Nothings focused their attention only on the immigrant flood. Abolitionists never advocated a black sanctuary, although John Brown did raise the issue. Every Northern state considered the question of black suffrage in the period before the Civil War. All either rejected it or took voting rights away from blacks. The North was no paradise for free blacks or escaped slaves, but at least it didn't have slavery.

70. **The correct answer is (C).** The nuclear accident occurred at Three Mile Island, a nuclear power plant on the Susquehanna River near Harrisburg, Pennsylvania. Two other choices were also environmental disasters. Love Canal was a suburban subdivision built on top of a former dump for toxic chemicals near Niagara Falls, New York. In the 1970s residents turned into environmental activists to publicize their plight. The oil supertanker *Exxon Valdez* ran aground on an Alaskan peninsula in 1989, spilling oil into the fragile, pristine waters.

71. **The correct answer is (E).** Marshall's decision in *Gibbons* v. *Ogden* (1824) asserted congressional control over interstate commerce even in the absence of federal legislation. The case involved a New York state grant of a monopoly for steamship navigation between New York and New Jersey. The Marbury case concerned judicial review. McCulloch established the constitutionality of the Bank of the United States and therefore of a liberal interpretation of the elastic clause. The Cohens case established federal review of state court decisions. The Slaughterhouse Case in 1873 began the narrow interpretation of the Fourteenth Amendment in regard to civil rights for blacks.

72. **The correct answer is (B).** The quotations are from the Rev. Walter Rauschenbusch, professor of church history at Rochester Theological Seminary from 1902 to 1918. His book, *Christianity and the Social Crisis* (1907), established him as one of the leaders of the Social Gospel movement. The principles of the evolutionary ladder did not necessarily apply to man, the highest creature on that ladder.

73. **The correct answer is (E).** These two projects set off the "transportation revolution." Route A is the Erie Canal, financed entirely by the state of New York. The federal government funded Route B, the National Road. Jackson vetoed the Maysville Road project because it lay entirely within a single state, Kentucky. Jackson's political enemy, Henry Clay, sponsored the bill, which helped doom the proposal. At the time there were hundreds of proposals in Congress for federal funding for internal improvements.

74. **The correct answer is (C).** The Rev. Martin Luther King, Jr., delivered this famous speech in 1963 on the steps of the Lincoln Memorial climaxing the massive March on Washington. He was awarded the Nobel Peace Prize in 1964.

75. **The correct answer is (B).** For many reasons, complete neutrality proved impossible to maintain after 1914. Choices I, II, III, and V all contributed to what eventually was a distinctly unneutral American position toward Germany. The League of Nations was established after the First World War.

76. **The correct answer is (D).** Social Security benefits were expanded and cut in half the poverty rate among those 65 and older.

77. **The correct answer is (E).** California entered the Union as a free state in 1850, but no slave state entered to maintain the balance in the Senate. The Missouri Compromise in 1820 brought in Missouri as a slave state and Maine as a free state and also established the 36° 30' line dividing the slave and free territories to the Rocky Mountains. A provision in the original Constitution ended the slave trade in 1808. The Confederate debt went unpaid after the Civil War.

78. **The correct answer is (B).** Until the 1840s Rhode Island continued to operate its state government under the 1663 colonial charter, which restricted suffrage to property owners and their eldest sons. Rebuffed by legal and constitutional efforts to expand suffrage, Thomas Dorr led a popular uprising that gave Rhode Island two governors, two legislatures, and a very small armed confrontation. The federal government avoided getting involved in the ensuing political mess. Luckily, the dissidents won their original demand for expanded suffrage in a few years. None of the other choices involve the fundamental nature of state governments. In a court case that evolved out of Dorr's Rebellion, *Luther* v. *Borden*, 1849, Chief Justice Taney declared, "This is a purely political question and must be left in the hands of the political branches of the government to decide." The enforcement of the constitutional guarantee of a republican form of state government rested with either the Congress or the president. There is no recourse to the federal courts if either of the other branches decides not to act.

79. **The correct answer is (A).** By the end of the 1880s immigrants from Southern and Eastern Europe outnumbered any other group. The Irish who fled the potato famine came in the 1840s. Chinese immigration disappeared in the 1880s following the 1882 Chinese Exclusion Act. By the 1880s the majority of immigrants lived in large cities, giving a distinct flavor to urban America. The second immigration act in 1924 (following the 1921 immigration act) used 1890 as a base for calculating the percentage of immigrants from each country permitted into the United States.

80. **The correct answer is (B).** The Hutchinson family—Will, Anne, and seven children—arrived in Massachusetts in 1634 following their minister, Cotton Mather. In England, Mather's theological thinking led him to emphasize the covenant of grace to minimize the harsher aspects of the Old Testament emphasis on punishment. Anne Hutchinson, deeply religious and intellectually astute, carried the emphasis forward logically to argue that God's grace could not be "earned" in a contractual sense. God granted salvation because God granted salvation; one could not earn merit points to enter into salvation. To many Protestants at this time, including Puritans, the outward signs of earning points were success and standing in the community. Therefore, Anne Hutchinson's thinking threatened the religious, economic, and social threads that bound everyone together in an orderly, godly community. She had to go!

When Indians attacked and killed Anne and almost all her family six years later on Long Island, the Puritan leaders knew God had endorsed their decision. One wonders what the outcome would have been if Anne's husband, Will, more interested in his merchant activities than theology, had switched places with her. When she was excommunicated from the Puritan church she was blasted, "You have stepped out of your place, you have rather been a husband than a wife, and a preacher than a hearer. You have been a naughty woman."

SAMPLE TEST C

U.S. History
Section I

Time—55 Minutes • 80 Questions

Directions: Each of the questions or incomplete statements below is followed by five suggested answers or completions. Select the one that is best in each case and then blacken the corresponding space on the answer sheet.

1. The agitation that led to the American Revolution stimulated an ongoing political debate and discussion over the principles of a republican society. Over the next fifty years, agreement evolved on the fundamental tenets of a republican society, which included all of the following EXCEPT

    (A) A person's private, personal activities and interests are outside the realm of the community's concern.

    (B) A balanced government is best because all classes and elements of society are represented.

    (C) The purposes of religion and education are to define, defend, and instruct the community on public virtue.

    (D) The people are the source of political power, the source of sovereignty.

    (E) Public officials are accountable to the people through frequent elections.

2. Which of the following statements about nineteenth-century politics is correct?

    (A) Between Lincoln's election in 1860 and Wilson's election in 1912, the Republican Party dominated national politics, winning the presidency in all but eight years and always having a comfortable margin in the Senate and the House of Representatives.

    (B) Andrew Johnson and Chester A. Arthur were the only presidents between 1860 and 1912 who were assassinated.

    (C) Between 1860 and 1912 only Grover Cleveland and Theodore Roosevelt were elected to two successive terms in the White House.

    (D) Between 1860 and 1896 most national presidential elections were hotly contested, resulting in narrow victories for the winner in both popular and electoral vote.

    (E) Between 1860 and 1896 the Republican and Democratic parties cornered all the popular enthusiasm, and third parties never attracted a sizable following nor won electoral votes.

Collection of Customs Revenues

3. These charts illustrate

    (A) the unfairness of mercantilism before 1767

    (B) British neglect of the mercantile system before 1767

    (C) the reasons behind the Boston Massacre incident

   (D)   the impact of Hamilton's protective tariffs

   (E)   the increase in the national debt during the Confederation period

4. A major difference between the Democratic Party of the 1830s during the period of Andrew Jackson and the Republican Party in the decade of the 1850s prior to the Civil War was that

   (A)   the earlier Democratic Party opposed slavery; the later Republican Party did not

   (B)   the earlier Democratic Party drew many supporters from among the rising Northern industrialists; the later Republican Party drew many supporters from Southern slaveowners

   (C)   the earlier Democratic Party opposed special economic legislation favoring one group over the other; the later Republican Party favored economic legislation to produce widespread economic opportunity

   (D)   the earlier Democratic Party was not supported by recent immigrants; the later Republican Party was supported by recent immigrants

   (E)   the earlier Democratic Party supported internal improvements at the federal government's expense; the later Republican Party argued that all internal improvements were the responsibility of local and state governments

5. "The last speaker alluded to this movement as being that of a few disappointed women. From the first years to which my memory stretches, I have been a disappointed woman. When, with my brothers, I reached forth after the sources of knowledge, I was reproved with 'It isn't fit for you; it doesn't belong to women.' Then there was but one college in the world where women were admitted, and that was in Brazil. I would have found my way there, but by the time I was prepared to go, one was opened in the young state of Ohio—the first in the United States where women and Negroes could enjoy opportunities with white men. I was disappointed when I came to seek a profession worthy an immortal being—

every employment was closed to me, except those of the teacher, the seamstress, and the house-keeper. In education, in marriage, in religion, in everything, disappointment is the lot of woman. It shall be the business of my life to deepen this disappointment in every woman's heart until she bows down to it no longer. I wish that women, instead of being walking showcases, instead of begging of their fathers and brothers the latest and gayest new bonnet, would ask of them their rights."

This speech was extemporaneously delivered in reaction to another speech at a national women's rights convention in Cincinnati in October, 1855. The speaker, who later married and kept her maiden name, was

   (A)   Elizabeth Cady Stanton

   (B)   Lucy Stone

   (C)   Jane Addams

   (D)   Frances Perkins

   (E)   Shirley Chisholm

6. What were the attractions of California and Texas for Americans before they became part of the United States?

   (A)   Texas was an area of excellent cotton land; California had outstanding harbors.

   (B)   Texas was an area for the cattle industry; California for the vegetable exporting industry.

   (C)   Texas was a haven for runaway slaves; California was an attraction for Mormons.

   (D)   Texas was an area for the cattle industry; California for mining gold.

   (E)   Texas offered an easy access to the booming Mexico market for American goods; California in our hands would keep Great Britain and France out of the West.

7. In 1883 an auction was held to raise funds for the Statue of Liberty. Many artists submitted art, poems, or essays. One in particular, "The New Colossus" by Emma Lazarus, has become closely identified with the Statue of Liberty. This short poem was not placed at the entrance of the Statue of Liberty, however, until sixty-two years later. Why?

(A) These years coincided with a period of mounting popular concern that too many "huddled masses" were entering our country.

(B) The statue was not completely finished until sixty-two years later.

(C) The poem was placed there as part of the celebration of the two hundredth anniversary of the Declaration of Independence.

(D) Squabbles over rival claims of authorship prevented the use of the poem until the litigation was resolved.

(E) Many Americans objected to using a poem written by a Socialist radical.

8. Established churches (tax-supported) existed in all of the colonies EXCEPT

(A) New Jersey and Massachusetts

(B) Pennsylvania and Rhode Island

(C) Virginia and South Carolina

(D) Maryland and Pennsylvania

(E) New York and Rhode Island

9. Most of the thirteen original colonies

(A) started as proprietary colonies and became royal colonies by the 1750s

(B) were successful in terms of their original plans within their first twenty years

(C) started as charter colonies and became royal colonies by the 1750s

(D) were formed as royal colonies

(E) purchased their charters from their proprietors

10. The decade of the 1920s was one of dramatic accomplishments in sports. Which of the following was NOT an accomplishment of this decade?

(A) Gene Tunney defeated Jack Dempsey to become the heavyweight champion of the world.

(B) Jim Thorpe, later voted the most outstanding athlete of the first half of the twentieth century, won the decathlon at the Olympics and was later stripped of his medals for earlier playing semi-professional baseball.

(C) Red Grange, "the Galloping Ghost," starred as a football player at the University of Illinois and in the newly formed professional National Football League.

(D) Gertrude Ederle was the first woman to swim the English Channel.

(E) Babe Ruth hit 60 home runs in a single season.

11. All of the following curtailed freedom of speech or expression EXCEPT

(A) Lincoln's suspension of habeas corpus during the Civil War

(B) the gag rule in the 1830s and early 1840s

(C) the Sedition Act, 1918

(D) McCarthyism during the 1950s

(E) British writs of assistance in the early 1760s

12. In 1783 when the United States achieved its independence from Great Britain, much of North America was claimed by other nations. Which of the following correctly matches the nation and the area it claimed in 1783?

(A) Spain, Russia, Great Britain—Area B

(B) Sweden—Area E

(C) France—Area A

(D) France—Area D

(E) Great Britain—Area C

13. Two seemingly unconnected entrepreneurs in the years after the Second World War actually pursued business practices that were quite similar. Their innovations changed American business. The key to the business success of both Ray Kroc and William Levitt was

    (A) standardization of their product

    (B) franchising to locally owned businesses

    (C) advertising

    (D) promotion through mailings to individual residences

    (E) corporate takeovers to buy other companies financed by corporate downsizing of the company's employees

14. Many groups pushed for free public education beginning in the 1830s. Which of the following incorrectly describes why a segment of American society pushed for free public education in the antebellum period?

    (A) Factory owners wanted education to instill habits of discipline to improve the work force and increase productivity.

    (B) Women argued for education so that in their future role as mothers they could instill moral values into their children.

    (C) Employers wanted the work force upgraded in terms of knowledge in order to compete with workers in foreign countries.

    (D) Reformers hoped that public education would reduce the adverse effects of the beginnings of industrialization.

    (E) Labor union leaders urged free public schools as a means of providing equality of opportunity for the working class.

15. The two major "oil" news stories of the 1970s were the Arab oil embargo, which resulted in a sharp increase in oil prices, and

    (A) a fight over drilling rights on the Continental Shelf

    (B) the building of the Alaskan Pipeline

    (C) the dependence of the U.S. on Japanese oil supplies

    (D) the Teapot Dome scandal

    (E) the Whitewater scandal

16. Which historian first labeled the years immediately preceding the writing and adopting of the Constitution the "critical period" of American history?

    (A) Frederick Jackson Turner

    (B) John Fiske

    (C) Charles A. Beard

    (D) George F. Kennan

    (E) W.E.B. DuBois

17. In a decision in 1896 the Supreme Court ruled that if blacks chose to believe that "enforced separation of the races stamps the colored race with a badge of inferiority, it is not by reason of anything found in the act, but solely because the colored race chooses to put that construction upon it." "We cannot say that a law which authorizes or even requires the separation of the two races in public conveyances is unreasonable,..." "If the civil and political rights of both races be equal one cannot be inferior to the other civilly or politically. If one race be inferior to the other socially, the Constitution of the United States cannot put them upon the same plane."

    What was the case?

    (A) *Brown* v. *Bd. of Education*

    (B) *Plessy* v. *Ferguson*

    (C) Civil Rights cases

    (D) Slaughterhouse cases

    (E) *Sweatt* v. *Painter*

18. In his message to Congress on December 2, 1823, Monroe asserted that

    (A) any new European colonization, including the transfer of colonies from one European power to another, required U.S. approval

    (B) a long range American policy goal was the removal of all European colonies from the New World

    (C) as a New World power the United States was entitled to participate in conferences involving major European powers

    (D) the political systems of the Old World were so different from those of the New World that any attempt to extend European political systems to the New World would be dangerous to the United States

(E)   the United States sympathized with Spain's attempt to reacquire her lost South American colonies, but would not tolerate any other European power's acquiring them

19. "The issue is Socialism versus Capitalism. I am for Socialism because I am for humanity. We have been cursed with the reign of gold long enough. Money constitutes no proper basis of civilization. The time has come to regenerate society—we are on the eve of a universal change."

This passage was

(A)   delivered by William Jennings Bryan in his Cross of Gold speech

(B)   spoken by President Grover Cleveland responding to J. Pierpont Morgan's offer to rescue the U.S. Treasury by selling gold to the treasury

(C)   written by Eugene V. Debs after being imprisoned following the Pullman strike

(D)   part of the Populist Party platform in 1892

(E)   spoken by Franklin Roosevelt as part of his inaugural address, March 4, 1933

20. All but one of the following is associated with the retail business in the three decades before 1910. Which is NOT associated with the retail business in this period?

(A)   Mail-order houses such as Montgomery, Ward & Co. and Sears, Roebuck & Co. expanded.

(B)   Brand name advertising such as Uneeda Biscuits began.

(C)   Chain stores such as the Atlantic and Pacific Co. (A & P) and Woolworth's 5 and 10 cent stores expanded.

(D)   Retailers concentrated more on rural than urban markets.

(E)   Mail-order houses opened retail stores in small and medium-sized cities.

21. The Supreme Court case of *Schechter Poultry Corp.* v. *U.S.*

(A)   upheld the constitutionality of the Agricultural Adjustment Act

(B)   involved a dispute over the right of the federal government to control a business exclusively engaged in intrastate commerce

(C)   involved the power of the federal government to enforce the newly enacted Meat Inspection Act

(D)   found the NIRA (National Industrial Recovery Act) unconstitutional because Congress had delegated some of its legislative powers to the executive branch

(E)   reversed the decision in *U.S. v. Butler*

22. What is the correct chronological order for the following disputes with Great Britain?

I.   Webster-Ashburton Treaty

II.   Caroline affair

III. Laird rams

IV.   Trent affair

(A)   I, II, III, IV

(B)   III, I, II, IV

(C)   II, I, IV, III

(D)   I, II, IV, III

(E)   IV, II, III, I

23. "He has waged cruel war against human nature itself, violating its most sacred rights of life and liberty in the persons of a distant people who never offended him, captivating and carrying them into slavery in another hemisphere, or to incur miserable death in their transportation thither. This piratical warfare, the opprobrium of *infidel* powers, is the warfare of the Christian king of Great Britain. Determined to keep open a market where MEN should be bought and sold, he has prostituted his negative [his veto power] for suppressing every legislative attempt to prohibit or to restrain this execrable commerce; and that this assemblage of horrors might want no fact of distinguished die, he is now exciting these very people to rise in arms among us, and to purchase that liberty of which he deprived them, by murdering the people upon whom *he* also obtruded them; thus paying off

former crimes committed against the *liberties* of one people, with crimes which he urges them to commit against the *lives* of another."

This paragraph was part of the approximately twenty-five percent of the original Declaration of Independence, as written by Thomas Jefferson, that was deleted before approval by the Continental Congress. Representatives from which two states demanded the removal of this particular paragraph?

(A) Massachusetts and Pennsylvania

(B) Virginia and New Jersey

(C) Virginia and Maryland

(D) Connecticut and New York

(E) Georgia and South Carolina

24. Which of the following was NOT an influential book that affected American economic thinking?

(A) John Kenneth Galbraith, *The Affluent Society*

(B) John Maynard Keynes, *The General Theory of Employment, Interest and Money*

(C) Adam Smith, *The Wealth of Nations*

(D) Thorstein Veblen, *The Theory of the Leisure Class*

(E) Gunnar Myrdal, *An American Dilemma*

25. The Second Great Awakening

(A) led to an interest in other reforms

(B) included millennialist movements such as the Millerites

(C) originated in the "Burned Over" district of western New York and the frontier

(D) especially appealed to young women

(E) was characterized by all of the above

26. "That the further introduction of slavery or involuntary servitude be prohibited, except for the punishment of crimes, whereof the party shall have been fully convicted; and that all children born within the said State, after the admission thereof into the Union, shall be free at the age of twenty-five years."

This brief amendment to a piece of pending legislation concerning the admission of a new state set off a crisis. What was the amendment and what was the crisis?

(A) Wilmot Proviso, Compromise of 1850

(B) South Carolina "Exposition and Protest," Compromise of 1833

(C) End of slavery proposed in Virginia legislature debates of 1831–1832, admission of West Virginia

(D) Tallmadge Amendment, Missouri Compromise

(E) Popular sovereignty for the territories, Kansas-Nebraska Act

27. "The [signers of the treaty] solemnly declare in the names of their respective peoples that they condemn recourse to war for the solution of international controversies, and renounce it as an instrument of national policy in their relations with one another.

"The [signers of the treaty] agree that the settlement or solution of all disputes or conflicts of whatever nature or of whatever origin they may be, which may arise among them, shall never be sought except by pacific means."

This quotation is from the

(A) Yalta Agreement

(B) Truman Doctrine

(C) SALT I Agreement

(D) Nuclear Test Ban Treaty

(E) Kellogg-Briand Treaty

28. Which was true of the life of the average person in the 1920s?

(A) The variety in the diet worsened as a result of the depression.

(B) The average home experienced a "second industrial revolution," leading to improved bathrooms and an increase in electrical appliances.

(C) The invention of and introduction of television widened everyone's information about the world.

(D) Women found that housework was less time-consuming because of the invention of new appliances for the home.

(E) Workers were more prone to join a labor union.

29. In the period of early industrialization from the 1830s to the 1850s,

    (A)   merchant capitalists initially used the "putting out" system to farm out piecework for people to do in their homes

    (B)   the work force was composed primarily of white males who could not find employment or could not afford to go west

    (C)   worker discontent as expressed through strikes was rare

    (D)   new technologies rapidly replaced older technologies

    (E)   entrepreneurs raised capital funds for expansion by relying on American investors who were wealthy millionaires

30. Which is NOT true about the nation's capital, Washington, DC?

    (A)   The vote to locate the capital on the Potomac River was part of the horsetrading of votes, Southern and Pennsylvanian, for Hamilton's plan for the federal government's assumption of the state debts.

    (B)   The original size of the District of Columbia was a 10×10 mile square astride the Potomac River with land granted by the states of Virginia and Maryland.

    (C)   The nation's capital was designed by a commission headed by a French engineer, Major Pierre L'Enfant.

    (D)   After a dispute the head of the commission to design Washington, DC, left, taking the plans with him; but, Benjamin Banneker, a free black who was a member of the commission, redrew the plans from memory.

    (E)   The Residence Act, the law that relocated the capital to Washington, DC, in 1800, provided that during the first ten years under the Constitution the nation's capital would be New York City.

31. In 1892 near the end of a lifetime of fighting for women's rights, a crusader summarized all her reasons:

    "The strongest reason for giving woman all the opportunities for higher education, for the full development of her faculties, her forces of mind and body; for giving her the most enlarged freedom of thought and action; a complete emancipation from all forms of bondage, of custom, dependence, superstition; from all the crippling influences of fear—is the solitude and personal responsibility of her own individual life. The strongest reason why we ask for woman a voice in the government under which she lives; in the religion she is asked to believe; equality in social life, where she is the chief factor; a place in the trades and professions, where she may earn her bread, is because of her birthright to self-sovereignty; because as an individual, she must rely on herself."

    She was

    (A)   Alice Paul

    (B)   Harriet Beecher Stowe

    (C)   Elizabeth Cady Stanton

    (D)   Lucretia Mott

    (E)   Abigail Adams

32. His presidency was marked by inactivity and great quotations, but the American people still loved him. His most famous quotes were: "The chief business of the American people is business," and "The man who builds a factory builds a temple.... The man who works there worships there." Who was this president?

    (A)   Warren G. Harding

    (B)   Woodrow Wilson

    (C)   Herbert Hoover

    (D)   Calvin Coolidge

    (E)   William Howard Taft

33. In 1949 the mood of the Cold War changed dramatically. For the next two years the news seemed to carry one crisis after another. Americans developed a siege mentality; communism seemed to be at the gates, threatening us everywhere. Which of the following was NOT part of the Cold War in the years from 1949 to 1951?

    (A)   The Alger Hiss trial

    (B)   The trial of Julius and Ethel Rosenberg

    (C)   The Soviet Union exploded its first atomic bomb

    (D)   The Korean War started

    (E)   The Truman Doctrine was announced

34. The antislavery reformer William Lloyd Garrison
    (A) was a promoter of the program of the American Colonization Society
    (B) advocated the immediate end of slavery
    (C) was primarily motivated by a desire to end racism and to establish a society of equals
    (D) opposed as impractical the ideas of some Northerners that the North should secede from the South
    (E) adopted an approach designed to minimize confrontation and hostility among Northerners so that they would concentrate on the intellectual ideas of his antislavery proposals

35. Which of the following is NOT true concerning the legislative programs of the presidency of Lyndon Johnson?
    (A) The Medicare program was begun.
    (B) Federal aid to public education increased.
    (C) Wage and price controls were introduced to guard against inflation.
    (D) The authority of the federal government over the states increased because many programs centralized decision making in the federal government.
    (E) Immigration laws were revised to end quotas based on national origins.

36. A common theme among travel narratives written by European visitors to the United States was the classlessness of American society. Crevecoeur, Lafayette, and others all commented on our lack of class distinctions. Lafayette wrote in 1777, "I will now tell you about the country and its inhabitants. They are as agreeable as my enthusiasm had painted them. Simplicity of manners, kindness, love of country and of liberty, and a delightful equality everywhere prevail. The wealthiest man and the poorest are on a level; and, although there are some large fortunes, I challenge anyone to discover the slightest difference between the manners of these two classes respectively toward each other."

    This characteristic of American society later became a cornerstone in the theories of a historian who trumpeted the role of the frontier as a leveling, equalizing factor in American development. The historian was

(A) Frederick Jackson Turner
(B) William Dunning
(C) John Fiske
(D) Charles Beard
(E) George Bancroft

37. Born in England of Quaker parents, he participated in both the American and the French revolutions through his inflammatory writings. Who is described?
    (A) Marquis de Lafayette
    (B) Thaddeus Kosciusko
    (C) Baron von Steuben
    (D) Thomas Paine
    (E) John Paul Jones

38. "The Communist threat is a global one. Its successful advance in one sector threatens the destruction of every other sector.

    "Apart from the military need, as I saw it, to neutralize sanctuary protection given the enemy north of the Yalu, I felt that military necessity in the conduct of the war made necessary:

    (1) The intensification of our economic blockade against China.

    (2) The imposition of a naval blockade against the China coast.

    (3) Removal of restrictions on air reconnaissance of China's coastal areas and of Manchuria.

    (4) Removal of restrictions on the forces of the Republic of China on Formosa, with logistical support to contribute to their effective operations against the Chinese mainland. . . .

    "War's very object is victory, not prolonged indecision."

    Who made this speech on April 19, 1951?
    (A) Harry Truman after the invasion of South Korea
    (B) Republican candidate Thomas Dewey after the fall of China to the communists
    (C) General Westmoreland during the Vietnam War
    (D) Harry Truman issuing the Truman Doctrine
    (E) General MacArthur after being relieved of his command in the Korean War

39. The trial of former vice-president Aaron Burr for treason in Richmond in 1807 is most important and most significant in American history because

(A) it exposed his scheme to seize control of Louisiana

(B) it showed the political reasons why Burr had challenged Hamilton to a duel

(C) it revealed the proposed New England Confederacy, the Federalist plan to have New England and New York secede from the United States

(D) Chief Justice John Marshall firmly established the Constitution's definition of treason

(E) it exposed the duplicity of Hamilton's behind-the-scenes attempt to help elect Burr president over Thomas Jefferson in the House of Representatives voting in the election of 1800

40. Title IX of the Education Amendments of 1972

(A) provided federal funds for audio-visual equipment for public schools

(B) provided federal funds for the construction of science labs to boost scientific knowledge to permit American students to catch up to Russian technological gains

(C) stimulated efforts to improve the study of foreign languages

(D) provided federal funds to improve secondary vocational education programs to make American graduates more competitive with the workers of other nations

(E) outlawed imbalanced gender-based funding in intercollegiate athletic programs

List One	List Two	List Three
1. New York City	1. Philadelphia	1. New York City
2. Philadelphia	2. New York City	2. Philadelphia
3. Boston	3. Boston	3. Baltimore
4. Baltimore	4. Charleston, SC	4. Boston
5. Cincinnati	5. Baltimore	5. New Orleans
6. New Orleans	6. Salem, MA	6. Charleston, SC
7. St. Louis	7. Newport, RI	7. Washington, DC
8. Pittsburgh	8. Providence, RI	8. Salem, MA
9. Louisville, KY	9. Marblehead, MA	9. Albany, NY
10. Albany, NY	10. Gloucester, MA	10. Richmond, VA

41. These three lists rank the cities in the United States in order from the largest to the tenth-largest city according to the census. Based on what you know about the growth of and changes in the American economy between 1790 and 1850, which of the choices identifies the lists by census year?

(A) 1850, 1790, 1820

(B) 1790, 1820, 1850

(C) 1790, 1850, 1820

(D) 1820, 1790, 1850

(E) 1820, 1850, 1790

42. "A group of frontier States entered the Union with democratic provisions respecting the suffrage, and with devotion to the nation that gave them their lands, built their roads and canals, regulated their territorial life, and made them equals in the sisterhood of States. At last these Western forces of aggressive nationalism and democracy took possession of the government in the person of the man who best embodied them, _____"

Who, according to historian Frederick Jackson Turner, was the "man who best embodied" the forces and characteristics of the frontier West?

(A) William Jennings Bryan

(B) Andrew Jackson

(C) Abraham Lincoln

(D) Theodore Roosevelt

(E) Daniel Webster

43. The North American continent was explored by many different nations and settled at many different points. What is the correct order in which permanent settlements appeared within the modern boundaries of the United States and Canada?

    (A) Jamestown, Quebec, St. Augustine, Plymouth, Santa Fe

    (B) St. Augustine, Santa Fe, Quebec, Jamestown, Plymouth

    (C) Plymouth, Jamestown, St. Augustine, Santa Fe, Quebec

    (D) Quebec, Santa Fe, St. Augustine, Plymouth, Jamestown

    (E) St. Augustine, Jamestown, Quebec, Santa Fe, Plymouth

44. This cartoon was used in support of

    (A) recruiting soldiers for the First World War to silence radical opposition to the draft

    (B) overcoming opposition to joining the League of Nations

    (C) the Texas revolution against Mexico

    (D) the Albany Plan of Union and independence from Great Britain

    (E) the formation of the Confederacy when the South seceded

45. "The price which society pays for the law of competition, like the price it pays for cheap comforts and luxuries, is also great; but the advantages of this law are also greater still, for it is to this law that we owe our wonderful material development, which brings improved conditions in its train. But, whether the law be benign or not, we must say of it, as we say of the change in the conditions of men to which we have referred: It is here; we cannot evade it; no substitutes for it have been found; and while the law may be sometimes hard for the individual, it is best for the race, because it insures the survival of the fittest in every department. We accept and welcome, therefore, as conditions to which we must accommodate ourselves, great inequality of environment, the concentration of business, industrial and commercial, in the hands of a few, and the law of competition between these, as being not only beneficial, but essential for the future progress of the race."

    Which of the following would NOT have supported this statement?

    (A) William Graham Sumner

    (B) Herbert Spencer

    (C) Henry George

    (D) John D. Rockefeller

    (E) Andrew Carnegie

46. The Tredegar Iron Company in Richmond, Virginia, is most significant in the history of the antebellum South because in 1847

    (A) the company decided to begin manufacturing cannons, which later provided a vital source to the Confederacy

    (B) it furnished the arms needed to end Nat Turner's revolt

    (C) a successful strike caused the company to shut down, leading Southerners to channel their future investments into cotton production rather than industrial development

    (D) the company began using slave labor, proving that slavery was an institution adaptable to industrial needs

    (E) the company announced that it did not need the favorable protection granted by the protective tariff, undercutting the claims of Northern industrialists that a high protective tariff was vital to American industrial development

47. Which of the following were events in our foreign relations with Japan?

    I.   Burlingame Treaty

    II.   San Francisco School Board incident

    III. Gentlemen's Agreement

    IV.   Tampico landing

    V.   Insular Cases

    (A) II and III only

    (B) I, II, III, and V only

    (C) I, III, and V only

    (D) II, III, and V only

    (E) II and IV only

48. The positions of loose construction and strict construction of the Constitution were first established in letters written by Hamilton and Jefferson to President Washington. The letters concerned

    (A) the issue of creating a Bank of the United States

    (B) our obligations to France under the Treaty of 1778

    (C) consolidating the national, state, and foreign debt and paying them at face value

    (D) an appropriate response to the Whiskey Rebellion

    (E) Jefferson's decision to purchase Louisiana

49. In the history of the civil rights movement, the Montgomery bus boycott is most significant because

    (A) Rosa Parks refused to surrender her seat and was arrested

    (B) nonviolent civil disobedience methods were adopted

    (C) the momentum shifted from a legalistic movement centered in the courts to a popular-based movement in the streets

    (D) the Rev. Martin Luther King, Jr., led the boycott

    (E) for the first time the president supported the civil rights movement

50. In their writing of the Constitution, the Founding Fathers were strongly influenced by the ideas of an Englishman and a Frenchman. These were, respectively,

    (A) John Locke and de Tocqueville

    (B) Edmund Burke and Lafayette

    (C) Alexander Hamilton and Montesquieu

    (D) James Madison and Lafayette

    (E) John Locke and Montesquieu

51. Gross National Product, GNP, is a measuring tool used by economists to judge the total output of a nation. The term applies to the grand total of all the goods and services produced in a nation in one year. Another economic statistic, the national debt, measures the indebtedness of the federal government, what the federal government has borrowed and owes in bonds. Which of the following statements about the GNP and the national debt during the 1980s is true?

    (A) The GNP languished due to slow growth, and the national debt increased by doubling.

    (B) The GNP doubled, and the national debt tripled.

    (C) The Democratic-controlled Congress reduced the national debt under the two Republican presidents, while the GNP grew slowly.

    (D) Two tax cuts pushed through Congress by Democratic presidents stimulated the economy, tripling the GNP and reducing the national debt.

    (E) Neither the national debt nor the GNP changed much from the trends of the previous two decades.

52. From 1865 to 1900 city dwellers faced many problems. Which was NOT an urban problem in this period?

    (A) Clogged downtown streets congested with streetcars, pedestrians, and horses

    (B) A lack of open space for parks

    (C) A lack of clean water and inadequate sewerage facilities

    (D) An influx of blacks moving out of the South into northern cities, creating large black ghettos

    (E) Reliance upon a politically chosen police force to maintain order

53. In the presidential campaign of 1968,

    (A)   the Republican Party captured the White House and control of both houses of Congress

    (B)   two presidential candidates, Martin Luther King, Jr., and Robert F. Kennedy, were assassinated

    (C)   the Democratic Party was divided and fragmented

    (D)   foreign policy issues were insignificant

    (E)   the major political issue was economic stability and economic growth

54. As president he set aside nearly one hundred fifty million acres as national forest land; convinced Congress to pass the Newlands Act to provide federal funding for dams and reclamation projects; and convened the nation's first governors' conference on conservation. He was

    (A)   William McKinley

    (B)   Theodore Roosevelt

    (C)   Franklin Roosevelt

    (D)   George Bush

    (E)   Woodrow Wilson

55. Which of the following statements is NOT true concerning diplomatic events in this area from 1945 to 1990?

    (A)   Country F invaded Kuwait in 1990, leading to Desert Storm in 1991.

    (B)   A communist threat to countries E and B convinced President Truman to announce the Truman Doctrine.

    (C)   Country K built the Aswan Dam with financial aid from the Soviet Union.

    (D)   President Carter's Camp David Accords in 1979 led to a peace treaty between countries A and K.

    (E)   A revolution in country C brought the Ayatollah Khomeini to power and presented the United States with a hostage situation after a mob stormed the U.S. embassy.

56. The American Revolution, broadly defined, is the second-most popular topic for writers and readers of American history (the Civil War is number one). Participants and later historians argued over what the Revolution was and what it meant. John Adams, writing in 1818, offered a personal perspective:

    "But what do we mean by the American Revolution? Do we mean the American war? The Revolution was effected before the war commenced. The Revolution was in the minds and hearts of the people. . . . This radical change in the principles, opinions, sentiments, and affections of the people, was the real American Revolution."

    Why had the British colonists become "Americans" in their "minds and hearts" by the 1770s? Select the explanation that does NOT apply.

    (A)   Colonial participation in England's wars against France and Spain embittered the colonists and diminished the image of the British army and the individual British soldier, such as the American capture of the French fort at Louisbourg in 1745 and its subsequent return to the French at the peace treaty.

    (B)   The growing perception among the colonists in their visits to England that American society was morally superior to English society.

    (C)   The increasing American reliance upon written constitutions and charters, a standard against which to judge acts and actions, as opposed to the British theory that the "constitution" was all the laws and acts and traditions of Great Britain, which, therefore, could be changed.

    (D)   The rise of the lower house of the colonial assemblies in the sense that the colonists increasingly felt that taxes and laws affecting property should come from the legislative body closest to the taxpayer, the colonial assembly, rather than from parliament.

(E)   The publication of Noah Webster's *An American Dictionary of the English Language* proved to Americans that they were evolving toward their own distinct dialect and were creating a distinct American culture.

57. Which best explains the rise of political parties in the 1790s?

(A)   Hamilton's and Jefferson's personal dislike for one another

(B)   A continuation of the Loyalists-Revolutionaries split of the Revolutionary War era

(C)   A continuation of the division of those for and against (the Antifederalists) the ratification of the Constitution

(D)   The desire of Washington for two distinct viewpoints on policy issues so that he could evaluate the issues to select the better course of action

(E)   Differing ideology and viewpoints accented by disagreements over the establishment of a national bank; the payment of the foreign, national, and state debts; our foreign policies; and the Alien and Sedition Acts

58. Between 1870 and 1900 the number of women in the work force increased dramatically—in manufacturing, from 364,097 to 1,380,469; in transportation and communications, from 1,050 to 42,181; and in clerical occupations, from 1,910 to 187,053. Which of the following was a characteristic accompanying this increase in the number of women working?

(A)   Working reinforced the trend, which began with industrialization, of women seeing themselves primarily as mothers.

(B)   Most of the women entering the work force were middle-class women seeking professional fulfillment.

(C)   Most women joining the work force saw themselves as beginning lifelong careers as workers supplementing the family income.

(D)   For immigrant women, ethnic background, cultural traditions, and the order of their group's arrival in the United States all affected choice of type and place of work performed.

(E)   Most working women were recently married young women who were working to pay for the mortgage.

59. The New Deal of Franklin Roosevelt inaugurated the "welfare state," which theoretically established a floor below which society will not permit its citizens to fall and a ceiling above which individuals should not be permitted to rise. Four of the following are aspects of the "welfare state." Which is NOT?

(A)   Veterans' benefits

(B)   Unemployment compensation

(C)   Personal progressive income tax

(D)   Aid to dependent children

(E)   Corporate progressive income tax

60. Bruce Barton's *The Man Nobody Knows* (1925) differed from William Stead's *If Christ Came to Chicago* (1894) and Charles Sheldon's *In His Steps* (1897) in that Barton's book

(A)   was part of the Social Gospel movement

(B)   reconciled business ethics and Christian teachings

(C)   condemned big businessmen for not doing enough to aid the poor

(D)   concerned advertising and politics, whereas the other two concerned religion

(E)   was part of the muckraking tradition

61. "The man over there says that women need to be helped into carriages, and lifted over ditches, and to have the best place everywhere. Nobody ever helps me into carriages, or over mud-puddles, or gives me any best place! And ain't I a woman?

"Look at me! Look at my arm! I have ploughed and planted, and gathered into barns, and no man could head me! And ain't I a woman? I could work as much and eat as much as a man—when I could get it—and bear the lash as well! And ain't I a woman? I have born thirteen children, and seen them all sold off to slavery, and when I cried out with my mother's grief, none but Jesus heard me! And ain't I a woman?"

This speaker had interrupted another speaker at a women's rights convention in Akron in 1851. Who was the person who gave this electrifying extemporaneous speech to the convention?

(A) Harriet Beecher Stowe

(B) Peggy Eaton

(C) Sojourner Truth

(D) Harriet Tubman

(E) Dorothea Dix

62. Which post-Second World War ally threatened the solidarity of the Western alliance by opposing Great Britain's entry into the Common Market and by forcing the removal from its soil of NATO headquarters?

(A) France

(B) China

(C) Japan

(D) Germany

(E) The United Nations

63. The map above

(A) illustrates the division between the Frostbelt and the Sunbelt

(B) illustrates why so many presidential candidates came from the Midwest in the latter half of the nineteenth century

(C) graphically distorts the approximate electoral vote

(D) shows why the Populist Party worried professional politicians in the Democratic and Republican parties

(E) is distorted to overrepresent the wealthy states

64. Which Supreme Court decisions concerned the principle that the Sixth and Fourteenth amendments guaranteed the right to legal counsel in criminal prosecutions and that the Fifth Amendment guaranteed the right to remain silent and not to incriminate oneself?

I. *Gideon* v. *Wainwright*, 1963

II. *Escobedo* v. *Illinois*, 1964

III. *Miranda* v. *Arizona*, 1966

IV. *Baker* v. *Carr*, 1962

V. Bakke case, 1978

(A) I and V only

(B) II, III, and IV only

(C) I, IV, and V only

(D) I, II, and III only

(E) II, III, and V only

65. Which of the following was NOT true concerning the creation of the National Association for the Advancement of Colored People, the NAACP?

(A) It grew out of the Niagara Movement, a 1905 convention of black leaders.

(B) It supported the programs and philosophy of Booker T. Washington.

(C) The immediate impetus for it sprang from a race riot in Springfield, Illinois, within sight of Lincoln's tomb.

(D) Many of the whites behind it were the descendants of abolitionists.

(E) It used the methods of publicity and suing in court to achieve its objectives.

66. In the policies they followed, Eisenhower, Nixon, and Reagan all emphasized

(A) stricter regulation of big business

(B) shifting some responsibilities from the federal government to the state and local governments

(C) reducing American responsibilities as the leader of the coalition of free nations

(D) expanding the New Deal programs

(E) reducing the federal deficit by cutting defense spending

67. Which of the following women is NOT correctly matched to the activity for which she was "the first"?

(A) Geraldine Ferraro—the first woman nominated by a major political party for the vice presidency

(B) Sally Ride—the first woman astronaut

(C) Sandra Day O'Connor—the first woman appointed to the Supreme Court

(D) Frances Perkins—the first woman to win the Nobel Peace Prize

(E) Emily Post—the first woman to write a standard etiquette book for the middle class

68. "Every contract, combination in the form of trust or otherwise, or conspiracy, in restraint of trade or commerce among the several States, or with foreign nations, is hereby declared to be illegal. Every person who shall make any such contract or engage in any such combination or conspiracy, shall be deemed guilty of a misdemeanor, and, on conviction thereof, shall be punished. . . .

"Every person who shall monopoly, or attempt to monopolize, or combine or conspire with any other person or persons, to monopolize any part of the trade or commerce among the several States, or with foreign nations, shall be deemed guilty of a misdemeanor, and, on conviction thereof, shall be punished."

The law from which this quotation is taken

(A) proved difficult to enforce against big business

(B) passed Congress by a close vote after a bitter struggle

(C) represented a new departure and a new direction in governmental policy

(D) continued the tradition of the Clayton Antitrust Act

(E) was part of the New Deal legislation

69. When the Founding Fathers wrote the Constitution they provided a fixed term of office for the president. One of the curious effects of holding presidential elections every four years is that we hold them even during periods of national crisis or war. Which of the following correctly describes a wartime presidential election?

(A) In 1864 during the Civil War, President Abraham Lincoln won reelection by narrowly defeating his opponent, General George McClellan.

(B) In 1944 during the Second World War, President Franklin Roosevelt decisively defeated Governor Thomas Dewey of New York for the second time.

(C) In 1916 while the First World War raged in Europe, President Woodrow Wilson defeated former President Theodore Roosevelt and his Progressive (Bull Moose) Party.

(D)   In 1952 during the Korean War, the Republican candidate General Dwight David Eisenhower defeated the Democratic incumbent, Harry S. Truman.

(E)   While the Vietnam War continued, President Lyndon Johnson lost to the Republican Ronald Reagan in 1968.

70.   Which of the following is true concerning the Salem witch trials in 1693?

  I.   Trials for witchcraft were more common in America than in Europe; 20 died at Salem alone and over 300 were accused of witchcraft just in colonial New England.

  II.   The accusers were mostly young girls and the accused were mostly older women, indicating generational strife.

  III.   The whole incident, accusations and trials, took place in an uncertain, unstable, confused political atmosphere for the Massachusetts Bay colony, after the deposing of Sir Edmund Andros and the Dominion of New England.

  IV.   One important factor was a geographical split within Salem, as reflected in old quarrels over the selection of a minister, caused by economic changes creating a western agricultural oriented farm region and a more commercially oriented eastern region.

  V.   A large number of the accused were "feme sole," or "women alone," who threatened the male-dominated society because they were widows who owned property or the sole family survivors who stood to inherit property.

(A)   I, II, III, IV, and V

(B)   I, II, and V only

(C)   I, III, and IV only

(D)   II, IV, and V only

(E)   II, III, IV, and V only

71.   The efforts of urban reformers in the late nineteenth century were greatly aided by a fundamental change

(A)   in the policies of the Roman Catholic Church when Pope Leo XIII issued his 1893 Papal encyclical, *Rerum Novarum*

(B)   in the European origins of the immigrants, shifting from Northern and Western Europe to mostly Southern and Eastern Europe

(C)   in thinking among intellectuals when Darwin published his book, *The Origin of Species*

(D)   in the prohibitionist movement away from prohibition and toward temperance

(E)   in thinking in favor of providing increased opportunities for blacks living in Northern cities

72.   What was the new policy adopted by the federal government in a treaty signed at Fort Laramie, Wyoming, in 1851?

(A)   To create schools such as the Carlisle Indian School to educate Native Americans (Indians) so as to eventually integrate them into American society

(B)   To give each Native American (Indian) a farm, similar to that available under the Homestead Act, so that Native Americans (Indians) would become individual farmers

(C)   To assign the Plains Indians areas that would be specifically reserved for each tribe, ending free movement across the prairies and ending intertribal warfare

(D)   To assign every tribe to a reservation in Oklahoma, the new Indian territory

(E)   To control trade between whites and Native Americans (Indians) by channeling it through the Bureau of Indian Affairs

73.   Which of the following is an idea of Woodrow Wilson's that came to be an accepted part of United States foreign policy after 1945?

(A)   Nonrecognition of revolutionary governments will lead to the downfall of such offensive governments.

(B)   The security of the United States is best preserved through collective security.

(C)   Isolation has kept us out of past European wars and will keep us out of future European wars.

(D)   The World Court is the best forum to settle international disputes.

(E)   Arbitration treaties between nations provide a much needed period for tempers to cool.

74.   In 1911 in the Standard Oil Case, the Supreme Court ruled that a "rule of reason" must be applied to distinguish between good trusts and bad trusts; because when Congress passed the legislation involved in the case it really intended to apply "the standard of reason which had been applied at the common law and in this country in dealing with subjects of the character embraced by this statute, . . ."

What was the law under which this case arrived at the Supreme Court?

(A)   Jim Crow laws

(B)   Sherman Antitrust Act

(C)   Interstate Commerce Act

(D)   National Industrial Recovery Act

(E)   Pendleton Act

75.   "My fellow citizens . . . I must speak to you about the serious situation that has arisen in Little Rock.... In that city, under the leadership of demagogic extremists, disorderly mobs have deliberately prevented the carrying out of proper orders from a federal court. Local authorities have not eliminated that violent opposition and, under the law, I yesterday issued a proclamation calling upon the mob to disperse.

"This morning the mob again gathered in front of the Central High School of Little Rock, obviously for the purpose of again preventing the carrying out of the court's order relating to the admission of Negro children to that school.

"Whenever normal agencies prove inadequate to the task and it becomes necessary for the executive branch of the federal government to use its powers and authority to uphold federal courts, the President's responsibility is inescapable.

"In accordance with that responsibility, I have today issued an Executive Order directing the use of troops under federal authority to aid in the execution of federal law at Little Rock, Arkansas."

Who was the governor of Arkansas who provoked this confrontation and who was the president who met the challenge?

(A)   Orvil Faubus and Dwight D. Eisenhower

(B)   George Wallace and John F. Kennedy

(C)   George Wallace and Richard Nixon

(D)   Strom Thurmond and Harry Truman

(E)   Lester Maddox and Lyndon Johnson

76.   Which is NOT true concerning the Alien and Sedition Acts?

(A)   They were used by the president to silence his political opponents, the Federalist newspaper editors.

(B)   They gave the president the power to imprison or to deport aliens dangerous to the national welfare.

(C)   They raised the residency requirement from five to fourteen years for naturalized citizenship.

(D)   They provided fines and imprisonment for those who spoke or published "false, scandalous, and malicious writing or writings against the government of the United States" or Congress or the president.

(E)   They grew out of the public anger at the undeclared naval war with France, the XYZ affair, the influx of Irish and French fleeing the abortive Irish Revolution of 1798 and the French Revolution of the 1790s.

77.   After the First World War, the American economy suffered from high unemployment. After the Second World War, the American economy avoided high unemployment. Which of the following did NOT contribute to avoiding high unemployment after the Second World War?

(A)   The G.I. Bill took thousands of veterans out of the labor force.

(B)   Many women left the labor force because they considered their Second World War service to be a temporary patriotic duty.

(C)   The Employment Act of 1946 committed the federal government to following policies to achieve full employment.

(D)   Maintaining a peacetime army after the Second World War required many in the armed forces, unlike the experience after the First World War.

(E)   The depression following the Second World War was not as severe as the one following the First.

78.   Political scandals in the late nineteenth century, between 1865 and 1890, included

(A)   Watergate and the Peggy Eaton affair

(B)   the Whiskey Ring and Teapot Dome

(C)   Teapot Dome and Crédit Mobilier

(D)   the Whiskey Ring and Crédit Mobilier

(E)   the Yazoo land deal and the Whiskey Ring

79.   During the late nineteenth century the American home and family benefited greatly from innovations in food preparation and food processing. Which of the following individuals is NOT correctly matched to his or her area of accomplishment?

(A)   Fannie Farmer—her cookbook was the first to standardize measurements in meal preparation in teaspoons, tablespoons, cups, and so forth.

(B)   Gustavus Swift—he shipped meat and meat by-products to Eastern cities in refrigerated railroad cars, increasing the variety of meat and reducing the cost.

(C)   H.J. Heinz—he canned pickles, vegetables, and fruits and developed prepared food products such as ketchup.

(D)   Philip Armour—he developed the citrus fruit industry and brought low-priced citrus fruits to urban markets.

(E)   Gail Borden—he developed condensed milk and canned milk, which freed everyone from the need to acquire fresh milk daily.

80.   The 1735 trial of John Peter Zenger

(A)   was a victory for the colonial argument against the British use of writs of assistance for search warrants

(B)   helped establish freedom of religion, as guaranteed in the 1649 Act of Toleration

(C)   was a milestone in the development of freedom of the press

(D)   grew out of the simple issue of a commission for a justice of the peace in Washington, DC, and established the principle of judicial review

(E)   established the clear definition of treason that was later incorporated into the Constitution: levying war against the United States, or in adhering to their enemies, giving them aid and comfort, testified to by two witnesses to the same overt act

Answer Key

1. A	17. B	33. E	49. C	65. B
2. D	18. D	34. B	50. E	66. B
3. B	19. C	35. C	51. B	67. D
4. C	20. D	36. A	52. D	68. A
5. B	21. D	37. D	53. C	69. A
6. A	22. C	38. E	54. B	70. E
7. A	23. E	39. D	55. D	71. A
8. B	24. E	40. E	56. E	72. C
9. A	25. E	41. A	57. E	73. B
10. B	26. D	42. B	58. D	74. B
11. E	27. E	43. E	59. A	75. A
12. A	28. B	44. D	60. B	76. A
13. A	29. A	45. C	61. C	77. E
14. C	30. E	46. D	62. A	78. D
15. B	31. C	47. A	63. B	79. D
16. B	32. D	48. A	64. D	80. C

Explanatory Answers

1. **The correct answer is (A).** In the late twentieth century, the concept of republicanism surfaced to explain and complicate much of the writing of American history about the era from the American Revolution into the nineteenth century. An exact definition is slippery, but two basic concepts persist. First, the individual has the responsibility to practice self-denial, or virtue. "The sacrifice of individual interests to the greater good of the whole formed the essence of republicanism and comprehended for Americans the idealistic goal of their Revolution." (Gordon S. Wood, *The Creation of the American Republic, 1776–1787.*) No individual had the right to place his own interests above those of the community. Your own business was not your own business if it conflicted with the community's values. An accompanying set of values emphasized the preeminence of the "public good." Property holders, who could exercise true independent thought and action, had a responsibility to become involved in the civic life of the community, alert for the first signs of corruption or the fatal attraction of luxury. Women, unable to participate openly in the political process, nevertheless played an important public role by instilling the correct republican values into their children—the sons to participate and the daughters to pass on to their children.

2. **The correct answer is (D).** The Republicans won the presidency for all but eight years between 1860 and 1912, but they rarely controlled both houses of Congress. A quick glance at the presidents gives the impression that Republicans dominated from 1860 to 1912. A closer look doesn't support that conclusion. Lincoln, Garfield, and McKinley were assassinated in this period. Lincoln, Grant, and McKinley were all reelected. Third parties won many popular and electoral votes between 1860 and 1896, especially the Greenback Labor Party in 1880 and the Populist Party in 1892. Lincoln in 1860, Hayes in 1876, Garfield in 1880, and Cleveland in 1892 all won the presidency with less than 50 percent of the total popular vote for all candidates. The electoral vote count in 1876 was Hayes 185, Tilden 184.

3. **The correct answer is (B).** Before 1767 it cost the British more to collect the customs duties than the total sums they collected! After 1767 the British made a determined effort to collect their taxes, and the resulting ill will helped fuel the revolutionary spirit.

4. **The correct answer is (C).** Economic opportunity was a major thrust for both the Democrats in the 1830s and the newly formed Republicans in the 1850s. The Democrats wanted to end special economic privileges granted by governments and to take government out of the business of giving one group or class an artificial advantage, as shown by the Bank war and the Charles River Bridge decision. The Republicans wanted to expand economic opportunity by using government to open up new opportunities for everyone, as in the example of the Homestead Act. The Democrats never opposed slavery. The Republicans seemed hostile to the institution and received no support from slaveholders, but Republicans generally made few explicit statements beyond those against the issue of the expansion of slavery into the territories. The Whig Party in the 1830s attracted the Northern industrialists. The immigrant vote flocked to the earlier Democratic Party, but not to the Republican Party in the 1850s, at which time the former Know-Nothings were a strong presence. By 1860 the Republicans advocated a liberal immigration policy, mainly to insure a ready supply of workers for industry. The Democratic Party of Jackson opposed internal improvements at federal government expense, but not the Republicans who sponsored the transcontinental railroad.

5. **The correct answer is (B).** Lucy Stone jumped from her seat to respond to the insinuation that the women's rights movement involved only a few disappointed women. Lucy married the prominent abolitionist and reformer Henry Blackwell in 1855 in a ceremony that shocked many. They rewrote the marriage vows to reflect their commitment to an egalitarian marriage. Both were later instrumental in establishing the National American Woman Suffrage Association in 1869.

6. **The correct answer is (A).** Long before gold was discovered in California, every country eyed its harbors and its access to the East Asia markets. China was to be the next growth area for American goods. One historian called this the "myth of the China market." It is still part of our thinking. Despite the popular Hollywood image of Texas as dry cattle ranges, eastern Texas is excellent farm land. When Sam Houston arrived in 1833, he wrote to President Jackson that Texas was "the finest country to its extent upon the Globe." Cheap (or cheaper) land has attracted American farmers since 1607.

7. **The correct answer is (A).** The poem was placed in an inconspicuous spot inside the Statue of Liberty in 1903. The events associated with the Second World War and the beginning of the Cold War caused Americans to embrace both the poem and the myth that this had always been a land with open arms for the "huddled masses."

8. **The correct answer is (B).** William Penn believed in the liberty of conscience. He had often been jailed in England for espousing such an utterly unthinkable idea. If people think for themselves, of what need are rulers? Roger Williams, kicked out of Massachusetts by the civil and religious authorities, also practiced religious toleration. The next best choice is Maryland and Pennsylvania because of the Maryland Act of Toleration in 1649. This law was actually a vain attempt by Catholics to protect their own freedom of worship in the face of overwhelming Protestant migration into Maryland. The Protestants gained control of the colonial assembly and virtually nullified the Act of Toleration five years after it had passed.

9. **The correct answer is (A).** Five of the original thirteen began as proprietary colonies and became royal colonies: North Carolina, South Carolina, Georgia, New York, and New Jersey. Three began as charter colonies and became royal colonies: Virginia, Massachusetts, and New Hampshire. Maryland began as a proprietary colony and became a royal colony but was restored to proprietary status in 1715. Delaware and Pennsylvania remained proprietary colonies. Rhode Island and Connecticut were charter colonies.

10. **The correct answer is (B).** All happened in the twenties except for Jim Thorpe's accomplishments. He won his medals at the 1912 Olympics in Stockholm and lost them shortly afterward.

11. **The correct answer is (E).** The writs of assistance tried to curtail smuggling, not speech. James Otis eloquently attacked the writs in a Massachusetts court suit, but British authorities upheld their use. The gag rule placated Southern congressmen by prohibiting the reading in Congress of abolitionist

petitions. The offensive (to Southerners) petitions could still be presented to Congress, but not read. Lincoln's suspension of habeas corpus during the Civil War is not well known. He imprisoned 15,000 civilians for disloyalty or sedition and suppressed over 300 newspapers for criticizing the war. The 1918 Sedition Act, actually an amendment to the Espionage Act of 1917, jailed pacifists and socialists for opposing the war effort. McCarthyism saw communists sprinkled throughout American society. They could be easily identified by their liberal leanings. If you were not a rabid anticommunist, you were suspect.

12. **The correct answer is (A).** Area B is the Oregon Territory, which was claimed by Spain, Russia, and Great Britain. Within a short time the United States would also lay claim to the area, based on the voyages of Captain Gray to the mouth of the Columbia River in 1792 and the Lewis and Clark expedition in 1803–1806. Spain surrendered her claim in the Florida Treaty or Transcontinental Treaty of 1821, also called the Step Treaty because of its appearance while defining the western boundary of the Louisiana Purchase. Russia relinquished her claim to Oregon in 1824 and withdrew to Alaska; thus, Area C is Russia's. Area A still belonged to Spain. Remember, France seized the Louisiana Territory from Spain shortly before selling it to the United States. Canada, Area D, was held by Great Britain. The island of Greenland, Area E, was and still is the possession of Denmark.

13. **The correct answer is (A).** Ray Kroc's McDonald's owed its success to standard products. No matter where you go, you can expect a McDonald's hamburger to be the same. Even locally owned McDonald's franchises must purchase their supplies from McDonald's, ensuring standardization. William Levitt revolutionized the home construction industry with Levittowns, planned communities. He mass-produced suburban houses that all looked the same. Songwriter Malvina Reynolds criticized the suburbs' "ticky tacky houses" in "Little Boxes," "they're all made out of ticky tacky and they all look just the same." Both proved that Americans want low-priced quality even if the product lacks individuality.

14. **The correct answer is (C).** The drive for free public education came from many sources for different reasons. Labor leaders and reformers sincerely believed that only free education offered a means of improvement, both individual and societal. In 1830 the Philadelphia Workingmen's Committee reported "that until the means of equal instruction shall be equally secured to all, liberty is but an unmeaning word, and equality an empty shadow, whose substance to be realized must first be planted by an equal education and proper training in the minds, in the habits, in the manners, and in the feelings of the community." While industrialists and factory owners saw a general link between education and economic progress, they saw an immediate benefit in a labor force taught self-discipline by the schools. Such workers more willingly accepted the regimen of the factory and the discipline of the clock. School books, such as McGuffey's Readers (which sold 122 million copies in the nineteenth century) were loaded with moral lessons and maxims. The fear of America falling behind because its workers cannot compete internationally belongs to the 1980s and 1990s, not to the earlier era.

15. **The correct answer is (B).** The discovery of the largest potential oil supply in North America on Alaska's North Slope led to a fight over the impact of a 789-mile pipeline on Alaska's fragile environment. In 1973–74 the pipeline was built, with a terminal at Valdez, Alaska.

16. **The correct answer is (B).** John Fiske wrote *The Critical Period of American History* in 1888 to counter the widespread popular notion that the recent Civil War was the most critical event in American history. The popular thinking of the time was that the United States had barely survived. Not so, said Fiske, it was an earlier period that had almost finished the United States as a nation, that during the Articles of Confederation. "The dangers from which we were saved in 1788 were even greater than the dangers from which we were saved in 1865."

17. **The correct answer is (B).** The quotes are from *Plessy* v. *Ferguson*, the case that established the "separate but equal" doctrine permitting separate public accommodations based upon race.

18. **The correct answer is (D).** This question requires a knowledge of what the Monroe Doctrine actually stated. First, any attempt by European powers to extend their monarchical political system to the Americas is dangerous to our uniquely republican principles. Second, there will not be any new European colonization in the American continents, nor the transfer of colonies from one European power to another. Third, the United States will not interfere in existing European colonies in the Americas. Fourth, the United States will not participate in strictly internal European affairs.

19. **The correct answer is (C).** Do not be fooled by the references to gold in the passage; Bryan and Morgan are incorrect. The only socialist among the choices is Eugene V. Debs. Imprisoned after the fiasco of the Pullman strike in 1894, Debs read socialist literature and emerged from jail a confirmed socialist. He helped organize the Socialist Party in 1901. His most successful campaign for the presidency garnered almost one million votes while he was an inmate in the Atlanta Federal Penitentiary, sentenced under the Sedition Act of 1918.

20. **The correct answer is (D).** Retailers concentrated on expanding urban markets rather than the static rural markets, although mail order catalogs opened new vistas for rural folks.

21. **The correct answer is (D).** The Supreme Court objected to Congress handing too much of its powers to the executive branch. Even a national emergency such as the Great Depression did not warrant rewriting the Constitution to place primary responsibility for fighting the depression in the hands of the President. The Butler case invalidated the AAA, the Agricultural Adjustment Act. The Meat Inspection Act passed in 1906 as part of the Progressive era.

22. **The correct answer is (C).** The Caroline affair in 1837–1838 strained U.S.-British relations. American supporters of an abortive Canadian revolution transported supplies to the rebels on the ship *Caroline*. Canadian militia crossed to the American side of the Niagara River and burned it. Passions and retaliations continued for several years. The Webster-Ashburton Treaty in 1842 settled the border between Maine and New Brunswick, a sticky situation dating from the Revolutionary War. In the Trent affair in 1861, a U.S. ship stopped the British steamer *Trent* and removed two Confederate commissioners, James Mason and John Slidell. Secretary of State Seward later ordered the two released because even if the two were guilty of treason, the United States didn't have the right to commandeer a British ship in order to capture them. The Laird rams were Confederate ships being built in a private British shipyard for the South in 1863. After the U.S. minister, Charles Francis Adams, complained, the British government seized the ships as a violation of Great Britain's neutrality.

23. **The correct answer is (E).** Before the invention of the cotton gin in 1793, many Southerners wanted to restrain the slave trade or even abolish slavery. Two states with a growing need for slave labor, Georgia and South Carolina, vehemently objected to this paragraph. The volatile topic of slavery entrapped Jefferson himself. He freed a few slaves at his death; economic necessity would permit nothing else.

24. **The correct answer is (E).** The full title of Myrdal's book is *An American Dilemma: The Negro Problem and Modern Democracy* (1944). The book illustrated the huge gap between professed democratic ideals and actual practices, especially in regard to race relations. Adam Smith's *The Wealth of Nations* (1776) was the first to present laissez-faire systematically. Veblen's *The Theory of the Leisure Class* (1899) attacked the values of capitalism and business, differentiating between industry and business. He added "conspicuous consumption" to economic thinking when he linked status to consumption patterns. Keynesian economics advocated manipulating the economy through fiscal policy (governmental taxing and spending policies) and monetary policy (controlling the money supply). In bad economic times the government should use deficit spending to stimulate the economy. When the economy begins to move too fast a tax increase cools it off. *The General Theory of Employment, Interest and Money* was published in 1936, but his fundamental ideas had been published earlier. Galbraith's *The Affluent Society* (1958) questioned ignoring the quality of life in social, educational, and cultural matters inherent in the Keynesian emphasis on private production of material goods.

25. **The correct answer is (E).** The Second Great Awakening grew out of frontier revivals and the religious turmoil in the "burned-over" district of western New York (so-called because repeated revivals swept over the area, like grass fires coming one after the other across a field). Methodist ministers like Charles G. Finney led the attack on sin. Man was a free moral agent, able to consciously choose good over evil in all its devious manifestations, hence the push to reform every aspect of society. This emotional message appealed to young women who became involved in many other reforms, especially the antislavery movement. Making the world a better place would surely speed up the Second Coming of Christ.

26. **The correct answer is (D).** New York Representative Tallmadge introduced this amendment in 1819 to limit the expansion of slavery. Note that no slave would have been freed under Tallmadge's provision. All children born of slaves would become free at age twenty-five. The ensuing debate—both public and congressional—was settled by the Missouri Compromise.

27. **The correct answer is (E).** The quote is from the Kellogg-Briand Treaty, drafted in 1928 and ratified by the Senate, 85–1, in January 1929. The Kellogg-Briand Treaty outlawed war. That's why there have been no wars since 1929! Seriously, the Senate clearly understood that this treaty was a philosophical statement not binding on any nation because no one was responsible for enforcing the treaty. The same day the Senate approved the treaty it appropriated funds for fifteen new cruisers. This toothless document was resurrected for the Nuremberg Trials. One of the charges against the Nazi war criminals was violation of the Kellogg-Briand Pact.

28. **The correct answer is (B).** The "second industrial revolution" of the twenties introduced more consumer goods and greatly increased the number of homes with electricity. By 1929 two-thirds of all homes had electricity. Many homes used the new electric appliances and also installed modern bathrooms. By 1925 the economy produced five million enameled bathroom fixtures each year. Housewives had more electric gadgets, but rising standards actually increased the amount of housework for the average home. Television was invented in this decade but widespread use lay far into the future, after the Second World War. Wider use of trucks brought more fruits and vegetables to market, greatly improving the average diet. Union membership declined, fueled by the disastrous strikes of the Red Scare and by the crafty response of corporations that introduced company unions and some benefits.

29. **The correct answer is (A).** The piecework of the "putting-out" system first characterized early industrialization. We did not leap into an industrial economy or society. Too much is made in history books of new inventions and innovations in the production process. Antebellum industrialization was uneven, with bottlenecks in the production process constantly being created as other bottlenecks were solved. Traditional workers often opposed industrialization, using strikes to fight the introduction of new machinery and entrepreneurial attempts to "speed-up" production. For this reason, early industrialists recruited pliant farm girls, such as at Lowell. New technology did not automatically replace the old, as any modern economist would argue it should. Instead factory owners replaced machines as they wore out. Their economic thinking is best described as "more hands, more profits." They did not grasp such simple capitalistic concepts as economies of scale or per unit cost. State governments and foreign investors frequently provided capital funds for economic enterprises. No other source existed. By 1860 there appears to have been only four millionaires in the United States, an inadequate source for investment dollars. After the Civil War, industrialization would be much different.

30. **The correct answer is (E).** For the first ten years the capital was moved from New York City to Philadelphia. This secured the votes of the large Pennsylvania delegation in Congress for the assumption of the state debts. Philadelphians were certain that the federal government would never leave sophisticated, urbane Philadelphia for a swamp on the Potomac!

31. **The correct answer is (C).** The date is too early for Alice Paul and too late for Lucretia Mott, who died in 1880. Abigail Adams, who died in 1818, had been the wife of John Adams, the second president. Harriet Beecher Stowe was not sympathetic to the women's movement, but she was still alive in 1892, dying in 1896. Elizabeth Cady Stanton died in 1902. Active to the end of her life, she was helping to write what would eventually be the six-volume *History of Woman Suffrage*.

32. **The correct answer is (D).** Calvin Coolidge was the perfect president for the twenties. The public wanted neither liberal reform nor active government. They got their wish in Coolidge, who embodied the pro-business stand of the Republican Party and the voting public.

33. **The correct answer is (E).** The Truman Doctrine came very early in the Cold War. It was announced in 1947 in support of the fight against communist guerrillas in Greece and to counter the Soviet Union's threat against Turkey.

34. **The correct answer is (B).** William Lloyd Garrison's message was confrontational, clear, and consistent; he demanded the immediate end of slavery. Like many abolitionists, he knew better what he hated than what he wanted for America's future. His single focus was the institution of slavery rather than the slave or the free black. He fought against slavery, not to end racism or to achieve equality. Garrison even advocated Northern secession from the South to protect Northerners from the contamination of interacting with evil slaveholders. Northern secession, of course, would have left the slaves trapped in a slave-based society with virtually no criticism of the institution. Garrison fought against one particular sin, the sin of slavery. He opposed colonization schemes as primarily a means for Southern slaveowners to protect slavery by ridding the South of free blacks.

35. **The correct answer is (C).** Medicare, federal aid to education, and revised immigration laws were all part of LBJ's Great Society, which increased the power of the federal government by shifting more decision making to Washington, DC. The 1960s was one of the most prosperous decades in American history. There was no need for wage or price controls. The later Nixon administration began wage and price controls in the early 1970s to combat inflation.

36. **The correct answer is (A).** Frederick Jackson Turner's famous 1893 essay, "The Significance of the Frontier in American History," argued that the frontier experience molded and shaped American character and values more than any other factor.

37. **The correct answer is (D).** Three foreigners gave distinguished service to the American Revolution. Lafayette participated in both revolutions, but not as a pamphleteer. Von Steuben drilled the new troops at Valley Forge. Kosciusko served as the chief engineer in the army. John Paul Jones was the hero of the American navy and later led the Russian navy. Paine wrote *Common Sense* and other incendiary pamphlets. Distressed by the calm at the end of the American Revolution, he traveled to England to incite revolution there. Bitterly disappointed, he was revived when the mob stormed the Bastille. Unable to read or write French, he joined the French Revolution and was elected to the revolutionary legislature.

38. **The correct answer is (E).** During the Korean War, General MacArthur disputed the concept of a limited war and argued for an attack against the Chinese mainland. Truman relieved him of his command for publicly criticizing the Commander in Chief. In a speech before Congress, MacArthur delivered his famous quote, "In war there can be no substitute for victory." But in the nuclear age, it's possible there can be no victory.

39. **The correct answer is (D).** Aaron Burr is one of the most interesting and intriguing characters in American history. After holding several state and national offices, he became Thomas Jefferson's vice-presidential candidate in 1800. Prior to the Twelfth Amendment, each elector in the electoral college voted for two for the presidency, with the second highest becoming the vice-president, provided that both had a majority. Jefferson and Burr tied for the most votes, although everyone knew who was the party's nominee for president. The decision then shifted to the House of Representatives, which just

happened to be controlled by the Federalist Party. There Burr's longtime New York rival and foe, Alexander Hamilton, worked to prevent Burr's theft of the presidency. Out of favor with Jefferson and facing an uncertain political future, Burr flirted with a vague secession scheme organized by some New England Federalists, the New England Confederacy. Burr was to win the governorship in 1804 and deliver New York into the New England Confederacy. Hamilton again undercut Burr's efforts, helping to defeat Burr's bid for the governorship, which led to their duel in 1804 in which Burr killed Hamilton. Although he was still the vice-president until March 4, 1805, the beginning of Jefferson's second term, Burr began involvement in various vague, shifting schemes apparently hoping to result in his control of Mexico, some Southern states or territories, or whatever opportunity presented itself. He was arrested for treason, and his trial in 1807 at Richmond was presided over by John Marshall, the Chief Justice of the United States, who was riding circuit. Everyone was alarmed by Burr's activities and saw him, and others like him, as a threat to the fragile nation. Marshall, however, used the trial to strictly enforce the Constitution's definition of treason—two witnesses to an overt act—solidly establishing the principle that in the United States the government could not easily use the accusation of treason to remove and attack those it deemed dangerous.

40. **The correct answer is (E).** Women's sports programs were greatly underfunded and often unavailable in many colleges. Title IX addressed the imbalance. After court decisions weakened the law, it was revitalized by the Civil Rights Restoration Act of 1988.

41. **The correct answer is (A).** At the end of the colonial period, Philadelphia was the nation's largest city. By 1820 New York City eclipsed Philadelphia due to its role as the nation's number one seaport. List Two contains too many New England cities to be other than 1790. One-half of the population lived in New England in 1790, and New England claimed six of the nation's top ten. Also note that every city is on the coast. List One also contains the midwestern cities that grew as population expanded into the Mississippi Valley. New Orleans could not be on the 1790 list, we had not yet purchased Louisiana. By 1870 the list would be New York City, Philadelphia, Brooklyn, St. Louis, Chicago, Baltimore, Boston, Cincinnati, New Orleans, and San Francisco.

42. **The correct answer is (B).** Turner's great symbol of the frontier West was Andrew Jackson. Some other historians have disagreed, seeing Jackson as himself a political creation of Jacksonian Democracy, a movement he symbolized rather than led or contributed to.

43. **The correct answer is (E).** The correct order is St. Augustine, 1565; Jamestown, 1607; Quebec, 1608; Santa Fe, 1609–1610; and Plymouth, 1620. These are the successful settlements that lasted. The list of failures is very long and includes attempts by each settling nation.

44. **The correct answer is (D).** This is the cartoon that appeared in Ben Franklin's newspaper, the *Pennsylvania Gazette,* in 1754. Paul Revere revived it eleven years later as a call to unity against the Stamp Act, and it became a frequent appeal in the years leading up to the revolution.

45. **The correct answer is (C).** This paragraph is from "The Gospel of Wealth," an essay written by Andrew Carnegie in 1889. His position that competition is essential to society would have been enthusiastically supported by all except Henry George. William Graham Sumner, a Yale professor, is best remembered for *What Social Classes Owe to Each Other* (1883). Herbert Spencer, an English proponent of Darwinism and good friend of Carnegie, published his ideas in *Social Statics*. John D. Rockefeller wiped out competition in an innovative, ruthless style. Henry George's *Progress and Poverty* championed the single tax to resolve the widening gap between wealth and poverty. The single tax would absorb all unearned increment on land value, and end the necessity for any other tax. Thus, taxes would be paid by society's increased wealth, not by any individual.

46. **The correct answer is (D).** The nation's fourth largest iron works, the Tredegar Iron Company, began to purchase slaves as workers. By the Civil War slaves constituted over one-half of the company's large work force. This experiment proved that slavery was not an institution linked only to agricultural

production, doomed eventually to die out. Slaves could also be industrial workers. Lincoln raised this possibility in his campaigns to frighten Northern workers.

47. **The correct answer is (A).** Following the San Francisco earthquake of 1906, the school board caused an uproar by designating a special school for older Japanese boys. The incident raised hackles in Japan that were finally pacified by the Gentleman's Agreement in 1907. Japan promised to no longer issue passports to Japanese headed for the United States, and the United States promised not to exclude specifically Japanese from American soil. The 1868 Burlingame Treaty between the United States and China recognized China's sovereignty and territorial integrity in exchange for continued Chinese immigration into the United States, with the stipulation of possible withholding of naturalization for Chinese immigrants. Woodrow Wilson landed the Marines at Tampico in 1914, part of the almost unfathomable strife between the United States and Mexico in this period. The Insular Cases in 1901 and 1902 concerned the question of the Constitution following the flag. Did natives of newly acquired territory automatically enjoy full rights under the Constitution? The Supreme Court ruled that not all constitutional rights applied.

48. **The correct answer is (A).** Jefferson's letter of February 15, 1791, and Hamilton's letter of February 23, 1791, were two of three opinions Washington requested on the constitutionality of the Bank of the United States. Attorney General Randolph actually submitted two letters, one against the bank and one equivocal. Jefferson's letter and Hamilton's letter are the classic summaries of the strict and loose construction theories.

49. **The correct answer is (C).** Until the Montgomery bus boycott the NAACP's court suits were the basis of the civil rights movement. The Brown decision was just one of a series of cases putting constant pressure on legal segregation. But with Montgomery, the scene of confrontation shifted out of the courts and into the streets. It was never the same again; now popular pressure forced Congress and the president into action.

50. **The correct answer is (E).** Montesquieu's *The Spirit of Laws* (1748) declared that "separation of powers" and "checks and balances" best protected individual liberties in a republic. John Locke's *Second Treatise on Government* (1689) expounded the theory that man in nature inherently possessed certain rights such as life, liberty, and property. Governments are established by choice in the manner of a contract. Should the government break its obligations to the contract, the people are released from their obligations to the government or are free to rebel. Thus, the people are the ultimate source of political authority.

51. **The correct answer is (B).** The numbers for 1980 and 1989 are as follows: GNP, $2,670,600,000,000 to $5,151,300,000,000; and national debt, $908,503,000,000 to $2,866,188,000,000.

52. **The correct answer is (D).** The mass migration of blacks out of the South would come later, after these years.

53. **The correct answer is (C).** Martin Luther King, Jr., and Robert Kennedy were both assassinated in 1968, King in April and Kennedy in June, but only Kennedy was running for the presidency. Martin Luther King, Jr., never sought political office or political appointment. Badly split over the Vietnam War, civil rights, and LBJ's domestic programs, the Democratic Party limped into the election year and lost the election. The 1968 Democratic Party convention in Chicago is easily one of the most bitter and raucous political party conventions in our history. Democratic nominee Hubert Humphrey lost to Richard Nixon but the Democrats still controlled both houses of Congress. The 1960s constituted an incredibly prosperous decade; economic issues never entered the campaign.

54. **The correct answer is (B).** Both in and out of the presidency, Theodore Roosevelt publicized the nation's need to conserve its natural resources and natural beauty.

55. **The correct answer is (D).** Country A is Libya and K is Egypt, with whom Israel (not labeled) signed the 1979 Camp David Peace Accords. The other nations are correct: F is Iraq; E and B are Greece and Turkey; and C is Iran.

56. **The correct answer is (E).** Webster's dictionary did not appear until after the American Revolution, in 1828. In 1782 he published his *Spelling Book*, which sold over 15 million copies in his lifetime and 90 million by 1890! In a 1768 letter to his friends in England, Sam Adams tried to explain the American assertion, "in all free states, the constitution is fixed." There are some things even parliament cannot change. As James Otis said in "Rights of the British Colonies Asserted and Proved," "To say the parliament is absolute and arbitrary is a contradiction. The parliament cannot make 2 and 2, 5; Omnipotency cannot do it." In other words, some principles of government transcend even parliament and king. Government is by its very nature limited.

57. **The correct answer is (E).** Some historians have seen the origins of political parties in the personal clash between Hamilton and Jefferson. Although the two disliked one another, this alone didn't generate political parties. Historians by nature are always looking for the roots of something. In a nutshell this is the "germ theory of history," the belief that everything grows from a source, and with sufficient investigation we can find that source. Thus some historians see the continuation of splits in the Revolutionary War era and the Confederation period as the source behind the development of political parties. But political parties need programs based on issues, fundamental ideologies, continuous organization, central leadership, and a cadre of faithful workers. These all came into existence as the issues of the 1790s sparked controversies.

58. **The correct answer is (D).** The full story of working women in this era is in Sarah Eisenstein, *Give Us Bread but Give Us Roses: Working Women's Consciousness in the United States, 1890 to the First World War*. For many women, working was their first major social experience outside their traditional biological and moral role as a mother. The work force was overwhelmingly lower class and immigrant. The outstanding middle class reformers such as Jane Addams get into the history books, but the daily grind was more the lot of the lower classes. Working was a temporary step for single women after attending school and before marriage, or so most thought. Many factors determined the particular industries to which various immigrant groups were attracted, such as newly emerging industries that coincided with their arrival and cultural traditions that looked askance at interaction with males outside of the family.

59. **The correct answer is (A).** The progressive income tax, both personal and corporate, theoretically shifts an ever increasing burden upon those most able to pay and helps redistribute income. Unemployment compensation is a right only for those who have worked; it cushions their loss of income and keeps them as consumers to prevent endangering other parts of the economy. Aid to dependent children protects a segment of the population that has no political voice or clout. Veterans' benefits have nothing to do with the welfare state. In theory, they are compensation deserved by veterans in consideration for their service to the nation. Veterans' benefits stem from political pressure by lobby groups in our population that have virtually no opposition. By the 1930s the cost of Civil War veterans' benefits had exceeded the cost of the Civil War itself.

60. **The correct answer is (B).** Bruce Barton was an advertising genius who invented Betty Crocker, a nonexistent specialist in the new field of home economics. He also wrote *The Man Nobody Knows* which depicted Christ as the ultimate successful businessman who created a world-class organization with twelve associates plucked off the streets. Barton was trying to link business methods and Christian doctrines and practices. In the other two books the authors suggested that Christ would be shocked at the attitudes and conditions of modern life and indirectly laid the blame upon the values and practices of businessmen.

61. **The correct answer is (C).** The speaker was Sojourner Truth. She never learned to read or write, but with her stage presence, passion, and voice she was exceedingly effective in front of an audience. She leaped onto the stage after ministers had opposed women's rights on the grounds of the manhood of Christ and the lesser intellect of women. Responding to the comment that "Christ wasn't a woman!" Truth demanded, "Where did your Christ come from? From God and a woman!" Her response alarmed

many women in the audience. They feared that their cause would be linked with other causes and tarred by the press as an abolitionist subterfuge or an attack on religion.

62. **The correct answer is (A).** Under President Charles de Gaulle, France experienced a revival of nationalism and asserted its traditional role as a leader in European affairs. Great Britain was regarded as too involved with its former colonies and with the United States to be a true European nation. Thus, for years France blocked Great Britain's entry into the emerging European economic organization for Europe, the European Common Market. Moving the headquarters of NATO removed an obnoxious American presence from French soil.

63. **The correct answer is (B).** Any map distorted to reflect relative population by states also indicates the electoral college distortion. A quick glance at the map shows why Ohio was the "mother of presidents" and why so many presidential candidates came from the Midwest. The Midwest was a strong power base from which to build a political coalition. The map also shows why Populism never really had a chance at national power. The Populist states together were insignificant in total population and in electoral college voting.

64. **The correct answer is (D).** The Gideon case granted the right of free counsel for poor defendants accused in state felony prosecutions. The Escobedo and Miranda cases dealt with the right to counsel and protection against self-incrimination. *Baker* v. *Carr* involved legislative reapportionment. The Bakke case concerned reverse discrimination.

65. **The correct answer is (B).** The NAACP endorsed the programs and philosophies of Booker T. Washington's critics, especially as expressed by W.E.B. DuBois. The Niagara Movement grew out of an attempt to create an alternative to Washington's accommodationist philosophy. The 1908 race riot in Springfield awakened the offspring of some abolitionists to the work that still needed to be done. One was Oswald Garrison Villard, a direct descendant of William Lloyd Garrison. W.E.B. DuBois was for decades the editor of *The Crisis*, the NAACP publication.

66. **The correct answer is (B).** None of these three Republican presidents advocated reducing the defense budget. They all recognized an increased American responsibility to lead the Free World, but their methods for carrying out that responsibility varied. The three generally tried to reduce the scope of New Deal programs. Despite a few spectacular antitrust suits, big business was not strictly regulated by them. The common thread among them was their desire to reduce federal responsibility for many social, educational, and welfare programs.

67. **The correct answer is (D).** Frances Perkins was the first woman to serve as a member of the president's cabinet, as Secretary of Labor under FDR. The first woman to win the Nobel Peace Prize was Jane Addams, the founder of Hull House, the Chicago settlement house. Early in her career as a reformer, Jane Addams pushed hard for an end to war. In 1907 she wrote *Newer Ideals of Peace*. When the First World War broke out, she worked hard for an end to the hostilities. While others embraced the American entry and war effort in 1917, Jane Addams was a lonely voice in opposition. For fifteen years after the war, she headed the Women's International League for Peace and Freedom. She is best remembered by history for Hull House. She was best known by contemporaries for her peace efforts. She shared the 1931 Nobel Peace Prize with Nicholas Murray Butler, the president of Columbia University.

68. **The correct answer is (A).** This is from the Sherman Antitrust Act passed in 1890. The act sailed through the House of Representatives unanimously and through the Senate 52–1. Only innocuous laws pass Congress by these margins. The Sherman Act passed Congress so easily because it did not introduce new features into traditional interpretations of Anglo-American law. Combinations and conspiracies had always been illegal. The terms combination, trust, conspiracy, and monopolize were never defined in the act itself. What the Sherman Antitrust Act did was to establish a precedent for later, more effective legislation. The Clayton Antitrust Act in 1914 continued the tradition of the Sherman Act, not vice versa.

69. **The correct answer is (A).** Wilson defeated the Republican Charles Evans Hughes in 1916. The Bull Moose Party campaign was in 1912. The 1944 meeting between FDR and Dewey was their only meeting; Truman defeated Dewey in 1948 when he again won the Republican nomination. HST decided not to seek reelection in 1952; thus, Eisenhower defeated the Democratic governor of Illinois, Adlai Stevenson, in that year. Neither LBJ nor Reagan figured in the election of 1968. Hubert Humphrey lost to the Republican candidate Richard Nixon in 1968.

70. **The correct answer is (E).** Few events in American history can match the drama of the Salem witch trials. While accusations were not uncommon, actions by the authorities were, at least in America. Thousands of accused witches died in Europe during our colonial period. In the French province of Alsace, over five thousand died in a fifty-year span. In comparison, the Salem witch trials stand out in American history for what they were—an anomaly. Behind the accusations (assuming witches don't really exist!!) lurked a multitude of contributing factors. Everyone was on edge. Sir Edmund Andros and his hated Dominion of New England were gone, but what would the new rulers, William and Mary, grant to Massachusetts? And when would they finally get around to it? When the accused and the accusers are grouped and their individual and collective histories traced, several patterns jump out. There had been a growing east-west rupture for years, smoldering and intruding into other issues. In traditional New England (and throughout the colonies), women were powerless. Older women controlled young girls; in the close-knit community of Puritan New England, all older women disciplined all young girls. The original accusers were nine and eleven years old. Psychologically they may have been striking out against what they sensed was their source of powerlessness. Almost all the accused were old women and their accusers young girls. Colonial New England had a vision of the well-ordered society. Of course they rarely achieved that ideal, but variations immediately raised hostility. Independent women property holders existed outside the ideal image. Mix in some personal idiosyncrasies, bad tempers, and strange physical appearances and you could, in Salem in the 1690s, get a witch scare.

71. **The correct answer is (A).** The Roman Catholic Church, mainly influenced by fears of European radicalism, emphatically responded to the stirrings of liberal reform and radicalism. The wide-ranging papal encyclical, the Syllabus of Errorum issued by Pope Pius IX in 1864, attacked, among other things, ideas of liberal reform as socially dangerous and godless. Pius IX guided the Roman Catholic Church from 1846 to 1878, years marked by the tumultuous European revolutions of 1848. His statement was more of a warning than a policy or doctrinal statement. Catholic bishops in America followed his lead and denounced the Knights of Labor as too radical. The next pope, Leo XIII, 1878–1903, reversed the trend in 1891 in *Rerum Novarum* ("of modern things"), which addressed the conditions facing the working class. While he defended private property, Pope Leo XIII criticized capitalism for its adverse effects on the laboring class, its economic insecurity, and its poverty. While declaring that much of socialism was Christian in principle, he also criticized socialism for its opposition to religion. As a result, American Catholics now took a larger part in union activities and humanitarian efforts to aid the poor. The predominantly Protestant Social Gospel movement gained an official Catholic component.

72. **The correct answer is (C).** In 1849, the Department of the Interior was created and the responsibility for Indian affairs was transferred to it from the War Department. The fact that the War Department was primarily responsible for Indian affairs up to 1849 tells you much about the federal government's approach! President Zachary Taylor's political friend, Orlando Brown, became the Commissioner of Indian Affairs. Brown was apparently the first one to suggest confining each of the Plains tribes to specifically defined areas, as was done in 1851. This would clear the path for travel both for settlers moving west and for the transcontinental railroads.

73. **The correct answer is (B).** Wilson's advocacy of the League of Nations at the Versailles Conference was based upon the concept of collective security; that is, an attack on one nation is an attack on all. His ideas bore fruit in the United Nations, NATO, SEATO, and other such organizations. William

Jennings Bryan staunchly supported arbitration treaties, in which a third nation would decide the outcome of the dispute, but the concept never caught on.

74. **The correct answer is (B).** The law was the Sherman Antitrust Act, passed in 1890. Although the language of the act seems clear enough to us today, we must look at it in the context of the legal thinking of 1890. Many judges, lawyers, and politicians sincerely believed that the law added no new feature to prevailing English common law against combinations and conspiracies. Indeed, the overwhelming support for the Sherman Antitrust Act, only one negative vote in the entire Congress, is probably due more to the belief that it changed nothing than to the belief that trusts must be controlled. Legislation that passes Congress by almost unanimous margins is ordinarily legislation that doesn't really do anything. So, maybe the Supreme Court was right in 1911.

75. **The correct answer is (A).** The challenge to federal authority at Little Rock occurred in 1957, during Eisenhower's presidency. Eisenhower had not spoken out publicly in support of the Brown decision ordering the desegregation of public schools, and many diehards assumed he was on their side in opposition to desegregation. He personally deplored the Brown decision, privately saying that such things were matters of the heart and should not be forced. However, he disliked defiance of the federal government even more. Eisenhower took a strong stand at Little Rock. Southerners learned that they did not have a friend in the White House on stopping desegregation.

76. **The correct answer is (A).** Choice (A) is not correct because of the word "Federalist." If the statement were to read "Republican" newspaper editors it would be correct.

77. **The correct answer is (E).** The economy suffered inflation after the Second World War but not depression. The booming economy surprised many.

78. **The correct answer is (D).** The Whiskey Ring and Crédit Mobilier marred the political scene in the late nineteenth century. The Yazoo land deal took place in the 1790s. The other scandals are associated with the following: Andrew Jackson's administration, Peggy Eaton affair; Richard Nixon's administration, Watergate; and Warren G. Harding's administration, Teapot Dome.

79. **The correct answer is (D).** Philip Armour was in the same business as Swift, the meat-packing industry.

80. **The correct answer is (C).** In a series of newspaper articles, Zenger attacked Governor Cosby in New York. Zenger was arrested and was held incommunicado for ten months before his trial came up. Judge De Lancey, Governor Cosby's good friend, presided over the trial. Zenger's lawyer, the wily Philadelphia attorney Alexander Hamilton (no, not the future Secretary of the Treasury!) admitted that Zenger wrote the articles, but convinced the jury to acquit Zenger on the basis of the truth or falsity of the accusations that Zenger raised. This was a novel interpretation of the law. Hamilton argued that a free society needs a free press; in 1735, he was far ahead of his time. The case set no immediate precedent, but it did lead to bolder juries.

SAMPLE TEST D

U.S. History
Section I

Time—55 Minutes • 80 questions

Directions: Each of the questions or incomplete statements below is followed by five suggested answers or completions. Select the one that is best in each case and then blacken the corresponding space on the answer sheet.

1. Abolitionist organizations were formed to end slavery. The passage of the Thirteenth Amendment in 1865 achieved that goal. The American Anti-Slavery Society met in May, 1865, to discuss the question of whether they should continue to exist as an organization. Frederick Douglass urged them to continue to fight for black civil rights and the ballot:

   "Slavery has been fruitful in giving itself names. It has been called 'the peculiar institution,' 'the social system,' and the 'impediment,' as it was called by the General Conference of the Methodist Episcopal Church. It has been called by a great many names, and it will call itself by yet another name; and you and I and all of us had better wait and see what new form this old monster will assume, in what new skin this old snake will come forth."

   The abolitionists quietly disbanded, their objective realized. But in 1909 some of the grandchildren of the pre-Civil War abolitionists came together to create an organization to fight for black civil rights, whose need had been so prophetically foretold by Douglass. That twentieth century civil rights organization founded in 1909 and formally organized in 1910 was

   (A) the Urban League

   (B) PUSH (People United to Save Humanity)

   (C) the NAACP (National Association for the Advancement of Colored People)

   (D) CORE (Congress of Racial Equality)

   (E) SCLC (Southern Christian Leadership Conference)

2. Four of the following were characteristics of the colonial economy and colonial politics that continued into the Revolutionary War and Confederation era. Which characteristic did NOT continue into the latter era?

   (A) Tension between debtors and creditors

   (B) A scarcity of currency

   (C) Tension between Westerners and Easterners

   (D) Constitutional and political struggles between the lower houses of the state assemblies and the governors

   (E) Disputes among the states over western land claims

3. In the nineteenth century, slavery was attacked by abolitionists. Southerners defended the institution claiming that the Founding Fathers and the Constitution sanctioned slavery by putting it into the Constitution. What references to slaves or slavery appeared in the Constitution as originally written in 1787?

   I. The apportionment of taxes based on population, except for "three-fifths of all other persons"

   II. The provision in the Fourteenth Amendment that said that slaves were not citizens and therefore could not sue in court

   III. The provision for prohibiting the ending of the slave trade before 1808

   IV. The provision requiring the return of runaway slaves

   V. The preamble statement "That all men are created equal; that they are endowed by their Creator with certain unalienable rights," in which the Founding Fathers meant only white males

(A)   I, III, and IV only

(B)   I, II, III, IV, and V

(C)   II and V only

(D)   II, III, and V only

(E)   I, II, III, and IV only

4. Which of the following was a similarity between Shays' Rebellion and the Whiskey Rebellion?

(A)   Both alarmed conservatives throughout the nation.

(B)   George Washington put both down.

(C)   Both were caused by a protest over taxes.

(D)   Both occurred in Pennsylvania.

(E)   Both occurred during the government of the Articles of Confederation.

5. Rock music, called Rock 'n' Roll in the 1950s, grew out of many different sources. Which of the following is NOT a source of rock music in the 1950s?

(A)   A cohesive adolescent population appeared in the 1950s because more students stayed in school longer, creating a distinct purchasing sub-culture

(B)   Teenagers rebelled against the suburban emphasis on conformity

(C)   Southern Mississippi blues and country & western combined to create a Southern "rockabilly" sound

(D)   The black tradition of participatory gospel music and the beat over the melody combined with the blues to create a new sound that attracted whites

(E)   The music of the Beatles from England inspired imitation

6. The British considered the Sugar Act of 1764 to be an improvement over the Molasses Act of 1733 because

(A)   the tax rate was reduced

(B)   a determined effort was made to collect the new tax

(C)   the price of molasses was reduced, stimulating the rum trade

(D)   the earlier act was part of the mercantilist philosophy

(E)   colonial sugar was cheaper

7. In _____ Ida Tarbell began her first year at Allegheny College in Meadville, Pennsylvania. In her autobiography, *All in the Day's Work; An Autobiography*, she recalls that event.

"In _____, with misgivings in not a few minds, the admission of women to Allegheny was voted. This was the same year that the University of Michigan opened its doors to women, and two years before Cornell. In the six years before I entered ten women had graduated. When I came there were but two seniors, two juniors, and no sophomores. I was a lone freshman in a class of forty hostile or indifferent boys. The friendly ... professor charged with the care of 'young ladies' put it that I was 'Lost in the Wilderness of Boy'"

What, approximately, was the year?

(A)   1830

(B)   1790

(C)   1920

(D)   1870

(E)   1960

8. The majority of the Native American (Indian) tribes avoided involvement in the American War for Independence. But one tribe saw an opportunity. Led by Thayendanegea (or Joseph Brant in English), this tribe raided settlements on the New York and Pennsylvania frontier during the war to stop penetration of their lands. They were the

(A)   Creek

(B)   Sioux

(C)   Iroquois

(D)   Delaware

(E)   Seminoles

9. Which of the following statements concerning child labor laws and court decisions is NOT correct?

(A)   In *Bailey* v. *Drexel Furniture Co.* the Supreme Court invalidated the 1919 Child Labor Act on the grounds that the taxing provisions of the law went beyond the power to tax and were instead an attempt to regulate employment standards, which was clearly a police power of the states.

(B) In *Hammer* v. *Dagenhart* the Supreme Court invalidated the 1916 Child Labor Act on the grounds that child labor could only be regulated under the police power of the states, not by Congress under the commerce clause.

(C) The Child Labor Act of 1919, based upon the powers of Congress to tax, levied a special high tax on products produced by child labor, ten percent of a company's net profit.

(D) The 1916 Keating-Owen Child Labor Act, based upon the commerce clause of the Constitution, prohibited the interstate shipment of products produced by child labor.

(E) In *Adkins* v. *Children's Hospital* the Supreme Court invalidated the Maximum Hours Act of 1918, which prohibited the employment of children living in the District of Columbia. Since Congress is the legislature for the District of Columbia, which is not a state, the Supreme Court could not claim this was an infringement on the states' police power. Instead the act was invalidated as infringing upon the Fifth Amendment, the liberty of an individual to enter into a contract.

10. In his early political career he was a Republican state representative in the New York state legislature, an unsuccessful candidate for mayor of New York City, a member of the United States Civil Service Commission, and the head of the New York City Board of Police Commissioners. Who is described?

(A) Lyndon Johnson

(B) Woodrow Wilson

(C) Theodore Roosevelt

(D) John F. Kennedy

(E) William Jennings Bryan

11. Historians' opinions are colored by the political issues of their times. The following have been suggested by historians as a cause of the Civil War. Which explanation is LEAST associated with a particular time period and climate of historical writing?

(A) It was a dispute over slavery.

(B) It was a constitutional dispute over states' rights.

(C) It was caused by a needless emotional fanaticism on both sides.

(D) It was a struggle between two competing economic groups or classes for control of the federal government.

(E) It evolved out of the impact of sectional antagonism upon the national political party system.

12. During the Civil War she worked in the U.S. Patent Office. Shocked at the inability of the Union Army to care for the wounded, she quit her job and organized a voluntary system to provide medical supplies to Union doctors. After the Civil War she became interested in the International Red Cross and was one of the founders of the American Red Cross in 1881, serving as its president until 1904. She was

(A) Frances Perkins

(B) Amelia Jenks Bloomer

(C) Clara Barton

(D) Jane Addams

(E) Florence Nightingale

13. The Sheppard-Towner Act of 1921

(A) was aimed at reducing childbirth mortality rates and infant mortality rates

(B) was the first broad-based restriction on immigration into the U.S.

(C) provided federal funds for highway construction

(D) in reaction to the Red Scare restricted the right of labor unions to use the general strike as a tactic

(E) provided for the building of planned suburban communities such as Columbia, Maryland

14. Some actions by Congress require a simple majority; others require a two-thirds vote; and others require a three-fourths vote. Some actions apply to only one house of the Congress. Which of the following statements about votes in Congress is NOT correct?

    (A) A majority vote in both the House of Representatives and the Senate is needed to declare war.

    (B) A two-thirds vote in both the House of Representatives and the Senate is needed to pass a bill over the president's veto.

    (C) A two-thirds vote in only the Senate is needed to remove a president from office by impeachment.

    (D) A two-thirds vote in only the Senate is needed to ratify a treaty.

    (E) A two-thirds vote in both the House of Representatives and the Senate is needed to approve the appointment of cabinet members and federal judges.

15. President Ronald Reagan's economic proposals were dubbed "Reaganomics." Which of the following was NOT part of Reaganomics?

    (A) Increased defense spending

    (B) Supply-side economics

    (C) Cutting spending for social programs

    (D) Curbing the growth of social security spending

    (E) Tax reductions, especially for the wealthy

16. As a protest against the failure to include women during consideration of the Fifteenth Amendment, Susan B. Anthony led a group of women to the polls in 1872 in Rochester, New York. Since women's suffrage was illegal, she was arrested and fined. In court she blistered her accusers, claiming that women deserved the right to vote because they were citizens. Which of the following was NOT included in her arguments for women's suffrage?

    (A) People are born with natural rights that are not bestowed by a government; among these is the right to vote.

    (B) The preamble in the Constitution refers to "We, the people of the United States," not to "We, the white male citizens."

    (C) The passage by a state of a law to make sex a qualification for voting amounts to a bill of attainder and an ex post facto law, both of which are unconstitutional, because states had not up to that point specifically disenfranchised women.

    (D) Neither the tax laws nor the criminal laws specifically use or imply the word "male," and women are held accountable under them, so neither the Constitution nor suffrage laws should be assumed to apply solely to males; otherwise women could neither be forced to pay taxes nor could they be charged with crimes.

    (E) Granting women the right to vote would increase the number of middle class voters, reducing the impact of the immigrant vote.

17. Jeffersonian Democracy and Jacksonian Democracy most differed in

    (A) the belief that it was essential to limit federal spending

    (B) the belief that the Constitution limited the sphere of the federal government's powers

    (C) the degree to which Jefferson and Jackson contributed to the movements that carried their names

    (D) the belief that the winning political party was justified in using the spoils system to remove federal officeholders

    (E) their faith in the wisdom and goodness of the common people

18. The Federal Reserve Act of 1913

    (A) set up a banking system that successfully prevented future depressions

    (B) was intended to create a more elastic currency

    (C) ended the National Bank system started in 1863

    (D) represented a victory for Wall Street bankers and financiers

    (E) was similar to a suggestion proposed by Theodore Roosevelt during his administration

19. *Schenck* v. *U.S.* (1919) and *Abrams* v. *U.S.* (1919) both involved the question of whether or not the Espionage Act of 1917 and the Sedition Act of 1918 violated freedom of speech and press guaranteed by the First Amendment. The decision in *Schenck* v. *U.S.* was unanimous; Schenck's conviction was upheld. The decision in *Abrams* v. *U.S.* was 7–2. One Supreme Court justice wrote the majority opinion in the Schenck case, asserting that the true test of every act is "the circumstances in which it is done." Does the act constitute a "clear and present danger"? This same justice dissented in the Abrams case, claiming that Abrams's action did not constitute a "clear and present danger," and that the best protection for our society was a "free trade in ideas—that the best test of truth is the power of the thought to get itself accepted in the competition of the market." Who was this justice who drew a fine line defending free speech and press?

    (A) Oliver Wendell Holmes, Jr.

    (B) Earl Warren

    (C) Hugo Black

    (D) Louis Brandeis

    (E) William Howard Taft

20. Which was true concerning indentured servants during the colonial period?

    (A) One-third of all the white immigrants to Virginia and Maryland in the 1700s were indentured servants.

    (B) Most indentured servants were young married males with a wife and children and were seeking a farm at the end of their service.

    (C) Indentured servitude fulfilled its promise for most indentured servants, and they successfully gained freedom and a small farm at the end of their service.

    (D) Most indentured servants came from the lower social classes.

    (E) Indentured servants received land under the headright system while they were serving as indentured servants.

21. When newspaper editor John L. O'Sullivan and other Americans used the term "Manifest Destiny" in the 1840s, they included all of the following ideas EXCEPT

    (A) It was the destiny of the United States to gain control of the entire continent of North America.

    (B) The Anglo-American race was superior to Indians and to Mexicans.

    (C) We should grab the excellent harbors of California before Great Britain or France did, since both had designs on the area.

    (D) We needed revenge against Mexico for our defeats in the Mexican War at the Alamo, Goliad, and San Jacinto.

    (E) God gave a mission to Americans to expand the "area of freedom" and to restrict the "area of absolutism."

22. "You may well ask, 'Why direct action? Why sit-ins, marches, etc.? Isn't negotiation a better path?' You are exactly right in your call for negotiation. Indeed, this is the purpose of direct action. Nonviolent direct action seeks to create such a crisis and establish such creative tensions that a community that has constantly refused to negotiate is forced to confront the issue. . . . There is a type of constructive nonviolent tension that is necessary for growth. Just as Socrates felt that it was necessary to create a tension in the mind so that individuals could rise from the bondage of myths and half-truths to the unfettered realm of creative analysis and objective appraisal, we must see the need of having nonviolent gadflies to create the kind of tension in society that will help men to rise from the dark depths of prejudice and racism to the majestic heights of understanding and brotherhood. . . ."

    Who wrote this "Letter from the Birmingham City Jail" in 1963 explaining his philosophy to those who urged him to go slow?

    (A) Marcus Garvey

    (B) Martin Luther King, Jr.

    (C) Malcolm X

    (D) George Wallace

    (E) Jesse Jackson

23. In the case of *Minor* v. *Happersett,* the Supreme Court ruled
    - (A) that a political party was a private organization and was able to prohibit women from voting in a party primary
    - (B) that voting was not a right of citizenship and therefore denial of the right to vote is within the powers of a state government
    - (C) that the Fifteenth Amendment applied only to black males and not to women
    - (D) that both poll taxes and literacy tests were legal methods to restrict a specific group from being able to vote
    - (E) that states could prohibit women from serving as lawyers

24. Few events grip the American public's interest as much as the every-four-years contest for the presidency. The prize of the presidency stirs souls, leading many to seek their party's nomination. Two politicians from major parties won the nomination and sought the presidency in three different years, and lost. They are the only three-time losers among the major parties in the presidential sweepstakes. They are
    - (A) Ulysses S. Grant and Michael Dukakis
    - (B) James G. Blaine and Thomas Dewey
    - (C) Barry Goldwater and Walter Mondale
    - (D) Richard Nixon and Daniel Webster
    - (E) Henry Clay and William Jennings Bryan

25. Widely celebrated in American folklore and film, the great era of the cowboy, the roundup, and the open range was short-lived, ending in the 1880s. Which of the following was NOT a factor contributing to fundamental changes in the cattle kingdom by the 1880s?
    - (A) Farmers learned how to adapt their farming methods and crops to the conditions on the Great Plains.
    - (B) Severe weather conditions, harsh winters and drought, wiped out many cattle herds in that one decade.
    - (C) Joseph Glidden invented and marketed a new fence, barbed wire, which restricted the free movement of cattle across the plains.
    - (D) Competition for grassland arrived as sheep-raising moved into the Great Plains.
    - (E) Indian uprisings in the 1880s blazed across the Great Plains, making isolated ranching too dangerous.

26. "Whereas it appears that a state of war exists between Austria, Prussia, Sardinia, Great Britain, and the United Netherlands on the one part and France on the other, and the duty and interest of the United States require that they should with sincerity and good faith adopt and pursue a conduct friendly and impartial toward the belligerent powers:

    "I have therefore thought fit by these presents to declare the disposition of the United States to observe the conduct aforesaid toward those powers respectively, and to exhort and warn the citizens of the United States carefully to avoid all acts and proceeding whatsoever which may in any manner tend to contravene such disposition." This quotation is from
    - (A) a speech by Franklin Roosevelt after the beginning of the Second World War in Europe
    - (B) the Good Neighbor policy of Hoover, which was endorsed by Franklin Roosevelt
    - (C) Wilson's declaration at the outbreak of the First World War
    - (D) Washington's Neutrality Proclamation
    - (E) Jefferson's embargo on foreign trade

27. *Marbury* v. *Madison* established the principle of "judicial review" by declaring an act of Congress unconstitutional. What was the second occasion when the Supreme Court declared an act of Congress unconstitutional?
    - (A) The Dred Scott case
    - (B) *Worcester* v. *Georgia*
    - (C) *Cohens* v. *Virginia*
    - (D) *McCulloch* v. *Maryland*
    - (E) The Dartmouth College case

28. "The antitrust approach was abandoned in favor of regulating business by means of codes of fair practices, in the desire to balance production and consumption. The individual industry codes fixed production levels, wages, hours, and guaranteed workers the right to unionize." What has just been described?

    (A) New Frontier

    (B) Sherman Antitrust Act

    (C) President Nixon's wage and price controls

    (D) National Recovery Administration

    (E) Interstate Commerce Act

29. Which of the following is NOT correctly linked to her primary area of accomplishment or recognition?

    (A) Ann Lee—founder of the Shakers

    (B) Sarah Hale—publisher of the popular women's magazine *Godey's Lady's Book*

    (C) Dorothea Dix—organizer of the Seneca Falls women's convention

    (D) Prudence Crandall—opened a school for young black women in Connecticut

    (E) Angelina and Sarah Grimké—former slaveholders who attacked slavery

30. In what political party did Ignatius Donnelly, "Sockless Jerry" Simpson, Mary Ellen Lease, and James Weaver serve as the leadership?

    (A) Populist Party

    (B) Know-Nothings

    (C) Dixiecrats

    (D) Prohibitionist

    (E) Loco-Focos

31. The Equal Rights Amendment (ERA) failed to win the approval of enough states to become part of the Constitution. Four of the following contributed to the defeat of the ERA. Which did NOT?

    (A) Radicals within the women's movement made it seem beyond the mainstream of American life by denouncing traditional marriages, the capitalist economic system, and two-parent families.

    (B) Women labor leaders turned lukewarm in support because of a concern about the impact of the ERA on special legislation protecting women in the work force.

    (C) The abortion decision and the subsequent debate split the movement and joined the Stop-ERA movement to the antiabortion movement.

    (D) The draft registration bill, meant to apply equally to men and women, proposed in reaction to the invasion of Afghanistan, failed to pass Congress, thereby handing the women's movement an apparent defeat for an objective it had not sought and tarnishing women's push for equality.

    (E) Affirmative action court suits raised women's wages to the level of men's, making it seem unnecessary to add the ERA to the Constitution.

32. Henry David Thoreau's essay on "Civil Disobedience" profoundly influenced which set of leaders?

    (A) Daniel Webster and Henry Clay

    (B) John Calhoun and Horace Mann

    (C) Mahatma Gandhi and Martin Luther King, Jr.

    (D) Abraham Lincoln and Jefferson Davis

    (E) Stephen Douglas and Frederick Douglass

33. At the end of the War of 1812, Daniel Webster opposed the protective tariff. Fifteen years later he had switched his position to favoring protective tariffs. Why?

    (A) British dumping of low priced products after the War of 1812 ruined many American industries.

    (B) Webster supported Clay's American System in exchange for Clay's support of Webster's proposal for a Second Bank of the United States.

    (C) The Jeffersonian Democrats, who had originally opposed the concept of a protective tariff, changed to supporting protective tariffs and forced the Federalist Party to adopt the opposite position.

(D) Anger over Calhoun's "Exposition and Protest" turned most Northerners in favor of free trade.

(E) The base of the New England economy changed from shipping and commerce to industrial production.

34. One reaction against Franklin Roosevelt's court-packing proposal was the rise of a coalition in Congress linking conservative Southern Democrats and conservative Northern and Western Republicans. In 1964, a conservative Republican senator and his supporters won the Republican Party nomination, presented a conservative party platform, and hounded liberal Republicans out of the party. The result was the overwhelming defeat of the ideologically identifiable Republican Party in 1964, leading directly to the very antithesis of their intentions by guaranteeing liberal reform, which materialized in the "Great Society." Who was the Republican candidate who lost in 1964?

(A) Richard Nixon

(B) Dwight D. Eisenhower

(C) Barry Goldwater

(D) Ronald Reagan

(E) Thomas Dewey

35. In the antebellum period, as daily work for males became separated from the home and performed at a different location, what new role became the ideal for middle-class women?

(A) Women should pursue professional careers in medicine and in law as doctors and lawyers.

(B) Women should agitate and push for the right to vote.

(C) Women should supplement the family income by taking in piecework under the "putting out" system.

(D) Women should concentrate on raising the children and providing a moral, clean home as a refuge for their family.

(E) Women should use their new freedom to work in the abolitionist movement.

36. Which of the following statements is NOT true concerning U.S. foreign policy events in the Caribbean between 1950 and 1990?

(A) In 1954 the CIA helped overthrow a left-wing government in Country A.

(B) The United States had backed the dictator of Country F, Batista, but he was overthrown in 1959 by Fidel Castro, who then announced that he would establish a communist government.

(C) President Lyndon Johnson sent 20,000 U.S. Marines to Country C in 1965 to support a military junta that had overthrown a leftist government.

(D) President Reagan sent troops to Country E in 1983 to prevent the establishment of another Marxist government in the Caribbean, and President Bush sent American troops to Country G to seize the dictator, General Noriega, on drug-smuggling charges.

(E) Country H was part of the Iran-Contra affair in the Reagan administration, a complicated scandal in which the White House-controlled National Security Council illegally sold weapons to Iran to raise money to support Contra revolutionaries against the leftist Sandinista government in country H.

37. Which was an official organization created by the First Continental Congress rather than an unofficial organization that exerted pressure for political conformity in the years before the Revolutionary War began?

(A) Sons of Liberty

(B) The Association

(C) Circular Letter

(D) Committees of Correspondence

(E) Daughters of Liberty

38. "There are at the present time two great nations in the world . . . the Russians and the Americans . . . They have suddenly placed themselves in the front rank among the nations. . . .

"All other nations seem to have nearly reached their natural limits, and they have only to maintain their power; but these are still in the act of growth. All the others have stopped, or continue to advance with extreme difficulty; these alone are proceeding with ease and celerity along a path to which no limit can be perceived. The American struggles against the obstacles that nature opposes to him; the adversaries of the Russian are men. The former combats the wilderness and savage life; the latter, civilization with all its arms. The conquests of the American are therefore gained by the plowshare; those of the Russian by the sword. The Anglo-American relies upon personal interest to accomplish his ends and gives free scope to the unguided strength and common sense of the people; the Russian centers all the authority of society in a single arm. The principal instrument of the former is freedom; of the latter, servitude. Their starting-point is different and their courses are not the same; yet each of them seems marked out by the will of Heaven to sway the destinies of half the globe."

This astounding statement is from a book, *Democracy in America*, published early in the nineteenth century by a foreign observer. The author was

(A) Jenny Lind

(B) James Bryce

(C) Francis Trollope

(D) Lafayette

(E) Alexis de Tocqueville

39. The mass production and mass purchasing of automobiles led to many changes in American society. Which of the following did NOT happen in the 1920s as a result of the mass marketing of automobiles?

(A) Changes in dating customs

(B) Demands by the voting public for more governmental funds for highways

(C) The stimulation of industries connected to the automobile industry, such as batteries, steel, oil, glass, and rubber

(D) The development of a motel industry

(E) A decline in the population of large cities as people moved to the suburbs and small towns since they could now commute to work

40. The issue of loose versus strict interpretation of the Constitution first arose

(A) over Hamilton's proposal to create a Bank of the United States

(B) over Jefferson's decision to purchase Louisiana from Napoleon

(C) in the case of *Marbury* v. *Madison*

(D) over Hamilton's proposal to consolidate the national, foreign, and state debts and to pay them off at face value

(E) in the 1796 presidential campaign between the Federalist and Jeffersonian parties

41. "Man as a religious being and moral agent acts more or less in three general spheres or departments of effort and responsibility, viz.:—The individual, the social, and the civil or governmental spheres. . . . It follows, therefore, that there are individual duties, virtues, sins; social duties, virtues, sins; and governmental duties, virtues, sins. In each sphere our religious and moral obligations are the same. Right and wrong confront human beings at every step. To be perfect, one must think, say, and do what is right in each and all the spheres of responsibility named."

This statement by Adin Ballou, a reformer, explains the reform impulse of "perfectionism." In which period of reform was this statement made?

(A) Antebellum years

(B) Progressive Era

(C) Social Gospel

(D) New Deal

(E) Great Society

42. Which of the following was true of politics in the late nineteenth century from 1870 to 1900?

    (A) National issues generated more interest than local issues.

    (B) The spoils system was of little concern to voters.

    (C) The supporters of the two major political parties can be differentiated by cultural, ethnic, and religious criteria.

    (D) Racial issues played a minor role in Southern politics.

    (E) The supporters of and opponents of immigration restriction and parochial schools showed no ethnic or cultural distinctions because these issues tended to be class issues.

43. What was most responsible for the decrease in the Native American (Indian) population in the settled areas of North America during the colonial period?

    (A) Indians were drawn into European wars by the intricate, complex European diplomacy and often ended up on the losing side at the peace table, forcing them to move farther west.

    (B) The British army and the colonial militias periodically mounted campaigns to push the Indians out of specific areas in order to open these areas up for settlement.

    (C) European diseases devastated the Indian population because they had no inherited immunity to measles, chicken pox, mumps, and whooping cough.

    (D) The arrival of whites injected a disruptive new element into the delicate balance of power between the tribes, leading to an increase in tribal warfare.

    (E) The whites initially enslaved Indians and blacks, but after they had captured a large percentage of the Indian population they were forced to turn more toward black slaves rather than Indian slaves.

44. "[The members of a trade union] should know that the labor movement means more, infinitely more, than a paltry increase in wages and the strike necessary to secure it; that while it engages to do all that possibly can be done to better the working conditions of its members, its highest object is to overthrow the capitalist system of private ownership of the tools of labor, abolish wage-slavery and achieve the freedom of the whole working class and, in fact, of all mankind. . . .

    "The Socialist party is to the workingman politically what the trade union is to him industrially; the former is the party of his class, while the latter is the union of his trade.

    "The difference between them is that while the trade union is confined to the trade, the Socialist party embraces the entire working class, and while the union is limited to bettering conditions under the wage system, the party is organized to conquer the political power of the nation, wipe out the wage system and make the workers themselves the master of the earth."

    These quotes

    (A) were written by Eugene V. Debs when criticizing the aims and objectives of the AFL, the American Federation of Labor

    (B) came from a speech by Earl Browder, twice the Communist Party candidate for the presidency

    (C) refuted the thinking of the abolitionist and social reformer, Wendell Phillips

    (D) illustrate the dissatisfaction within the American Federation of Labor, which led to the creation of the CIO, the Congress of Industrial Organizations

    (E) are from the preamble to the constitution of the Americans for Democratic Action, ADA

45. The League of Women Voters grew out of what previous organization?

    (A) AAUW, American Association of University Women

    (B) National American Woman Suffrage Association

    (C) Girl Scouts of America

    (D) National Organization for Women

    (E) American Red Cross

46. Religious toleration developed by the end of the colonial period primarily because

    (A) no church was strong enough to gain dominance

    (B) the colonists saw the folly of Europe's bloody wars of religion

    (C) of the example of the Puritans coming to America for religious freedom

    (D) of Roger Williams's example of separating church and state to keep the government free from religious interference

    (E) of the English tradition of strict separation of church and state

47. "The timid man, the lazy man, the man who distrusts his country, the overcivilized man, who has lost the great fighting, masterful virtues, the ignorant man and the man of dull mind, whose soul is incapable of feeling the mighty lift that thrills 'stern men with empires in their brains'—all these, of course, shrink from seeing the nation undertake its new duties; shrink from seeing us build a navy and army adequate to our needs; shrink from seeing us do our share of the world's work by bringing order out of chaos in the great, fair tropic islands from which the valor of our soldiers has driven the Spanish flag. These are the men who fear the strenuous life, who fear the only national life which is really worth leading. . . ."

    Who gave this speech in 1899 a few months after he was elected governor of New York?

    (A) William McKinley

    (B) William Jennings Bryan

    (C) Theodore Roosevelt

    (D) Commodore Dewey

    (E) John Hay

48. Which of the following is most opposed to the concept of imperialism?

    (A) Northwest Ordinance

    (B) Treaty of Paris, 1898

    (C) Writings of Alfred Thayer Mahan

    (D) Dollar diplomacy

    (E) Manifest Destiny

49. Out of over one thousand individual items identified in the 1860 tariff customs reports, one city was the leader in all but seven American exports and all but twenty-four foreign imports. Which of the following was this leading U.S. seaport?

    (A) Boston

    (B) Philadelphia

    (C) Baltimore

    (D) New Orleans

    (E) New York City

50. "You may dispose of me very easily, I am nearly disposed of now. But this question is still to be settled—this Negro question, I mean; the end of that is not yet. You had better—all you people at the South—prepare yourselves for a settlement of this question."

    Who uttered this warning?

    (A) John Brown in 1859 after his unsuccessful raid at Harpers Ferry

    (B) William Lloyd Garrison in the first issue of *The Liberator* in 1831

    (C) Abraham Lincoln on the eve of issuing the Emancipation Proclamation in 1863

    (D) Nat Turner before being hanged for his revolt in 1831

    (E) Homer Plessy after the *Plessy* v. *Ferguson* decision in 1896 permitting "separate but equal" facilities

51. During the Civil War, after Southern congressmen and senators had withdrawn, the Republicans passed significant legislation that the Southerners had opposed. Which of the following were part of this legislation?

    I. Transcontinental railroad

    II. Morrill Land-Grant College Act

    III. Morrill Tariff

    IV. Homestead Act

    V. Federal Reserve Act

    (A) I, II, III, and IV only

    (B) II, III, and IV only

    (C) II, IV, and V only

    (D) I, II, III, IV, and V

    (E) I, III, and IV only

52. "The United States is better situated from a military standpoint than any other nation in the world. Even in our present condition of unpreparedness no foreign power is in a position to invade us today. If we concentrate on our own defenses and build the strength that this nation should maintain, no foreign army will ever attempt to land on American shores." Who would have objected to this 1941 statement?

    (A) Charles Lindbergh

    (B) Senator Gerald Nye

    (C) America First Committee

    (D) Franklin D. Roosevelt

    (E) Veterans of Future Wars

53. In comparing the experiences of African Americans in the northern urban ghettos in the early twentieth century with the experiences of immigrant groups in the late nineteenth century, historians have found significant differences. In what ways did the experience for African Americans differ from that for immigrant groups?

    (A) The percentage of African Americans who owned their homes in the ghetto was higher than it had been for immigrants.

    (B) The black community was held together by ethnic loyalties that cut across class lines, unlike the immigrants who developed few community institutions.

    (C) The practice of income pooling, sending all members of the family out to work in order to pool the family's income, was part of the black experience but not part of the immigrant experience.

    (D) Segregation and racial discrimination restricted the geographical area of the black ghetto, making it unable to expand, unlike the immigrant ghetto, which expanded so as not to be as crowded.

    (E) Blacks tended to live more with members of their nuclear family (father, mother, and children); immigrants came mainly as individuals rather than as members of a family, and therefore most lived as individuals outside a family setting.

54. In the 1960s and 1970s a political movement developed in opposition to what was perceived as the legacy of liberalism and liberal politics. Nicknamed the "Radical Right" by its opponents, the movement spawned a broad-based criticism of liberalism. Which of the following was NOT associated with the "Radical Right"?

    (A) The Moral Majority

    (B) Fundamentalists

    (C) Jerry Falwell

    (D) Television evangelists

    (E) Jimmy Carter

55. Before this war the income tax was levied against only 5 percent of the population. As a result of the financial demands of this war, the federal government passed two acts. The first substantially raised the number of people who had to pay a tax on their income, from 5 percent of the population to 74 percent of the population. The second act began the practice of withholding, collecting the income tax before the money reached the individual.

    What was the war that forever changed paydays for Americans?

    (A) First World War

    (B) Second World War

    (C) Korean War

    (D) Vietnam War

    (E) Spanish-American War

56. The Mayflower Compact is significant in the history of American political thought because

    (A) in it the people regarded themselves as the source of political power

    (B) in it the people agreed to be bound by the will of the majority

    (C) it was copied for the Massachusetts Bay Charter

    (D) in it church and state were separated

    (E) in it were provisions guaranteeing civil rights for women and blacks

57. In 1811 there were 88 state banks; in 1816, 256. What explains the increase in the number of state banks from 1811 to 1816?

   (A) The needs of the wartime economy during the War of 1812 demanded it.

   (B) New banks were established under the National Banking system.

   (C) Regional trade was stimulated by the building of canals.

   (D) Federalists replaced the Democrats and changed federal banking policies.

   (E) The restraining influence of the First Bank of the United States ended when its charter expired.

58. In a circular sent to farmers in 1867, Oliver H. Kelley brought attention to a new organization. "Its grand object is not only improvement in husbandry, but to increase the general happiness, wealth and prosperity of the country. It is founded upon the axioms that the products of the soil comprise the basis of all wealth; that individual happiness depends upon general prosperity, and that the wealth of a country depends upon the general intelligence and mental culture of the producing classes.

   "We ignore all political or religious discussions in the Order. . . . Its objects . . . are to advance education, to elevate and dignify the occupation of the farmer, and to protect its members against the numerous combinations by which their interests are injuriously affected."

   This organization was the

   (A) Ku Klux Klan

   (B) Populist Party

   (C) National Grange

   (D) American Farm Bureau Federation

   (E) Farmers' Alliance

59. The first college in the United States in the antebellum era to admit both blacks and women was

   (A) Harvard

   (B) Lane Seminary

   (C) Oberlin

   (D) Yale

   (E) West Point

60. In 1588 England defeated a major European rival, clearing the way for England to begin her efforts to colonize the New World. In the 1650s, England began to enact a series of Navigation Acts to secure control of her trade with her New World colonies. These Navigation Acts sprang from England's trade rivalry with a second European nation. Just prior to the American Revolution, England successfully defeated a third rival. England's rivals, in the order that England met the challenges, were

   (A) Prussia, France, Spain

   (B) Spain, the Netherlands, France

   (C) Portugal, Spain, France

   (D) France, the Netherlands, Spain

   (E) Spain, France, Russia

61. In the 1960s university students shed their passive image. Demonstrations, sit-ins, teach-ins, riots, and building takeovers showed that not all college students were interested in only beer, football, parties, and sex. Where was the initial student riot in the 1960s and what was the issue?

   (A) Students at the University of California at Berkeley clashed with administration officials over an attempt to close a "free speech" area beside the campus.

   (B) Four students at Kent State University were shot by the National Guard while protesting against the Vietnam War.

   (C) Students at UCLA joined nearby black residents in an urban riot in Watts in Los Angeles.

   (D) Nine black students tried to integrate a university in Little Rock, Arkansas, causing a riot.

   (E) Black students at Jackson State College in Mississippi rioted over a planned march by the KKK, which had been approved by the administration.

62. Both the Federalists and the Jeffersonian Republicans (or Democrats) were afraid of threats to the infant United States in the first decades of our nation's existence. However, they differed greatly over the sources of danger. Which of the following does NOT correctly match the party to what that party felt was a source of danger?

(A) Republicans—the executive branch and/or the Senate augmenting its powers

(B) Federalists—a majority in the House of Representatives enacting laws against the wealthy

(C) Federalists—an attack by Great Britain from Canada

(D) Federalists—an increase in Irish immigration

(E) Republicans—a large national debt

63. All of the following were crises during the Eisenhower administration EXCEPT

(A) the U-2 spy plane incident

(B) the building of the Berlin Wall

(C) the tension between Red China and Nationalist China in the Taiwan Straits

(D) the Suez Canal crisis

(E) the Lebanon crisis leading to the Eisenhower Doctrine

64. Four of the following were differences between the New England colonies and the Chesapeake colonies. Which of the following was NOT a difference that existed between the Chesapeake colonies and the New England colonies?

(A) The so-called plantation houses of the Chesapeake region were not as large, sturdy, or comfortable as the better built houses for the New Englanders because the Chesapeake settlers had so much more capital tied up in their labor force.

(B) The commercial cities of the Chesapeake Bay were larger than those of New England because the Chesapeake area was settled first.

(C) Due to the higher death rates in the Chesapeake region, marriages were, on average, longer in New England.

(D) The church played a central role in the life of New England but was less influential in the social and political life of the Chesapeake area.

(E) The average life span for women in the Chesapeake region was shorter than that in New England because the Chesapeake retained, for a much longer time, a frontier-like quality to its life in terms of health care and overall standard of living.

65. He created an embarrassing crisis for the U.S. government. A general in the U.S. Army, he invaded Spanish territory with a state militia when we were not at war with Spain and hanged two British citizens. His actions almost led to war with Great Britain and Spain. Cooler heads prevailed, though, and Spain, realizing she could not defend her possession, eventually ceded it to the United States. He was

(A) James Madison

(B) John Quincy Adams

(C) Commodore Dewey

(D) Theodore Roosevelt

(E) Andrew Jackson

66. Which of the following individuals is NOT correctly linked to his activities in regard to slavery?

(A) John Quincy Adams fought against the "gag rule" while serving as a representative in Congress after his term as president ended.

(B) William Penn, the founder of Pennsylvania, spoke out against Quakers owning slaves and gradually ended slave holding among Quakers.

(C) Theodore Dwight Weld published *The Bible Against Slavery* and *American Slavery As It Is*, which helped inspire Harriet Beecher Stowe to write *Uncle Tom's Cabin*.

(D) William Lloyd Garrison published an antislavery newspaper, *The Liberator*.

(E) David Walker, a free black, published *Appeal to the Coloured Citizens of the World*, a pamphlet that urged blacks to rebel.

67. "This bill will strike down restrictions to voting in all elections—Federal, State, and local—which have been used to deny Negroes the right to vote.

"This bill will establish a simple, uniform, standard which cannot be used however ingenious the effort to flout our Constitution.

"It will provide for citizens to be registered by officials of the United States government, if the state officials refuse to register them.

"It will eliminate tedious, unnecessary lawsuits which delay the right to vote. . . .

"The last time a president sent a civil rights bill to Congress it contained a provision to protect voting rights in Federal elections. That civil rights bill was passed after eight long months of debate. And when that bill came to my desk from Congress for my signature, the heart of the voting provision had been eliminated.

"This time, on this issue, there must be no delay, or no hesitation or no compromise with our purpose.

"We cannot, we must not refuse to protect the right of every American to vote in every election that he may desire to participate in. And we ought not, we must not wait another eight months before we get a bill. We have already waited a hundred years and more and the time for waiting is gone."

Who gave this speech to Congress urging the passage of a civil rights bill?

(A) Lyndon Johnson

(B) John F. Kennedy

(C) Abraham Lincoln

(D) Andrew Johnson

(E) Dwight D. Eisenhower

68. Upton Sinclair's chief purpose in writing *The Jungle* was to

(A) awaken the public to the horribly unsanitary conditions in meat-packing plants

(B) aid the plea for better housing for immigrant stockyard workers

(C) rally public support for the Meat Inspection Act and the Pure Food and Drug Act,

both of which were tied up in the Senate

(D) join other muckrakers in attacking the political corruption within the municipal government of Chicago

(E) advance the cause of socialism and fight against "wage slavery"

69. In 1872 a San Francisco dry-goods store owner received a letter from Jacob Davis, a tailor. Davis was seeking a business partner for a new type of sturdy pants with rivets in the pockets to make them stronger. In 1873 they began to market the pants with a leather patch guaranteeing a new pair if the seams didn't hold. Who became the business partner of Jacob Davis?

(A) Richard Sears

(B) Levi Strauss

(C) Denis Kearney

(D) Leland Stanford

(E) John Wanamaker

70. In the years from 1790 to 1860 the issue of federally funded internal improvements was a consistent political issue. Which of the following statements about internal improvements is NOT correct?

(A) In 1806, President Thomas Jefferson directed his Secretary of the Treasury Albert Gallatin to draw up a plan for federally funded roads and canals.

(B) President James Madison vetoed the Bonus Bill in 1817 because he had misgivings about its constitutionality.

(C) President Andrew Jackson vetoed the Maysville Road Bill in 1830 because it would have federally funded a road entirely within a single state, Kentucky.

(D) In the period from 1790 to 1860 the section that most consistently pushed for internal improvements was the South.

(E) Internal improvements at federal expense was part of Henry Clay's "American System."

71. "The fruits of the toil of millions are boldly stolen to build up colossal fortunes for a few, unprecedented in the history of mankind; and the possessors of these, in turn, despise the Republic and endanger liberty. From the same prolific womb of governmental injustice we breed the two great classes—tramps and millionaires. . . .

"We have witnessed for more than a quarter of a century the struggles of the two great political parties for power and plunder, while grievous wrongs have been inflicted upon the suffering people. We charge that the controlling influences dominating both these parties have permitted the existing dreadful conditions to develop without serious effort to prevent or restrain them. Neither do they now promise us any substantial reform."

These quotes are from a political party platform that was part of the presidential election of

(A) 1932

(B) 1924

(C) 1912

(D) 1892

(E) 1948

72. One of the most damaging pieces of antislavery literature was the narratives of escaped slaves or former slaves. Which of the following were written by escaped slaves or former slaves?

I. Olaudah Equiano, *The Interesting Narrative of the Life of Olaudah Equiano, or Gustavus Vassa, The African*

II. Frederick Douglass, *Narrative of the Life of Frederick Douglass*

III. Maria Monk, *Awful Disclosures*

IV. Harriet Beecher Stowe, *Uncle Tom's Cabin*

V. William Lloyd Garrison, *The Liberator*

(A) I and II only

(B) II and V only

(C) II and IV only

(D) II, III, IV, and V only

(E) I, III, and IV only

U.S. Exports to Belligerents during the First World War

	To Allies	To Central Powers
1914	$824,860,000,000	$169,289,000,000
1915	$1,991,747,000,000	$11,878,000,000
1916	$3,214,480,000,000	$1,159,000,000

73. What explains the figures in this chart?

(A) The United States increased its trade to the Allies in order to protect the value of its loans to the Allies.

(B) The United States remained neutral during the early years of the war until the Central Powers attacked our merchant ships as shown by the sinking of the U.S.S. *Lusitania*.

(C) British control of the seas effectively choked off trade with the Central Powers.

(D) The German invasion of Poland cut off the main potential trade access to Germany through Poland via Russia.

(E) The Japanese attack on Pearl Harbor caused American attention to focus more on defeating Japan than on helping the Allies.

74. The Virginia and Kentucky Resolutions

(A) led to the Alien and Sedition Acts

(B) were written by Alexander Hamilton, John Jay, and James Madison

(C) were endorsed by the Federalist Party

(D) raised the issue of state nullification of federal laws

(E) were part of the campaign rhetoric for the election of 1796 between John Adams and Thomas Jefferson

75. After the Constitution was written in 1787, it was sent to the states for ratification. Virginia narrowly approved the Constitution, 89–79. Who was the Virginia delegate to the Constitutional Convention who fought in Virginia against ratifying the Constitution because it lacked a Bill of Rights? His fight earned him the title, "Father of the Bill of Rights."

(A) Thomas Jefferson

(B) George Washington

(C) John Adams

(D) George Mason

(E) Sam Adams

76. In the middle of the twentieth century, the U.S. Senate identified the five senators it considered to have been the greatest of all time. Three of those selected served in the decades from 1810 to 1850. They also occupied other offices and positions in those years, but the service, influence, and significance of each in the Senate was truly distinguished. The three were

(A) Thomas Jefferson, James Madison, Andrew Jackson

(B) Henry Clay, John Calhoun, Daniel Webster

(C) Henry Clay, James Polk, Stephen Douglas

(D) George Washington, Andrew Jackson, Abraham Lincoln

(E) Robert Hayne, Daniel Webster, Thaddeus Stevens

77. "The problem of birth control has arisen directly from the effort of the feminine spirit to free itself from bondage. Woman herself has wrought that bondage through her reproductive powers and while enslaving herself has enslaved the world. The physical suffering to be relieved is chiefly woman's. Hers, too, is the love life that dies first under the blight of too prolific breeding. Within her is wrapped up the future of the race—it is hers to make or mar. All of these considerations point unmistakably to one fact—it is woman's duty as well as her privilege to lay hold of the means of freedom....

"The basic freedom of the world is woman's freedom. A free race cannot be born of slave mothers. A woman enchained cannot choose but give a measure of that bondage to her sons and daughters. No woman can call herself free who does not own and control her body. No woman can call herself free until she can choose consciously whether she will or will not be a mother."

This is an excerpt from *Woman and the New Race*, written by

(A) Sojourner Truth

(B) Susan B. Anthony

(C) Harriet Tubman

(D) Margaret Sanger

(E) Rachel Carson

78. "It is inconsistent with the spirit of neutrality for a neutral nation to make loans to belligerent nations, for money is the worst of all contrabands—it commands all other things... as a neutral government does all in its power to discourage its citizens from enlisting in the armies of other countries, it should discourage those who by loaning money would do more than they could by enlisting. The government withdraws the protection of citizenship from those who do enlist under other flags— why should it give protection to money when it enters foreign military service?"

This attitude by Secretary of State Bryan before the United States entered the First World War was later echoed in the

(A) Marshall Plan

(B) Fourteen Points

(C) Nye Committee investigations

(D) Atlantic Charter

(E) Lend-Lease Act

79. Only two Americans served as president at the birth of their country, George Washington and Jefferson Davis. Which of the following did both Washington and Davis face when they assumed the presidency of the United States and of the Confederate States?

I.   An empty treasury

II.   An alliance with a European country

III.   The immediate threat of war

IV.   Organized political party opposition in the national legislature

V.   A constitution that protected slavery

(A) II, III, and V only

(B) I, II, III, IV, and V

(C) I and III only

(D) I and V only

(E) II, IV, and V only

80. *King Kong, The Wizard of Oz, Gone With the Wind*, and Shirley Temple as a leading box-office attraction are all from which decade?

    (A) 1910s

    (B) 1920s

    (C) 1930s

    (D) 1940s

    (E) 1950s

Answer Key

1. C	17. C	33. E	49. E	65. E
2. D	18. B	34. C	50. A	66. B
3. A	19. A	35. D	51. A	67. A
4. A	20. D	36. B	52. D	68. E
5. E	21. D	37. B	53. D	69. B
6. B	22. B	38. E	54. E	70. D
7. D	23. B	39. E	55. B	71. D
8. C	24. E	40. A	56. B	72. A
9. E	25. E	41. A	57. E	73. C
10. C	26. D	42. C	58. C	74. D
11. A	27. A	43. C	59. C	75. D
12. C	28. D	44. A	60. B	76. B
13. A	29. C	45. B	61. A	77. D
14. E	30. A	46. A	62. C	78. C
15. D	31. E	47. C	63. B	79. D
16. E	32. C	48. A	64. B	80. C

Explanatory Answers

1. **The correct answer is (C).** The NAACP was founded in a 1909 meeting attended by DuBois and other blacks associated with the Niagara Movement and whites shocked by a race riot in Springfield, Illinois, within the shadow of Lincoln's grave. Many of those at the first meeting were descendants of abolitionists, including Garrison's grandson, Oswald Garrison Villard. The following year, 1910, a formal organization was created.

2. **The correct answer is (D).** Currency problems and clashes between debtors and creditors continued into the latter period. Shays' Rebellion is just one example. Tension between the tidewater and the frontier regions is illustrated by the Paxton Boys, Regulators, legislative disputes over appropriations for fighting Indians, and the relocation of state capitals to inland locations. Disputes over western lands were not resolved until after the Confederation period. The one characteristic that changed was the fighting between the lower houses and the governors. The lower houses won because eleven states rewrote their constitutions by 1777 to provide for a much weaker executive.

3. **The correct answer is (A).** Choice V is from the Declaration of Independence, not the Constitution. The Declaration of Independence is a spiritual statement of the values of America; it is not a legal document and has no legal standing in a court. Choice II is incorrect. The Dred Scott case in 1857 declared that slaves were not citizens and could not sue in court. The Fourteenth Amendment, passed after the Civil War, was carefully worded to wipe out the Dred Scott decision. Section 1 of the Fourteenth Amendment makes everyone born or naturalized in the United States a citizen of both his state and of the United States. Every American in effect has dual citizenship.

4. **The correct answer is (A).** The Whiskey Rebellion took place in 1794 in Pennsylvania. Shays' Rebellion took place in 1786 in Massachusetts during the Articles of Confederation. The Whiskey Rebellion protested against Hamilton's excise tax on whiskey, which was designed more to impress the inhabitants of the West with the power of the federal government than to raise revenue. Squeezed by creditors, Massachusetts farmers protested against court confiscations of their farms for nonpayment of debts. President Washington put down the Whiskey Rebellion, not Shays' Rebellion. Both uprisings alarmed conservatives across the nation.

5. **The correct answer is (E).** The Beatles invaded by song and in person in the next decade, the 1960s. They gratefully acknowledged their debt to "the King," Elvis Presley. Other early pioneers of rock and roll were Chuck Berry, Fats Domino, Little Richard, and Bill Haley and the Comets (earlier called the Saddlemen and then the Country Jive Band). Rock and roll, with its suggestive sexual overtones, shocked the music establishment, which was part of its appeal to teenagers. Frank Sinatra called it "the most brutal, ugly, desperate, vicious form of expression it has been my misfortune to hear." In 1950, for the first time in history, one-half of all students graduated from high school, which means that now over half stayed in school, out of the adult work force. Teenagers formed a distinct, large consumer group that spent millions of dollars on records.

6. **The correct answer is (B).** The tax rate was reduced from six pence to three, but that was not the most significant part of the Revenue Act of 1764 (the Sugar Act). The British were determined to collect this tax and to inaugurate a new policy of enforcing trade and navigation laws.

7. **The correct answer is (D).** Her autobiography is a delightful description of college life as seen through the eyes of a shy, intelligent young woman in a hostile atmosphere. One fad of the era was for women to be "pinned" to a fraternity. Fraternities vied with one another to corral the most attractive and acceptable young women. Not wishing to hurt anyone's feelings Ida accepted four pins and created a social faux pas by wearing all four at once to chapel! For a few months she was, in her words, a "social outcast."

8. **The correct answer is (C).** Indians were greatly confused by the civil war aspect of the American Revolution. Both governments, the English and the American, offered conflicting advice. Many tribes had suffered when their ally, France, had lost the French and Indian War, and they saw a potentially difficult situation in the Revolution. Unfortunately for the Iroquois, the Americans won. The Iroquois Confederacy never recovered its unity and strength. Thayendanegea had been educated at the New Hampshire Indian School, which later became Dartmouth College. He even briefly visited Great Britain in 1775–1776.

9. **The correct answer is (E).** *Adkins* v. *Children's Hospital* declared unconstitutional an act of Congress that authorized the Wage Board of the District of Columbia to establish minimum wages for women, not maximum hours for children.

10. **The correct answer is (C).** The accomplishments described were part of the early political career of Theodore Roosevelt.

11. **The correct answer is (A).** Southern apologists writing immediately after the Civil War claimed that the war was a constitutional squabble over states' rights. For this reason, some Southerners still prefer calling it the War Between the States. Progressive era historians emphasized economic and class struggle as themes in American history. Charles Beard saw two competing classes that just happened to also have been divided geographically into a planter aristocracy and a rising industrial class. The First World War, fought to save the world for democracy, left many intellectuals disillusioned. Historians now saw a needless fanaticism in all wars, especially apparent in the 1850s. The rise of a congressional conservative coalition in the late 1930s and the Dixiecrat revolt of 1948 led to a reexamination of the impact of sectionalism on national political parties in the late 1930s and the 1940s.

Slavery is the one interpretation that was always present as a secondary explanation or even primary cause of the Civil War. As Lincoln said in his second inaugural address, "All know that slavery was somehow the cause of the war." Historians may disagree over exactly how it caused the war; but it was the one indispensable ingredient of the Civil War.

12. **The correct answer is (C).** Clara Barton founded the American Red Cross. Her counterpart in Great Britain was Florence Nightingale. When Barton died in 1912, she was working to establish the Red Cross in Mexico.

13. **The correct answer is (A).** Our nation's first federally funded health care act, the Sheppard-Towner Act, provided prenatal clinics and public health centers in communities willing to put up matching

funds. The American Medical Association staunchly opposed the act; doctors in this era did not believe preventive medicine was a responsibility of the medical profession. How things have changed! It was thought that the newly enfranchised women would vote as a bloc so politicians listened attentively to their demand for this act. By the end of the decade it was apparent that women lacked any degree of cohesiveness as voters. That plus the steady opposition of the AMA led the politicians to terminate the act in 1929. Columbia, Maryland, was part of the federal government's greenbelt towns, planned communities to illustrate the advantages of planning over sprawl. But it was part of the New Deal.

14. **The correct answer is (E).** Two-thirds approval of the Senate only is needed for ratifying the nominations of cabinet members and federal judges.

15. **The correct answer is (D).** There are two theories about how to stimulate the economy. One advocates putting money into the hands of the poor and depending on the resulting demand for consumer goods to stimulate the economy. The second idea is to put more money into the hands of the wealthy who will expand the economy by investing their new funds in capital, thereby generating expansion. Since the supply of capital funds increases, this theory is called supply-side economics. Economists constantly debate which is more effective. Different economists line up on one side or the other on the basis of their political leanings, their vision of where the economy should go, and their individual philosophical assumptions. President Reagan opted for the second theory: increase the supply of capital rather than increase demand through consumer spending. His tax reductions especially benefited the rich. The 1981 and 1986 tax cuts granted a $69 tax reduction to those making $10,000 to $20,000. Those making $40,000 to $50,000 got a $1,000 cut; those making over $1,000,000, a $281,000 cut.

16. **The correct answer is (E).** This is a later argument, one that was added after the switch in the national origin of the average immigrant from northern and western Europe to southern and eastern Europe. Anthony even argued that women came under the Fifteenth Amendment prohibition against denying the vote because of "previous condition of servitude." She asserted that the legal and traditional position of women within marriage amounted to servitude. She was fined, but the court never tried to collect the fine because that would have given her the basis for an appeal to a higher court.

17. **The correct answer is (C).** Jefferson and Madison organized their party and built their following. Jacksonian Democracy existed before Jackson entered the scene. It is named for him because he came to symbolize the movement, but he had nothing to do with its origins or philosophy. Take Jefferson's ideas out of Jeffersonian Democracy and little is left. On the contrary, you might have trouble finding Jackson's intellectual contributions in Jacksonian Democracy.

18. **The correct answer is (B).** The Federal Reserve Act (Owen-Glass Act) created a new banking system to solve the dilemma of inelastic currency. The Federal Reserve Board controlled the decentralized system through twelve districts. Banks established under the 1863 National Bank System were required to join the Federal Reserve.

The new system was unable to prevent the great crash of 1929 and subsequent downturns in the economy. Wall Street tenaciously fought against the proposed system in the six-month-long congressional debate. Whereas Theodore Roosevelt avoided volatile issues like the tariff and currency inelasticity, Wilson charged ahead and won in both areas.

19. **The correct answer is (A).** Oliver Wendell Holmes, Jr., spent thirty years on the Supreme Court, where he became famous for the clarity and sharpness of his dissents, many of which later formed the basis for majority opinions.

20. **The correct answer is (D).** The reputation of Virginia and Maryland as graveyards held down the number of willing immigrants. Eighty percent of immigrants to these two colonies in the 1700s were indentured servants. The overwhelming majority of indentured servants were young, male, and single. In the seventeenth century high death rates virtually negated the dream of a farm at the end of one's service. The rates improved a little in the eighteenth century, but as the labor pool expanded masters

became more likely to use harsh methods or to literally work a servant to death. After all, from the owner's point of view he was purchasing a service rather than charitably providing an opportunity. Indentured servants frequently ran away. Most of the good land was already taken, so indentured servants found themselves unable to purchase a usable farm. Many became drifting day laborers. The headright system in the seventeenth century rewarded the American who paid for passage for someone, not the other way around. Usually he got fifty acres per person.

21. **The correct answer is (D).** I can almost hear the outcry from Texas! The battles of the Alamo, Goliad, and San Jacinto were part of the Texan Revolution, not the Mexican War. The first two were defeats, but San Jacinto was the victory under Sam Houston that ended the revolution and secured the independence of Texas. The author of the two phrases in choice (E) was Andrew Jackson, who was still alive in the early 1840s and, of course, favored expansion. There are only three natural harbors on the west coast, San Diego, San Francisco, and Seattle. Every nation wanted them; we got them.

22. **The correct answer is (B).** Rev. Martin Luther King, Jr., had been urged by his fellow white ministers to go slow, to not press integration. King responded with this letter explaining nonviolent resistance and why it was essential to not "go slow." Unless pressed, the cause of equal rights would never be negotiated, just avoided.

23. **The correct answer is (B).** Virginia Minor sued in a federal court claiming that she was denied one of her "privileges and immunities" guaranteed by the Fourteenth Amendment, specifically the right to vote. The Supreme Court ruled in 1875 that voting was not a right guaranteed by citizenship. Women were citizens; but states could still deny them the vote.

24. **The correct answer is (E).** Henry Clay complained that the Whigs only nominated him when the party didn't have a chance. He lost in 1824, 1832, and 1844. William Jennings Bryan lost in 1896, 1900, and 1908. Some historians would argue that for Bryan representing the peoples' wishes was more important than winning the presidency.

25. **The correct answer is (E).** In spite of the Battle of Wounded Knee in 1890, the Indian threat was already gone before 1880. Agriculturalist Hardy Campbell promoted his technique of dry farming, a method to farm areas with low rainfall, and immigrants introduced Russian wheat and other hardy crops that thrived on the plains. Mother nature cruelly sent exceptionally high rainfall in the 1870s, causing overexpansion into marginal farmland. During the next decade, rainfall fell below normal; and drought hit in 1885 and 1886. The winters were harsh, especially the fabled winters of 1886–1887 and 1887–1888. At one point it snowed for fourteen days. Cattle prices plummeted due to overexpansion, and small farmers were increasingly replaced by large corporate farms. Joseph Glidden invented his barbed wire fence in 1874, creating by far the most successful version of a woodless fence. With few trees on the Great Plains, fencing had presented a major difficulty until Glidden invented his barbed wire fence.

26. **The correct answer is (D).** This passage is from Washington's Neutrality Proclamation of April 22, 1793. The United States wanted to avoid getting involved in the European wars set off by the French Revolution. The Neutrality Proclamation is an excellent example of diplomatic double-talk; nowhere in the proclamation does Washington use the word "neutrality."

27. **The correct answer is (A).** The issue of the constitutionality of an act of Congress did not appear again until the Dred Scott case. The decision found the Missouri Compromise of 1820 unconstitutional because the 36° 30' line deprived citizens of their right to the use of their property (their slaves) without following due process of law. *Worcester* v. *Georgia* concerned federal treaty supremacy over a state law trying to push the Cherokee Indians westward. *Cohens* v. *Virginia* dealt with federal jurisdiction to review state court decisions to judge if they violated rights guaranteed under the Constitution. The decision in *McCulloch* v. *Maryland* asserted the national sovereignty of the federal government and the constitutionality of the Bank of the United States. Finally, the Dartmouth College case declared that the sanctity of a contract was beyond the will of the people as expressed through their state legislature.

28. **The correct answer is (D).** The National Recovery Administration, or NRA (the Blue Eagle), tried a partnership approach to stabilize the economy during the early years of the New Deal. Overproduction was the country's villain. Thus, production was controlled to reduce competition and to prevent waste. The "sick chicken" Schechter decision mercifully ended the hodgepodge of almost unenforceable regulations of the NRA.

29. **The correct answer is (C).** Dorothea Dix labored to improve the lot of the insane in the era before the Civil War. In many states she was the first woman to address the legislature. The organizers of the Seneca Falls Convention were Elizabeth Cady Stanton and Lucretia Mott.

30. **The correct answer is (A).** Political cartoonists had a ball with the leadership of the Populist Party in the 1890s. Mary Ellen Lease urged farmers to "raise less corn, and more Hell." Simpson was a poor farmer pushed to the forefront by Populism. Lease, Weaver, and Donnelly were perpetual reformers who moved into the Populist movement because it provided a forum and an audience. In the popular mind, outside of the Populist strongholds, the Populist leaders were seen as visionaries, dreamers, radicals, or lunatics.

31. **The correct answer is (E).** The first four played a role in defeating the ERA, at least in the eyes of the general public. Women's wage levels have never equaled those of men. Gains have been made, but equality is a long way off.

32. **The correct answer is (C).** Thoreau's essay served as a catalyst for Gandhi in India and for Martin Luther King, Jr. Without the concept of massive disobedience to an unjust law, neither movement would have succeeded as it did.

33. **The correct answer is (E).** In 1815 Webster, like most New Englanders, feared that a high tariff would inhibit shipping and commerce. By 1830, though, the region's future clearly lay in industrialization more than shipping, and protective tariffs protected American industries from foreign competition. Choice (A) did occur, but nationalism was not the reason for Webster's switch. Only the first part of choice (C) is correct. Political parties never determine their stands based on that of their opponents, and the areas of agreement between parties far outnumber those of disagreement. Free trade is the opposite of a protective tariff. Clay's American system included a Bank of the United States and a high tariff, with the proceeds being used to fund internal improvements. Webster didn't sell his support (or soul) to Clay nor to anyone else. (Ask your English teacher about the short story, "The Devil and Daniel Webster.")

34. **The correct answer is (C).** The Republican candidate was Senator Barry Goldwater of Arizona (nicknamed AuH_2O). He electrified his supporters in his acceptance speech by closing with "I would remind you that extremism in the defense of liberty is no vice! And let me remind you also that moderation in the pursuit of justice is no virtue!" He had voted against the Civil Rights Act of 1964 and against the Nuclear Test Ban Treaty. Conservatives loved him. He won only six states, and President Lyndon Johnson won a comfortable majority in Congress for his programs.

35. **The correct answer is (D).** The separation of work and home in the antebellum period led to a new ideal of the home as a refuge from the demands of the work environment. Wives were to provide a quiet haven for husbands who labored outside the home. Women should concentrate on the home and raising moral children, relieving the husband of these petty issues while he struggled in the emerging industrial, capitalist workplace.

36. **The correct answer is (B).** Country A is Guatemala; E Grenada; G Panama; H Nicaragua; and C the Dominican Republic. But F is not Cuba, where Castro took over creating a thorn in the sides of American policy makers. F is Puerto Rico.

37. **The correct answer is (B).** We hear of the others more often, but all were extralegal organizations opposing the British either politically or through enforcing boycotts. The only official opposition was

The Association, created by the First Continental Congress.

38. **The correct answer is (E).** Alexis de Tocqueville wrote the insightful *Democracy in America*. Frances Trollope, an English novelist, wrote a delightfully unflattering book, *The Domestic Manners of the Americans* (1832), pungently describing crude American social customs to amused or angered readers. James Bryce tried to explain the actual workings of the American political system in *The American Commonwealth* (1888), still widely quoted as an accurate analysis. Jenny Lind, the "Swedish Nightingale," captivated American audiences in her concert tour from 1850 to 1852. Promoted by P.T. Barnum, she captured the public's imagination and even inspired a collection of trunks and furniture.

39. **The correct answer is (E).** The suburban boom came later, after the Second World War in the 1940s. The automobile drastically altered dating customs, permitting young couples to escape the eyes of their elders. A whole collection of spin-off industries grew out of the automobile industry. At one time one out of every seven jobs was directly connected to the automobile industry.

40. **The correct answer is (A).** President Washington was uncertain about the constitutionality of the Bank of the United States, which passed Congress on February 8, 1791, and he asked for written opinions. The best two came from Secretary of the Treasury Hamilton and Secretary of State Jefferson. They remain the classic statements of loose and strict construction of the Constitution. Washington followed Hamilton's thinking and signed the bill creating the Bank. Hamilton's position was poured into judicial concrete in the McCulloch decision in 1819. In purchasing Louisiana in 1803 Jefferson swallowed his strict interpretation stance. The Constitution does not indicate who, if anyone, may purchase new territory for the United States. There wasn't time to pass a constitutional amendment to give the president authority, and the deal was too good to pass up.

41. **The correct answer is (A).** Ballou's statement is an excellent explanation of the impulses that drove reformers in the antebellum years. Man is a creation of God; man is part of God's holy plan. Therefore, if man will only strive for it, perfection is possible in all spheres of human activity. Most reformers also believed as a corollary that society's achievement of perfection on earth would speed up the Second Coming of Christ. Ballou established the cooperative community of Hopedale, an experiment in "practical Christianity," which lasted from 1840 to 1856.

42. **The correct answer is (C).** Local issues of race, immigration, prohibition, schools, and spoils dominated politics in this era. National issues were less clear. The economy was undergoing major changes while shifting from an agricultural to an industrial base. National politics reflected this confusion; local politics seemed more relevant to voters. Historians investigating the political loyalties of the late nineteenth century have identified cultural, ethnic, and religious criteria that differentiate groups of voters.

43. **The correct answer is (C).** The Europeans were greatly superior to the Native Americans in their resistance to disease. Indians were devastated by smallpox, measles, chicken pox, and other diseases, all of which were minor ailments to Europeans born with some inherited immunity. Indians had no immunity whatsoever. As much as 90 percent of the Native American population may have died, destroying their religious, political, economic, and military organization. For the full impact, see Alfred W. Crosby, Jr., *The Columbian Exchange: Biological and Cultural Consequences of 1492*. The unequal exchange of diseases is also a frequent theme in science fiction; the best known is H.G. Wells, *War of the Worlds*.

44. **The correct answer is (A).** Eugene V. Debs was the spokesman for the Socialist Party. The Socialists criticized Samuel Gompers and the American Federation of Labor for concentrating only on economic gains for workers. The Socialist Party's objectives included the overthrow of the capitalist system. The AFL never criticized capitalism; it just argued for a bigger slice of the pie. Many radical writers have called the AFL one of the strongest supporters of capitalism.

45. **The correct answer is (B).** With the ratification of the Nineteenth Amendment assured, the National

American Woman Suffrage Association voted in March, 1919, to create a new organization to press for legislation for women. Everyone, including women leaders and professional politicians, expected women to vote as a bloc for women's issues. Hence the need to continue some organization dedicated to women as a separate group of voters. That organization was the League of Women Voters. The expected togetherness of women voters never materialized. "Womenness" is too broad a category to hold a group together. This explains why the women's movement, like all other broadly based movements, has done much better with specific goals than with general ideals.

Actually, women gained only two distinct laws in the 1920s, the Sheppard-Towner Act, that provided medical care to children and to women, and the Cable Citizenship Act, which granted separate citizenship to women. Prior to this law, a woman could lose her citizenship if her husband did.

46. **The correct answer is (A).** Religion was only one reason for Europe's so-called wars of religion. Nationalism, economic rivalry, dynastic control, and the balance of power also played a role. For many policy makers of this era, religion was similar to later Cold War ideology. Wars over religion were bloody, but far from foolish to contemporaries. Puritans came for freedom from religious persecution for themselves, not religious freedom for everyone. Roger Williams wanted to separate church and state to maintain the purity of the church, not the state. The English have never separated church and state, although they practice religious freedom.

47. **The correct answer is (C).** The "strenuous life" is the trademark of Theodore Roosevelt, who believed that individuals and nations needed to rise to the challenges confronting them or sink into insignificance. His personal life was the "strenuous life." The author of twenty-two books, he practiced his own standard of the combined physically active and mentally alert life.

48. **The correct answer is (A).** The Northwest Ordinance promised America's "colonies," the Northwest territories, that they would not be colonies forever. Eventually they would be states equal to the original thirteen.

49. **The correct answer is (E).** An excellent harbor, proximity to European markets, a good location for business headquarters, and a wide hinterland all combined to make New York City the primary United States seaport, and not just in this period of history.

50. **The correct answer is (A).** This prophetic warning came from John Brown shortly before his execution for the unsuccessful raid on Harpers Ferry in October, 1859.

51. **The correct answer is (A).** The Republican Party platform for the 1860 campaign specifically mentioned four projects: a transcontinental railroad, a higher tariff, a national banking system, and a homestead act. The land-grant college idea had been pushed for years, especially by Midwesterners. Nicknamed the "Illinois idea," and sponsored by a Vermont senator, it finally passed Congress after the Southerners pulled out. Senator Jefferson Davis of Mississippi vehemently opposed the college land-grant law.

52. **The correct answer is (D).** Charles Lindbergh delivered this speech. Convinced that Germany was an overwhelming potential foe, he, and many others such as the America First Committee, urged the nation to avoid getting involved in Europe's wars. Senator Nye chaired the committee that investigated the "merchants of death" accusations about our involvement in the First World War. In the 1930s, college students started the Veterans of Future Wars hoping to get their bonuses while they were still alive. President Franklin Roosevelt recognized that the conflict in Europe involved larger issues than just American security.

53. **The correct answer is (D).** Racial discrimination hemmed in the black ghetto, making it more crowded and giving African Americans no options for home ownership outside the ghetto. Rents were high for single rooms and people moved often, creating instability. Those who managed to climb into the middle class proudly asserted all the differentiating trappings of their new class status. Class was more precious because it was so tenuous and uncertain. African Americans lacked the range of associational links that

immigrants had; therefore, their loyalty to community institutions and to the group was much weaker. Religion, history, nationalism, shared migration, links to the home country, and education were all stronger in the immigrant community. For years commentators simply likened the black experience in the ghetto to the immigrant experience. Blacks were just the "last of the immigrants," ran the argument. Just as immigrants pulled themselves up, so would blacks. Racism scuttled that similarity.

54. **The correct answer is (E).** Jimmy Carter was a fundamentalist Christian, but his political style and methods were those of a technocrat, one who applied managerial and technical solutions to a problem. The Radical Right tended to apply ideological or moral solutions to problems. The Moral Majority was an organization created in 1979 by the Reverend Jerry Falwell. Television evangelists raised millions of dollars for conservative candidates and pulled into political activities a group formerly uninvolved.

55. **The correct answer is (B).** The Revenue Act of 1942 increased the number of people who paid taxes and the Current Tax Payment Act of 1943 forever changed paydays. Now the income tax was, in the words of a Treasury Department official, "a people's tax." Almost everyone paid and all had their wages withheld.

56. **The correct answer is (B).** The Mayflower Compact was signed by forty-one male passengers aboard the Mayflower in November 1620. Since only about one-third of the passengers were members of the Leyden congregation and the ship was outside the boundaries of its land grant, the leaders had no legitimate means of controlling the company. The agreement committed everyone to following majority rule in their civil government. This document is one of the cornerstones of American political theory. Plymouth itself was never much of a colony, being eventually absorbed by Massachusetts.

57. **The correct answer is (E).** The First Bank of the United States was chartered in 1791 for twenty years. When Jefferson won the presidency, he and his followers merely tolerated the Federalist Bank, and in 1811 they quietly let it die. To their dismay they learned the economic value of the Bank in providing a reliable currency. They swallowed their ideology and chartered the Second Bank of the U.S. in 1816, again with a twenty-year charter.

58. **The correct answer is (C).** Oliver H. Kelley, a clerk in the U.S. Bureau of Agriculture, a forerunner of the Agricultural Department, started the National Grange of the Patrons of Husbandry in 1867. Originally conceived as a national fraternal organization, the local and state chapters later pursued political objectives to control or limit railroad monopolies, leading to the Granger cases such as *Munn v. Illinois*.

59. **The correct answer is (C).** Oberlin College in Ohio became a hotbed of abolitionism and radicalism in the 1830s, opening its doors first to women in 1833 and then to blacks in 1835. The college was also a station on the Underground Railroad.

60. **The correct answer is (B).** In 1588 England defeated the Spanish Armada. In the 1650s the Navigation Acts were aimed at the Dutch, who controlled much of the carrying trade (what we call shipping) throughout the world. Between 1754 and 1763 the British fought the French in the Seven Years' War, or, as it was called here, the French and Indian War.

61. **The correct answer is (A).** Choice (B) happened, but in 1970. The Little Rock incident took place in 1957 and involved nine high school students attempting to integrate Central High School. The campus of UCLA was not linked to the black residential area of Watts. The issue at Jackson State was the same as at Kent State, a protest against U.S. bombing of Cambodia during the Vietnam War.

62. **The correct answer is (C).** The Federalists tended to be pro-British or at least to see Great Britain as a political, social, and financial model worth emulating. The greater threat to the U.S. was not Great Britain but that wild nation ruled by irrational revolutionaries, France.

63. **The correct answer is (B).** The Berlin Wall was erected in August 1961 during Kennedy's administration.

64. **The correct answer is (B).** Every tidewater plantation in the Chesapeake region was accessible by an

ocean-going ship, so large towns or cities were unnecessary. Cities exist where they do because they are at a point of transshipment, where goods are changed from one form of transportation to another. Since transshipment was unnecessary in the Chesapeake Bay, so were cities, and commercial cities did not develop until after the colonial period. Williamsburg is a beautifully restored town, but it was a government center, and it bustled with activity only when the legislature was in session.

65. **The correct answer is (E).** Andrew Jackson chased Seminole Indians into Florida in 1818, precipitating a crisis. His actions raised many eyebrows, but they secured Florida for the United States. Ironically, Jackson's future political opponent, John Quincy Adams, supported him, and his future vice-president, John C. Calhoun, condemned him. In 1818 Calhoun was the Secretary of War and Adams the Secretary of State.

66. **The correct answer is (B).** William Penn never criticized slavery. Quaker criticism waited until John Woolman and Anthony Benezet spoke out against it beginning in the 1750s. Eventually their message virtually ended slavery among the Quakers.

67. **The correct answer is (A).** The emphasis on voting could be either era, Reconstruction or the "Second Reconstruction" of the 1950s and 1960s. The comment on the earlier civil rights bill reaching "my desk" shows that this president signed one a short time before. The remark that "We have already waited a hundred years and more" places the event in the Second Reconstruction. The speaker, therefore, must be president Lyndon Johnson, who gave this impassioned plea before submitting what became the Voting Rights Act of 1965.

68. **The correct answer is (E).** Upton Sinclair wrote *The Jungle* to dramatize the plight of the workers. As Sinclair later complained, "I aimed at the public's heart and hit it in the stomach." He hoped to arouse the public's sympathy for immigrant workers. Often mentioned and rarely read by students, *The Jungle* should be read as a work of literature and as a work of protest rather than as an exposé.

69. **The correct answer is (B).** Levi Strauss joined up with Davis to create the blue jeans that acquired the nickname "Levis." Richard Sears was a founder of Sears, Roebuck and Company. John Wanamaker was a Philadelphia merchant who pioneered the department store, standard prices, and money-back guarantee. Denis Kearney was a leader in California against Oriental immigration. Leland Stanford was the Central Pacific and Southern Pacific railroad magnate.

70. **The correct answer is (D).** The West most consistently pushed for internal improvements. Too much is made of the opposition of Thomas Jefferson to Alexander Hamilton's economic program. Jefferson distrusted the man more than he disliked the proposals, especially in regard to transportation. The National Road began in 1806 under Jefferson. He directed his Secretary of the Treasury, Albert Gallatin (who was also Madison's Secretary of the Treasury until 1814), to draw up a set of plans for "opening roads and making canals, together with a statement of the undertakings of that nature, which, as objects of public improvement, may require and deserve the aid of Government." Gallatin's Report reads like a blueprint for later canals and roads. It identifies all the essential routes. In the next few years, military expenditures gobbled up any anticipated revenue available for internal improvements. Ever the frugal spenders, neither Jefferson nor Madison pushed to increase revenues to begin internal improvements. Of the two, Madison was more doctrinaire and inflexible (which explains why Jefferson is considered the more successful president). Madison wanted a constitutional amendment to clearly grant the federal government the power to finance internal improvements. Instead he got the Bonus Bill, maneuvered through Congress by John Calhoun before his nationalism gave way to an ever increasing sectionalism. Madison vetoed the Bonus Bill in his last act as president. Internal improvements were part of Clay's idea to tie the sections together as markets. Jackson's veto of the Maysville Road Bill, sponsored by Clay, was politically motivated as well as constitutionally motivated. Jackson knew he was right constitutionally, but he also enjoyed revenge against his rival from the election of 1824. The West most consistently pushed for internal improvements in this era in order to get its produce to market.

71. **The correct answer is (D).** The quote is from the Populist Party platform, July 4, 1892. Every student of American history should read the preamble to the Populist Party platform.

72. **The correct answer is (A).** Olaudah Equiano's 1794 autobiography of his capture in Africa and his subsequent life as a slave was the first of the escape books and in many respects the best. Douglass published his narrative to prove that he had been a former slave. Too articulate for many disbelievers in the North, he had to prove that it was possible for an ex-slave to acquire all the education and manners of his civilized Northern critics! Publication forced him to flee to England where friends raised the money to purchase his freedom from his Maryland owner. Stowe and Garrison were both Northern whites. Maria Monk's *Awful Disclosures* published in 1836 is perfectly named. She claimed to be an escaped nun (she claimed that nuns were captured by the Roman Catholic Church and forced to be nuns). Her book inspired a Boston mob to attack a convent. How courageous! What she really proved was that an outrageous, untrue book could sell if it catered to the public's prejudices, in this case anti-Catholicism.

73. **The correct answer is (C).** Choices (D) and (E) apply to the Second World War, not to the First, although both contain incorrect statements. The United States was already reducing its trade with Germany long before the invasion of Poland, and after Pearl Harbor, the United States concentrated on defeating Germany rather than on defeating Japan. The *Lusitania* was a British ship. Loans to the Allies followed rather than preceded our increased exports. They began when the Allies encountered difficulty paying. It was British control of the seas that choked off trade with the continental Central Powers. The German submarine campaign was an attempt to equalize British naval surface power. It failed in the long run.

74. **The correct answer is (D).** The XYZ affair led to the Alien and Sedition Acts, which Jefferson and Madison blasted in the Virginia and Kentucky Resolutions in 1798. The issue of state nullification of federal laws was raised for the first time. But the Democratic-Republicans raised the issue more as part of their political campaign against the Federalists than as a constitutional or doctrinaire issue. The Hartford Convention in 1814 and Calhoun's "Exposition and Protest" cemented nullification into an abstract constitutional issue.

75. **The correct answer is (D).** That honor belongs to George Mason. Mason stood stubbornly for the inclusion of a Bill of Rights in the Constitution, refusing positions he was offered in the new government in return for his support of the ratification of the Constitution by the Virginia ratifying convention. Virginia ratified the Constitution by a vote of 89–79 and then proposed that the first order of business for the new government be the consideration of a Bill of Rights. The ten amendments quickly passed.

76. **The correct answer is (B).** Clay was from Kentucky, Calhoun from South Carolina, and Webster from Massachusetts. The other two were Robert Taft from Ohio who served in the Senate from 1938 to 1953 as "Mr. Republican," and the Progressive era reformer, Robert La Follette from Wisconsin.

77. **The correct answer is (D).** These quotes are from Margaret Sanger, the pioneer nurse who fought to restore a woman's right to obtain information about birth control, which right she had had prior to the passage of the federal Comstock Act in 1873. Before this law, both contraceptive aids and abortions were easily available and were widely used by many middle-class and working-class women. Sanger published a magazine, *The Woman Rebel*, beginning in 1914 and wrote a pamphlet on *Family Limitation*. Upon opening a clinic in Brooklyn in 1916, she was arrested for violating laws against even discussing birth control methods. She continued to fight. In 1936 the Supreme Court in *United States* v. *One Package* reinterpreted the Comstock Law to rule that contraceptives and birth control materials were no longer defined as obscene materials.

78. **The correct answer is (C).** In the 1930s, the Nye Senate Committee publicized the "merchants of death" interpretation of the reasons for United States involvement in the First World War. We entered to protect loans made by American banks to the Allies and to protect the profits of the arms manufacturers. The

Johnson Debt Default Act (1934) prohibited new loans to any foreign government that had not repaid its First World War debts. The Neutrality Acts of 1935, 1936, and 1937 tried to prevent a repetition of United States economic entanglement with one side during a foreign war. The Acts were one war too late.

79. **The correct answer is (D).** The treasury was empty in both instances, and both constitutions protected slavery. War loomed in 1861 for the South but not for the United States in 1789. We were allied with France in 1789, but the Confederacy could not find an ally. The Confederacy actually faced more political opposition in its congress than did the fledgling United States. Before Hamilton's program there really were no parties or distinct groupings or followings in the first Congress. Political opposition grew out of responses to Hamilton's ideas and coalesced into political parties as the decade went on.

80. **The correct answer is (C).** Even in the middle of the Great Depression, millions of Americans went to the movies, perhaps as an escape. Between 60 and 90 million attended weekly. Adding to the talking films begun in the late 1920s was the new attraction of color. Watch *The Wizard of Oz*—it begins in black and white and then bursts into color in Oz. The original book by Frank Baum sets the opening scene as gray and dreary and the movie faithfully follows.

SAMPLE TEST E

U.S. History

Section I

Time—55 minutes • 80 Questions

Directions: Each of the questions or incomplete statements below is followed by five suggested answers or completions. Select the one that is best in each case and then blacken the corresponding space on the answer sheet.

1. More than any other, this colony was the lengthened shadow of one man. He offered easy land terms of 50 free acres; laid out his principal city in checkerboard fashion to prevent a disaster similar to the Great Fire of London; and offered a sincere trust in humanity and religious freedom in his "Holy Experiment." What colony and founder are described?

   (A) New York—Peter Stuyvesant

   (B) Georgia—James Oglethorpe

   (C) Pennsylvania—William Penn

   (D) Maryland—Lord Baltimore

   (E) Massachusetts Bay—John Winthrop

2. The treaties that came out of the Washington Disarmament Conference in the early 1920s—the Five Power Naval Disarmament Treaty, the FourPowerTreaty, and the NinePowerTreaty—were consistent with previous American foreign policy in regard to the

   (A) Open Door Notes

   (B) Stimson Doctrine

   (C) mediation of the Russo-Japanese War

   (D) Versailles Treaty

   (E) Monroe Doctrine

3. The most important influence on the institution of slavery was the

   (A) cotton gin

   (B) gag rule

   (C) American Colonization Society

   (D) Underground Railroad

   (E) "Three-fifths" Compromise

4. "There are, in this case, all the essential constituent parts of a contract. There is something to be contracted about; there are parties, and there are plain terms in which the agreement of the parties, on the subject of the contract, is expressed. There are mutual considerations and inducements. The charter recites, that the founder, on his part, has agreed to establish his seminary in New Hampshire, and to enlarge it, beyond its original design, among other things, for the benefit of that province; and thereupon a charter is given to him and his associates, designated by himself, promising and assuring to them, under the plighted faith of the state, the right of . . . administering its concerns, in the manner provided in the charter. There is a complete and perfect grant to them of all the power of superintendence, visitation, and government. Is this not a contract?"

This quotation

   (A) is from Calhoun's "Exposition and Protest" opposing the Tariff of Abominations

   (B) is from Marshall's decision in *Gibbons* v. *Ogden*

   (C) is from a speech in favor of the Morrill Land-Grant College Act

   (D) illustrates the emotions and arguments of the Great Awakening

   (E) is from Daniel Webster's argument before the Supreme Court in the Dartmouth College case

5. If all of these five were transported back to the antebellum period, who would be most likely to approve of the "Cult of True Womanhood"?

   (A) Phyllis Schlafly

   (B) Betty Friedan

   (C) Carrie Nation

   (D) Gloria Steinem

   (E) Shirley Chisholm

6. Who practiced polygamy, organized an authoritarian political community, and separated themselves from outsiders?

   (A) Shakers

   (B) Mormons

   (C) Christian Scientists

   (D) Quakers

   (E) Amish

7. "If a nation shows that it knows how to act with reasonable efficiency and decency in social and political matters, if it keeps order and pays its obligations, it need fear no interference from the United States. Chronic wrongdoing, or an impotence which results in a general loosening of the ties of civilized society, may in America, as elsewhere, ultimately require intervention by some civilized nation, and in the Western Hemisphere the adherence of the United States to the Monroe Doctrine may force the United States, however reluctantly, in flagrant cases of such wrongdoing or impotence, to the exercise of an international police power."

   What foreign policy was based upon this statement?

   (A) Dollar diplomacy

   (B) "Watchful waiting" in Mexico

   (C) Good Neighbor policy

   (D) Open Door policy

   (E) Roosevelt Corollary

8. The Great Compromise during the writing of the Constitution involved

   (A) the creation of three separate branches of government—executive, legislative, and judicial

   (B) determining whether sovereignty rested with the states or the federal government

   (C) the respective powers of the House and Senate and representation in the Senate and the House

   (D) ending the slave trade after twenty years

   (E) whether or not only a majority vote was needed to tax imports

9. At different times in our nation's history a group of Americans has decided to go en masse to Washington, D.C., to publicize its cause and to pressure Congress and the president for action. All of the following link a "march on Washington" with the group's reason for marching EXCEPT

   (A) 1941, A. Philip Randolph—discrimination against blacks in defense industries

   (B) 1963, Martin Luther King, Jr.—racial justice and civil rights

   (C) 1894, Jacob Coxey—creation of federal government public works projects for the relief of the unemployed

   (D) 1930, the Bonus Army—antiwar protest by isolationists against increased defense spending

   (E) 1967, march on the Pentagon—antiwar protest against the Vietnam War

10. This act guaranteed the right of labor unions to organize and to bargain collectively, and it created the National Labor Relations Board to ensure fair and open campaigning by unions for initial union recognition and organization. Which act is described?

    (A) Clayton Act

    (B) Norris-LaGuardia Act

    (C) Taft-Hartley Act

    (D) Landrum-Griffin Act

    (E) Wagner Act

11. The legacy of Reconstruction included

    (A) the Solid South and the rise of the Redeemers or Bourbons

    (B) constitutional amendments to ensure black civil rights sometime in the future

    (C) the crop lien system and sharecropping

(D) expenditures for badly needed schools and roads

(E) all of the above

12. All of the following except one contributed to the adoption of Jim Crow laws in the South in the 1890s. Which of the following did NOT?

(A) A decline in the commitment of Northern liberals to civil rights for blacks

(B) The inability of the Southern Redeemer conservative governments to maintain control of Southern state governments

(C) The adoption of racism by Southern Populist radicals to counter conservative Redeemer use of racism to win political support

(D) Civil rights marches and agitation by Southern blacks, provoking white retaliation

(E) A series of Supreme Court decisions weakening the protection of civil rights granted by the Fourteenth Amendment

13. "His Catholic Majesty will permit the citizens of the United States, for the space of three years from this time, to deposit their merchandizes and effects in the port of New-Orleans, and to export them from thence without paying any duty than a fair price for the hire of the stores, and His Majesty promises either to continue this permission, if he finds during that time that it is not prejudicial to the interests of Spain, or if he should not agree to continue it there, he will assign to them, on another part of the banks of the Mississippi, an equivalent establishment."

This quotation is from

(A) the Treaty of Paris (1763) ending the French and Indian War (Seven Years' War)

(B) the Treaty of Paris (1783)

(C) Pinckney's Treaty with Spain

(D) the Clayton-Bulwer Treaty

(E) the Jay-Gardoqui Treaty

14. President Martin Van Buren endorsed the Independent Treasury plan that

(A) ordered payment of land purchases in specie

(B) advocated the creation of a new Bank of the United States

(C) advocated the creation of a Federal Reserve banking network

(D) provided for federal depositories independent of private or state banks

(E) deposited federal revenues in "pet banks"

15. Who defended his business practices as a necessary survival of the fittest? "The American Beauty Rose can be produced in the splendor and fragrance which bring cheer to its beholder only by sacrificing the early buds which grow up around it. This is not an evil tendency in business. It is merely the working out of a law of nature and a law of God."

(A) Matthew Josephson

(B) J. Pierpont Morgan

(C) John D. Rockefeller

(D) William Jennings Bryan

(E) Andrew Carnegie

16. Which was NOT part of the politics of 1865 to 1900?

(A) "Waving the bloody shirt"

(B) The Grand Army of the Republic (GAR)

(C) Crédit Mobilier

(D) Mugwumps

(E) Loco-Focos

17. It is impossible for us to know how many colonists attended church services. We do know, however, how many church buildings existed in 1775. The largest single denomination had only 668 out of 3,142 buildings. Knowing what you do about religion in colonial America, which of the following would be arranged in order from highest number to lowest number of church buildings?

(A) Congregational, Anglican, Quaker, Catholic

(B) Anglican, Catholic, Mennonite, Quaker

(C) Catholic, Huguenot, Methodist, Congregational

(D) Quaker, Lutheran, Jewish synagogues, Dunker

(E) Catholic, Presbyterian, Anglican, Moravian

18. Franklin Roosevelt put together a coalition of different groups that became the backbone of the Democratic Party for the next thirty years. FDR's Democratic Party coalition included all of the following EXCEPT

(A) Southerners

(B) suburbanites

(C) blacks

(D) urban political machines

(E) labor

19. All of the following contributed to the causes of the Mexican War EXCEPT

(A) the election of 1844

(B) the spot resolutions

(C) Mexican anger over the Republic of Texas

(D) American designs on California

(E) private claims of U.S. citizens against Mexico

20. Of the following, which correctly lists rank order, from largest to smallest, of ethnic groups in the United States according to the census of 1790?

(A) English, African, Scots and Scotch-Irish, German

(B) English, German, Scots and Scotch-Irish, African

(C) English, Scots and Scotch-Irish, African, German

(D) Scots and Scotch-Irish, English, German, African

(E) German, English, Scots and Scotch-Irish, African

21. The 1850s were marked by an intense North-South debate over the issue of slavery in the territories, yet the census of 1860 listed only seven slaves in the Nebraska territory and two in the Kansas territory. What explains the contradiction between the actual number of slaves in the Kansas and Nebraska territories and the intensity of the dispute?

(A) Slaveholders expected to move into Kansas and Nebraska when opposition to slavery in that area decreased.

(B) The issue of slavery in the territories had become an important symbol to both sections and an indication of the future direction of the economy and the nation.

(C) The Lecompton Constitution safeguarding slaveholders had not yet been adopted.

(D) John Brown's raid on Harpers Ferry led to the Pottawatomie massacre, causing slaveholders to retreat to Missouri.

(E) Slavery was tied to cotton production, which was impractical in the Kansas and Nebraska territories.

22. Which famous American woman is NOT correctly matched to her accomplishment?

(A) Jane Addams founded Hull House, one of the first settlement houses in America.

(B) Mary Lyon, pioneering woman educator, founded Mount Holyoke.

(C) Susan B. Anthony advocated women's suffrage.

(D) Frances Willard advocated better treatment of the insane before the Civil War.

(E) Frances Perkins was the first woman cabinet member, Secretary of Labor under FDR.

23. Executive Office, State of _____ July 6, 18 ___

    Hon. XXXX, President of the United States,

    Sir: "Your answer to my protest involves some startling conclusions and ignores and evades the question at issue—that is, that the principle of local self-government is just as fundamental in our institutions as is that of Federal supremacy. . . .

    "You calmly assume that the executive has the legal right to order Federal troops into any community of the United States, in the first instance, whenever there is the slightest disturbance, and that he can do this without any regard to the question as to whether that community is able and ready to enforce the law itself. Inasmuch as the executive is the sole judge of the question as to whether any disturbance exists in any part of the country, this assumption means that the executive can send Federal troops into any community in the United States at his pleasure, and keep them there as long as he chooses....

    "You say that troops were ordered in . . . upon the demand of the post-office department, and upon representations of the judicial officers of the United States that process of the courts could not be served, and upon proof that conspiracies existed."

    This letter was written by a state governor to

    (A) Cleveland during the Pullman strike
    (B) Eisenhower during the Little Rock crisis
    (C) Washington during the Whiskey Rebellion
    (D) Jackson during the nullification crisis
    (E) Truman after he dismissed General MacArthur

24. Which of the following statements contradicts Jefferson's philosophy of government?

    (A) That government is best which governs the least.
    (B) The presidency should have little pomposity or ceremony.
    (C) A strong army is essential to defend liberty.
    (D) Freedom of speech is essential in a republic.
    (E) The will of the majority must by accepted.

25. In the 1912 presidential campaign, Woodrow Wilson urged his New Freedom, Theodore Roosevelt his New Nationalism. Which of the following statements about these two economic philosophies is correct?

    (A) Wilson won the election and put his philosophy into legislation and into practice.
    (B) Roosevelt won the election and put his philosophy into legislation and into practice.
    (C) In the next seventy years, the federal government's approach to big business and antitrust followed the New Nationalism philosophy.
    (D) New Deal economic policies were mainly a continuation of New Freedom policies.
    (E) They were both copied from Eugene V. Debs' program for the economy.

State Representation in 18th Century
Representative Bodies

(The number of representatives from the colonies/states who signed the following documents and who served in the First Congress.)

	Albany Plan of Union	Dec. of Indep.	Art. of Confed.	Const. of 1787	First Congress under the Const.
NH	2	3	2	2	3
Mass	7	5	6	2	8
Conn	5	4	5	2	5
RI	2	2	3	0	1
NY	4	4	4	1	6
NJ	3	5	2	4	4
PA	6	9	5	8	8
DE	0	3	3	5	1
MD	4	4	2	3	6
Vir	7	7	5	3	10
NC	4	3	3	3	5
SC	4	4	5	4	5
GA	0	3	3	2	3

full suffrage granted by 1914

no suffrage granted by 1918

26. What is the best conclusion to draw from these figures?

   (A) Colonists followed virtual representation in practice despite their protests to Great Britain.

   (B) Representation in political conventions was apportioned by population as much as possible.

   (C) Drawing a conclusion is difficult because some delegates did not sign the documents for personal and political reasons.

   (D) The majority of the delegates to the Constitutional Convention did not sign that document.

   (E) Most of the signers of one document signed the other documents.

27. The Camp David Accords, agreed to under the leadership of President Carter, led to peace in the Middle East between

   (A) Iran and Iraq

   (B) Afghanistan and the Soviet Union

   (C) Lebanon and Israel

   (D) Israel and Egypt

   (E) the Soviet Union and the United States

28. The proper title for this map is

   (A) "Women's Suffrage Movement"

   (B) "Manhood Suffrage in the Era of Jacksonian Democracy"

   (C) "Black Suffrage During Reconstruction"

   (D) "Jim Crow Laws and Black Suffrage"

   (E) "Suffrage Laws and the Populist Movement"

29. Which of the following statements concerning mercantilism is accurate?

   (A) Laissez-faire was a basic concept in mercantilism.

   (B) Mercantilism seriously retarded the development of a wide range of colonial industries.

   (C) Americans were economically hurt by the laws requiring all imperial trade to be carried in British ships manned by British sailors.

   (D) The British government controlled and directed economic activities to benefit the national state rather than the colonies or individual British citizens.

   (E) A nation increases its national wealth by importing more goods than it exports.

30. The following is the electoral college vote for president in the second race between John Adams and Thomas Jefferson: Jefferson, 73; Aaron Burr, 73; John Adams, 65; Charles Pinckney, 64; and John Jay, 1. Which of the following statements is true?

    (A) This election was held in 1796.

    (B) This election led to the adoption of the Twelfth Amendment.

    (C) Because of the tie the president was selected by the Senate, as specified by the Constitution.

    (D) This presidential campaign was Jefferson's reelection to the presidency.

    (E) The major issue of this election was the impressment of American sailors.

31. The first talking motion picture was

    (A) *The Jazz Singer*

    (B) *Rebel Without a Cause*

    (C) *Gone with the Wind*

    (D) *Birth of a Nation*

    (E) *Bridge over the River Kwai*

32. Which statement describes American social structure in the Age of Jackson, 1820–1850?

    (A) American society became more aristocratic.

    (B) Social mobility increased and economic equality increased.

    (C) Social mobility increased and economic inequality increased.

    (D) There was social rigidity and an increase in economic inequality.

    (E) There was social rigidity and an increase in economic equality.

33. The Dawes Act

    (A) made Native Americans (Indians) citizens

    (B) established the reservation system

    (C) pushed the Native Americans (Indians) further west

    (D) failed in its intended purpose

    (E) led to the publication of *A Century of Dishonor*

Percentage Margin of Victory by the Winning Presidential Candidate Over His Nearest Opponent, by States

	1828	1832	1836	1840	1844
Massachusetts	66	30	9	16	12
Connecticut	50	20	1	11	5
New York	2	4	9	4	1
Pennsylvania	33	16	4	1	2
Virginia	38	50	13	1	6
North Carolina	47	70	6	15	5
Kentucky	1	9	6	29	8
Tennessee	90	90	16	11	1
Mississippi	60	77	2	7	13
Indiana	13	34	12	12	2
Illinois	34	37	10	2	12
Missouri	41	32	21	14	17
Total Average	36%	36%	11%	11%	9%

Percentage of Adult White Males Voting in Presidential Elections

1824: 26.5%	1836: 55.2%
1828: 56.3%	1840: 78.0%
1832: 54.9%	1844: 74.9%

34. The figures from these two tables support the statement that

    (A) Andrew Jackson's campaigns in 1840 and 1844 stimulated high voter interest.

    (B) Voter participation increased as presidential elections within individual states became more hotly contested.

    (C) Jacksonian Democracy dramatically increased the number of voters.

    (D) Issue-oriented presidential campaigns such as the election of 1840 stimulated high voter turnout.

    (E) The antislavery movement changed voting patterns.

35. Which labor group pursued limited objectives, excluded intellectuals, avoided politics, and avoided broad social aims?

 (A) American Federation of Labor

 (B) Knights of Labor

 (C) American Railway Union

 (D) National Labor Union

 (E) Socialist Party

36. Four of the following contributed to the passage of the Immigration Acts of 1921 and 1924. Which did NOT?

 (A) Results of I.Q. tests given to American soldiers during the First World War

 (B) Resentment of workers against foreign immigrants' taking jobs away from Americans by their willingness to work for low wages

 (C) A belief, caused by two short postwar depressions, that the nation's pool of labor was already overcrowded

 (D) The belief that those immigrants already in the country were not adequately Americanized

 (E) A desire to resume the prewar policy of restrictive quotas after the First World War

37. Which is true of both the Korean War and the Vietnam War?

 (A) Both led to a change in the party occupying the White House.

 (B) It is possible to establish the day on which the first enemy military action took place in each war.

 (C) In both wars the United States took over after a long unsuccessful struggle by an ally.

 (D) The United Nations entered both wars and branded North Korea and North Vietnam as aggressors.

 (E) The United States had stated clearly that it would defend South Korea and South Vietnam if attacked.

38. Which New Deal agency no longer exists?

 (A) Agricultural Adjustment Administration (AAA)

 (B) Securities and Exchange Commission (SEC)

 (C) Federal Housing Administration (FHA)

 (D) Federal Deposit Insurance Corporation (FDIC)

 (E) Tennessee Valley Authority (TVA)

39. *The Star-Spangled Banner*

 (A) became the national anthem immediately after the War of 1812 ended when Congress officially adopted it

 (B) was written to celebrate the heroic defense of Washington, DC, during the War of 1812

 (C) celebrated the greatest American victory of the War of 1812, Jackson's victory over the British at New Orleans

 (D) was written to celebrate the defense of Baltimore during the War of 1812

 (E) was written to honor George Washington when he died in 1799

40. "The Dixiecrats deserted him over the issue of civil rights for blacks. Thousands of his potential supporters swung to Henry Wallace's Progressive Party. His major opponent came from New York and had been the presidential candidate four years before. And yet, somehow he won."

 Who is being referred to?

 (A) Jimmy Carter in 1976

 (B) Richard Nixon in 1968

 (C) Franklin D. Roosevelt in 1932

 (D) John F. Kennedy in 1960

 (E) Harry Truman in 1948

41. The Thirteenth, Fourteenth, and Fifteenth Amendments to the Constitution

 (A) were necessary to secure the civil rights of the freedmen

 (B) completed the political proposals of William Lloyd Garrison

 (C) were widely supported in the North

(D) were passed because of Andrew Johnson's strong support

(E) were passed and ratified as a group

42. Inside the United States, the Second World War was responsible for many social and economic changes. Which of the following did NOT occur during the Second World War?

(A) The number of women working increased

(B) Population patterns shifted as large numbers of people moved around within the United States

(C) Labor union membership declined in total numbers as restrictions on striking went into effect

(D) Big business became more concentrated as war contracts went to large corporations and many small businesses went out of business

(E) Colleges and universities became more closely linked to the federal government through dependence on defense research grants

43. The dotted lines on the map represent the

(A) canal routes used by entrepreneurs

(B) National Road linking the states together

(C) new territory in the Louisiana Purchase

(D) extent of the frontier line for 1800 and 1830

(E) lines for the Proclamation of 1763

44. "The sympathies of the Democratic Party, as shown by the platform, are on the side of the struggling masses who have ever been the foundation of the Democratic Party. There are two ideas of government. There are those who believe that, if you will only legislate to make the well-to-do prosperous, their prosperity will leak through on those below. The Democratic idea, however, has been that if you legislate to make the masses prosperous, their prosperity will find its way up through every class which rests upon them.

"You come to us and tell us that the great cities are in favor of the gold standard; we reply that the great cities rest upon our broad and fertile prairies. Burn down your cities and leave our farms, and your cities will spring up again as if by magic; but destroy our farms and the grass will grow in the streets of every city in the country."

This speech came from

(A) the campaign of William Jennings Bryan for the presidency in 1896

(B) the campaign of Franklin D. Roosevelt for the presidency in 1932

(C) the campaign of Theodore Roosevelt for the presidency in 1912

(D) the attempt by McNary and Haugen to secure price supports for farmers in the 1920s

(E) FDR in support of a second Agricultural Adjustment Act after the first was declared unconstitutional

45. A historian compared tax lists for the years 1687 and 1771. What changes do you think he found in the Boston of 1771 compared to the Boston of 1687?

(A) An increase in the number of indentured servants entering Boston from abroad

(B) A decline in the number of people considered poor and propertyless

(C) A more stratified social structure

(D) An economy controlled by large land-owners rather than by merchants

(E) A stable population with little geographical, occupational, economic, or generational mobility

46. The first social critic influenced the reforms of his era with two books, *How the Other Half Lives and The Battle With the Slum*. The second critic shaped reform in his era with *The Other America*. These two intellectual reformers and critics of American society were

(A) Jacob Riis and Michael Harrington

(B) Lincoln Steffens and John Kenneth Galbraith

(C) Edward Bellamy and Bruce Barton

(D) Alfred Thayer Mahan and Gunnar Myrdal

(E) Upton Sinclair and Ralph Nader

47. Four of the following were considered to be conservationists. Who was NOT considered a friend of conservation?

(A) John Muir

(B) Theodore Roosevelt

(C) Gifford Pinchot

(D) Franklin Roosevelt

(E) Richard Ballinger

48. What made it possible for the United Nations to defend South Korea when the latter was attacked in 1950?

(A) The Soviet Union was boycotting the United Nations in protest of its refusal to give a seat to Communist China.

(B) The Soviet Union did not use its veto power because it was concerned about the rise of Communist China as a rival.

(C) The Korean War was a local struggle, and neither the United States nor the Soviet Union considered it part of the Cold War.

(D) The Soviet Union was boycotting the United Nations in order to test the latter's response to a carefully orchestrated scheme—the preplanned invasion by a communist country of an ally of the West.

(E) South Korea was entitled to protection as a member of the United Nations.

49. Which of the following statements about the process of amending the Constitution is correct?

(A) The original Constitution did not provide for a means of amendment.

(B) The Constitution can be amended by a two-thirds vote of both the Senate and the House of Representatives and by the approval of two-thirds of the state legislatures.

(C) The states can bypass the federal government by forcing Congress to call a national convention to propose an amendment (if requested by the legislatures of two-thirds of the states) and by approving the proposed amendment with three-fourths of the state conventions.

(D) Proposed constitutional amendments need the approval of the House of Representatives and the Senate and the president's signature before amendments can be submitted to the states for ratification.

(E) Through the power of judicial review, the federal courts have the power to declare an amendment unconstitutional.

50. Which was true of free blacks living in the North during the thirty years prior to the Civil War?

(A) All Northern states granted free blacks the right to vote

(B) Public facilities were integrated

(C) Economic opportunities for employment matched those given to recent immigrants

(D) Free public education was open to blacks

(E) Racial tensions often exploded into riots

51. "All men are, by nature, equal and free: No one has a right to any authority over another without his consent: all lawful government is founded on the consent of those who are subject to it: Such consent was given with a view to ensure and to increase the happiness of the governed, above what they could enjoy in an independent and unconnected state of nature."

This quotation from James Wilson is an example of the

(A) doctrine of nullification

(B) philosophy of natural rights

(C) philosophy of rugged individualism

(D) Southern states' rights point of view

(E) rhetoric of Populism

52. "The existence of an area of free land, its continuous recession, and the advance of American settlement westward, explain American development."

Which of the following is NOT part of the theories of the author of this quotation?

(A) The westward movement influenced the development of American character.

(B) Our frontier was a steady movement away from the influence of Europe.

(C) Successive waves of frontiers—a trader's frontier, a rancher's frontier, a miner's frontier, and a farmer's frontier—swept over the unsettled lands during the westward movement.

(D) Part of our frontier heritage was the acquisition of habits of wastefulness in regard to national resources.

(E) The frontier introduced two economic classes, and therefore the underlying cause of all major events in American history was economic, class competition.

53. As defined by John C. Calhoun, the doctrine of nullification

(A) said that both the highest federal court and the highest state court had to agree on the constitutionality of a federal law

(B) gave a majority of states, by vote of their state legislatures, the power to declare an act of Congress null and void

(C) stated that any individual state could on its own authority declare a federal law unconstitutional and therefore unenforceable

(D) called for two presidents, one from the North and one from the South, either of whom could nullify a federal law

(E) applied only to tariff laws and revenue laws

54. When Europeans arrived, they found the continent of North America occupied. Which of the following were tribes of Native Americans (Indians) who lived in the future United States?

(A) Arawak, Creek, Osage, Miami

(B) Apache, Aztec, Hopi, Paiute

(C) Cheyenne, Crow, Inca, Sioux

(D) Lenape, Maya, Narraganset, Oneida

(E) Choctaw, Mohawk, Pueblo, Shawnee

55. U.S. foreign policy in the 1920s most resembled the decade from 1800 to 1810 in which of the following arenas?

(A) Territorial expansion

(B) Involvement in the armed conflicts of Europe

(C) Commitment to the pursuit of diplomacy by peaceful means

(D) Interest in events in the Pacific

(E) Disarmament

56. After the Second World War, older black organizations were challenged by the rise of new, more confrontational groups. Which of the following belong to postwar confrontational black organizations?

(A) National Association for the Advancement of Colored People (NAACP) and Student Nonviolent Coordinating Committee (SNCC)

(B) Southern Christian Leadership Conference (SCLC) and Student Nonviolent Coordinating Committee (SNCC)

(C) Urban League and Congress of Racial Equality (CORE)

(D) Southern Christian Leadership Conference (SCLC) and Urban League

(E) National Association for the Advancement of Colored People (NAACP), Southern Christian Leadership Conference (SCLC), and Congress of Racial Equality (CORE)

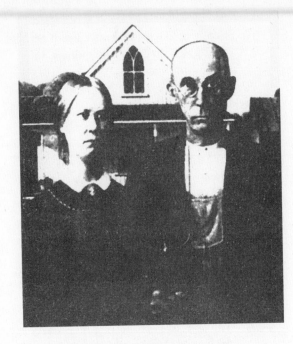

57. Who painted this Midwestern couple?

(A) John James Audubon

(B) Ben Shahn

(C) Andrew Wyeth

(D) Grant Wood

(E) Thomas Eakins

58. The Intolerable Acts, also called the Repressive Acts,

(A) closed all American ports until the tea from the Boston Tea Party was paid for

(B) punished the colonists for the Stamp Act Congress

(C) extended the Canadian border down to the Ohio River

(D) led to the First Continental Congress

(E) were in retaliation for the Boston Massacre

59. During the years of the Great Depression and the New Deal, blacks

(A) benefited equally with whites in the programs of the New Deal because Franklin Roosevelt refused to sanction discrimination

(B) did not continue to migrate to northern cities because there were no jobs

(C) benefited from the civil rights bills passed by Congress with Franklin Roosevelt's urging

(D) tended to vote for the Republican Party because the Democratic Party did not support policies beneficial to blacks

(E) benefited from having a friend in the White House, Eleanor Roosevelt, who could speak and act independently in support of black goals

60. The Supreme Court case of *Myers* v. *U.S.* in 1925 said that the president had the power to fire anyone appointed to a position in the executive branch, even a position that required Senate approval for appointment. This decision vindicated the position taken by

(A) Andrew Jackson in regard to the spoils system

(B) Thomas Jefferson in regard to impeaching Federalist judges

(C) Woodrow Wilson in regard to the Versailles Treaty

(D) Andrew Johnson in opposition to Radical Republicans

(E) the Hartford Convention during the War of 1812

61. "Neither of the two parties shall conclude either truce or peace with Great Britain without the formal consent of the other first obtained; and they mutually engage not to lay down their arms until the independence of the United States shall have been formally or tacitly assured by the treaty or treaties that shall terminate the war."

This passage is Article VIII of the Treaty of Alliance of 1778 between France and the United States. The United States did not keep its pledge to France as stipulated in Article VIII. It instead signed a peace treaty without conferring with France. Why?

(A) The United States did not want to get involved with the French Revolution.

(B) The United States discovered that France and her ally Spain were eager to prevent the United States from gaining control of the territory extending from the Appalachian Mountains to the Mississippi River.

(C) Since French military and naval aid did not amount to much help, the United States did not feel obligated to follow the treaty.

(D) No British troops were left in the United States after the capture of Cornwallis's army, and the British quickly gave in before we had an opportunity to consult with our ally, France.

(E) Washington's Neutrality Proclamation, April 22, 1793, abrogated the Treaty of 1778.

62. The conservative branch of the Republican Party recaptured the White House in the 1920s. How did the Republicans deal with the Progressive legacy of federal regulatory legislation?

(A) They quietly permitted the legislation that created the regulatory agencies to expire.

(B) They supported new legislation to weaken the powers of the regulatory agencies.

(C) They captured control of the regulatory agencies by appointing conservatives as administrators or commission members.

(D) They joined forces with New Dealers to improve and to update the old regulatory legislation.

(E) They abolished the federal regulatory agencies.

63. The center of the manufacturing of cotton textiles switched from New England to the South between the 1880s and the 1950s because

(A) New England Irish and Italian immigrants refused to work in the textile mills

(B) New England changed its textile emphasis to wool production

(C) cheap Southern labor and lower taxes enticed the textile industry to move to the South

(D) the Arab oil embargo drove up New England industrial costs

(E) Southern blacks were once again permitted to work in the textile mills, as they had during slavery

64. Why did Lyndon Johnson make a decision not to run for reelection in 1968?

(A) He narrowly won (which many considered a virtual defeat) in the early New Hampshire Democratic primary against Senator Eugene McCarthy.

(B) His deescalation of American involvement in Vietnam angered too many people and jeopardized his reelection.

(C) His previous presidential election had been very close, giving him grounds to expect defeat if this election was going to be close.

(D) The objectives of the War on Poverty and the war in Vietnam had been achieved.

(E) His potential Republican opponent, Richard Nixon, looked unbeatable.

65. She revolutionized the role of First Lady. While her husband was president, she wrote a column for a newspaper, "My Day"; promoted the careers of talented women; and worked openly for civil rights for blacks, something her husband could not do. Later she represented the United States in the United Nations and chaired the President's Commission on the Status of Women, which led to the Equal Pay Act. Who was this pioneering First Lady?

(A) Lady Bird Johnson

(B) Jackie Kennedy

(C) Rosalynn Carter

(D) Eleanor Roosevelt

(E) Hillary Clinton

66. Which two presidential candidates were bitterly attacked because they were Catholics?

(A) Thomas Dewey and Adlai Stevenson

(B) Walter Mondale and Lyndon Johnson

(C) Al Smith and John F. Kennedy

(D) Herbert Hoover and Dwight David Eisenhower

(E) Jimmy Carter and John F. Kennedy

67. "Once lead this people into war and they'll forget there ever was such a thing as tolerance. To fight you must be brutal and ruthless, and the spirit of ruthless brutality will enter into every fiber of our national life, infecting Congress, the courts, the policeman on the beat, the man in the street."

Wilson's prophecy at the outbreak of the First World War in Europe came true in regard to all of the following EXCEPT

(A) the Chicago race riot, 1919

(B) the Palmer raids

(C) the Espionage Act of 1917 and the Sedition Act of 1918

(D) the reaction to the steel strike of 1919

(E) the Volstead Act

68. Four of the following correctly match a reformer to the area of reform. Which does NOT?

(A) Dorothea Dix—treatment of the mentally ill

(B) Lucretia Mott—women's rights

(C) Horace Mann—education

(D) Neal Dow—temperance

(E) Roger B. Taney—labor unions

69. Why was there so much colonial opposition to the Tea Act of 1773?

(A) The East India Company was granted a monopoly control over the sale of tea in the colonies.

(B) The act raised taxes on tea.

(C) British troops accompanied the British merchants who came to sell the tea.

(D) The tea tax was passed in retaliation for the Boston Tea Party.

(E) The act raised the price of tea.

70. Which of the following is NOT correctly linked to an event that occurred during his presidential administration?

(A) Peace Corps started—Kennedy

(B) Marshall Plan—Franklin Roosevelt

(C) U-2 incident—Eisenhower

(D) Iranian hostage crisis—Carter

(E) SALT I Agreement—Nixon

71. "Three distinct motives are apparent in the groupings of the buildings. Those about the Grand Basin—the Administration, Manufactures, Agriculture, Machinery, Electricity, Mines, and also the Art Building—are essentially dignified in style; those lying farther to the north—the Horticultural, Transportation [designed by Louis Sullivan], and Fisheries—being less formal, blend readily with the more or less homelike headquarters buildings of the States and foreign governments, which are grouped among the trees of the extreme northern portion of the grounds. Upon the Midway... no distinct order is followed, it being instead a most unusual collection of almost every type of architecture known to man—oriental villages, Chinese bazaars, tropical settlements, ice railways, the ponderous Ferris wheel, and reproductions of ancient cities. All these are combined to form the lighter and more fantastic side of the. . . ."

What is David Burnham describing in this *Handbook*?

(A) The original plans for the layout of Washington, D.C.

(B) The New York City World's Fair in 1939

(C) The 1893 Chicago World's Fair

(D) The 1876 Centennial in Philadelphia

(E) The first amusement park at Coney Island, New York

72. "*Pervasive discrimination and segregation* in employment, education and housing, which have resulted in the continuing exclusion of great numbers of Negroes from the benefits of economic progress.

"*Black in-migration and white exodus*, which have produced the massive and growing concentrations of impoverished Negroes in our major cities, creating a growing crisis of deteriorating facilities and services and unmet human needs.

"*The black ghettos*, where segregation and poverty converge on the young to destroy opportunity and enforce failure. Crime, drug addiction, dependency on welfare, and bitterness and resentment against society in general and white society in particular are the result."

This quotation from the *Report on Civil Disorders* identified the reasons behind the race riots in the 1960s. The report was the work of the

(A)   Urban League

(B)   Kerner Commission

(C)   NAACP

(D)   Warren Commission

(E)   Niagara Movement

73. "In the future days, which we seek to make secure, we look forward to a world founded upon four essential human freedoms.

"The first is freedom of speech and expression, everywhere in the world.

"The second is freedom of every person to worship God in his own way, everywhere in the world.

"The third is freedom from want, which, translated into world terms, means economic understanding which will secure to every nation a healthy peace-time life for its inhabitants, everywhere in the world.

"The fourth is freedom from fear, which, translated into world terms, means a worldwide reduction of armaments to such a point and in such a thorough fashion that no nation will be in a position to commit an act of physical aggression against any neighbor, anywhere in the world."

Who gave this "Four Freedoms" speech?

(A)   Wendell Wilkie

(B)   Woodrow Wilson

(C)   Franklin Roosevelt

(D)   Winston Churchill

(E)   Herbert Hoover

74. Both France and Great Britain violated American neutral rights in the years preceding the War of 1812. What consideration influenced the United States to go to war against Great Britain rather than France?

(A)   British violations caused the loss of American lives; the French violations only cost property losses.

(B)   The Federalist Party, which controlled Congress, tended to be anti-British.

(C)   It was easier for the United States to attack British territory than to attack French territory.

(D)   The French respected our embargo; the British did not.

(E)   President Adams had already chastised France in the undeclared naval war of the late 1790s; this time he decided to attack Great Britain.

75. Which of the following was NOT used by Southerners in defense of the institution of slavery?

(A)   Northern wage workers toiling in the factories were treated more inhumanely.

(B)   The curse on Cain for killing his brother Abel began the degradation of blacks.

(C)   Slavery was essential to the agricultural system of the South, which produced crops requiring extensive hand labor.

(D)   Slavery existed in the Bible and was never criticized by Christ, the Disciples, or the Old Testament prophets.

(E)   The Constitution protected slavery in the South, and abolished it only north of the Ohio River and the Mason-Dixon line.

76. In just one year, 1807–1808, American imports dropped from $138 million to $57 million. American exports dropped from $108 million to $22 million. Why?

(A)   Britain tightened its impressment of American sailors, driving American shipping from the seas.

(B)   Macon's Bill No. 2 restricted American trade to every nation except Great Britain and France.

(C)   Jefferson's embargo curtailed American shipping.

(D)   Napoleon's Berlin and Milan decrees cut off continental Europe from American shipping.

(E)   The undeclared naval war with France made shipping too dangerous.

77. Who drew this nineteenth-century political cartoon attacking boss rule in New York City?

    (A) William Seward

    (B) Thomas Nast

    (C) William Marcy Tweed

    (D) Fiorello La Guardia

    (E) Seth Low

78. Which colony was established as a buffer against the Spanish colonies and to give the poor and unfortunate a chance for a new start in life?

    (A) Maryland

    (B) Georgia

    (C) Nova Scotia

    (D) Pennsylvania

    (E) Plymouth

79. In his sociological study, *The Levittowners*, about a planned suburb in New Jersey, Herbert Gans found a local society characterized by "the equality of men and women, the power of the child over his parents, the importance of voluntary association, the social functions of the church, and the rejection of high culture" and "the adherence to the traditional virtues: individual honesty, thrift, religiously inspired morality, Franklinesque individualism, and Victorian prudery." His description of suburban society is most reminiscent of

    (A) Sloan Wilson's *The Man in the Gray Flannel Suit*

    (B) Alexis de Tocqueville's *Democracy in America*

    (C) Theodore Dreiser's *Sister Carrie*

    (D) William H. Whyte's *The Organization Man*

    (E) Willa Cather's *My Antonia*

80. "Brother, Can You Spare a Dime?" and "Can I Sleep in Your Barn Tonight, Mister?" were popular hit songs during

    (A) 1917

    (B) the Civil War

    (C) the Second World War

    (D) 1932

    (E) the 1960s

Answer Key

1. C	17. A	33. D	49. C	65. D
2. A	18. B	34. B	50. E	66. C
3. A	19. B	35. A	51. B	67. E
4. E	20. A	36. E	52. E	68. E
5. A	21. B	37. A	53. C	69. A
6. B	22. D	38. A	54. E	70. B
7. E	23. A	39. D	55. C	71. C
8. C	24. C	40. E	56. B	72. B
9. D	25. C	41. A	57. D	73. C
10. E	26. C	42. C	58. D	74. C
11. E	27. D	43. D	59. E	75. E
12. D	28. A	44. A	60. D	76. C
13. C	29. D	45. C	61. B	77. B
14. D	30. B	46. A	62. C	78. B
15. C	31. A	47. E	63. C	79. B
16. E	32. D	48. A	64. A	80. D

Explanatory Answers

1. **The correct answer is (C).** William Penn founded his "Holy Experiment" in Pennsylvania. The American environment usually forced drastic alterations in the original plans of the founders. Pennsylvania was an exception.

2. **The correct answer is (A).** American policy in the Far East was based upon the philosophy of the Open Door Notes: maintain an autonomous China with all nations having equal trade access. Japan offered the greatest threat to China and to U.S. possessions in the Far East, and for this reason the treaties tried to curtail Japanese power.

3. **The correct answer is (A).** Before the cotton gin many Southerners speculated how the South could get rid of its useless slave system. Eli Whitney's invention made the question moot for the foreseeable future. The cotton gin cemented both cotton and slavery in the South.

4. **The correct answer is (E).** The Dartmouth College case, *Dartmouth College* v. *Woodward* (1819), concerned an attempt by the New Hampshire legislature to replace the board of trustees of Dartmouth College and, in effect, to take control of the institution. The Supreme Court invalidated the seizure, finding the original charter to be a contract beyond the power of the legislature to alter unilaterally. In his argument before the Supreme Court, Daniel Webster made his famous remark "It is, sir, as I have said, a small college, and yet there are those that love it."

5. **The correct answer is (A).** "The Cult of True Womanhood" emphasized domesticity, piety, purity, and submissiveness as the attributes of a true woman. The modern antifeminist, Phyllis Schlafly, would approve of these virtues. Betty Friedan, author of *The Feminine Mystique* (1963), was the first president of NOW, the National Organization for Women. Gloria Steinem has also been a feminist leader. Carrie Nation was a militant prohibitionist who went from town to town with her trusty axe, busting up one bar after another. Shirley Chisholm, the first black woman elected to the House of Representatives in 1968, once said that being a woman presented more obstacles to her career than being black.

6. **The correct answer is (B).** Polygamy separates Mormons from the others. Shakers separated the sexes, even married couples. Christian Scientists eschewed modern medicine for God's healing power

through prayer. The Mormons left for Utah, then a territory of Mexico, to find a home where no one would ever bother them. In quick succession came the Mexican War, the Mexican Cession, and the California gold rush, and their isolation evaporated.

7. **The correct answer is (E).** Theodore Roosevelt's Corollary to the Monroe Doctrine (1904) asserted that the United States had the right to intervene to punish "chronic wrongdoing," meaning fiscal mismanagement of international borrowing. The Monroe Doctrine had said European powers could not intervene; the Roosevelt Corollary said the United States could.

8. **The correct answer is (C).** The Great Compromise, or Connecticut Compromise, established a two-house federal legislature with the numbers in the Senate based on equal representation for each state and those in the House of Representatives based on population. It reconciled the conflict between the Virginia Plan and New Jersey Plan. The other choices involve other compromises made during the writing of the Constitution.

9. **The correct answer is (D).** Two marches dealt with racial injustice. A. Philip Randolph's threatened march led to FDR's Executive Order 8802, which stated that "there shall be no discrimination in the employment of workers in defense industries or Government. . . . " The 1963 march helped push two civil rights bills through Congress, the Civil Rights Act of 1964 and the Voting Rights Act of 1965. The march on the Pentagon in 1967 was one of the highlights of the antiwar peace movement. Coxey's army in 1894 was one of the first pushes for federal public works projects to provide employment during downturns in the economy. Coxey lived to see his idea triumph in the New Deal and was occasionally a guest of honor at White House dinners. The veterans of the First World War were promised pensions to begin in 1945. Out of work in 1932 because of the Great Depression, these veterans, the Bonus Army, reasoned that Congress should move the date up. Congress balked, and president Hoover tried to wait them out. Hoover ran out of patience, and fears of revolution mounted. U.S. Army soldiers, led by General Douglas MacArthur, routed the veterans.

10. **The correct answer is (E).** This New Deal law was the Wagner Act, also known as the National Labor Relations Act, which passed Congress in 1935. The Supreme Court found the act constitutional in the case of *NLRB* v. *Jones and Laughlin Steel Corp*. The Clayton Act (1914), nicknamed labor's Magna Carta, exempted labor organizations from antitrust laws, although subsequent court decisions weakened that protection. The Norris-LaGuardia Act (1932) prohibited yellow dog contracts and restricted injunctions in regard to boycotts, picketing, and strikes. The Taft-Hartley Act (1947) outlawed closed shops, permitted right-to-work laws (which could locally get rid of the union shop), and established a cooling-off period for strikes involving the nation's security (deemed so by a federal judge). The Landrum-Griffin Act (1959) attempted to control labor union corruption and to ensure internal democratic procedures within unions.

11. **The correct answer is (E).** Political Reconstruction ended when the Bourbons, or Redeemers, took control of state governments. For almost one hundred years afterward, the South voted Democratic, hence the term Solid South. Impoverished land-rich planters and the abundance of poor whites and ex-slaves combined to create sharecrop farming in the South. The planters, who had controlled prewar state legislatures, had spent very little in order to keep their own taxes down. This attitude had helped make the prewar South backward, and in many respects the South had been an underdeveloped country preoccupied with race. Much good came out of Reconstruction. Many schools and roads were built. Another legacy was the constitutional promise to grant civil rights to blacks. It may not sound like much of an achievement, but thereafter blacks had only to get whites to obey existing laws, not to rewrite the laws. That is why the American experience cannot be compared with recent events in South Africa.

12. **The correct answer is (D).** In the late nineteenth century Northern liberals began to acquiesce to Southern racism. Many were exhausted by their unsuccessful effort to secure civil rights; others were seduced by the racist implications of imperialism and Darwinism. The Redeemer governments proved to be even more corrupt than the Reconstruction governments from which they rescued the South.

Challenged by the rising Populist movement, the Redeemers increasingly raised the specter of race to maintain their power. Poor whites abandoned their black allies and proved even more effective racists. Meanwhile, successive Supreme Court decisions weakened the commitment to civil rights. The Slaughterhouse Cases (1873) and the Civil Rights Cases (1883) helped create the atmosphere that led to the Plessy decision. Civil rights marches were a much later development.

13. **The correct answer is (C).** Pinckney's Treaty granted the United States the right of deposit at New Orleans in the 1790s. In the 1850 Clayton-Bulwer Treaty, the United States and Great Britain promised one another not to build an isthmian canal without the other's permission. In the proposed Jay-Gardoqui Treaty under the Articles of Confederation in the 1780s, the United States surrendered the right of navigation on the lower Mississippi River in exchange for increased commerce with Spain. The treaty never materialized due to Southern opposition.

14. **The correct answer is (D).** After the destruction of the Second Bank of the United States, provision had to be made for federal monies. Jackson's policy of depositing federal funds in pet banks was too politically oriented. Van Buren's Independent Treasury Act (1840) created subtreasuries controlled by the federal government. Each subtreasury served as a depository for federal funds; none operated as a bank nor performed any banking functions. One year later the Whigs repealed the Independent Treasury Act, but Polk revived it in 1846. With minor changes it lasted until the Federal Reserve Act in 1913.

15. **The correct answer is (C).** John D. Rockefeller defended his business practices with this famous quote. A cartoonist pictured Rockefeller pulling all the buds off a rose bush except for one, his Standard Oil Company.

16. **The correct answer is (E).** "Waving the bloody shirt" was a favorite tactic of Republican candidates in the post-Civil War era. "Vote as you shot." As one wag explained it, not every Democrat was a traitor, but every traitor (Southerner) was a Democrat. Therefore, as a voter you should vote Republican and only Republican. The GAR, or Grand Army of the Republic, was an organization of Union veterans. Their pension demands solved the vexing problem of how to spend the huge treasury surplus built up by high tariff rates. The Crédit Mobilier scandal accompanied the building of the first transcontinental railroad. Mugwumps were high-principled Republicans who could not bring themselves to support the unscrupulous Blaine in 1884. Instead they threw their support to the Democrat Cleveland. The Loco-Foco faction of the Democratic Party in the Jackson period supported economic reforms against banks, monopolies, and tariffs. Loco-Focos were mostly New York radicals.

17. **The correct answer is (A).** In 1775 one-half of the colonists lived in New England, the home of the Puritan, or Congregational, Church. The Anglican Church, or Church of England (Episcopal Church), was the official church in six colonies. Most Quakers lived in heavily populated Pennsylvania and New Jersey. Catholic historians refer to the colonial era as the penal period, for at one time or the other every colony had some form of anti-Catholic legislation. Very few Catholics lived in colonial America. The ranking for the churches named in the question is as follows:

Congregational:	668	Catholic:	56
Presbyterian:	588	Moravian:	31
Anglican:	495	Dunker:	24
Quaker:	310	Mennonite:	16
Lutheran:	150	Huguenot:	7
Methodist	65	Jewish synagogues:	5

The complete list is in Clinton Rossiter's *The First American Revolution*, a paperback edition of part of a larger work, *Seedtime of the Republic*.

18. **The correct answer is (B).** Suburbia was always the citadel of Republicans. As suburban areas grew in the 1950s–1970s, the Republican Party's strength increased. If intellectuals and academics were added to the remaining four groups, you would have the nucleus of FDR's coalition.

19. **The correct answer is (B).** The spot resolutions were attempts by Whigs in Congress to embarrass President Polk after he had asked for a declaration of war based upon the claim that Mexico had "shed American blood upon American soil." Whig Congressman Abraham Lincoln and others introduced resolutions asking the president to point out the "spot" on the map where American blood had been shed. The "spot" of the incident, of course, lay entirely within disputed territory, not on American soil.

20. **The correct answer is (A).** The largest ethnic group is the English. Blacks were second. Historians estimate that in colonial America blacks made up as much as 25 percent of the total population. Nineteenth-century European white immigration reduced the percentage of blacks in American society. The natives of Scotland are Scots, not Scotch. The Scots who left Scotland for Northern Ireland and then later migrated to America are called Scotch-Irish.

21. **The correct answer is (B).** Choice (E) is tricky. It explains why some historians consider the issue of slavery in Kansas and Nebraska to have been foolish, but it doesn't explain why Northerners and Southerners became so upset over a "foolish" issue. The future direction and tone of the nation was being decided. Slavery became a powerful symbol meaning different things to people in each section. Don't assume that slavery could never have been adapted to a use other than agriculture. The Lecompton Constitution, which proposed that Kansas enter the Union as a slave state, was ultimately rejected by the voters of Kansas. John Brown's raid on Pottawatomie Creek took place in 1856, prior to his 1859 raid on Harpers Ferry.

22. **The correct answer is (D).** Frances Willard was for years the driving force behind the WCTU, the Women's Christian Temperance Union. She also worked to obtain women's suffrage.

23. **The correct answer is (A).** This letter was written by Governor John Peter Altgeld to President Cleveland. The best clue is the reference to the federal mail, the pretext for Cleveland's ordering of federal troops to put down the Pullman strike. The issue of constitutionality in federal-state confrontations is invariably raised by the losing state.

24. **The correct answer is (C).** Jefferson disapproved of a large federal army, believing that the state militias could effectively defend the United States from invasion. The defense of Washington, D.C., in the War of 1812 proved otherwise. Jefferson believed a strong army was a threat to liberty because of the threat of a possible coup led by generals and because a standing army could so easily enforce the arbitrary whims of the executive.

25. **The correct answer is (C).** New Nationalism emphasized regulating big business; New Freedom wanted to break up monopolies. Wilson won the election and pushed the Clayton Antitrust Act and the Federal Trade Commission through Congress. He slowly shifted his approach in practice, however, to regulation rather than antimonopoly. For the next seventy years, the policy of the federal government was one of regulation of big business. Despite some spectacular isolated antitrust suits, the federal government's approach toward business has been regulation rather than antitrust. One historian wrote an article in the 1950s entitled, "Whatever Happened to the Antitrust Movement?" Debs was the candidate of the Socialist Party. His prescription for American business differed radically.

26. **The correct answer is (C).** The British political system espoused virtual representation, every member of Parliament represented every British citizen everywhere. The Americans practiced actual representation, each member of a legislative body represented the people who put him there. Now you see why the British couldn't make any sense of the American argument of "No taxation without representation." Each colony or state is generally represented at the meetings. The colonists followed actual representation, in theory and in practice. The First Congress under the Constitution is the only body apportioned by population. A comparison with the other numbers indicates that the colonists and states did not

apportion their representative bodies strictly. Thirty-nine of the fifty-five delegates to the Constitutional Convention signed the Constitution, a majority. Most of the signers of the Declaration did not sign the Constitution. Only six—Benjamin Franklin, George Read, James Wilson, George Clymer, Robert Morris, and Roger Sherman—signed both. Some historians have suggested that the Declaration was the work of radicals and the Constitution of conservatives. Too much can be made of this; the correct answer is probably the years between the two signings. The documents have almost a separate and individual existence. It is too artificial to try to uncover threads linking them together.

27. **The correct answer is (D).** President Carter personally mediated a peace agreement between two suspicious enemies, Egypt and Israel. The Camp David Accords in 1978 set the stage for a 1979 peace treaty. Egypt became the first Middle East Arab nation to accept the existence of Israel.

28. **The correct answer is (A).** The map shows "The Women's Suffrage Movement." Note that women's suffrage was a western movement beginning in Wyoming. The conservative Southern states held out the longest.

29. **The correct answer is (D).** Laissez-faire, first articulated by Adam Smith in his 1776 book *The Wealth of Nations*, advocated a philosophy of freeing individuals from government restrictions so that each person could pursue his self-interest. Mercantilism, an earlier philosophy, advocated governmental control of economic activities to increase the national wealth. A few colonial industries were hampered by British restrictions, but the number of restrictions was small and enforcement was lax. Examples are the restrictions in the Woolens Act (1699), the Hat Act (1732), and the Iron Act (1750). Before 1776 the colonists were British citizens. They benefited from the Navigation Acts' restricting trade to British ships and British crews. Seventy-five percent of colonial trade was carried in colonial ships. A nation gains wealth by exporting more than it imports, thereby maintaining a favorable balance of trade and piling up money in the treasury.

30. **The correct answer is (B).** This is the election of 1800, the second race between John Adams and Thomas Jefferson. Adams had won in 1796. The Constitution originally stipulated that each presidential elector was to vote for two individuals. The person who received the most votes, provided that he received more than half, was the president. The recipient of the second highest number of votes was the vice-president, provided that he also received more than half the votes. Everyone in America knew Jefferson was the presidential candidate and Burr the vice-presidential candidate. But, technically, they tied for the presidency. The tie between Jefferson and Burr forced the election into the House of Representatives, which was controlled by the Federalists. After a long rancorous debate, Jefferson won. The Twelfth Amendment, which changed the method of selecting the president, was adopted in recognition of the need for changing the election machinery. Now the electors specified a vote for president and for vice-president, and no repetition of the election of 1800 was possible. The Twelfth Amendment also ended the possibility of a president and vice-president from different political factions, as had happened in 1796.

31. **The correct answer is (A).** An early full-length motion picture, *Birth of a Nation,* in 1915 portrayed the Ku Klux Klan as a benevolent organization that saved the South during Reconstruction. The first talking motion picture, however, was *The Jazz Singer* in 1927, with Al Jolson. The other films are classics from later decades.

32. **The correct answer is (D).** The myth of the Jacksonian Era is that economic equality increased. It did not. Recent research indicates a rigidity in social mobility and an increase in economic inequality. The post-Civil War era was characterized more by social mobility.

33. **The correct answer is (D).** The Dawes Severalty Act (1887) tried to dissolve the Native American (or Indian) tribes by dividing tribal lands among individual Indians, 160 acres per family, 80 acres to single adults. The word "severalty" means owning something free of joint interest; in other words, free from tribal limitations or restrictions. To prevent fraud, the land could not be sold for twenty-five years. The

act failed in its intended purpose of breaking up the tribes and turning Indians into individual farmers because the Indians didn't want to be individuals. Helen Hunt Jackson's eloquent book *A Century of Dishonor* (1881) marked the beginning of the agitation that culminated with the Dawes Act. Whites made the cultural mistake of assuming that Indians really wanted to be like them. Indians were finally made full citizens in 1924.

34. **The correct answer is (B).** To say that one of the characteristics of Jacksonian Democracy was high voter turnout is too simplistic. Voter participation increased during the Jacksonian period only as presidential elections within each state became more hotly contested. Interest and excitement within each state increased as that particular state became part of the national political campaign. When each candidate seemed to have a fighting chance within a particular state, interest shot up. Not until the Whig Party generated a real threat to the Democrats did voter interest peak. High voter interest was not a cause of Jacksonian Democracy, it was a characteristic of Jacksonian Democracy.

35. **The correct answer is (A).** Samuel Gompers, the founder of the AFL, once summarized the AFL philosophy succinctly as "more" for its members. The AFL, fearing that the solidarity of the labor movement would be dissipated by ideological concerns, spurned involvement in larger issues.

36. **The correct answer is (E).** There had never been a policy of restriction of immigrants prior to the First World War. The other factors all added fuel to the discussion of "raising a fence" around the Statue of Liberty. The fence went up in the 1921 act and was perfected in 1924 and 1927.

37. **The correct answer is (A).** The wars played a major role in the outcome of the elections of 1952 and 1968, both of which replaced the party in the White House. In 1952 the Democrats lost to Eisenhower; in 1968 to Nixon. In both elections the incumbent Democratic president did not run for reelection. The Korean War began on a specific day; the Vietnamese did not. The United States took over after the French left Vietnam. The United Nations branded North Korea as the aggressor; no such action ever accompanied the Vietnam War. We had treaty obligations to defend South Vietnam but not South Korea. On the eve of North Korea's invasion, the secretary of state curiously excluded South Korea from the United States defense perimeter in the Far East. Truman reacted because he saw a repetition of the same events that had sparked the Second World War.

38. **The correct answer is (A).** The Supreme Court declared the AAA unconstitutional in the case of *U.S. v. Butler*.

39. **The correct answer is (D).** The defense of our nation's capital during the War of 1812 was a disaster and a disgrace. Over 70,000 militiamen were called to defend the city; only 6,000 showed up. They fled with the first shots. *The Star-Spangled Banner* was written by Francis Scott Key while he was temporarily detained during a prisoner exchange during the bombardment of Fort McHenry, which guarded the entrance to Baltimore's harbor. The words were later set to a popular English drinking song; that is why it is so difficult for a single person to hit all the notes. George Washington was widely eulogized when he died. The most memorable accolade came from Robert E. Lee's father, Henry Lee, "first in war, first in peace, and first in the hearts of his countrymen."

40. **The correct answer is (E).** Harry Truman defied all odds by winning reelection in 1948. The Republican candidate, Thomas Dewey, was considered such a shoo-in that he had already begun to select his cabinet. The Democratic Party was split three ways, but somehow Truman triumphed in one of the greatest upsets ever.

41. **The correct answer is (A).** William Lloyd Garrison was satisfied with the Emancipation Proclamation and the Thirteenth Amendment because all he sought was the immediate end of slavery. By the end of the Civil War the Thirteenth Amendment was widely supported in the North, but not the Fourteenth and Fifteenth. Slavery was a sin, but political or social equality was unacceptable to many in the North. Popular acceptance of the doctrine of the equality of the races is a mid-twentieth-century concept. President Andrew Johnson disapproved of the Fourteenth and Fifteenth amendments, but the president plays no role whatsoever in the

amending process. The later two amendments were passed because the actual implementation or operation of the previous one revealed specific defects that had to be corrected. The amendments went into effect as follows: Thirteenth, December 18, 1865; Fourteenth, July 28, 1868; and Fifteenth, March 30, 1870.

42. **The correct answer is (C).** Labor union membership increased during the war. Strikes were illegal, but recruiting labor union members was not, and union membership doubled.

43. **The correct answer is (D).** The lines are the frontier line for 1800 and 1830. One hint is that Kentucky and Tennessee were two of the first three states added to the union.

44. **The correct answer is (A).** The quotation is from the famous "Cross of Gold" speech by William Jennings Bryan in the presidential campaign of 1896.

45. **The correct answer is (C).** The colonial period lasted from 1607 to 1776. Many broad generalizations about colonial society need qualification. By the 1770s, the number of indentured servants among immigrants was much lower. In many respects the colonists were beginning to think of themselves as a Europeanized, crowded society. As cities grew the ranks of urban poor more than doubled in size, creating a shifting, propertyless mass of workers. Most broad generalizations concerning colonial society do not apply to the cities. Only five percent of the population lived in cities. From the beginning, the sea trade dominated the Boston economy. By the 1770s the Boston social structure was more stratified, but one's position in that structure was not guaranteed. Geographic, occupational, and generational mobility opened theoretical opportunities for all.

46. **The correct answer is (A).** Jacob Riis's two books, published in 1890 and 1902, stirred up Progressive urban reformers. Michael Harrington's book in 1962 focused attention on the hidden poor, those who had fallen through the cracks in the expanding American good life. *The Other America* was one impetus for LBJ's War on Poverty.

47. **The correct answer is (E).** Naturalist John Muir was instrumental in the establishment of Yosemite National Park and the National Forest system. Both Roosevelts were well-known conservationists in and out of the White House. Gifford Pinchot served as Chief Forester in Theodore Roosevelt's administration. He continued in his post in the Taft administration, but his good friend and boss, James Garfield, was replaced as secretary of the interior by Richard Ballinger. The impetuous Pinchot clashed with Ballinger over his plans to sell federal land set aside for conservation. Ballinger was legally correct in his actions, but he seemed to be selling out the nation's conservation effort to corporation interests.

48. **The correct answer is (A).** The Soviet Union was boycotting the United Nations Security Council as a protest against the refusal of the United Nations to shift Nationalist China's (Taiwan) seat to Communist China. The invasion apparently took the Soviet Union by surprise. (One historian has suggested that it was all planned, but the evidence is still missing.) Unable to veto due to its absence, the Soviet Union watched helplessly as the machinery of the United Nations quickly operated in the manner envisioned by its founders. Dozens of U.N. members sent troops or supplies. None of the nations left "temporarily" divided by the Second World War received seats in the United Nations. East and West Germany finally acquired seats in 1973. After conquering South Vietnam, Vietnam joined the United Nations in 1977. North and South Korea still don't belong.

49. **The correct answer is (C).** There are two methods of proposing an amendment to the Constitution and two methods of ratifying an amendment. An amendment is proposed by a two-thirds vote of each house of Congress, or by a national convention called by Congress when requested by two-thirds of the state legislatures. A proposed amendment can be ratified by three-fourths of the state legislatures or by the conventions of three-fourths of the states. The president plays no role in the amendment process. By definition, any part of the Constitution is constitutional, and an amendment can't be ruled unconstitutional.

50. **The correct answer is (E).** Free blacks and escaped slaves suffered greatly in the antebellum North, facing discrimination and segregation in jobs, housing, schools, and public facilities. The New England

states granted suffrage to blacks but most of the other Northern states did not. Pennsylvania took black suffrage away in the 1840s. Earlier, New York removed the property requirement for all except blacks. Southern slaveowners delightedly read newspaper accounts of the frequent Northern race riots to their slaves. The message was, Stay here, you are better off. But Southern slaves still understood that Northern blacks were not property and that they had some legal protections and rights.

51. **The correct answer is (B).** This quotation by James Wilson represents the philosophy of natural rights during the Revolutionary period. The most succinct summary is found in the preamble to the Declaration of Independence. Read it!

52. **The correct answer is (E).** The quotation is from the writings of historian Frederick Jackson Turner, who is most famous for his essay, "The Significance of the Frontier in American History." Choice (E) is part of an argument of Charles Beard, who stressed the economic interpretation of American history. Turner claimed that the frontier experience was the great equalizer of social classes. The demands of the environment stripped away the veneer of culture and civilization and made each man equal to every other.

53. **The correct answer is (C).** Calhoun's doctrine of nullification gave a state the authority to declare an act of Congress null and void. The only means to overcome a state's nullification was for three-fourths of the states to meet in a special convention to pass a specific ordinance against nullification. Calhoun was convinced that it would be too difficult to garner three-fourths of the states. Calhoun's theory of concurrent majority called for two presidents, one for each majority: the majority from the North and the majority (in the South) of the South. To Calhoun majority rule meant plunder of the minority. Only institutional safeguards could protect each majority, North or South.

54. **The correct answer is (E).** The Arawaks lived on the islands of the Caribbean on Cuba, Hispaniola, and Jamaica; the Aztecs lived in Mexico; the Incas in Peru; and the Mayans in the Yucatan peninsula of Mexico.

55. **The correct answer is (C).** The two decades are similar in their attempts to achieve American objectives by peaceful means. Between 1800 and 1810, Jefferson and Madison used the Embargo Act, the Nonintercourse Act, the Chesapeake affair, and Macon's Bill No. 2 to try to avoid war. The Washington Naval Disarmament Conference; the Four, Five, and Nine Power treaties; and the Kellogg-Briand Pact indicate the diplomatic objectives and methods in the twenties.

56. **The correct answer is (B).** The NAACP and the Urban League were founded around 1910. CORE grew out of a meeting of Chicago militants in 1942. The post-Second World War organizations are the Southern Christian Leadership Conference (1957) and the Student Nonviolent Coordinating Committee (1960).

57. **The correct answer is (D).** This is Grant Wood's *American Gothic*, painted in 1930. Wood used his sister and his dentist to show the harsh life and simple values of his Iowa neighbors.

58. **The correct answer is (D).** The Boston Massacre took place much earlier, in 1770. After the Boston Tea Party in December 1773, the British responded with the Intolerable Acts, which closed the port of Boston; revoked the Massachusetts charter; took from the popularly elected assembly the power to appoint the governor's council, and gave it to the king; restricted town meetings to one a year; and moved trials for British officials out of Massachusetts. Widespread concern among the other colonies led to the convening of the First Continental Congress.

59. **The correct answer is (E).** New Deal programs were locally administered, so New Deal programs in the South continued to discriminate against blacks. In Jacksonville, Florida, the relief money was distributed according to a formula based on each race's percentage of the population. This heavily discriminated against blacks because they were a disproportionately higher percentage of the unemployed and therefore more in need. The migration northward continued; the South seemed void

of hope, economically and socially. The first civil rights bill to pass Congress after Reconstruction passed in 1957. Blacks had already started to shift their voting from the Republican Party to the Democratic. As one black leader said, "Turn Lincoln's portrait to the wall." In the 1930s blacks began voting overwhelmingly Democratic, a pattern that still continues. Blacks sensed that they had a friend in the White House in FDR; they knew they had one in Eleanor. The realities of Congress, where Southern Democrats controlled key committee positions, made it impossible for FDR to campaign openly for equal rights. He could not risk losing the support of the committee chairmen for his New Deal programs.

60. **The correct answer is (D).** Most of the articles of impeachment against Andrew Johnson concerned his violation of the Tenure of Office Act. This act expressly prohibited the president from firing any person appointed to a position that required Senate approval. Always willing to accept a belligerent challenge, Johnson promptly fired Secretary of War Stanton. Johnson was impeached but was not found guilty. The vote against him was 35–19, but since a two-thirds majority was necessary for conviction, he was saved by one vote.

61. **The correct answer is (B).** The American negotiators—Benjamin Franklin, John Jay, and John Adams—signed the separate peace because the French and Spanish seemed too eager to hem in the infant United States along the Atlantic coast. Anxious to wean the United States from her alliance with France, the British offered generous boundary terms, including the area to the Mississippi River. Despite textbook exaggerations of George Rogers Clark's exploits, the U.S. claim to the trans-Appalachians was quite poor. The French Revolution didn't start until the end of the decade. The Peace of Paris took place in 1783 (with a preliminary treaty in 1782) long after the defeat at Yorktown in 1781. The United States would never have won the Revolutionary War without massive amounts of French aid and supplies. When General Cornwallis surrendered at Yorktown the British still had 50,000 soldiers in the colonies. The United States didn't defeat Great Britain; Great Britain intelligently gave up a hopeless cause.

62. **The correct answer is (C).** Conservative Old Guard Republicans took control of the regulatory agencies by putting conservatives on the boards and in the agencies. Conservatives in the Reagan administration followed the same tactic. Trying to abolish the boards and agencies involves a fight with Congress. It is much easier to negate the effectiveness of agencies from the inside.

63. **The correct answer is (C).** Cheap labor and low taxes drew the textile industry out of New England and into the South. Each new wave of New England immigrants worked in factories and mills before being replaced with newer and cheaper immigrants. Not a lack of labor but the cost of labor pulled textiles out of New England. Only a few slaves worked in industry in the South before the Civil War. The textile labor force was made up chiefly of poor whites.

64. **The correct answer is (A).** Lyndon Johnson narrowly won the New Hampshire Democratic primary in a contest against Senator Eugene McCarthy of Wisconsin, an antiwar critic, showing that he was very vulnerable and might not even win renomination. The War on Poverty may have been over, but the Vietnam War was not. Johnson had creamed Barry Goldwater in 1964; victory in 1968 looked more difficult. Nixon won an overwhelming victory in his reelection bid in 1972, but his victory over Humphrey in 1968 was very close. Nixon later deescalated American involvement in Vietnam.

65. **The correct answer is (D).** Eleanor Roosevelt was nicknamed "Eleanor Everywhere." She also was responsible for getting the use of the Lincoln Memorial for Marian Anderson's famous concert after the DAR, the Daughters of the American Revolution, refused to let a black use their concert hall. The Equal Pay Act of 1963 legislated equal pay for equal skill and responsibility. In some fields that is easy to judge. A teacher is a teacher, male or female. However, in many areas the concept proved difficult to apply. By the 1970s and 1980s women leaders raised the idea of "comparable worth," equivalent pay for equivalent or similar jobs. For example, driving a truck may require the same level of skill and

knowledge as operating a restaurant dishwasher. Therefore, a female truck driver should receive the same pay as a male dishwasher. That concept is incredibly difficult to apply. It works as long as only one source ranks the jobs by difficulty. Put more people to the task and consensus evaporates.

66. **The correct answer is (C).** A whisper and smear campaign confronted both Al Smith in 1928 and John F. Kennedy in 1960. The truth is that no Democrat, Catholic or Protestant, could have beaten Hoover in 1928. In 1960 Kennedy's Catholicism apparently helped him more than it hindered. Catholic ethnic voters tended to live in large urban areas, which increased Kennedy's urban vote total and gave him a better chance of capturing an entire state's electoral vote.

67. **The correct answer is (E).** The Espionage Act and the Sedition Act were both examples of governmental intolerance. The steel strike, the Boston police strike, the coal strike, the Seattle general strike, and the Palmer raids were all part of the Red Scare of 1918–1921, one of the periods of intolerance. Intolerant of only liquor, the Volstead Act implemented prohibition. Even habitual drinkers looked forward to prohibition as a great social experiment to build a better future society. Ten years later prohibition may have been revealed to be foolish, but it was not so considered at its inception.

68. **The correct answer is (E).** Roger B. Taney (pronounced Tawney) was the fourth Chief Justice of the United States, serving from 1836 to 1864. Helping Jackson during the Bank War, he drafted the bank veto message and removed the deposits from the bank. As Chief Justice he is best remembered for two decisions: the Charles River Bridge decision (1837) protected the community's rights from monopoly grants to corporations and entrepreneurs; the Dred Scott case (1857) invalidated the Missouri Compromise and the Compromise of 1850, and infuriated Northerners.

69. **The correct answer is (A).** Monopoly control over the sale of tea angered the colonists, particularly merchants. The tax remained steady for over six years at three pence per pound. The British troops were already here; remember the Boston Massacre, March 5, 1770? The tea was consigned to American merchants for sale. The Boston Tea Party, December 16, 1773, was caused by anger over the Tea Act, not the reverse. Because the East India Company had been granted a monopoly, it was able to lower the price of tea in the colonies, and the new price was lower than smuggled tea.

70. **The correct answer is (B).** The Marshall Plan was part of Truman's administration.

71. **The correct answer is (C).** Two hints indicate that it is the Chicago World's Fair in 1893, commemorating the four hundredth anniversary of Columbus (I know, they were off by a year!). David Burnham and Louis Sullivan were two outstanding architects of that era. Sullivan was not pleased with the overall tone and direction of American architecture that resulted from the Chicago Fair. He later charged that the fair had set back American architecture for a generation. Sullivan advocated the union of the new technology made possible by new materials, such as steel, and the need to create an outward and inward form that expressed emotions and feelings. The new office skyscrapers could be both functional and magnificent. Sullivan took his cue from nature, "form follows function." "All things in nature have a shape, that is to say, a form, an outward semblance, that tells us what they are, that distinguishes them from ourselves and from each other." Burnham had shown a preference for European styles rather than the emerging American architectural styles. The fair had a separate Woman's Building that presented, as the artist Candace Wheeler wrote, "a man's ideal of woman— delicate, dignified, pure, and fair to look upon." Two murals on the walls depicted "The Primitive Woman" by Mary MacMonnies and "Modern Woman" by Mary Cassatt. In the first, the woman was welcoming her man home from the rigors of the hunt; in the second, modern woman pursued art, music, and dance. Blacks fared much worse. They were excluded from participation in planning and administration, from the construction crews, and from the exhibits. Blacks organized a special "Colored People's Day," a "Jubilee," and invited the former abolitionist Frederick Douglass to speak. Fortunately, Douglass was an official representative from Haiti. He characterized the fair as "a whited sepulcher." Native Americans were included only as the primitive peoples whom Columbus encountered.

72. **The correct answer is (B).** The Kerner Commission, headed by the governor of Illinois, looked at the reasons for black discontent in the 1960s. The Niagara Movement was the forerunner of the NAACP. The Warren Commission investigated the circumstances surrounding the assassination of John F. Kennedy.

73. **The correct answer is (C).** Franklin D. Roosevelt delivered this eloquent speech in January 1941. It remains today a succinct summary of the universal aspirations of people all over the globe.

74. **The correct answer is (C).** Canada attracted the Americans in two ways, as a prize of war and as a means of attacking the British. No method existed for the United States to attack France unless we attacked only French shipping. Since Great Britain had virtually driven French shipping from the seas, our options were severely limited. British violations aggravated the Americans more, for impressment was frustrating and humiliating. We were driven to war by steady diplomatic humiliation.

75. **The correct answer is (E).** Southerners defended slavery with the Bible. It is true that the institution of slavery is not criticized in the Bible. In ancient times a conquered people were enslaved as war booty, as when the Jews were carried into Babylon. The Cain and Abel story was often used by Southerners. After confronting Cain for killing Abel, God punished Cain by putting a mark on him and his descendants. By reading between the lines and stretching their imaginations, Southerners reasoned that Cain was turned into a black man for punishment. The comparison between the conditions for the worst Northern factory workers and the conditions for the best slaves was fair and was often used by Southerners. Very few could imagine anything other than an agricultural South. "King Cotton" blinded them to any other possible crop or industry. The Constitution did not specifically protect slavery in the South, although the three-fifths clause and the 1808 date abolishing the slave trade seem to condone slavery. The Northwest Ordinance abolished slavery in the Old Northwest. Individual state action abolished slavery north of the Mason-Dixon line.

76. **The correct answer is (C).** All of these statements are true for the fifteen years preceding the War of 1812. In 1807–1808 Jefferson's embargo stymied shipping. Be able to put the changing American, French, and British policies prior to the War of 1812 into chronological order.

77. **The correct answer is (B).** The cartoonist Thomas Nast undermined Boss Tweed's control. Even illiterate New York City immigrants understood Nast's scathing cartoons.

78. **The correct answer is (B).** James Oglethorpe led a group of associates who founded Georgia in 1733 for the relief of jailed debtors and for fortifying the southern frontier against Spanish Florida.

79. **The correct answer is (B).** The emphasis on equality, voluntary association, the social character of churches, the rejection of culture, and the emphasis on public morals are also in *Democracy in America*, published in the 1830s.

80. **The correct answer is (D).** These two songs were popular in 1932 because they conveyed the popular feelings of the period. If you can, find some people who lived through the Depression and ask them to tell you their personal histories. You may be surprised at the depths of deprivation and fear in the early years of the Depression.

NOTES

NOTES